Geoff Harcourt
Source: Tony Jedrej, *Cambridge Evening News*

CAPITAL CONTROVERSY, POST-KEYNESIAN ECONOMICS AND THE HISTORY OF ECONOMIC THOUGHT

Geoff Harcourt has made substantial and wide-ranging contributions to economics in general, and to post-Keynesian economics in particular. In this volume more than forty leading economists pay tribute to and critically evaluate his work.

In particular, contributions focus on:

- debates in the area of capital theory
- the development of post-Keynesian economics and the 'Cambridge tradition'
- major figures in the history of economic thought including Marx, Keynes and Sraffa

The contributors represent a wide range of schools in economics, and include Nobel Laureates Paul Samuelson and Robert Solow.

Philip Arestis is Professor of Economics at the University of East London.

Gabriel Palma is Lecturer in Economics in the Faculty of Economics and Politics, University of Cambridge.

Malcolm Sawyer is Professor of Economics in the School of Business and Economic Studies, University of Leeds.

ROUTLEDGE FRONTIERS OF POLITICAL ECONOMY

CAPITAL CONTROVERSY, POST-KEYNESIAN ECONOMICS AND THE HISTORY OF ECONOMIC THOUGHT

Essays in Honour of Geoff Harcourt
Volume One

Edited by
Philip Arestis, Gabriel Palma
and Malcolm Sawyer

London and New York

First published 1997
by Routledge
11 New Fetter Lane, London EC4P 4EE

Simultaneously published in the USA and Canada
by Routledge
29 West 35th Street, New York, NY 10001

Reprinted 2002

Transferred to Digital Printing 2003

Routledge is an imprint of the Taylor & Francis Group

Typeset in Times by Solidus (Bristol) Limited
Printed and bound in Great Britain by
Biddles Short Run Books, Kings Lynn

British Library Cataloguing in Publication Data
A catalogue record for this book is available from the British Library

Library of Congress Cataloging in Publication Data
Capital controversy, post Keynesian economics and the history of economic
thought : essays in honour of Geoff Harcourt /
edited by Philip Arestis, Gabriel Palma, and Malcolm Sawyer.
p.   cm. — (Routledge frontiers of political economy, ISSN 1359–7914 : 6)
Includes bibliographical references and index.
1. Capital–History.   2. Keynesian economics–History.
3. Markets–History.   4. Unemployment–History.   5. Economic policy–History.
I. Arestis, Philip.   II. Palma, J. Gabriel.
III. Sawyer, Malcolm C.   IV. Harcourt, Geoffrey Colin.   V. Series.
HB501.C24224   1966
332′.041–dc20   96-15332
ISBN 0–415–13391–2

CONTENTS

CONTENTS

CONTENTS

CONTENTS

FIGURES

TABLES

CONTRIBUTORS

Heinz W. Arndt, Australian National University, Canberra, Australia
Mauro Baranzini, Centro di Studi Bancari, Vezia-Lugano, Italy
William J. Baumol, New York University, United States of America
Christopher Bliss, University of Oxford, England
Heinrich Bortis, Université de Fribourg, Switzerland
A. W. Bob Coats, University of Nottingham, England
Avi J. Cohen, York University, Toronto, Canada
Bernard Corry, Queen Mary and Westfield College, University of London, England
Lilia Costabile, Universita degli Studi di Napoli Federico II, Italy
Paul Dalziel, Lincoln University, New Zealand
William Darity, Jr, University of North Carolina, Chapel Hill, United States of America
Paul Davidson, University of Tennessee, Knoxville, United States of America
John B. Davis, Marquette University, Milwaukee, United States of America
Phyllis Deane, University of Cambridge, England
Robert Dixon, University of Melbourne, Australia
Sheila C. Dow, University of Stirling, Scotland
Helmar Drost, York University, Toronto, Canada
John Eatwell, New School, New York, United States of America
Christopher A. Gregory, Australian National University, Australia
Peter Groenewegen, University of Sydney, Australia
Harald Hagemann, Universität Hohenheim, Stuttgart, Germany
Omar F. Hamouda, Massachusetts Institute of Technology, United States of America
John Hatch, University of Adelaide, Australia
Geoffrey M. Hodgson, University of Cambridge, England
Hans E. Jensen, University of Tennessee, Knoxville, United States of America
John E. King, La Trobe University, Australia
Heinz D. Kurz, Institut für Volkswirtschaftspolitik, Graz, Austria
Michael S. Lawlor, Wake Forest University, Winston-Salem, North Carolina, United States of America
Andrea Maneschi, Vanderbilt University, Nashville, United States of America

Maria Cristina Marcuzzo, Università di Roma, 'La Sapienza', Italy
Luigi L. Pasinetti, Università Cattolica Sacro Cuore, Milan, Italy
Mark Perlman, University of Pittsburgh, United States of America
Ray Petrides, Murdoch University, Australia
Stephen Pratten, University of Cambridge, England
Colin Rogers, University of Adelaide, Australia
Alessandro Roncaglia, Università di Roma, 'La Sapienza', Italy
Robert Rowthorn, University of Cambridge, England
Thomas K. Rymes, Carlton University, Ottawa, Canada
Neri Salvadori, Università di Pisa, Italy
Paul A. Samuelson, Massachussetts Institute of Technology, Cambridge, United States of America
Roberto Scazzieri, Università degli Studi, Bologna, Italy
Robert M. Solow, Massachussetts Institute of Technology, Cambridge, United States of America
John K. Whitaker, University of Virginia, Charlottesville, United States of America

FOREWORD

Nice guys don't finish last; they are never finished

I first met Geoff on a balmy evening in the Easter vacation of 1966 while in Cambridge (where else?) attending a curious gathering called the London Oxford Cambridge seminar. In those halcyon days, before the SSRC had got off the ground and study groups were twinkles in no one's eyes, this was the only forum for research students and interested faculty to meet at some sort of 'national' level. We were standing for some reason in a narrow lane (Mill Lane? Laundress Lane?) and fell to talking with each other after a day long set of seminars. Our Cambridge hosts were terribly condescending; but for a young man recently come from the USA the atmosphere was quite amusing. They seemed to speak of Maynard as if he was about to come around the corner. Geoff was a recently naturalized Cantabrigian but, all the same, a decent Australian applied economist. We immediately got along very well and have done so ever since. He, in the meantime and despite one or two escapes, has been in Cambridge all these years while I have been at the LSE man and boy *sans* escape for thirty-one years.

Over these years the map of economics, and indeed that of the Cambridge economics faculty, has changed. LSE, on the other hand, has remained by and large the same place, though some persons have passed on and others have taken their place. LSE has been mainstream, mathematical, technical, unworried by controversies, undivided into camps, utterly devoted to publishing in a small set of journals. At the same time, it is a very tolerant place. It has looked on with amusement while I have lurched between econometrics, Marxian economics, Hayek, Keynesian controversies and, as long as I publish in a refereed journal, has let me be. Geoff has traversed no fewer and if anything many more avenues: accounting, post-Keynesian economics, capital theory controversies, Australian political economy, Sraffa, Marx, Marshall, the Vietnam War; and who knows what he will yet get into. But he has done this in a combative atmosphere. Doing economics at Cambridge is like being a Christian during the English Civil War; you can't just be a Christian. You have to identify yourself as to what sect, what party, what faction you belong to. Your views on the non-substitution theorem are as important as a marker for the rest of your world-view, on everything from beer or sherry to the stance on Vietnam, as your views on transubstantiation were in seventeenth-century England.

Yet, through it all, Geoff has sailed with a smile and a robust attitude and a lot of writing. After many storms, Cambridge has becalmed (before yet another storm?). Indeed, Old Cambridge (like old Labour), is being marginalized in New Cambridge (New Labour), which is becoming very much like the LSE. Old Cambridge survives in a few individual pockets of resistance in Cambridge (Geoff being one of the sturdiest) and in various outposts in Italy, India, Australia.

In this Festschrift essay I briefly want to ask why it is that, relative to its position in economics in the mid-1960s when I first met Geoff, Cambridge economics (and not all economics taught in Cambridge is Cambridge economics) has failed to maintain its pivotal position. Why have the burning issues of those days – capital theory controversy, left Keynesianism, the political economy of socialism, growth and accumulation theory – lost their urgency? Much of the answer is, of course, in the way the world has materially changed. But ideas do matter. Was it something endogenous to Cambridge or something exogenous – the power of the Establishment, the weight of positivist methodology, the American dominance of the profession – that undermined the Cambridge programme?.

Recall that in the 1950s and 1960s Cambridge was part and parcel of the Establishment. The serried ranks of Marshall lecturers, the visitors who came across to keep the capital controversy going, the worldly influence of Kaldor and Kahn and Austin Robinson, will say that the power of the Establishment certainly was not the factor. Indeed, at the other end of the political spectrum Chicago was feeling more beleaguered in those days than Cambridge was. In both cases the corresponding party was the other Cambridge. But, while Chicago has emerged triumphant and imposed its methods and models on the world of economics, Cambridge has waned.

Seeking an endogenous explanation, I venture (taking my life in my hands no doubt) to suggest that the internal contradictions within the three Cambridge revolutions caused great problems for Cambridge. At the same time, the theoretical debates distracted attention away from the central task of economics: the study of real-world problems and an attempt to solve them. Indeed, Geoff's writings describe this trajectory extremely well, though I do not thereby mean to make him the fall guy. He is the nice guy in this story.

The three Cambridge revolutions are (in my view, as Geoff reminded us in *The Social Science Imperialists* against any false objectivity) Sraffa 1926, which spawned the imperfect-competition literature; Keynes 1936, which is obvious; and the Joan Robinson–Piero Sraffa revolution of 1956–60. (I am bracketing the Accumulation of Capital with Production of Commodities deliberately.) When I first met Geoff it was the last of the three revolutions which was in its world-conquering phase. But Cambridge was also fighting the bastard Keynesians who were deviating from the true path of the 1936 revolution – the Americans. Since these apostates swore by competitive microeconomics, the 1926 revolution could also be thrown at them.

The 1936 revolution was leading to the most practical and applied work. Geoff's earliest papers on the historical cost versus replacement cost accounting of profits plump for the benighted Accountant despite the fact, as he himself later argues, that the Accountant gets it wrong in the golden age. But why should any applied economist have cared about the golden age? That is the space in which Irving Fisher will live happily with Joan Robinson. Keynes was, after all, interested in the short run; perhaps the sequence of temporary equilibria but hardly steady states. But the latest revolution was taking Cambridge away from its task of defending the 1936 revolution. When, in the inflationary 1970s, the monetarist attack came, Cambridge was too absorbed in the third revolution to take up arms against the new enemy in defence of Maynard (with the honourable exception of Nicholas Kaldor, a most un-Cambridge Cambridge economist).

As if that were not bad enough, the Robinson–Sraffa revolution, though failing to unseat neoclassical orthodoxy, got its one success in undermining Marxian economics at the hands of Ian Steedman. Thus, 'objectively speaking', as we used pretentiously to say in those heady days, the effect of the third revolution was bad for the left, while, at the same time, the post-Keynesian refurbishment of the Keynesian edifice used the 1926 revolution via imperfect competition and Kalecki to expose Keynes as being inconsistent in his macro and his micro theory. *The General Theory* was rewritten in oligopolistic/imperfectly competitive terms with Kalecki as our hero rather than Keynes. In my view, uncertainty and the nature of a monetary economy are enough to sustain Keynes against Walras or Lucas, but this was not the approach taken. Keynes's model was rejected and refurbished. Thus, the Keynesian front was split in the dark days of monetarist attack.

Worse was to come – though, to his credit, while Geoff has dabbled with golden ages and Kaleckian mark-ups, he has never been part of this further step. This was the turning of the Sraffa 1960 logic against Keynes. In Garegnani's argument about long-run output, Keynes was castigated for lacking logical coherence. Indeed Keynes had failed to be Ricardo! The Anglo-Italian tendency finally undermined Keynes by denying him his triumph against his arch-enemy Ricardo. Ricardo captured Cambridge once again, having briefly lost it in 1936. By 1986, Cambridge had scuttled Keynes. Indeed, the Lucas critique of Keynes is not all that different, because the long-run equilibrium and golden ages, free of uncertainty and rational-expectations equilibria, are just first cousins if not Siamese twins.

So Keynes's idea that economists would become like dentists was not to be. Economists became philosophers and metaphysicians wanting logical certainties, rigorous, unique equilibria. Capital intensity reversals and reswitching crowded out simple issues like inflation and unemployment and incomes policies (which to Geoff's credit as an Australian he has always been interested in). Walrasian economics has always been engaged in this quest, as the other book published in 1960 – Debreu's *Theory of Value* – demonstrated.

FOREWORD

But neoclassicals are vulgar economists. They carry on their applied work unmindful of logical inconsistencies. They swing from Cobb Douglas technology to Leontieff technology, assume perfect competition or oligopolistic pricing, make capital malleable or not as the applied problem demands. (The Chicago ones are slightly more finicky.) The important point in economics, as Alfred Marshall understood, is not to get it right but to solve the problem at hand with an appropriate model and then move on. Cambridge got bogged down in the search for the Holy Grail of complete consistency between theory and applications, confusing the day-to-day and the Golden Age, turning on itself. The last paper of Joan Robinson (Robinson 1980, 1985), which was published posthumously, very much reflected the regret at the diversion of efforts.

But, despite being occasionally diverted by steady states, Geoff has continued to take interest in the here and now. He still cares about fuller employment, about incomes policies, about finding another chink in the arguments against socialism. When I last met him in Cambridge his talk was of regret at the defeat of the Australian Labor Party in the election and the paper he was writing, developing the ideas of Wilfred Salter to arrive at a high-wage policy consistent with full employment. Long may he live and battle.

Meghnad Desai

REFERENCE

Robinson, J. (1980, 1985), 'Spring cleaning', mimeo, Cambridge, published as 'The theory of normal prices and the reconstruction of economic theory', in G. R. Feiwel (ed.) *Issues in Contemporary Macroeconomics and Distribution*, London: Macmillan.

GEOFF HARCOURT:
A TRIBUTE

For anyone working in the economics faculty at Cambridge, as I used to, Geoff was a central figure. Almost always to be found in his office, he was so genuinely friendly.

With a very broad range of interests in economic analysis, he was willing to provide help and advice to anyone wishing to prepare work for publication. He knew most of the faculty and was always ready to be consulted, ready to provide advice and information about whom to consult about any particular economic issue and about who might be helpful on specific subjects. Though steadily working himself, he was always ready to discuss any aspect of particular issues of economics. I always felt free to drop by his office and discuss with him whatever topic I was interested in working on. He always responded with useful suggestions. He never gave one the feeling that one was interfering with his own interests or projects.

I always felt he constituted a kind of centre to consult about who might be helpful on a wide range of topics. I never felt that I was unduly impinging on his time for work on his own projects. I almost never came to the faculty, for any purpose, without stopping at his office and having a pleasant and often highly informative communication with him on a variety of topics in economics.

Richard Goodwin
University of Siena, Italy

INTRODUCTION

This is one of two volumes published to celebrate the major contributions Geoff Harcourt had made to the discipline of economics and to post-Keynesian economics in particular. During his illustrious career, Geoff has gained enormous respect and admiration from colleagues and friends of varied persuasions, as is amply evidenced by the contributions to these two volumes.

Geoff Harcourt, 'an Australian patriot and a Cambridge economist' in his own words,[1] was born in Melbourne on 27 June 1931. At school he wanted to be a vet – he has always loved birds and other animals – and mostly did science. He took some economics only to 'make up the numbers', as he puts it, but did very well at it, and very badly at physics, so that luckily for us and unluckily for all the animals in the world, he proceeded to do economics at the University of Melbourne. It was Cambridge-oriented economics that he studied there, which he has loved ever since.

It was clear, even at that early stage in Geoff's academic life, that great things were going to happen in the future. His undergraduate dissertation was a clear pointer to the future. Oligopolistic price theory, with firms having as their objective the 'desire for secure profits as much as maximum profits', was integrated with the macroeconomic system of Keynes's *General Theory*, in an attempt to study the behaviour of Australian companies during the Great Depression. Effective demand, especially investment, pricing under conditions of imperfect competition, applied economics and more, were all there. The main ingredients of his undergraduate dissertation were clearly visible in his master's degree dissertation, although its theme was a radically different one, namely a pilot survey of income and saving in Melbourne.

In late July 1955 he and Joan married, 'lived happily ever after', and left Melbourne in mid-August for King's College, Cambridge – where else, indeed? Geoff's Ph.D. turned out to be a study of the economic implications of using historical cost accounting procedures for price formation in a period of inflation, which inevitably entailed implications for measuring income for dividend and tax purposes. It was at this time that Geoff acquainted himself with Robinson's *The Accumulation of Capital*, then newly published. Indeed, he read a paper on the main propositions of the book to three consecutive sessions of the research students seminar, chaired by Robin Marris. Joan Robinson attended the third session. She actually did not think much of that group of students with the exception of 'a chap called Harcourt'. *The*

Accumulation of Capital provided the *core* which has inspired Geoff's contributions to economics, and his teaching. This is not difficult to understand now, perhaps, given the influence on both Joan Robinson and Geoff Harcourt of the writings of Smith, Ricardo, Marx, Marshall, Keynes, Kahn, Kalecki and Sraffa.

Geoff returned to Australia after his Ph.D. at Cambridge, to take up his first lecturing job in the Department of Economics at the University of Adelaide. It was there that he met Eric Russell, his greatest mentor and friend in Australia. On Geoff's own admission he learned a great deal from Eric, including theory, applied economics and policy as it relates to the real world, and how to teach undergraduates economics. He lectured on Kaldor's economics and wrote a critique of Kaldor's theories of distribution and growth as they had been developed by that time. That critique concentrated on the pricing behaviour of the consumption and investment goods sectors, and focused essentially on the full-employment assumption adopted by Kaldor. It essentially argued that the full-employment assumption required strong conditions on pricing behaviour in the two sectors in order for the distributive mechanism to work and for Kaldor's growth models to behave in the intended way. Geoff argued that it was better to drop the un-Keynesian full-employment assumption in favour of keeping the distribution mechanism, a more realistic and relevant aspect of Kaldor's theoretical framework. At about this time he wrote 'The accountant in a golden age', published in 1965 (*Oxford Economic Papers*), which is perhaps his best-known paper after the 1969 *Journal of Economic Literature* survey.

In 1963 Geoff returned to Cambridge on a year's study leave. His interest in oligopolistic industries continued and these aspects of his work were the central focus of the paper published in the *Economic Record* (1965) on the determination of employment and the distribution of income in a two-sector model in the short period. That paper was presented at a seminar the audience of which included, among others, all the famous Cambridge economists of the time. It was in a sense the apotheosis of his enduring concern with, and maturity of his interest in, the idea of oligopoly, which had occupied him since his undergraduate years. This concern is further reflected in his often-quoted paper with Peter Kenyon in *Kyklos* (1976). Not surprisingly, Geoff has come to view the *Economic Record* contribution as his favourite theoretical paper. The seminar must have been a resounding success, for soon after it he was offered a lecturing job in the faculty which he accepted for only three years – he did not wish to let Adelaide University down – and before he knew it, he was elected to a Fellowship in Trinity Hall. The paper he presented at that seminar provided the impetus for a stream of important and influential contributions, with a distinctly strong post-Keynesian thread running through them. These included the choice of technique papers, the best known of which appeared in the *Economic Journal* in March 1968.

Geoff has always been concerned with making the assumptions of the problem in hand explicit and with bringing out the limitations as well as the illuminations of the relevant analysis. An excellent example of this is his *Economic Activity* (with P. H. Karmel and R. H. Wallace, 1967), a book based on a lecture course on Keynesian economics and one that Geoff considers as 'a clear and unpretentious account of the "state of the art" at the time'. The time was the end of 1966 and Geoff was leaving Cambridge for Australia. That was also the era of the Vietnam War and Australia's role in it. Those events and Geoff's political involvement had a profound impact upon him, especially upon his views on the relationship between ideology and analysis. No longer could they be separated in his writings and teaching.

In the midst of all that political fervour, Geoff 'took time off' to write his first piece on the capital controversy for the *Journal of Economic Literature*. The favourable feedback on that paper encouraged Geoff to push on within the area and no fewer than four further papers materialized. The then editor of Cambridge University Press was very impressed by that vast output and asked Geoff to put them together in a book. The first draft was ready, in Geoff's words, 'in two months flat (out!)'. Published in May 1972, under the well-known title *Some Cambridge Controversies in the Theory of Capital* (with subsequent editions in most major languages), the book contained two themes. The first was a critique of the concept of using price as an indication of scarcity in distribution theory, and the second was a methodological critique of utilizing differences to study change. A year's study leave in 1972–3 was spent at Clare Hall as a Visiting Fellow. During that time Geoff gave a number of seminars on the capital debate book, with his afterthoughts being published in *Oxford Economic Papers* in 1976, with the apt title, 'The Cambridge controversies: old ways and new horizons – or dead end?'. It was also then that he formed a close friendship with Tom Asimakopulos (they had already met at Cambridge in the 1950s), which lasted until the latter's premature death in May 1990.

Geoff returned to Adelaide University in 1973. The golden age of capitalism was coming to an end by then, soon followed by the stagflation of the 1970s and the monetarist era. Australia did not stand outside the trend. In 1975 the government there introduced monetarist policies accompanied by confrontationist attitudes between government, capital and labour. Although Geoff had already spent some time drawing out the policy implications of the capital theory debate, the Australian experience gave him a new platform on which to formulate his economic policy views more cogently. At the heart of those ideas was a set of economic policies designed to reduce inflation slowly while maintaining high levels of employment and external balance. Furthermore, redistribution through public-sector policies was seen as the quid pro quo for trade union acceptance of incomes policies. Fiscal and monetary policies were to aim at influencing the level and the rate of growth of economic activity. Nationalization of key industries including financial intermediaries would boost investment, and a fixed exchange rate adjusted from time to time would ensure external balance. When the Australian Labor Party (ALP) was returned to power in 1983, the Accord between trade unions and the government must have owed a great deal to those ideas propounded by Geoff as the economist on the ALP's National Committee of Enquiry in 1978, in the form of background discussion papers. They are still on Geoff's agenda and he has taken them a step further recently in a number of contributions.

In the mid-1970s Geoff developed a new interest in writing intellectual biographies. He has written a steady stream of them, which he has admitted to enjoying enormously – a clear indication of his love of and concern for fellow human beings. Some of this material may very well form the nucleus of the major task he first began when he returned to Cambridge in 1982 (to a teaching post in the Faculty of Economics and Politics and a Fellowship at Jesus). It is to write the intellectual history of Joan Robinson and her circle, and to show the connections between their contributions and those of the classical economists, Marx, and Keynes, as well as of contemporaries whom Joan Robinson and her circle influenced. The project is not finished yet, for good reasons which have to do with Geoff's continuing concern with a number of developments both in economic theory and in economic policy in the real world. But above all, it is *A 'Second Edition' of The General Theory*, which he is co-editing with Peter Riach and hopes to bring out in 1996, sixty years after the publication of *The General Theory*, that has taken up much of his time. This is an exciting publication which is intended to tell us what Keynes would have written in the late 1930s had he known what those who succeeded him were to contribute on a number of aspects of *The General Theory* in the post-war period. 'Putting Keynes back at the forefront of the debate' is the essential purpose of the book. And just to show the world that he has not run out of steam as a surveyor of the passing scene, Geoff published a paper entitled 'Reflections on the developments of economics as a discipline', a piece about the Nobel Prize winners up to Debreu. It was published in the *History of Political Economy* in 1984.

Since he last returned to Cambridge in 1982, Geoff has been at the centre of the teaching of and research in macroeconomics. He has also been instrumental in the development of the graduate programme in the Faculty of Economics and Politics, and has systematically been the most popular Ph.D. supervisor.

We have tried in this introduction to offer an inevitably short summary of Geoff Harcourt's academic life and work. Just as Mark Perlman has done recently in a preface to a selection of Geoff's essays, we have tried to look into Geoff's four groups of contributions:[2]

1 works analysing contemporary economic theoretical problems;
2 works synthesizing states of debates in economic theory;

3   works having a distinctly biographical flavour and pertaining to various contemporary economics; and

4   works pertaining to economic and allied social policies.

Of course this convenient list does not pretend to cover the full range of material covered in Geoff's massive output of books and papers.

We are delighted, but not surprised, that on 13 June 1994 Geoff was awarded one of the highest Australian honours of Officer in the General Division of the Order of Australia (AO), for 'service to economic theory and to the history of economic thought'. Well done Australia! And yet Geoff still flourishes as a Reader at Cambridge (he is Reader in the History of Economic Theory, *ad hominen*), and enjoys himself as ever. Our greatest regret, and his, we are sure (though he has never shown it at all), is that despite his achievements, national and international recognition, and his vast contributions to the discipline of economics, he has been denied a full professorship – although his old university in Adelaide did bestow upon him in 1988 the title of Professor Emeritus. This, of course, continues the famous Cambridge tradition of being less than generous in awarding professorships, as, for example, the failure to so honour Piero Sraffa, Maurice Dobb, Richard Goodwin, Luigi Pasinetti and others, or the late concessions of professorships to Joan Robinson and Nicky Kaldor.

The editors of this book are exceptionally grateful for Geoff's help, encouragement and friendship throughout the years. The speed by which *constructive* comments are generously provided on manuscripts and papers, the breadth and depth of them, his unfailing availability at the other end of the telephone, his writings and contributions to conferences from which we, and so many others, have benefited are just some of the ways in which we have gained through knowing him. We are honoured to have had a long association with so great a figure as Geoff Harcourt. Many have benefited from his warm hospitality to visitors to Cambridge. The two volumes we have put together are intended to mark our enormous respect and admiration for such a great friend. We are sure that these sentiments are completely shared by all the contributors to the two volumes, and indeed by many others who would have liked to have contributed but unfortunately were unable to do so.

There is another aspect of Geoff's skills that makes him almost unique in academia. He was a player of Australian Rules football in an amateur capacity. That he was still playing such a physically demanding game at the age of 47 is no mean feat. As befits an Australian, he was also a keen player of cricket until a recurring back injury and then his four recent brushes with death put him out of the game – only temporarily, we are delighted to say. Undeterred by the back injury, he ran the Cambridge half-marathon in the mid-1980s, and every day now he goes on a long bike ride. Despite his recent illness, his resilience is such that he is as sparkling as he has ever been. Geoff often jokes about those incidents, but then, being intelligently funny is yet another characteristic of his good nature. This ability adds even more to his humane approach, not just to his economics but also to his fellow human beings, especially his friends.

No introduction of this kind should come to an end without at least a mention of the quiet, and yet dynamic and effective, person who we know has played a central and critical role in supporting what Geoff has managed to achieve in his life. This is, of course, Joan, who has been a reliable and tremendously supportive partner in Geoff's life. She has also been an extremely good and warm friend to all of us, all these years. She, and Wendy, Robert, Timothy, Rebecca, their respective partners and the recent addition of a grandchild (thanks to Wendy and Claudio Sardoni), complete a very happy family indeed.

Nor should we fail to mention Geoff's religious and political convictions, which are central to his economics. It is very pleasing to see how well these three aspects – religion, politics and economics – mesh in his recent paper, 'A "modest proposal" for taming speculators and putting the world on course to prosperity'. They combine with his unfailing compassion for his fellow women and men to give expression to his real feelings about humanity.

Special thanks must go to the contributors for their willingness to respond to our comments and suggestions with forbearance and good humour. Thanks are also extended to the secretaries of the Department of Economics at the University of East London, June Daniels and Christine Nisbet, and the secretary of the School of Business and Economic Studies at the University of Leeds, Eleanor Lynn, for their generous assistance. Finally, Alan Jarvis and his staff, as always, have provided excellent support throughout the period it took to prepare both volumes.

Philip Arestis, Gabriel Palma and Malcolm Sawyer

NOTES

1   All the quotes from Geoff Harcourt in the introduction are from his entry in P. Arestis and M. Sawyer (eds) (1992) *A Biographical Dictionary of Dissenting Economists*, Aldershot: Edward Elgar, pp. 232–41.

2   The four groups are quoted from the preface (written by Mark Perlman) to G. C. Harcourt (1995) *Capitalism, Socialism and Post-Keynesianism*, Cheltenham: Edward Elgar.

1

A CAMBRIDGE ECONOMIST *BUT* AN AUSTRALIAN PATRIOT

John Hatch and Ray Petrides

INTRODUCTION

When we were approached separately to contribute to Geoff Harcourt's sixty-fifth birthday Festschrift we had a like-minded response. Why not write about his impact on Australian economics and policy? This, it seemed to us, would redress the balance which had emphasized his work in Cambridge and his own description of himself as a 'Cambridge economist' (Harcourt 1992a). Of course he has always stressed, sometimes to the irritation of his more stuffy colleagues, that despite living for many years in Cambridge he remains an 'Australian patriot' (Harcourt 1995a), and one who has aggressively retained his interest in Australian politics, economics and sport and the Australian accent to go with it.

In some respects Geoff is something of an enigma. Although much of his interest and writing in economics has been at the most fundamental and broad level, he still retains an interest in local and small-scale issues. This dichotomy is indeed the very soul of the man and the scholar.

We had observed and participated in an exciting epoch of some twenty years at the University of Adelaide when Geoff Harcourt and his colleagues built a department of excellence and achievements in economics. From those earliest years Geoff was seen as the mentor of many fresh faces in the profession: guiding, encouraging and pushing people into new research fields. He rapidly became one of the best-known economists in Australia and surely the most sought-after reader of the preliminary and rudimentary research efforts of numerous fledgling economists. This was not only because of his boundless energy and enthusiasm, but also because of his great generosity of spirit and his willingness to find positive elements in even the roughest of drafts. Many an outstanding career in economics was launched by this willing and unstinting sacrifice of time and effort to guide the work of others.

Interestingly, and in a sense surprisingly, Geoff never really built a school or 'dynasty' in Adelaide. At times he himself seemed to regret this, and indeed it is reasonable to speculate that his final agonizing decision to leave his beloved department was partly based on this failure to build a school. Although his colleagues loved and valued him, few joined him in his academic niche. Why was this? First, Geoff was so complex in his values, and so eclectic, that few could define his position. This is not to say that he is inconsistent, rather that he is tolerant, flexible and able to recognize the merit of a wide range of views. Such characteristics do not appeal greatly to real ideologues, or even joiners. It has been Geoff's fate to be admired by many, but joined by few. We believe that he may have been the more influential for this.

Second, Geoff is not an organizer in the narrow sense. He is interested in ideas and in people in general, rather than in political and strategic groupings. He always tries to see other people's views and usually discerns some merit in them – always in the people and sometimes in the views. This is not the stuff of narrow ideologies and academic in-fighting. At the same time he was devoting his energy to his own work in both post-Keynesian economics and the related policy issues flowing from it. He also found time to be active in teaching and administration, and for several years to lead the powerful and effective anti-Vietnam War movement in South Australia. In what follows, we wish to touch in more detail on some of this and, we hope, throw further light on why he is probably the best loved (an unusual adjective to describe any economist) and one of the best-known Australian economists.

THE MELBOURNE YEARS

When he arrived in Melbourne University Geoff Harcourt was searching for a political and social philosophy and for a discipline in which they could be embedded. Over the next four years while he studied for an honours degree in economics he found democratic socialism and Christian socialism, and what subsequently became a large and distinguished niche in economics (see Harcourt 1995a for details). Of course, he was an outstanding undergraduate, gathering numerous prizes and awards, some of which helped to finance his years of study and allowed him to buy his way out of a commitment to become a state school teacher of economics.[1]

This practical background lies behind his desires in most of his writing to illuminate economic questions which will have some policy relevance. He was indeed fortunate that the Commerce Faculty at Melbourne, apart from one or two members, had a preference for and some links with Cambridge and the economics of Keynes.[2] By the time he reached his fourth (honours) year at university his views on the role of economics in providing explanations of 'how particular societies work' and how to 'produce desirable results for ordinary people' (Harcourt 1992b: 9) were already coalescing. Over the years those views developed and matured, and some of his best work focused on purely theoretical issues, but there is no doubt that his earliest emphasis on

2

economics generating welfare-increasing policies underlies virtually every-thing he has written.

This approach to economics can be seen in his earliest sustained piece of writing, which was a 30,000-word thesis submitted in partial fulfilment of the requirements for the B.Com. degree with honours (Harcourt 1953). It is of interest for its own sake but also because it contained themes which are echoed in much of his later writing. By his fourth year at university he was clearly brimming with confidence, and this is discernible in the exuberant, assertive, almost brash style of parts of the thesis. But he believed he had something worthwhile to say and he expressed it in the strongest possible terms. He noted that the *General Theory* assumptions of perfect competition in a closed economy were inappropriate for considering provisions for depreciation by firms operating under other market conditions. Taking his lead from K. W. Rothschild's well-known 1947 paper 'Price theory and oligopoly', he attempted to examine Keynes's analysis of the depreciation provisions of firms and their impact on investment and aggregate demand under oligopolistic conditions. He brought his training in accountancy to bear in attempting to develop propositions about the actual behaviour of firms under the depressed economic conditions associated with the 1929–33 Depression. A sample of firms across the spectrum of Australian industry were examined to test the relatively vague propositions (not identified as hypotheses) which emerged from his theoretical discussion. The conclusions to the thesis were both modest and agnostic in contrast to the earlier parts, but he established a pattern of seeking practical policy implications for much of his subsequent work.

Of course the more general problem of integrating Keynes into a largely oligopolistic world has still not been solved. Geoff is one of those still wrestling with the problems (an example is his recent paper delivered at the 1995 Adelaide Conference of Economists), where he stresses that Keynes in the latter part of the twentieth century needs to be seen in the context of the global economy and in the context of at least a 'simplified' oligopoly model. Surely the fact that Keynes conceived his theories in a competitive world, albeit one of practical competition, not pure or perfect competition, is not sufficient reason for abandoning his insights. One might as well abandon Darwin because he did not fully understand and incorporate modern genetics! Geoff has not made this mistake; he knows a good theory when he sees it. He is not uncritical of Keynes's theories and he is well aware of the gaps in them and the changes in the world which have rendered them at times inapplicable. However, he also cherishes the great insights, which are, with intelligent adaptations, as useful today as they were in the 1920s and 1930s.

After his honours degree and before departing for Cambridge he was employed as a research assistant for the Ritchie Research Professor in Economics at the University of Melbourne and also wrote an M.Com thesis, 'Pilot survey of savings in Melbourne'.[3] Variants of the theme he first developed in his undergraduate days appear in his Cambridge Ph.D. thesis, which he has described as 'mainly applied' (Harcourt 1995a). Because of his better-known work on the Cambridge controversies and related themes it sometimes comes as a surprise that Geoff Harcourt's economics often had an applied and policy flavour to it. When he returned to the University of Adelaide to a lecturing position his research orientation, though reflecting the strong Cambridge influences, continued to emphasize the application of theory to policy.

ADELAIDE AND CAMBRIDGE: THE SYNTHESIS

Arriving in Adelaide at the age of 27 in 1958, initially to fill the position of research assistant, he was allowed to work on the completion of his Ph.D. and a little later that year he was appointed to a lectureship in economics. Almost immediately he began to establish a pattern of participation in academic activities, one which has characterized the rest of his career. It was the remarkable combination of academic talent, dedication to his subject matter and enormous energy combined with his empathetic nature, tolerance of almost every shade of opinion and the mix of democratic socialist and Christian socialist views which began to shine through. As we have said earlier, he did not always have the full agreement of his colleagues on either academic or political issues but his tolerance, patience and willingness to carry a heavy workload meant that most of the time he had their support. Many high-powered economists who later rose to prominence were recruited by the professor and head of the Adelaide Department, P. H. Karmel, at Geoff's instigation. To the students he was able to display a virtuoso knowledge of economics, peppered with fresh insights and delivered with enthusiasm and sincerity. And even at the earliest stage of his career he was urging and encouraging students to venture widely and to take an occasional risk in their studies. He was unstinting in the time and effort he would devote to students as long as they were conscientious in their own efforts. This helpful and generous nature is his most abiding characteristic, and one which has endeared him to countless students.

In Adelaide in 1958 he gave a few lectures based on his new interest in Joan Robinson's *The Accumulation of Capital* (1956). In the following year he was entrusted with giving some of the economic theory lectures to advanced students, and most importantly in 1960 he took over the first-year lectures on Keynesian economics. Out of this course emerged a textbook on Keynesian economics (Harcourt *et al.* 1967).[4] During this time he was cementing his friendship with Eric Russell, 'my friend and mentor' (Harcourt 1992a: Ch. 18) and being influenced by him to take an eclectic approach to the analysis of economic problems, while always maintaining his social democratic ideals. Out of this emerged Geoff's middle-way approach to the 'post-energy crisis' problems of advanced capitalist economies and the view that ideology and analysis are indissolubly mixed (see later).

After six years in Adelaide he went back to Cambridge on sabbatical leave which stretched to an absence of over three years as he accepted a lectureship in the Faculty of Economics and Politics and a teaching fellowship at Trinity Hall. By now he was gaining increasing recognition at Cambridge and elsewhere as his publications came under notice. In 1965 the University of Adelaide wisely recognized the merit of his academic performance by promoting him to a readership at the relatively youthful age of 34 while he was still on unpaid leave. A few months after his return from Cambridge at the end of 1966 he was appointed to a personal chair, an honour reserved for outstanding academic achievement and one which is awarded only after the close scrutiny of a group of academic peers.

ADELAIDE – AN AUSTRALIAN ECONOMIST

In 1967 began a period of the most frenetic activity as he combined an academic career played out in the international as well as the Australian sphere with political leadership of the South Australian-based Campaign for Peace in Vietnam (CPV).[5] Now that he was a professor he approached his role of instigating, encouraging and nurturing the research of all about him even more seriously. Apart from continuing to carry a large lecturing and administration load he also took on the supervision of more than his fair share of Master's and Ph.D. students. Invariably he stressed the positive aspects of their work, often 'making a fuss' of what they produced even if it was in rudimentary form. His approach was even-handed, providing encouragement regardless of the views and methodologies adopted and whether they were theoretical or applied.

For almost twenty years, excluding various absences, he organized the Monday Workshop programme at Adelaide and later the Thursday joint seminar with the economists at Flinders University. There was a well-established institution of taking an academic visitor to lunch and dinner, and usually including members of both departments. The atmosphere created was one of friendly, open inquiry, one of an excited seeking after knowledge and insights. Debates and discussions begun in the seminar room were continued in the same amicable atmosphere in the Adelaide tearoom throughout the week.

It is perhaps worth mentioning here the rather extraordinary tearoom culture which was built significantly around Geoff's personality.[6] It was intensely democratic. One of us well recalls a bizarre incident in which a very recent but confident product of the English public school system, who had just arrived to do a doctorate, debated vigorously with Harcourt in full public view and then proceeded to insult him; albeit intellectually. Geoff and the man became good friends, but continued to disagree vigorously, mainly in this case in the tearoom. More seriously, the tearoom was a forum for ideas, a clearinghouse for scandal and gossip, and a wonderful safety valve. Geoff was at its centre, though others graced it. Visitors were astonished at the good-humoured vigour, and many a visitor from North America or elsewhere has bemoaned the fact that there was no such institution back home. As with St Crispin's Day, not to be there at 11 or 4 was to be ashamed, despised and in considerable danger. The tearoom transcended all factions, and indeed seemed for years to preclude them.

There was a downside. Although outsiders – non-economists – were welcomed, some felt greatly intimidated and approached the place like a child on the first day at school. Geoff's love affair with the tearoom was formally recognized in September 1995 when, in his presence, the room was named the G. C. Harcourt Room. It is a measure of the man that we suspect that he would sooner have this modest room named after him than some grand but anonymous building.

The flow of visitors at this time was truly astonishing and must in the main be attributed to Harcourt's networking, though he of course would never use that modish word! They included Harry Johnson, Joan Robinson, Sir John and Lady Hicks, Colin Clark, Pheobus Dhrymes, a very young Ron Jones, Kenneth Boulding (twice), to name but a few. Politicians occasionally dropped in, among them Jim Cairns and our present Governor-General, Bill Hayden. None was spared the tearoom experience. To come to Adelaide to give a seminar was a sought-after guernsey (Australian slang for invitation), as Geoff would say.

His joint editorship of *Australian Economic Papers* (he was first appointed joint editor in 1967), his offices in the South Australian branch of the Economic Society and his presidency of the Australian Economic Society also brought him into frequent communication with a wide range of academics and further enhanced his reputation for providing inspiration as well as sympathetic advice and guidance.

The publication of Harcourt's remarkable assessment of the Cambridge controversies (1972) saw the final cementing of his international recognition and reputation. In the political sphere he had wound down his activities in the CPV in order to find time to write on the Cambridge controversies, but the election of a Labor government in December 1972 and the almost immediate withdrawal of Australian forces from Vietnam dramatically changed the political landscape. His major academic legacy from this period was the reinforcement of his long-held view that *politics and economics are intertwined and that any pretence to the contrary should be exposed*. As a result he tended to express his views more forcefully than hitherto. The euphoria associated with the new Labor government was also wearing away, the growth rate of the Australian economy slowed dramatically and the inflation rate rose above 15 per cent in 1973 and 1974, partly for internal reasons and partly for reasons connected with the first energy crisis of 1973. Here was a fresh opportunity to become involved in the policy debates and to press the implications of his post-Keynesian views.

At Economic Society meetings in 1974 and early 1975 he began to advocate the reintroduction of wage indexation, which had been excised from the centralized wage setting system about 1960. In fact the Labor government succeeded in persuading the Australian Arbitration Commission (as it was then known) to reinstate indexation as part of its wage-fixing policy from the third quarter of 1975. But in December 1975 the Labor government was defeated, to be replaced by a conservative government which adopted and extended the apparently monetarist policies introduced in the last Labor budget in 1975. The case for a coherent post-Keynesian policy cried out to be made and Geoff, along with some colleagues from Adelaide and Flinders Universities, set about making it.[7]

In a paper published in the *Australian Accountant* (1974, reprinted in Harcourt 1986) he set out the bare bones of his view of policy, which came to be known with reference to the collective view as the Adelaide Plan. The 'rampant' Australian inflation was analysed from a Keynesian perspective, identifying the excess demand elements, the cost–push elements associated with wage norms and expected inflation, other distributional factors linked to trade union behaviour, and forces emanating from a non-competitive market structure and small open economy effects with a (relatively) fixed exchange rate. The policy proposal which he favoured was the introduction of indexation not only for money wages but also for pensions. In support of this he implicitly relied on Keynes's analysis of the labour market and especially the issue of the maintenance of real income and the removal of expectations-related uncertainty about it. The price index used to adjust wages (and pensions) should be appropriately adjusted for exchange rate movements and in the light of the major distortion of relativities which had occurred with the inflation explosion of the previous few years. Indexation should be applied only to the equivalent of the minimum wage. In the three months after this paper was written the group behind the Adelaide Plan had emerged with a more comprehensive set of proposals (Harcourt 1986: 245–9; see also Nieuwenhuysen and Drake 1976). The most notable feature of their argument, apart from a confident assessment of the inflationary situation now as being 'wage–price and wage–wage' (Harcourt 1986: 248) which called for proportional indexation of wages, was the view that reductions in the level of aggregate demand were inappropriate in the circumstances.

While Geoff was involved in the grander development of macro policy, he still had time for reflection on more philosophical matters. As the computer revolution developed in the 1970s, there was much speculation about the impact of the new technology on employment levels. In 1978 the *Bulletin* (a weekly Australian news magazine) published the views of a dozen or so economists on this vexed issue of technological unemployment. They were universally optimistic except for Geoff. Harcourt and one of the present authors, who, to quote the *Bulletin*, 'accept that in the past technical change has not created major unemployment and so economists have become "complacent", they believe that computerisation may destroy so many simple jobs, for those whose innate abilities are limited and whose education is narrow or incomplete'. They go on to suggest that 'we may be facing permanent technological unemployment on a previously unthought of scale'. It is not fashionable (yet) twenty years later to attribute consistently high unemployment to this factor, but one suspects that the 'village idiot' effect is a valid component of persistent unemployment and that Geoff's intuition was right. We should note that recognition of the 'village idiot' effect does not show a lack of compassion, but rather a true appreciation of reality. Sweeping jobs and the like are important in providing work for those who through no fault of their own cannot achieve high-level skills and may be sidelined in a technological society.

In 1977 the second massive electoral defeat for the Australian Labor Party led to the appointment of a National Committee of Inquiry on which Geoff Harcourt was invited to serve in his capacity as economist. Here he began to coalesce his views on the policy mix for a mixed economy (Harcourt 1979), and in a semi-political document they were stated with greater force and less analysis than subsequent statements elsewhere. Capitalist economies, he argued, referring to the Keynes–Minsky thesis, were inherently unstable so he took as his starting point the need for an interventionist government policy which directed its attention to distributional issues including the private–public composition of output. Central to his policy approach was the role assigned to incomes policy. This was to be pursued through the arbitral tribunals and be combined with 'both fiscal and monetary policy and be consistent with the rate of growth expected as resources are reallocated and restructuring takes place' (Harcourt 1979: 58). Longer-term policies would promote the development of an infrastructure, and reform should always take account of the impact on the weak and disadvantaged. Thus his approach to the dismantling of the tariff was extremely cautious, almost agnostic.

There is no doubt that the question of the tariff and protection more generally has caused Geoff more agony than most issues. Clearly, economic theory, and indeed the central dogma of economics, unambiguously suggests free trade. However, common sense and humanity decree that there will be losers from free trade, at least during the adjustment period, and the adjustment period in practice may be very long or even for ever. It is a matter of head and heart, but heart is not always wrong. Geoff supported the Whitlam government's tariff reduction policy (1972–5), but now has some regrets about this. In retrospect he would advocate a selective mix of protection and export promotion, though he freely admits that the right mix is elusive. Once again, we see his lack of dogma and his recognition of the essential complexity of economic policy. Not for him the easy and unquestionable solution.

This approach to the vexed free trade problem, which of course has

8

recently been highlighted by crises in the current account, has been addressed by Geoff in several recent papers. Always his humanity and concern for the welfare of others shines through. In several papers in the late 1970s and early 1980s he provided for his policy approach a detailed analytical base, one which was at once in close touch with contemporary economic developments but still retained its Keynesian roots (see especially Harcourt and Kerr 1980; Harcourt 1982). When the Australian Labor Party was elected in March 1983 it adopted a set of policies reflecting the debates to which he had been an important contributor. The centrepiece of its policies was an indexation-based incomes policy which continued to evolve and adapt over the government's term of office. Despite the protestations of the uninhibited free-market economists to the contrary, it is one policy which has been judged as highly successful.

In the wider international sphere, and from his new home in Cambridge, Geoff has welcomed the collapse of the Soviet hegemony, but has not seen this as an *unambiguous* endorsement of Western capitalism. His position has always been that capitalism works, but that it can work much more fairly and better, and that it is the economist's role to see that this happens. This is exemplified in his recent 'offshore' contributions to Australian economic debate, most obviously in his Donald Horne address (Harcourt 1992b) and in a recent paper (Harcourt 1993). In both of these Geoff pursues broad themes in an Australian context.

As a patriot Geoff wants Australia to lead the charge. He himself has contributed greatly to this end and his legacy lives on in the writings of many sometimes relatively obscure scholars. Perhaps Geoff's greatest asset is his optimistic and generous view of humanity, which in the long run beguiles both supporters and opponents.

NOTES

1   One of Geoff's favourite stories against himself relates to an aptitude test which to the best of our memory, wrote him off for intellectual pursuits and suggested that he might aspire to become a chicken farmer! Presumably his Jewish background precluded him from being a 'pig farmer'!

2   At the time this was probably the case to varying degrees at most Australian universities, while the economists who dominated the policy-making departments of the Australian Public Service had also enthusiastically embraced Keynesian economics.

3   Incidentally, during this time he was twice short-listed but did not win a Rhodes Scholarship. For this we must now be eternally grateful. After all, he might have gone to the other place!

4   The course on which the book was based was first taught by P. H. Karmel, who was appointed professor of economics at the age of 27. Harcourt and Wallace followed Karmel in teaching the course but Harcourt's strong Keynesian influence can be seen in the chapters written by him.

5   He has estimated that he spent two and a half days a week on the CPV 'as well

as having a full teaching load, jointly editing *Australian Economic Papers ...*' (Harcourt 1992a: 5) and fulfilling, sometimes in the breach, family duties. In addition he was a long-standing member of the Australian Labor Party and the Howard League for Penal Reform, not to mention his continuing interest in sport in almost all its forms.

6 It should be noted that the intellectual atmosphere which Geoff helped to create did not owe its existence to the collection of Harcourt clones. In fact, the surprising aspect to an outsider was the extent to which his colleagues disagreed with his 'post-Keynesian' views on economics and with his campaign for peace in Vietnam. See our earlier comments on this.

7 Apart from Geoff other academics (at the time) most actively involved included the late Eric Russell, Barry Hughes and Philip Bentley. From the political arena only Ralph Willis, currently (July 1995) the Treasurer in the Keating Labor government, was a participant.

REFERENCES

Harcourt, G. C. (1953) *The 'Reserve' Policy of Australian Companies during the Depression: A Study of Oligopoly in Australia over the Period 1928 to 1934*, Melbourne, University of Melbourne.

—— (1972) *Some Cambridge Controversies in the Theory of Capital*, Cambridge: Cambridge University Press.

—— (1979) 'Economic issues and the future of Australia', in *Australian Labor Party, National Committee of Inquiry*, Flinders University, Adelaide: Australian Political Studies Association Monograph no. 23.

—— (1982) 'Making socialism in your own country', reprinted in Harcourt, G. C., *Controversies in Political Economy: Selected Essays*, ed. O. F. Hamouda, New York: New York University Press.

—— (1986) *Controversies in Political Economy: Selected Essays*, ed. O. F. Hamouda, New York: New York University Press.

—— (1992a) *On Political Economists and Modern Political Economy. Selected Essays of G. C. Harcourt*, ed. C. Sardoni, London: Routledge.

—— (1992b) 'Markets, madness and a middle way', *The Second Annual Donald Horne Address*, Melbourne, 1992, also published in *Australian Quarterly* 64(1): 1–17.

—— (1993) 'A large G & T', *Australian Labour Review* 148: March 34–6, and in an extended version as 'Macroeconomic policy for Australia in the 1990s', *Economics and Labour Relations Review* 4(2): 167–75.

—— (1995a) 'Recollections and reflections of an Australian patriot and a Cambridge economist', *Banca Nationale del Lavoro Quarterly Review* 58: 225–53.

—— (1995b) 'Doing economics', Workshop on Realism in Economics, unpublished: 1–13.

Harcourt, G. and Kerr, P. (1980) 'The mixed economy', in J. North and P. Weller (eds) *Labor: Directions for the Eighties*, Sydney: Ian Novak Publishing.

Harcourt, G. C., Karmel, P. H. and Wallace, R. H. (1967) *Economic Activity*, Cambridge: Cambridge University Press.

Nieuwenhuysen, J. and Drake, P. (eds) (1976) *Essays on Australian Economic Policy*, Melbourne: Melbourne University Press.

Robinson, J. (1956) *The Accumulation of Capital*, London: Macmillan.

Rothschild, K. W. (1947) 'Price theory and oligopoly', *Economic Journal* 57: 299–320.

2

NOTES ON THE SURPLUS APPROACH IN POLITICAL ECONOMY

Heinrich Bortis

[The purpose of economics is] to make the world a better place .... [Economics is] very much a moral as well as a social science and very much a handmaiden of progressive thought. It is really the study of the processes whereby surpluses are created ..., how they are extracted, who gets them and what [is done] with them.

(Harcourt 1986: 5)

INTRODUCTION

The surplus approach in political economy is intimately linked up with the Ricardian theory of value and distribution. Labour time measures the value of the social product, and its division net of land rents (which are determined by the marginal principle) into wages and profits is governed by the surplus principle: fundamentally, the natural wage rate and hence the wage sum are governed by an institutional mechanism and profits appear as a residual, that is, a surplus. The distributional aspect of the surplus principle is closely associated with the production and the use of the surplus. Part of the gross produce is, and indeed must be, used up in the social process of production; that is, as intermediate products, necessary wages and depreciation of fixed capital. The remaining social produce, the social surplus, is at the free disposal of society and might consist of luxury consumption goods or goods serving cultural and social purposes, investment goods or goods required by the state.

The surplus approach was first systematically put to use by François Quesnay in the various versions of his *tableau économique*, where the surplus showed up as *produit net*, that is, rents accruing to the landowners. Later on it dominated classical political economy. Indeed, surplus labour incorporated in profits and rents played a fundamental role in the theoretical systems of David Ricardo and Karl Marx. Subsequently, this principle 'has been submerged and forgotten since the advent of the "marginal" method' (Sraffa 1960: v). Currently, the surplus approach is re-emerging with the slow but steady rise of classical political economy in association with the Keynesian principle of effective demand.

The surplus principle is associated with political economy, not with economics. Political economy deals with the functioning of the socio-economic *system*; economics is concerned with the *behaviour* of producers and consumers, which may be coordinated by the market or by the principle of effective demand according to whether a neoclassical or a Keynesian standpoint is taken. Hence the surplus principle is essentially a *social* principle. To bring to the open the meaning of this proposition with respect to the basic content and method in political economy is the main purpose of this chapter. Moreover, it will be argued that the surplus principle also has an ethical dimension. A few methodological points will also be taken up. However, I first provide some reasons as to why the surplus principle should be put at the place of its rival, namely the marginal principle.

FROM THE MARGINAL TO THE SURPLUS APPROACH

Neoclassical economic theory – the tradition of economic reasoning initiated by Jevons, Walras, Marshall and Menger – is ultimately based upon a single principle (Schumpeter 1954: 998ff.), namely the marginal principle embodied in marginal utilities, marginal products and marginal costs. The principle is intimately associated with the rational, that is, the profit- and utility-maximizing behaviour of economic agents. Their actions are coordinated by the market; that is, the supply and demand apparatus. The market mechanism is supposed to solve all the important economic problems, most importantly value, functional distribution and employment. With sufficient competition an automatic and inherent tendency towards a full-employment equilibrium is expected to prevail.

The starting point of neoclassical theorizing is *exchange*. This emerges from the structure of Walras's *Éléments* (Walras 1874 [1952]). In sections II and III of this work individuals are assumed to be endowed with certain quantities of goods. Utility-maximizing exchange leads to new endowments. Production and distribution are treated subsequently (ibid.: sect. IV) and emerge as an application of exchange. In equilibrium the 'factor prices' equal the corresponding marginal productivities. The 'factors of production' – land, labour and capital – all stand on the same footing within the linear process of production, where they are somehow transformed into final products.

Several corollaries are associated with the neoclassical view. First, exchange is supposed to bring about 'social harmony' in the sphere of distribution; this precludes us from questioning distributional outcomes since functional income distribution is regulated by an objective, even natural mechanism. Moreover, with the social product being distributed on the basis of the marginal principle, the social and circular process of production (*à la* Leontief–Sraffa) and the associated notion of the social surplus do not enter the scene in neoclassical theory. This in turn points to the individualistic nature of neoclassical or liberal economic theory. All economic phenomena are explained on the basis of the optimizing behaviour of individuals. Here the *social* appears as an interaction between individuals. Social processes in the proper sense – the pursuit of a common aim by complementary means requiring cooperation and organization – are not essential to liberal theory. The 'social', most importantly social institutions, is relegated to the framework surrounding the market.

There are serious problems with the demand-and-supply approach first suggested by Adam Smith (Dobb 1973: 47). These are ultimately associated with the fact that production is not a sphere of application of exchange, but is a genuinely social and circular process in the sense of Quesnay, Ricardo, Marx, Leontief, Sraffa and Pasinetti (Pasinetti 1977, 1981, 1993). Systematic criticism of the modern neoclassical theory of value and distribution along these lines started with Sraffa's discussion of the laws of return in the 1920s (Sraffa 1926) and with his *Production of Commodities by Means of Commodities* (Sraffa 1960), which is basic to the capital theory debate of the 1960s. Luigi Pasinetti initiated this debate between the two Cambridges (Pasinetti 1977: 169–77, especially 171 n9), and Geoffrey Harcourt actively took part in it and produced the definitive assessment (Harcourt 1972).

The capital theory debate produced a clear-cut result: there are no regular associations between so-called factor prices and factor quantities. Hence supply and demand cannot solve the great economic problems – value, functional income distribution and employment – in the long run and on a fundamental level (that is, on the level of principles), though it may do so temporarily on the level of appearances. Most importantly, this implies that even under ideal conditions, namely those of perfect competition, prices do not correspond to marginal costs, distribution cannot be regulated by the marginal principle and there is no inherent tendency towards a full-employment equilibrium brought about on the 'labour market'. Hence if production and reproduction is conceived as a social process (*à la* Leontief–Sraffa–Pasinetti) with the scale of activity determined by effective demand and hence fixed, 'the marginal product of a factor (or alternatively the marginal cost of a product) would not merely be hard to find – it just would not be there to be found' (Sraffa 1960: v). The Ricardian–Marxian theory of production and its modern developments – mainly exemplified by Sraffa – is about *proportions* that must be there if the social process of production is to go on smoothly. This implies that within the process of production only *relative* quantities and *relative* prices are determined (Pasinetti 1981: 23 n30). Since changes in the *scale* of production are not considered and the scale cannot be varied at will, marginal products cannot enter the picture.

Even if regular long-period relationships between prices and quantities existed, there would be problems with neoclassical theory. In the real world the position of demand and supply curves inevitably depends upon legal, socioeconomic and political institutions. A socially inappropriate institutional set-up may prevent a full-employment equilibrium from coming into being. This raises the question as to the institutional set-up in line with a market equilibrium. The problem involved is so complex that it seems to defy any solution.

The difficulties related to marginal economic theory in general and to the marginal theory of distribution in particular would suggest abandoning the neoclassical approach and taking up classical and Keynesian political economy, particularly the surplus approach to distribution complemented by the principle of effective demand. Hence the starting point in economic theorizing should not be the individual and exchange but society and production. This means that the social state of affairs, the *social* in short, is not just an interaction between autonomous individuals based on explicit and implicit contracts and hence something derived, as is the case in neoclassical economics. The *social* as is embodied in a monetary production economy and pictured by classical and Keynesian political economy is a state of affairs of its own and is characterized by the common aim to be achieved and the complementary functions to be exercised; the latter require coordination and cooperation. In this sense each enterprise is a social entity. The same is true of the circular process of production, which is perhaps the most important social macro-institution in modern societies.

Hence, the *social* is a part–whole relationship between social classes and society and is as such prior to individuals and their behaviour. This implies that individuals are not in a position to act at all without the presence of a social or institutional foundation. Institutions enable individuals to reach permanently individual and social aims in all spheres of life. Examples of institutions are enterprises and associations of various kinds, but also money and finance and the legal system. A classical arrangement of institutions was proposed by Marx: economic institutions – production, money and finance and the market – form the material basis of society on which an institutional superstructure may be erected, comprising political, legal, social and cultural institutions. Hence society may be conceived of as a structured set of institutions which represents the social structure. The complementarity and interdependence of institutions make society a structured entity possessing laws of its own. One of these social laws is precisely the surplus principle.

THE SURPLUS PRINCIPLE AND THE CONTENT OF POLITICAL ECONOMY

Since production is a social process, the surplus emerging from production is also a social phenomenon; hence the notion of *social surplus*. In this section

14

we first consider some general characteristics of the surplus principle. This is to examine the production, distribution and use of the social surplus. In the second place we briefly consider how value is connected with the surplus principle and deal with the interaction between the scale of economic activity (that is, the level of employment) and the size of the surplus.

The surplus approach can perhaps be characterized most appropriately by considering the production of the surplus in principle, that is, on the most fundamental level, where, for example, the particular conditions of production are abstracted from (Marx 1867 [1974]: 192–330). The productive labour force in the consumption and investment goods sectors requires a certain quantity of goods to reproduce itself, that is, necessary consumption goods, and to reproduce the means of production, that is, replacement investment. To produce these necessary goods a certain amount of labour time, for example person-years, is required. The remaining labour time may be devoted to producing necessary goods and services for unproductive workers and employees in other spheres of production or of the service sector in the broadest sense of the word, including services provided by the state. The latter goods and services represent the surplus, here defined in physical terms, which is, in principle, at the free disposal of society and may, as such, be used for non-necessary and luxury consumption, for accumulation (net investment), social and cultural purposes and for state activities, such as education, administration, the legal system, infrastructure and defence. Hence the surplus consists of all the goods that are at the free disposal of society.

Unproductive labour is of course unproductive only in a technical, not in a social sense. This type of labour, though it does not contribute to the production of the surplus directly, contributes to the proper functioning of society and hence to the production of the surplus indirectly, for example through a well-functioning legal system and through an education system which enhances technical progress and thereby contributes to increasing the volume of the surplus.

The essentially social nature of the surplus means that distribution of incomes in general and of the surplus in particular are equally social issues. Distribution is 'the principal problem in Political Economy' (Ricardo 1821 [1951]: 5). Ricardo was the first to express analytically the social nature of distribution, which he perceived as a complex social problem involving intricate part–whole relationships, that is, relationships between social classes and society as a whole. His approach to deal with distribution was based upon the function in society of the great income categories, that is, wages, profits and rents. For example, the natural wage rate or 'the natural price of labour is that price which is necessary to enable the labourers ... to subsist and to perpetuate their race, without either increase or diminution' (ibid.: 93). The natural wage is determined not economically, that is, by markets, nor by physiological conditions, but by society, that is, social institutions:

It is not to be understood that the natural price of labour, estimated even in food and necessaries, is absolutely fixed and constant. It varies at different times in the same country, and very materially differs in different countries. It essentially depends on the habits and customs of the people.

(ibid.: 96–7)

The market wage rate is of secondary importance:

The market price of labour is the price which is really paid for it, from the natural operation of the proportion of the supply to the demand . . . . However much the market price of labour may deviate from its natural price, it has, like commodities, a tendency to conform to it.

(ibid.: 94)

With the natural wage rate determined, profits are a residual, i.e. part of the surplus, determined on marginal land: 'in all countries, and all times, profits depend on the quantity of labour requisite to provide necessaries for the labourers, on that land or with that capital which yields no rent' (ibid.: 126). The social function of profits is to ensure the accumulation of capital which may, in turn, act favourably upon the level of the natural wage rate (ibid.: ch. xi). Land rents are another part of the surplus and are socially far less useful since they are mainly devoted to luxury consumption. Consequently, Ricardo always advocated that the interest of the country required cheap food, associated with small rents, low money wages and large profit volumes. Clearly, distribution is in Ricardo's view a matter of proportions, that is, a set of part–whole relationships. The question is how a *given* social product ought, in a first step, to be divided into wages and the surplus and how the surplus is to be distributed subsequently.

With the income shares given, the determination of structures, particularly the wage structure, represents another important distributional problem. In the labour theory of value, which is inevitably associated with the surplus principle, the structure of wages is linked with the determination of the reduction coefficients. The latter govern the socioeconomic status of the various categories of labour if either the entire economy is considered or the individual workers on the enterprise level. Among the empirical work done in this domain, Phelps Brown's (1977) *Inequality of Pay* is certainly one of the most important attempts to come to grips with the determination of the wage structure.

The problems associated with the determination of the shares of wages, profits and rents in income and of the wage structure point to the immense complexity of the distributional problem. This is so because distribution is a genuinely social problem, where proportions or part–whole relations play a fundamental role.

Distribution is the fundamental problem in political economy in the sense

16

that distribution is logically prior to other issues in political economy, such as value and employment. Regarding value, Dobb argues that in

> the system of determination envisaged by Ricardo ... there was a crucial sense in which distribution was *prior* to exchange: namely, that price-relations or exchange-values could only be arrived at *after* the principle affecting distribution of the total product had been postulated.
> (Dobb 1973: 169; emphasis in original)

The prices of production are determined once the real wage rate or the rate of profit is fixed.

The relationship between distribution and the prices of production can perhaps be explained best by considering the Sraffian price system. To render the system of prices of production determinate either the real wage rate or the rate of profit has to be determined outside the production system (Pasinetti 1977: 73). Some classical economists opted for determining the real wage rate; specifically, Ricardo argued that the natural wage rate was governed by institutional factors (Ricardo 1821 [1951]: 93ff); here profits appear as a residual. Modern post-Keynesian economists argue that the rate of profits is determined by the rate of growth (e.g. Pasinetti 1962). Other theoretical justifications for the rate of profit could be provided. For example, profits could, in a Marshallian vein, be considered the earnings of management (Marshall 1920: 596–628), justified by the inherent difficulties of coordination arising in any genuinely social institution – such as the firm – constituting more than the sum of its parts.

Once functional income distribution is determined, a two-sided link between the surplus principle and the principle of effective demand associated with a theory of the scale of employment emerges. On the one hand, the share of the surplus (profits, and rents on non-reproducible goods, that is, land, privileges and special skills) in national income is a determinant of economic activity (that is, output and employment): a higher surplus share is, in principle, associated with a lower employment level and vice versa. Since less is consumed out of the surplus than out of necessary wages, the demand for consumption goods increases if income is redistributed in favour of wages, which, in principle, is associated with higher output and employment levels. This emerges from the supermultiplier relation (Bortis 1984: 600, relations 12 and 13), which states that the long-period level of output and employment is governed by a set of institutionally determined long-period effective demand components.

On the other hand, long-period effective demand governs the volume of the surplus. Permanent unemployment means that the volume of the surplus (profits and rents) is reduced. Indeed, if the supermultiplier formula (ibid.: 600, relation 12) is solved for the surplus volume, the latter depends on the volume of output and employment, which is basically governed by the export multiplier (the reciprocal of the import coefficient times the terms of trade) on the level of government expenditures, on the long-period investment volume that is required to maintain the productive capacities determined by the foreign trade mechanism and, finally, on the reciprocal value of the leakage coefficient associated with property income, that is, the sum of the tax and of the saving ratio. This mechanism of surplus determination implies that there would be profits even if there was no net investment; in this case the volume of net profits would equal government expenditures multiplied by the reciprocal of the profit tax coefficient.

ETHICAL IMPLICATIONS OF THE SURPLUS PRINCIPLE

The social sciences are ethical or moral sciences because each social action or each social phenomenon embodies an ethical dimension, in the same way as a body implies weight. In this vein Keynes wanted 'to emphasize strongly the point about economics being a moral science' (letter to Harrod, 16 July 1938, Keynes 1973: 300). Two points ought to be noted in this context. The first is on the meaning of ethics in the social sciences, the second about the relationship between ethics and the real world.

In the social sciences it is necessarily social or political ethics that is relevant, not individual ethics. The latter is about ethically correct behaviour regarding individual aims or regarding the relations between individuals, as are associated with explicit or implicit contracts, for example. The former, however, is associated with the ethically appropriate organization of society. Here the notion of the common weal or of the public interest is basic. The common weal would imply a social state of affairs such that each individual could realize his or her natural dispositions and abilities. A most important component of the common weal is the socially appropriate organization of the material basis of a society, that is, the process production, the distribution of the surplus, markets and the monetary and financial system. This in turn implies that employment and distribution are central issues in political or social ethics. The common weal is a fundamentally social notion since the various social institutions, that is, the material basis (production, distribution, exchange and money), and the political, legal, social and cultural super-structure are essentially complementary. This gives rise to complex part–whole relationships between the different spheres of social life and the common weal.

The ethical nature of the social sciences shows up most forcefully in the concept of *distributive justice*, which embodies the ethically appropriate relationship between the incomes and income shares accruing to individuals and social groups and total (national) income. This objectively given but largely unknown notion would imply ethically correct income shares and reduction coefficients determining the wage structure, and represents a part–whole relationship. If distributive justice were realized, prices based on labour

18

values would represent just prices, as is the case, for example, with Pasinetti's natural prices (Pasinetti 1981, 1993). Just prices would in turn be associated with justice in exchange which represents *commutative justice*. This notion is related to behaviour, whereas distributive justice is associated with the social system.

The common weal and the real world are linked up with the notion of *alienation* in the sense Marx coined it in his *Paris Manuscripts* (Marx 1844 [1973]: 510ff.). Alienation may perhaps be grasped most easily if it is conceived of as the gap that exists between the real world and the social preconditions for the common weal. Marx clearly perceived that, basically, alienation was related not to the behaviour of individuals but the functioning of the system. For him, economic alienation (for example, alienation occurring in the economic sphere) was fundamental. He argued that the institution of private property was the basic cause of alienation (ibid.: 523ff.). In hindsight this is a very fragile argument. Indeed, one can plausibly argue with Aristotle and Aquinas that private property is a highly important social institution which induces individuals to behave responsibly, to care about things and hence to prevent the squandering of scarce natural resources. Keynes's views on the basic defects of capitalist systems seem more plausible than Marx's: 'The outstanding faults of the economic society in which we live are its failure to provide for full employment and its arbitrary and inequitable distribution of incomes' (Keynes 1936 [1973]: 372).

Thus the real world and the common weal are linked by the concept of alienation, which implies that a social situation embodying the common weal would correspond to the ethically appropriate form of the same real-world situation. Hence each reduction of alienation or each social improvement which tends to approach some social situation to the common weal has a social ethical dimension. This also holds if inappropriate social and economic policies are pursued which widen the gap between the common weal situation and some actually prevailing situation. Since society is an entity made up of a complementary system of institutions – that is, the material basis and the institutional superstructure – the common weal and system-caused alienation are essentially social notions encompassing the entire society. This in turn implies that the social sciences which deal with the functioning of socio-economic systems are essentially moral sciences.

In this view the surplus principle is crucially important in social or political ethics for two basic reasons. First, the distribution of the surplus is a fundamental social problem *per se*. Without a socially acceptable distribution of the surplus the orderly functioning of a society is threatened in the short or long term. A second reason is provided by the link existing between the surplus principle and the principle of effective demand as expressed by the supermultiplier relation (Bortis 1984). A more equal distribution of income and wealth is, in principle, associated with higher output and employment levels and, eventually, larger *volumes* of the surplus. Schumpeter perhaps rightly thought that the close link between distribution and the scale of economic activity was the essence of the Keynesian revolution: '[Keynes's] doctrine ... can easily be made to say both that "who tries to save destroys real capital" and that, *via* saving, "the unequal distribution of income is the ultimate cause of unemployment". *This* is what the Keynesian Revolution amounts to' (Schumpeter 1946: 517).

METHODOLOGICAL ISSUES

Two broadly related methodological points are important in this context. The first is linked to the social nature of the surplus principle; the second to the theory of knowledge, with which it is associated.

The surplus principle is essentially of a social nature: distribution is a part–whole relationship with relations between individuals and social classes on the one hand and society on the other, and not a symmetric relation between individuals, as is portrayed by the neoclassical factor markets. In this view the fundamental issue is 'functional' income distribution; that is, the distribution of national income among social classes or into broad income categories in the form of wages, profits and rents. The important point is about the social function of these income categories. For example, Ricardo argued that wages ensure the maintenance of the labour force; the natural wage which would keep the population constant is a sociological datum. Or else, the social function of profits was to provide finance for accumulation. Since rents were largely spent on luxury consumption goods, which are not very useful socially, Ricardo advocated a redistribution of incomes from rents to profits.

The determination of the structure of wages, profits and rents is also a social issue embodying part–whole relationships. Here, the structure of wages as is implicitly based on Ricardian–Marxian reduction coefficients is particularly important.

Hence the social nature of distribution leads to sociological or institutional distribution theories of immense complexity since the whole of the institutional set-up of society is involved directly or indirectly, including trade unions, the state, customs and habits, power relations and others. John Stuart Mill in his *Principles of Political Economy*, published in 1848, perhaps expressed best the basic idea underlying the sociological or institutional theory of income distribution:

> The laws and conditions of production of wealth partake the character of physical truths. There is nothing optional or arbitrary in them. It is not so with the Distribution of Wealth. That is a matter of human institution solely.... The distribution of wealth ... depends on the laws and customs of society. The rules by which it is determined, are what the opinions and feelings of the ruling portion of the community make them, and are very different in different ages and countries; and might

still be more different, if mankind so chose.

(quoted in Baranzini and Scazzieri 1986: 37)

The institutional determination of distribution, though very simple in principle, becomes of organic complexity in the real world since all institutions of a society enter the scene directly or indirectly. This is due to the fact that society may be conceived of as a set of interrelated and complementary institutions and thus forms an entity governed by laws of its own, such as the surplus principle of distribution and the principle of effective demand. The organic complexity of societies implies that causation (for example, the determination of distributional shares and structures) is also organically complex. To explain some concrete distributional outcome requires not only a knowledge of theoretical principles; familiarity with the situation being considered is also necessary.

The fact that societies are specific entities characterized by particular institutional set-ups implies that market equilibria are of a secondary importance, mainly because the position of demand and supply curves – if they existed! – depends upon institutions other than the market. The relevant equilibria in political economy are *system equilibria*, represented by Sraffian-type prices of production, long-period output levels governed by the supermultiplier relation (Bortis 1984) and institutionally determined distributional outcomes along the lines indicated by the surplus principle.

Knowledge about social phenomena in general and about the surplus principle in particular is always probable in Keynes's sense (Keynes 1921 [1971]). Objective truth exists but our knowledge of it is always imperfect or reliant on probability to a greater or lesser degree. Knowledge flows from two sources: from the consideration of principles and from empirical and historical observation, but of these the former seems more important, as a quick glance at the history of economic theory shows. Indeed all the great authors have written on principles.

CONCLUDING REMARKS

On account of its essentially social character the surplus principle is intimately connected with political economy and does not fit into a system of economics which is based on the marginal principle. More specifically, the surplus principle is basic in Ricardo's sociological or institutional distribution theory. This is perhaps the most important reason why Ricardo called his main work *Principles of Political Economy and Taxation*. The marginal principle, however, is essentially individualistic: the individual economic agents are supposed to get their share of the national product without social institutions and arrangements acting as intermediaries. The marginal principle is associated with the view that the optimizing behaviour of individuals in the economic domain is, under competitive conditions, coordinated in a *socially* sensible way by the – anonymous – market mechanism. Consequently Marshall entitled his book *Principles of Economics*.

Geoffrey Harcourt, as a pupil of Joan Robinson, is, quite naturally, one of the most prominent critics of the marginal principle (Harcourt 1972). There is little doubt that the capital theoretic critique has contributed to putting the surplus principle of distribution to the fore again. This opens exciting perspectives. The surplus principle leads immediately to the Ricardian–Sraffian prices of production (Pasinetti 1977) and to Pasinetti's natural system (Pasinetti 1981, 1993). Value and distribution deal with proportions that must be fulfilled to enable the process of production and reproduction to go on in a technically and socially orderly way. However, the surplus principle may be combined easily with the Keynesian principle of effective demand (Bortis 1984). This means dealing with the scale of economic activity. Subsequently, interactions between proportions and scale may be investigated. More specifically, this may mean dealing with the interactions between distribution and the employment level. All this would amount to synthesizing the classical proportions-based and the Keynesian scale-based strands of thought in a great system of classical–Keynesian political economy which, in a Keynesian vein, would constitute a branch of social ethics. As one of the most eminent post-Keynesian political economists, Geoffrey Harcourt has made a substantial contribution to this undertaking.

REFERENCES

Baranzini, M. and Scazzieri, R. (eds) (1986) *Foundations of Economics: Structures of Enquiry and Economic Theory*, Oxford: Basil Blackwell.

Bortis, H. (1984) 'Employment in a capitalist economy', *Journal of Post Keynesian Economics* 6(4): 590–604.

Dobb, M. (1973) *Theories of Value and Distribution since Adam Smith: Ideology and Economic Theory*, Cambridge: Cambridge University Press.

Harcourt, G. C. (1972) *Some Cambridge Controversies in the Theory of Capital*, Cambridge: Cambridge University Press.

—— (1986) *Controversies in Political Economy: Selected Essays of G. C. Harcourt*, ed. O. F. Hamouda. Brighton: Wheatsheaf.

Keynes, J. M. (1921 [1971]) *A Treatise on Probability*. London: Macmillan.

—— (1936 [1973]) *The General Theory of Employment, Interest and Money*, in *The Collected Writings of John Maynard Keynes*, vol. 7, London: Macmillan for the Royal Economic Society.

—— (1973) *The General Theory and After*: Part II, *Defence and Development*, in *The Collected Writings of John Maynard Keynes*, vol. 14, London: Macmillan for the Royal Economic Society.

Marshall, A. (1920) *Principles of Economics*, 8th edition, London: Macmillan.

Marx, K. 1844 [1974] 'Ökonomisch–philosophische Manuskripte aus dem Jahre 1844', in Marx–Engels, *Werke, Ergänzungsband*, Berlin: Dietz-Verlag.

—— 1867 [1973] *Das Kapital*, vol. 1, Berlin: Dietz-Verlag.

Pasinetti, L. L. (1962) 'Rate of profit and income distribution in relation to the rate of economic growth', *Review of Economic Studies* 29: 267–79.

—— (1977) *Lectures on the Theory of Production*. Basingstoke: Macmillan.

—— (1981) *Structural Change and Economic Growth: A Theoretical Essay on the Dynamics of the Wealth of Nations*, Cambridge: Cambridge University Press.

—— (1993) *Structural Economic Dynamics: A Theory of the Consequences of Human Learning*, Cambridge: Cambridge University Press.

Phelps Brown, H. (1977) *The Inequality of Pay*, Oxford: Oxford University Press.

Ricardo, D. (1821 [1951]) *On the Principles of Political Economy and Taxation*, ed. Piero Sraffa with the collaboration of Maurice Dobb, Cambridge: Cambridge University Press.

Schumpeter, J. A. (1946) 'John Maynard Keynes, 1883–1946', *American Economic Review* 36: 495–518.

—— (1954) *History of Economic Analysis*, London: Allen & Unwin.

Sraffa, P. (1926) 'The laws of return under competitive conditions', *Economic Journal* 36: 535–50.

—— (1960) *Production of Commodities by Means of Commodities*, Cambridge: Cambridge University Press.

Walras, L. (1874 [1952]) *Éléments d'économie politique pure ou Théorie de la richesse sociale*, Paris: Librairie Générale de Droit et de Jurisprudence.

3

THE SAVINGS DEBATE IN AUSTRALIA AND THE MEANING OF CAPITAL

Paul Dalziel

Looking back with hindsight from the early 1990s, we may say that the capital theory controversies of the 1950s to 1970s related not so much to the *measurement* of capital as to its *meaning* (Harcourt, 1976). Related to this perspective is the following question: what is the appropriate method with which to analyse processes occurring in capitalist economies (especially those related to production, distribution and accumulation)?

(Harcourt 1994a: 29)

Geoffrey Harcourt begins his entry in *A Biographical Dictionary of Dissenting Economists* by describing himself as 'an Australian patriot and a Cambridge economist' (Arestis and Sawyer 1992: 232). The description is well founded. Apart from his own important contributions to post-Keynesian economics, Harcourt is renowned for his surveys and commentaries on the 'Cambridge controversies in the theory of capital' (see Harcourt 1969, 1972, 1976, 1994a), and a long absence from his home country has not dulled his passionate interest in Australian economic policy issues (see Harcourt and Kerr 1980; Harcourt, 1982, 1992) These two strands in Harcourt's professional career were appropriately recognized when, in the 1994 Queen's Birthday Honours List, he was made an officer in the General Division of the Order of Australia, to the delight of his friends and colleagues.

Australian economic policy and Cambridge capital theory are also brought together in this chapter, written to honour Geoffrey Harcourt's contributions to economics on the occasion of his sixty fifth birthday. Its focus is a current issue in Australian policy debates, namely whether the Australian government should take steps to encourage a higher domestic aggregate saving rate. As will be discussed shortly, the proponents of this policy are motivated by an expectation that a higher saving rate will produce faster capital accumulation without unsustainable increases in overseas debt. It will be argued in this chapter that such an expectation relies on a particular view of the *meaning* of capital, and, as the quotation at the head of the chapter observes, the issue of what 'capital' means lies at the heart of the Cambridge controversies – a point often made by Joan Robinson (see Robinson 1975: vi, for example). It will be further argued that the view of the meaning of capital held by those advocating a higher saving rate in Australia is inappropriate, and that a correct view based on the analysis of the Cambridge school leads to very different policy conclusions.

This chapter also addresses the second question highlighted by Harcourt in the above quotation: what is the appropriate method with which to analyse processes occurring in capitalist economies? It does this by adopting a diagrammatic version of process analysis recently described by Meade (1993) and used in Dalziel and Harcourt (1994) and Dalziel (1996) in related contexts. Process analysis is a methodology with an honourable history in economic thought, but one which seems to have fallen into general disfavour in orthodox economic modelling (see, for example, Chick 1984; Cottrell 1986; Earl 1990, ch. 10; Dalziel 1995: ch. 3 for recent discussions). The method's approach is to suppose some initial event, and then to analyse the processes that occur as a result. Following the Cambridge understanding of the meaning of capital, the initial event in the analysis below is investment expenditure, and the subsequent discussion traces the implications for income, saving, consumption, imports and exports.

THE ARGUMENT FOR RAISING AUSTRALIA'S SAVING RATE

The proposal that government policy should aim to increase the level of national saving in Australia has been argued most forcefully by FitzGerald (1993) in a recent report commissioned by the Australian Federal Treasurer. The FitzGerald Report reviews household saving, provision for retirement policies, business saving and government fiscal strategies, before setting out a national saving strategy for Australia. The need for such a strategy is motivated in the report by a number of concerns. The first is that the level of national saving in Australia 'is now at its lowest level this century other than in the "national emergencies" of the two World Wars and the Great Depression' (FitzGerald 1993: 2). The second is that continued growth 'will require sustained strong flows of investment [that] will in turn require strong flows of saving' (ibid.: 4). The third is that a level of overseas debt that is already high means that 'Australia cannot grow with strong investment funded by raising foreign debt further (relative to GDP) indefinitely' (ibid.: 6). Finally, demographic trends mean that 'Australia has not only a national saving problem but also a need for strong retirement saving' (ibid.: 8).

Post-Keynesian readers will recognize that FitzGerald's second concern (which in many ways underlies the other three) is completely at odds with what Keynes called the most fundamental of his conclusions within this field; namely, that 'the investment market . . . can never become congested through shortage of saving' (Keynes 1937: 222). This point has been made by

Trethewey (1994) in a critique of the FitzGerald Report, by Harcourt and Kitson (1993: 440) in a similar American context, and more generally by a number of writers after Asimakopulos (1983) argued otherwise in the *Cambridge Journal of Economics* (see Bibow 1995; Dalziel 1996; Harcourt *et al.* 1995 for recent summaries of this debate). This chapter will not repeat that analysis, but will instead concentrate on the FitzGerald Report's third point of concern, namely that inadequate domestic saving leads to current account deficits in the balance of payments, and hence to rising overseas debt.

The FitzGerald Report's justification for its concern about the current account is derived from the income and expenditure identities of the National Income Accounts:

$$W + P + T \equiv C_p + C_g + I_p + I_g + X - M \qquad (3.1)$$

where W is after-tax wage income, P is after-tax profit income, T is total direct and indirect tax revenue, C is consumption expenditure, I is investment expenditure, the subscripts p and g denote the private and government sectors respectively, X is exports and M is imports. Private-sector saving is defined to be $W + P - C_p$, denoted S_p, while public-sector saving, S_g, is defined to be $T - C_g$. Hence equation (3.1) can be rearranged to read:

$$M - X \equiv (I_p - S_p) + (I_g - S_g) \qquad (3.2)$$

As Trethewey (1994: 23) observes, equation (3.2) 'is based on national accounting identities which say nothing about cause and effect'. Nevertheless, the approach taken in the FitzGerald Report (sect. 2.3, pp. 36–9) is to project a possible path for each of the four variables on the right-hand side of equation (3.2), and to use these projections to calculate the outlook for Australia's saving–investment imbalance, and hence for its current account deficit. Thus, it is assumed that the difference between investment and saving determines the current account deficit, as is explicitly claimed on p. 8 of the report (see also chart 1.8 on p. 9). The projections produce 'a continuing widening of the saving and investment gap – that is, a widening current account deficit' (p. 39), and the remainder of the report is devoted to analysing how Australia might raise domestic saving to support stronger ongoing growth, by recommending ways in which government policy could raise the underlying structural rate of saving from about 18 per cent of GDP to as high as 23 per cent. In particular, the report urges greater fiscal restraint at both state and Commonwealth levels.

The credibility and feasibility of the recommendations have been questioned (see especially Black 1994; Horne 1994), but this is not the line of criticism pursued in this chapter. Instead, the following sections address the more fundamental issue raised by the report's methodology (which is by no means unique to either the FitzGerald Report or to the savings debate in Australia): namely, whether it is realistic to *assume* that a current account deficit is determined by the difference between the independent behaviour of domestic investment and domestic saving. This, it turns out, depends on 'the meaning of capital'.

THE MEANING OF CAPITAL

In keeping with the Australian and Cambridge theme of this chapter, the conflicting views about the meaning of capital can be introduced by considering two publications that appeared exactly forty years ago, one written by an Australian economist, Trevor Swan, and the other written by a Cambridge economist, Joan Robinson. Both authors were concerned with the analysis of capital accumulation, and indeed Swan (1956) makes several references to Robinson (1956). Both have become foundational items in the literature, with the former giving rise to the Swan–Solow neoclassical growth model (see also Solow 1956) and the latter remaining an important building block in the post-Keynesian theory of economic growth (see, for example, the importance attached to it in Eichner and Kregel's famous 1975 survey, especially p. 1295). Consider, first, Joan Robinson's view of the process of capital accumulation, summarized in the following quotation:

> The accumulation of capital over the long run takes place as the result of decisions to invest made in a succession of short-period situations, for every day the sun rises upon an economy which has, that day, a particular who's who of capital goods in existence, and a particular state of expectations based upon past experience and the diagnosis of current trends.
>
> (Robinson 1956: 198)

Because capital accumulation depends on *investment* decisions, which in turn depend on expectations, capital accumulation is a very uncertain business in Robinson's model. Indeed, when Robinson comes to consider the benchmark case in which technical progress is neutral, the time pattern of production is invariant, there are no financial constraints and entrepreneurs are content to accumulate at the same proportional rate as in the past, she describes this example as 'a golden age' to indicate 'that it represents a mythical state of affairs not likely to obtain in any actual economy' (ibid.: 99). The focus of her work, therefore, is on the behaviour of *entrepreneurs* – the people who make the investment expenditure decisions. If entrepreneurs pursue capital accumulation with vigour, something approaching the golden age is possible (ibid.: 213), but if competition is blunted and the urge to accumulate slackens as the capital stock increases, the economy is liable to fall into a state of stagnation (ibid.: 176).

Consider now the approach taken by Trevor Swan, summarized in the following quotation:

27

In a given state of the arts, the annual output Y depends on the stock of capital K and the labour force N, according to the constant-elasticity production function $Y = K^\alpha N^\beta$. With constant returns to scale, $\alpha + \beta = 1$. The annual addition to the capital stock is the amount saved sY, where s is a given ratio of saving to output (or income).

(Swan 1956: 334–5)

Because capital accumulation depends on *saving* decisions, and because it is assumed explicitly that 'effective demand is so regulated ... that all savings are profitably invested, productive capacity is fully utilized, and the level of employment can never be increased merely by raising the level of spending' (ibid.: 335; see Solow 1956: 91 for a similar statement), capital accumulation proceeds smoothly in Swan's model. In particular, the equilibrium output:capital ratio is shown to be stable, so that 'the given rate of growth of labour thus determines the equilibrium growth rate of the whole economy, while the saving ratio determines the output–capital ratio at which equilibrium will occur' (Swan 1956: 336). The focus of Swan's work, therefore, is on the behaviour of *savers*, and he shows, for example, that an increase in the saving ratio from 5 to 10 per cent would cause output per head and the wage rate to be higher in the new equilibrium, whereas the output:capital ratio and the profit rate would be lower (ibid.: 337).

These two quotations represent radically different views of capital accumulation that could be just as readily illustrated by any number of references in the post-Keynesian and neoclassical literatures of the past forty years. In Robinson's world-view, priority is given to the investment decisions of entrepreneurs (which then determine aggregate saving), whereas in Swan's world-view, priority is given to the saving decisions of income earners (which then determine aggregate investment). Since everyone knows that actual investment always equals actual saving (by definition), however, and since planned investment must equal planned saving in any sort of macroeconomic equilibrium, the reader might object that the contrast just described is simply two ways of approaching the same phenomenon. This is not so. At the heart of the contrast is two very different understandings of the nature of capital.

For Joan Robinson, the stock of capital is made up of specific buildings, plant, machinery and so on, each example of which is more or less purpose-built for its particular line of production. This has two implications. First, it means that for an individual entrepreneur, if 'the market for the type of production concerned shrinks unexpectedly, the value of the capital goods falls or vanishes completely' (Robinson 1956: 5–6). This is what makes investment so uncertain, and hence is why the expectations of entrepreneurs are critical in determining capital accumulation. Second, the income flows that generate the saving flows to accommodate new capital formation cannot occur *until* the investment expenditure has taken place. Hence, 'it is necessary to guard against the confusion of thinking of rentier thriftiness as providing finance for investment' (ibid.: 276); it is only when the new factory (for example) has been built that the associated saving can take place (a point to which the discussion below will return in the context of international capital flows).

For Trevor Swan, on the other hand,

> capital is made up of a large number of identical Meccano sets, which never wear out and can be put together, taken apart, and reassembled with negligible cost or delay in a great variety of models so as to work with various combinations of Labour and Land, to produce various products, and to incorporate the latest technical innovations illustrated in successive issues of the Instruction Book.
>
> (Swan 1956: 344)

In this case, the role of the entrepreneur virtually disappears, or at least is greatly simplified to finding the least-cost combinations of labour and capital to produce the required volume of output, which is assumed to be maintained at its full-employment level (as cited above). Given these assumptions, it is then not unreasonable for the neoclassical growth model to suppose that the number of Meccano sets produced each period is set by the level of voluntary saving out of full-employment income. To say that it is not unreasonable, however, is not the same thing as saying the supposition is realistic.

In fact, the supposition is not realistic. The year 1991–2, for example, in which national saving reached its low of 16 per cent of GDP (the experience which led to the concerns recorded in the FitzGerald Report), was also a year in which the official unemployment rate in Australia reached 10.5 per cent on its way to a peak of 11.3 per cent in December 1992, so that Trevor Swan's full-employment assumption was not even approximately satisfied. Instead, the Australian experience of that period is easy to explain using the standard Keynesian theory of a recession triggered by a fall in investment production as real interest rates were raised by policymakers to combat inflation (adversely affecting 'animal spirits'). The slowdown in capital accumulation implied by the fall in investment meant that the economy had a reduced capacity to absorb saving, which no policy to increase the saving rate could have overcome.

The starting point of this chapter, therefore, is a claim that it is Joan Robinson's view of capital that is the more realistic one, and is the one that is relevant for macroeconomic advice. That is, if policymakers are concerned to increase economic growth, the focus of their attention should be on the investment decisions of entrepreneurs rather than on the saving decisions of income earners. Further, the remainder of the chapter will argue that it is this same misconceived focus on saving behaviour (rather than on capital goods production) that leads to the widespread concern about current account deficits in the balance of payments and to the unsound policy conclusions found in studies such as the FitzGerald Report.

A PROCESS ANALYSIS

In this and the following section, the problem under review is analysed using a diagrammatic version of process analysis. Before the analysis is presented, a number of preliminary remarks may be useful. First, to simplify matters but without loss of generality it will be assumed that the domestic country experiences a balance of payments current account deficit with the rest of the world. Domestic country variables will be denoted by upper-case symbols and rest-of-the-world variables by the equivalent lower-case symbol. Again in keeping with the focus on the meaning of capital, a distinction will be made between international trade in capital goods and international trade in consumption goods. Finally, only net transactions will be considered, so that the domestic economy is assumed not to export any capital goods and only foreign residents are assumed to hold some portion of their saving outside their own economy.

Consider Figure 3.1, which is divided into halves. The left-hand side depicts the process of expenditure and income flows in the domestic country

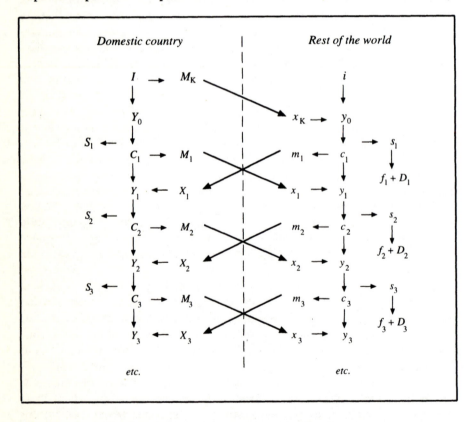

Figure 3.1 A process analysis with international capital flows

30

after a certain level of domestic investment expenditure, I, while the right-hand side depicts the flows in the rest of the world after its investment expenditure, i. The possibility of international trade in capital goods, however, means that a country's investment expenditure need not be the same as its investment production. Suppose that the domestic economy imports capital goods to the value of M_K (which must equal the value of capital goods exported from the rest of the world, x_K). Then the income earned by factors of production in the domestic capital goods industries is given by:

$$I - M_K = Y_0 \qquad (3.3)$$

Y_0 is the domestic income earned in the initial round of the process analysis, as shown in the second row of the left-hand side of Figure 3.1. Out of this income, households purchase consumption goods and services, denoted C_1, and the remainder is saved, S_1. International trade in consumption goods means that some of this consumption expenditure will leak into imported goods, M_1, causing an increase in exports, x_1, in the rest of the world. In many models, it is traditional to assume that the marginal propensity to consume and the marginal propensity to import are fixed fractions of income, but these restrictions are not necessary in this general model. The consumption expenditure on domestic goods $(C_1 - M_1)$ plus exports (X_1) brought about by imports into the rest of the world equals the amount of income generated at the end of the first round of the multiplier process, Y_1. This income in turn creates further consumption and saving flows (with the associated international trade), so that in every round of the process, $r \geq 1$, the following relationship holds:

$$I - M_K = \sum_{j=1}^{r} S_j + \sum_{j=1}^{r} (M_j - X_j) + Y_r \qquad (3.4)$$

That is, at every point in the process, the initial level of investment production is distributed among accumulated voluntary saving, accumulated current account deficits in consumption goods and the income generated in the latest round not yet spent or voluntarily saved. Eventually (or perhaps asymptotically) a round occurs in which all income is saved both domestically and in the rest of the world. At this point, domestic consumption and exports are zero, and so the multiplier process stops. Y_r in equation (3.4) is zero in this final round, and, using non-subscripted symbols to denote the values of the accumulated variables, the analysis reveals that:

$$I - M_K = S + (M - X) \qquad (3.5)$$

The analysis for the rest of the world is similar, with one important additional element. In every round, foreign income earners hold their savings, s, in some combination of their own countries' financial assets, f, and debt issued by residents of the domestic economy, D. The process analysis then shows that:

$$i + x_K = y_0 \tag{3.6}$$

$$= \sum_{j=1}^{r} s_j + \sum_{j=1}^{r} (m_j - x_j) + y_r \qquad \text{for every round } r \geq 1 \tag{3.7}$$

$$= s + (m - x) \tag{3.8}$$

$$= (f + D) + (m - x) \tag{3.9}$$

Finally, equilibrium in the domestic economy's foreign exchange markets requires that its current account deficit must be matched by capital account inflows; that is:

$$M_K + M - X = D \tag{3.10}$$

These equations, and the flows recorded in Figure 3.1, now allow a discussion of the causes of current account deficits, and what impact policies to increase an economy's aggregate national saving rate may have on a persistent deficit.

DISCUSSION OF THE ANALYSIS

To begin the discussion of the process analysis in the previous section, note that equations (3.5) and (3.8) produce within a global economy context the standard Keynesian result that investment expenditure generates an equal amount of voluntary saving through the multiplier process (see, for example, Keynes 1936: 63–5; Meade 1993; Dalziel and Harcourt 1994). This is obtained by adding equation (3.8) to equation (3.5) and eliminating the offsetting sides of international trade transactions:

$$I + i = S + s \tag{3.11}$$

Thus, in a global context, it remains true that 'the investment market ... can never become congested through shortage of saving' (Keynes 1937: 222). Saving is induced by investment expenditure, again lending support to the post-Keynesian emphasis on investment decisions by entrepreneurs as the primary focus for explaining the accumulation of capital. There remains, however, the question of how the saving is distributed between domestic and foreign residents.

This question can be approached in two steps. First, substitute equation (3.10) into equation (3.9) to obtain:

$$i = f \tag{3.12}$$

Equation (3.12) is a result of the assumption that only net transactions are considered in this analysis. It means that the value of the accumulated saving of foreign residents in financial assets of their own countries is equal to the value of their aggregate investment expenditure. The second step is to note from equations (3.5) and (3.10) that:

$$I = S + D = S + (M_K + M - X) \tag{3.13}$$

Allowing for the non-partitioning into private-sector and government-sector variables, equation (3.13) is easily converted into equation (3.2), which is the national income accounting identity underlying the FitzGerald Report. Note, however, that equation (3.13) has not been derived from the national income accounting identity, but is the outcome of a process initiated by the investment expenditure, $I + i$. This allows some dangers to be highlighted of introducing policies intended to increase saving in order to reduce a current account deficit.

First, it may be that the current account deficit has occurred because of the need to finance the purchase of imported capital goods. Suppose, for example, that:

$$D = M_K \Leftrightarrow M = X \tag{3.14}$$

Putting equation (3.14) into equations (3.5) and (3.8) then reveals that domestic saving equals domestic production of capital goods ($S = I - M_K$) and saving in the rest of the world equals its production of capital goods ($s = i + x_K$). This outcome does not seem a cause for policy concern. It means that residents in the country that produces capital goods retain equity in those capital goods, even if a portion is exported to another location (where presumably it is able to generate a higher rate of return than in its country of origin). Such transactions suffer the usual problems of uncertainty that affect all capital accumulation, but should not raise any additional concerns about fairness or sustainability in the capital-importing country.

It may be, however, that the size of the current account deficit is larger than can be accounted for by the net level of capital good imports, in which case the import of consumption goods must be greater than the export of consumption goods (that is, $M > X$). The analysis in Figure 3.1 allows a clear description of the process by which this occurs. First, receivers of income from production in the domestic country use some of that income to purchase imported consumption goods. This provides income to the rest of the world, of which only a portion is used to purchase exported consumption goods; the remainder is used to purchase a share in the equity of the capital goods produced in the domestic country. Thus, the distribution of saving is weighted towards foreign residents in excess of their share of capital good production.

In this setting, policies that succeeded in increasing the domestic country's rate of saving might reduce the current account deficit, by reducing the level of imports of consumption goods in each round of the process analysis in Figure 3.1. To that extent, the policy framework suggested by the FitzGerald Report in Australia (for example) may appear to have some merit. Before such a conclusion is accepted, however, policymakers should consider some very important caveats revealed in the above process analysis that are overlooked in analyses based on national income accounting identities alone.

First, the domestic residents who purchased the imported consumption goods could have instead purchased more equity in the country's capital stock (that is, they could have increased their saving), but chose not to do so. Similarly, the overseas residents who purchased equity in the domestic country could have instead purchased more exported consumption goods, but again chose not to do so. Hence, there may be a presumption that the resulting allocation of saving is economically efficient, in the sense that the people involved presumably believed that their actions were to their own advantage. This is the line of reasoning (developed within a neoclassical framework) proposed by Pitchford (1990), the most widely known advocate of the status quo in the foreign debt debate in Australia.

Second, the process by which an increase in domestic saving reduces the external deficit has serious side-effects. In particular, a rise in the saving rate means that expenditure is reduced. This is necessary, of course, to produce the desired fall in expenditure on imports, but it also involves a reduction in the level of expenditure on domestically produced consumption goods. Thus incomes are reduced, both in the domestic country and in the rest of the world (the latter because of the drop in exports). The overall result is a standard example of the paradox of thrift: efforts to increase the rate of saving produce the same level of aggregate saving, albeit perhaps distributed in a way more acceptable to domestic policymakers, but at a lower level of global economic activity.

Third, the relationship that a decline in domestic expenditure will lead to an improvement in the current account deficit relies on the *ceteris paribus* assumption that there is no offsetting behavioural change on the part of trading partners. In fact, the process analysis reveals that there are likely to be at least some offsetting effects, since the fall in incomes in the rest of the world as the domestic economy reduces its imports can be expected to reduce expenditure in the rest of the world on domestic exports. Consideration must also be given to exchange rate effects. In an extreme case, for example, where the volume of domestic equity and debt purchased by overseas residents, D, is predetermined, the exchange rate would rise until the fall in imports was matched by the same fall in exports, leaving the aggregate deficit unchanged.

These caveats suggest that efforts to increase a country's national saving rate may not be effective in eliminating a balance of payments current account deficit, and that, even if such attempts do have the desired effect, there are likely to be adverse side effects on the level of domestic and international economic activity, unless steps are taken at the same time to offset them.

CONCLUSION

The current policy debate about the national saving rate in Australia has provided the context for this chapter, but the chapter's fundamental premise has far wider application. That fundamental premise concerns the meaning of capital; in particular, this chapter has adopted the post-Keynesian view that capital accumulation (investment) is not the *result* of saving, as in neo-classical growth models, but rather provides an *outlet* for saving. Once the decision has been made about the level of investment production, policies affecting variables such as wages, profits, international trade, inflation, private saving and public saving can influence only the distribution of saving, and not its level. In a modern capitalist economy, of course, conflict over the distribution of saving (and the subsequent distribution of control over the means of production) is no small matter, and hence it should come as no surprise when a government becomes concerned about a persistent balance of payments deficit and its associated loss of saving to foreign residents.

The process analysis of this chapter, however, does not support the view that policies to raise the domestic saving rate will always be appropriate to meet such a concern. In the first instance, the analysis suggests that a distinction should be made between capital goods and consumption goods in a country's balance of payments. This is because a country that is running an external deficit in order to finance the import of capital goods has no grounds for complaint – the saving is accruing to the country that is producing the capital goods.

If, on the other hand, a country is operating an external deficit to finance net imports of consumption goods, there remains the question of whether or not there are better-targeted policies available for reducing excess imports than simply increasing aggregate domestic saving. The process analysis reveals two possible candidates. The first is an effort to increase the proportion of domestic consumption expenditure that is spent on domestically produced goods rather than on imported goods. This would increase domestic incomes, and hence domestic saving, although at the expense of incomes in the rest of the world (and so is still subject to the third concern discussed at the end of the previous section). Alternatively, efforts could be made to increase the level of consumption expenditure in surplus countries, especially where import barriers reduce the volume of consumption expenditure on goods produced in deficit countries. Indeed, this second option is the approach advocated recently by Geoffrey Harcourt (1994b). Its advantage is that it increases the overall level of global economic activity while at the same time tackling the balance of payments problems experienced by deficit countries.

ACKNOWLEDGEMENTS

The genesis of the ideas presented in this chapter lies in discussions I had with Geoffrey Harcourt while I was his guest in the Faculty of Economics and Politics at the University of Cambridge during the first half of 1994. Those discussions led to a paper, Dalziel and Harcourt (1994), which first extended the model in Dalziel (1995) to international capital flows. I am particularly grateful to Geoffrey Harcourt both for his hospitality and for his insightful comments on my research during and after my sabbatical leave in Cambridge. I am also happy to acknowledge again the contributions of my colleagues Peter Earl and Amal Sanyal to the ideas discussed here, and the written comments on an earlier draft by Geoffrey Harcourt, James Juniper and the editors.

REFERENCES

Arestis, P. and Sawyer, M. (eds) (1992) *A Biographical Dictionary of Dissenting Economists*, Aldershot: Edward Elgar.

Asimakopulos, A. (1983) 'Kalecki and Keynes on finance, investment and saving', *Cambridge Journal of Economics* 7(3–4): 221–33.

Bibow, J. (1995) 'Some reflections on Keynes's finance motive for the demand for money', *Cambridge Journal of Economics* 19(5): 647–66.

Black, T. (1994) 'The FitzGerald Report on national saving: economic utopia or economic stagnation?', *Economic Papers* 13(2): 10–16.

Chick, V. (1984) 'Monetary increases and their consequences: streams, backwaters and floods', in A. Ingham and A. M. Ulph (eds) *Demand, Equilibrium and Trade: Essays in Honour of Ivor F. Pearce*, London: Macmillan.

Cottrell, A. (1986) 'The endogeneity of money and money-income causality', *Scottish Journal of Political Economy* 33(1): 111–20.

Dalziel, P. (1995) 'Inflation and endogenous money: a process analysis', unpublished manuscript, Lincoln University.

—— (1996) 'The Keynesian multiplier, liquidity preference and endogenous money', *Journal of Post Keynesian Economics* 18(3): 311–31.

Dalziel, P. and Harcourt, G. C. (1994) 'A note on Mr Meade's relation and international capital movements', mimeo, Lincoln University and Cambridge University.

Earl, P. (1990) *Monetary Scenarios: A Modern Approach to Financial Systems*, Aldershot: Edward Elgar.

Eichner, A. S. and Kregel, J. A. (1975) 'An essay on post-Keynesian theory: a new paradigm in economics', *Journal of Economic Literature* 13(4): 1293–314.

FitzGerald, V. W. (1993) *National Saving: A Report to the Treasurer*, Canberra: Australian Government Publishing Service.

Harcourt, G. C. (1969) 'Some Cambridge controversies in the theory of capital', *Journal of Economic Literature* 7(2): 369–405. Reprinted in Harcourt, G. C. (1986) *Controversies in Political Economy: Selected Essays of G. C. Harcourt*, ed. O. F. Hamouda, Brighton: Wheatsheaf.

—— (1972) *Some Cambridge Controversies in the Theory of Capital*, Cambridge: Cambridge University Press.

—— (1976) 'The Cambridge controversies: old ways and new horizons – or dead end?', *Oxford Economic Papers* 28(1): 25–65. Reprinted in Harcourt, G. C. (1992) *On Political Economists and Modern Political Economy: Selected Essays of G. C. Harcourt*, ed. C. Sardoni, London: Routledge.

—— (1982) 'Making socialism in your own country', 12th annual John Curtin Memorial Lecture. Reprinted in Harcourt, G. C. (1986) *Controversies in Political Economy: Selected Essays of G. C. Harcourt*, ed. O. F. Hamouda, Brighton: Wheatsheaf.

—— (1992) 'Markets, madness and a middle way', 2nd Donald Horne Address. Reprinted in Harcourt, G. C. (1995) *Capitalism, Socialism and Post-*

Keynesianism: Selected Essays of G. C. Harcourt, Aldershot: Edward Elgar.

—— (1994a) 'Capital theory controversies', in P. Arestis and M. Sawyer (eds) *The Elgar Companion to Radical Political Economy*, Aldershot: Edward Elgar.

—— (1994b) 'A "modest proposal" for taming speculators and putting the world on course to prosperity', *Economic and Political Weekly* 29: 2490–2. Reprinted in Harcourt, G. C. (1995) *Capitalism, Socialism and Post-Keynesianism: Selected Essays of G. C. Harcourt*, Aldershot: Edward Elgar.

Harcourt, G. C. and Kerr, P. (1980) 'The mixed economy', in J. North and P. Weller (eds) *Labour: Directions for the Eighties*, Sydney: Ian Novak.

Harcourt, G. C. and Kitson, M. (1993) 'Fifty years of measurement: a Cambridge view', *Review of Income and Wealth* 39(4): 435–47.

Harcourt, G. C., Roncaglia, A. and Rowley, R. (eds) (1995) *Income and Employment in Theory and Practice: Essays in Memory of Athanasios Asimakopulos*, London: Macmillan.

Horne, J. (1994) 'Raising national saving: the FitzGerald Report', *Economic Papers* 13(2): 1–9.

Keynes, J. M. (1936) *The General Theory of Employment, Interest and Money*, London: Macmillan. Reprinted in *The Collected Writings of John Maynard Keynes*, vol. 7, London: Macmillan for the Royal Economic Society, 1973.

—— (1937) 'The "ex ante" theory of the rate of interest', *Economic Journal* 47 (188): 663–9. Reprinted in *The Collected Writings of John Maynard Keynes*, vol. 14, London: Macmillan for the Royal Economic Society, 1973.

Meade, J. (1993) 'The relation of Mr Meade's relation to Kahn's multiplier', *Economic Journal* 103(418): 664–5.

Pitchford, J. (1990) *Australia's Foreign Debt: Myths and Realities*, Sydney: Allen & Unwin.

Robinson, J. (1956) *The Accumulation of Capital*, London: Macmillan.

—— (1975) *Collected Economic Papers*, 2nd edn, vol. 2, Oxford: Blackwell.

Solow, R. M. (1956) 'A contribution to the theory of economic growth', *Quarterly Journal of Economics* 70(1): 65–94.

Swan, T. W. (1956) 'Economic growth and capital accumulation', *Economic Record* 32(96): 334–61.

Trethewey, M. (1994) 'Does low saving restrain investment? A note relevant to the FitzGerald Report from a "Keynesian" perspective', *Economic Papers* 13(2): 17–26.

4

KEYNESIAN MACROECONOMICS AND THE CAPITAL DEBATES

Colin Rogers

INTRODUCTION

Geoff Harcourt is perhaps best known for his contribution to the capital theory debates of the 1950s, 1960s and 1970s. However, another important element of Geoff's wide-ranging interests is his long-standing contribution to the debate on the economics of Keynes; as witnessed, for example, by two of his publications in the 1980s (Harcourt 1985, 1987) and his more recent editorial role in *The General Theory* (second edition) (Harcourt and Riach, 1996). The links between these two elements of Geoff's work are, in the minds of many, somewhat obscure. Consequently, it is the intention of this chapter to draw attention to the relationship between the capital debates and Keynesian economics.

There are several strands to this relationship. First, as has been argued by Rogers (1989) and others, mainstream Keynesian economics is open to the Cambridge critique of neoclassical capital theory so meticulously documented by Harcourt (1972). Second, by adopting neoclassical capital theory Keynesian macroeconomics surrendered any attempt to explain long-period equilibrium and found itself reduced to the use of rigidities (which had in any event been rejected by Keynes) in an attempt to explain unemployment in the short rather than the long term. Third, and by implication, points one and two suggest that to rehabilitate Keynesian economics it will be necessary to abandon neoclassical capital theory and the neoclassical explanation of long-period equilibrium. This chapter revisits these issues by drawing on more recent work by Steedman (1994).

The chapter is arranged as follows: the next section, 'Keynesian and neoclassical macroeconomics', outlines the relationship between the IS–LM model and neoclassical capital theory along the lines presented by Backhouse (1981). The intention is to highlight the relationship between the loanable funds theory of the rate of interest, neoclassical growth theory and mainstream Keynesian economics. The section after that then reviews the limits to neoclassical capital theory and the final section draws out some implications for Keynesian macroeconomics.

KEYNESIAN AND NEOCLASSICAL MACROECONOMICS

The relationship between Keynesian (short-period) macroeconomics, as represented by the IS–LM model, and neoclassical capital theory, represented by the neoclassical growth model, was demonstrated very neatly in a somewhat neglected paper by Backhouse (1981). The discussion which follows will briefly highlight the features of the Backhouse analysis relevant to the theme of this chapter.

Backhouse's intention in writing the paper was to integrate the two elements of macroeconomics that had previously been treated as distinct: the IS–LM analysis of short-period equilibrium and the neoclassical growth theory for long-period equilibrium. To a large extent this dichotomy still exists in the textbooks, although at the more advanced level the short-period IS–LM perspective has been abandoned entirely in favour of the growth perspective.

The model consists of a market for goods, money and two factor inputs: labour and 'capital'.

The labour market

The production function has the traditional form in which output, Y, is a function of the capital stock, K, and employment, E:

$$Y = F(K, E) \tag{4.1}$$

The production function is assumed to exhibit all the usual neoclassical properties but it differs from the common neoclassical specification by including E, employment, rather than the labour force, N. This minor variation allows for the existence of unemployment (or over-full employment) in a Keynesian interpretation of the labour market in which the 'demand' for labour determines employment. The labour force grows at the rate n and N excludes any 'natural' unemployment; that is, the labour supply curve coincides with the labour force, N. With a production function that is homogeneous of degree 1 the production function may be written in per capita terms as:

$$y = F(k, e) \tag{4.2}$$

Employment is determined by the usual profit-maximizing condition, $w/p = F_e$. Note that the neoclassical or market-clearing case occurs only when $e = 1$ and for values of $e \neq 1$ the marginal product of labour, F_e, differs from the full-employment marginal product. Disequilibrium in the labour market may occur in the short period if money wages are fixed and price level is such that the real wage differs from the market-clearing level.

The goods market

Equilibrium in the goods market occurs when $y = c + i$.[1] Each of these elements is modelled in the traditional fashion. Consumption per capita is assumed to be a constant fraction, $1 - s$, of income:

$$c = (1 - s)y \qquad (4.3)$$

Investment consists of two elements: replacement and new. New investment is analysed in typical Keynesian Tobinesque fashion as dependent on the difference between the marginal product of capital, $dy/dk \equiv F_k$ and the real rate of interest, r.[2] If $r = F_k$ then replacement investment maintains the capital:labour ratio, k, constant. Hence, in per capita terms, the investment function is given by:

$$i = [\phi(F_k - r) + n]k \qquad (\phi' > 0) \qquad (4.4)$$

The money market

The money market is presented in standard Hicksian–Tobin fashion with money demand a function of the nominal rate of interest, r, wealth per capita, Ω, and nominal income per capita, py. With the money supply measured in per capita terms, equilibrium in the money market is written as:

$$m = L(py, \Omega, r) \qquad L_{py} > 0, L_\Omega > 0, L_r < 0 \qquad (4.5)$$

Per capita wealth, Ω, is given by:

$$\Omega = m + qpk \qquad (4.6)$$

where q is Tobin's 'valuation ratio of equities to the value of capital at reproduction cost' (Backhouse 1981: 176). The relationship is written as:

$$q = F_k/r \qquad (4.7)$$

Long-period equilibrium is described as the situation where $q = 1$ so the short period is characterized by the condition $F_k \neq r$.

Short- and long-period equilibrium solutions to the model

As Backhouse demonstrates, long-period equilibrium in the model may coincide with the steady-state solution generated by the neoclassical growth model. To see this, substitute equations (4.2), (4.3) and (4.4) into the goods market equilibrium condition to produce:

$$sF(\ldots) = \phi(F_k - r)k + nk \qquad (4.8)$$

In long-period equilibrium wages growth, $\dot{w}$, and growth in the capital:labour ratio, $\dot{k}$, are zero; that is, both $\dot{w} = 0$ and $\dot{k} = 0$ and $e = q = 1$. In addition, in the steady state, equation (4.8) may be written as:

$$sF(k^*,1) = nk^* \qquad (4.9)$$

where k^* is the steady-state capital:labour ratio and $r^* = F_k(k^*,1)$. Expression (4.9) is the familiar steady-state equilibrium solution from a Solow-type neoclassical growth model, $sy^* = nk^*$ (Backhouse 1981: 179).

A short-period equilibrium solution to the model is derived by fixing w and k, the money wage and the capital:labour ratio. To return to expression (4.9), this can now be solved for employment, e, as a function of the rate of interest, r, given the values for w and k. That is, a version of the IS curve is derived and can be shown to have a negative slope in (e,r) space. In similar fashion, the relationship between (e and r) implied by the money market can be derived from expressions (4.6) and (4.7) to produce an orthodox LM curve with a positive slope. (See Backhouse 1981 for a complete discussion.) A short-period equilibrium solution to the model can now be illustrated as in Figure 4.1.[3] The $\dot{w} = 0$ and $\dot{k} = 0$ loci divide the space into four quadrants in which the dynamic behaviour of w and k are as illustrated.

Given values for k and w a short-period equilibrium is illustrated at E in which disequilibrium exists in both the capital and labour markets. This situation is often described as Keynesian (Backhouse 1981). Unemployment exists as $e_0 < 1$ and $q > 1$ as the marginal product of capital, $F_k 0$, on the $\dot{k} = 0$ locus, exceeds the rate of interest, r_0, determined by IS–LM. The existing capital stock is smaller than the cost-minimizing–profit-maximizing stock so that the capital stock will increase over time.

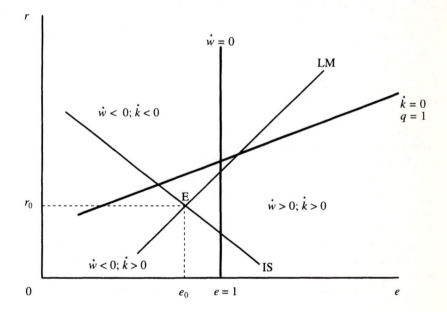

Figure 4.1 Keynesian short-period equilibrium

41

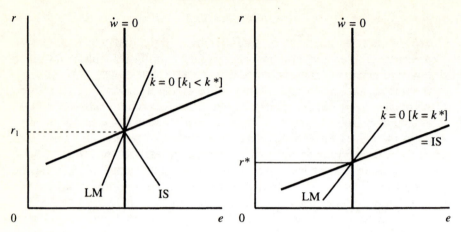

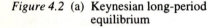

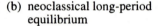

Figure 4.2 (a) Keynesian long-period   (b) neoclassical long-period
equilibrium   equilibrium

Keynesian and neoclassical long-period equilibria are illustrated in Figure 4.2. Long-period equilibrium is attained as falling money wages shift the IS and LM curves to the right and the increasing capital stock shifts the $\dot{k} = 0$ locus down ($F_{kk} < 0$). A Keynesian long-period equilibrium is illustrated in Figure 4.2(a) and occurs when $e = q = 1$. However, this is not necessarily the neoclassical steady state as k_1 may not be consistent with k^*. It is only when expression (4.9) holds that the neoclassical steady state is achieved. Only then is *the* natural rate of interest, r^*, consistent with the natural rate of unemployment implied by the definition of e.

Note also that the neoclassical model lacks an independent IS curve as it is an assumption of the neoclassical world that $F_k = r$, always, so that the IS curve coincides with the $\dot{k} = 0$ locus (Backhouse 1981).

Now it is apparent that so long as Keynesian economists adopt the neoclassical analysis of long-period equilibrium as the specification of the long period towards which their short-period equilibria tend, albeit sluggishly, they have implicitly taken on board neoclassical capital theory. Consequently the Keynesian long-period equilibrium illustrated in Figure 4.2(a) must ultimately coincide with the neoclassical long-period equilibrium in Figure 4.2(b). The mechanism driving this part of the adjustment process is neoclassical capital theory in terms of which saving 'finances' investment to generate the natural rate of interest, r^*. Whenever $k < k^*$, forces in the neoclassical capital market ensure that k is driven to equality with k^*. This process also ensures that the capital market delivers *the* natural rate of interest, r^*, in both neoclassical and Keynesian long-period equilibrium.

The capital market

The capital market is not examined in any detail by Backhouse but it is apparent that if it has properties analogous to those of the labour market firms would employ capital up to the point where the marginal product of capital equals the rate of interest. That is, $F_k = r$. In terms of Tobin's valuation ratio, $q = 1$. In the neoclassical version of the model this condition holds continuously. However, in the Keynesian or short-period version of the model the capital stock is treated as fixed so the nominal rate of interest produced in the IS–LM model (= real rate in the absence of inflation) inevitably produces a situation where the marginal product of capital differs from the rate of interest, given the level of employment. This means that investment will occur and alter the capital stock to achieve the condition $F_k = r$. As Sargent (1987: ch. 1) puts it, the Keynesian version of the model arises from the assumption that there is no perfect market in which firms can purchase additional capital (or sell redundant capital) and it is in this sense that the capital market differs from the labour market in neoclassical theory. Capital is firm specific but labour is not. Note also that $q = 1$ at various levels of output and employment but the model achieves full long-period equilibrium only when $e = q = 1$.

Of particular interest is the fact that the adjustment mechanism in this version of the neoclassical growth model is consistent with the loanable funds theory of the rate of interest. The loanable funds theory rests on the existence of a capital market in which the forces of productivity and thrift determine the natural rate of interest. Thus, whenever $sy > nk$ the excess supply of saving is associated with a *fall* in the natural rate of interest, and the process continues until real saving and investment are equated at r^*. Conversely, if $sy < nk$ the natural rate of interest *rises*. It is this loanable funds theory that underlies both Keynesian and neoclassical theories of long-period equilibrium in the Backhouse analysis. (For a discussion of the relationship between the loanable funds theory and Tobin's q see Rogers (1989).) Hence the neoclassical growth model also provides analytical foundations consistent with the loanable funds theory of the natural rate of interest. However, as we shall see, this is a very special result which goes by the board even in a one-commodity model with fixed capital.

LIMITS TO NEOCLASSICAL THEORY

Some of the difficulties facing Keynesian economics as a result of adopting the analytical framework outlined in the previous section are well known. In particular, Keynesian economics is reduced to the analysis of frictions and rigidities despite the fact that Keynes argued that flexibility of wages and prices would not solve the problem of persistent unemployment in a *laissez-faire* economy. However, the implications for Keynesian economics of adopting neoclassical capital theory have not been thoroughly investigated (see Rogers 1989). Consequently, the comments which follow are intended to stimulate interest in such an investigation.

To begin with some background, it is well known that the neoclassical parables consist of the following propositions:

$$dy/dk > 0; \ dk/dr < 0; \ dk/dw > 0; \ dw/dr < 0 \text{ and that } F_k = r \equiv dy/dk = r$$

The capital debate, in which Geoff Harcourt participated, demonstrated that these parables could not be generalized beyond a one-commodity world: the corn model. More recently Steedman (1994) has taken a closer look at a one-commodity world that differs from the corn model in an apparently trivial way: some of the output is durable and lasts more than one period. This model can be described as a 'one-commodity fixed-capital model' in which the single commodity is either consumed or used to produce output. In the latter case it is called a 'machine' and operates for a fixed number of periods at constant efficiency to produce output, at which point it expires ('depreciation by sudden death'). Despite the simplifying assumptions, the model would seem to be more useful than the traditional corn model as a starting point for neoclassical capital theory. However, it turns out that some of the key neoclassical parables still break down, and this undermines the neoclassical and Keynesian stories told in the previous sections.

To see this, consider Steedman's (1994) analysis of the aggregate neoclassical production function $y' = f(m)$, where y' is gross output and m is the number of machines per worker. The function is well behaved and workers receive a real wage w (measured in terms of new output and paid *ex post*), and all the machines last for t years.[4] The uniform rate of interest is r and the annuity formula, $a(r)$, is a function of r and t, and $a'(r) = a''(r) > 0$.[5] If c represents consumption per employed worker and $n =$ is the steady growth rate, then:

$$w + a(r)m = y' \tag{4.10}$$

and:

$$c + a(n)m = y' \tag{4.11}$$

From the national accounting identities $y \equiv w + rk \equiv c + nk$ the value of capital per worker, k can be determined as:[6]

$$k = m \left[\frac{a(r) - a(n)}{r - n} \right] \qquad r \neq n \tag{4.12}$$

If the aggregate production function is interpreted to represent a case where there are infinitely many production techniques all involving the same t, the following relationships between k, r and y result.

To begin with, the relationship between k and r is not as straightforward as is implied by the neoclassical parables, even in Steedman's version of the one-commodity model. Differentiating the accounting identity with respect to r generates:

$$dy/dr = (k + dw/dr) + r\, dk/dr \qquad (4.13)$$

which implies that $dy/dr < r(dk/dr)$ as $(k + dw/dr) < 0$. Thus if $dk/dr < 0$ then $dy/dr < 0$ also and if $dk/dr > 0$ the sign of dy/dr cannot be determined in a qualitative analysis. Also, on rearranging equation (4.13) to produce:

$$[dy/dk - r]dk/dr = [k + dw/dr] < 0 \qquad (4.14)$$

it follows that if $dk/dr < 0$ as per the neoclassical parable then $dy/dk > r$ must obtain (Steedman 1994: 305).

The difficulties do not stop here, however, and further insight is obtained by rewriting equation (4.12) as $k = mv$ (where v = the quantity in square brackets) and making the substitutions to produce $y = [y' - a(n)m + nvm]$ and differentiating both k and y with respect to m to produce:

$$dk/dm = v + m(dv/dm) = v(1 + \varepsilon) \qquad (4.15)$$

and:

$$dy/dm = a(r) - a(n) + nv + nm(dv/dm = v(r + n\varepsilon) \qquad (4.16)$$

where $\varepsilon = (dv/dm)(m/v)$. It then follows that:

$$dy/dk = \left[\frac{r + n\varepsilon}{1 + \varepsilon} \right] \qquad (4.17)$$

Consequently, as ε is never positive it follows from equation (4.15) that $dk/dr < 0$ if and only if $-1 < \varepsilon < 0$.[7] Similarly, from equation (4.16) it follows that $dy/dr < 0$ if and only if $-(r/g) < \varepsilon < 0$. Finally, it is apparent from equation (4.17) that $dy/dk = r$ and only if $n = r$. Consequently, it is not inevitable that the parables apply even in a one-commodity 'fixed-capital' world.

In a one-commodity durable-capital world the relationship between y, n and k (and by implication r and w) may be quite different from that suggested by the parables. Steedman (1994) shows that it is a simple matter to construct an example in which an increase in n fundamentally changes the relationship between y and k and $dk/dr > 0$. In Steedman's example, at a growth rate $n = 0$, $dy/dk < 0$ as r rises but at a higher rate of steady growth the relationship between y and k changes from $dy/dk > 0$ to $dy/dk < 0$ as r increases.

IMPLICATIONS FOR KEYNESIAN MACROECONOMICS

The implications of these results for the neoclassical–Keynesian analysis of pp. 39–42 are as follows. The first appears initially to be positive. The

Keynesian or short-period specification of the investment function which relies on $dy/dr \neq r$ applies in all states except when the steady-state golden rule holds; that is, $r = n$. However, on reflection, this implies that in general it is not possible for the Keynesian model to get on to the $k = 0$ locus in the Backhouse version of the Keynesian model. Alternatively the $k = 0$ locus collapses to a point where $r = n$; that is, only when the golden rule applies.

Second, as the relationships between y, r, k and w all exhibit properties that differ from the parables there is no reason to expect that the adjustment processes described earlier will apply. For example, from expression (4.8) the neoclassical relationship between steady-state y, s, n and k (and implicitly r and w also) is given by $sy^* = nk^*$. A notional increase in n reduces y^*, k^* and w^*, and increases r^*, while an increase in s increases y^* and k^* and w^* and reduces the natural rate of interest, r^*. By comparison, in the Steedman one-commodity world an increase in s will be associated with an increase in k as well as r^*, and y^* may increase or decrease depending on the configuration of the rate of interest and the rate of steady growth. All of these results are possible in a one-commodity durable capital model.

Consequently these results imply that there is no general mechanism in neoclassical capital theory which is consistent with the loanable funds theory of the rate of interest. The fact that $sy \neq nk$ does not imply that the real rate of interest will fall if $sy > nk$ or that it will rise when $sy < nk$. The loanable funds mechanism, in terms of which an excess supply of saving will depress the real rate of interest and an excess demand for saving will increase it, is a story which cannot in general be told. Thus, although the neoclassical model may be stable in the sense that it converges to a steady state whenever $sy \neq nk$ and that a steady-state or natural rate of interest, r^*, may exist, we cannot deduce anything in general from this about the behaviour of the real rate of interest. Steedman shows in his one-commodity world that $dk/dr > 0$ even if the relationship between sy and nk appears normal. The behaviour of r is independent of the relationship between sy and nk. Thus the loanable funds story based on the market forces of productivity and thrift to generate the natural rate of interest cannot be generalized even to Steedman's one-commodity world.

The link between these results, Keynesian economics and Keynes's *General Theory* is indirect but operates through the theory of the rate of interest. In his correspondence with Harrod, Keynes (1973: 552) made it clear that in his opinion the classical theory of the rate of interest should be discarded *in toto* as it was incapable of rehabilitation in any shape or form! The classical theory of the rate of interest to which Keynes was referring is of course the theory in terms of which the forces of productivity and thrift determine the natural rate – the loanable funds theory. It is this theory which was adopted from Wicksell and which Keynes applied in the *Treatise* and of which Robertson remained an ardent supporter. And it is this theory which is adopted by mainstream Keynesians. With the benefit of hindsight, it is now apparent that it is this loanable funds theory of the rate of interest which collapses in the face of the capital critique. Steedman's illustration is simply another example of why the loanable funds story lacks sound theoretical foundations in neoclassical capital theory. Although it cannot be claimed that Keynes was cognizant of the finer points of modern capital theory, his uncanny instinct for spotting the flaws in classical theory appears prescient.

CONCLUDING REMARKS

Much of the Keynesian macroeconomics which grew out of the neoclassical synthesis implicitly incorporated neoclassical capital theory as the basis for long-period analysis but the implications of this adoption have generally been neglected. Nevertheless, it is now apparent that Keynesian macroeconomics relies on neoclassical capital theory to generate its long-period equilibrium solutions. The capital debates, both new and old, have, however, exposed the limitations of neoclassical capital theory. Consequently, more recent Keynesian theories which graft short-period perspectives on to what is essentially a neoclassical long-period analysis will be subject to the limitations exposed by the capital critique. Keynesians of all shades should exploit these insights to better ground their short- *and long-period* analysis in a framework not subject to the capital critique.

ACKNOWLEDGEMENT

I am grateful to Geoff Harcourt, T. K. Rymes and James Juniper for helpful suggestions. Any remaining errors are my own.

NOTES

1   To simplify matters, the role of the government incorporated by Backhouse is excluded.
2   The real rate of interest equals the nominal rate of interest as expected inflation is zero.
3   The general expressions for the IS, LM and $\dot{k} = 0$ loci are as follows:

$$e = \eta(r; k, w) \qquad \eta_r < 0, \eta_k \lessgtr 0, \eta_w < 0 \qquad \text{(IS)}$$
$$r = \mu(e; k, w) \qquad \mu_e < 0, \mu_k \lessgtr 0, \mu_w < 0 \qquad \text{(LM)}$$
$$r = F_k(k, e) \qquad F_{ke} > 0 \qquad \dot{k} = 0$$

4   The assumption that all methods of production involve the same t is made to avoid the possibility of reswitching (Steedman 1994: 303–4).
5   The annuity formula is

$$a(r) \equiv \left[\frac{r(1 + r)^t}{(1 + r)^t - 1} \right]$$

6   The relation between y and y' is given by

47

$$y = y' - m \left[\frac{ra(n) - na(r)}{r - n} \right]$$

where the expression in square brackets represents depreciation per worker.

7 Note that $dk/dr = (dk/dm)(dm/dr)$ and that $dm/dr < 0$.

REFERENCES

Backhouse, R. E. (1981) 'Keynesian unemployment and the one-sector neoclassical growth model', *Economic Journal* 91: 174–87.

Harcourt, G. C. (1972) *Some Cambridge Controversies in the Theory of Capital*, Cambridge: Cambridge University Press.

—— (ed.) (1985) *Keynes and His Contempories*, London: Macmillan.

—— (1987) 'Theoretical methods and unfinished business', in *The Legacy of Keynes*, Nobel Conference XXII, ed. D. Reese, New York: Harper & Row.

Harcourt, G. C. and Riach, P. (eds) (1996) *The General Theory²*, London: Routledge.

Keynes, J. M. (1973) *The General Theory and After*. Part 1, *Preparation*, in *The Collected Writings of John Maynard Keynes*, ed. D. Moggridge, vol. 12, London: Macmillan for the Royal Economic Society.

Rogers, C. (1989) *Money Interest and Capital*, Cambridge: Cambridge University Press.

Sargent, T. J. (1987) *Macroeconomic Theory*, 2nd edition, New York: Academic Press.

Steedman, I. (1994) '"Perverse' behaviour in a "one commodity" model', *Cambridge Journal of Economics* 18: 299–311.

5

RESWITCHING, SOCIAL DISCOUNT RATE AND ENVIRONMENTALISM

A note

William J. Baumol

It has been recognized by others that environmentalists often display a curious bias in favour of the use of high discount (interest) rates in cost–benefit calculations. This seems odd, because the preoccupation of pro-environment groups with preservation of our natural heritage for the distant future should lead us to expect them to favour low discount rates. For, of course, a low discount rate means that the future is valued highly, relative to the present and, as a practical matter, it favours selection of those activities whose benefits are more heavily concentrated at later dates. A reasonable explanation in terms of political realities has already been offered and this chapter will provide what can, perhaps, be considered little more than a reformulation of that explanation rather than an alternative. However, that reformulation provides a strong formal foundation for the discussion, connects it with an important literature in capital theory with which Harcourt is associated, and yields a model which, I believe, is helpful in dealing both with analytic issues and with application.

The basic model is a simple formulation of a standard reswitching phenomenon, and may, perhaps, represent one of the more persuasive illustrations of the significance of reswitching in practice. The prototype scenario involves a proposal to construct, at high initial cost, a dam which can be expected to generate electricity for, say, 100 years. However, the dam will flood a canyon and, hence, destroy its amenity value for ever. Thus, the project has social costs which occur predominantly in the initial period and in the distant future. Only in intermediate periods are positive benefits generated. This is the time pattern of net returns that characterizes the standard reswitching examples. In this case the construction project is ruled out in terms of benefits and costs if the interest rate is either very high or very low, and that offers environmentalist opponents of the dam a strategic choice which they often make in the way that has already been indicated.

The model, as we will see, enables one to deal with such phenomena as growth in amenity value that occurs as population expands, with the effects of taxation and other institutional influences upon the opportunity cost of resources derived by the public sector from particular private sources, and it enables us to see the implications of some procedures proposed by Feldstein for proper use of the social discount rate.

THE PROTOTYPE MODEL

It is easy to formulate the model which has just been described. To deal with it in its simplest form, we assume that the annual amenity value of the canyon is constant over time, and that the same is true of the flow of benefits from the dam. Then, for convenience, we define one period as the length of time needed to construct the dam, and use the following notation:

C = the cost of construction of the dam;
B = the benefit (net value of the electricity) that flows from the dam per period during its operating life;
A = the amenity value of the canyon per period;
h = the number of years the dam is expected to remain in operation;
i = the interest rate; and
D = $1/(1 + i)$ = the discount factor.

The net value of the investment in the dam is given by

$$V = -C + \sum_{t=1}^{h} D^t B - \sum_{t=0}^{\infty} D^t A$$

$$= -(C + A) + \sum_{t=1}^{h} D^t (B - A) - \sum_{t=h+1}^{\infty} D^t A \quad (5.1)$$

or (by the standard algebra of discounting)

$$V = -(C + A) + (B/i)[1 + i - 1/(1 + i)^h] = A/i \quad (5.2)$$

From equation (5.1) it is clear that as $i \to \infty$ we obtain

$$\lim_{i \to \infty} V = -(C + A) < 0$$

That is, if the interest rate is very high only the immediate cost and amenity loss will matter and the project cannot be justified.

Similarly, from equation (5.1), if $i \to 0$ so that $D \to 1$ we have

$$\lim_{i \to \infty} V = -C + hB - tA = -\infty$$

That is, with no discounting of any future costs or benefits, the loss of amenity value for the indefinite future becomes overwhelming so that the project must, once again, fail the cost–benefit test.[1] It follows that there must exist a range of low values of i and another set of high values of i at which the project will be rejected. On the other hand, for some intermediate value of i, call it i^*, the project will be acceptable, by equation (5.2), if

$$B > [(C + A)i^* + A]/[1 + i - 1/(1 + i^*)^h] > 0 \qquad (5.3)$$

Thus, if equation (5.1) is the correct representation of V for some particular project, and equation (5.3) is satisfied, we have a reswitching case; that is, a case in which there exists a multiplicity (at least two) of solutions for the project's internal rate of return.

THE ENVIRONMENTALIST STRATEGY

Given their assumed objective – to prevent the project from being carried out – the environmentalists then have a choice between advocacy of a high interest rate and advocacy of a low interest rate for the purpose. If they look beyond the immediate issue, it is clear that their goal is apt to be furthered by the lower rate. For at some other time they may, for example, seek approval of something like a project involving a current investment to help preserve for use in the distant future a resource that would otherwise deteriorate. The fact that its outlay is current and its benefits lie far in the future means that only a low interest rate will permit this proposal to pass a cost–benefit test.

Yet, in practice, environmental groups have often made the other choice and sought to halt dam construction by claiming that the pertinent interest rate is very high. The reason is the difficulty of providing a reliable and persuasive estimate of the amenity value, A, or even of documenting its existence. All too often it is simply brushed aside in a cost–benefit calculation in practice and treated as though it were negligible and hence best taken to be zero. There have even been cases in which those opposed to the environmentalists have claimed that A is negative – that the dam will improve on nature and increase the amenity value of the site. If such a judgement is accepted for political or other reasons it is clear that only a high discount rate can be relied upon to prevent construction of the dam.

EXTENSION OF THE MODEL

Our construct lends itself easily to incorporation of some complications. For example, suppose that the amenity value of the canyon, rather than being a fixed number per year, is taken to have a fixed value per (representative) visitor or per potential visitor (its option value) and that the number of visitors or potential visitors grows in proportion to population which, in turn, grows at the steady rate g per period. Then if A_0 is the total amenity value in the initial period, in period t the amenity value, in discounted present value, will be given by

$$A_t = A_0 \left(\frac{1 + g}{1 + i} \right)^t \equiv A_0 S^t \tag{5.4}$$

which will be a convergent series if $g < i$ so that $S < 1$. That is, so long as population grows at a rate lower than the (real) rate of interest, the basic calculation will not be materially affected. The only significant change in expression will occur in equation (5.2), where, because

$$\sum_{t=1}^{\infty} S^t = \frac{1}{1 - S} - 1 = \frac{S}{1 - S}$$

$$= \frac{1 + g}{1 + i} \bigg/ \left(1 - \frac{1 + g}{1 + i} \right) = 1 \bigg/ \left(\frac{1 + i}{1 + g} \right) - 1 = \frac{1 + g}{i - g}$$

we now have

$$V = -(C + A) + (B/i)[1 + i - 1/(1 + i)^h] - A_0 \frac{i + g}{i - g} \tag{5.2*}$$

The analysis then proceeds precisely as before. If $A_0 = A$ the lower reswitching point presumably will occur at a higher value of i than when g equals zero, because the last (amenity value) term has a larger present value than before and so can outweigh the positive middle term before the interest rate is nearly as close to zero.

Of course, if $g > i$ the $A_0 S^t$ series does not converge and then the proposed project will be ruled out at *any* interest rate.

Clearly, it is not only the amenity value which may vary with t. The flow of benefits from the dam, B_t, may also change with time, and the construction outlays may, perhaps, be spread over time and overlap with B_t. The corresponding changes in the model are obvious enough and no more need be said about them.

However, the possibility of such modifications may help to throw light on a pertinent controversy over the way in which the appropriate discount rate should be chosen.

SOME ARGUMENTS FOR A HIGH INTEREST RATE

Those who advocate a relatively high interest rate for cost–benefit calculations have cited many grounds for support of their position. Here, I will consider only those that relate to the opportunity cost of the resources the public project would withdraw from the private sector. It has been held by Harberger and others (including myself) that taxes on corporate profits serve

52

to raise that opportunity cost. I have also suggested that the opportunity cost is increased by the likelihood that the private risk of an investment exceeds its social risk.

The tax on corporate profits which, for illustrative simplicity, I take to be 50 per cent, affects matters in the following way. Suppose the public rate of time preference is 10 per cent, meaning that individuals will not provide funds to an enterprise unless its expected rate of return to them is 10 per cent. Then a firm that hopes to avail itself of the capital market must invest only in projects whose expected return (before taxes) is at least 15 per cent. Since taxes are a transfer, not a real social cost, it follows that any resources withdrawn from the corporate sector must incur an opportunity cost of 15 per cent. That is, if those resources were devoted to a public project returning, say, only 12 per cent, society would suffer a net loss of 3 per cent. Hence, so the argument runs, the proper discount rate for public projects is (at least) the 15 per cent pre-tax return on corporate investments.

The argument relating to risk is analogous. Suppose corporations require a 4 per cent risk premium so that they will invest only in projects with an expected return of 19 per cent. To the stockholder the project's risk may be substantial. But if many firms and government enterprises undertake such projects at the same time, then from the point of view of the economy – that is, society as a whole – the insurance principle will apply, provided, of course, that the risks of the different projects are independent. Then the marginal social risk cost of such a project is close to zero. This means that to society a corporate project with an expected yield of 19 per cent should be treated as having a riskless yield of that magnitude. The opportunity cost of withdrawal of resources from that project and their removal to the public sector must then be evaluated at 19 per cent. This is the argument which asserts that the proper discount rate to be used in such cases is 19 per cent.[2]

In sum, such arguments suggest that the proper discount rate for a government project is not our illustrative 10 per cent time preference rate of the general public but something considerably higher, reflecting the opportunity cost of resources taken from the private sector as a whole. For, according to this view of the matter, any lower discount rate will result in approval of government projects which cause a net reduction in general welfare because they take away more consumers' and producers' surplus than they contribute[3].

THE FELDSTEIN MODIFICATIONS

Feldstein (1970) has suggested, however, that the preceding analysis is not quite valid. He points out that there are two decisions at stake, and that by dealing explicitly with only one of them the discussion is somewhat misleading and yields a calculation that is incorrect.

The choice of discount rate for government projects does, indeed, affect two decisions: first, the allocation of resources between the public and private sector, and, second, the allocation of public-sector resources between projects with short-term and distant pay-offs. Now, the preceding discussion has treated the interest rate as though its sole use were the former. But if that rate is chosen so as to elicit optimal decisions as between public and private investment it may well be set at a level which leads to incorrect decisions on durability of public investments. To achieve correct decisions on the two issues, one therefore needs two instruments, not one. Moreover, as Feldstein tells us, a second instrument is available for the purpose. The interest rate is the tool which is, by its construction, ideally adapted to deal with the second type of decision: the choice between longer-term and shorter-term projects. It should, therefore, be reserved for that purpose, and the correct interest rate for that task is the consumers' time preference rate, the 10 per cent in our example.

Next, to prevent this step from biasing decisions in favour of indefensible public projects, their opportunity cost should indeed be taken into account. But this should be done not by modifying the interest rate figure, but by making appropriate deductions from the benefit figures, the B_t. If in year t there is a gross benefit B_t but this transfer of funds exacts a net opportunity cost N_t, the appropriate benefit figure becomes $B_t^* = B_t - N_t$. In this way, the calculation retains the requisite degrees of freedom and can yield appropriate choices on both of the decisions to be made.

Our model can help to bring out the pertinence of these observations. In our scenario, the public sector removes C dollars in resources which, say, involves a net opportunity loss of L per dollar per annum. But the project also yields a flow of benefits, of which, say C_t flows to the corporate sector in period t, thus serving in effect to amortize the public sector's 'debt' to the business sector. Thus, in period t the outstanding value of that debt is

$$C - \sum_{s=1}^{t} C_s$$

and the corresponding opportunity loss from the public sector's employment of business resources is $L_t = L(C - \sum C_s)$. Therefore, the correct way of taking this into account, according to Feldstein, is to take as the benefit figure for year t, $B_t^* = B_t - L_t$, leaving the interest rate to equal the time preference figure.

This conclusion's persuasiveness is increased by the observation that the stream of opportunity losses, the L_t, has no necessary and predetermined time path. The actual time path that emerges from the circumstances, whatever it may be, is correctly reflected in the Feldstein procedure. However, in the procedure described earlier, which makes all adjustments through the interest rate, an artificial time path of the L_t is implicitly forced on the calculation. To see this, let i_p represents the pure time preference interest rate, and let r be the increment added to it to represent the opportunity costs we have been discussing. Then the interest rate used in this calculation is $i = i_p + r$, so that the present value of B_t^* is taken to be $B_t^*[1/(1 + i_p + r)]$. This asserts, in effect, that

$$L_t(1/(1 + i_p)] = B_t^*[1/(1 + i_p + r)] - B_t[1/(1 + i_p)]$$

which yields an L_t figure that need have no relation to the true value of L in year t.

CONCLUDING COMMENT

Approaches in economic analysis have a gratifying way of finding powerful applications in arenas distinct from those for which they were originally formulated. The fruitful debate on reswitching offered substantial illumination to capital theory, its original domain. This chapter has sought to show that analytic tools that played an important role in the reswitching discussion also shed light on other economic issues. In particular, it has shown why environmental economists, despite their concern over the distant future, need not follow the obvious course in the choice of discount rate they advocate for benefit–cost analysis. Though a low discount rate may serve to give greater weight to future benefits *vis-à-vis* those that are more immediate, high discount rates may be equally effective in protecting our heritage from destructive current projects. This is so because of the reswitching phenomenon, the possibility that both a high and a low discount rate can yield the same present-value figure for a given project. This observation opens the way to a choice between the two rates on grounds of political feasibility or other practical considerations.

ACKNOWLEDGEMENT

I am most grateful to the Centre of Policy Studies at Monash University under whose sponsorship this note was written.

NOTES

1   This is true even if the time horizon, h^*, is finite, provided that $h^*B < h^*A + C$.
2   If part of the public-sector project's resources is derived from other sources with a lower opportunity cost, the appropriate discount rate, on this view, will be correspondingly lower. It will, in fact, be a weighted average of the pertinent opportunity costs, with the weights equal to the proportion of the funds derived from each source.
3   Although the preceding argument is quite persuasive I suspect it will not be confirmed fully by a rigorous analysis. The problem is that we are faced here with a second-best problem. Optimality requires that a dollar of resources invested by an individual have the same social marginal yield as the same resources invested by a firm. But differences in tax treatment of firms and individuals drives a wedge between the two, as we have seen. Thus, the overall optimality conditions for the economy are unavoidably violated, and the most desirable of the attainable

decisions for the public sector must be second-best. However, as we know, second-best calculations are not straightforward, and simple rules such as those discussed in the text generally do not get us there. In any event, without an explicit calculation of the second-best solution we cannot be confident that the rules just enunciated are precisely those that are required. On this issue see Usher (1969).

REFERENCES

Feldstein, M. S. (1970) 'Choice of technique in the public sector: a simplification', *Economic Journal* 53(320): 985–90.
Usher, D. (1969) 'On the social rate of discount: comment', *American Economic Review* 59: 925–9.

6

THE PRODUCTIVITY OF WORKING AND WAITING

Static and dynamic aspects of the capital controversy[1]

Thomas K. Rymes

INTRODUCTION

The measurement of technical progress or total factor productivity has three basic variants. In the traditional, neoclassical or Hicksian variant, all measurable inputs are treated alike. In particular, no distinction is drawn between inputs which are non-reproducible and those which are reproducible – that is to say, those which are simultaneously inputs and outputs of the economic system. Elsewhere[2] I argue that the failure of the traditional measures of multifactor productivity to distinguish between non-reproducible and reproducible inputs involves logical contradiction and results in potentially severe understatements of the measured rate of technical advance.[3] A second variant of measured technical progress is the neo-Ricardian construct, which rigorously takes into account the reproducibility of all forms of capital inputs. For economies in which throughout this chapter non-reproducible inputs such as land and exhaustible natural resources[4] are ignored, this concept conceives of all non-reproducible inputs as being drawn from one class of primary inputs, human labour or 'working'.[5] In the neo-Ricardian conception, capital vanishes as a class of primary inputs. The third variant of the measurement of technical progress is one based on the concept advanced by Harrod. Harrod's concept of technical progress also rigorously distinguishes between non-reproducible and reproducible inputs, with the former consisting of two classes of primary inputs, 'working' and 'waiting'.[6] Neutral technical progress in Harrod, sometimes incorrectly designated as purely labour augmenting, results in equi-proportional increases in the efficiency or augmentation of working and waiting. Progress is biased in Harrod's sense when it is either relatively working- or waiting-using. The concept of working in Harrod is the familiar one of labour, expressed in natural units. But what is the concept of waiting in Harrodian technical progress? Can it be expressed in natural units? Is the concept operational? These are the questions which this chapter tries to answer.[7] In contrasting Harrod's concepts and measures of primary inputs and technical progress with the other variants, issues in capital theory are joined.

If the class of labour inputs is the only primary input in the neo-Ricardian (or Marxian?) conception of technical progress, then in a steady state and, *a fortiori*, in traverse analyses of temporary equilibria, net rates of return to capital in excess of rates of growth involve exploitation,[8] since consumption out of returns to capital represents 'take-out' by inputs not truly primary. The ownership of the services of capital should be taken out of individual and placed into collective hands. The state could save all the returns to capital such that the net rate of return would equal the rate of growth. There would be no need for the private owners of capital to consume since they provide no primary input.[9] Moreover, the concept of waiting implies that net rates of return are determined by 'productivity and thrift', static arguments which the neo-Ricardians, mindful of the Cambridge capital conroversy, are not inclined to accept. More fundamentally, there is disagreement over the relative importance of objectivist versus subjectivist conceptions of cost. The objectivists or neo-Ricardians insist that all inputs and outputs, both in terms of prices and quantities *and* in terms of levels and proportionate rates of change, must be in 'natural' or objective units.[10]

Neo-Austrians insist that all cost is subjective and cannot be objectively measured, and question the meaning of any empirical construct in economics.[11] Keynesians, particularly Harrod (and to some extent Robinson[12]), follow the Marshallian tradition, attempting to retain what is valuable from both objectivist and subjectivist approaches to quantitative economics.

THE MEASUREMENT FRAMEWORK

Reproducible capital is simultaneously an input and output of modern capitalist economic systems. The appropriate measurement framework then is the Leontief–Sraffa–Pasinetti, or input–output, flow accounts (for some arbitrary time period). The simple, well-known framework used here is

$$\mathbf{AQ + C + GDQ = Q}$$
$$[\mathbf{\mathit{I} - (A + GD)}]^{-1}\,\mathbf{C = Q}$$

for quantities,

$$\mathbf{B}[\mathbf{\mathit{I} - (A + GD)}]^{-1}\,\mathbf{C = BQ = \tilde{L}}$$

for labour,

$$\mathbf{RD}[\mathbf{\mathit{I} - (A + GD)}]^{-1}\,\mathbf{C = GDQ = RK = \tilde{K}}$$

for 'capital', and

$$\mathbf{WB}[\mathbf{\mathit{I} - (A + RD)}]^{-1} = \mathbf{P}$$

for prices. The simple framework used here does not stress the vintage problem of durable capital goods and the joint production problems associated with stocks of goods-in-process. The durability of the capital goods is, however, captured by treating capital consumption (or depreciation) as part of the matrix of the intermediate inputs per unit of gross output coefficients, A. The phenomenon of growth in capital stocks is captured by the matrix $\mathbf{GD}$, an element of which is $g_{ij}d_{ij}$, the capital stock produced in activity i owned in activity j per unit of the gross output of activity j multiplied by the respective net growth rate. The vectors $\mathbf{C}$ and $\mathbf{Q}$ are consumption and gross output vectors by activity.

The Leontief–Sraffa–Pasinetti equations

$$[I - (A + \mathbf{GD})]^{-1}\, \mathbf{C} = \mathbf{Q}$$

and

$$\mathbf{B}[I - (A + \mathbf{GD})]^{-1}\, \mathbf{C} = \mathbf{BQ} = \bar{\mathbf{L}}$$

are well known. The latter is the flow of the services of labour or working which is associated with vectors of final consumption and gross outputs directly ($\mathbf{BC}$), indirectly ($\mathbf{BAQ}$) to maintain the associated capital stocks, and hyper-indirectly ($\mathbf{BGDQ}$) to provide for growth in the associated capital stocks. Thus the matrix

$$\mathbf{B}[I - (A + \mathbf{GD})]^{-1}$$

is the set of coefficients showing the amount of working which must be done directly to produce present consumption, indirectly by maintaining the capital stocks, and hyper-indirectly by building up the capital stocks for the future. The designation of working as $\bar{\mathbf{L}}$ is to remind us that working is a primary input; it does not appear anywhere as part of the produced outputs and inputs of the economy.

Up to this point, there is no disagreement between the neoclassical, neo-Ricardian and Harrodian concept of primary inputs. When we turn to the expression

$$\mathbf{RD}[I - (A + \mathbf{GD})]^{-1}\, \bar{\bar{\mathbf{C}}} = \mathbf{RDQ} = \mathbf{RK} = \tilde{K}$$

differences appear.

Begin with the neoclassical concept first. The quantity relations set out are from accounts in which prices cancel out 'along the rows'.[13] Consider an entry in $\mathbf{RD}$ before the price cancellation has occurred, i.e. in the matrix $\mathbf{PRD}$. A typical entry is

$$P_i R_{ij} K_{ij} / Q_j$$

where $P_i R_{ij}$ is the net return or net rental for the *service* flow of the capital good (per unit of output) which is metered or indexed or represented by the net stock of capital (per unit of output). The net capital stock is then the proxy for the service flow rendered by the stock[14] – as is seen for the case of inventories. Just as it is meaningful to measure the service of working or labour, one can, in neoclassical analysis, measure the services of capital goods. One thinks of the degree of utilization of fixed plant, but it is clear that inventory stocks provide buffer services by being stocks *on hand*. The neoclassical conception is then that the stocks of capital are measures of services which are priced by the net rentals, the P_iR_{ij} terms.[15]

The neo-Ricardian case can be seen when the prices cancel 'along the rows' and, if we assume that net rates of return on any capital good are the same regardless of the activity with which it is associated – that is, $R_{ij} = R_i$ for all j, then the net rates of return also cancel 'along the rows' and the expression

$$RD[I - (A + GD)]^{-1} \ C = RDQ = RK = \tilde{K}$$

would appear as

$$DI[I - (A + GD)]^{-1}C = DQ = K$$

where K is the vector of capital stock services which are clearly reproducible by the economic system. Indeed, the relation

$$AQ + C + GDQ = Q$$

could be written as

$$AQ + C + GD[I - (A + GD)]^{-1} \ C = Q$$

so that the required services associated with the growing stocks would have been taken into account. All that would be left, after the services of the capital stock have been thus accounted for, would be the primary inputs of working which are not *produced* by the economic system and which cannot be treated similarly to the endogenous services of the capital goods. The neo-Ricardians are correct to treat the services of the capital goods and the stocks of the depreciated capital goods as non-primary inputs but are incorrect when they argue that working or labour is the only primary input, that no primary input is associated with capital.

In the Harrodian case, households, individually or collectively, own the capital stocks, and carry, maintain and augment such stocks; that is, they are supplying the services of waiting associated with such stocks. The labour input, the working, is also owned and supplied by households in the same way. An institutional question is whether the working and waiting are supplied privately or collectively. In the neoclassical and neo-Ricardian cases, the stocks are imperfect indicators of the flow of services of the capital goods. The difference between the two is that the neoclassical theorists draw no distinction, as inputs, between the services of working and the flow services of the capital stocks, whereas the neo-Ricardians clearly and correctly treat working as primary and non-reproducible while the flow services of the capital inputs are intermediate and reproducible. In the Harrodian case the opportunity cost of the flow services called waiting, associated with the ownership of capital goods, is that they must be carried, maintained and augmented. (The willingness of households to wait more than would be involved in merely maintaining the stocks is taken into account by the GD matrices as components of net final demand.) Similarly the flow of time not consumed is the measure of the flow of 'working'. There is no requirement that different capital goods be indexed or aggregated into homogeneous flows of waiting. There need be no homogeneous flows of 'working' and 'waiting'. If a capital good has a price, a net rental, twice that of a second good, it means that there is twice as much carrying, or twice the waiting, compared with the second goods. It is exactly analogous to the case of heterogeneous households where the labour of one sells at twice per year the labour as another: the former is said to be supplying twice the working as the latter. The twice is not based on some physical measure, however; it is prices which yield the cardinality.

Waiting, then, is equivalent to working. The willingness of households to wait and to work, and therefore the supply of waiting and working, are a function of net rates of return and real wage rates. Changes in them may therefore be induced by changes in such prices. Waiting and working cannot be produced, however – they are non-reproducible and therefore primary. Waiting and working are the two classes of primary inputs or factors of production in Harrodian concepts of total factor productivity.

This has always been implicitly understood in neoclassical and Keynesian analyses. An optimal neoclassical growth model has the steady-state conditions, $q_k(k) - \delta = R = n + n' + \sigma$, where $n + n'$ is the steady-state rate of growth of working and waiting, n, plus the Harrodian rate of technical progress, n', and σ is the rate of time preference. The gross marginal physical product of capital, $q_h(k)$, adjusts so that R equals $n + n' + \sigma$, and does not determine it. The economy has the stock of capital it has because there is sufficient waiting to carry it, k, to maintain it, δk, and to augment it, $(n + n')k$, the net price of such waiting being $R = n + n' + \sigma$. A greater flow of waiting would be associated with a lower σ and R. In the parable part of the story, this would be associated with a higher k and lower $q_k(k)$. The parable part of the story is derived from the fundamentals and is not essential to it. In Keynesian growth literature, one has

$$R = n + n'/s_\pi = n + n' + \sigma$$

where s_π is the fraction of waiting income saved. If $s_\pi = 1$, then $\sigma = 0$ and, at this level, the neoclassical and Keynesian arguments are the same. In both cases savings represent the opportunity cost of carrying the capital goods, and, whereas the capital goods are reproducible, the waiting is not.

THOMAS K. RYMES

THE MEASUREMENT OF TOTAL FACTOR PRODUCTIVITY

In the foregoing there are unchanging technologies. There is no reason to expect, for instance, that an increase in waiting (which would take the form of increased savings and increased expenditures on new or the maintenance of certain types of capital goods) would necessarily be associated with an increase in some aggregate real stock of capital goods or an increase in some aggregate flow of waiting. Capital goods are heterogeneous; so are waiting and working. All the possibilities associated with the Cambridge capital controversy hold. The problem with the capital input is *not* that shown in a comparison of techniques drawn from a given multi-technique technology but rather arises in the context of technical progress. How to measure that technical change in Harrodian terms is the matter before us.

With respect to the labour input or working, the measure of neutral Harrod progress, where the *same* rate of progress occurs in each activity, would be

$$\mathbf{B}^*[\mathbf{I} - (\mathbf{A} + \mathbf{GD})]^{-1}\,\mathbf{C}^* = \mathbf{B}h^{-1}[\mathbf{I} - (\mathbf{A} + \mathbf{GD})]^{-1}\,\mathbf{C}h = \mathbf{B}h^{-1}\,\mathbf{Q}h = \bar{L}$$

where all the $\mathbf{B}$ coefficients are reduced and all the elements of $\mathbf{C}$ and $\mathbf{Q}$ are raised in the same proportion h.

With respect to prices, we would have

$$\mathbf{W}^*\,\mathbf{B}^*[\mathbf{I} - (\mathbf{A} + \mathbf{RD})]^{-1} = \mathbf{W}h\,\mathbf{B}h^{-1}\,[\mathbf{I} - (\mathbf{A} + \mathbf{RD})]^{-1} = \mathbf{P}$$

so that for unchanging real net rates of return, the rise in $\mathbf{W}$ will be offset exactly by the fall in the coefficients of $\mathbf{B}$.

With respect to the capital input, divergences appear between the neo-Ricardian and Harrodian measures of technical progress. If the capital inputs are treated as reproducible in the neo-Ricardian way, then we have

$$\mathbf{RD}[\mathbf{I} - (\mathbf{A} + \mathbf{GD})]^{-1}\,\mathbf{C}h = \mathbf{RDQ}h = \mathbf{K}h$$

that is, that $\mathbf{C}$ and $\mathbf{K}$ must rise together for an unchanging $\mathbf{R}$. In Harrodian language, a neutral technical advance will be a state where, with $\mathbf{R}$ constant, the output–capital ratio will remain unchanged. Harrod also defined a neutral advance as a state where, again with $\mathbf{R}$ constant, the output–waiting ratio would rise *pari passu* with the output–working ratio. A technological advance, neutral in the Harrod sense, within the time structure of production means that flows of waiting in every activity for every horizon can carry, maintain and augment a growing flow of services of reproducible capital goods. Thus, we would have

$$\mathbf{RD}h^{-1}\mathbf{I} - (\mathbf{A} + \mathbf{GD})]^{-1}\,\mathbf{C}h = \mathbf{RD}h^{-1}\,\mathbf{Q}h = \tilde{\mathbf{K}}$$

so that the ratio of waiting to working remains unchanged.

Why is the operator h^{-1} applied to the $\mathbf{D}$ matrix outside the inverse and not to the one insider? The $\mathbf{D}$ matrix inside the inverse conceives of capital as output, the **D** matrix pre-multiplying the inverse indexes capital as an input. The $\mathbf{D}h^{-1}$ formulation reveals that the growing stocks of commodities as inputs require less waiting to produce, carry and augment. Because of advances in efficiency, more can be produced with given flows of working, just as larger stocks of capital can be carried, maintained and accumulated with given flows of waiting. The larger capital stocks are aggregate measures for the services of capital goods, and so the services of waiting are augmented, are made more efficient, by the technical progress. Given flows of waiting can carry, maintain and augment larger stocks of capital. Harrod neutral technical progress augments the services of working and waiting. It is not just labour augmenting, nor is it just waiting augmenting. It augments both. How is Harrod technical progress to be measured? Although the operational matters have been dealt with extensively elsewhere (cf. note 2), they may be briefly set out. The static column accounts for any activity, say j, in our relations would be

$$WL_j + R_j P_i K_{ij} + P_i M_{ij} + P_j M_{jj} = P_j Q_j$$

Where lower-case letters represent proportionate rates of growth, the Harrod measures of this rate of technical progress, using standard Divisia index number formulation, would be

$$q_j - \frac{[WL_j(l_j)}{P_j Q_j} + \frac{R_j P_i K_{ij}}{P_j Q_j}(k_{ij} - h_i) + P_i M_{ij}(m_{ij} - h_i)$$

$$+ \frac{P_j M_{jj}}{P_j Q_j}(m_{jj} - h_j)] = h_j = \frac{[WL_j}{P_j Q_j}(w) + \frac{R_j P_k K_{ij}}{P_j Q_j}(r_j + p_i + h_i)$$

$$+ \frac{P_i M_{ij}}{P_j Q_j}(p_i + h_i) + \frac{P_j M_{jj}}{P_j Q_j}(p_j + h_j)] - p_j$$

where the neoclassical measures would have $h_{i\ \text{not}\ =\ j} = 0$.

Consider the expression $k_{ij} - h_i$. It measures the proportionate rate of growth of the net stock of capital in activity j produced in activity i 'deflated' by the Harrod rate of technical progress in activity i. The expression $m_{jj} - h_j$ measures the proportionate rate of growth of activity j's output used by itself (it could equally represent the stock of goods-in-progress in activity j) 'deflated' by the Harrod rate of technical progress in activity j. The growing flows and stocks of reproducible commodities are 'deflated' to reflect the fact that it now requires less working and waiting to produce them. Consider finally the expression $r_j + p_i + h_i$. It shows the proportionate rate of growth of the net rental to be paid in activity j for the services of the capital goods reproducible in activity i 'inflated' by the Harrodian rate of technical progress in activity i. Why inflated? The prices of the primary inputs, working and waiting, can rise faster than the prices of what such primary inputs, directly and indirectly, produce because of the technical progress. It is clear then that $k_{ij} - h_i$ is the proportionate rate of change in the services of waiting in activity j indexed by the net stock of capital k_{ij} adjusted for the improvement in the efficiency in the activities producing the capital goods. If it takes less waiting to maintain and augment such capital goods then the capital goods themselves are being produced more efficiently. It is also immediate that such measures can be obtained only if we can measure Harrod rates of technical progress simultaneously for all activities – and this is what Leontief–Sraffa–Pasinetti accounts permit us to do.[16]

CONCLUSION

I have indicated what are the concepts of working and waiting in Harrodian measures of technical progress and how they are indexed or measured in a world exhibiting technical progress.

In papers mentioned in note 2, I have indicated the major theoretical problems confronting the implementation of Harrodian measures. In a static situation of unchanging technology, the various stocks of capital goods are measures of both simultaneously the services of the capital goods and the rates of saving or the measure of the services of carrying such capital goods or waiting. In a dynamic situation of technical progress, these two measures part company. The changing stocks of capital goods, as indexes of the services of the capital goods, are increasing because of the technical progress (that is, the growing stocks of the capital goods are not a separate source of growth but are produced by the advance in technology). The changing stocks of capital goods – all produced means of production – must be deflated by the Harrodian rates of technical progress (indeed, such rates of technical progress cannot be derived without this simultaneous 'inflation') to obtain changes in the flows of waiting. The rise of the capital stocks relative to waiting is precisely a measure of the fact that, because of the augmentation of the efficiency of waiting, owners of capital goods can now carry more, maintain more and, in forgoing present consumption at the same rate, augment and acquire more capital goods than before, so acquiring higher real incomes.[17]

In the introduction, the potential understatement of the rate of technical progress involved in the traditional neoclassical measures was noted. To conclude this chapter, this aim is illustrated by numbers drawn from a study by Cas and Rymes (Table 6.1). For the whole period covered by the study, the Harrodian measures show an average annual rate of increase of 1.7 per cent, whereas the traditional neoclassical measures show only 1.2 per cent, 30 per cent lower. For the period up to 1973, the mean rate of increase for the Harrod measures is 2.6 per cent, whereas the traditional measures show 1.9 per cent again about 30 per cent lower. Both measures show the sharp fall in measured total factor productivity or technical progress in Canada since the mid-1970s.

Table 6.1 Annual rates of growth, aggregate multifactor productivity in Canada, 1961–80

	Harrodian	Neoclassical
1961–2	6.9	5.1
1962–3	2.8	2.2
1963–4	3.3	2.4
1964–5	2.3	1.8
1965–6	2.0	1.6
1966–7	−0.3	−0.6
1967–8	4.2	3.2
1968–9	2.2	1.6
1969–70	−0.2	−0.2
1970–1	1.8	1.5
1971–2	2.5	2.0
1972–3	3.6	2.7
1973–4	−1.6	−1.4
1974–7	−1.9	−1.8
1975–6	2.9	2.6
1976–7	−0.1	−0.1
1977–8	−0.3	−0.1
1978–9	0.9	0.7
1979–80	0.3	0.2

Source: Cas and Rymes 1991: Table I–1

The difference in the measures is striking, and one is driven to decide which is the theoretically correct measure of technical progress. The Harrodian one seems superior for a better understanding of the processes by which the efficiencies of working and waiting are enhanced in any overall study of capital accumulation and technical progress in modern economies.

In the foregoing, I have been assuming that the 'working and waiting' supplied by individuals are fully employed. The Keynesian problem, however, suggests that 'working and waiting' may not be fully employed. An increase in waiting may take the form of attempting to hold not additional capital goods but rather additional amounts of the social convention called money and may result in a fall in productivity advance as unemployment of working and waiting results. The social convention called money introduces the question of the institutional form into the analysis. In general, however, we know very little about the relationship between institutional form, when money is concerned, and technology,[18] and even less about the connection between institutional form and technical progress.

NOTES

1 I presented a paper 'Conceptual and empirical problems in the Harrod–Robinson–Read measurement of technical change in Canada' to the International

Colloquium on Technical Change, University of Manchester, 11–13 September 1985. Professor Ian Steedman reiterated concern, which he had kindly expressed previously in correspondence, over the concept of waiting employed in my theoretical and empirical work on productivity measurement. In this chapter, I hope to explain the concept more clearly and allay perhaps the concern which he has, and no doubt others have. Professor Harcourt holds the view that the real rate of return to capital is determined not by overall capital intensity conditions but, in steady states for example, rather by growth rates and propensities to save or to wait. He supported my criticisms of Hicks–Solow measures and my argument for their replacement by Harrod measures of multifactor productivity. See his review of my book (Rymes 1971) in *Economic Journal*, June 1972. This chapter attempts to show that the Harrod measures are not based on any aggregate measures of waiting. Questions about the significance of Keynesian unemployment of 'working and waiting', which always concerned Professor Harcourt, and the satisfactory incorporation of the role of money in measures of the productivity of working and waiting remain, however, to be answered. I am indebted to Geoff Harcourt and René Durand for comments on earlier drafts.

2 The original argument was expressed in Rymes (1971) and later developed further (Rymes 1972, 1983). First empirical measures appeared in Rymes (1986); and more extensive empirical measures of Harrodian technical progress at the aggregate and detailed industry levels are provided in Cas and Rymes (1991).

3 The predicted understatement of the traditional measures is borne out by the Canadian estimates presented in the Cas–Rymes study. The understatement of the rate of technical progress by the neoclassical measures has also been shown by Hulten (1979) and is involved in the Domar aggregation procedures used by Hulten (1978). See also Hulten (1992).

4 I have elsewhere explored some of the problems involved in measuring technical progress when attention is paid to exhaustible natural agents. See Rymes (1993).

5 The most rigorous statement of such technical progress is found in Pasinetti (1981). See also Bertram Schefold (1976).

6 Harrod (1961: 300–4; 1936: 24) discusses the difference between waiting and commodity or reproducible capital. Joan Robinson, though adapting Harrod's concept of technical progress because of its correct treatment of reproducible inputs, did not accept waiting as a primary input. See Robinson (1962: Essay III; 1969: 310). Professor Larry Read, who showed how the Harrod concept of technical progress could be made operational, accepts a non-labour class of primary inputs (cf. Read (1961, 1968). The connection between Read's work and the Harrod theory is set out in Rymes (1983).

7 I shall not, except tangentially, consider the neoclassical or Hicksian concept of technical progress since I have criticized it exhaustively elsewhere (see the references in note 2). The logical flaws in it are also dealt with by Steedman (1983, 1985). It should be noted, as well, that Hicks appeared to have doubts about his earlier *Theory of Wages* conception; cf. Hicks (1973). He argued (p. 120 n. 3), 'It will therefore be noticed that on this plane of discourse there can by definition be no reswitching. Every technique to which a switch is made is a new technique. In practice, isn't it?' A variant of the Hicksian measure is illustrated by recent attempts to distinguish between technological progress and efficiency change or innovations and 'catching up', the Farrell–Salter approach. (See Perelman 1995.) Since it is costly to install and update technology, it cannot be argued without such a theory of costs just how much 'catching up' there is to do at any time. This variant does not deal with the basic issue raised in this chapter.

8 See, for example, Hicks (1985: 308–9).

66

9 I am indebted to Professor Marc Lavoie, Université d'Ottawa, for discussions on this point. I think this was Joan Robinson's complaint about the concept of 'waiting' as a factor of production, namely, that no one individual need receive consumption to provide it (cf. Robinson 1971: 10). Yet the problem with the state argument is that an institutional form is introduced into the discussion without taking into account the theoretical position that the technical conditions of production are not independent of the choice of costly institutional form. On this, see Coase (1994).

10 Robinson (1973: 127). In a letter to Professor A. Asimakopulos dated 11 July 1971, Sraffa, responding to Asimakopulos's query about the role of demand in *Production of Commodities by Means of Commodities*, states, 'I take it that the drama is enacted on Marshall's stage where the claimants for influence are utility and cost of production. Now utility has made little progress (since the 1870s) towards acquiring a tangible existence and survives in textbooks at the purely subjective level. On the other hand, cost of production has successfully survived Marshall's attempt to reduce it to an equally evanescent nature under the name of "disutility", and is still kicking in the term of hours of labour, tons of raw materials, etc. This, rather than the relative slope of the two curves, is why it seems to me that the "influence" of the two things on price is not comparable' (Asimakopulos 1988: 142).

11 See, for instance, Buchanan (1969) and O'Driscoll and Rizzo (1985).

12 See Robinson (1979).

13 One of the difficulties associated with joint production is that, of course, the prices do not cancel out 'along the rows'.

14 I ignore changes in capacity utilization in this chapter until the conclusion.

15 If one wrote of the gross rentals for the services of the capital goods, one would have $P_i(R_{ij} + \delta_{ij})K_{ij}/Q_j$, where δ_{ij}, the rate of depreciation of the ith capital good in the jth activity, part of the intermediate input–output coefficients in A, means that $R_{ij} + \delta_{ij}$ is the gross rate of return.

16 Modern input–output accounts now permit empirical estimates of Harrodian rates of multifactor productivity advance both at the activity and aggregate economy level. See Cas and Rymes (1991).

17 Setting aside the question of the interdependence between technology and institutional form, suppose firms' saving and investing are permitted by the willingness of persons to hold claims on the firms. With Harrod-neutral technical progress, with unchanging net rates of return to capital and relative goods prices, the real value of the claims on the firms will rise as the efficiency of the waiting, supplied by the households in accommodating the capital accumulation of the firms, is increasing. Real wages and real returns to waiting will be rising equally, as exhibited by rising real wage rates and real rising prices of the equity claims on the growing net stocks of capital as the efficiency of the working and waiting supplied by individuals in the economy is enhanced by technical progress.

18 For one beginning see Rogers and Rymes (forthcoming).

REFERENCES

Asimakopulos, A. (1988) 'Keynes and Sraffa: visions and perspectives', *Investment, Employment and Income Distribution*, Cambridge: Polity Press.

Buchanan, J. (1969) *Cost and Choice: An Inquiry in Economic Theory*, Chicago: University of Chicago Press.

Cas, A. and Rymes, T. K. (1991) *On Concepts and Measures of Multifactor Productivity in Canada*, Cambridge: Cambridge University Press.

Coase, R. (1994) 'The institutional structure of production', *Essays on Economics and Economists*, Chicago: University of Chicago Press.

Harrod, R. (1936) *The Trade Cycle*, Oxford: Clarendon Press.

―――― (1961) 'The neutrality of improvements', *Economic Journal* 71: 300–4.

―――― (1972) 'Review of Rymes (1971)', *Economic Journal* 82.

Hicks, J. (1973) *Capital and Time*, Oxford: Clarendon Press.

―――― (1985) 'Sraffa and Ricardo: a critical review', in G. A. Caravale (ed.) *The Legacy of Ricardo*, Oxford: Blackwell.

Hulten, C. R. (1978) 'Growth accounting with intermediate inputs', *Review of Economics Studies* 34: 511–18.

―――― (1979) 'On the "importance" of productivity change', *American Economic Review* 69: 126–36.

―――― (1992) 'Accounting for the wealth of nations: the net versus gross output controversy and its ramifications', *Scandinavian Journal of Economics, Supplement* 94: 9–24.

O'Driscoll, G. and Rizzo, M. J. (1985) *The Economics of Time and Ignorance*, Oxford: Blackwell.

Pasinetti, L. L. (1981) *Structural Change and Economic Growth*, Cambridge: Cambridge University Press.

Perelman, S. (1995) 'R & D, technical progress and efficiency change in industrial activities', *Review of Income and Wealth* 41: 349–66.

Read, L. M. (1961) 'The measurement of total factor productivity', Dominion Bureau of Statistics, mimeo.

―――― (1968) 'The measurement of total factor productivity appropriate to wage–price guidelines', *Canadian Journal of Economics* 1: 349–58.

Robinson, J. (1962) 'Essay III: A model of technical progress', in *Essays on the Theory of Economic Growth*, London: Macmillan.

―――― (1969) *The Accumulation of Capital*, 3rd edition, London: Macmillan.

―――― (1971) 'Marx, Marshall and Keynes', *Collected Economic Papers*, vol. 2, Oxford: Blackwell.

―――― (1973) 'Economics today', *Collected Economic Papers*, vol. 4, Oxford: Blackwell.

―――― (1979) 'Garegnani on effective demand', *Cambridge Journal of Economics* 3(2). Reprinted in Eatwell, J. and Milgate, M. (eds) (1983) *Keynes' Economics and the Theory of Value Distribution*, London: Duckworth.

Rogers, C. and Rymes, T. K. (forthcoming) 'Keynes's monetary theory of value and modern banking', in G. Harcourt and P. Riach (eds) *The Second Edition of The General Theory*, London: Routledge.

Rymes, T. K. (1971) *On Concepts of Capital and Technical Change*, Cambridge: Cambridge University Press.

―――― (1972) 'The measurement of capital and total factor productivity in the context of the Cambridge Theory of capital', *Review of Income and Wealth* 18: 79–108.

―――― (1983) 'More on the measurement of total factor productivity', *Review of Income and Wealth* 34: 297–316.

―――― (1986) 'The measurement of multifactorial productivity in an input–output framework: new Canadian estimates', in A. Franz and N. Rainer (eds) *Problems of Compilation of Input–Output Tables*, vol. 2, Vienna: Schriftenreihe der Österreichischen Statistischen Gesellschaft.

―――― (1993) 'Some theoretical problems in accounting for sustainable consumption', in A. Franz and C. Stahner (eds) *Approaches to Environmental Accounting*, Berlin: Physica-Verlag.

Schefold, B. (1976) 'Different forms of technical progress', *Economic Journal* 86: 806–19.

Steedman, I. (1983) 'On the measurement and aggregation of productivity increase', *Metroeconomica* 35: 223–33.

——— (1985) 'On the impossibility of Hicks-neutral change', *Economic Journal* 95: 746–58.

7

FIXED CAPITAL AS A PROBLEM IN JOINT PRODUCTION

Some historical considerations

Peter Groenewegen

In their review of Sraffa's *Production of Commodities by Means of Commodities*, Harcourt and Massaro point out that

> the interest in joint production [in Part II of Sraffa's book] lies 'in its being the genus of which Fixed Capital is the leading species'. Treating fixed assets as joint products one year older when they are counted in the means of production introduces as many extra unknowns (that is, prices of fixed assets) as there are years in the economic life time of the fixed assets concerned (Sraffa does not make clear what determines these life times). Each industry is therefore divided into processes which are distinguished one from another by the ages of the fixed assets in their means of production and total output. The equations of these processes provide the additional equation needed to solve for the prices of the fixed assets.
>
> (Harcourt and Massaro 1964: 450)

In this way, the prices imputed to the fixed assets in the production process imply an annual charge for the use of the fixed capital enabling full replacement of the asset and payment of the competitive, uniform profit rate on the value of fixed assets employed. This Sraffa formulation is quite general. The prices for the asset, which change year after year, allow the appropriate depreciation to be calculated on an annual basis irrespective of the pattern of productive efficiency of the machine.

The approach to fixed capital in Sraffa's book easily generates some reflections on classical political economy. These arise from Sraffa's inspiration for this unusual treatment of fixed capital from an impressive list of classical authors: Torrens, Ricardo, Malthus and Marx (Sraffa 1960: 94–5). As Pasinetti (1977: 2–4, 24–6; 1980: esp. xiv–xv) has pointed out, 'this is one of the more interesting innovations of the classical theories'.

Sraffa explained that the notion of treating fixed capital as a form of joint production seems to harmonize with the 'classical picture of an agricultural system where the annual product, in Smith's words, naturally divides itself into two parts, one destined for replacing a capital, the other for constituting a revenue' (Sraffa 1960: 94, referring to Smith 1776 [1976]: I, p. 332, IIiii4). However, as Sraffa also points out, the treatment of fixed capital as a case of joint production by taking the residual part of the fixed capital as part of the produce was first explicitly suggested by Torrens, from where it was adopted by Ricardo, Malthus and, via Malthus, by Marx. After these authors, the method 'seems to have fallen into oblivion' until its resurrection by Sraffa in part II of his book.[1]

The above raises a number of historical questions about aspects of classical political economy and its subdivisions. Three periods can be identified in the classical writings during the gradual transformation of what Pasinetti (1980: xiv) calls the 'pre-classical concept of national wealth understood as a stock'. Quesnay's discovery of the concept of fixed capital as part of the analysis of the annual reproduction of wealth is one. Another is the adoption of the joint product approach by Torrens in 1818. A further phase in capital theory is the disappearance of this view, which coincides with the decline of the classical period as defined by Marx (see Groenewegen 1987). These breaks are probably associated with the gradual metamorphosis of the items constituting fixed capital in actual practice, something which would have exerted influence on a treatment of fixed capital by economic writers. Whether this is the case or not is something requiring explanation in the light of the subsequent return by the marginalists to either the traditional stock view of the matter (Pasinetti 1980: xiv) or to an exclusive circulating capital view.

The subject matter of this chapter follows these historical phases. The next section looks at the treatment of capital as stock in the literature before 1750. After that, the treatment of the subject in the second half of the eighteenth century is examined. The following section looks at the various presentations of the joint production treatment of fixed capital, with special reference to Torrens's pioneering discussion in 1818. A final section offers some conclusions.

TREATMENT OF FIXED CAPITAL BEFORE 1750

The treatment of 'stock' in the early literature was largely confined to either a loosely defined mercantile notion, or an accounting concept of capital in terms of the resources invested in a business. As a shorthand for accumulated wealth, the word 'stock' began to be quite widely used in the second half of the seventeenth century (e.g. Coke 1670: 5; Child 1690: 154). Barbon and North identified stock with trading, drawing parallels between stocklords and landlords, and defining the components of stock as 'Goods, that is, Mettals, Manufactures' (Barbon 1690 [1934] 20; [North] 1691 [1954]: 517–18). This general position persisted until the middle of the eighteenth century. The accounting concept is illustrated in the definition of 'capital' provided by Postlethwayt:

> Capital, amongst merchants, bankers and traders signifies the sum of money which individuals being to make up the common stock of partnership, when it is first formed. It is also said of the stock which a merchant at first puts into trade, for his account. It signifies likewise the fund of a trading company or corporation, in which sense the word stock is generally added to it. Thus we say, *the capital stock of a bank*, etc.
>
> (Postlethwayt 1751: I, p. 448)

Petty (1691 [1965]: 251–2) appears to have used the word 'capital' only once, referring to 'the Hollanders Capital in the *East India* Company', an application of the accounting concept of shareholders' funds. Boisguilbert (1697: 167) at one stage mentions capital in the context of productive investment in farming and trade, as a sum of money lent for that purpose; earlier he used it in the sense of general property (ibid.: 165, 167). Richard Cantillon (1755 [1931]: 202, 204, 220) uses the word 'capital' to describe the principal of a loan to an undertaker who uses it productively; in a later chapter, he used the word 'avances' in a domestic industry situation (lace production), where the capital is used to pay the wages of spinners, lace-makers and a portion (left unspecified) of those who have made their tools (ibid.: 226).[2]

More interesting are the implicit definitions of the political arithmeticians when estimating national wealth. Good examples are Petty (1665 [1965]) and King (1697 [1936]). Both estimate part of the national wealth (particularly that associated with the landed wealth) by capitalization of the annual income (Petty 1665 [1965]: 105–10; King 1697 [1936]: 61). When they enumerate the main items of wealth (excluding land and people), they first mention housing, then shipping, then cattle, then coined gold and silver, then 'Wares, Merchandizes, Utensils of Plate and Furnitures . . .' (Petty 1665 [1965]: 106–7 – cf. Petty 1691 [1965]: 302–5; King 1697 [1936]: 61 – indicates that shipping for him included 'other Carriages, Engines and Instruments in Trade, Arts and Imployments'.) This suggests that by the end of the seventeenth century the major forms of 'fixed capital' were buildings, shipping and cattle, whereas tools and machines formed only a small part of the national capital stock. Hence depreciation would have presented itself as the necessary repairs of the physical wear and tear in buildings and shipping and the physical replacement of (working) cattle. Other tools and instruments of trade were too insignificant for their depreciation to have posed a visible problem.

Deane and Cole (1969: 270) report that King's total estimate of English and Welsh national capital (about £310 million excluding coin and household goods) is made up of two-thirds in the form of land, 17.5 per cent in housing 8 per cent in cattle, and the remaining 10 per cent in 'Shipping and other Carriages, Engines and Instruments of Trade, Arts and employment on Naval and Military stores (including defence works), Foreign and Domestic Wares,

Commodities and Provisions'. If engines and instruments of trade were the same proportion in that part of capital stock (as enumerated in the quotation) as in 1760, then this item approximated only £3.9 million or 1.25 per cent of the English capital stock in 1688 (estimated from data in Mathias and Postan 1978: 42, 58). Since this proportion was likely to have been lower in 1688 than in 1760, engines and instruments were clearly not very important for seventeenth-century economic observers. However, when landed wealth is, more appropriately, excluded from the capital stock, this proportion rises to 3.5 per cent.

NOTIONS OF CAPITAL FROM 1750 TO 1800

During the second half of the eighteenth century, notions of capital and stock underwent a significant change, much of it associated with Quesnay's work. By contrast, British work on the subject remained in the earlier style. An example is that of Tucker (1774 [1973]: 184–5, 187), who implicitly identifies capital with a 'stock of wealth' or the resources invested in a business. Steuart (1767) is similar. He saw borrowing 'for carrying on trade' as more 'relative to the merchant than to the manufacturer [that is, artisan]' and argued that 'the first matter [raw materials], and the instruments of manufacture' could only be considered as objectives in a production loan transaction (II, p. 137).

The modern concept of capital, including that of fixed capital, originates with the works of Quesnay. He clearly formulated these concepts within the analysis of production expressed through the national accounting framework underlying his analysis of annual reproduction. The significance of Quesnay's major contribution and its practical application was grasped by Turgot:

> M. Quesnay was the first to establish the correct notion of the revenue, when he learnt to distinguish the *gross product* from the *net* product, and not to include the profits of the cultivator in the *net* product. . . . M. Quesnay has developed the mechanism of agriculture which is based entirely on very large original advances and requires in addition annual advances which are equally necessary. It is therefore necessary to deduct from the sale of the produce: first, all the expenses or *annual advances*; secondly, the interest of the original advances; thirdly, their maintenance and the replacement of their inevitable decay, at least equal to the interest; fourthly, the subsistence and reasonable profit of the entrepreneur farmer and his agents, the wages of their labour and of their industry.
>
> (Turgot 1763 [1973]: 102–3)

Particularly relevant is Turgot's reference to Quesnay's treatment of the part of the gross revenue (gross product) destined to replace the capital or the advances. Annual advances or circulating capital had to be totally replaced; for original advances or fixed capital only that part required for the 'maintenance and the replacement of their inevitable decay' had to be reproduced from the annual product. However, Physiocratic writings do not contain statements showing that the Physiocrats *explicitly* treated that part of the fixed capital (original advances) not needing to be replaced as part of the annual product of society.

The joint-product method of dealing with fixed capital, however, can easily be accommodated by, for example, Quesnay's product calculations in the 1766 version of the *'tableau économique'*. Its data (Quesnay 1766a [1958]: 794–802) provide for a capital stock at the start of the period of 13 milliards of which 10 milliards are the original advances (fixed capital) for the productive (agricultural) class, 2 milliards the annual advances or circulating capital of this class and 1 milliard the annual advances of the sterile class. This investment yields a gross product on Quesnay's accounting of 7 milliards; 5 milliards in the agricultural sector sufficient to replace 2 milliards of annual advances plus the 1 milliard of the original advances, since Quesnay assumed that the stock of fixed capital (original advances) depreciates at an annual rate of 10 per cent. Net revenue is then put at 2 milliards, the difference between gross product and capital reproduction in the agricultural sector.[3] If Quesnay had used the joint-product approach for fixed capital, then gross product of the agricultural sector is a joint product of 14 milliards (5 milliards of agricultural produce and 9 milliards of left-over fixed capital) which likewise reproduces the capital stock (10 milliards of fixed capital and 2 milliards of circulating capital) plus 2 milliards of net product. However, neither Quesnay nor for that matter, Turgot and Adam Smith ever produced such a picture of joint production in which left-over fixed capital is included as part of the annual product flow in the accounting framework.

As suggested in the next section, the explicit introduction of the joint-production treatment of fixed capital seems to have been inspired by the complexities for value theory from the use of fixed capital in production. Why were such complexities ignored by eighteenth-century writers, who recognized the importance of fixed capital as part of their analyses and who identified the problem of depreciation within the process of reproduction and the setting of necessary prices which ensured that reproduction? Is this difference associated with the changing forms this capital was perceived to take? Discussion of the types of fixed capital identified by Quesnay, Turgot and Smith in their writings is needed to answer these questions.

Quesnay provides relatively little discussion of the characteristics of fixed and circulating capital and no catalogue of their components. In a footnote to the *'Analyse'* (Quesnay 1766a [1958]: 795 n2) he clearly distinguished between annual and original advances, his terminology for circulating and fixed capital. The latter is worth in total five times the value of the required annual advances, while the interest calculated on the original advances is designed to cover both depreciation costs and the risks incurred in making the investment. Depreciation is defined as the continual repairs required to keep the stock of original advances intact (ibid.: 798). The components of advances must be largely inferred from his descriptions of agricultural reproduction costs, as in his article *Farmers* (Quesnay 1756 [1983]: 14–15).[4] However, when demonstrating that advances do not consist of money, Quesnay presents a brief catalogue of their physical composition: 'Survey the farms and the workshops and see what are the properties of these so precious advances. You will find buildings, cattle, seed, raw materials, furniture and instruments of all kinds' (1766b [1958]: 846).

In a discussion of advances in manufacturing and agriculture, Turgot (1766 [1977]: 69–76, esp. 69–71) listed capital requirements which included buildings, cattle and tools and instruments as the major forms of original advances, circulating capital (annual advances) being confined to the wages fund and the supply of raw materials. Turgot also included of infrastructure: 'canals, markets and buildings of every kind'. The distinction between these types of advance rested on the (annual) production period: annual advances had to be totally reproduced within that period, whereas only a portion (assumed to be 10 per cent by Quesnay) of the original advances had to be reproduced.

Adam Smith both advanced and retrogressed on this discussion. 'Fixed capitals' are defined by him as 'improvement of land, useful machines and instruments of trade, or suchlike things as yield a revenue or profit without changing masters'. Smith also indicated that 'different occupations require very different proportions between the fixed and the circulating capitals employed in them', and later added to fixed capital 'the acquired and useful abilities of all the inhabitants or members of the society' (Smith 1776 [1976]: bk II, ch. 1, paras 5, 6 and 17). Smith also argued that the expense of maintaining the fixed capital 'must be excluded from the net revenue', and this expense is compared to that of repairs in a private estate (ibid.: bk. II, ch. 2, paras 6 and 8). He did not, however, develop the notion of depreciation of fixed capital to any extent apart from explicitly excluding it, and the stock of fixed capital, from the annual revenue.

Quesnay, Turgot and Smith show a clear awareness of a category of fixed capital in the form of buildings and cattle (but also, especially in the case of Smith, including machines). More importantly, although Quesnay, Turgot and Smith grasped the general concept of depreciation and its association with the durability of capital, they failed to appreciate the analytical problems it raised. They treated depreciation as part of the technical data and not as an economic problem to be explained. This was perhaps appropriate at a time when simple repairs were all that was required in order to keep the dominant forms of fixed capital intact. This question is taken up further in the concluding section.

PETER GROENEWEGEN

THE CLASSICAL JOINT-PRODUCT APPROACH TO FIXED CAPITAL

Sraffa clearly stated that the explicit joint-product treatment of fixed capital originated with Torrens's critical comments on Ricardo's theory of value (Torrens 1818 [1984]). In this critique, among other things Torrens also wished to demonstrate his own value proposition (more fully developed in Torrens 1821 [1965]: 25–42) that capitals of equal value, even if of unequal durability, produce equal values provided that the residual value of the fixed capital is included in the final product. Assume that wool production requires a fixed capital of $1,500 and that circulating capital (for wages and raw materials) requires $500; silk production requires $500 of fixed capital and $1,500 of circulating capital. With depreciation of the fixed capital at 10 per cent, the principle that equal values of capital ($2,000 in both cases) produce equal values appears to be violated if the only relative values of wool and silk are considered. The value of the first equals $850 ($500 to replace circulating capital, $150 for the depreciation of fixed capital plus $100 for profits on total capital) whereas the price of silk is $1,750 (being $1,500 for wages and raw materials or the replacement of circulating capital, $50 for depreciation of fixed capital and likewise $200 for profit.) If residual fixed capital – $1,350 for wool production and $450 for silk production – is included in the product, then Torrens's proposition is true and equal capitals of $2,000 produce equal products of $2,200 given the rate of profit of 10 per cent. This proposition, when repeated in Torrens (1821 [1965]) was criticized by Ricardo (1823 [1951]: 393–5), who argued that this argument required a clear definition of equal capitals when they consisted of heterogeneous commodities. This could be done only in value terms. Moreover, given the time dimension in the value of capital, it also required the assumption of equal time periods for the employment of the fixed capitals.

In the writings of these nineteenth-century economists, the emphasis had shifted to manufactures. Hence, the dominant form of fixed capital in their analyses is undoubtedly the machine. This can be demonstrated from Ricardo's *Principles*, whose fixed-capital illustrations invariably emphasize machines, a major form of investment in a rich country (1821 [1951]: 266, cf. pp. 42 and 30–1). Ricardo was aware that the distinction between fixed and circulating capital is simply one of degree, depending as it does on its durability relative to the particular production process under consideration (ibid: 31, 150). At the same time, the problems raised by different durability of capital in both the theory of value and of distribution plagued Ricardo more and more. This included problems of depreciation (ibid.: 30–8; his use of Torrens's method as a simplification occurs on p. 33). Ricardo's final paper (Ricardo, (1823 [1951]) explained why the method of Torrens, which he had briefly used in the third edition of the *Principles* (1821 [1951]: 33), did not solve the value problems in which he himself was interested. It begged the question of capital valuation (Ricardo 1823 [1951]: 383–95). The value of the fixed capital and the value of the residual product were treated as data by Torrens rather than unknowns (see Torrens 1821 [1965]: 27–9).

Malthus also adopted the Torrens joint-product method, from Torrens's *Essay on the Production of Wealth* (1821 [1965]). Malthus (1823: 11) specifically ascribed it to Torrens. Two years later, he repeated the argument in a footnote to a paper written in 1825 (published as Malthus 1829: 174n), this time without acknowledgement. He later elaborated on the subject in the content of the theory of the profits.

> The reader will be aware that if we reckon the value of the fixed capital employed as a part of the advances, we must reckon the remaining value of such capital at the end of the year as a part of the annual returns. Without a correction of this kind it would appear that in those departments of industry in which the greatest quantity of fixed capital had been applied, the value of the capital compared with the value of the produce had been the greatest, from which it would seem to follow that the rate of profits had been the lowest; but though the capitalist naturally considers the whole of what he employs in production as capital advanced; yet in reality his annual advances consist only of his circulating capital, the wear and tear of his fixed capital with the interest upon it, and the interest of that part of his circulating capital which consists of the money employed in making his annual payments as they are called for.
>
> (Malthus 1836: 169)

In the third edition of his *Elements*, James Mill introduced Torrens's joint-product method as a simplification of language and, hence, of great advantage on a priori grounds:

> The case of fixed and of circulating capital may be treated as the same, by merely considering the fixed capital as a product, which is regularly consumed and replaced, by every course of productive operations. The capital, not consumed, may be always taken, as an additional commodity, the result of the productive process.
>
> (Mill 1826 [1966]: 251)

Neither Malthus nor Mill seems to have appreciated Ricardo's criticism of Torrens's joint-product method. Torrens, as Ricardo (1823 [1951]) explicitly noted, could not adequately explain the meaning of equal capitals which produced the equal values in his theory. Five years earlier, Ricardo had similarly exposed a counter-example from Torrens's pen because Torrens, in assuming equal capitals because the capitals under consideration were fixed capital of *equal duration*, had neglected the fact that they were of unequal value (1818 [1951]: 310–13, esp. 311–12). Neither were published until their discovery by Sraffa among the Mill–Ricardo papers.

CONCLUDING REMARKS

The solution to the capital value problem in the joint-product method was not discovered by the classical economists, but had to await Sraffa's analysis, apart from some exceptions noted earlier.[5] The abandonment of Torrens's method can be largely explained by the fact that its apparent simplicity did not really solve the problems raised by fixed relative to circulating capital. As Mill (1826 [1966]: 251) implied, it simply suppressed it. Jevons was to do this again when he argued:

> the notion of capital assumes a new degree of simplicity as soon as we recognise that what has been called a part is really the whole. Capital ... consists merely in the aggregate of those commodities which are required for sustaining labourers of any kind of class engaged in work.
>
> (Jevons 1879: 223)

This simplification sustained the early developments of marginalist theory, especially its Austrian variant, by doing away with the distinction between fixed and circulating capital for all practical purposes. The method of treating all capital as circulating capital remained an important premise of much of the marginalist theory of capital.

Marx, on the other hand, favourably mentioned the Torrens joint-production method of treating fixed (i.e. constant) capital. In *Capital*, Marx quoted the method as described by Malthus, using it to demonstrate that the part of fixed (constant) capital 'advanced for the production of value' equals the difference between the value of fixed capital at the beginning and at the end of the period remaining as part of the output of the process ([1867 [1959]: 213 and n1). Earlier, Marx (1862–3 [1972]: 71–2) had mentioned Torrens's joint-production method as something of interest.

This leaves the question of whether the rise and fall of Torrens's method was associated with changes in the perception of the components of fixed capital by early-nineteenth-century writers. Such a different perception can in fact be observed: machinery did not become very prominent in the category of fixed capital in the literature until the nineteenth century. This reflects in the rise in relative importance of machinery in the national capital stock between 1760, the 1830s and 1860. At 1851–60 replacement cost, the value of industrial machinery and equipment rose from £9 million in 1760 to £61 million in 1830 and to £160 in 1860, a relative rise from 3.6 per cent (1760) to 7.0 per cent (1830) and 15.2 per cent (1860) of total productive capital (Mathias and Postan 1978: 42).

From this historical evidence, it is reasonable to suggest that the rise of machines also transformed depreciation and the problem of maintaining fixed capital intact from a relatively simple physical problem of repairs into a major value problem. The following hypothesis seems not unwarranted. The unimportance of machinery in national capital stock initially made the depreciation problem not very important. More detailed analysis of fixed capital by the Physiocrats and Smith gave the problem greater prominence but saw it solved by simple depreciation rules such as Quesnay's 10 per cent formula. Greater emphasis on value considerations, together with greater prominence of machines, inspired the joint-production solution by Torrens. It failed to meet the problem satisfactorily, as Ricardo pointed out. The method stayed (James Mill and Malthus) and was noted by Marx. Subsequently, many marginalists tended to assume the problem away. Since then, depreciation has remained a difficult problem, often solved by practical rules, sometimes by convenient theory. As indicated by Harcourt and Massaro (1964), the rehabilitation of Torrens's idea of the joint-production method provides a theoretically satisfactory solution to a difficult and important problem, which much of Harcourt's earlier work (1982: Part I) on accounting procedures and company behaviour under inflationary conditions had tried to address.[6]

ACKNOWLEDGEMENT

I am indebted to Tony Aspromourgos for useful comments. These historical observations on joint production supplement those of Kurz (1986 [1990]).

NOTES

1   I can find no hint of the Torrens method in the first edition of McCulloch's *Principles*, nor in the lengthier treatment of the subject by J. S. Mill. On the use of joint production by von Neumann, Koopmans and Leontiev, see Schefold (1987: 1030–1).

2   Such tools tended to be not very expensive, either for the spinner or the lace-maker. The portion of this cost as part of the advance in this case can imply either an interest, depreciation charge; cf. below, on Quesnay. Postlethwayt (1751: I, p. 116) was also familiar with the concept of advance. Higgs's translation often uses the word 'capital' to translate the French *fonds* or adds it gratuitously to some passages to give Cantillon a more modern flavour.

3   It is unnecessary to deal with the manufacturing (sterile) sector which, in the Physiocratic system, is assumed not to yield a net product.

4   These costs include 'interest on the stock for outlays on the purchase of horse, ploughs, carts, and other landed advances', an ambiguous phrase which can mean either depreciation (as Quesnay implied in Quesnay (1766a [1958]) or the necessary cost of capital investment. See my introduction to Quesnay (1756 [1983]: xvi).

5   In the last sentence of note 1 above.

6   I recall here my initial surprise when seeing Geoff Harcourt at a Canberra sitting organized by the Mathews Committee on Taxation and Inflation in 1974. This discussed the effects on business tax liability of inflation on stock and other

capital replacement values. Until then, I had (wrongly) associated him only with strict theoretical debate on capital, distribution and growth.

REFERENCES

Barbon, N. (1690 [1934]) *A Discourse of Trade*, a reprint of economic tracts, ed. Jacob Hollander, Baltimore: Johns Hopkins Press.

Boisguilbert, P. Pesant de (1697) *Le Détail de la France*, n.p., n.p.

Cantillon, R. (1755 [1931]) *Essai sur la nature du Commerce en Général*, London: Macmillan.

Child, J. (1690) *A Discourse of Trade*, London.

Coke, J. (1670) *A Discourse on Trade*, London.

Deane, P. and Cole, W. A. (1969) *British Economic Growth 1688–1959*, Cambridge: Cambridge University Press.

Groenewegen, P. (1987) 'Marx's conception of classical political economy: an evaluation', *Political Economy: Studies in the Surplus Approach* 3(1): 19–35.

Harcourt, G. C. (1982) *The Social Science Imperialists: Selected Essays*, ed. P. Kerr, London: Allen & Unwin.

Harcourt, G. C. and Massaro, V. G. (1964) 'Mr Sraffa's production of commodities', *Economic Record* 40(91): 442–54.

Jevons, W. S. (1879) *Theory of Political Economy*, London: Macmillan.

King, G. (1697 [1936]) *On the Naval Trade of England anno 1688 and the National Profit then Arising Thereby*, in G. E. Barnet (ed.) *Two Tracts by Gregory King*, Baltimore: The Johns Hopkins Press, 1936.

Kurz, H. (1986 [1990]) 'Classical and early neo-classical economists on joint production', in H. Kurz, *Capital, Distribution and Effective Demand*, Cambridge: Polity Press.

Malthus, T. R. (1823) *The Measure of Value Stated and Illustrated*, London: John Murray.

—— (1829) 'On the measure of the conditions necessary to the supply of commodities', in *Transactions of the Royal Society of Literature of the United Kingdom*, vol. 1, London: John Murray.

—— (1836) *Principles of Political Economy*, London: William Pickering.

Marx, K. (1862–3 [1972]) *Theories of Surplus Value Part III*, London: Lawrence & Wishart.

—— (1867 [1959]) *Capital*, vol. 1, Moscow: Foreign Languages Publishing House.

Mathias, P. and Postan, M. M. (1978) *Cambridge Economic History of Europe*, vol. 7. Cambridge: Cambridge University Press.

Mill, J. (1826 [1966]) *Elements of Political Economy*, 3rd edition. Reprinted in Mill, J., *Economic Writings of James Mill*, ed. De Winch, Edinburgh: Oliver & Boyd.

[North, D.] (1691 [1954]) *Discourses upon Trade*, reprinted in *Early English Tracts on Commerce*, ed. J. R. McCulloch, Cambridge: Cambridge University Press.

Pasinetti, L. L. (1977) *Lectures on the Theory of Production*, London: Macmillan.

—— (1980) *Essays on the Theory of Joint Production*, London: Macmillan.

Petty, W. (1665 [1965]) *Verbum Sapienti*. Reprinted in Petty, W., *Economic Writings of Sir William Petty*, ed. C. H. Hull, New York: Kelley.

—— (1961 [1965]) *Political Arithmetick*. Reprinted in Petty, W., *Economic Writings of Sir William Petty*, ed. C. H. Hull, New York: Kelley.

—— (1691 [1965]) *Political Arithmetick*. Reprinted in Petty, W., *Economic Writings of Sir William Petty*, ed. C. H. Hull, New York: Kelley.

Postlethwayt, M. (1751) *The Universal Dictionary of Trade and Commerce*, London.

Quesnay, F. (1756 [1983]) *Farmers*, Reprints of Economic Classics, series 2, no. 2, ed. P. Groenewegen, Sydney: Department of Economics, University of Sydney.

—— (1766a [1958]) 'Analyse de la formule arithmétique du tableau Économique', in *François Quesnay et la Physiocratie*, vol. 2, Paris: Institut National d'Études Démographiques (INED).

—— (1766b [1958]) 'Dialogues sur le commerce', in *François Quesnay et la Physiocratie*, vol. 2, Paris: INED.

Ricardo, D. (1818 [1951]) 'Fragments on Torrens', in *Works and Correspondence of David Ricardo*, vol. 4, ed. P. Sraffa, Cambridge: Cambridge University Press.

—— (1821 [1951]) *Principles of Political Economy and Taxation*. Vol. 1 of *Works and Correspondence of David Ricardo*, ed. P. Sraffa, Cambridge: Cambridge University Press.

—— (1823 [1951]) ['Absolute value and exchangeable value'], in *Works and Correspondence of David Ricardo*, vol. 4, ed. P. Sraffa, Cambridge: Cambridge University Press.

Schefold, B. (1987) 'Joint production in linear models', in J. Eatwell, M. Milgate and P. Newman, *The New Palgrave: A Dictionary of Economics*, vol. 2, London: Macmillan.

Smith, A. (1776 [1976]) *An Inquiry into the Nature and Causes of the Wealth of Nations*, ed. R. H. Campbell and A. S. Skinner, Oxford: Clarendon Press.

Sraffa, P. (1960) *Production of Commodities by Means of Commodities by Means of Commodities: Prelude to a Critique of Economic Theory*, Cambridge: Cambridge University Press.

Steuart, J. (1767) *An Inquiry into the Principles of Political Oeconomy*, London: A Millar & T. Cadell.

Torrens, R. (1818 [1984]) 'Strictures on Mr Ricardo's doctrine respecting exchangeable value', in R. Torrens, *The Economists Refuted (1808) and Other Early Writings*, Reprints of Economic Classics series 2, no. 3, ed. P. Groenewegen, Sydney: Department of Economics, University of Sydney.

—— (1821 [1965]) *An Essay on the Production of Wealth*, New York: Augustus M. Kelley.

Tucker, J. (1774 [1973]) *Four Tracts on Political and Commercial Subjects*, tract I, in R. L. Meek (ed.) *Precursors of Adam Smith*, London: Everyman's University Library.

Turgot, A. R. J. (1763 [1973]) 'Plan for a paper on taxation', in *The Economics of A. R. J. Turgot*, ed. P. D. Groenewegen, The Hague: Martinus Nijhoff.

—— (1766 [1977]) 'Reflections on the production and distribution of wealth', in *The Economics of A. R. J. Turgot*, ed. P. D. Groenewegen, The Hague: Martinus Nijhoff.

8

BÖHM-BAWERK'S LETTERS TO J. B. CLARK

A pre-Cambridge controversy in the theory of capital

Avi J. Cohen and Helmar Drost

INTRODUCTION

The Cambridge capital theory controversies acquired an identity in large part due to Geoff Harcourt's (1972) masterful chronicle and analysis. The Cambridge controversies, however, were only the most recent in a long tradition of capital theory controversies. There were extensive debates between Eugen von Böhm-Bawerk, J. B. Clark and Irving Fisher at the turn of the century, and between Frank Knight, Friedrich von Hayek and Nicholas Kaldor in the 1930s. These earlier, pre-Cambridge capital theory controversies still lack a coherent narrative, let alone a comprehensive analysis of Harcourt's standard.

This chapter fills part of the missing narrative of the Böhm-Bawerk–Clark controversy.[1] That controversy was carried out largely in print, but also in private correspondence. While Clark's letters to Böhm-Bawerk seem to have been destroyed in Second World War Allied bombing raids (Beach and Bostaph 1982), thirteen of Böhm-Bawerk's letters to Clark are preserved in the John Bates Clark Papers in the Rare Book and Manuscript Library of Columbia University (Böhm-Bawerk 1889–1908). The letters, written in German, to our knowledge have never been published. Our English translation appears in this chapter.

In order to place the letters in context, we first present a chronology of the Böhm-Bawerk–Clark controversy and a brief theoretical overview of key issues. The letters do not significantly alter the interpretation of the published controversy, but they do add richness and texture. As part of the published record, the letters will, we hope, be of use to historians of economics interested in Böhm-Bawerk, Austrian economics, capital theory, and the spread of the marginal revolution from the realm of demand and utility to the realm of production. This small contribution is made in honour of Geoff Harcourt, himself a keen student and accomplished practitioner of the history of economic theory.

CHRONOLOGY

Böhm-Bawerk's *Positive Theory of Capital* first appeared in German in 1889. It generated enormous interest and was quickly translated into English by William Smart (Böhm-Bawerk 1891b). Clark's theory of capital appeared in a series of articles (1888, 1889a, 1890a, 1891, 1892) which were later consolidated in *The Distribution of Wealth* (1899).

Clark, who spoke German from his studies in Heidelberg with Karl Knies, wrote two brief and relatively approving reviews of Böhm-Bawerk's work (Clark 1889b, 1890b). The critical debate began with Clark's (1893) attack on Böhm-Bawerk, then moved to private correspondence and the pages of the *Quarterly Journal of Economics (QJE)*. With two articles each in 1895, agreements and disagreements became clearly focused, but the disputants temporarily withdrew from debate with key differences unresolved. Böhm-Bawerk's energies shifted to his work for the Austrian Finance Ministry. He rejoined the debate in the 1906 *QJE* with a delayed response to Clark's *Distribution of Wealth* (1899). After four articles between 1906 and 1907, the debate ended without resolution. Table 8.1 presents a complete chronology of the published debate.

Not surprisingly, many of the unresolved issues, involving problems of

Table 8.1 Chronology of the Böhm-Bawerk–Clark debate

Böhm-Bawerk (1890a) [1884] *Capital and Interest: A Critical History of Economic Thought*	Clark (1895b) 'Real issues concerning interest' Response to Böhm-Bawerk (1895b)
Böhm-Bawerk (1891b) [1889] *Positive Theory of Capital*	Clark (1899) *The Distribution of Wealth*
Clark (1889b) Review of Böhm-Bawerk (1889)	Böhm-Bawerk (1906) 'Capital and interest once more: I. Capital vs. capital goods' Rebuttal of Clark (1899)
Clark (1890b) Book note on Böhm-Bawerk (1890a)	
Clark (1893) 'The genesis of capital' Attack on Böhm-Bawerk (1891b)	Böhm-Bawerk (1907a) 'Capital and interest once more: II. A relapse to the productivity theory' Continuation of Böhm-Bawerk (1906)
Böhm-Bawerk (1895a) 'The positive theory of capital and its critics – I' Rebuttal of Clark (1893)	Clark (1907a) 'Concerning the nature of capital: a reply' Response to Böhm-Bawerk (1906, 1907a)
Clark (1895a) 'The origin of interest' Response to Böhm-Bawerk (1895a)	
Böhm-Bawerk (1895b) 'The origin of interest' Response to Clark (1895a)	Böhm-Bawerk (1907b) 'The nature of capital: a rejoinder' Response to Clark (1907a)

integrating time and production into an equilibrium framework, resurfaced in the capital theory controversies of the 1930s and between the two Cambridges.

THEORETICAL OVERVIEW

Despite a few crucial differences, Böhm-Bawerk's and Clark's theories have remarkable similarities. The similarities stem from a shared conception of capital as both first, heterogeneous, concrete capital goods, and second, a monetary fund of value which is homogeneous, malleable and perfectly mobile. Clark distinguishes between concrete capital goods and a monetary fund of 'true capital'. Böhm-Bawerk spends most of *Positive Theory of Capital* discussing concrete capital goods, but in his quantitative model of interest rate determination (Book IV), capital takes the form of a homogeneous subsistence fund consisting of one wage good commodity, denominated in money.

Despite this shared conception of the dual nature of capital, Clark ignores completely Böhm-Bawerk's treatment of a subsistence fund of capital. Throughout the debate, it is as if Clark never read Book IV of Böhm-Bawerk's work, even though Clark's (1889b: 344) first review of Böhm-Bawerk's work mentions that 'A special feature of [*Positive Theory*] is its treatment of capital as a fund for future consumption.' Clark's 'oversight' exaggerates their differences, creating the impression of a polar opposition between Clark's emphasis on the fund of true capital and Böhm-Bawerk's emphasis on concrete capital goods.

Both authors accept the (diminishing marginal) productivity of concrete capital goods, but attribute it to different abstract concepts. Böhm-Bawerk attributes the productivity of capital to the influence of time. The third of his famous reasons for interest is the increased productivity of more 'roundabout' or time-using methods of production. He develops the concept of the period of production as a measure of capital, and claims it is uniquely and inversely related to the marginal productivity of capital. Clark attributes the productivity of capital to the effects of true capital, which is a permanent, timeless fund.

Böhm-Bawerk and Clark share similar analyses of concrete capital goods. They part company over Clark's belief that characteristics of concrete capital goods are only secondary for understanding interest. Clark's primary explanation of interest centres around his additional concept of true capital, a concept Böhm-Bawerk (1907a: 282) rejects entirely as a 'mythology of capital'. Their key disagreements all relate to the concept of true capital and the way in which it, together with Clark's explicitly static framework, purges time from the analysis. Böhm-Bawerk sees his primary advances as centred around the roles of time: periods of production, the productivity of roundabout methods using capital goods, and positive time preference. Clark explains interest in a totally timeless fashion, rooting it in the technical productivity of a permanent fund of true capital.

Clark identifies sharply and concisely the fundamental differences between their theories (although still ignoring Böhm-Bawerk's subsistence fund of capital):

[Böhm-Bawerk's theory] studies only concrete instruments. It measures the period that their action defines, and reduces interest to an *agio* due to the particular intervals of time that are thus measured. [My own theory] recognizes these instruments and their qualities, but gives a cardinal place to the study of that permanent capital which the endless succession of instruments constitutes. It defines the interest problem in terms of that fund, and makes the rate to be the fraction of itself that the fund annually creates. It is a productivity theory; and it relegates the separate periods of production to a subordinate place.

(Clark 1895a: 258)

This brief overview should provide enough background to help make sense of the letters that follow. Where possible, we have added references [in square brackets] and notes to guide the reader to sources referred to in the letters.

Innsbruck, 26 March 1889

Esteemed Colleague,

Please receive my sincere thanks for your kind letter as well as your articles [Clark 1889a; probably also 1888]. I have read them immediately with the greatest interest. I have the impression that our analyses of capital and labour have many similarities. We are both convinced that the problems of interest and wages have to be solved *simultaneously*; we both have the same theoretical starting point, the theory of final utility; and our approaches are very similar in many other respects.

I very much like your exposition [Clark 1889a] regarding the 'marginal field of employment' and the elasticity of the labour market (pp. 44–50); likewise the analogous exposition regarding the marginal field of capital (for example p. 55); further, the extension of the law of diminishing returns to the field of production. You will have encountered the same ideas in slightly different form in my book.

The only difference between us appears to lie in a different view of the function of capital. You (and Mr. Wood [1888]) describe the choice as between the use of capital and the use of labour. I describe the choice as between the use of labour in longer or shorter production periods. If I am not mistaken, it is this latter view which really gets to the bottom of the matter and which at the same time provides an explanation not only for the level but also for the *origin* of the interest on capital which in your case and Mr. Wood's case appears to be assumed as something given. But perhaps I may be mistaken.

I am very happy that we have established professional contact and I hope that this relationship will become a lasting one.

Respectfully, your faithful colleague

E. Böhm-Bawerk

*

Innsbruck, 9 May 1889

Dear and Esteemed Sir,

Returning from a longer trip, I only have found the time today to thank you for sending me your 'Philosophy of Value' [must mean *Philosophy of Wealth* (Clark 1886)] and for your two very kind letters.

Your 'Philosophy of Value' has been extremely interesting to me. I can only congratulate you on the clarity and originality with which you have expressed the most important ideas of the theory of value; and it certainly does not diminish your contribution if, by coincidence, some people in Europe unknown to you have developed the same basic ideas.

In any case, we both are on common ground regarding the theory of value. And I am especially glad that this common ground extends also to the field of interest on capital. Over the last months I have received numerous expressions of approval regarding my new theory of interest; but very few have given me as much pleasure as yours. In academic life, judgements should not be counted but should be weighted, and to this extent the judgement of *one* man who, like you, has worked independently on the same problem, who knows from his own experience all of the difficulties and then extends his agreement, weighs as heavily as a dozen judgements of ordinary economists.

It is a rather strange coincidence that we Austrians concur with you Americans in so many of our scientific ideas. In the theory of value you concur with the Austrian *Menger* and his successors. In the theory of capital I concur with you and with Professor *Patten* [1889] who in his article regarding the 'fundamental idea of capital', has expressed similar ideas, though still in a slightly rudimentary way. I consider this coincidence as a good indication of the correctness of our simultaneously developed theories.

What I think about the state of present American economics has been recently expressed in an article which will be published in one of the next issues of the Conrad'sche Jahrbücher [*für Nationalökonomie und Statistik*]. Unfortunately, the article was already sent before I received your last letters through which I came to learn about your 'Philosophy of Value'.

Yours faithfully,
E. Böhm-Bawerk

*

Innsbruck, 11 July 1889

Dear Professor Clark,

Thank you cordially for your kind letter as well as for your honourable assessment of my book in the Political Science Quarterly [Clark 1889b].

I am extremely anxious to know the complete exposition of your theory and I would be indeed very glad if you, starting from a different origin, arrive at the same or at least almost the same conclusions; it would be the best indication that we both have found the truth.

With your concluding remark [Clark 1889b] you are absolutely correct: the series of inputs which indirectly serve the final production of a commodity is indeed infinite. This has not escaped my attention either. Yet, for the calculation of the 'production period', as I understand the term, the absolute length of the period between the first input and the completion of the consumption commodity is irrelevant. This period would always be *infinitely* long. It is the *average* which is relevant, as I have elaborated on pp. 94–96. And this *average* production period is always finite and, in most cases, not very large.

Moreover, in praxis it is not so much the absolute length of the (average) *production period* that counts, but the occurrence of particular *extensions* of the production period. If an entrepreneur considers whether to use instead of 10 manual labourers, one machine which, for example, requires a labour input of 20 man years, he does not have to know, and in fact he will never know, how long the total production period will be during which he, together with his raw material suppliers and tools suppliers, etc., produces output. He will only calculate how much additional product he can obtain through a particular *extension* of the production period and, that will correspondingly determine his behaviour in the market for 'present goods'.

Only for a few *theoretical* considerations is it necessary to look at the complete (*average*) production period (for example, in the analysis of the relationship between subsistence fund and production period). Even here, as I believe, the theoretical considerations will not be altered because of the practical difficulty of accurately calculating the length of the production period. I don't believe that any of my final conclusions will become incorrect as a result of the points you raised – however, I am open to being corrected on this matter.

I am sending, at the same time, by book post, a short article in the *Conrad'sche Jahrbücher* [*für Nationalökonomie und Statistik*] which I wrote several months ago but has appeared only now.

Yours truly and faithfully,

E. Böhm-Bawerk

*

St Gilgen, 13 September 1889

Dear Professor Clark,

I have read with great interest your kind letters of July 15 and August 14. I am very glad that our opinions are the same on so many points, not only regarding 'capital and interest' and 'final utility', but also regarding the correct research methodology.

I have read the first article of Mr. Giddings [1889] regarding the production cost of capital. As spirited as his discussion may be, I cannot agree with his basic ideas. I believe that every economist has to decide whether the value of inputs ('costs') is ultimately the *cause* or the *result* of the value of outputs. I personally am of the opinion that the latter is the case and that the ultimate cause of the value of goods is not derived from costs but from final utility; and therefore any explanation of value phenomena which *ends* with costs appears unsatisfactory to me.

I am looking forward with great anticipation to your own exposition regarding 'capital and interest'.

E. Böhm-Bawerk

*

Vienna, 17 February 1890

Dear Professor Clark,

I too have read the article of Mr. Giddings [1890] with great interest without being able to agree with him. I believe that Mr. Giddings has not correctly understood *my* theory and, on my part, I cannot agree with *his* theory in its most important point; namely, that the interest on capital is explained by the supposedly *greater* costs of capitalist production.[2]

A few days ago, I wrote extensively to Mr. Bonar on this matter. He intends to reply to Mr. Giddings' article in the Quarterly Journal and will probably use in his reply ideas from my correspondence [Bonar 1890; Böhm-Bawerk 1890b]. You will, therefore, probably see in the next issue of the Quarterly Journal an extensive version of my views on Mr. Giddings' theory.

A few days ago I sent you an article from Conrad's Jahrbücher which deals with the question of methodology [probably Böhm-Bawerk 1890c].

It would interest me very much to know whether you share my objections to Mr. Giddings' theory or whether you disagree with his theory for different reasons.

Yours truly and faithfully,

E. von Böhm-Bawerk

P.S. My address is now: *Vienna* III, Beatrixgasse 14[B], Austria

*

Vienna, 19 November 1890
[Postcard]

Many thanks for the interesting articles! I am very anxious to read the major work which you promise at the end of your article on the 'law of wages' [Clark 1890a].

Yours faithfully,

E. Böhm-Bawerk

*

Vienna, III, Beatrixgasse 14[B],
19 January 1891

Dear Professor Clark,

I must express my regret that I still have not had the pleasure of meeting you personally. I attended the seminar of Knies in Heidelberg from *October 1875* to *July 1876*, that is, one year later than when you participated in the seminar. An American by the name Coppock participated in the seminar at the same time as I did (and Professor Wieser in Prague). I have not heard anything from him and it appears that he did not join academia.

A few days ago I received a letter from Mr. Henry Carey Baird, a relative of the famous economist. He has read, in Smart's translation [Böhm-Bawerk 1890a:

153–161], my slightly-too-strident critique of the theory of interest of his relative, and is very infuriated and intends to reply to it. May I ask you to tell me *very honestly* whether impartial economists in America also find my critique of Carey unfair or excessively strident? Perhaps you will be so good as to also tell me whether, as I assume, the English translation of my book contains the *original* quotations of Carey from his Principles of Social Science, 1858. I did not quote from the original, but from the German translation of *Adler*, 1863. I sincerely hope that the German translation on which I based my critique was precise and accurate.

Yours truly and faithfully,

E. Böhm-Bawerk

*

Vienna, 6 April 1891

Dear Professor Clark

Thank you very much for your repeated and kind correspondence. It is a relief to know that I am not alone in my opinion regarding Carey's theory of interest.

I was extremely pleased by the recent honour of being elected an honourable member of the American Economic Association. I consider this honour especially high because of my increasing esteem of the importance and the progress of American [economic] science.

I am sending by 'book-post' an offprint of my article on the 'Austrian Economists' [Böhm-Bawerk 1891a]. I really didn't want to write this article. It is always embarrassing to speak about oneself and one's own group. It is very difficult to emphasize the importance of the *issues* with which one wrestles without giving the impression of immodesty about the *people* involved.

Yours faithfully,

E. Böhm-Bawerk

*

Vienna, 24 September 1891

Dear Professor Clark,

I am writing today only to apologize for my long delay in answering your kind letter of 29 June.

I have been away during the summer for several months and I have been, since my return, burdened with pressing work in a way that lead to a complete neglect of my personal correspondence. I would like to respond to your proposed discussion with appropriate care and therefore will have to wait until I have some free time.

Yours faithfully,

E. Böhm-Bawerk

*

Vienna, 15 December 1893

Dear Professor Clark,

Your article [Clark 1893] on 'The Genesis of Capital', for which I thank you very much, has been of great interest to me. My impression can be summarized briefly as follows: the difference which separates us is indeed much smaller than it appears, but undoubtedly there is a difference.

What separates us, in a nutshell, is your distinction between 'true capital' and 'capital goods', which I personally consider as superfluous and indeed dangerous. But I don't believe that this difference in our theoretical premises has to have, or actually does have, important practical implications for the positive content of our doctrines.

I believe that you attach too much importance to the fact that I use the example of 'goods of same kind and number' to demonstrate the difference in value between present and future goods. In fact, it was not my intention to attach particular importance to the identity of certain goods and I don't believe that any part of my theory would require, as a necessary premise, such an emphasis on a *concrete type of goods*. However, I had to confine myself to commodities of the same type only for the technical reason that a demonstration of the effect of time is impossible with a comparison of goods of different types. The sentence, 'Present goods are more valued than future goods' obtains its particular meaning only through the fact that I compare *otherwise identical* goods, that is, goods of the same type. For example, a present pound of gold is more valuable than a future pound of iron, would be a statement that would have nothing in common with my idea.

I am, therefore, also able to agree essentially with large parts of your article; for example, your description of true capitalists and quasi-capitalists (pp. 302–304) as well as your concluding sentences (pp. 313–315).

I also would like, in particular, to point out that, in my opinion, a capitalist will not value a driving horse of 1893 five percent higher than a driving horse of 1894; the capitalist, according to his subjective circumstances, very often does not value present goods higher than future ones, but frequently profits only from exchange situations that turn the estimation of *other* people for his present good, more importantly his present *money*, to his advantage (See, for example, p. 279, second volume of the English edition of my Positive Theory).

After having spent much time with work of a different nature, I intend to devote the year 1894 again to the theory of capital and I hope that this year will provide an opportunity to exchange my views with yours in public.

In the meantime, once again many thanks and greetings and 'happy Christmas'!

Yours faithfully,
E. Böhm-Bawerk

*

E. Böhm-Bawerk
Vienna, III, Beatrixgasse 14[B]
10 September 1894

Dear Professor Clark,

Thank you very much for your kind letter which I enjoyed reading; I am hurrying to respond to the two questions which you addressed to me.

1.) I completely share your opinion 'that an increase of wages with no change in the wants scale (of the labourers) would shorten the working day'. However, in my opinion, the validity of this statement depends, as I have expressed in my article [Böhm-Bawerk 1894 (in German)], on the often referred to premise that the working day is completely flexible and that its length is brought into accordance with the marginal utility of the last effort-requiring unit of time.

I believe that nowhere in my article have I made a claim which is in conflict with the above thesis. However, I have neglected, and I did so deliberately, to refer to this statement in my numerical examples simply because the examples would have become even more complicated and, for the majority of readers, hardly understandable. The general conclusions which I wanted to illustrate with my examples would, in any case, not have changed.

2.) I also completely agree with your view that poor and rich buyers of labour will pay the same for a unit of labour (of the same type). I believe that nowhere did I claim the opposite or made the opposite assumption; in those paragraphs which probably aroused your doubts (for example, page 216, 217, 219), I have always stated only that the rich would, if 'necessary' (p. 218 last line), or in an 'extreme case' (p. 219, fifth line) be 'inclined', or be 'able', to pay a higher price. In my view, the higher purchasing power of the rich only guarantees the acquisition of labour and of the products of labour at the *general market price* vis-à-vis those excluded by their *lower* purchasing power; the level of purchasing power of the potential buyer is important, 1. for the determination of the general market price, and 2. for the selection of the actual *buyer* from the many individuals who *desire* the commodity.

By the way, my article [Böhm-Bawerk 1894] is supposed to appear soon in English translation in the 'Annals of the American Academy'; perhaps in the October issue if the translation is completed by then.

With best regards,
Yours faithfully,
E. Böhm-Bawerk

*

E. Böhm-Bawerk
Vienna, III, Beatrixgasse 14[B]
6 January 1905

Dear Professor Clark,

After several years of an extremely burdensome government appointment, during which I had to abandon totally all academic work I have finally found my freedom again which I will use above all to acquaint myself with the main contributions to economic theory over the last five to six years.

I have just started to read your interesting book on 'The Distribution of Wealth' (1899) and have noticed in the introduction that a second volume on the 'Dynamics of Distribution' was supposed to follow. I have not yet seen this second volume and I cannot remember having seen any announcement of its publication or any review of it.

Could you please tell me briefly whether the second volume has appeared and, if so, when, and by whom it was published.

Thanking you in advance for your kind response, I am faithfully yours,

E. Böhm-Bawerk

*

E. Böhm-Bawerk
Vienna, III, Beatrixgasse 14[B],
1 March 1908

Dear Professor Clark,

Thank you very much for your last letter and your regards. I have, in the meantime, completed reading your 'Essentials' [Clark 1907b]. The book contains innovative and important ideas in an area which is yet to be explored in economics. I am happy to tell you that I agree in almost all important parts with your convincing exposition. Indeed, it appears to me that there is much more in common in our approaches to analysing economic phenomena than there are differences. Certainly, progress in science almost always requires that one discusses those matters on which one does not agree rather than those on which one holds a common view!

The 'Essentials' will be reviewed in our Vienna Journal by Dr. Schumpeter, who is presently in Egypt.

I enjoyed hearing about the academic career of your son. I congratulate Mr. John Maurice Clark, on having been introduced to economic theory by such a father, and I congratulate his father on having such an assistant at his side!

With best regards for father and son,

Yours always faithfully,

E. Böhm-Bawerk

NOTES

1   See Cohen (1993) for a more detailed chronicle and analysis of the Böhm-Bawerk–Clark controversy. That paper is part of a book in progress (inspired by Harcourt (1972)) entitled *Capital Controversy from Böhm-Bawerk to Bliss: History versus Equilibrium*.

2   Giddings's 1889 and 1890 articles generated another controversy over capital and interest. Giddings challenged Böhm-Bawerk's utility and time preference explanation of the origin of interest, advancing instead a fallacious cost-of-production explanation. The chronology of the articles in this controversy is: Bonar (1888, 1889a), Giddings (1889), Bonar (1889b), Giddings (1890), Bonar (1890), Böhm-Bawerk (1890b), Giddings (1891), Green (1891) and Bilgram (1891).

REFERENCES

Beach, W. and Bostaph, S. (1982) 'The mystery of the mislaid MSS, or raiders of the lost arc(hives)', *The History of Economics Society Bulletin* 3(2): 27–9.

Bilgram, H. (1891) 'The interest controversy', *Quarterly Journal of Economics* 5(3): 375–7.

Böhm-Bawerk, E. von (1884) *Geschichte und Kritik der Kapitalzins-Theorien*. Innsbruck: Wagner.

—— (1889) *Kapital und Kapitalzins. Zweite Abteilung: Positive Theorie des Kapitals*. Innsbruck: Wagner.

—— (1889–1908) Thirteen letters to J. B. Clark, in the J. B. Clark Papers, Box 1, Rare Book and Manuscript Library, Columbia University.

—— (1890a) *Capital and Interest: A Critical History of Economic Theory*, trans. William Smart, London: Macmillan.

—— (1890b) 'Professor Giddings on the theory of capital', *Quarterly Journal of Economics* 4(3): 347–9.

—— (1890c) 'Historical *vs.* deductive political economy', *Annals of the American Academy of Political and Social Science* 1(2): 244–71. Originally appeared as 'Zur Literaturgeschichte der Staats- und Sozialwissenschaften', *Jahrbücher für National-alökonomie und Statistik* 54: 75–95. Reprinted in Böhm-Bawerk, E. von (1968) *Gesammelte Schriften von Eugen von Böhm-Bawerk*, ed. F. X. Weiss, Frankfurt: Verlag Sauer & Auvermann.

—— (1891a) 'The Austrian economists', *Annals of the American Academy of Political and Social Science* 1(3): 361–84. Reprinted in Böhm-Bawerk, E. von (1962) *Shorter Classics of Eugen von Böhm-Bawerk*, South Holland, IL: Libertarian Press.

—— (1891b) *Capital and Interest: Positive Theory of Capital*, trans. William Smart, London: Macmillan.

—— (1894) 'Der letzte masstab des güterwertes', *Zeitschrift für Volkswirtschaft, Sozialpolitik und Verwaltung* 3: 185–230. English translation as 'The ultimate standard of value', *Annals of the American Academy of Political and Social Science* (1894) 5(2): 149–208. Reprinted in Böhm-Bawerk, E. von (1962) *Shorter Classics of Eugen von Böhm-Bawerk*, South Holland, IL: Libertarian Press.

—— (1895a) 'The positive theory of capital and its critics – I', *Quarterly Journal of Economics* 9(2): 113–31.

—— (1895b) 'The origin of interest', *Quarterly Journal of Economics* 9(4): 380–7.

—— (1906) 'Capital and interest once more: I. Capital vs. capital goods', *Quarterly Journal of Economics* 21(1): 1–21.

—— (1907a) 'Capital and interest once more: II. A relapse to the productivity theory', *Quarterly Journal of Economics* 21(2): 247–82.

—— (1907b) 'The nature of capital: a rejoinder', *Quarterly Journal of Economics* 22(1): 28–47.

Bonar, J. (1888) 'The Austrian economists and their view of value', *Quarterly Journal of Economics* 3(1): 1–31.

—— (1889a) 'The positive theory of capital: a review article', *Quarterly Journal of Economics* 3(3): 336–51.

—— (1889b) 'The cost of production of capital', *Quarterly Journal of Economics* 4(1): 81–3.

—— (1890) 'Professor Giddings on the theory of capital', *Quarterly Journal of Economics* 4(3): 346–7.

Carey, H. C. (1858) *Principles of Social Science*, Philadelphia: J. B. Lippincott & Co.

Clark, J. B. (1886) *The Philosophy of Wealth: Economic Principles Newly Formulated*, Boston: Ginn & Co. [2nd edition 1887].

—— (1888) 'Capital and its earnings', *Publications of the American Economic Association* [Monographs] 3(2): 7–69.

—— (1889a) 'Possibility of a scientific law of wages', *Publications of the American Economic Association* 4(1): 39–63.

—— (1889b) 'Review of Böhm-Bawerk', *Political Science Quarterly* 4(2): 342–6.

—— (1890a) 'The law of wages and interest', *Annals of the American Academy of Political and Social Science* 1(1): 43–65.

—— (1890b) Book note on *Capital and Interest* (vol. 1, Smart translation), *Annals of the American Academy of Political and Social Science* 1(2): 310–12.

—— (1891) 'Distribution as determined by a law of rent', *Quarterly Journal of Economics* 5(3): 289–318.

—— (1892) 'The ultimate standard of value', *Yale Review* 1(4): 258–74.

—— (1893) 'The genesis of capital', *Yale Review* 2(4): 302–15.

—— (1895a) 'The origin of interest', *Quarterly Journal of Economics* 9(3): 257–78.

—— (1895b) 'Real issues concerning interest', *Quarterly Journal of Economics* 10(1): 98–102.

—— (1899) *The Distribution of Wealth*, New York: Macmillan.

—— (1907a) 'Concerning the nature of capital: a reply', *Quarterly Journal of Economics* 21(3): 351–70.

—— (1907b) *The Essentials of Economic Theory as Applied to Modern Problems of Industry and Public Policy*, New York: Macmillan.

Cohen, A. J. (1993) 'The mythology of capital or of equilibrium?: the Böhm-Bawerk/Clark controversy', York University Department of Economics Working Paper, 93–7, April.

Giddings, F. H. (1889) 'The cost of production of capital', *Quarterly Journal of Economics* 3(4): 503–7.

—— (1890) 'The theory of capital', *Quarterly Journal of Economics* 4(2): 172–206.

—— (1891) 'The growth of capital and the cause of interest', *Quarterly Journal of Economics* 5(2): 242–8.

Green, D. I. (1891) 'The cause of interest', *Quarterly Journal of Economics* 5(3): 361–5.

Harcourt, G. C. (1972) *Some Cambridge Controversies in the Theory of Capital*, Cambridge: Cambridge University Press.

Patten, S. N. (1889) 'The fundamental idea of capital', *Quarterly Journal of Economics* 3(2): 188–203.

Wood, S. (1888) 'A new view of the theory of wages', *Quarterly Journal of Economics* 3(1): 60–86.

9

THE FATE OF THE CAMBRIDGE CAPITAL CONTROVERSY

Geoffrey M. Hodgson

In 1960, Piero Sraffa published a slim volume of 96 pages that was over thirty years in the preparation. The central proposition of the work is that there is no measure of capital independent of distribution and prices. *Production of Commodities by Means of Commodities* constituted a devastating logical attack on the aggregate production function of neoclassical theory and theories of supply, distribution and growth based upon it.

A few years earlier, Joan Robinson (1953) had asked the forbidden question: how is capital to be measured? Sraffa drove home the argument that there was no independent measure. A physical measure is useless unless capital consists of a single good, or uniform bundle of goods. A price measure is impossible unless there is a prior set of relative prices. But, in a capitalist system, such prices depend on the rate of profits. If the production function is a function of 'capital' and this is measured in price terms, then the view that this function leads to a determination of the rate of profits involves circular reasoning.

In such terms, Sraffa's work was a highly destructive *internal* critique of the type of neoclassical theory which made extensive use of aggregate production functions, in application to theories of supply, growth and distribution in particular. It showed that such aggregate production functions with 'capital' as a single factor were unfounded on any general theory in which there were heterogeneous capital goods, including fixed capital. They could represent no more than an imaginary world where there were no machines or raw materials, other than a mythical, single and ubiquitous common substance – the fabled 'Ricardian corn'.

More than a third of a century later, however, aggregate production functions are still common in both the textbooks and the core journals of mainstream economics. Why is this so? This chapter is written with that question in mind and may help contribute to a full answer. A full explanation must involve not only the internal logic of the theories and debates but also the culture and institutions of the economics profession itself.

Clearly, I can do no more than to touch upon these issues here. Neither is it possible to enter into all the technical controversies that took place, particularly over the nature and measurement of capital (Harcourt 1972, 1994; Ahmad 1991) and the Marxian labour theory of value (Steedman 1977; Steedman *et al.*, 1981). Indeed, any attempt to do so would tempt readers to skip to the next chapter in this volume, such is the general familiarity of the book's likely readers with the debris of those past debates. Instead, the purpose of this chapter is to place the Sraffian opus in the wider context of the theoretical development of economics and of the evolution of the economics profession itself. Perhaps in this way some new lessons can be learnt.

Notably, the survival of the aggregate production function after the Sraffian attack is not a simple story of deafness and inertia on the part of orthodoxy. Leading American neoclassical economists such as Paul Samuelson (1966, 1989) were involved in the capital theory debates and eventually conceded much ground to the Sraffians.

The technique adopted here is to consider the fate of Sraffa's *Production of Commodities* in the light of its recorded citations in the academic journals. The first section, 'The production of citations by means of citations', considers the slow take-off of *Production of Commodities* and the capital theory debates of the 1960s. The following section, 'Revolting cites', addresses the heyday of that work, from the early 1970s to the mid-1980s. Then, in 'Building cites for a new heterodoxy', notable attempts to synthesize Sraffa with Keynes are addressed. The final section, 'Out of cite – out of mind', concludes the chapter by considering the subsequent decline in attention to Sraffa and his legacy.

THE PRODUCTION OF CITATIONS BY MEANS OF CITATIONS

With all its faults and shortcomings, the use of the data in the *Social Science Citations Index* (*SSCI*) has become established as one of the best methods of assessing the impact of a scholarly work. A large number of the more well-established academic journals are regularly analysed for the number of times the articles within them cite particular works. Currently, in the subject area of economics alone, well over 100 journals are used to obtain these data. In the other social sciences there are many more. All the 'core' economics journals are present on this list, along with a number of publications specializing in heterodox approaches.

The citation data for Sraffa's *Production of Commodities by Means of Commodities* are presented in Figure 9.1. A citation figure of 15 indicates that the *Production of Commodities* has been cited 15 times in that year, by all journals on the *SSCI* list, including both economics and non-economics journals.

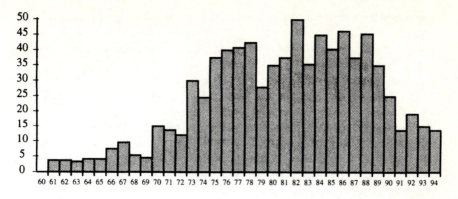

Figure 9.1 Yearly number of *Social Science Citation Index* citations of Sraffa's
Production of Commodities

Several points are worthy of note. First, it was not until ten years after its appearance that annual citations to *Production of Commodities* reached double figures. This is a remarkably poor start, given the theoretical significance of the work. The 'incredibly long gestation period' (Harcourt 1972: 14) of this volume prior to publication was followed, after birth, by an equally incredible decade of neglect.

Second, it is in the 1970s and 1980s that citations to the work reach their highest levels. However, the highest citation level of 49, achieved in 1982, is itself relatively low for a work of this stature and importance.

Finally, there has been a precipitous fall in citations to the work since 1988, reaching consistently low levels since 1991. This fall is even more severe if account is taken of the fact that the overall annual volume of social science citations has multiplied several times over since 1960. In sum, there has been a decade of delayed recognition, followed by two decades of moderate attention, followed by neglect in the early 1990s.

What can be the explanations of the delayed ascent, moderate rise and precipitous fall of the impact of Sraffa's classic, as measured by citations? Part of an answer can be obtained by considering the publications associated with the debates around Sraffa's work. Shortly after it was published it received two lengthy and positive reviews, by Meek (1961) and Robinson (1961). However, neither of these reviews was in a top-ranking economics journal.[1]

In 1961 two notable followers of Sraffa – Joan Robinson from Cambridge and Piero Garegnani from Italy – visited the Massachusetts Institute of Technology and engaged in controversy with Samuelson. One result was the famous attempt by Samuelson (1962) to rescue orthodoxy with the 'surrogate production function'. His article was published in the UK-based *Review of Economic Studies*, which is generally regarded as one of the core economics journals.[2] In it Samuelson made a brief reference to Sraffa. However, even

97

this mention by a future Nobel laureate did not immediately improve the flow of citations to Sraffa's book.

Indeed, Sraffa was not always the main character in the early capital theory debates. Much of the early controversy was over the use of aggregate production functions in Swan's (1956) and Solow's (1956) neoclassical models of growth and distribution (Ahmad 1991: ch. 4; Harcourt 1972: chs 2–3).

The mid-point of the 1960s had passed before the debates over capital reversing and reswitching began in earnest and drew attention to Sraffa's book. Notably, a number of anti-neoclassical articles on these themes appeared in a symposium in the prestigious (and US-based) *Quarterly Journal of Economics* (*QJE*). They included works by Garegnani (1966), Morishima (1966), Pasinetti (1966) and Robinson and Naqvi (1967). In retrospect, the publication of these articles in the *QJE* was of enormous significance for the capital controversy. One wonders how different the story might have been if this one core journal had not opened its pages to these strange and controversial imports from Europe.

In the *QJE* symposium Samuelson conceded much of the argument with a co-authored recantation (Levhari and Samuelson 1966) and his milestone 'summing-up' article (Samuelson 1966). The possibility of capital reversing and reswitching had been established, undermining the notion of a 'well-behaved' production function.

Even then, citations of *Production of Commodities* remained at a very low level for another five years. It is impossible to be sure, but it is likely that two journal publications are largely responsible for raising the profile of the work in the early 1970s.[3] The first, and probably most important, was the survey of the capital controversies by Geoff Harcourt in the *Journal of Economic Literature* (*JEL*) in 1969. This extended the Cambridge (UK) attack from the *QJE* bridgehead across the Atlantic and reached a strategically significant core journal – published by the American Economic Association – which has consistently scored highest in terms of citation impact.[4] Harcourt (1972) followed this with the definitive monograph on the capital theory debates of the 1960s, which must have added to the impact of his *JEL* article.

The second journal article was Garegnani's (1970) *coup de grâce* against the aggregate production function. This appeared in the *Review of Economic Studies*, reportedly despite the earlier wishes of its editors. Garegnani showed that the typical textbook picture of a 'well-behaved' production function was based on highly restrictive and implausible assumptions. Garegnani's article was quickly reprinted in a widely circulated reader produced by Penguin and edited by Hunt and Schwartz (1972). Along with the publication of related Penguin readers by Harcourt and Laing (1971) and Sen (1970), all this helped the capital theory debates to reach wider audience.

Accordingly, and probably as a consequence of these publications in the

1969–72 period, the number of citations received by *Production of Commodities* jumped from an annual average of 4.9 in the years 1961–9 to 15 in 1970 and 30 in 1973.

REVOLTING CITES

The mood of the times should not be forgotten: 1968 and all that. Protest and political turmoil in many developed Western countries spilled over into academia with an intensified questioning of established assumptions and approaches. In particular, there was a massive growth in interest in Marxism in general and Marxian economics in particular.

Sraffa had been an intimate friend of Antonio Gramsci and had Marxian sympathies. *Production of Commodities* was widely viewed as rehabilitating both classical economics and the economics of Marx. Nevertheless, Sraffa's editorship of the collected works of Ricardo brought suspicion upon him as a 'neo-Ricardian' from the more 'fundamentalist' adherents of Marx.

In 1975 Ian Steedman published a demonstration of the possibility of 'positive profits with negative surplus value' in the *Economic Journal*. Using a Sraffian framework, Steedman had undermined the labour theory of value. Steedman (1977) extended this argument and critique in an influential book. In the contemporary context of high academic interest in Marxism an enormous controversy erupted (Harcourt 1982a; 1982b: ch. 14). This may have done a great deal to improve the citation rate of *Production of Commodities*, but – as Steedman was the first to acknowledge – it did little to repulse neoclassical orthodoxy or to build a positive theoretical alternative. Indeed, Steedman's main object had been to purge the heterodox economists of 'obscurantism'. This was seen as a necessary ablution before a rigorous theoretical alternative could be developed.

Critical and open-minded heterodox economists were faced with a dilemma: the theoretical status of the Sraffian system itself. Two very different points of view emerged. One group saw the work of Sraffa and his followers as primarily an internal critique of neoclassical theory that had exposed logical inconsistencies and faulty foundations. In this view the significance of Sraffa's work was still important but primarily destructive of orthodoxy. A second group saw Sraffa as providing much more: a common foundation for a new heterodox economic theory embracing the insights of Marx, Keynes, Kalecki and others. The Sraffian approach was seen as providing an appropriate foundation for the analysis of the essential workings of the capitalist mode of production. This latter group are dubbed here the 'constructivist' Sraffians.[5]

BUILDING CITES FOR A NEW HETERODOXY

The leading 'constructivist' Sraffians were John Eatwell, Piero Garegnani and Murray Milgate.[6] In a number of publications in the late 1970s and early 1980s they argued that the Sraffian framework was a secure foundation for the Keynesian theory of effective demand (Garegnani 1978, 1979a; Eatwell and Milgate 1983). However, this meant interpreting Keynes in 'long-period' rather than 'short-period' terms. It also involved the downplaying of the key concepts of uncertainty and expectation in Keynesian analysis.

This was in great contrast to other Keynesians who had emphasized problems of uncertainty and had argued that the economy cannot be captured by a static analysis. Whereas Garegnani (1979b: 183), echoed by Eatwell (1979, 1983), denied a 'central role to uncertainty and expectations', others, such as Davidson (1972), Loasby (1976), Minsky (1976 and Shackle (1974), saw uncertainty and expectations as being central both to the work of Keynes and to developments based upon it.

The fact that Sraffa's long-period analysis represents a major amendment to Keynes's theory was admitted by Sraffian theorists themselves. For instance, Garegnani (1979b: 183) insisted that the 'short-period character of Keynes theory' is a weakness. Following this, Eatwell stated that there are 'many parts of *The General Theory* which either do not address or ... directly contradict the notion of long-period theory ... it frequently appears that Keynes is simply presenting a theory of ... short-period positions' (1983: 271–2).

As early as 1973, Robinson was expressing some misgivings about the exclusive focus of the Sraffian constructivists on the long period: 'In reality,' she wrote, 'all the interesting and important questions lie in the gap between pure short-period and long-period analysis' (Robinson 1973: 60). By 1980 her differences with the constructivists had become even more clear, as Harcourt related in an incisive account of this episode:

> in her debates with Garegnani, and with Eatwell and Milgate, Joan Robinson used her views on the inadmissibility of long-period comparisons for describing processes, which she developed in her critique of neoclassical theory, to criticise the central stress by these authors on the notion of centres of gravitation or long-period positions.
>
> (Harcourt 1985: 106)

Sraffian 'values' or 'prices of production' were rejected because they could not be incorporated in a theory which was set in historical time (Robinson 1974, 1979, 1980; Bhaduri and Robinson, 1980).

Robinson also asked what was the meaning of the normal rate of profits in long-period analysis: does it mean 'what the rate of profit on capital will be in the future or what it has been in the past or does it float above historical time as a Platonic Idea?' (1979: 180). Garegnani replied that the normal rate of profits is located in the present:

> It corresponds to the rate which is being realised *on an average* (as between firms and over time) by the entrepreneurs who use the dominant technique ... it is also the rate of profits which that present experience will lead entrepreneurs in general to expect *in the future* from their current investment.
>
> (Garegnani 1979b: 185)

This response suggests that long-period analysis is a short-period one as well, for the long-period average is seen to bear upon short-period decisions. But how do entrepreneurs *know* what the average rate of profits is, or whether the rate of profits in their own enterprise is above or below it? How can entrepreneurs form expectations of a future rate of profits on the basis of this present average rate of profits, which is unperceived and unknown? Even if it were known, why should entrepreneurs assume that it would remain the same in the future? These questions are neither raised nor answered in the Garegnani–Eatwell–Milgate extension of Sraffian theory.

It is also questionable whether a Sraffian world of fixed coefficients can represent the long period if this is meant to include capital accumulation and technological change. Sraffian theorists have suggested that these phenomena can be encompassed by the comparative–static analysis of the switching of techniques. But as Robinson put it:

> It is a mistake in methodology to compare two technical systems ... and then to switch one to the other. A switch is an event in historical time which has to be accounted for by introducing historical causation in the story. This is where Sraffa leaves us and hands us over to Keynes.
>
> (Robinson 1980: 134)

Technological change is a process, through time, with future consequences which are rarely known with any precision in the present. It involves, for instance, investment in research and development, where the payoffs are essentially uncertain, and changes in the social relations of production resulting from industrial struggles or the reorganization of work. A static matrix of Sraffian input–output coefficients cannot represent these processes.

Furthermore, it was not simply key Keynesian concepts such as uncertainty and expectations that were the casualties of this attempt to build a theory upon Sraffian foundations. The very emphasis on *physical* inputs and outputs in the Sraffa system neglected questions of learning and knowledge which had been given little attention by orthodoxy and heterodoxy alike. Robinson (1975: vii) hinted at them after she belatedly stumbled across Veblen's (1908) critique of neoclassical capital theory.[7] In any adequate sense, it is difficult to relate knowledge and learning to the physical coefficients of the Sraffa system, just as the personal transformations involved in the learning, cognitive and innovative processes fit uneasily with the agent driven mechanistically to maximize utility with given preference functions.[8]

Finally, the Sraffian approach does not offer a theory of human agency and interaction. It simply suggests that the long-period positions will somehow reflect and affect the expectations and actions of agents, without explaining how the average rate of profits and long-period prices are attained. Whatever the strengths of Sraffian analysis, particularly its destructive critique of neoclassical and Marxian theories of value and capital, this lack is a serious weakness. In consequence, it cannot be claimed that Sraffian analysis provides an adequate or entirely appropriate foundation for heterodox theory.[9]

Sraffian theory was also criticized in an article by Hahn in the *Cambridge Journal of Economics*. Against 'the followers of Sraffa', Hahn argued that 'there is no correct neo-Ricardian proposition which is not contained in the set of propositions which can be generated by orthodoxy . . . the neo-Ricardian attack *via* logic is easily beaten off' (1982: 353). If true, this would much diminish both the destructive and constructive versions of Sraffian theory.

In fact, the more careful Sraffians had always made it clear that their attack was effective against the *aggregate* neoclassical production function only. Other, disaggregated versions of neoclassical theory, such as general equilibrium theory of the genre of Arrow and Hahn (1971), were not vulnerable to such a critique. In these models, capital could be treated as heterogeneous and disaggregated. Formally, Hahn was right in suggesting that his version of general equilibrium theory could also generate 'badly behaved' aggregate production functions, reswitching and other curiosa. But the Arrow–Hahn type of theory had not been the foundation of Solovian and other models in which capital as a single factor of production entered as an input. Instead, aggregate production functions abound.

Further, the possibility that general equilibrium theory could generate similarly 'perverse' results did not imply that Sraffian theory was of lesser importance. In fact, if Hahn is right, then general equilibrium theory is a special case of Sraffian analysis, rather than the other way round. General equilibrium theory involves *additional* assumptions, such as individual utility maximization, which are not present in Sraffian analysis and thus confer upon it a more general status.

The Sraffian constructivists hinted that they held to a different model of human behaviour, based on habits and rules rather than the utility maximizer of neoclassical theory. Such an approach was began in the institutionalism of Thorstein Veblen and John Commons. But neither the links to institutionalism, nor a specific theory of human action along these lines, were developed by the constructivists. If they had been, things might have been different. The behavioural core of constructivist Sraffian theory remained empty.

In the mid-1980s the constructivist project had hardly started. However, rather than rising to the challenge, its protagonists left it in its unfinished state. This virtual abandonment of the project needs to be explained. Did the criticisms of Robinson and others make their mark? Mongiovi, a younger member of the constructivist group, declared almost a decade later that the theoretical research programme engendered by Sraffa's work 'is still in the early stages of development' (1992: 544). Indeed, despite the expenditure of much ink and paper, it has remained more or less in that state for much over a decade, and faith has been lost in the constructivist promise.

OUT OF CITE – OUT OF MIND

Ironically, for mainstream economists, general equilibrium theory was soon to become a falling star. However, Sraffian theory was not a major force behind this shift. Part of the motivation behind the development of post-war general equilibrium theory had been to develop the microfoundations for economics as a whole. Key developments in the 1970s thwarted this project. Although they were not given due attention at the time, they eventually played a role in transforming mainstream microeconomic theory and bringing general equilibrium theory down from its pedestal.

In the 1970s, Sonnenschein (1972, 1973a, 1973b), Mantel (1974) and Debreu (1974) showed that, starting from the assumption of individual utility maximization, the excess demand functions in an exchange economy can take almost any form. There is thus no basis for the assumption that they are generally downward-sloping. This problem is essentially one of aggregation when individual demand functions are combined. The consequences for neoclassical general equilibrium theory are devastating (Kirman, 1989). As Rizvi puts it, the work of Sonnenschein, Mantel and Debreu is quite general and is not restricted to counter-examples:

> Its chief implication ... is that the hypothesis of individual rationality, and other assumptions made at the micro level, gives no guidance to an analysis of macro-level phenomena: the assumption of rationality or utility maximisation is not enough to talk about social regularities. This is a significant conclusion and brings the microfoundations project in [general equilibrium theory] to an end.
>
> (Rizvi 1994a: 363)

Hahn immediately accepted the consequences, and compared the impact of the Sonnenschein *et al.* results with the Sraffian critique:

> The neo-Ricardians ... have demonstrated that capital aggregation is theoretically unsound. Fine.... The result has no bearing on the mainstream of neoclassical theory simply because it does not use aggregates. It has a bearing on the vulgar theories of the textbooks.... Results most damaging to neoclassical theory have recently been

proved by Debreu, Sonnenschein and Mas-Collel.

(Hahn 1975: 363)

On the whole, however, the problems raised by Sonnenschein *et al.* were not given sufficient attention by either orthodox or heterodox theorists at the time.

Rizvi (1994a: 361) saw the later appearance of Shafer and Sonnenschein's (1982) review of the Sonnenschein-type aggregation problems as crucial in bringing the issue to the notice of the profession.[10] Notably, the issues were previously ignored in two books which had addressed the microfoundations project: these by Harcourt (1977) and Weintraub (1979). Quickly after 1982, however, the pursuit of general equilibrium theory and the neoclassical microfoundations project were abandoned by many in the mainstream avant-garde.

Notably, the Sraffian critique contributed little to this development. Nor did it influence the new alternative mainstream paradigm: game theory. Rizvi (1994b: 3–4) argues that the rise of game theory in the 1980s was due primarily to the 'decreasing returns' of Arrow–Debreu–McKenzie general equilibrium analysis and the arbitrariness and existence problems exposed by Sonnenschein and others. Game theory filled the vacuum.

The Sraffian critique not only was bypassed, but became irrelevant for the new core theory of neoclassicism. Sraffian results have no apparent critical effect on game theory. Losing their status even as internal criticisms of the mainstream core, they became less and less relevant.

This is not to suggest that all mainstream theorists were as rigorous as Sonnenschein or as agile as Hahn. The great majority simply ignored both the capital theory debates and even the Sonnenschein results. Versions of aggregate production functions abound and are central to recent and fashionable developments such as real business cycle theory and endogenous growth theory. For many, it is as if the capital controversy had never happened.

What morals can be drawn from this tale? In lieu of a conclusion a few can be suggested:

1   The fate of theory is not a matter of cold logic alone. The slow reception and relatively weak impact of the Sraffian critique of neoclassical theory was due in part to its origin outside the top American universities that have dominated post-1945 economics research. Even its Cambridge pedigree was not good enough. *Production of Commodities* became prominent only after the appearance of key contributions in core economics journals, notably the *Quarterly Journal of Economics*, and after it had been given attention by leading American economists, notably by Samuelson.

2   There was more to the increase of interest in the 1970s in Sraffa's works than their intrinsic logic. They became tied up with the wave of political

radicalism that swept Western universities and the associated debates around Marxian economics.

3   The Sraffian constructivists never developed a widely accepted theoretical system to rival the neoclassical one. Attempts to do this by Eatwell, Garegnani and others faltered, probably in controversy over the interpretation of Keynes's legacy. In particular, because no alternative theory of human agency was proposed to replace the idea of individual utility maximization, the centre of the neoclassical system remained unchallenged. The Sraffian assault on neoclassical theory was directed largely at aggregate production functions and left much of the citadel intact.

4   Ironically, neoclassical general equilibrium did eventually suffer devastating blows in the 1980s, when Sonnenschein and others demonstrated key problems of aggregation starting from individual utility maximization. Cold logic did then have an effect, but only when it was directed at core propositions and the central microfoundations project of mainstream theory. The Sraffian critique had failed to do this.

5   From the outset, whether conceived as an internal critique of neoclassical economics or the foundation of an alternative paradigm, Sraffian economics had no theory of individual human action and no story concerning the actions of agents and their consequences. It thus had nothing to say about these key causal relations with an economic system. This defect always left it vulnerable by comparison with mainstream theory, which does embody a theory of human action, whatever its faults.

6   Further, the identification of the stationary-state parameters governing distribution in an economic system (namely the technological coefficients and the real wage) is not itself an exploration into causal relations and processes. Sraffian analysis replicates the deductivist methodology that dominates mainstream economic theory. As a critique of orthodoxy, the Sraffian approach is thus disabled.

The fate of Sraffian theory and the capital controversy is both a tragedy and an object lesson for all those committed – like the economist in whose honour this chapter is written – to a better and more humane economics and a basis for economic policies that may contribute to the building of a better world.

ACKNOWLEDGEMENT

I am very grateful to Philip Arestis, Geoff Harcourt and Malcolm Sawyer for comments on an earlier draft of this chapter.

NOTES

1   See also Harcourt and Massaro (1964).
2   The most famous and widely used definition of a core journal in economics is given by Diamond (1989). However, Diamond's list uses imperfectly specified

105

criteria, and a more recent and rigorous alternative is provided by Burton and Phimister (1995).

3   The brevity of this list may be questioned. Note also Pasinetti (1969). Bhaduri's (1969) important critique of Samuelson's surrogate production function made no reference to Sraffa and did not use a Sraffian framework of analysis.

4   For an explanation of 'citation impact' and specific citation impact figures see *SSCI*'s regularly published *Journal Citations Reports*.

5   According to Roncaglia (1991), there are three constructivist approaches within Sraffian economics, the 'Smithian' (Sylos–Labini), the 'Ricardian' (Pasinetti), and the 'Marxian' (Garegnani). Attention is concentrated on the latter category, which is arguably the closest to, and the most reliant upon, Sraffa's work.

6   This section draws from material published by Hodgson (1989). Earlier, Hodgson (1982) had written in a 'constructivist' spirit. But this is a transitional work, and by the time of its appearance its author had abandoned the constructivist Sraffian project for institutionalism (see Hodgson (1988) for its later development).

7   Veblen was one of the first to point out that the concept of the 'amount of capital' can be derived only through a process of valuation: 'The value involved is, like all value, a matter of imputation' (Veblen 1919: 371; see also pp. 196–7). He thus hints at the problem of circular argumentation much later identified by Robinson and Sraffa. Veblen rejected the 'factors of production' approach in its entirety, seeing production as being as much to do with 'the accumulated, habitual knowledge of the ways and means involved . . . the outcome of long experience and experimentation' (Veblen 1919: 185–6). See also Hodgson (1994).

8   Instead, it has been the evolutionary and institutional frameworks of Nelson and Winter (1982), Dosi *et al.* (1988), Lundvall (1992) and Morroni (1992) that have brought the issues of knowledge, learning and innovation to the fore.

9   Duménil and Lévy (1987) attempted to construct a more dynamic model based on Sraffian foundations. However, objections still remain: crucial problems of information and knowledge are assumed away. For more on the limitations of the Sraffa–Keynes synthesis see Harcourt and O'Shaughnessy (1985).

10 See also Duffie and Sonnenschien (1989).

REFERENCES

Ahmad, S. (1991) *Capital in Economic Theory: Neo-classical, Cambridge and Chaos*, Aldershot: Edward Elgar.

Arrow, K. J. and Hahn, F. H. (1971) *General Competitive Analysis*, Edinburgh: Oliver & Boyd.

Bhaduri, A. (1969) 'On the significance of recent controversies in capital theory: a Marxian view', *Economic Journal* 79(3): 523–9. Reprinted in Harcourt, G. C. and Laing, N. F. (eds) (1971) *Capital and Growth*, Harmondsworth: Penguin, and in Bhaduri, A. (1993) *Unconventional Economic Essays*, Oxford: Oxford University Press.

Bhaduri, A. and Robinson, J. (1980) 'Accumulation and exploitation: an analysis in the tradition of Marx, Sraffa and Kalecki', *Cambridge Journal of Economics* 4(2): 103–15. Reprinted in Bhaduri, A. (1993) *Unconventional Economic Essays*, Oxford: Oxford University Press.

Burton, M. P. and Phimister, E. (1995) 'Core journals: a reappraisal of the Diamond list', *Economic Journal* 105(2): 361–73.

Davidson, P. (1972) *Money and the Real World*, 1st edn, London: Macmillan.

Debreu, G. (1974) 'Excess demand functions', *Journal of Mathematical Economics* 1(1): 15–21.

Diamond, A. M., Jr (1989) 'The core journals of economics', *Current Contents* (1) (2 January): 4–11.

Dosi, G., Freeman, C., Nelson, R., Silverberg, G. and Soete, L. (eds) (1988) *Technical Change and Economic Theory*, London: Pinter.

Duffie, D. and Sonnenschein, H. (1989) 'Arrow and general equilibrium theory', *Journal of Economic Literature* 27: 565–98.

Duménil, G. and Lévy, D. (1987) 'The dynamics of competition: a restoration of the classical analysis', *Cambridge Journal of Economics* 11(2): 133–64.

Eatwell, J. (1979) *Theories of Value and Employment*, London: Thames Papers in Political Economy. Reprinted in Eatwell, J. and Milgate, M. (eds) (1983) *Keynes' Economics and the Theory of Value and Distribution*, London: Duckworth.

—— (1983) 'The long-period theory of employment', *Cambridge Journal of Economics* 7(3/4): 269–85.

Eatwell, J. and Milgate, M. (eds) (1983) *Keynes' Economics and the Theory of Value and Distribution*, London: Duckworth.

Garegnani, P. (1966) 'Switching of techniques', *Quarterly Journal of Economics* 80: 554–67.

—— (1970) 'Heterogeneous capital, the production function and the theory of distribution', *Review of Economic Studies* 37: 407–36. Reprinted in Hunt, E.K. and Schwartz, J. G. (eds) (1972) *A Critique of Economic Theory*, Harmondsworth: Penguin.

—— (1978) 'Notes on consumption, investment and effective demand: I', *Cambridge Journal of Economics* 2(4): 335–53. Reprinted in Eatwell, J. and Milgate, M. (eds) (1983) *Keynes' Economics and the Theory of Value and Distribution*, London: Duckworth.

—— (1979a) 'Notes on consumption, investment and effective demand: II', *Cambridge Journal of Economics* 3(1): 63–82. Reprinted in Eatwell, J. and Milgate, M. (eds) (1983) *Keynes' Economics and the Theory of Value and Distributing*, London: Duckworth.

—— (1979b) 'Notes on consumption, investment and effective demand: a reply to Joan Robinson', *Cambridge Journal of Economics* 3(2): 181–7. Reprinted in Eatwell, J. and Milgate, M. (eds) (1983) *Keynes' Economics and the Theory of Value and Distribution*, London: Duckworth.

Hahn, F. H. (1975) 'Revival of political economy: the wrong issues and the wrong arguments', *Economic Record* 51: 360–4.

—— (1982) 'The neo-Ricardians', *Cambridge Journal of Economics* 6(4): 353–74.

Harcourt, G. C. (1969) 'Some Cambridge controversies in the theory of capital', *Journal of Economic Literature* 7: 369–405.

—— (1972) *Some Cambridge Controversies in the Theory of Capital*, Cambridge, Cambridge University Press.

—— (ed.) (1977) *The Microeconomic Foundations of Macroeconomics*, Boulder, CO: Westview Press.

—— (1982a) 'The Sraffian contribution: an evaluation', in I. Bradley and M. Howard (eds) *Classical and Marxian Political Economy: Essays in Honour of Ronald L. Meek*, London: Macmillan.

—— (1982b) *The Social Science Imperialists: Selected Essays*, ed. P. Kerr, London: Routledge & Kegan Paul.

—— (1985) 'On the influence of Piero Sraffa on the contributions of Joan

Robinson to economic theory', *Economic Journal (Conference Papers)* 96: 96–108.
—— (1994) 'Capital theory controversies', in P. Arestis and M. Sawyer (eds) *The Elgar Companion to Radical Political Economy*, Aldershot: Edward Elgar. Reprinted in Harcourt, G. C. (1995) *Capitalism, Socialism and Post-Keynesianism: Selected Essays*, Cheltenham: Edward Elgar.
Harcourt, G. C. and Laing, N. F. (eds) (1971) *Capital and Growth*, Harmondsworth: Penguin.
Harcourt, G. C. and Massaro, V. G. (1964) 'Mr Sraffa's production of commodities', *Economic Record* 40: 442–54. Reprinted in Bradley, I. and Howard, M. (eds) (1982) *Classical and Marxian Political Economy: Essays in Honour of Ronald L. Meek*, London: Macmillan.
Harcourt, G. C. and O'Shaughnessy, T. J. (1985) 'Keynes' unemployment equilibrium: some insights from Joan Robinson, Piero Sraffa and Richard Kahn', in G. C. Harcourt (ed.) *Keynes and His Contemporaries*, London: Macmillan.
Hodgson, G. M. (1982) *Capitalism, Value and Exploitation: A Radical Theory*, Oxford: Martin Robertson.
—— (1988) *Economics and Institutions: A Manifesto for a Modern Institutional Economics*, Cambridge: Polity Press; Philadelphia: University of Pennsylvania Press.
—— (1989) 'Post-Keynesianism and institutionalism: the missing link', in J. Pheby (ed.) *New Directions in Post-Keynesian Economics*, Aldershot: Edward Elgar. Reprinted in Hodgson, G. M. (1991) *After Marx and Sraffa: Essays in Political Economy*, London: Macmillan.
—— (1994) 'Capital theory', in G. M. Hodgson, W. J. Samuels and M. R. Tool (eds) *The Elgar Companion to Institutional and Evolutionary Economics*, vol. 1, Aldershot: Edward Elgar.
Hunt, E. K. and Schwartz, J. G. (eds) (1972) *A Critique of Economic Theory*, Harmondsworth: Penguin.
Kirman, A. P. (1989) 'The intrinsic limits of modern economic theory: the emperor has no clothes', *Economic Journal (Conference Papers)* 99: 126–39.
Levhari, D. and Samuelson, P. A. (1966) 'The nonswitching theorem is false', *Quarterly Journal of Economics* 80(4): 503–17.
Loasby, B. J. (1976) *Choice, Complexity and Ignorance: An Enquiry into Economic Theory and the Practice of Decision Making*, Cambridge: Cambridge University Press.
Lundvall, B.-Å. (ed.) (1992) *National Systems of Innovation: Towards a Theory of Innovation and Interactive Learning*, London: Pinter..
Mantel, R. (1974) 'On the characterization of aggregate excess demand', *Journal of Economic Theory* 12(2): 348–53.
Meek, R. (1961) 'Mr Sraffa's rehabilitation of classical economics', published simultaneously in *Science and Society* 25: 139–56 and *Scottish Journal of Political Economy* 9: 119–36. Revised and reprinted in Meek, R. (1967) *Economics and Ideology and Other Essays*, London: Chapman & Hall.
Minsky, H. P. (1976) *John Maynard Keynes*, London: Macmillan.
Mongiovi, G. (1992) 'Piero Sraffa', in P. Arestis and M. Sawyer (eds) (1992) *A Biographical Dictionary of Dissenting Economists*, Aldershot: Edward Elgar.
Morishima, M. (1966) 'Refutation of the nonswitching theorem', *Quarterly Journal of Economics* 80: 520–5.
Morroni, M. (1992) *Production Process and Technical Change*, Cambridge: Cambridge University Press.
Nelson, R. R. and Winter, S. G. (1982) *An Evolutionary Theory of Economic Change*,

Cambridge, MA: Harvard University Press.

Pasinetti, L. L. (1966) 'Changes in the rate of profit and switches of techniques', *Quarterly Journal of Economics* 80(4): 503–17.

—— (1969) 'Switches of technique and the "rate of return" in capital theory', *Economic Journal* 79: 508–25. Reprinted in Harcourt, G. C. and Laing, N. F. (eds) (1971) *Capital and Growth*, Harmondsworth: Penguin.

Rizvi, S. A. T. (1994a) 'The microfoundations project in general equilibrium theory', *Cambridge Journal of Economics* 18(4): 357–77.

—— (1994b) 'Game theory to the rescue?', *Contributions to Political Economy* 13: 1–28.

Robinson, J. (1953) 'The production function and the theory of capital', *Review of Economic Studies* 21(1): 81–106. Reprinted in Robinson, J. (1960) *Collected Economic Papers*, vol. 2, Oxford: Basil Blackwell, and in Harcourt, G. C. and Laing, N. F. (eds) (1971) *Capital and Growth*, Harmondsworth: Penguin.

—— (1961) 'Prelude to a critique of economic theory', *Oxford Economic Papers* 13: 7–14. Reprinted in Robinson, J. (1975) *Collected Economic Papers*, vol. 3, 2nd edn, Oxford: Basil Blackwell, and Hunt, E. K. and Schwartz, J. G. (eds) *A Critique of Economic Theory*, Harmondsworth: Penguin.

—— (1973) 'Ideology and analysis', in *Sozialismus Geschichte und Wirtschaft: Festschrift für Eduard Marz*, Vienna: Europaverlags AG. Reprinted in Robinson, J. (1979) *Collected Economic Papers*, vol. 5, Oxford: Basil Blackwell.

—— (1974) *History versus Equilibrium*, London: Thames Papers in Political Economy.

—— (1975) *Collected Economic Papers*, vol. 3, 2nd edn, Oxford: Basil Blackwell.

—— (1979b) 'Garegnani on effective demand', *Cambridge Journal of Economics* 3(2): 179–80. Reprinted in Eatwell, J. and Milgate, M. (eds) (1983) *Keynes' Economics and the Theory of Value and Distribution*, London: Duckworth.

—— (1980) *Further Contributions to Modern Economics*, Oxford: Basil Blackwell.

Robinson, J. and Naqvi, K. A. (1967) 'The badly behaved production function', *Quarterly Journal of Economics* 81: 579–91.

Roncaglia, A. (1991) 'The Sraffa schools', *Review of Political Economy* 3(2): 187–219.

Samuelson, P. A. (1962) 'Parable and realism in capital theory: the surrogate production function', *Review of Economic Studies* 39: 193–206. Reprinted in Harcourt, G. C. and Laing, N. F. (eds) (1971) *Capital and Growth*, Harmondsworth: Penguin.

—— (1966) 'A summing up', *Quarterly Journal of Economics* 80: 568–83. Reprinted in Harcourt, G. C. and Laing, N. F. (eds) (1971) *Capital and Growth*, Harmondsworth: Penguin.

—— (1989) 'Remembering Joan', in G. R. Feiwel (ed.) *Joan Robinson and Modern Economic Theory*, London: Macmillan.

Sen, A. K. (ed.) (1970) *Growth Economics*, Harmondsworth: Penguin.

Shackle, G. L. S. (1974) *Keynesian Kaleidics*, Edinburgh: Edinburgh University Press.

Shafer, W. and Sonnenschein, H. (1982) 'Market demand and excess demand functions', in K. J. Arrow and M. D. Intriligator (eds) *Handbook of Mathematical Economics*, vol. 2, Amsterdam: North-Holland.

Solow, R. M. (1956) 'A contribution to the theory of economic growth', *Quarterly Journal of Economics* 70(1): 65–94. Reprinted in Sen, A. K. (ed.) (1970) *Growth Economics*, Harmondsworth: Penguin.

Sonnenschein, H. (1972) 'Market excess demand functions', *Econometrica* 40(3): 549–63.

—— (1973a) 'Do Walras's identity and continuity characterize the class of community excess demand functions?', *Journal of Economic Theory* 6(4): 345–54.

—— (1973b) 'The utility hypothesis and market demand theory', *Western Economic Journal* 11(4): 404–10.

Sraffa, P. (1960) *Production of Commodities by Means of Commodities: Prelude to a Critique of Economic Theory*, Cambridge: Cambridge University Press.

Steedman, I. (1975) 'Positive profits with negative surplus value', *Economic Journal* 85(1): 114–23.

—— (1977) *Marx after Sraffa*, London: NLB.

Steedman, I., Sweezy, P. M. *et al.* (1981) *The Value Controversy*, London: NLB.

Swan, T. W. (1956) 'Economic growth and capital accumulation', *Economic Record* 32: 334–61.

Veblen, T. B. (1908) 'Professor Clark's economics', *Quarterly Journal of Economics* 22(1): 147–95. Reprinted in Veblen, T. B. (1919) *The Place of Science in Modern Civilisation and Other Essays*, New York: Huebsch [reprinted 1990 with a new introduction by W. J. Samuels, New Brunswick: Transaction], and in Hunt, E. K. and Schwartz, J. G. (eds) (1972) *A Critique of Economic Theory*, Harmondsworth: Penguin.

—— (1919) *The Place of Science in Modern Civilisation and Other Essays*, New York: Huebsch. Reprinted 1990 with a new introduction by W. J. Samuels, New Brunswick: Transaction.

Weintraub, E. R. (1979) *Microfoundations*, Cambridge: Cambridge University Press.

10

KEYNES'S MACRO THEORY OF PROFITS*

Robert Dixon

INTRODUCTION

Few have done more to remind us of the continuing relevance of the ideas of Kalecki and Keynes than Geoff Harcourt. In the context of the present chapter it is especially important to note Geoff's role in exploring and formalizing the link between theories of pricing and aggregate profits on the one hand and theories of income and employment determination on the other. This is seen most clearly in his outstanding *Economic Record* (1965) paper[1] in which he showed how the traditional short-period Keynesian model could be adapted to incorporate decisions on price setting and choice of technique, with the result that the distribution of income as well as the level of employment can be determined by the model, and also in Chapter 3 of the *Cambridge Controversies* (1972) where it is shown, *inter alia*, that the relationship between the real wage and the marginal product of labour (and thus the level of unemployment) depends upon the balance between aggregate investment and aggregate saving. At the centre of both works lies the idea that profitability and the functional distribution of income are, in some essential way, macroeconomic phenomena.

In this chapter I look in some detail at one specific aspect of macro distribution theories, namely Keynes's macro theory of profits. It is my contention that Keynes's much-neglected model is actually very rich in dynamics and policy insights, and complements Kalecki–Harcourt type models in particular very nicely. I will attempt to demonstrate that Keynes's macro theory of profits underpins the analysis of aggregate income and employment equilibrium in *The General Theory* (Keynes 1973a) and I will argue that recognizing this adds important insight into some key elements in that work.

The substantive part of the chapter is arranged into four sections. The first deals with the theory of profits to be found in the *Treatise on Money* (Keynes 1971) (and other work by Keynes written in the early 1930s). The second section looks at the important role of the macro theory of profits in his *General Theory of Employment, Interest and Money* (Keynes 1973a). Among other things, I argue that for Keynes, macro demand shocks *are* profit shocks and it is for that reason that aggregate output and employment respond in a predictable way to variations in aggregate demand. The third section argues that, in this context at least, Keynes was a 'mild' rational-expectations theorist, a matter often overlooked when people write about Keynes and uncertainty and expectations. The last section offers some concluding remarks.

KEYNES'S MACRO THEORY OF PROFITS IN THE *TREATISE ON MONEY*

For the reader familiar with the writings of Robinson and Kalecki, Keynes's macro theory of profits[2] may be best developed as follows. Assume a classical two-sector model with no consumption out of profits but with some savings out of wages. Given this, the two sectors which make up the model are a wage-goods producing sector (denoted by the subscript wgs), which produces goods and services for workers and their families to consume, and a capital-goods producing sector (denoted by the subscript cgs). We will assume that the only (operating) costs of production in each sector are its own labour costs. Profits,[3] P, in the wage-goods sector will be equal to the revenue of that sector (given the assumption that there is no consumption out of profits, this will be equal to current expenditure on wage goods, C) less the value of wages, W, paid out in that sector as a cost of production. Thus[4]

$$P_{wgs} = C - W_{wgs} \qquad (10.1)$$

with

$$C = (1 - s_w)(W_{cgs} + W_{wgs}) \qquad (10.2)$$

where s_w is the propensity to save out of wages. Substitution of equation (10.2) into (10.1) yields

$$P_{wgs} = (1 - s_w)(W_{cgs} + W_{wgs}) - W_{wgs}$$

which may be written as

$$P_{wgs} = W_{cgs} - s_w(W) \qquad (10.3)$$

where

$$W = W_{cgs} + W_{wgs}$$

This is to say that the level of profits received by firms in the wage-goods sector depends upon the balance between the size of wage outlays by firms in the other sector, the capital-goods sector, W_{cgs}, and the savings of the public, $s_w(W)$, or, as Keynes puts it, 'profits on the production and sales of consumption goods are equal to the difference between the cost of new investment and savings' (Keynes 1971: 124).[5]

Since the amount spent on new capital goods, I, is equal to $P_{cgs} + W_{cgs}$, and P is equal to $P_{cgs} + P_{wgs}$, it is easily seen that

$$P = I - s_w(W) \qquad (10.4)$$

And so we may say that 'the total profits on output as a whole are equal to the difference between the *value* of new investment and savings' (ibid.).

The *Treatise on Money* (and in particular the first volume) is concerned primarily with the connection between the money supply, banking policy and interest rates on the one hand and the level of output as a whole and the price level of consumer goods, on the other. The nexus between profits and investment is the core of the *Treatise* and offers the possibility of a dynamic analysis, because 'profits (or losses) having once come into existence become, as we shall see, a cause of what subsequently ensues; indeed, the mainspring of change in the existing economic system' (ibid.: 126). As we have just seen, movements in aggregate profits are linked by Keynes to discrepancies between investment and the savings of the public. It is by altering the balance between investment and savings that stabilization policy, and in particular interest rate policy, is able to work. In the *Treatise* he presents a summary of his argument about the dynamics of the business cycle and the role of monetary policy which runs:

> As a rule, the existence of profit will provoke a tendency towards a higher rate of employment and of remuneration for the factors of production; and vice versa. By varying the price and quantity of bank credit the banking system governs the value of investment; upon the value of investment relatively to the volume of savings depend the profits or losses of the producers.
>
> (ibid.: 163f).

Essentially the same arguments are presented in Keynes's Harris Foundation lectures, given in Chicago in 1931 (1973b: 352–8). The analysis of the slump, its causes and possible cures are set out there in terms of the Treatise Model. In Lecture 2 he summarizes his approach as follows:

> When the value of current investment is greater than the savings of the public, the receipts of the entrepreneurs are greater than their costs, so they make a profit; and when, on the other hand, the value of current investment is less than the savings of the public, they make a loss. That is my secret, the clue to the scientific explanation of booms and slumps which I offer you.
>
> (ibid.: 353f)

In Lecture 3 he argues that the problem of recovery is essentially a problem of re-establishing the volume of investment to its pre-slump level and he identifies three lines of approach to achieve this. The first involves the restoration of confidence. The second line of approach 'consists in new construction programs under the direct auspices of the government or other public authorities'. And the third line of approach 'consists in a reduction of the long-term rate of interest' (ibid.: 364). He concludes by saying that although it is desirable to advance along all three fronts simultaneously, it is a 'vital necessity' for the long-term interest rate to fall (ibid.).[6]

One thing that these texts reveal is that for Keynes the macro theory of profits was acting as the foundation for his policy analysis. This is also to be seen in one of Keynes's *Essays in Persuasion*, titled 'The Great Slump of 1930' (see Keynes 1972: 126–34), and in a series of articles in *The Times* in 1933 entitled 'The means to prosperity'. There he argues that in order for the level of activity to expand, business investment will have to increase, but 'business enterprise will not seek to expand until *after* profits have begun to recover' (ibid.: 354; emphasis in original). Thus the first step in dealing with the slump must be increased 'governmental loan-expenditure' (ibid.).

THE MACRO THEORY OF PROFITS AND *THE GENERAL THEORY*

To neglect the *Treatise on Money* as a work in its own right is one thing, but unfortunately commentators on Keynes have also almost completely neglected the role of the macro theory of profits in *The General Theory of Employment, Interest and Money*. One reason for this is the tendency for people to see *The General Theory* in isolation from the *Treatise*. This is unfortunate, because *The General Theory* contains a number of explicit references to Keynes's macro theory of profits; indeed, Keynes made the link between the *Treatise* and *The General Theory* quite clear. For example, near the beginning of *The General Theory* he offers a brief summary of the theory of employment to be worked out in the following chapters:

> The outline of our theory can be expressed as follows ... to justify any given amount of employment there must be an amount of current investment sufficient to absorb the excess of total output over what the community chooses to consume when employment is at that given level. For unless there is this amount of investment, the receipts of the entrepreneurs will be less than is required to induce them to offer the given amount of employment. It follows therefore, that, given what we shall call the community's propensity to consume, the equilibrium level of employment ... will depend on the amount of current investment.
>
> (Keynes 1973a: 27).

Elsewhere he writes:

> the new argument [he means the argument of *The General Theory*] ... is essentially a development of the old. Expressed in the language of my *Treatise on Money*, it would run: the expectation of an increased excess of investment over saving, given the former volume of employment and

114

output, will induce entrepreneurs to increase the volume of employment and output.

(ibid.: 78)

In a draft of *The General Theory* he added:

> Both arguments depend on the discovery, if it can be called such, that an increase in the sum of consumption and investment will be associated with an increase in entrepreneurs' profit and that the expectation of an increase in entrepreneurs' profit will be associated with a higher level of employment and output. The significance of both my present and my former arguments lies in their attempt to show that the volume of employment is determined by the efforts of the entrepreneurs to maximise the excess of investment over saving as defined in my *Treatise on Money*.

(Keynes 1973b: 437)

The connection between the macro theory of profits, the notion of profits as a 'mainspring of change' and the analysis of the commodities market in Keynes's post-*Treatise* work persists well beyond the publication of *The General Theory of Employment, Interest and Money* in 1936. In an article in *The Times* in 1937 titled 'How to avoid a slump', (obviously) written after his *General Theory* was published, Keynes says, 'the production of investment goods tends to fluctuate widely, and it is these fluctuations which cause the fluctuations, first of profits, then of general business activity, and hence of national and world prosperity' (1982: 386.) Even later, in the preface to the French edition of *The General Theory*, written in 1939, he writes (1973a: xxxiii), 'we can calculate . . . what level of output and employment is in profit-equilibrium with a given level of new investment'.

One of the best ways to see the nature of the link (and the importance of the link) between the macro theory of profits to be found in the *Treatise* and the analysis of the commodities market to be found in *The General Theory* and elsewhere is by reminding ourselves that in *The General Theory* 'wage-units' are used to deflate all variables, including aggregate demand and aggregate supply.

If we begin from a position of 'equilibrium' (in the *General Theory* sense of a balance between aggregate demand and supply) and allow for an autonomous increase in aggregate demand measured in wage-units given the level of aggregate supply, this automatically implies an equivalent increase in current (and expected) profits, and it is this which acts as the 'mainspring of change'.

Consider the following simple model.[7] We assume that the propensity to save out of profits is unity and the propensity to save out of wages is zero. Given these assumptions, aggregate profits receipts in money terms in any period will equal the money value of investment expenditure in that period

115

$$P = I$$

Let aggregate demand, AD, in money terms be given by

$$AD = C + I = w_m L + I \qquad (10.5)$$

where L is the number employed and w_m is the money wage rate. Measured in wage-units, aggregate demand may be expressed as

$$AD/w_m = (C/w_m) + (I/w_m) = L + I/w_m \qquad (10.6)$$

Likewise, the value of profits in wage-units will be given by

$$P/w_m = I/w_m$$

It follows that, given the wage-unit and the level of employment, any autonomous increase in aggregate demand measured in wage-units (and in this model that amounts to any increase in the value of investment measured in wage-units) must be accompanied by an equivalent increase in profits, as, given our assumptions, if the increased demand is realized,[8] it will generate revenues to firms in excess of their current wages bills. What happens consequent upon this initial stimulus to variables such as output and employment is dependent upon a number of things, not the least of which is what happens to the wage-unit (and to price-cost margins). The main point to be understood, though, is that *for Keynes an autonomous demand (expenditure) shock is a profits shock.*

The foregoing also explains the reason for the use of wage units in *The General Theory*, and demonstrates the importance of the device. The use of wage-units should not be neglected, and nor should we believe that we could just as easily use some other (e.g. a price) deflator instead of wage-units. To do so would be to throw out a key part of the analysis.

KEYNES AS A RATIONAL-EXPECTATIONS THEORIST

Following Muth (1961: 316), rational expectations may be loosely defined as informed predictions of future events which are essentially the same as the predictions provided by relevant economic theory, given the information available to the agents. It is my contention that Keynes's agents in the *Treatise* are rational in this, rather mild, Muthian sense.

In considering the implications (and especially the policy implications) of his macro theory of profits in the *Treatise*, Keynes supposes that entrepreneurs forecast changes in the level of their profits by attempting to form expectations of the future balance between aggregate saving and aggregate investment and the consequences of this for the demand for their particular products.[9] Keynes argues that in order to forecast the balance between savings and investment, it is necessary for entrepreneurs to form expectations of

116

future monetary (banking) policy. This view, which is essentially a rational-expectations approach, is most clearly stated in the section dealing with the behaviour of entrepreneurs in Chapter 11 of the *Treatise on Money*. There, Keynes writes:

> production takes time and in so far as entrepreneurs are able to forecast the relation between saving and investment [it is this] which influences them in deciding the scale on which to produce and the offers it is worthwhile to make to the factors of production.
>
> (Keynes 1971:143)

He goes on to say:

> All the same, accurate forecasting in these matters is so difficult and requires much more information than is usually available, that the average behaviour of entrepreneurs is in fact mainly governed by current experience supplemented by such broad generalisations as those relating to the probable consequences of changes in bank rate, the supply of credit and the state of the foreign exchanges.
>
> (ibid.: 144)

In other words, entrepreneurs render uncertain decisions tractable by evaluating the performance of the macroeconomy (using certain indicators, especially the long-term bank rate). Given the definition of rational expectations set out above, it is clear that Keynes is a proponent of 'rational' expectations in this context because entrepreneurs are assumed to be behaving as if they are familiar with the fundamental equations of the *Treatise*. For this reason I think a case can be made for saying that Keynes, not Wicksell, can be regarded as *the* early precursor to the rational expectations idea (cf. McCallum 1980: 717).

Nor is this view (that individuals make rational forecasts of future macro balances based on their knowledge of relevant economic theory) entirely absent from *The General Theory*. We find there Keynes telling us that individual entrepreneurs form '*expectation(s) of the sum* of the proceeds resulting from consumption and investment respectively on various hypotheses' (1973a: 77; my emphasis), and we have already noted the passage in *The General Theory* where he writes that 'the expectation of an increased excess of investment over saving, given the former volume of employment and output, will induce entrepreneurs to increase the volume of employment and output' (ibid.: 78; my emphasis). Not that this view went unchallenged by his contemporaries. One of Keynes's most perceptive critics, Ralph Hawtry, objected to the idea of aggregating the plans of a number of individuals. In his book *Capital and Employment*, Hawtry writes, 'there are difficulties in the conception of an aggregate of plans or expectations ... [they] are states of mind of individuals [and as such] are of varying degrees of incompleteness and uncertainty, and extend to varying future periods of time' (1952: 161). In commenting on drafts of *The General Theory* Hawtry repeatedly expressed his concern at Keynes's desire to quantify expectations of aggregate demand (proceeds). There is a well-known and often-cited passage on expectations which appears in a footnote on p. 24 of *The General Theory* where Keynes writes:

> By his expectations of proceeds I mean that expectation of proceeds which, if it were held with certainty, would lead to the same behaviour as does the bundle of vague and more various possibilities which actually makes up his state of expectation when he reaches his decision.
>
> (Keynes 1973a: 24)

This passage was inserted as a result of Hawtry's criticisms of the drafts of *The General Theory* (Keynes 1973b: 596).

CONCLUDING REMARKS

It seems to me that, through the macro theory of profits of the *Treatise*, *The General Theory* has its origins in Malthusian economics; that some of the central ideas in the *Treatise* can be expressed in modern 'Kaleckian' form; that those ideas can be seen also to constitute an essential element in *The General Theory*; that Keynes, at least in the *Treatise* (but also, in my view, in *The General Theory*) was an early proponent of rational expectations (as defined by Muth); and that to put wage-units aside is to lose the insight that for Keynes macro demand shocks are profit shocks. More generally, I would argue, the *Treatise* and *The General Theory* must be seen as forming a coherent whole.

ACKNOWLEDGEMENTS

I am grateful to Tony Aspromourgos and John Creedy for their helpful comments on an earlier version of this chapter.

NOTES

1   Harcourt's 1965 paper is based on an earlier critique of Kaldor (Harcourt 1963).
2   In post-Keynesian writing one often finds reference to the 'widow's cruse', Keynes's notion that expenditure on consumption out of profits itself becomes a source of revenue to firms over and above the wages they have paid out and so serves to boost aggregate profits. As a result, 'profits ... are a widow's cruse which remains undepleted however much of them may be devoted to riotous living' (Keynes 1971: 125). For most of us that is all we ever hear of Keynes's theory of aggregate profits. But for Keynes himself, the widow's cruse was really a very minor element of his theory; he actually refers to it as a 'peculiarity ... which we may note in passing' (ibid.). It is unfortunate that the widow's cruse is the only reference which most of us find to Keynes's macro theory of profits (and for that matter to the *Treatise on Money*) because Keynes's theory of profits

is actually deserving of detailed study in its own right and ought not merely be treated as a footnote or a historical aside while we rush to get on to the models of Kalecki or Kaldor.

3   I am not following the *Treatise* definitions here. In the *Treatise*, profits are defined as 'the difference between the actual remuneration of entrepreneurs and their normal remuneration', where 'normal' means 'that rate of remuneration which ... would leave them under no motive either to increase or to decrease their scale of operations' (Keynes 1971: 111f).

4   We are assuming that stocks of wage-goods either do not exist or are unchanging over time.

5   By 'cost of new investment' he means the wages outlaid by firms in the capital goods sector.

6   Following the Harris Foundation lectures in Chicago in 1931, Keynes took part in a seminar discussion on the topic 'Are wage cuts a remedy for unemployment?' Keynes analyses their effect by asking: How will wage cuts affect the investment–saving balance? He says the net effect will depend upon whether, on balance, the effect of the wage cut upon investment offsets its effect upon saving (1973b: 368ff.). He also mentions that possibility that even if wage cuts could 'do the job', the required cut may be so great as to threaten social harmony (ibid.: 371f.). This is a point he mentions time and time again whenever he discusses (and invariably rejects) wage cuts as a possible remedy for the slump.

7   The following draws heavily on the appendix to Chapter 7 in Dixon (1988).

8   Keynes would say 'is effective'.

9   At times, in both the *Treatise* and *The General Theory*, Keynes seems to confuse 'individuals expectations of an aggregate'. with the 'aggregate of their expectations or expected values'. Hawtry, one of his most perceptive critics, objected to this notion of formulating expectations of an aggregate. He wrote to Keynes on 6 December 1930: '[you say] "that entrepreneurs forecast the relationship between saving and investment in its effect on the demand for their product". But this does not represent what is in their minds. What each tries to forecast is the demand for his own product. Even if he is acquainted with your fundamental equations, he must still recognise that the demand for his product is affected by factors other than a difference between saving and investment' (Keynes 1973b: 168). Actually, strictly speaking this is not a valid criticism of Keynes's text because he makes sufficient assumptions to ensure that all markets expand and contract together as the aggregate level of activity expands and contracts.

REFERENCES

Dixon, R. (1988) *Production, Distribution and Value*, Brighton: Wheatsheaf Books.

Harcourt, G. C. (1963) 'A critique of Mr Kaldor's model of income distribution and economic growth', *Australian Economic Papers* 2: 20–36.

—— (1965) 'A two sector model of the distribution of income and the level of employment in the short run', *Economic Record* 41: 103–17.

—— (1972) *Some Cambridge Controversies in the Theory of Capital*, Cambridge: Cambridge University Press.

Hawtry, R. (1952) *Capital and Employment*, 2nd edition, London, Longmans, Green & Co.

Keynes, J. (1971) *A Treatise on Money 1: The Pure Theory of Money*, London: Macmillan for the Royal Economic Society. (Volume 5 of the *Collected Writings of John Maynard Keynes*.)

—— (1972) *Essays in Persuasion*, London: Macmillan for the Royal Economic

Society. (Volume 9 of the *Collected Writings*.)

────── (1973a) *The General Theory of Employment, Interest and Money*, London: Macmillan for the Royal Economic Society. (Volume 7 of the *Collected Writings*.)

────── (1973b) *The General Theory and After:* Part 1, *Preparation*, London: Macmillan for the Royal Economic Society. (Volume 13 of the *Collected Writings*.)

────── (1982) *Activities 1931–1939: World Crises and Policies in Britain and America*, London: Macmillan for the Royal Economic Society. (Volume 21 of the *Collected Writings*.)

McCallum, B. (1980) 'Rational expectations and macroeconomic stabilisation policy: an overview', *Journal of Money, Credit and Banking* 12: 716–46.

Muth, J. (1961) 'Rational expectations and the theory of price movements', *Econometrica* 29: 315–35.

11

PROFIT AND RENT IN A MODEL OF CAPITAL ACCUMULATION AND STRUCTURAL DYNAMICS

Mauro Baranzini and Roberto Scazzieri

INTRODUCTION

When Geoff Harcourt arrived at King's College, Cambridge, in the Michael-mas term of 1955, the early contributions by John Maynard Keynes had already sparked off a number of important investigations in the field of long-run economic dynamics and capital theory. Joan Robinson was busy putting the final touches to her *Accumulation of Capital* (1956), Nicholas Kaldor was about to publish his seminal papers on the theory of income distribution and growth (1956, 1957), and Piero Sraffa was about to conclude his long and final journey through classical and Ricardian economics which eventually led to the publication of *Production of Commodities by Means of Commodities* in 1960.

Geoff Harcourt's early interest in savings formation, taxation, earnings rates and in the trade cycle in general has been a precious background for fully appreciating the macroeconomic framework of Joan Robinson and Michal Kalecki, and Nicholas Kaldor's seminal contributions to the long-run dynamics of a capitalist economy. In particular, in his first year as a young graduate he went 'to Joan Robinson's lectures on what was to become *The Accumulation of Capital* [1956], often with Tom Asimakopulos and Keith Frearson' (Harcourt 1995: 10). On the other hand, Sraffa's reconsideration of classical economic theory had a profound influence on him and alerted him in the early 1960s to the relevance of structural and compositional features when considering economic dynamics.

Geoff Harcourt's earlier contributions to economics seem to reflect his dual emphasis on both macroeconomic features of an expanding system and the foundations of structural analysis. This is shown by his early papers on the Kaldorian growth model (1963, 1965a) and his paper written jointly with Vincent Massaro on the role of subsystems in Sraffa's circular economy

(1964a). Geoff Harcourt tells us that the latter was read and reread by Sraffa himself, and published with his blessing; and this was even more true of the review article, written jointly with Vincent Massaro, of *Production of Commodities by Means of Commodities* published in the *Economic Record* (Harcourt and Massaro 1964b).

The two above strands of enquiry were put together in masterly fashion in the survey article 'Some Cambridge controversies in the theory of capital' (Harcourt 1969) and subsequently extended in the volume with the same title published by Cambridge University Press in 1972, which Harcourt finished while at Trinity Hall, Cambridge. This painstaking work has been a point of access to this relevant and wide-ranging area of analysis for an entire generation of scholars; and by the numerous hints provided has been the starting point for numerous research programmes. One example may suffice: when commenting on the Kaldor–Pasinetti model of profit determination and income distribution, Harcourt stresses the importance of the assumption of the equality between the rate of profits and the rate of interest earned by workers on their savings, and asks himself what would be the implications of the relaxation of such an assumption (1972: 217). On the basis of this hint many contributions would follow over the subsequent twenty years (see Baranzini 1991: 56–8).

In this chapter we draw upon the original Kaldor growth model (1956), as refined by Luigi Pasinetti (1962), in order to investigate features of structural economic dynamics which may have relevant implications for the long-run distribution of income and wealth among socioeconomic classes. In this way, we shall take up a theme closely related to Joan Robinson's emphasis upon the fine structure of rents along an expanding path characterized by 'technological disequilibria' with the coexistence of techniques of different degrees of efficiency (see Robinson 1956: bk. 2; Quadrio-Curzio 1993), and to Harcourt's original remark on the significance of the equality between the rate of profit and rate of interest (1972: 217).

The post-Keynesian view of long-run distribution of income and wealth, as expounded by Kaldor and Pasinetti, retains the basic structure of classical economic theory while investigating its scheme of causal determination: profits are associated with the requirements of steady growth while wages become a residual. A natural step would seem to be that of resuming a view of the economy in which a third class (not considered by Kaldor or Pasinetti) is introduced; in our case a class of *rentiers* whose income may be derived from both profits and rent. This assumption gives the model more flexibility and makes it more compatible with a vision of the economic system emphasizing technological rigidities and market imperfections, as these features are often associated with the existence of distinct incomes or social classes.

The basic results for two-class growth models may be summarized as follows. Assuming full employment and steady-state growth, Pasinetti (1962) showed that, if workers receive wage and profit payments and capitalists profit payments only, then the long-run equilibrium rate of profits, P, is equal to the natural rate of growth, n, divided by the capitalists' propensity to save, s_c ($P/K = n/s_c$). The rate of profits is therefore independent of the workers' propensity to save and of the production technology; moreover, this outcome makes the share of profits in national income independent of the workers' propensity to save.

A possible way of generalizing the original two classes–two incomes model has been suggested by Pasinetti (1977: 58). Pasinetti's proposal consists in considering a model with two classes of savers (the class of workers and the class of capitalists and *rentiers*) and three categories of income (wages, profits and rents). It is argued that the equilibrium rate of profits is determined (provided, of course, that Samuelson and Modigliani's (1966) dual theorem does not apply) by the formula $r = g_n/(1 + \delta)s_c$, where r and g_n are the rate of profits and the natural rate of growth respectively, s_c is the saving propensity of the capitalist–*rentier* class, and δ is the 'long-run ratio of total rent to capitalists' profits' (Pasinetti 1977: 58). The validity of Pasinetti's result is, however, limited to the case in which total rent is a constant proportion of capitalists' profits. Otherwise, 'a *steady state* path would not exist, and we would be outside the scope of this type of analysis' (ibid.; emphasis in original).

To our knowledge, no attempt seems to have been made so far to consider the long-run income distribution along the steady-state, full-employment path of an economy which starts the accumulation process with three categories of income (wages, profits and rents) and three classes characterized by different propensities to save (those of workers, capitalists and *rentiers*). The aim of this chapter is to introduce a simple model for the analysis of that case and to derive a first set of results on the possible steady states of such an economy.

THE BASIC ASSUMPTIONS OF THE MODEL

Let us consider an economic system in which total net income, Y, is divided into wages, W, profits, P, and rent, R. Total net savings will also be divided into three categories: workers' savings, S_w, capitalists' savings, S_c, and *rentiers'* savings, S_r.

Workers receive wage and profit payments, the latter in the form of interest on their accumulated savings. Capitalists are pure profit-earners. *Rentiers* receive interest on their accumulated savings and, at the same time, receive a rent. The latter includes all kinds of incomes which are not the remuneration of labour, at the current wage rate, and do not derive from accumulated savings. It follows that the term 'rent' will refer, in the present framework, to a range of incomes which may include, among others, Ricardian rents and monopolists' profits. Such a general formulation is justified by the fact that one purpose of our analysis is that of studying those characteristics of steady-state growth which do not depend on the differences among all such incomes. In addition, it may be important to stress that the purpose of our chapter is to focus on the long-run distribution compatible with steady growth so that our conception of rent is independent of any particular assumption about production technology. For instance, our long-term steady-state conditions have to be satisfied in the cases both of decreasing and of constant-returns technology.

Let now s_w, s_c and s_r denote the saving propensities of workers, capitalists and rentiers respectively (where $0 \leq s_w < s_c$, $s_r \leq 1$); the classes are supposed intergenerationally stable. Denoting by P_w, P_c and P_r the amount of profits received respectively by workers, capitalists and *rentiers*, and by K_w, K_c and K_r the capital stock owned by the same classes, we have

$$S_c = s_c P_c = s_c r K_c \tag{11.1}$$

$$S_w = s_w (P_w + W) = s_w (r K_w + r K_w \theta) \tag{11.2}$$

$$S_r = s_r (P_r + R) = s_r (r K_r + r K_r \delta) = s_r \phi K_r \tag{11.3}$$

where the variables r and δ are the rate of profits and the long-run ratio of total rent to rentiers' profits (R/P_r) respectively.[1] (From now on we set $\phi = r(1 + \delta)$ the long-run ratio of *rentiers'* income to their capital stock.)

EQUILIBRIUM GROWTH

In this section we shall study the conditions which need to be satisfied in order to have equilibrium full-employment growth. The system will remain in dynamic equilibrium if and only if

$$I = S \tag{11.4}$$

where I is investment. Substituting from the savings functions and denoting, for analytical convenience, by $W + r K_w$ the income of the workers, by $r K_c$ the income of the capitalists and by ϕK_r the income of the *rentiers*, we can write relation (11.4) as

$$I = s_w (W + r K_w) + s_c r K_c + s_r \phi K_r \tag{11.5}$$

The aggregate savings ratio is then given by

$$s = s_w + (s_c - s_w) r \frac{K_c}{K} \frac{K}{Y} + (s_r - s_w) \phi \frac{K_r}{K} \frac{K}{Y} \tag{11.6}$$

We must now find a suitable expression for K_c/K and K_r/K. In the long run the capital stock owned by each category of savers must be proportional to their savings (otherwise a steady-state balanced growth path would not exist) so that

$$\frac{K_c}{K} = \frac{S_c}{S} = s_c P_c / I = \frac{s_c}{s_c - s_w} \frac{(s_c - s_w)P_c}{I}$$

$$= \frac{s_c}{s_c - s_w} \frac{I - s_w Y - (s_r - s_w)\phi K_r}{I} \tag{11.7}$$

$$\frac{K_r}{K} = \frac{S_r}{S} = s_r \phi K_r / I = \frac{s_r}{s_r - s_w} \frac{(s_r - s_w)\phi K_r}{I}$$

$$= \frac{s_r}{s_r - s_w} \frac{I - s_w Y - (s_c - s_w)r K_c}{I} \tag{11.8}$$

From these relations we can derive the equilibrium capital share of the three classes. First, by substituting the right-hand side of equation (11.8) into (11.7), after the necessary manipulations, we obtain (where $n = I/K$, the natural rate of growth)

$$\frac{K_c}{K} = \frac{s_c}{s_c - s_w} \frac{\left(n - s_w \frac{Y}{K}\right)(n - s_r\phi)}{n^2 - s_c s_r \phi r} \tag{11.9}$$

Introducing (11.9) into the right-hand side of (11.8) and rearranging, we obtain

$$\frac{K_r}{K} = \frac{s_r}{s_r - s_w} \frac{\left(n - s_w \frac{Y}{K}\right)(n - s_c r)}{n^2 - s_c s_r \phi r} \tag{11.10}$$

Hence the equilibrium capital share of the workers' class will be given by

$$\frac{K_w}{K} = 1 - \frac{K_c}{K} - \frac{K_r}{K} = 1 - \frac{n - s_w \frac{Y}{K}}{n^2 - s_c s_r \phi r}\left(s_r \frac{n - s_c r}{s_r - s_w} + s_c \frac{n - s_r\phi}{s_c - s_w}\right) \tag{11.11}$$

Substituting the right-hand side of equation (11.6) into the well-known Harrod–Domar equilibrium condition $s/n = K/Y$, we obtain

$$n = \frac{Y}{K}\left[s_w + (s_c - s_w)r\frac{K_c}{K}\frac{K}{Y} + (s_r - s_w)\phi\frac{K_r}{K}\frac{K}{Y}\right] \tag{11.12}$$

into which we introduce relations (11.9) and (11.10), so obtaining, after the necessary manipulations, the following expression:

125

$$\left(r - \frac{n}{s_c}\right)\left(n - s_w \frac{Y}{K}\right)\left(\phi - \frac{n}{s_r}\right) = 0 \qquad (11.13)$$

which is satisfied when one of the following relations (or combination of them) holds:

$$r = n/s_c \qquad (11.14a)$$

$$Y/K = n/s_w \qquad (11.14b)$$

$$\phi = n/s_r \qquad (11.14c)$$

Relation (11.14a) is the well-known 'Cambridge equation', originally formulated by Kaldor (1956) and Pasinetti (1962) for the case in which national income is made up by profits and wages only. Relation (11.14b) corresponds to the Meade–Samuelson and Modigliani dual theorem.

Relation (11.14c) may be defined as the *rentiers'* long-run equilibrium. In this case the long-run ratio of *rentiers'* income to their capital stock, ϕ, is equal to the natural rate of growth divided by the propensity to save of the *rentiers'* class; it is therefore independent of the technology of production and of the propensities to save of the other classes. As shown below, in this case the capitalists' share of capital stock must equal zero, so that only the workers and the *rentiers* will own a positive share of capital and will contribute to the process of accumulation. From relations (11.3) and (11.14c) it follows that $\phi = n/s_r = r(1 + \delta)$; the implications of this result will be discussed in detail below.

As shown in Table 11.1, the solutions obtained cannot hold simultaneously, and the respective capital share of the three classes is obtained by inserting equations (11.14a), (11.14b) and (11.14c) into (11.9), (11.10) and (11.11).

These results are, to a certain extent, paradoxical. The workers' class, which in the neo-Keynesian model of income distribution receives a residual

Table 11.1 Long-run capital share of the three classes

Long-run equilibrium condition	K_w/K (workers' share)	K_c/K (capitalists' share)	K_r/K (rentiers' share)
$r = n/s_c$	$s_w \dfrac{s_c Y/K - n}{n(s_c - s_w)}$	$s_c \dfrac{n - s_w Y/K}{n(s_c - s_w)}$	0
$Y/K = n/s_w$	1	0	0
$\phi = n/s_r$	$s_w \dfrac{s_r Y/K - n}{n(s_r - s_w)}$	0	$s_r \dfrac{n - s_w Y/K}{n(s_r - s_w)}$

income, cannot be squeezed out of the model and will always hold a positive fraction of the capital stock (at least, as long as s_w is positive). On the other hand, the capitalist class and the *rentier* class (which, whenever they contribute a positive share of overall savings, maintain a strategic importance in the determination of the distribution of income) can maintain a positive capital share only for one of the three equilibria (11.14a), (11.14b) and (11.14c).

When dropping one of the three steady-state conditions, (11.14a), (11.14b) and (11.14c), one might go back and redefine the initial model; however, this will not be done here since the corresponding steady state is exhaustively described by the solutions which apply in each particular case.[2]

EQUILIBRIUM GROWTH AND INCOME DISTRIBUTION WHEN THE RENTIERS' LONG-RUN EQUILIBRIUM APPLIES

The determination of the rate of profits and the distribution of income for the case in which Pasinetti's theorem (11.14a) or Meade's and Samuelson and Modigliani's dual theorem (11.14b) apply (that is, when the savings required by the long-run equilibrium are provided by workers and capitalists or by workers only) have been exhaustively treated in the literature.

In this section we shall focus on relation (11.14c), for which the long-run equilibrium savings are provided by workers and *rentiers* only. Within this framework we shall consider (a) the distribution of income between the two classes, (b) the equilibrium value of the rate of profits, and (c) the distribution of income among wages, profits and rent.

Distribution of income between social classes

When equation (11.14c) applies, $K_c/K = 0$ and the capitalists cannot exist in the long run; we may thus write

$$Y = + rK_w + \phi K_r \qquad (11.15)$$

In this case, since $\phi = n/s_r$ and $K_r = s_r K[n - s_w Y/K]/[n(s_r - s_w)]$, the share of *rentiers'* income in national income is now given by

$$Y_r/Y = \phi K_r/Y = \frac{n\dfrac{K}{Y} - s_w}{s_r - s_w} \qquad (11.16)$$

which, under the assumption of a given technology, makes the share of *rentiers'* income a function of exogenous variables only (the natural rate of growth, the capital:output ratio and the propensities to save of the workers and *rentiers*). Hence changes in δ, the long-run ratio of total rent to *rentiers'* profits, do not affect the *rentiers'* income share.

It is worth noting that a higher propensity to save on the part of the workers and *rentiers* will both have a negative effect on the *rentiers'* income share. Although the former outcome is not surprising, the latter might seem somewhat paradoxical. But $\phi = n/s_r$ and K_r/K both correlate negatively with s_r; which means that a higher propensity to save on the part of *rentiers* forces down their long-run income : capital stock ratio and, at the same time, reduces their share of capital; the combined effect of these two factors compresses the equilibrium share of *rentiers'* income.

The workers' income share is now given by

$$Y_w/Y = (W + rK_w)/Y = 1 - \phi \frac{K_r}{Y} = \frac{s_r - n\dfrac{K}{Y}}{s_r - s_w} \tag{11.17}$$

which is a function of exogenous variables only. Since the workers' income share has been defined as a residual, its partial derivatives with respect to the two propensities to save have the same *modulus*, but opposite sign as compared with those concerning relation (11.16). It is also worth mentioning that the workers' income share is independent of δ, the long-run ratio of total rent to *rentiers'* profits. This means that δ cannot influence the distribution of income between social classes, although it may influence the distribution of income among wages, profits and rent, as we shall see below.

The long-run equilibrium rate of profits

In order to describe how the rate of profits is determined in the long-run equilibrium, it is worth discussing the implications of equation (11.14c) with respect to the relationship between r (the rate of profits) and δ (the long-run ratio of total rent to *rentiers'* profits, R/P_r), bearing in mind that in this case the capitalists' share of capital is zero and that only workers and *rentiers* contribute a positive share of overall savings. From relations (11.3) and (11.14c) we obtain

$$\phi = n/s_r = r(1 + \delta) \tag{11.18}$$

which yields the following value for the long-run equilibrium interest rate (earned by workers and *rentiers*)

$$r = \frac{n}{s_r(1 + \delta)} \tag{11.19}$$

This expression is a function of the parameters n (the natural rate of growth),

128

s_r (the *rentiers'* propensity to save) and δ (the long-run ratio of total rent to *rentiers'* profits). It is hence independent of the behavioural parameters of the worker class and of the technology of production. This outcome, which was obtained by Pasinetti (1977: 58) in a different framework, reinforces the validity of the Cambridge equation since it confirms the strategic importance of that class of individuals who are not wage receivers, in spite of the fact that in this case the class under consideration receives an income which is not entirely derived from capital accumulation.

Distribution of income among wages, profits and rent

We now turn our attention to the share of wages, profits and rent in national income. When equation (11.14c) applies, and $K_c/K = 0$, total profits, P, are given by

$$P = r(K_w + K_r) = rK \tag{11.20}$$

and from equation (11.19) the share of profits can be written as

$$P/Y = rK/Y = \frac{nK/Y}{s_r(1 + \delta)} \tag{11.21}$$

which is exogenously determined by the parameters n, K/Y, s_r and δ, but is independent of the saving behaviour of the workers' class. Hence the behavioural parameters of the workers' class, although influencing the distribution of income between *rentiers* and workers, cannot influence the share of profits in national income.

From relations (11.14c) and (11.19), total rent, in the long-run equilibrium under consideration, is given by

$$R = rK_r\delta = K_r \frac{n\delta}{s_r(1 + \delta)} \tag{11.22}$$

which yields

$$R/Y = \frac{n\delta}{s_r(1 + \delta)} \frac{K_r}{K} \frac{K}{Y} = \frac{\delta}{1 + \delta} \frac{n\dfrac{K}{Y} - s_w}{s_r - s_w} \tag{11.23}$$

Hence the share of rent in national income is a function of parameters only, among which are the propensities to save of both classes. This means that the worker class, though not influencing the share of profits, can affect the share of total rent which, by definition, accrues to *rentiers* only.

The share of wages will hence be a residual once the shares of profits and rent have been determined.

CONCLUSIONS

At this point our results allow some conjectures about the dynamic path which would be followed by an economy approaching one of the three steady states which have been described, starting from a situation in which workers, capitalists and *rentiers* contribute together to the process of capital accumulation. On each of the three traverses, one or two classes of savers are bound to disappear, since the coexistence of the three classes is impossible in the steady state. Such an outcome may appear to show some similarity with what happens in Ricardo's three-class model of capital accumulation, where workers, capitalists and *rentiers* may coexist only along the traverse towards the stationary state (characterized by a marginal productivity of labour equal to the natural wage rate). A similar outcome may occur in the foregoing model, but rests upon an entirely different basis, for no assumption of diminishing returns has been made so far, and the accumulation process alone would be responsible for the disappearance of one class of savers.

The results of the section headed 'Equilibrium growth', above, deserve further comment, since they point to a phenomenon which seems to have passed unnoticed so far. In the case considered in that section, capital accumulation is based on the savings of workers and *rentiers*, where *rentiers'* income is derived from rent and accumulated savings, and workers' income is derived in part from wages and in part from the accumulation made in the past. Under such conditions, it has been shown that the type of income distribution compatible with full-employment equilibrium growth is determined by the natural rate of growth and by the *rentiers'* propensity to save, and that there is one degree of freedom in solving the model, with regard to the determination of the interest rate, r, and of the ratio of total rent to *rentiers'* profits, δ. In order words, the condition for equilibrium growth determines the ratio of *rentiers'* total income to the *rentiers'* capital stock, but leaves indeterminate the composition of their income between rent and interest on accumulated savings.

Such an indeterminacy may be eliminated by taking the ratio of total rent to *rentiers'* profits as exogenously fixed, provided equation (11.14c) is satisfied. In this case it is possible to determine the system's interest rate, and the distribution of income consistent with equilibrium, full-employment growth. This result may appear somehow surprising, since it suggests that, when equilibrium savings are provided by workers and *rentiers* only, the condition to be satisfied relatively to the distribution of income among wages, profits and rent is more flexible than in the case when the equilibrium savings are provided by workers and pure capitalists. The reason for this is that the long-run equilibrium condition $\phi = n/s_r = r(1 + \delta)$ is related only to the ratio of *rentiers'* total income to their capital stock; so that it becomes possible to allow for a trade-off between rent and *rentiers'* profits. It may be worth mentioning that, according to Pasinetti (1977: 58), the long-run ratio of total rent to the profits earned by his capitalists–*rentiers* (a class which corresponds to our *rentiers*) has to be constant in the steady state. This result is a consequence of expressing the long-run equilibrium condition in terms of the rate of profits, *r*. Once we refer to the *rentiers'* long-run ratio between total income and their capital stock, it becomes apparent that changes in δ may still allow the maintenance of a given full-employment path, provided the interest rate varies accordingly.

The above analysis brings to the fore a number of remarkable features of the dynamic path that may be followed by a capitalist economy that is subject to intense structural dynamics, and thus bound to show a pattern of differentiation among the flows of income and wealth, with the emergence of rent as a category of income characteristically associated with technological disequilibria and market asymmetries. In particular, our investigation has shown the inherent instability of the three-class configuration (workers, capitalists, *rentiers*) and the existence of alternative long-run equilibria corresponding to different socioeconomic structures. One case (that of the coexistence of capitalists and workers) corresponds to the classical situation of a capitalist economy. Another case (workers only) corresponds to a worker-owned economy in which pure capitalists have disappeared, so making room for the classes of wage-earners and rent-earners. The latter socioeconomic structure (which is compatible with a long-run growth equilibrium) points to the possibility of some kind of 'capitalists' euthanasia' along an expanding path, a situation to be compared with Keynes's '*rentiers'* euthanasia' within the framework of a mature and sluggish economic system (see Keynes 1936: ch. 24).

NOTES

1 Relation (11.3) may seem at odds with the established view that rent does not derive from the ownership of a capital stock. It is hence important to stress that it is simply an *ex post* analytical relation which does not represent the process of rent determination; it refers instead to the link which exists between rent and the rentiers' capital stock when rentiers contribute a positive share of overall savings.

2 In this chapter we confine ourselves to the study of the necessary conditions for long-run steady-state growth. A further line of research might include the analysis of what happens outside the steady state when the three classes have different ranges of saving propensity and ratios of outside income to return on accumulated saving in order to see the eventual domination of capital's share by particular classes.

BIBLIOGRAPHY

Baranzini, M. (1975) 'The Pasinetti and the anti-Pasinetti theorems: a reconciliation', *Oxford Economic Papers* 27: 470–3.

—— (1991) *A Theory of Wealth Distribution and Accumulation*, Oxford: Clarendon Press.

Baranzini, M. and Harcourt, G. C. (1993) *The Dynamics of the Wealth of Nations: Essays in Honour of Luigi Pasinetti*, London: Macmillan.

Harcourt, G. C. (1963) 'A critique of Mr Kaldor's model of income distribution and economic growth', *Australian Economic Papers* 2: 20–36.

—— (1965a) 'A two-sector model of distribution of income and the level of employment in the short run', *Economic Record* 41: 103–17.

—— (1965b) 'The accountant in a golden age', *Oxford Economic Papers* 17: 66–80.

—— (1969) 'Some Cambridge controversies in the theory of capital', *Journal of Economic Literature* 7: 369–405.

—— (1972) *Some Cambridge Controversies in the Theory of Capital*, Cambridge: Cambridge University Press.

—— (1995) 'Recollections and reflection of an Australian patriot and a Cambridge economist', *Banca Nazionale del Lavoro Quarterly Review* 194: 225–54.

Harcourt, G. C. and Massaro, V. G. (1964a) 'A note on Mr Sraffa's sub-systems', *Economic Journal* 74: 715–22.

—— (1964b) 'Mr Sraffa's *Production of Commodities*', *Economic Record* 40: 442–54.

Kaldor, N. (1956) 'Alternative theories of distribution', *Review of Economic Studies* 23: 83–100.

—— (1957) 'A model of economic growth', *Economic Journal* 67: 591–624.

Keynes, J. M. (1936) *The General Theory of Employment, Interest and Money*, London: Macmillan.

Meade, J. E. (1963) 'The rate of profits in a growing economy', *Economic Journal* 73: 665–74.

—— (1966) 'The outcome of the Pasinetti process: a note', *Economic Journal* 76: 161–5.

Pasinetti, L. L. (1962) 'The rate of profit and income distribution in relation to the rate of economic growth', *Review of Economic Studies* 29: 267–79.

—— (1974) *Growth and Income Distribution: Essays in Economic Theory*, Essay 6, Cambridge: Cambridge University Press.

—— (1977) 'Growth and income distribution: answering Professor Stiglitz's questions', in Morishima, M. 'Pasinetti's *Growth and Income Distribution* Revisited', *Journal of Economic Literature* 17: 56–61.

Quadrio-Curzio, A. (1993) 'Comment', paper presented at the International Conference 'Joan Robinson: The Passion for Reason', held at the Einaudi Foundation, Turin, December.

Robinson, J. (1956) *The Accumulation of Capital*, London: Macmillan.

Samuelson, P. A. and Modigliani, F. (1966) 'The Pasinetti paradox in neoclassical and more general models', *Review of Economic Studies* 33: 269–302; see also the following comments by L. L. Pasinetti, J. Robinson, N. Kaldor and K. Sato, and the reply by the two authors.

Scazzieri, R. (1993) *A Theory of Production*, Oxford: Clarendon Press.

Sraffa, P. (1960) *Production of Commodities by Means of Commodities*, Cambridge: Cambridge University Press.

132

12

UNEVEN DEVELOPMENT AND THE RATE OF PROFIT

Robert Rowthorn

INTRODUCTION

There has been an extensive, and sometimes heated, debate on the validity and significance of Marx's famous theory of the so-called falling tendency of the rate of profit. Most of the debate, in modern times, has been concerned with one particular aspect of this theory, namely the relationship between real wages, the choice of technique and the rate of profit. Other, equally important, features of Marx's theory have been largely neglected. This chapter seeks to rectify that imbalance. It presents two quite distinct versions of Marx's theory, both of which have textual support in Marx's own writing. One version is based on the neoclassical notion of the diminishing marginal productivity of investment. The other version is based on the idea of uneven technological development, whereby the sectors producing means of production experience slower productivity growth than sectors which use these means of production. Such uneven development will normally cause means of production to become more expensive in comparison to final output, and under certain conditions the result will be a fall in the rate of profit. The chapter argues that both versions of Marx's theory are equally plausible and both may potentially explain temporary reductions in the rate of profit. However, neither can convincingly explain why such a fall should be permanent. The chapter also considers some empirical and historical evidence relevant to Marx's theory.

MARX'S THEORY

Marx begins his analysis by considering what he calls 'the general rate of profit', which is defined as follows. Let L be the total amount of labour performed in the capitalist sector during a given period, in return for which workers receive wages containing V units of labour. The amount of surplus value which workers create is given by $S = L - V$, and the general rate of profit is equal to:

$$r = \frac{S}{C + V} \tag{12.1}$$

where C is the value of 'constant' capital employed in production (equipment, buildings, materials, etc.). This formula is not an arbitrary invention of Marx. A similar formula is used in reality by individual capitalists in evaluating the return they receive on their own investments.[1] The formula also indicates the ability of capital to finance growth from its own profits: if all surplus value is invested, the value of total capital $(C + V)$ grows at a proportionate rate r. Thus, the rate of profit indicates the capacity of capital for 'self-expansion'.

Before examining Marx's formula for the rate of profit, let us write it in the following more convenient form:

$$r = \frac{\dfrac{S}{V}}{\dfrac{C}{L}\left(1 + \dfrac{S}{V}\right) + 1}$$

where, as above, $L = S + V$. This can be written:

$$r = \frac{e}{k(1 + e) + 1} \tag{12.2}$$

where $e = S/V$ and $k = C/L$. The ratio k can be interpreted in a variety of ways and has a variety of names. Conventionally, it is interpreted as an index of the capital intensity of production, indicating the value of constant capital employed by the average worker, and this is how we shall interpret it.[2] The question of names is more difficult, because there is no agreed terminology and Marx's own use of terms in this area is rather obscure. In what follows, I shall refer to k as the capital coefficient.[3]

Looking at equation (12.2) makes it is clear that the rate of profit depends on two magnitudes: the rate of surplus value e and the capital coefficient k. Marx argued that variations in the capital coefficient are of great importance and may in themselves account for a secular decline in the rate of profit. In the course of development, he argues, there is a secular increase in the 'volume' or, as Marx calls it, the 'mass' of capital employed per worker. The average worker operates with an ever greater amount of equipment, transforming an ever greater quantity of material and producing ever more output per unit of time. Other things being equal, such an increase in the *volume* of constant capital per worker would cause the *value* of capital per worker to rise. With a given rate of surplus value, this in turn would cause the rate of profit to fall. This is the essence of Marx's argument and his objection to Ricardo's view that all variations in the rate of profit stem from variations in the rate of surplus value. Marx's argument is neatly summarized in the following quotation:

> The law of the falling rate of profit, which expresses the same or even a higher rate of surplus value, states, in other words, that any quantity of the average social capital, say, a capital of 100, comprises an ever larger portion of means of labour and an ever smaller portion of living labour. Therefore, *since the aggregate mass of living labour operating the means of production decreases in relation to the value of these means of production*, it follows that the unpaid labour and the portion of value in which it is expressed must decline as compared to the value of capital advances.
>
> (Marx 1966: 215–16 (my emphasis))

COUNTERACTING INFLUENCES

Having established a basic tendency for the rate of profit to fall, Marx considers the various influences which may counteract this tendency and help maintain the rate of profit. To understand the logic of his argument, suppose that means of production can be classified into two types: (a) instruments of labour, such as buildings, machinery and the like; and (b) raw materials, semi-finished goods and other 'objects of labour'. For simplicity, I shall refer to the former as 'machinery' and the latter as 'materials'. Let Q_1 and Q_2 be index numbers representing, respectively, the real volume of machinery and materials; and let λ_1 and λ_2 be the average unit labour values of machinery and materials. The total value of constant capital in use is given by:

$$C = Q_1\lambda_1 + Q_2\lambda_2 \tag{12.3}$$

and, hence:

$$\frac{C}{L} = \frac{Q_1}{L} \cdot \lambda_1 + \frac{Q_2}{L} \cdot \lambda_2 \tag{12.4}$$

This expression for k can be simplified by writing:

$$q = \left(\frac{Q_1}{L}, \frac{Q_2}{L}\right)$$

$$\lambda = (\lambda_1, \lambda_2)$$

Following Marx, we shall call q the 'technical composition of capital', because it indicates the real volume of capital per worker. Substituting in equation (12.4), it follows that:

$$k = q\lambda' = q_1\lambda_1 + q_2\lambda_2 \tag{12.5}$$

135

Thus, the capital coefficient is obtained by multiplying the technical composition of capital by the vector of unit labour values. Substituting in equation (12.2), we obtain an alternative formula for the rate of profit:

$$r = \frac{e}{q\lambda'(1 + e) + 1} \qquad (12.6)$$

The logic of Marx's argument can be restated as follows. In the course of development, the technical composition of capital, q, has a tendency to rise. If unit values λ are given, this implies an increase in the capital coefficient k ($= q\lambda'$). And if the rate of surplus value, e, is given, such an increase in k will cause the rate of profit to fall. From this logic, and from equation (12.6), we can immediately identify three types of counteracting influence which may prevent a fall in the rate of profit:

1 factors that reduce the extent to which q rises in the course of development. Among these, Marx mentions 'economies in the employment of constant capital', which reduce the real volume of equipment or materials required for production; and the establishment of 'new lines of production', such as luxury goods or services which are labour intensive and have a low technical composition.

2 factors that 'change the elements of constant capital' and thereby reduce the unit value of machinery, materials and other means of production. In equation (17) this implies a reduction in the vector λ. Marx mentions a variety of ways whereby constant capital is cheapened and we shall consider these below.

3 factors that increase the rate of surplus value, e. Marx mentions the following ways of achieving this: lower real wages; longer hours of work; or more intense work – all of which worsen the lot of the worker; and reducing the value of wage goods by importing cheaper food and other items from abroad or else improving production methods at home.

Thus, there are three types of counteracting influence: those which prevent an increase in q; those which reduce λ; and those which raise e. The first two determine how the capital coefficient, k, changes in the course of development. Marx's falling rate of profit theory is distinguished from that of Ricardo by his stress on the capital coefficient. Although Marx does on occasion consider variations in e, these are analytically of secondary importance compared to the more fundamental variations in k, which are the hallmark of his long-run theory. Indeed, for much of the time Marx assumes e is constant, which allows him to focus exclusive attention on the really important variable k. I shall now follow the same procedure and assume that e is constant. Later, we shall consider what happens when e varies. Note that in a dynamic economy, where labour productivity is rising, the assumption that e is constant will normally imply that real wages are increasing.

In considering the behaviour of k, we shall assume that the technical composition of capital q rises continuously in the course of development – because the average worker either operates more machinery or processes more materials per unit of time; and we shall consider how far such an increase is offset by reduction in the value of means of production (as indicated by the vector λ). We shall ignore the unusual case of a reduction in q.

UNEVEN DEVELOPMENT

Technical change is always uneven in its impact, varying from one sector of the economy to another in nature, extent and timing. Since these various sectors are component parts of the same coherent whole, the result is a form of development known as 'combined and uneven development'. To analyse the implications of such development is impossible within the confines of a one-sector model of the kind used above. I shall therefore employ the more complex model whose basic equations are shown in Table 12.1. The economy is divided into three sectors: sectors 1 and 2, which produce means of production, and sector 3, which produces consumer goods. Goods produced in sector 1 are called 'goods of type 1', and those produced in sector 2 are called 'goods of type 2'. There is a hierarchical relationship between the various sectors: goods of type 1 are used in the production of all goods, including type 1 goods themselves; goods of type 2 are used in the production of other goods, but not used, either directly or indirectly, in their own production; finally, consumer goods, as their name suggests, are not used in production at all. This threefold classification may seem arbitrary at first sight, but in fact it has a definite justification. It makes explicit the three major kinds of economic linkage between sectors which are theoretically possible. The model contains the conceptual elements required for understanding more complex interdependencies.[4]

For the most part, the equations shown in Table 12.1 are self-explanatory, the assumptions and notation being merely an extension of those already used in the previous one-sector model. To produce one unit of good i requires l_i units of labour, b_{i1} units of type 1 goods and b_{i2} units of type 2 goods. Because type 2 goods do not enter either directly or indirectly into their own production, both $b_{12} = 0$ and $b_{22} = 0$. We assume that production takes 1 year and type i goods last for n_i years. Equations (12.7) show how the value of each commodity is determined, equations (12.8) and (12.9) respectively show the technical composition and the capital coefficient in each sector, and equations (12.12) combine these sectoral ratios to form economy-wide aggregates.

Looking at equations (12.7), one obvious feature stands out: the value of each commodity depends on the technical coefficients in its own sector and those above it in the hierarchy, but not on sectors below it in this hierarchy. Thus, λ_1 depends only on the coefficients in sector 1, λ_2 depends only on the

Table 12.1 A multisectoral model

Structural values

$$\text{type 1 goods: } \lambda_1 = \ell_1 + \frac{b_{11}}{n_1}\lambda_1$$

$$\text{type 2 goods: } \lambda_2 = \ell_2 + \frac{b_{21}}{n_1}\lambda_1 \tag{12.7}$$

$$\text{consumer goods: } \lambda_3 = \ell_3 + \frac{b_{31}}{n_1}\lambda_1 + \frac{b_{32}}{n_2}\lambda_2$$

Technical compositions by sector

$$q_1 = (b_{11}/\ell_1, 0)$$

$$q_2 = (b_{21}/\ell_2, 0) \tag{12.8}$$

$$q_3 = (b_{31}/\ell_3, b_{32}/\ell_3)$$

Capital coefficients by sector

$$k_1 = \frac{b_{11}}{\ell_1}\cdot\lambda_1$$

$$k_2 = \frac{b_{21}}{\ell_2}\cdot\lambda_1 \tag{12.9}$$

$$k_3 = \frac{b_{31}}{\ell_3}\cdot\lambda_1 + \frac{b_{32}}{\ell_3}\cdot\lambda_2$$

Economy-wide ratios

$$q = \frac{L_1}{L}\cdot q_1 + \frac{L_2}{L}\cdot q_2 + \frac{L_3}{L}\cdot q_3 \tag{12.10}$$

$$k = \frac{L_1}{L}\cdot k_1 + \frac{L_2}{L}\cdot k_2 + \frac{L_3}{L}\cdot k_3$$

where L_i is total employment in sector i and $L = L_1 + L_2 + L_3$.

---

coefficients in sectors 1 and 2, and λ_3 depends on the coefficients in all three sectors. This hierarchical structure has important implications for the behaviour of capital coefficients. To explore these implications, let us take the various sectors one at a time and see what happens when techniques of production change. In each case we shall assume that the technical composition rises in the sector concerned, whereas the unit value of output in this sector falls.

Consider first what happens if the technical composition rises in sector 3; that is, if b_{31}/l_3 or b_{32}/l_3 increases. This reduces λ_3, the unit value of consumer goods, but has no effect on λ_1 and λ_2, the unit values of means of production. Since λ_1 and λ_2 are unaffected, the capital coefficient in sectors 1 and 2 remains unchanged. However, in sector 3 itself the capital coefficient rises. The reason is obvious: individual means of production have the same value as before, but each worker in sector 3 is using more means of production, so the total value of means of production per worker in this sector must be greater. Arithmetically, this argument can be expressed as follows. The capital coefficient in sector 3 is given by:

$$k_3 = \frac{b_{31}}{l_3}\lambda_1 + \frac{b_{32}}{l_3}\lambda_2$$

Since λ_1 and λ_2 are given, an increase in b_{31}/l_3 or b_{32}/l_3 will lead to an increase in k_3. Thus, an increase in the technical composition of capital in the sector producing consumer goods increases the capital coefficient in this sector (the value of means of production per worker), but has no effect on the capital coefficient in other sectors of the economy.

Consider what happens if the technical composition rises in sector 2. This reduces the unit value of type 2 goods and thereby reduces the capital coefficient in sector 3. However, it has no effect on the unit value of type 2 goods and, as a result, the capital coefficient in sector 1 remains unchanged. In sector 2 itself the capital coefficient rises. The reason for this is obvious. More type 1 goods per worker are used in this sector, and each of these goods has the same unit value as before. Since type 1 goods are the only means of production used in this sector, the result is an increase in the capital coefficient in sector 2.

Consider, finally, what happens if the technical composition rises in sector 1. This reduces the value of type 1 goods supplied to the rest of the economy and, in consequence, the capital coefficient in sectors 2 and 3 falls. In sector 1 itself the situation is more complex. Because this sector produces its own means of production, we have two counteracting forces to consider. On the one hand, more means of production are used per worker; but, on the other hand, these means of production are cheaper. The final impact of technical change on the capital coefficient depends on which of these forces is the stronger. In the present case, the capital coefficient in sector 1 is given by:

$$k_1 = \frac{b_{11}}{1 - b_{11}/n_1} \tag{12.11}$$

There are two distinct situations to consider. First, there is the transition from handicraft to modern production, during which the technical composition rises from approximately zero to some positive amount. Such a transition is

139

always accompanied by an increase in the capital coefficient in sector 1. Once the transition to modern production is complete, however, the situation is different. A further increase in the technical composition no longer implies an automatic increase in the capital coefficient and the latter may rise or fall, depending on the precise nature of the technical change in question. If there is a revolutionary 'capital-saving' innovation, then b_{11} will fall and so, as a rule, will the capital coefficient in sector 1 (see equation (12.11)). The opposite will be the case if investment is of the 'capital-using' variety: b_{11} will rise and so too will the capital coefficient in sector 1.

The above discussion is summarized in Table 12.2. As we move down this table, the impact of technical change becomes ever more ambiguous. At the top is the consumer goods sector. Unless offset by some technical change elsewhere in the economy, a rise in technical composition in this sector always leads to a rise in the capital coefficient of the economy as a whole. For other sectors, which produce means of production, the situation is quite different. The capital coefficient may rise in certain sectors, but it will also fall in others, and the final outcome will depend on the relative strength of these two effects. Indeed, in case (b) – that of further development in an already mechanized sector 1 – technical change may cause the capital coefficient to fall in all sectors of the economy at once. This will occur when there is a capital-saving innovation in sector 1 whose effect is to reduce the amount of equipment required per unit of output.

So far we have assumed that technical change occurs in one sector of the economy at a time. In reality, however, technical change may occur in several different sectors of the economy at once, in which case the various capital coefficients will be subject to opposing forces. Consider, for example, the

Table 12.2 Effects of technical change on capital coefficient[a]

	Effect on capital coefficient in:			
Rise in technical composition[b] in:	Sector 1 (type 1 goods)	Sector 2 (type 2 goods)	Sector 3 (consumer goods)	Whole economy
Sector 3 (consumer goods)	0	0	+	+
Sector 2 (type 2 goods)	0	+	−	?
Sector 1 (type 1 goods)				
(a) transitional stage[c]	+	−	−	?
(b) further development[d]	?	−	−	?

[a] Capital coefficient = value of constant capital per worker
[b] Technical compositon = real 'volume' of constant capital per worker
[c] Transitional stage = shift from handicraft production (i.e. technical composition very low) to modern production (i.e. technical composition high)
[d] Further development = further increase in technical composition when production is already organized on a modern basis (i.e. when the technical composition is already fairly high)

capital coefficient in sector 3 of the simple economy considered above. A rise in the technical composition in this sector means that the average worker uses more equipment and materials than before. *Ceteris paribus*, such an increase in the real volume of constant capital per worker will also imply an increase in the value of constant capital per worker (the capital coefficient). This is the basic tendency. On the other hand, suppose there is simultaneously a technical change in the sectors which supply equipment and materials to sector 3, as a result of which these items fall in unit value. This establishes a counter-tendency whose effect is to reduce the capital coefficient in sector 3. What eventually happens to this coefficient depends on the relative strength of tendency and counterdependency. If the former is stronger, the capital coefficient will rise, whereas if the latter is stronger, this coefficient will fall. A similar argument can be applied to sector 2, whose capital coefficient is also subject to opposing forces. In each case, a rising capital coefficient is an indication of uneven development, of lagging technical progress in the sectors which produce means of production.

The overall capital coefficient, k, is a weighted average of the sectoral coefficients (see equation (12.10)). Its behaviour depends partly on what happens to individual sectoral coefficients and partly on the relative weight of the various sectors in the economy as a whole. Assume, for the moment, that the weights are given. We can distinguish several interesting possibilities. Suppose there is a wave of innovations which begins in sector 1 and gradually spreads forwards through sector 2 to sector 3, until eventually the whole economy is transformed. To see what happens we need merely consult Table 12.2. At first, there may be some increase in the capital coefficient in sector 1, but there also will be a significant reduction in capital coefficients in others sectors of the economy. As a result, the overall capital coefficient, k, is unlikely to rise immediately and may even fall. After a time, however, the locus of innovation will swing from sector 1 towards sector 2 and then, finally, to sector 3. As this happens, the balance of forces will gradually shift, until those making for a higher capital coefficient become dominant and k starts to rise. So, in this example, the sequence of events is as follows: the overall capital coefficient, k, is at first stable or else falls as production methods in sector 1 are transformed, and then later k rises as the locus of innovation shifts to other sectors.

The sequence of events is quite different if innovation begins at the consumer goods end, in sector 3, and spreads backwards to sectors 1 and 2. This case can again be analysed by consulting Table 12.2. At first, the overall capital coefficient will rise. After a time, however, the locus of innovation will shift to other sectors; means of production will become cheaper and the capital coefficient will stabilize or may even fall. Thus, depending on which sector it strikes first, a wave of innovations may cause the capital coefficient to rise or fall in the course of development. The two cases are illustrated in Figure 12.1.

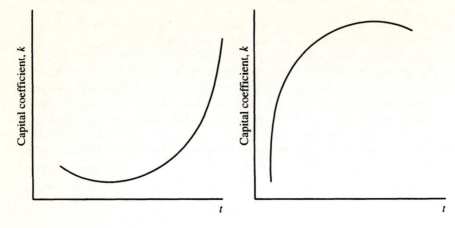

Figure 12.1 Effects of a wave of innovation
  (a) Innovation begins in sector 1 (basic   (b) innovation begins in sector 3
       means of production)   (consumer goods)

TWO BASIC MECHANISMS

The preceding discussion has revealed two basic mechanisms which can account for a rising capital coefficient and a falling profit rate. On the one hand, there is the conventional mechanism of declining investment productivity, referred to by Keynes as the 'declining marginal productivity of capital'. We have examined this mechanism in detail in the context of a one-sector model, but it is obviously of general relevance. In no matter what sector it occurs, a decline in investment productivity in a particular sector will tend to increase the capital coefficient both in the sector itself and in other sectors of the economy which it supplies with inputs.

An alternative mechanism which may account for a rising capital coefficient is associated with uneven development, in which technical progress in the sectors producing means of production lags behind technical progress in the sectors using means of production. This causes the unit values of means of production to rise relative to those of output in general, and the result is an increase in the overall capital coefficient. Such even development is frequently ignored in Marxist discussions of the falling rate of profit, yet it was central to Marx's own writings on this subject, and is often very important in practice.

Table 12.3 gives some evidence about what happened in the advanced capitalist countries in the final phase of the long post-war boom when there was widespread concern about declining profitability in manufacturing industry. The first two columns show the capital:output ratio in manufacturing industry for the two periods 1960–3 and 1970–3; both capital stock and

Table 12.3 The capital coefficient in manufacturing, 1960–73

	Gross capital: output ratio at current prices		Percentage change	Components of percentage change	
	Average 1960–3 (1)	Average 1970–3 (2)	1960–3 to 1970–3 (3)	Real capital per unit of output[a] (4)	Relative price of capital goods[b] (5)
Canada	2.22	2.36	+6.3	−8.8	+16.0
France[c]	1.91	1.76	−8.1	−29.5	+30.0
Germany	1.44	1.67	+15.6	−8.1	+7.0
UK	2.57	3.18	+23.6	+5.8	+17.0
USA	1.21	1.35	+11.7	−11.2	+25.9

Source: OECD National Accounts, OECD Flows and Stocks of Fixed Capital
[a] Real capital per unit of output = gross capital: output ratio at constant prices.
[b] Relative price of capital goods = price index of gross fixed capital ÷ price index of value added.
[c] Output includes mining and utilites

output are measured in current prices. Despite certain conceptual problems, this ratio is a reasonable proxy for what I have called the 'capital coefficient'.[5] From the table, we see that in all but one country the capital : output ratio measured in current prices rose substantially between 1960–3 and 1970–3. This provides support for the Marxist idea of a rising capital coefficient.

The table also gives some indication as to why the capital coefficient increased. Column (4) measures how much was due to the declining physical productivity of capital, and column (5) measures how much was due to the rising price of capital inputs as compared to final output. In three of the five countries shown, the physical productivity of capital actually improved over the period, and the increase in the capital coefficient was entirely the result of a shift in relative prices. In the remaining countries, Germany and the UK, capital productivity declined, but even here relative price shifts were important. In every country shown, capital goods became more expensive in comparison with final output. This change in relative prices was probably the result of slower technical progress in the sectors producing capital goods as compared to the sectors which use them. Thus, the evidence suggests that, during the period in question, uneven sectoral development was a more important factor than declining capital productivity in explaining what happened to the capital coefficient in the manufacturing sector.

CAUSAL FACTORS

The various reasons for uneven development between sectors can be classified roughly under three headings: 'nature', 'technology' and 'organization'. Let us consider these in turn.

143

Nature

As Ricardo argued long ago, natural factors may cause production to become progressively more difficult as accumulation proceeds. For example, in agriculture, inferior land may be brought into cultivation as the economy expands; similarly, in mining, lower-grade ores or more inaccessible mineral deposits may be exploited. Natural factors may also inhibit development in a more subtle way, not by making production absolutely more difficult, but by acting as a drag: holding back the sector concerned and preventing it from developing as fast as other, more dynamic sectors. It may be intrinsically more difficult to raise labour productivity in certain kinds of agriculture or mining than in, say, manufacturing. However, although valid up to a point, this argument should be treated with caution. The extent to which nature acts as a constraint on production depends on the current state of technology. Declining or lagging labour productivity in sectors such as agriculture or mining is as a much a result of technological failure as of natural limits. With the evolution of technology, natural limits may be overcome and lagging sectors may become the most dynamic. Natural limits are never absolute and should always be viewed in relation to the prevailing technology.[6]

Technology

There are several other ways in which technology is relevant in the present context. We have already mentioned the idea of a pool of inventions which is gradually depleted in the course of development. As this pool is depleted, it may become progressively more difficult to raise output, either in particular sectors or right across the entire economy, and the result may be a gradual increase in the capital coefficient. This is one possibility. Another possibility is uneven technological development. From the very start, the new technology may be biased towards particular sectors of the economy. Suppose, for example, there is a new technology which leads to revolutionary new production methods in the consumer goods sector, but has only a relatively minor effect on other sectors. Thus, means of production will become relatively more expensive through the course of time, as compared to consumer goods. As a result, the capital coefficient will rise in the consumer goods sector and also, probably, in the economy as a whole.

Organization

The third set of reasons why the capital coefficient might rise in the course of development are associated with the organization of production. To exploit the full potential of a certain technology and to revolutionize methods of production may require radically new forms of economic organization. For example, in an economy of small, independent producers it may be impossible to employ large-scale, highly mechanized techniques of production. To utilize such techniques effectively may require the elimination of most of the existing producers and the concentration of production in a few hands. Until this is done the sector concerned may stagnate. A similar phenomenon may arise even in sectors which are already organized on a capitalist basis. Every radically new technology requires new forms of organization and work practices. Forms of organization and practices appropriate to a previous epoch of production become outdated; they become an obstacle to the application of new technology and further economic development. Until this obstacle is removed, the new technology cannot be effectively applied. Moreover, quite apart from its implications for the application of new technology, the form of organization may also obstruct full development of old technologies. In the course of a long boom, for example, the organizational structure of an economy may become sclerotic and inflexible, and all kinds of work practices may develop which obstruct change and prevent the full exploitation of already well-known techniques. If this is a fairly universal phenomenon throughout the economy, there may be a general fall in the productivity of investment. On the other hand, if sclerosis is confined to certain sectors, the result will be uneven development, whereby the sclerotic sectors lag behind their more dynamic counterparts. Either way, for reasons discussed earlier, the outcome may be a rise in the capital coefficient either in key sectors or throughout the economy as a whole.

It is clear that there are a wide variety of natural, technological and organizational reasons why the capital coefficient may rise at a certain stage of development, and why such a rise may be associated with growing problems which culminate in crisis and depression. However, one should not make a fetish of this coefficient. Certainly, the capital coefficient did rise during the final phase of the long post-war boom, and this was apparently one of the factors accounting for the fall in the average rate of profit which occurred in most of the advanced capitalist countries during this period. But there were other, equally important factors at work, such as the squeeze on profits caused by higher wages, higher taxes and, at the very end, in 1972–3, higher primary product prices.[7] Moreover, the recent long-boom is by no means typical. In the preceding long-boom, before the great crash of 1929, for example, the capital coefficient did not rise at all. This is tacitly recognized, even by Ernest Mandel, one of the strongest advocates of the view that long-waves are associated with huge swings in the capital coefficient.[8] Thus although movements in the capital coefficient may help to explain why capitalist development alternates between long phases of prosperity and depression, they are not the only factor to consider. Not every major depression is preceded by an increase in the capital coefficient; and even when such an increase does occur, it may not always be of decisive importance.

So much for the theory of long waves. What about the ultimate destiny of capitalism, the permanent decline in the rate of profit which Marx occasionally hints at, and which his famous disciple Henryk Grossman made the foundation of his theory of collapse (*Zusammenbruch*) (Grossman, 1929)? Here it is difficult to be anything but extremely sceptical. Nothing I have said in this chapter supports the idea of a *permanent* rise in the capital coefficient and consequential permanent fall in the rate of profit. Nor does it suggest that ever greater difficulty will be experienced in holding down the capital coefficient and keeping the rate of profit up to the level required for accumulation.

ACKNOWLEDGEMENTS

I should like to thank the following people who have commented on various drafts of this chapter: H. Chang, D. J. Harris, M. Itoh, M. Landesmann, R. C. O. Matthews, N. Okishio and R. P. Smith. A longer version of the chapter is contained in Landesmann (1996).

NOTES

1   Capitalist accounting is done in prices and not values. However, in present context this distinction is of minor importance, and the arguments which follow could easily be restated using prices instead of values.

2   Such an interpretation is only strictly valid under certain conditions about hours of work, holidays and shiftwork, etc. Throughout this paper I assume that there is no shiftwork and that the average worker performs exactly 1 unit of labour during the accounting 'year'. Under these conditions k is exactly equal to the value of constant capital per worker. Under more general assumptions, this may not be the case. Suppose that N workers are required to operate the constant capital, that there are m production shifts and that each worker performs on average h units of labour per year. Then $L = mhN$ and hence

$$k = \frac{C}{L}$$

$$= \frac{1}{mh} \cdot \frac{C}{N}$$

where C/N is the value of constant capital per worker. It is clear that $k = C/N$ if and only if $mh = 1$. If the latter condition does not hold, then k and C/N will be numerically different. Moreover, variations in m and h may lead to divergent behaviour on the part of k and C/N. Indeed, k and C/N may even move in opposite directions. For example, a rise in C/N might be accompanied by an even greater rise in m, reflecting an extension of shiftworking, in which case k would fall. In the present chapter such complications are ignored.

An alternative interpretation for the ratio k is as follows. The total amount of new value created during the current period is equal to L. This is *net* output measured in value terms. Since C is constant capital, measured in value terms, it follows that:

$k = C/L =$ value of constant capital/value of net output

Thus, k measures, in value terms, the amount of constant capital which is required to produce one unit of net output during the current period. For this reason, it is sometimes called the 'capital:output ratio measured in value terms'.

3 Readers who object to this terminology may substitute some alternative expression such as the 'capital:output ratio in value terms' or the 'ratio of dead to living labour'.

4 Note that the distinction between type 1 and type 2 goods does not correspond directly to any obvious empirical classification. As a rough guide one might think of type 1 goods as machinery and type 2 goods as raw materials, but this would be only a very crude approximation.

5 As explained in note 3, the capital coefficient is the 'capital:output ratio' measured in value terms. If current prices are proportional to values, the capital coefficient is exactly equal to the capital:output ratio measured in current prices.

6 Available historical evidence suggests that over the long run most extractive industries, in particular agriculture and mining, have experienced above-average growth rates of labour productivity. For evidence on this point see Barnett and Morse (1963) and Barnett (1979).

7 For a discussion of these other factors see, for example, Rowthorn (1981).

8 See Mandel (1975: 131, sect. 6). Note that Mandel's discussion is cast in terms of the value composition of capital, C/V, whereas we are talking about the capital coefficient, k ($k = C/L$). However, this is a minor difference which does not affect the substance of the argument. The two ratios are closely related to each other, as can be seen from the following equation:

$$\frac{C}{V} = \frac{CL}{LV} = \frac{C}{L}\left(\frac{V+S}{S}\right) = \frac{C}{L}\left(1 + \frac{S}{L}\right) = k(1+e)$$

Provided e is roughly constant, movements in C/V will mirror those in k. Differences will arise only when e varies a great deal.

REFERENCES

Barnett, H. J. (1979) 'Scarcity and growth revisited', in V. K. Smith (ed.) *Scarcity and Growth Reconsidered*, Baltimore: Johns Hopkins University Press.

Barnett, H. J. and Morse, C. (1963) *Scarcity and Growth*, Baltimore: Johns Hopkins University Press.

Grossman, H. (1929) *Das Akkumulations und Zusammenbruchsgesetz des kapitalistischen Systems*, Leipzig: Verlag von C. L. Hirschfield.

Landesmann, M. (1996 forthcoming) *The Structural Dynamics of Market Economies*.

Mandel, E. (1975) *Late Capitalism*, London: New Left Books.

Marx, K. (1966) *Capital*, vol. 3, Moscow: Progress Publishers.

Rowthorn, R. (1981) 'Late capitalism', in R. Rowthorn, *Capitalism, Conflict and Inflation*, Lawrence & Wishart, London.

13

THE RATE-OF-RETURN DEBATE

An afterglow

Harald Hagemann

INTRODUCTION

Harcourt's 1969 survey article on the Cambridge controversies in the theory of capital, which shortly afterwards was expanded to a book (Harcourt 1972), is surely his best-known paper. In these classical writings, the contributions of his 1955–8 Cambridge classmate and close friend Luigi Pasinetti[1] to the capital theory debates played a major role. Of course, the well-known contributions of his other Cambridge classmate Pierangelo Garegnani and the latter's attacks against the neoclassical view of a downward-sloping demand curve for aggregate value capital were also appropriately recognized. But our festee, more than other participants in the debate, paid elaborate attention to Solow's modern reformulation of Fisher's concept of the rate of return on investment and Pasinetti's critique of it.[2] It was not only post-Keynesian economists like Pasinetti and Harcourt, heavily influenced by Joan Robinson and Sraffa, but also neoclassical economists such as Ferguson who interpreted Solow's approach as an attempt to corroborate essential findings of the *aggregate* version of neoclassical theory, based on the macroeconomic production function, by means of a linear multisectoral model: 'The situation appeared almost hopeless for aggregate neoclassical theory until a seminal breakthrough by Solow established the grounds for resurrecting aggregate capital theory' (Ferguson 1972: 175).

Solow's concept of the *social* rate of return (SRR) is defined solely in terms of changes in consumption streams: the perpetual 'gain' in consumption is compared to the 'sacrifices' in consumption during the transition period. It was Pasinetti (1969) who early on directed attention to the fact that the 'costs' of the transition, in general, do not consist only of sacrifices in consumption but additionally of physical quantities of particular capital goods of the old technique α that cannot be reused with the new technique β. Such wastages of capital goods may constitute a *second* type of cost even in the stationary economy. Furthermore, as will be shown below, there may be a third type of cost, namely technological unemployment of the labour force during the transition phase, a type of cost which hitherto has been neglected in the literature on the SRR but is in the very centre of Pasinetti's more recent writings (1981, 1993).

What was Solow's original intention in seeking to present the rate of return as 'the central concept in capital theory' (1963: 16)? It can be seen from numerous statements in his De Vries Lectures (ibid.: 25, 34 and 36) that his main aim in constructing a 'capital theory without capital' was to evade the criticism of the neoclassical concept of 'capital'. The neoclassical notion of capital, being under vehement attack, was abandoned by Solow in favour of the 'social rate of return on saving' concept. Thus the development of the rate-of-return concept must be basically understood as an attempt to form a surrogate for the marginal productivity of capital in a world with heterogeneous capital goods. In such a world, the marginal productivity of capital can no longer be determined as a physical magnitude; that is, independently of the rate of profit (the wage rate) and prior to the determination of the system of relative prices. The parallels with Samuelson's attempt to replace the original production function with a surrogate are unmistakable.[3] In both cases it is intended that vital results of the Clark–Ramsey parable should be 'rescued' in a world of heterogeneous capital goods. However, the capital reversing and reswitching debate has clearly shown that this is impossible. The rate of profit cannot generally be explained with the help of the social rate of return on investment or by marginal productivity theory. Nell maintains that 'Solow explicitly disavows any interest in *determining* the rate of profit' (1975: 811; emphasis in original), and this no doubt agrees with Solow's later position, reached after much 'learning by debating' (see Solow 1976: 71–2). This view, however, is in stark contrast to Solow's earliest statement, where he explicitly said that he was trying to formulate 'a *theory of interest rates*, not a theory of capital' (1963: 16; my emphasis). Later on he still considered the equality between the interest rate in competitive equilibrium and the social rate of return on investment as at least 'part of an explanation . . . of the rate of profit' (Solow 1970: 427–8). Neoclassical economists such as Hahn, working within the framework of general equilibrium theory, do not even support this claim; rather they emphasize that the rate of interest (rate of profit) can only *measure* the rate of return (or the marginal productivity of capital), not that the rate of return can *explain* the rate of profit.[4]

THE EFFICIENT TRANSITION PATH

Solow's SRR concept can be sketched most simply by means of the fundamental duality relation between the wage–profit frontier and the consumption–investment frontier. Assume that there are two techniques, α and β, whose respective frontiers intersect (at least) once (see Figure 13.1).[5] With the prices of commodities of the two techniques given at the switch point values of the wage rate, w^*, and the rate of profit, r^*, the technique with the higher consumption per capita (i.e. technique β) also has the higher capital intensity in price terms, k. This follows from

$$k^{\iota} = \frac{c^{\iota} - w^*}{r^* - g} \tag{13.1}$$

where $\iota = \alpha, \beta$. This holds true for the stationary economy ($g = 0$, $c = c_{max}$) as well as for the growing economy ($g > 0$), provided that the latter is on the right side of the Golden Rule of Accumulation with the growth rate, g, being smaller than the profit rate, r (e.g. $g = \bar{g} < r^*$). In order to obtain the higher consumption per capita ($c^{\beta}(\bar{g}) > c^{\alpha}(\bar{g})$) and ($c^{\beta}_{max} > c^{\alpha}_{max}$), society's changeover from technique α to technique β, therefore, can be accomplished, if at all, only by means of additional savings investment. The necessary sacrifices in consumption can be either *direct* sacrifices – that is, consumption goods of the current output which are not consumed but used for productive purposes – or *indirect* sacrifices – that is, consumption goods that are given up by the diversion of resources from the production of consumer goods to the production of capital goods.

Now it is clear that a transition path leading from technique α to technique β need not exist, and, if it does exist, it need not be efficient in the sense that all resources (including labour) are permanently fully employed and that there

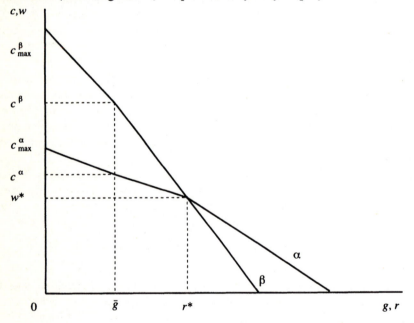

Figure 13.1 Efficiency curves

150

does not exist any other path with a higher consumption per head in any one of the periods of the transition phase. Yet Solow's theorem rests decisively on the assumption that such an efficient transition path exists. In order to form an opinion on the relevance of Solow's theorem one has to consider the conditions under which such a path exists.

It is well known since Bharadwaj's excellent study (Bharadwaj 1970) that two techniques which are equiprofitable at a given wage rate, w^*, may use and produce *different* types of commodity; in particular, different types of means of production.

If at least one pure capital good used with technique α cannot be reused with technique β, capital goods wastages are unavoidable. Hence the transition path is inefficient and Solow's theorem does not hold.

If technique β uses at least one means of production which is not produced by technique α the transition may be impossible or inefficient. It is impossible if the 'new' capital good cannot be produced by means of a sort of *prototype* process of production using the 'old' capital goods of technique α. Yet if such a process exists, the transition path is inefficient since this prototype process can be assumed to be inferior to the corresponding process of production of this new capital good of technique β. (If it were not inferior, society would change over not to technique β but to a technique γ using this process.) In this case, however, Solow's idea of a switch point transition breaks down: the economy which wants to change over to technique β *en route* has to apply an inferior technique with a lower rate of profit and prices that are higher than switch-point prices.[6] The re-evaluation of the whole capital stock, which Solow obviously wanted to bypass by means of confining his analysis to switch point transitions, is thus inevitable.

Hence it follows that Solow's theorem does not hold if the two techniques produce and use different types of capital goods, whereas it may hold otherwise. In accordance with Solow, I therefore restrict the analysis to the narrow class of transitions between two techniques using and producing the *same* types of commodity. In this case a transition path always exists, though it may be inefficient.

Some of the confusion inherent in the SRR debate has its roots in the fact that the disputants proceed from different views of the underlying system of production and consumption. In particular, there seems to be a considerable divergence of opinion with regard to the character of the n commodities of the multisectoral economy producing with single-product industries. Whereas Solow seemingly assumes that *all* commodities serve equally well for production *and* consumption purposes,[7] Pasinetti (1969: 514) presupposes that some (up to $n - 1$) commodities cannot be consumed; that is, they are strictly intermediate products. In order to clarify the problems in question, one should distinguish between three types of products:

151

1 pure capital goods, i.e. commodities which can be used only for productive purposes;
2 combined capital and consumption goods, or double-purpose goods; and
3 pure consumption goods, i.e. commodities which cannot be used as means of production.

Modifying one of Joan Robinson's puns (1970: 312), we may differentiate between commodities of the *steel*, the *steel&leets* and the *leets* categories; for short, the *s*, the *s&l* and the *l* categories.

We are now prepared to state in detail the conditions for an efficient transition path. According to this classification of commodities the vector of gross outputs $x = [x_1, \ldots, x_m, x_{m+1}, \ldots, x_{m+k}, x_{m+k+1}, \ldots, x_n]$ can be decomposed into

$$\boldsymbol{\eta} = [x_1, \ldots, x_m, 0, \ldots, 0]$$

$$\boldsymbol{\xi} = [0, \ldots, 0, x_{m+1}, \ldots, x_{m+k}, 0, \ldots, 0]$$

and

$$\boldsymbol{\varphi} = [0, \ldots, 0, x_{m+k+1}, \ldots, x_n]$$

where the first m commodities out of n are of the s type, the following k commodities are of the $s&l$ type, and the last $n - m - k$ commodities are of the l type. Since pure capital goods cannot be consumed, we have for each vector of consumption goods $z = [z_1, \ldots, z_n]$

$$z_1 = \ldots = z_m = 0$$

The length of the transition process leading from technique α to technique β is assumed to be T periods ($1 \leq T < \infty$). In period $t = 0$ the economy is on a steady-state path exclusively using technique α, i.e.

$$x_0^\beta = 0 \tag{13.2}$$

x_0^α, L_0 and z_0 are the steady-state values respectively of gross outputs (intensities of the n sectors), of the quantity of labour employed, and of consumption goods produced in period 0 by means of technique α. At the end of the transition phase, in period T, the economy has reached the new steady-state path using exclusively technique β. Thus

$$x_T^\alpha = 0 \tag{13.3}$$

En route the economy produces its annual output by means of linear combinations of the $2n$ production processes of the two techniques. The transition from period $t - 1$ to period t is controlled by the choice of activity levels of the two techniques in period t, x_t^α and x_t^β. With the activity levels given, the quantity of labour employed and the vector of consumption goods produced in period t are determined by

$$L_t = x_t^\alpha l^\alpha + x_t^\beta l^\beta \tag{13.4}$$

and

$$z_t = \xi_{t-1}^\alpha + \varphi_{t-1}^\alpha + \xi_{t-1}^\beta + \varphi_{t-1}^\beta - (\xi_t^\alpha + \varphi_t^\alpha)A^\alpha - (\xi_t^\beta + \varphi_t^\beta)A^\beta \tag{13.5}$$

respectively.[8] l^ι is the column vector of direct labour inputs of technique ι ($\iota = \alpha, \beta$) and A^ι is the $n \times n$ matrix of circulating capital input coefficients $[a_{ij}^\iota]$, where a_{ij}^ι denotes the input of commodity i needed to produce one unit of commodity j in technique ι.

The choice of activity levels now has to fulfil the condition of *full employment of the labour force*

$$L_\iota = (1 + g)L_{t-1} \tag{13.6}$$

and the condition of *full employment of all pure intermediate products* ('full capacity growth')

$$\eta_t^\alpha A^\alpha + \eta_t^\beta A^\beta = \eta_{t-1}^\alpha + \eta_{t-1}^\beta \tag{13.7}$$

Moreover, an efficient transition sequence is characterized by the fact that it cannot be dominated, with regard to its consumption sequence, by another feasible development with the same initial and final states and subject to the same availability of the services of the sole non-produced factor labour. In addition, the consumption goods vector in each period has to be at least as great as to cover some socially determined subsistence level of society in the respective period, i.e.

$$z_t \geq z_0^{\min} (1 + g)^t \tag{13.8}$$

In order to find necessary conditions for a consumption-efficient transition path in $T + 1$ periods one can formulate the discrete optimal control problem as a vector-valued convex optimization problem with equality and inequality constraints in the $[2n(T + 1)]$-dimensioned Euclidian space. The abstract maximum-principle for these problems provides the wanted necessary existence conditions for such a path. The result, however, is not very instructive with regard to the properties of technologies which render possible an efficient transition path. Therefore I shall merely show by means of a simple two-sectoral example that even in the case where both techniques use and produce the same set of commodities an efficient transition path need not exist and hence Solow's theorem need not hold.

Assume that only two commodities are produced, commodity 1 being of the s type and commodity 2 of the $s\&l$ type. The technology of the economy thus can be described by

$$A^\iota = \begin{bmatrix} a_{11}^i\, a_{21}^i \\ \\ a_{12}^i\, a_{22}^i \end{bmatrix}, l^\iota = \begin{bmatrix} l_1^\iota \\ \\ l_2^\iota \end{bmatrix} \begin{matrix} \} \ s\text{-type commodity} \\ \\ \} \ s\&l\text{-type commodity} \end{matrix} \qquad (\iota = \alpha, \beta)$$

If the relation between the input quantities of the pure capital good 1 and labour is *higher* in *both* processes of production of technique α than in the respective processes of technique β; that is, if

$$\left[\frac{a^{\alpha}_{11}}{l^{\alpha}_1}, \frac{a^{\alpha}_{12}}{l^{\alpha}_2}\right] > \left[\frac{a^{\beta}_{11}}{l^{\beta}_1}, \frac{a^{\beta}_{12}}{l^{\beta}_2}\right]$$

then wastages of commodity 1 are inevitable on society's way from technique α to technique β.[9] A reduction in technique α's activity levels unequivocally sets free greater amounts of the pure intermediate product 1 relative to labour than can be absorbed by technique β (see Figure 13.2). Labour is the scarce resource and pure capital goods necessarily become redundant. The transition path, although compatible with full employment of labour, is incompatible with full capacity growth. Hence Solow's theorem does not hold.

If, on the other hand, the relation between the input quantities of the pure capital good 1 and labour is *lower* in *both* processes of technique α than in the respective processes of technique β, the condition of full employment of labour will of necessity be violated when the economy changes over to β. In this case the pure capital good is the scarce resource; the technological conditions, though compatible with full capacity utilization, involve to some extent the unemployment of labour. Again, Solow's theorem does not hold.

Obviously, with more complicated systems of production and consumption it is possible that both certain amounts of some pure capital goods and a

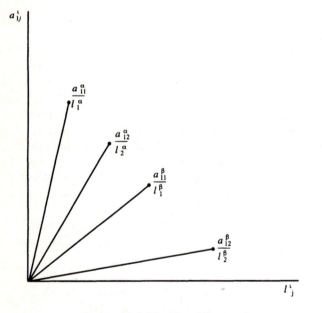

Figure 13.2 Machine–labour ratios

154

certain amount of labour may become redundant in the transition process. This is the case if one of the m strictly intermediate products turns out to be a 'bottleneck' factor which prevents the smooth diversion of resources from technique α to technique β. Thus the costs of the transition, in general, consist of sacrifices in consumption, of capital-good wastages, and of some technological unemployment of labour.

CONCLUDING REMARKS

Pasinetti had claimed that Solow's theorem of the rate of return property of the rate of profit is a mere 'tautological assertion' which proved nothing:

> After *calling* 'social rate of return' the rate of profit at which two economic systems are equally profitable one should not be surprised to find that the social rate of return so defined is indeed, in all circumstances, equal to the rate of profit at which the two economic systems are equally profitable.

> (Pasinetti 1969: 526)

This position, which had been shared by Harcourt,[10] was not only criticized by Bliss (1975: 234, n7) as 'nonsensical' and later by Hahn (1982: 372) as 'wrong', but also criticized by Nell, who substantiated his criticism in contrasting the rate of return which results from a concrete transition process with the switch-point rate of profit as defined by a comparison of two alternative long-run equilibria which are equally profitable.[11] Solow did not arrive at the rate of return through comparisons of equilibrium positions but understood it as that interest rate which discounts to zero the stream of consumption differences associated with the transition. This surely is not a tautology.[12] However, Solow discussed only a very narrow class of transitions, namely those that take place at switch points of two production systems. Hence the two systems share the same rate of profit and a common price system. But the fact that the two steady-state equilibria share the switching price system does not automatically imply that one can move resources from one to the other without any price changes. As has been shown in the previous section, adjustment costs, owing to the fact that some of the heterogeneous capital goods used with the old technique can neither be used with the new technique nor consumed, have to be excluded, as has technological unemployment during the transition phase. Solow succeeded because he introduced into his model a particular type of *capital malleability* which is a prerequisite to the deduction of his theorem. In contrast, Pasinetti (1969) assumed that redundant capital goods cannot be reused in any way so that they would be entirely wasted if the transition were to take place, with the consequence that the kind of result Solow was seeking does not materialize. Capital-good wastages caused by the transition imply a switch-point rate of return, δ^*, falling short of the switch-point rate of profit, r^*. Solow's reply to this criticism reads: 'I have tacitly assumed that no capital goods ever have to be "discarded" because they are redundant or appropriate to only one of the two techniques' (1970: 426). The latter also comprises the fact that Solow exclusively dealt with the special case where both techniques use the same commodities and did not investigate the more general class of transitions between systems with different basic products. Thus I cannot agree with Burmeister and van Long's statement that Solow 'has proved that *under quite general conditions* this social rate of return equals the interest rate' (1977: 306; my emphasis).

As Solow's analysis assumes that the transition from one technique to another takes place at a switch-point, the real wage rate and the rate of profit remains constant. With the rate of growth being given, it follows from equation (13.1) for the capital intensity in price terms, k, that the transition to the technique with the higher consumption per capita implies also an increase in k. This transition involves an increase in the sum of profits as well as in the share of profits, as can easily be seen from the definition of the ratio of the share of profits to the share of wages:

$$\frac{P}{W} = \frac{r^* K}{w^* L} = \frac{r^*}{w^*} k \tag{13.9}$$

Even with the rate of profit being constant, the capitalists, nevertheless, are interested in the transition because of the rising sum and share of profits. However, where there is a will there is not automatically a way. For it is possible that the voluntary sacrifices in consumption by profit receivers do not suffice to provide amounts of the means of production in exactly the proportions necessary for a one-period transition into a new steady state. Harcourt reminded us that 'Solow confined himself to models of centrally planned economies' (1982: 264). In reading Solow one gets the impression, however, that he introduces the central planner as a *deus ex machina* when questions are raised as to who initiates and controls the transition process.[13] The switch from a capitalist to a planned economy corresponds to the methodological switch from the comparison of semi-stationary equilibria to the analysis of transition processes. Thus I agree with Harcourt's verdict that Solow was 'treading . . . a very slippery path indeed between technocracy and the working of competitive market economies' (1972: 111). In a situation as described before, the central planner must compel the workers to restructure their consumption. Thus workers can be affected by the change, although the real wage rate remains constant in the switch-point transition. With a classical saving function, the central planner thus plays a role as an advocate of the interests of the profit receivers. One may agree with Solow's statement that 'there is nothing in the introduction of consumer preferences that has to paper over class differences' (1976: 70). But one may also doubt whether Solow's SRR concept can be regarded as a variant of general equilibrium theory when the effects on individual welfare through enforced consumption sacrifices and enforced extra consumption of particular commodities are neglected. From the point of view of general equilibrium theory with the preference side not chopped off, as in Nuti (1974), it can be argued that the sacrifices in consumption of some commodities decreed by the central planner may imply higher losses in utility than the gains in utility from simultaneously decreed extra consumption of other commodities. The permanent validity of the switch-point price system assumed by Solow thus cannot turn our attention away from the fact that, in contrast to the long-run equilibria before and after the transition, *during* the transition process these prices do not always indicate scarcity and reflect individual preferences – or, as Bliss has put it, 'Solow's type of analysis and the kind of result he seeks will fail where a change in prices is necessary for the switch of resources' (1975: 234, n7).

Whereas the 'unobtrusive postulate' that a fall in the rate of profit will lead to a technique with a higher capital intensity was at the very centre of Pasinetti's attack, Solow claimed that 'I have never in rigorous work adopted Pasinetti's "unobtrusive" postulate.... In any case, when I speak of "neo-classical capital theory in its full generality" I am certainly not referring to this construction of Pasinetti's' (1970: 424). Ferguson's hope, quoted above, that Solow's SRR concept would establish the grounds for resurrecting *aggregate* capital theory certainly has not materialized.

The champions of 'neo-classical capital theory in its full generality', which may be traced back to Malinvaud's classical 1953 paper, on the other hand, were annoyed that both Pasinetti and Solow had restricted their analysis to cases with a constant rate of interest (profit). Bliss's remarks (1975: 230–5), in which he stressed *generalized* marginal rates of substitution between consumption forgone now and incremental consumption gained in the future as the fundamental concept, and Hahn's essay against the neo-Ricardians (1982) are particularly perceptive. Whereas Hahn, a colleague of our festee in Cambridge, became bored with capital theory, many contributors to this volume might hope that the challenge by Bliss and Hahn would be taken up by younger economists with the same competence and enthusiasm as Geoff Harcourt displayed almost thirty years ago.

NOTES

1 See Harcourt (1995: 232–5) and Baranzini and Harcourt (1993).
2 See chs 3 and 4 of Harcourt (1972), and sect. VI in the 'afterglow' of the Cambridge controversies (Harcourt 1975), respectively in the revised version (Harcourt 1976) or the most recent 'afterglow' of the Pasinetti Festschrift (Baranzini and Harcourt 1993: 9–12).
3 See also Solow's statement: 'We have collaborated in this field for so long that it is impossible for me to say whether any given idea originated with him, with me, or in between' (Solow 1963: 6).
4 Cf. Hahn's new preface to his doctoral thesis (1972: 1–10).

5   To be able to plot the dual functions of both techniques into one diagram, both the wage rate, w, and consumption per head, c, of the two techniques have to be expressed in terms of the self-same commodity basket.

6   Of course, only the prices of those commodities which are common to both techniques can be compared.

7   Solow does not state this assumption explicitly. Nevertheless, it seems to be implicit in most of his arguments; see particularly Solow (1967: 32) and Solow (1970: 426–7).

8   Equation (13.5) implies that those quantities of the double-purpose goods which are 'superfluous' with regard to productive purposes in the next period are transferred to the respective consumer goods markets which are supposed to be in a position of permanent equilibrium.

9   In spite of the above (partial) intensity constellation with respect to the s-type commodity, technique β, nevertheless, may have the higher capital intensity in price terms ($k^\beta > k^\alpha$) provided that its two processes require sufficiently greater amounts of the $s\&l$-type commodity than technique α. Technique β, therefore, may have the higher consumption per capita and society has thus a motive to make the switch.

10 'Solow's analysis reflects the fact that at switch points investment in either technique yields *by definition* a rate of return equal to the switch-point rate of profits, which is also the rate of profits at which prices have been computed' (Harcourt 1972: 168).

11 See equations (4) and (5) in Nell (1975: 810).

12 See Hagemann (1977: chs 3–5) for a more detailed analysis.

13 Pasinetti had argued that 'the State, as such, cannot consume: consumption can be carried out only by individuals' (1962: 277). It is known and partly contradicts Pasinetti's apodictic formulation that central planners and their bureaucrats are not beings without needs. Their consumption narrows the consumption possibilities of the rest of society until the transition is accomplished and the bureaucrats, in defiance of Parkinson's law, disappear again. Solow has some motive for neglecting such administrative costs connected with the transition process, as the rate-of-return property of the rate of profit depends on the assumption of costless adjustment.

BIBLIOGRAPHY

Baranzini, M. and Harcourt, G. C. (eds) (1993) *The Dynamics of the Wealth of Nations: Growth, Distribution and Structural Change. Essays in Honour of Luigi Pasinetti*, London: Macmillan.

Bharadwaj, K. R. (1970) 'On the maximum number of switches between two production systems', *Schweizerische Zeitschrift für Volkswirtschaft und Statistik* 106: 409–29.

Bliss, C. J. (1975) *Capital Theory and the Distribution of Income*, Amsterdam: North-Holland.

Brown, M., Sato, K. and Zarembka, P. (eds) (1976) *Essays in Modern Capital Theory*, Amsterdam and New York: North-Holland.

Burmeister, E. (1968) 'The social rate of return in a linear model', *Weltwirtschaftliches Archiv* 101: 255–71.

Burmeister, E. and Ngo van Long (1977) 'On some unresolved questions in capital theory: an application of Samuelson's correspondence principle', *Quarterly Journal of Economics* 91: 289–314.

Dougherty, C. R. S. (1972) 'On the rate of return and the rate of profit', *Economic Journal* 82: 1324–50.

—— (1980) *Interest and Profit*, London: Methuen.

Eatwell, J. (1976) 'Irving Fisher's "rate of return over cost" and the rate of profit in a capitalistic economy', in M. Brown, K. Sato, and P. Zarembka (eds) *Essays in Modern Capital Theory*, Amsterdam and New York: North-Holland.

Ferguson, C. E. (1972) 'The current state of capital theory: a tale of two paradigms', *Southern Economic Journal* 39: 160–76.

Garegnani, P. (1970) 'Heterogeneous capital, the production function and the theory of distribution', *Review of Economic Studies* 37: 407–36.

Hagemann, H. (1977) *Rate of Return und Profitrate*, Meisenheim: Anton Hain.

Hahn, F. H. (1972) *The Share of Wages in the National Income: An Inquiry into the Theory of Distribution*, London: Weidenfeld & Nicolson.

—— (1982) 'The neo-Ricardians', *Cambridge Journal of Economics* 6: 353–74.

Harcourt, G. C. (1969) 'Some Cambridge controversies in the theory of capital', *Journal of Economic Literature* 7: 369–405, reprinted in Harcourt, G. C. (1986) *Controversies in Political Economy: Selected Essays by G. C. Harcourt*, ed. O. F. Hamouda, Brighton: Wheatsheaf.

—— (1972) *Some Cambridge Controversies in the Theory of Capital*, Cambridge: Cambridge University Press.

—— (1975) 'The Cambridge controversies: the afterglow', in M. Parkin and A. R. Nobay (eds) *Contemporary Issues in Economics*, Manchester: Manchester University Press.

—— (1976) 'The Cambridge controversies: old ways and new horizons – or dead end?', *Oxford Economic Papers* NS 28: 25–65; reprinted in Harcourt, G. C. (1982) *The Social Science Imperialists: Selected Essays by G. C. Harcourt*, ed. P. Kerr, London: Routledge & Kegan Paul.

—— (1982) *The Social Science Imperialists: Selected Essays by G. C. Harcourt*, ed. P. Kerr, London: Routledge & Kegan Paul.

—— (1986) *Controversies in Political Economy: Selected Essays by G. C. Harcourt*, ed. O. F. Hamouda, Brighton: Wheatsheaf.

—— (1995) 'Recollections and reflections of an Australian patriot and a Cambridge economist', *Banca Nazionale del Lavoro Quarterly Review* 194: 225–54.

Malinvaud, E. (1953) 'Capital accumulation and the efficient allocation of resources', *Econometrica* 21: 233–68.

Morishima, M. (1969) *Theory of Economic Growth*, Oxford: Oxford University Press.

Nell, E. J. (1975) 'The black box rate of return', *Kyklos* 28: 803–26.

Nuti, D. M. (1974) 'On the rates of return on investment', *Kyklos* 27: 345–69.

—— (1976) 'Discussion', in M. Brown, K. Sato and P. Zarambka (eds) *Essays in Modern Capital Theory*, Amsterdam: North-Holland.

Pasinetti, L. L. (1962) 'Rate of return and income distribution in relation to the rate of economic growth', *Review of Economic Studies* 29: 267–79.

—— (1969) 'Switches of technique and the "rate of return" in capital theory', *Economic Journal* 79: 508–31.

—— (1970) 'Again on capital theory and Solow's "rate of return"', *Economic Journal* 80: 428–31.

—— (1981) *Structural Change and Economic Growth: A Theoretical Essay on the Dynamics of the Wealth of Nations*, Cambridge: Cambridge University Press.

—— (1993) *Structural Economic Dynamics: A Theory of the Economic Consequences of Human Learning*, Cambridge: Cambridge University Press.

Robinson, J. (1970) 'Capital theory up to date', *Canadian Journal of Economics* 3: 309–17.

Samuelson, P. A. (1962) 'Parable and realism in capital theory: the surrogate production function', *Review of Economic Studies* 29: 193–206.

Solow, R. M. (1963) *Capital Theory and the Rate of Return*, Amsterdam: North-Holland.

—— (1967) 'The interest rate and transition between techniques', in C. H. Feinstein (ed.) *Socialism, Capitalism and Economic Growth: Essays Presented to M. Dobb*, Cambridge: Cambridge University Press.

—— (1970) 'On the rate of return: reply to Pasinetti', *Economic Journal* 80: 423–8.

—— (1976) 'Discussion', in M. Brown, K. Sato and P. Zarembka (eds) *Essays in Modern Capital Theory*, Amsterdam: North-Holland.

14

THE SOCIAL 'BURDEN' OF HIGH INTEREST RATES[1]

Luigi L. Pasinetti

The rate of interest is a highly conventional, rather than a psychological, phenomenon. For its actual value is largely governed by the prevailing view as to what its value is expected to be.

(Keynes, 1936: 203)

LOOKING BACK AT DOMAR

Towards the end of the Second World War, when economists began to figure out possible scenarios for post-war economic development and policy, Evsey Domar (1944), in a well-known article, created a stir by arguing that not only a high level of public debt, but also a *continuous growth* of public debt, and thus persistent deficit spending, could be sustainable, provided that a vigorous process of economic growth were maintained. His arguments came down to something that sounds almost obvious today: whereas in a stationary economy continuous growth of the public debt is impossible, as it inevitably leads to an explosive situation, in a steadily growing economy the public debt can indeed grow indefinitely, provided that its rate of growth is kept within the constraints of the rate of growth of the national product. Their ratio can thereby remain stable indefinitely.

Domar's aim was to examine the 'burden' of the public debt for the community as a whole, in terms of the level of the tax rate that it would be necessary to impose in order to pay the interest.

Domar's numerical examples, and tables, may look cumbersome and incomplete, but they are significant. He implied steady-state debt to income ratios of the order of no less than 200 or 300 per cent! And he considered rates of interest of the order of 2 or 3 per cent, which were taken for granted at the time. With rates of growth of national income of the order of 2 or 3 per cent, he could conclude that the 'burden' of the debt would in fact turn out to be rather small, under various hypotheses.

The immediate post-war two decades seemed to vindicate Domar's contention. But the crises of public finance that have characterized almost all industrial countries in the late 1970s and 1980s suggest a reconsideration of the problem.

As becomes clear from the following, the relevant magnitudes to concentrate on are the levels of interest rates.

A COMPARATIVE DYNAMICS EXERCISE

We may abandon Domar's cumbersome methods and carry out a few simple exercises of comparative dynamics, confronting alternative paths of steadily growing economic systems, which differ only as to interest rates; the relevant magnitudes all grow at the same percentage rates, and the relevant ratios remain stable.

We can calculate the 'burden' for the community – in Domar's terms, the tax rate, t, which is the amount of taxation as a proportion of national income, Y, which the government would have to impose in order to pay the interest due on the outstanding public debt, D. We may suppose that the government aims at keeping the debt to national income ratio (D/Y) constant on the growth path. We can thus find out what budget deficit, G, in absolute terms and as a proportion of national income, the government can afford to have, compatibly with the payment of interest on the debt and constancy of the D/Y ratio.

Clearly, if g is the rate of growth of Y, so that

$$\Delta Y = gY, \tag{14.1}$$

the government can afford a budget deficit, and thus an increment of the public debt, of

$$G = \Delta D = gD, \tag{14.2}$$

while keeping the D/Y ratio constant. Total interest to be paid will be

$$iD, \tag{14.3}$$

where i is the interest rate. Thus, with a government deficit of gD, and the D/Y ratio kept constant, the amount that must be raised by taxation is the difference between (14.3) and (14.2). In other words, the tax rate that must be imposed in order to pay the interests on the debt, while keeping the D/Y ratio constant, is given by

$$t = (i - g)D/Y. \tag{14.4}$$

This is the steady-state 'social burden' of the public debt.

It should be noticed that the rate of inflation does not make any difference to these simple formulae. The growth rate and the interest rate both contain a real component and a nominal component (due to the increase of the general price level). But we are considering the ratio of debt to income; the nominal component, by appearing in both the numerator and the denominator, cancels out.

It emerges quite clearly from equation (14.4) that the crucial factor in the whole picture is represented by the difference $(i - g)$; that is, by the difference between the rate of interest and the rate of growth.[2]

Let us consider, very briefly, the three possible cases that may arise.

Case (a): $i = g > 0$

This represents the 'golden rule' of capital accumulation case: most elegant and simple.

In this case, the public budget can be permanently in deficit and the public debt can thereby increase indefinitely, but national income increases at the same rate (g), so that the D/Y ratio remains constant. Another way of looking at this case is to say that the government budget has a deficit which is wholly due to interest payments. If considered *net of interest payments*, the deficit (what has also been called the 'primary' deficit) is zero. Since $i - g = 0$, then, from equation (14.4), $t = 0$. The interest is paid through deficit spending, but it can simply be cumulated with the debt, without any need to impose any tax to pay for it. The growth of national income balances the growth of the public debt. Although the debt is increasing indefinitely, the burden of the debt for the community as a whole is nil, whatever the level the D/Y ratio may be. For the tax-paying community, it is as if there were no debt!

Case (b): $g > i > 0$

In this case, the situation, for the tax-paying community, is even more favourable than in case (a).

The interest paid on the debt, if accumulated with the debt itself, makes it grow at a rate i which is *lower* than rate g of growth of the national income. Thus a further growth of the debt, at rate $(g - i)$, is possible without worsening the D/Y ratio. In this case, the government deficit, given by equation (14.2), compatible with constancy of the D/Y ratio, even allows a *primary* deficit equal to $(g - i)D$. The 'burden' of the debt for the community as a whole becomes negative. It becomes a subsidy! As appears from equation (14.4), not only is it not necessary to impose any tax to pay for the interests, but in fact the community is afforded a subsidy or, if you like, the correspondent of a *negative* tax. It may sound paradoxical, but we should realize that the higher the level of the public debt the higher the deficit, as given by equation (14.2), which the government can afford to undertake without worsening the D/Y ratio. From another point of view, the negative tax – that is, the subsidy – for the tax-paying community is the higher, the higher is the level of the (stable) D/Y ratio!

Case (c): $i > g > 0$

This is the case that, alas, seems to have become more relevant recently. Expressions (14.1), (14.2) and (14.3) give, in this case too, the growth of income, the size of the deficit compatible with constancy of the D/Y ratio, and the size of the interest payments, respectively. It may be interesting to point out that there always is room for a permanent government deficit of size gD, as long as $D > 0$. In other words, the existence of a public debt allows the government to run a *permanent* budget deficit that is compatible with a constant D/Y ratio. But, in this case, the government budget, net of interest payments – that is the *primary* budget – must be *in surplus* by an amount equal to

$$(i - g) D \tag{14.5}$$

which entails the imposition of a positive tax (since $i > g$), given by

$$t = (i - g)D/Y \tag{14.4}$$

This represents, in Domar's terms, the steady-state 'burden' of the national debt.

We are faced, quite clearly, with a situation which is the reverse of that of the previous case, case (b). The primary government surplus, expression (14.5), necessary in order to keep the D/Y ratio constant, is the higher, the higher is the difference $(i - g)$ between the interest rate and the growth rate. And similarly, the tax, expression (14.4), which it becomes necessary to impose in order to pay for the interests and keep the D/Y ratio constant is the higher, the higher is the D/Y ratio.

POST-WAR EXPERIENCE

The comparative dynamics exercise of the previous section refers, of course, to abstract, steadily growing paths. In practice, economies will never be on steady, permanently growing paths. Yet the significance of such paths, as standards of reference, is undeniable.

If we look back at what actually happened after the Second World War, we find that the unprecedented and extraordinary economic growth of the industrial countries in the 1950s and 1960s was associated with government demand management, vigorous growth of national incomes, strong capital accumulation, low unemployment, but also with *low interest rates*. Keynes's idea of an 'euthanasia' of the *rentier* seemed convincing for some time. The general 'convention' about interest rates seemed to work in the sense of keeping them low. The central banks seemed to behave in such a way as to keep interest rates as low as possible, even if that entailed some (possibly moderate) rate of inflation. Within this framework, 'Keynesian' policies worked splendidly, and practically no government faced any serious problem of public finance.

A radical change took place in the late 1970s.[3] The trigger for the change is normally taken as being the oil crises – external events – which speeded up the upward movement of the price levels in general. It must also be added, however, that trade unions failed completely to understand the role they should have played in a 'Keynesian' framework of near-full employment. The result was substantial cost–push inflation (not Keynesian demand–pull!). This had a dramatic effect on events. No wonder the 'monetarist' critiques to the hitherto accepted 'Keynesian' policies became convincing. These critiques were partly justified, but misdirected. In any case, they had strong effects. Perhaps the most striking of such effects, an effect that persists today, has been the radical change which has taken place in the 'convention' about interest rates.

Everywhere, interest rates shot up dramatically.

It may be interesting to look at this event in an indirect way: as it has been reflected in the monumental scholarly work on the history of interest rates that Sidney Homer published in the USA. This work was published in 1963 and, from Homer's analysis, it appeared quite clearly that 'prime market rates of interest' (usually government bonds) of the order of 2 or 3 per cent had become, in the last few centuries, almost a general rule in the advanced industrial countries. When, in 1977, Homer published a second edition of his work, he was baffled by the striking changes that had taken place. Yet he could still write, in the preface to the second edition:

> When a historian attempts to record and discuss a span of many centuries, indeed millennia, it would seem unlikely that the events of a single decade or so would require a wholly new perspective and hence a significant revision. And yet, during the fourteen years that have elapsed [since the previous edition] interest rates, both here and abroad, have made more history than they did in the several preceding centuries.

Only a few years later, a third edition of the work appeared necessary and had to be brought out. Sidney Homer having died in the meantime (in 1983), a pupil of his, Richard Sylla, was entrusted with the task. On the very first page of the new edition, Sylla thought he should warn the reader:

> The spectacular rise in interest rates during the 1970's and early 1980's pushed many long-term market rates on prime credits up to levels never before approached, much less reached, in modern history. A long view, provided by this history, shows that recent peak yields were far above the highest prime long-term rates reported in the United States since 1800, in England since 1700, or in Holland since 1600. In other words, since modern capital markets came into existence, there have never been

such high long-term rates as we recently have had all over the world.

(Homer and Sylla 1991: 1)

If Keynes is right in thinking that interest rates are largely governed by a 'convention', we must surely agree that such a convention has recently changed! The major point seems to be that the central banks have come to regard the interest rates as the tool which they can use to deal with inflation.

Perhaps this is the most dramatic change that has happened recently – not only in monetary policy, but in public policy in general. The effects on the public finances of industrial countries are there to be seen.

VULNERABILITY TO HIGH PUBLIC DEBT

The size of the public debt and the size of government budget deficits have become subjects of common concern to all governments.

It is usual to blame the politicians, who are always too easily prone to public spending. This alertness to the dangers of easy spending is no doubt a welcome attitude. Any decision on deficit spending should be carefully scrutinized and in all cases carefully justified.

Yet the roots and nature of the impending dangers are not always clearly perceived. Why is it that deficit spending is to be so much frowned upon today, whereas it was not so much of a danger in the good old 'Keynesian' days of the 1950s and 1960s? It is too easy to avoid answering the question and simply say that it was the Keynesian 'profligacy' of those decades that has created the basis for our present predicaments.

The comparative dynamics exercise presented earlier in the chapter is very simple and of course concerns abstract steady-state paths, yet it should suffice to open our eyes.

Case (a) shows that stable debt to income ratios – even of the order of magnitude of 300 per cent or more, as considered by Domar – entail no burden for tax-payers as long as the rate of interest to be paid on government bonds does not exceed the rate of growth of national income.

Case (b) shows something further. When the rate of interest is lower than the rate of growth, the deficit compatible with a constant D/Y ratio is the higher, the higher is the debt, which seems to me to help to show how easy it is, in such a situation, to fall into the perverse tendency to widen deficit and debt. (It brings to mind situations of the early 1970s, when high inflation blew up the rates of growth and interest, pushing the former above the latter, and even causing negative *real* rates of interest.)

Conversely, case (c) should alert us that, as soon as the rate of interest is allowed to exceed the rate of growth, the public finances of any country are becoming *increasingly vulnerable to the size of the debt to income ratio*.

It is significant that the Maastricht Treaty, born in an era of high interest rates, has fixed two specific parameters in this respect: a debt to income ratio of 60 per cent and a government budget deficit of 3 per cent. It is not difficult to realize that these two parameters are connected, as they are consistent with a steady-state rate of growth of national income of 5 per cent (say $1\frac{1}{2}$ per cent in real terms and $3\frac{1}{2}$ per cent in nominal terms). As may be seen from expression (14.2), by dividing through by Y, the deficit compatible with a (stable) D/Y equal to 60 per cent is precisely 3 per cent. If the excess of the rate of interest over the rate of growth were of 2 points, then (on a steady growth path), the 'social burden' (that is, the tax to be imposed in order to pay the interest) would be a mere 1.2 per cent of national income, as is shown by equation (14.4) – a reasonably bearable level. The two Maastricht parameters seem to have been devised for supposedly 'safe' economies (such as, for example, Germany).

But as soon as the D/Y ratio is allowed to increase, the consequences become serious. For example, in Italy, a debt to income ratio of the order of 120 per cent is at present creating major problems of public finance – not only because a doubling of the D/Y ratio (with respect to the Maastricht standard) also doubles, *ceteris paribus*, the 'social burden' of the debt (on a steadily growing path), but also because, in fact, things do *not* remain equal; they induce a vicious circle. The fact that the D/Y ratio is reputed to be too high, with respect to the conventional Maastricht parameters, induces the so-called 'financial markets' to impose higher interest rates than those prevailing for the 'safe' countries. In this way, the difference $(i - g)$ is compelled to be 2 or 3 (in some cases 4) points wider than the one prevailing for the 'safe' countries. We learn from our exercise (see equation (14.4)) that, with a D/Y ratio of 120 per cent, when $(i - g)$, instead of being of the order of say 2 points, as it is for the 'safe' countries, is increased to the order of, say, 5 points, the 'burden' of the debt – that is, the tax to be imposed in order to pay the interest – turns out to be of the order of 6.25 per cent! This means that, on a steady-state growth path, no less than 6.25 points of the tax pressure is to be devoted simply to paying the interest!

This vulnerability is commonly attributed to the high size reached by the debt. It is, in fact, due to the high level reached by interest rates.

WHAT LEVEL FOR THE RATE OF INTEREST?

But what is an appropriate level for the rate of interest?

Questions of this type, which had been debated for centuries, have – quite surprisingly – disappeared from today's economic discussions. In earlier times, moral philosophers thought it their duty to search for a standard on the basis of which they would be able to say when interest was no longer 'interest' and was becoming 'usury'.[4] Today's positivistic attitude leads us to avoid the problem entirely, and to retreat into a sort of passive acceptance of the dictates of the 'financial markets'.

Keynes was bold enough to state his view on the 'convention' on the rate of interest; and to dream a more attractive world, in which low interest rates could induce capital saturation, full employment, and a level of welfare that could free our grandchildren from the atavistic yoke of economic want. (Keynes 1930).

For two decades, after the war, the dream seemed a reasonable one to entertain. It was spoiled by our inability to invent (national and international) institutions appropriate to allow us to deal with inflation without using interest rates as a tool.

The social burden of the high interest rates is thus upon us, and it is by no means light.

A revenge of the *rentier*? It may well simply be another aspect of the century-old unresolved conflict on income distribution.

NOTES

1   An Italian version of this paper – with substantially the same arguments, though presented differently – will appear in vol. 3 of *Studi in onore di Siro Lombardini*, forthcoming. Financial support from the Italian Research Council (CNR, 95.01936.CTIO) is gratefully acknowledged.
2   An application of this exercise to the Italian situation of the late 1980s was proposed in a note of mine (see Pasinetti 1989).
3   A Keynesian interpretation of the successions of international 'conventions' behind the post-war movements of interest rates is presented in an interesting work by Ciocca and Nardozzi (1993).
4   I have dared to propose a discussion on this in Pasinetti 1993: ch. 6.

REFERENCES

Ciocca, P. and Nardozzi, G. (1993) *L'alto prezzo del danaro: un 'interpretazione dei tassi di interesse internazionali*, Bari: Laterza; English translation forthcoming, from Oxford University Press.

Domar, E. (1944) 'The "burden of the debt" and the national income', *American Economic Review* 34: 798–827.

Homer, S. (1963) *A History of Interest Rates*, New Brunswick, NJ: Rutgers University Press (2nd edition, 1977).

Homer, S. and Sylla, R. (1991) *A History of Interest Rates*, 3rd edition, New Brunswick, NJ: Rutgers University Press.

Keynes, J. M. (1930) 'Economic possibilities for our grand-children, in *Nation and Atheneum*, October; reprinted in *The Collected Writings of John Maynard Keynes*: vol. 9, *Essays on Persuasion*, London: Macmillan, 1972.

—— (1936) *The General Theory of Employment, Interest and Money*, London: Macmillan.

Pasinetti, L. L. (1989) 'A note on the evaluation of public deficits: net or gross of interest?', *BNL Quarterly Review* 170: 303–11.

—— (1993) *Structural Economic Dynamics: A Theory of the Economic Consequences of Human Learning*, Cambridge: Cambridge University Press.

15

MARX, KEYNES AND SRAFFA
Conflicting attitudes towards political economy
William Darity, Jr

There is a time element which perhaps cannot be treated on a 3rd dimension. But Time is a common enemy to us all. I believe that like the rest of us you have had your faith in supply curves shaken by Piero. But what he attacks are just the one-by-one supply curves that you regard as legitimate. His objections do not apply to the supply curve of output – but Heaven help us when he starts thinking out objections that do apply to it!
(Joan Robinson in a letter to Keynes dated 10 May 1932, in Keynes 1973b: 378)

The habit of representing surplus-value and value of labour-power as fractions of the value created – a habit that originates in the capitalist mode of production itself, and whose import will hereafter be disclosed – conceals the very transaction that characterizes capital, namely the exchange of variable capital for living labour-power, and the consequent exclusion of the labourer from the product. Instead of the real fact, we have the false semblance of an association, in which labourer and capitalist divide the product in proportion to the different elements which they respectively contribute toward its formation.
(Marx 1967: vol. 1, p. 533)

Those who have resisted the elegant, siren-like lure of neoclassical economics have been fortunate in not having been forced to reinvent the wheel in mounting opposition to orthodoxy. Instead, they have been able to find refuge in the shadows cast by three figures of enormous and enduring intellect: Karl Marx, Piero Sraffa and John Maynard Keynes. Each of their legacies stakes out definite paths away from the 'mainstream'.

However, each of their legacies provides markedly different and largely irreconcilable views on the weaknesses of neoclassicism. In addition, each legacy represents a distinctive attitude towards classical political economy as well. Through an exploration of their respective approaches towards classical economics we can gain a deeper understanding of the relationships between the perspectives of Marx, Sraffa and Keynes. In examining their attitudes towards the classical school we can grasp the unity in their positions as heretical voices, but we also can grasp the disunity in their respective critiques of the dominant brand of economics still practised today.

Indeed, the disunity is sufficiently deep that the argument of this chapter is self-consciously intended as a antidote for those heterodox economists who tend to blend the trio indiscriminately. To this day neoclassicism remains the dominant wisdom. However, only one of the three, Keynes, posed a challenge to the orthodoxy that, at least for a time, gained somewhat broad acceptance among English-speaking economists.

Of course, Marx never had the opportunity to confront the neoclassicals directly. The divide in economics between classicism and neoclassicism came in the 1870s, after Marx was finished with the bulk of the preparation of the portions of *Capital* he was to complete before his death in 1883 (Bharadwaj 1978: 26–7). We are left only to speculate about Marx directly confronting the work of Jevons, Marshall, Menger, Edgeworth, Walras, J. B. Clark and their numerous kith and kin with his viperish wit and insight.

However, Marx actually had posed a critique of the 'new' economics *before* its consolidation! Marx identified the outlines of the emerging neoclassical tradition – the alchemist's brew of utilitarianism, marginalism and curves of supply and demand – in what he characterized as a degenerative plunge into 'vulgar' political economy by the orthodox post-Ricardians. Ricardo had, in Marx's estimation, pushed political economy to its *scientific* limits – limits which it could not go beyond within its own frame of analysis. Marx turned outside political economy – outside the limits of 'economics' proper – to seek a critique external to its premises.[1] This permitted him to burst through the limits (Marx 1969: 164–9). In the process Marx chastised those who were in retreat from Ricardo's achievements. For the 'vulgar' economists did no more than mouth, apologetically, the bourgeois class's own platitudes about its own activities, cloaked in academic jargon: 'The vulgar economist does practically no more than translate the singular concepts of the capitalists who are in the thrall of competition, into a seemingly more theoretical and generalized language, and attempt to substantiate the justice of these conceptions' (Marx 1967: vol. 3, p. 231).

Marx attributed the decline in classical economics to the accurate perception on the part of the bourgeoisie that the Ricardian economics was being appropriated by the working class for its own objectives. Thus, Marx (1967: vol. 1, p. 15) argued, it became necessary for the capitalists to push economics in a safer direction:

In France and in England the bourgeoisie had conquered political power. Thenceforth, the class-struggle, practically as well as theoretically, took on more and more outspoken and threatening forms. It sounded the death knell of scientific bourgeois economy. It was thenceforth no longer a question, whether this theorem or that was true, but whether it was useful to capital or harmful, expedient or inexpedient, politically dangerous or not. In place of disinterested inquiries, there were hired prize-fighters, in place of genuine scientific research, the bad conscience and the evil intent of apologetic.

In proceeding with his own construction of the appropriate method for the study of capitalist society, Marx made a fundamental abstraction between the interdependent spheres of circulation and of production. The latter sphere was the site of the creation of surplus value and the locus of exploitation in 'bourgeois society'. His caustic description of the former sphere – the sphere of circulation or the 'market system' – rings strongly with the themes that were soon to occupy the neoclassicals: 'This sphere [the sphere of simple circulation] that we are deserting, within whose boundaries the sale and purchase of labour-power goes on, is in fact a very Eden of the innate rights of man. There alone rules Freedom, Equality, Property, and Bentham' (Marx, 1967: vol. 1, p. 176). Unlike the classicals, especially Smith and Ricardo, who struggled to sense the phenomena below the surface, the vulgar economists were enamoured only with the outward appearance of things (Marx, 1969: esp. 164–6).

The vulgar economists, the immediate predecessors of the neoclassical school, were, in a sense, the *easy* targets for Marx. Although it is evident, on the basis of Marx's dismissal of vulgar economics, that he would have little positive to say about the scientific merits of contemporary economics, it also is evident that he would not view it as the most important object of criticism. Marx's project sublated classical political economy, represented in its highest form in Marx's estimation by Ricardo's contributions. Here lay, in his eyes, the substantive statement of bourgeois economics.

Moreover, Marx's critique was not intended to push classical economics 'forward'; rather his intent was to identify its limitations so severely as to indicate that it required fundamental reconstruction and transformation into an entirely different scheme of thought. Marx's plaudits for Ricardo stemmed not from the admiration born of disciplehood but from the healthy respect the gladiator feels for the strongest combatant in the arena (Pilling 1980: 17–22).

Sraffa, however, never explicitly detected the fundamental intellectual antagonism in the positions taken up by Ricardo and Marx. For Sraffa, Marx was a member of the classical school. This is evident by Sraffa's remarks on the inattention given to the theory of value early in the twentieth century in contrast with the intense attention given to such matters in the prior century:

[The difference felt by the majority of economists nowadays in regard to the theory of the value] is justified by the fact that this theory, more than any other part of economic theory, has lost much of its direct bearing upon practical politics, and *particularly in regard to doctrines of social changes, which had formerly been conferred upon it by Ricardo and afterwards by Marx, and in opposition to them by bourgeois economists.*

(Sraffa 1926: 535; my emphasis)

171

Marx, in contrast, characterized Ricardo as the 'last great representative' of classical political economy or 'bourgeois economy', thus setting his own project apart from Ricardo's (Marx 1967: vol. 1, p. 14).

In Sraffa's treatment, both Ricardo and Marx become mere 'radical' economists – with Marx falling in tow as a sophisticated and faithful developer of Ricardo's economics.[2] For Sraffa, the classical school stretched from Smith to Marx, providing a viable alternative to bourgeois economics which Sraffa identified with the marginalist method. Whereas Marx's target was the entire sweep of political economy, in all its branches and tendencies, Sraffa's target was the type of political economy that developed since the 'great divide' of the 1870s.

In fact, Sraffa returned to classical political economy – centring his interpretation of classical economics on the notion of an economic surplus – to forge an alternative to neoclassicism. Effectively Sraffa turned backward chronologically to push economics 'forward', beyond a host of puzzles that had come to trouble the supply and demand theorists. Sraffa set as his task the reconstruction of economics on a basis independent from the neoclassical approach with which he was most familiar, the Marshallian economics, a task which Eatwell for one, believes he accomplished: 'In the surplus approach [of the classicals] the difficulties, and peculiarities, encountered by neoclassical economists do not arise, and in consequence it provides a much firmer foundation for all aspects of economic theory and not only for the theory of value' (1982: 223–4). Even if Sraffa's (1960: 93–5) location of Marx within the classical school was misplaced, he had at least done a thorough and complex reading of Marx. Nevertheless, it remained a reading of Marx from the perspective of an economist, albeit a politically 'radical' economist with an astonishing intellect.

Keynes, unlike Sraffa, apparently had not done a thorough reading of Marx. His scattered published remarks on Marx are largely dismissive. Keynes's (1936: 32) most famous act of derogation of Marx is his relegation of Marx, with Silvio Gesell and Major Douglas, to the 'underworld' of monetary cranks and under-consumptionists whose primary merit was, in Keynes's eyes, their efforts to keep effective demand doctrine alive.[3]

Perhaps Keynes's (1963: 297–311) attachment to political liberalism kept him from devoting much attention to the alleged ideological godfather of the Soviet experiment, an experiment toward which Keynes was plainly hostile.[4] Perhaps Keynes was influenced excessively by Marshall's attitude toward Marx.[5] Regardless, there is no direct link from Marx's work into Keynes's. There may have been an indirect link via Sraffa. Sraffa was, after all, a member of Keynes's 'circus' – although, apparently, not as major a participant in Keynes's efforts to prepare *The General Theory* as Richard Kahn, Joan Robinson and Roy Harrod. But the influence of Marx on Keynes, if there at all, had to be coloured by Sraffa's particular interpretation of Marx's work.

172

As for Keynes's attitude toward classical economics, he saw continuity where Sraffa saw a gulf. This again may reflect the influence of Marshall, who minimized the presence of divisions in the development of economics. Sraffa (see 'Introduction' 1978: 1–3), unlike Keynes, was not a pupil of Marshall's, completing his training in economics in Italy prior to his arrival in Cambridge in 1921. Keynes clustered among those he called 'the classical economists' not only 'Ricardo and James Mill and their *predecessors*' but also 'the *followers* of Ricardo, those, that is to say, who adopted and perfected the Ricardian economics, including (for example) J. S. Mill, Marshall, Edgeworth, and Prof. Pigou' (Keynes 1936: 3 n1; emphases in original).

According to Keynes, the singular failure of this essentially unbroken chain of economists from James Mill and Ricardo up through 'Prof. Pigou' was its lack of a theoretically adequate account for long-lasting unemployment. Keynes's intended project thus became narrower still than that of either Marx or Sraffa. After all, Keynes explicitly accepted the 'classical theory' of full employment.[6] What was missing for Keynes was a theory sufficiently general to explain the persistence of unemployment and to explain the behaviour of an economy under such conditions. That was the hole he intended to fill.

The irony is, of course, that in charting such a course Keynes's theory could be shown to cast doubt on the 'classical theory' under *all* conditions, particularly given the implications of his long-period analysis of employment. Still Keynes himself made no such claim, thus making his theory amenable to a broader acceptance among economists than either Marx or Sraffa could have expected, especially given the publication of *The General Theory* in the midst of the Great Depression.

Thus Marx, Sraffa and Keynes present three distinct attitudes toward classical political economy. Marx viewed the classical approach, especially in Ricardo's hands, as the highest form attainable by economics. Incipient neoclassicism in the form of vulgar economics was the inferior brand, in his eyes, but *all* political economy – including the classical approach – demanded overthrow. Sraffa shared a belief in the inferiority of neoclassical economics when compared with classicism, but for theoretical reasons quite different from Marx's. As a result, Sraffa undertook a rehabilitation of economics on the basis of the classical approach rather than the overthrow of economics as a whole.

Finally, Keynes, unlike either Marx or Sraffa, largely accepted Marshall's idealism. From this vantage point, economics was conceived of as steadily improving in terms of logical coherence and rigour as its development progressed from Ricardo to 'the Prof'. The neoclassical approach appears indistinguishable from Ricardian economics to Keynes. All of it comprised 'classical economics' in his eyes. The fatal flaw was the ongoing divorce of this increasingly refined system of logical analysis from reality – in particular its inability to comprehend a crisis of massive unemployment.

This detailed preliminary exegesis on Marx's, Sraffa's and Keynes's perspectives on classical economics provides a background to the discussion that follows. Each of their respective positions on methodology will be taken up in the remainder of the chapter. A preliminary understanding of their respective stances *vis-à-vis* the classical school is a vital prelude to understanding their positions on the nature of scientific method.

With regard to methodology there are three topics that will be considered: Marx's, Sraffa's and Keynes's objects of enquiry; the nature of their respective critiques; and their respective views on the relationship between the scientific content of concepts and empirical material.

Marx was explicit about the character of his project in *Capital* – an exploration of 'the capitalist mode of production, and the conditions of production and exchange corresponding to that mode'.[7] The task of the scientist thus becomes the discovery of the basic tendential characteristics of the development of the mode of production under study. Therefore, for Marx, his ultimate objective was to identify the laws of motion of capitalism – those 'tendencies working with iron necessity towards inevitable results' (1967: vol. 1, p. 8). When all is said and done, Marx presents three laws of motion of capitalism in *Capital* which are expressions of the same essential process: the law of the centralization of capitals, the law of relative surplus population, and the law of the tendency of the rate of profit to fall.[8] These laws embody the basis for Marx's claim that the capitalist mode of production, like all previous social modes of production, would experience a finite history.

This object plainly lay outside the domain of political economy. Marx adamantly sought to isolate the historical specificity to capitalism of the phenomena that so attracted the attention of the economists – the phenomena that, in effect, created the economists. Again, in contrast, Sraffa's object of enquiry lay squarely within the field of political economy. Sraffa sought to construct a consistent theory of exchange value and distribution without reference to the doctrine of supply and demand. Of necessity, his research project became an investigation of the determinants of relative prices – a subject of secondary importance to Marx's project. Marx's extensive use of tableau in volume 2 of *Capital* was intended to provide an abstract representation of the general form of circulation activities in a capitalist economy, of which the generation of relative prices was but a part. Sraffa's focus on relative prices made this aspect of his research much the same as that of the neoclassicists; his focus on distribution pressed his object back toward that of Ricardo and the classical school.

Keynes's object was the construction of a pragmatic – that is, policy relevant – theory of unemployment. He therefore undertook a search for the characteristics of the dominant economics – the tradition in which he continuously reminded his audiences he 'had been brought up' – that prevented or blocked investigation into the sources of the Great Depression. He (Keynes 1973a) found his answers in the inadequate treatment of the nature of uncertainty and, correspondingly, an inadequate comprehension of what he called a 'monetary production economy'. Keynes launched his most withering assault on what he viewed as a key implicit or explicit assumption of the 'classical economics': the neutrality of money.

With each of the three, the level of critique posed for economic theory is related intimately to the nature of their object of enquiry. Marx was not concerned primarily with the purely logical shortcomings of Ricardian economics; rather he sought out its ideological content to identify its foundations in the material and concrete circumstances of Ricardo's time. This is reflected in turn in Marx's attitude towards the presence of contradictions in classical political economy. The following observations by Geoffrey Pilling are pertinent:

> [John Stuart] Mill started with Ricardo's work as a purely abstract system of thought, ignoring the (contradictory) reality which this system expressed. Driven on by the criticism of Ricardo's opponents (the leading one of whom was Malthus) and also sensing that Ricardo's work was in contradiction with reality; Mill tried to eliminate the contradictions of Ricardian political economy. What he tried to achieve says Marx . . . was 'formal, logical consistency'. . . .
>
> Now Marx's attitude to the undoubtedly real contradictions of the Ricardian system was quite different. In the first place, he grasped the true *source* of these contradictions. It lay not in the error of Ricardo's *thought*, but expressed the contradictory economic and social phenomena which Ricardo in his theory was seeking to express.
>
> (Pilling 1980: 32; my emphasis)

Pilling then juxtaposes Marx's dialectical method against the method of formal logic characteristic of political economy. This juxtaposition does not mean that Marx produced an illogical theory, but that Marx's point of entry into the analysis of capitalism originated from an entirely different philosophical basis from that of the classicals. A passage from the third volume of *Capital* that gives special clarity to Marx's dialectical use of contradictions is the following explication of aspects of the law of the tendency of the rate of profit to fall:

> it is but a requirement of the capitalist mode of production that the number of wage-workers should increase absolutely, in spite of its relative decrease. Labour-power becomes redundant as soon as it is no longer necessary to employ it for 12 to 15 hours daily. A development of labourers, i.e., enable the entire nation to accomplish its total production in a shorter time span, would cause a revolution, because it would put the bulk of the population out of the running. This is another manifestation of the specific barrier of capitalist production, showing also that capitalist production is by no means an absolute form of the

development of the productive forces and for the creation of wealth, but rather that at a certain point it comes into collision with this development. This collision appears partly in periodical crises, which arise from the circumstance that now this and that portion of the labouring population becomes redundant under its old mode of unemployment. The limit of capitalist production is the excess of the labourers. The absolute spare time gained by society does not concern it. The development of productivity concerns it only in so far as it increases the surplus labour-time of the working-class, but not because it decreases the labour-time for material production in general. *It moves thus in contradiction.*

(Marx 1967: vol. 3, pp. 263–4; my emphasis)

Further, as Pilling (1980: 34) points out, Marx's dialectical method permitted him to make statements that would appear as sheer nonsense to the formal logician; for example, Marx's claim that the emergence of the 'full-grown capitalist must take place, both within the sphere of circulation and without it'.

Sraffa, by way of contrast, initiated his critique of the Marshallian neoclassical school on grounds of logical inconsistency. In his brilliant 1926 *Economic Journal* paper, Sraffa posed what appeared as an intractable dilemma for the neoclassicists. If one firm within an industry is not the exclusive user of a factor, it is not in fact a fixed factor for the firm. Under general conditions of free or perfect competition, each firm would be faced with a perfectly elastic supply of all factors. This obviates the presence of increasing costs and the determinant basis for the construction of 'short-run' rising industry supply curves.

On the other hand, if the purchases of an individual firm raised the factor's price, this would contradict the assumed existence of free competition. The dilemma arose, according to Sraffa (1926: 536–7), because of Marshall's faulty attempt to graft the classical law of diminishing returns, which was solely in 'reference to land' and 'adequate in its own right', on to a theory of relative prices rooted in the interplay of supply and demand. Diminishing returns and free competition were not logically compatible, argued Sraffa.

The Marshallian theory left no room for increasing returns under conditions of free competition, either, except for those cases of external economies 'external of the firm' and 'internal to the industry'. Thus, as Sraffa observed, 'The only economies which could be taken into consideration would be such as occupy an intermediate position between these two extremes; but it is just in the middle that nothing, or almost nothing is to be found.' (1926: 540).

These conundrums and inconsistencies associated with the neoclassical conception of the competitive determination of relative prices led Sraffa to advocate the closeting of the Marshallian partial method. In an exchange on these matters with Dennis Robertson, Sraffa's final comment is telling:

> [Mr. Robertson and I] seem to be agreed that the theory cannot be interpreted in a way which makes it logically self-consistent and, at the same time, reconciles it with the facts it sets out to explain. Mr. Robertson's remedy is to discard mathematics, and he suggests that my remedy is to discard the facts; perhaps I ought to have explained that, in the circumstances, I think it is Marshall's theory that should be discarded.[9]
>
> (Sraffa 1930: 93)

Sraffa did appear to leave room for an assault on the problem of the formulation of prices under competition via the method of general equilibrium, although he expressed scepticism about its capacity, at least at its state of development in the 1920s, to resolve the puzzles:

> When we proceed to a further approximation, while keeping to the path of free competition, the complications do not arise gradually as would be convenient; they are present themselves simultaneously as a whole. If diminishing returns arising from a 'constant factor' are taken into consideration, it becomes necessary to extend the field of investigation so as to examine the conditions of simultaneous equilibrium in numerous industries: a well-known conception, whose complexity, however, prevents it from bearing fruit, at least in the present state of our knowledge, which does not permit of even much simpler schemata being applied to the study of real conditions.
>
> (Sraffa 1926: 541)

Sraffa did suggest that even the general equilibrium strategy could not incorporate increasing returns into a system assuming perfect competition: 'If we pass to external economies, we find ourselves confronted by the same obstacle, and there is also the impossibility of confining within statical conditions the circumstances from which they originate' (ibid.). Thus, he anticipated the restrictive convexity assumptions embedded in contemporary models of competitive general equilibrium.

Given the failure of neoclassicism to produce a satisfactory analysis of relative prices under conditions of free competition, Sraffa gravitated back towards the classical system and its emphasis on cost-determined 'natural' or 'normal' prices. The classical system, in Sraffa's hands, required no particular assumption about returns to scale (see Eatwell 1977). This agenda, which evidently occupied close to forty years of Sraffa's (1926: p. 541) research, is foreshadowed in the following sentence: 'And so, as a simple way of approaching the problem of competitive value, the old and now obsolete theory which makes it dependent on the cost of production alone appears to hold its ground as the best available.'

The fulfilment of the agenda finally surfaced with the publication of

Sraffa's (1960) *Production of Commodities by Means of Commodities*. There is also a clear foreshadowing of the direction Sraffa was to take in *Production of Commodities* in his remarkable introduction to Ricardo's *Principles*. Here Sraffa (1951: xiii–lxii) can be found discussing the surplus, the wage–profit nexus, the standard commodity and the invariable standard of value.

Sraffa's introduction to Ricardo's *Principles* indicated how deeply he had probed to identify the *logical* shortcomings of the classical system. Quite early, presumably in the 1920s, Sraffa had concluded that Marshallian economics was beset by hopeless inconsistencies, but the logical weaknesses of Ricardian economics could be remedied by a careful reinterpretation. Thus Sraffa, unlike Marx, sought to 'complete' the classical project on its own terms – to salvage it from obsolescence by demonstrating that it can successfully explain relative prices under competitive conditions whereas the neoclassical theory is unable to do so.[10]

Keynes's critique proceeds at an entirely different level from either Marx's or Sraffa's. For Keynes, the weakness of the dominant theory centred on its policy irrelevance. It was no longer a useful guide to understanding or explaining the performance of the industrial economies.

Keynes complained about 'the completeness of the Ricardian victory', commenting on how the

> professional economists, after Malthus, were apparently unmoved by the lack of correspondence between the results of their theory and the facts of observation – a discrepancy which the ordinary man has not failed to observe, with the result of his growing unwillingness to accord to economists the measure of respect which he gives to other groups of scientists whose theoretical results are confirmed by observation when they are applied to the facts.
>
> (Keynes 1936: 32–3)

Thus Keynes's critique of orthodoxy was empirical – a type of critique that is instrumental in understanding his negative assessment of Tinbergen's econometric results in the 1930s.

In a letter to Roy Harrod, Keynes (1973b: 2) indicates that for him progress in economics was dependent on the development of models that more and more closely approximate reality. The purpose of the statistician was not to identify fixed parametric coefficients in models, as Keynes (1973b: 285–320) believed Tinbergen had done, but to test the situational relevance of the model:

> it is of the essence of the model that one does *not* fill in real values for the variable functions. To do so would make it useless as a model. For as soon as this is done, the model loses its generality and its value as a mode of thought. That is why Clapham with his empty boxes was barking up the wrong tree and why Schultz's results, if he ever gets any,

178

are not very interesting (for we know beforehand that they will not be applicable to future cases). The object of statistical study is not so much to fill in missing variables with a view to prediction, as to test the relevance and validity of the model.

(Keynes 1973b: 296)

The key point is that the terms of Keynes's critique of orthodoxy were not based primarily upon the identification of errors in the reasoning behind its construction:

Our criticism of the accepted classical theory of economics has consisted not so much in finding logical flaws in its analysis as in pointing out that its tacit assumptions are seldom or never satisfied, with the result that it cannot solve the economic problems of the actual world.

(ibid.: 378)

Thus Keynes's critique proceeded by arguing that the dominant brand of economics did not facilitate the solution of real-world social problems. Although Sraffa desired an empirically relevant theory, his critique principally was motivated by the identification of intractable problems in the formal logic of the neoclassical system and the belief that the problems in formal logic that had plagued the classical system could be resolved. Marx, though not suggesting that a sound theory should be empirically empty nor illogical, did not focus on these considerations as establishing a fundamental critique. His starting point was instead an identification of the 'real-world' or material conditions that produced the development of classical political economy in the first place. Neither Sraffa nor Marx was particularly anxious to advance theory to assist status-quo policymakers, a definite aim of the intensely policy-motivated Keynes.

The final aspect of Marx's, Keynes's and Sraffa's positions on methodology to be addressed here is their views on the relationship between their theoretical concepts and empirical material. Specifically, did they believe that to be 'scientific', concepts must bear a direct correspondence to data that can be extracted from the real world by direct observation?

Keynes, for one, never addressed this issue explicitly. There are clues to his position in his comments on a League of Nations study group's report entitled *Statistics Relating to Capital Formation*. Here Keynes (1973b: 280) argued that fundamental theoretical issues concerning the operation of the economic system must be resolved before the statistician can meaningfully subject the concepts to measurement. It matters a great deal, Keynes points out, in the construction of data series on savings, whether savings are construed as becoming available for finance immediately or only with a time-lag. The implication is that given a sound theory for guidance, empirical analogues for 'macroeconomic' concepts such as savings, investment and consumption can

179

be found in carefully constructed national income accounts.

Nevertheless, a word of caution is pertinent. Keynes's emphasis on subjective uncertainty has a 'metaphysical' quality about it, lending a non-quantitative flavour to his treatment of expectations that is at complete odds with the efforts of contemporary applied econometricians. Thus subjective uncertainty itself cannot be observed directly, nor can it be calibrated. What is observable is the *manifestations* of its presence. In addition, crucial concepts in Keynes's development of his *General Theory* such as aggregate demand price and aggregate supply price are strictly within the minds of the 'enterprisers' – also lacking direct empirical correspondence and perhaps lacking even indirect empirical correspondences. Much the same is true of Keynes's marginal efficiencies.

Sraffa, however, seems to have felt that theoretical constructs are superior if they can be measured statistically, although that is not the sole criterion for evaluation of their worth. In a discussion of a paper presented by John Hicks at the International Economics Association meetings in 1958 on the capital measurement controversy, Sraffa (1961: 305) made a distinction between measurement 'in which the statisticians were mainly interested' and 'measurement in theory'. He elaborated on the significance of this distinction as follows:

The statisticians' measures were only approximate and provided a suitable field for work in solving index number problems. The theoretical measure required absolute precision. Any imperfections in these theoretical measures were not merely upsetting, but knocked down the whole theoretical basis. One could measure capital in pounds or dollars and introduce this into a production function. The definition in this case must be absolutely water-tight, for with a given quantity of capital one has a certain rate of interest so that the quantity of capital was an essential part of the mechanism. One therefore had to keep the definition of capital separate from the needs of statistical measurement which were quite different. The work of J. B. Clark, Böhm-Bawerk and others was intended to produce pure definitions of capital, as required by their theories not as a guide to actual measurement. *If we found contradictions then these pointed to defects in the theory, and an inability to define measures of capital accurately.* It was on this – the chief failing of capital theory – that we should concentrate, rather than on problems of measurement.

(Sraffa 1961: 305–6; my emphasis)

Sraffa thus committed himself to the view that proper development of theory must take priority over statistical measurement – development of theory free of logical contradiction. He acknowledged that 'the usefulness of a theory lay in its explanatory value' and suggested that one can be interested in theory even if one cannot 'fit actual figures into it'. (1961: 306). None the less, the inability to measure the concepts satisfactorily was taken by Sraffa (1961: 306) as a signal of theoretical inadequacy:

> if one could not get the measures required by the theorists' definitions, this was a criticism of theory, which the theorists could not escape by saying that they hoped their theory would not often fail. If a theory failed to explain a situation it was unsatisfactory.
>
> (ibid.)

Sraffa, on this basis, might be viewed as more intensely an empiricist than even Keynes, although both of them reveal a substantive awareness of the theory-laden nature of 'facts'.

Marx, in contrast with both Keynes and Sraffa, took a blatantly *anti-empiricist* stance – although by no means did he take an *anti-empirical* stance. For Marx the purpose of science was to construct concepts that need not correspond directly to observable categories of real-world phenomenon. Scientific concepts themselves were invisibles; what was visible were the manifestations of their operation. Thus Marx placed a clear emphasis on theory as an a priori construction for appropriation of empirical material.

At the heart of Marx's method was a procedure of abstraction that continuously pushed the analyst to penetrate deeper and deeper beneath the surface of things. In Marx's words, 'In the analysis of economic form ... neither microscopes nor chemical reagents are of use. The force of abstraction must replace both' (1967: vol. 1, p. 8). In volume 3 of *Capital* Marx was even more blunt: 'all science would be superfluous if the outward appearance and the essence of things coincided' (ibid.: vol. 3, p. 817). Marx's analytical method, at least in presentation, moved continuously from 'higher' to 'lower' levels of abstraction – from the unseen to the seen – as he developed a science of history.

Those who do not comprehend Marx's conception of science are also unable to comprehend his law of the tendency of the rate of profit to fall and his countertendencies to the law. Therefore, it could be a misplaced enterprise to seek to 'test' Marx's law by measuring statistically a 'rate of profit' and then examining whether it displays a pattern of secular decline. Like his concepts of value, surplus value and rate of exploitation, Marx's pure rate of profit was a-empirical or pre-empirical. What would be observable is the surface manifestations of the working out of the law and its countertendencies in the forms of, for example, ever-increasing mechanization of production, the secular decrease in the length of the working day, the ongoing superfluity of a part of the working class, and late nineteenth-century imperial expansion by Western nations.

The interpretation of Marx's method adopted here is close in many respects to the position taken by Fine and Harris. The following observations from their book *Rereading Capital* are pertinent here:

181

When Marx refers to an economic law he explicitly means a tendency.... But the meaning of a tendency is understood differently by different writers. One meaning ... is that if one collects data on the rate of profit over a definite period of history one will observe a definite downward trend (or regression line). We shall call this an 'empirical tendency.' A second meaning is that if one *abstracts* from the counteracting influences one identifies an 'underlying' direction of movement of the rate of profit. This interprets a tendency as a proposition developed at a certain level of abstraction which by itself yields no general predictions about actual movements in the rate of profit. Actual movements depend on a complicated relationship between the tendency and the counteracting influences which have been abstracted from – their particularly balance at particular times. We shall call this an 'abstract tendency.' The latter is Marx's concept of the law of the TRPF [tendency of the rate of profit to fall]. The observable effect of the law cannot be a simple tendency for the actual rate of profit (in value or price terms) to fall. The effects of the law (which, being constructed from the law at a lower level of abstraction) must be the effects of the complex contradictions between the tendency of the rate of profit to fall and the counteracting influences ...

The TRPF can only appear through its effects derived from its articulation with the counteracting influences, and these in turn can only be examined in relation to the TRPF. In short, the law of the TRPF is an abstract and not an empirical tendency.

(Fine and Harris 1979: 64–5)

What joins Keynes, Marx and Sraffa was a mutual rejection of the orthodox economics of their time (and of our time). But in a sense that is perhaps the most that joins them. They charted vastly different projects for research: Marx sought to dissect, demolish and transform political economy into a science of history instead of a 'better' economics; Sraffa sought to salvage economics by retrieving its classical/Ricardian foundations; and Keynes sought to convert economics into a genuinely policy-relevant enterprise by giving it a substantive theory of unemployment. Their projects necessarily were associated with vastly different critiques of orthodoxy, and their attitudes towards the scientific status of concepts displayed heterogeneity as well.

They all came to terms with classical political economy: Marx launching a profound assault, Sraffa embracing it, and Keynes dismissing it as other-worldly until it could be modified to treat real-world crises. In coming to terms with it, they were all touched by it and found it to be more worthwhile as a target or as a tradition to utilize than the neoclassical economics.

Marx 'coquetted' with the classicals' language, transforming its terminology into images that stripped bare the inner essence of capitalism. He absorbed its puzzles not to resolve them so much as to comprehend what were the real conditions that had produced such conundrums. He used their concept of competition, grappled with the valuelessness of credit, and exposed their inability to settle 'the machinery question'. In producing his own answer to the latter problem Marx revealed why unemployment is a persistent feature of capitalism.

Sraffa had no intention of overturning classical political economy. Instead his aim was to give it a rigour and elegance that could give it clear superiority over the muddled neoclassical economics. In some respects, Sraffa's project *de facto* was the least subversive of economics as a whole of the three!

Keynes's critique grew more subversive than perhaps even he intended. For as the full implications of his theory unfolded, microeconomics could not take Keynes seriously and remain the same. Either it would have to change radically or Keynes's economics would have to be deradicalized by an insistence that it must have 'microfoundations'. Subjective uncertainty could absorb and overwhelm the whole of economics, if it was allowed to get out of hand. The economists tended to accept Keynes's charge to think about unemployment in a more serious fashion without accepting the full consequences of his theory. Only Marx, in refusing to save 'economics', began with the goal of posing a *fundamental* intellectual challenge to all of political economy. And only Marx remains entirely unacceptable as a serious intellectual contender by most American economists. Although many have never tried to understand Sraffa and many have not really understood Keynes, both Sraffa and Keynes bear mantles of legitimacy never granted to Marx. That is, again, because Marx refused to become an 'economist', while nevertheless being the finest historian of the development of political economy up to his time.

ACKNOWLEDGEMENTS

I should like to acknowledge many helpful criticisms and suggestions from both Bobbie Horn and Michael Pyne in the development of this chapter – although each of them would have written a contribution much different from this one.

NOTES

1 See, for example, the terrain J. S. Mill carved out for economics in his *Principles of Political Economy* (Mill 1965).
2 Various economists influenced by Sraffa have also taken the position that there is no major discontinuity between Marx and Ricardo. For example, Walsh and Gram (1980) observe, 'In the later work of Marx, classical English political economy had thus reached its final nineteenth century expression' (p. 115). They also describe Marx 'as the last great figure in the tradition of classical political economy' (p. 123). John Eatwell has continued to attempt to demonstrate, time

and again, the compatibility between Marx and Ricardo. The most comprehensive of these efforts was his 1974 essay 'Controversies in the theory of surplus value: old and new'. What all fail to do is to explain Marx's own resistance to this sort of characterization of his work in relationship to Ricardo's.

For a strong statement of the position that Marx and Ricardo are in fundamental opposition see Suzanne de Brunhoff (1973). De Brunhoff's essay stimulated Eatwell's (1974) efforts. See also de Brunhoff's (1974) reply to Eatwell. For another recent effort to distance Marx from Ricardo see Wolff *et al.* (1982).

3 The late Dudley Dillard, in a paper presented in December 1982 at the Keynes–Marx Centennial panel at the American Economic Association meeting in New York City, 'Keynes and Marx', suggested that Keynes took Marx quite seriously because he adopted Marx's description of the capitalist circuit of exchange, $M–C–M^1$. In the ensuing discussion, however, Donald Moggridge observed that Keynes 'cannibalized' the idea from manuscripts submitted to the *Economic Journal* by left-wing British economists rather than obtaining it from a direct reading of Marx. Moreover, Moggridge added, Keynes never even sent the manuscripts out to be refereed.

4 Still, Keynes was close to the younger generation of Apostles, a secret society at the University of Cambridge, which included many who were openly enthusiastic about communism and several who served as Soviet spies. See Moggridge (1992: 470).

5 Keynes's mentor makes mention of Marx in only three places in his most renowned work. See the eighth edition of Marshall's *Principles of Economics* (1920: 417, 487–8, 647). It is impossible to determine to what extent Marshall's superficial insights reflect the inadequacy of his study of Marx or a tactical decision to distort Marx's views. In all fairness, it should be noted that only vol. 1 of *Capital* was available in English translation throughout most of Marshall's academic career, appearing in 1887, a mere three years before the first edition of Marshall's *Principles*.

6 If stabilization measures could maintain 'full employment', the classical economics would be relevant again; Keynes (1936: 378) wrote, 'if our central controls succeed in maintaining an aggregate volume of employment corresponding to full employment as nearly as is practicable, the classical theory comes into its own again from this point onwards'.

7 See Marx's 'Preface to the first German edition' (1967: vol. 1, p. 8).

8 For a superb analysis of Marx's laws of motion in capitalism from a methodological standpoint see Rosdolsky's *Making of Marx's 'Capital'* (1977: esp. 282–312, 376–82, 398–411).

9 Of course, Sraffa's recommendation might have opened the door for a debate over the actual content of 'Marshall's theory' and the relationship between Marshall, Keynes and Sraffa.

10 Unfortunately, many of Sraffa's disciples, more so than Sraffa himself, have failed to recognize the distance between Ricardo and Marx. They therefore tend to see the logical weaknesses in Ricardo's work as carrying over into Marx's (e.g. Eatwell 1974: 282 or Steedman 1977) in the form of the 'transformation problem'. The separateness of Ricardo's and Marx's problematic eludes them altogether. For a critique of the Sraffians on these matters, although they are careful to add that the criticism applies least to Sraffa himself, see Himmelweit and Mohun (1978: 87–8). They also suggest that Sraffian and Ricardian economics are not identical!

REFERENCES

Bharadwaj, (1978) *Classical Political Economy and the Rise to Dominance of the Supply and Demand Theories*, Calcutta: Orient Longman.

de Brunhoff, S. (1973) 'Marx as an a-Ricardian: value, money, and price at the beginning of Capital', *Science and Society*, pp. 421–9.

—— (1974) 'Controversies in the theory of surplus value: a reply to John Eatwell', *Science and Society* 37(4): 478–82.

Eatwell, J. (1974) 'Controversies in the theory of surplus value: old and new', *Science and Society* 37(3): 281–303.

—— (1977) 'The irrelevance of returns to scale in Sraffa's analysis', *Quarterly Journal of Economics* 15: 61–8.

—— (1982) 'Competition', in I. Bradley and M. Howard (eds) *Classical and Marxian Political Economy: Essays in Honor of Ronald L. Meek*, London: Macmillan.

Fine, B. and Harris, L. (1979) *Rereading Capital*, New York: Columbia University Press.

Himmelweit, S. and Mohun, S. (1978) 'The anomalies of capital', *Capital and Class* 6: 67–105.

'Introduction to Sraffa' (1978) *New Left Review* 112: 62–4.

Keynes, J. M. (1936) *The General Theory of Employment, Interest, and Money*, London: Macmillan.

—— (1963) 'A short view of Russia (1925)', in *Essays in Persuasion*, New York: W. W. Norton.

—— (1973a) *Collected Writings*, vol. 13, ed. D. E. Moggridge, London: Macmillan.

—— (1973b) *Collected Writings*, vol. 14, ed. D. E. Moggridge, London: Macmillan.

Marshall, A. (1920) *Principles of Economics*, 8th edition, London: Macmillan.

Marx, K. (1967) *Capital*, 3 vols, New York: International Publishers.

—— (1969) *Theories of Surplus Value*, Part 2, London: Lawrence & Wishart.

Mill, J. S. (1965) *Collected Works of John Stuart Mill*, vols 2 and 3, Toronto: University of Toronto Press.

Moggridge, D. E. (1992) *Maynard Keynes: An Economists' Biography*, London: Routledge.

Pilling, G. (1980) *Marx's Capital: Philosophy and Political Economy*, London: Routledge & Kegan Paul.

Rosdolsky, R. (1977) *The Making of Marx's 'Capital'*, London: Pluto Press.

Sraffa, P. (1926) 'The laws of returns under competitive conditions', *Economic Journal* 86: 535–50.

—— (1930) 'Reply to Robertson', *Economic Journal* 40: 89–93.

—— (1951) 'Introduction' to *The Works and Correspondence of David Ricardo*: vol. 1, *On the Principles of Political Economics and Taxation*, ed. P. Sraffa, Cambridge: Cambridge University Press.

—— (1960) *Production of Commodities by Means of Commodities*, Cambridge: Cambridge University Press.

—— (1961) 'The discussion of Professor Hicks' paper', in F. A. Lutz and D. C. Hague (eds) *The Theory of Capital*, IEA Proceedings, New York: St Martin's Press.

Steedman, I. (1977) *Marx after Sraffa*, London: New Left Books.

Walsh, V. and Gram, H. (1980) *Classical and Neoclassical Theories of General Equilibrium: Historical Origins and Mathematical Structure*, Oxford: Oxford University Press.

Wolff, R., Roberts, B. and Callari, A. (1982) 'Marx's (not Ricardo's) "Transformation problem": a radical reconceptualization', *History of Political Economy* 14(4): 564–82.

16

ISOLATING SOURCES OF STERILITY IN MARX'S THEORETICAL PARADIGMS

Paul A. Samuelson

INTRODUCTION

Keynes (1919, 1931, 1933) was both scathing and patronizing on Marx, the writer of 'an obsolete textbook which I know to be not only scientifically erroneous but without interest or application to the modern world' and the spawner of the 'turbid rubbish of the Red bookshops'. Joan Robinson (1942) came to think otherwise, not only offering an expository primer on Marx but also arguing (inconclusively in my close reading of her and Kalecki) that Marx led Michal Kalecki to an early and independent anticipation of Keynes's *General Theory*. (On my summing up, Kalecki by 1933 had arrived about where Kahn had been in 1931, but *no* mechanisms that he could have read in the several million words of Karl Marx paralleled or particularly resembled Kalecki's attained profit–income multiplier mechanisms.) Keynes humoured Joan's Marx book but conceded no merit in its object.

Keynes never explicated the grounds for his rejection. Nor is there evidence known to me that he ever devoted a month to study of Marx. Like Keynes, an American economist of my post-1931 generation was never assigned an *economic* text of Marx (beyond *The Communist Manifesto* and vol. 1 of *Capital*, and these in social science survey courses). No undergraduate or graduate courses were offered at Harvard and the University of Chicago – or I daresay at any of the Big Ten state universities – prior to 1940 when Paul Sweezy and Joseph Schumpeter gave occasional seminars at Harvard. Chance alone caused me to read John Strachey's *The Coming Struggle for Power* and *The Nature of the Capitalist Crisis* when they came out in the 1930s; and these amateurish exercises did not serve as a spectre haunting the pre-war college seminars. Of course, students were attracted in droves to left-wing groups by the Great Depression, but mostly these recruits belonged to departments of sociology, history and mathematics rather than vulgar economics. Also, as I have learned from reading scores of intellectuals' autobiographies, few who joined up with the red flag felt any compulsion to master the intricacies of C–M–C– ... and *Mehrwert*. Just as most natural philosophers had yet to cut the pages of their copies of Newton's *Principia*, being content to know that the truth was embalmed in its Latin, so it was enough for most radicals to know that the Master had proved in six solid volumes of scholarship the bankruptcy of the capitalist system and of mainline political economy. I must add that, later, when I came to sample viewpoints of Marxists on Marx, they tended to agree on two things: other Marxists did not have it quite right, but each of them did own the correct version.

George Bernard Shaw is a case in point. He was seen reading simultaneously in the British Museum the scores of Wagner and Marx's *Capital* (in its French edition – all that was available at that time to an educated Anglo-Saxon). Shaw claimed that Hyndman, the leader of British Marxians, had never read *Capital* and that he himself had a monopoly understanding. Alas, as Philip Wicksteed quickly demonstrated, Shaw's understanding was skin-deep and easily peeled off him in a conversion to Jevonism, which itself was not very thick.

Bertrand Russell, possessor of an independent income, did devote a visiting year to Germany to evaluate Marxism. His post-mortem was that Marx's critique lacked cogency. I looked up the book he published on the subject of social democracy, but could not convince myself that Russell was ever able to pass a 1955 MIT exam on the subject. What he did infer, and not incorrectly, was that there could not be found in Marx's text a cogent refutation of Mill–Marshall economics.

Schumpeter professed to admire Marx. As his longtime student and friend, I always wondered whether the verb 'professed' should be replaced by the word 'pretended'. On almost every point – and I would artfully confirm this by contriving innocent questions for him – Schumpeter came out with cause-and-effect conclusions 180 degrees different from Marx's. (Example: Marx believed technological change undermined full employment; Schumpeter thought such fears exaggerated. Schumpeter thought capitalism *economically* stable; its very *successes* (!) would undermine it sociologically.) When required to write the foreword to a book on Schumpeter and Marx, I (1970) had to conclude lamely that Schumpeter admired Marx for his chutzpah, his wish to create a dynamic theory of everything. With friends like that, Marx had no need for an enemy, which was what used to be said by orthodox Marxists about Joan Robinson and her 1942 primer on Marx. (During the McCarthy witch-hunt in the USA, Joan once said to me, 'I understand that in Washington you get into J. Edgar Hoover's bad files if you purchase a copy of my Marx primer. And after all it's a book *against* Marx's labour theory of value.')

It is well known that Böhm-Bawerk more than once published critiques of Marx. I have not been a great admirer of Böhm-Bawerk's kind of pedantry. But in this matter I have never thought he has been accorded simple justice. One, Böhm was critical toward *all* writers not of his name, and his captiousness is not so much ideological as logical and terminological. Moreover, his simple points cut deep and have never been refuted or even rebutted. He is boringly complete, but then completeness and boringness are part of his customary style when dealing with English dons, orthodox churchmen, radical Europeans, or mathematical economists like Irving Fisher. The Böhm–Hilferding boxing match I cannot score for Hilferding.

That leaves Ludwig von Bortkiewicz. Twice in 1907 he analysed the relationships of 'the rate of surplus value paradigm' to 'the rate of profit paradigm'. Bortkiewicz is widely interpreted to have in some sense vindicated something novel and valuable in Marx's alternative paradigm to mainstream economics. However, when you follow through in detail the exact steps of Bortkiewicz's mathematics, you discover that he is showing precisely how to extricate yourself from Marx's detour and get back to where mainstream economics always had been. He took his clue from the little-known 1898 pre-Sraffian analysis of Vladimir Dmitriev, an obscure Russian reader of Ricardo. Dmitriev was the first to solve the Quesnay riddle of input–output, and his solution is that of Leontief, von Neumann, Sraffa, Smith, Ricardo and Böhm-Bawerk.

To prove this, let Jack's labour produce the corn, which with Bill's labour produces the finished loaf of bread. In that case the 'exploitation' of workers' wages from the competitive presence of positive interest rates is crystal clear, and gains nothing from going to a *bad* approximation given by an idiosyncratic Marx labour theory of value. (When corn itself needs corn input as well as labour input, the Ricardo–Stigler '93 per cent labour theory of value' can easily become an *infinitely* bad approximation for the P_{bread}/P_{corn} and wages/profits ratios.)

I have not forgotten the 'transformation problem' *à la* Marx, Tugan-Baranowsky, Winternitz, Dobb, Meek and Seton. By all odds Francis Seton's 1957 version is the most comprehensive and conclusive, and Marx's *Mehrwert* paradigm receives no shred of defence from it.

The real Trojan horse in the Red bookshops has been Piero Sraffa's 1960 classic *Production of Commodities by Means of Commodities*. Ian Steedman's 1977 *Marx after Sraffa* tells that story. What would be deemed unacceptable by Marxians from Dmitriev or Debreu may sneak in from a non-admirer of J. B. Clark and Böhm-Bawerk.

After this extensive introduction I turn to my business of the day, to try to discern in detail how Karl Marx was thrown off an understanding of (a) the laws of motion of capitalism (and the mixed economy and the planned–bureaucratic state), (b) the laws of distribution of the social product between wages and property returns, (c) the trends in degree of income and wealth inequality (Gini–Pareto parameters), (d) the *ex ante* and *ex post* divergences and convergences of economic development by region, and (e) the avoidance of chronic mass unemployment.

If you sample Marx texts, say in Sweezy's 1942 classic or Robinson's contemporaneous introduction, and find the gleanings unrewarding, good scholarly procedure entitles you to follow Keynes's example and ignore the subject. However, around 1955 I volunteered mentally for the duty to investigate whether the subject was truly as lacking in merit as seemed thought to be the case. (Mark Twain: Wagner is not as bad as he sounds.) My curiosity was not so well rewarded as to make me want, for that reason, to stay the course; but the fact that some billions of humans then did claim to be followers of Marx's vision did carry weight with me – just as the rather eccentric Judeo–Christian–Islamic doctrines acquire importance when a billion folk think they do. I sensed no personal affect in either eschewing Marxian economics or studying it. But I would joke in seminars that those who had attained reputation as mainstream economists could only gain a second reputation if they could uncover new, certifiable merit in the Marxian paradigm. If!

In actual fact, colleagues and friends thought it strange of me to waste good tennis time on so irrelevant a subject. Indeed, when I first lectured at Yale on the transformation problem, the overflow crowd evaporated away at first whiff of matrix algebra; and the hardy remnant of economist dons and graduate students were suspicious that it was all a Samuelson put-on and hoax. No one understood my demonstration that Bortkiewicz's algorithm was literally a way to get rid of Marx's invariant $(p_j - c_j)/v_j$ paradigm and, after a fresh start, calculate the quadratic or nth-degree polynomial equations for capitalistic [price$_j$/wage] vector elements in function of the interest rate. When a Marxist 'transformed properly', it was literally a process of 'erase and start again' and not an insightful stepping-stone to complicated reality. Meek and Dobb went to their graves without having a clue to this damning logic; and if Morishima ever understood this fact about 1907 Bortkiewicz, I know not where he has said so.

Let me end this long introduction with the admission that at the end of the day I never could find analytical pearls in Marx to cast before orthodox economist swine. As will be made clear, *Capital*'s volume 2 tableaux of reproduction and balanced exponential growth represented Karl Marx's sole contribution to economic theory. See my 1974 contribution to the Lloyd Metzler Festschrift where I justify this. Still, here his formulation generically avoids error only when organic compositions of capital are all equal and when nothing new could possibly come from the *rate of surplus value (Mehrwert)* innovations.

In sum, at its heart Marx's paradigm was hopelessly flawed. For the rest of this chapter I sample the constructive task of identifying where and how Marx got thrown off understanding of why, and to what degree, wages fall short of the whole of aggregate income; of what trends tend to raise or lower profit shares; and why dynamic planning has need for the signalling of competitive market price and for the mechanism of self-interest incentives.

190

(In the famous debate over socialist planning by means of decentralized auctioneer planning – by Lerner and Lange against Mises and Hayek – it was Hayek who was the victor since necessary information will evaporate away in the absence of real-thing markets. More on this later.)

FALLACY NUMBER ONE IN (YOUNG) MARX

Before Karl Marx was a Marxian economist, both he and Friedrich Engels independently arrived at the uninformed view that mid-nineteenth-century Europe had attained to a stage of technological plenty sufficient to support comfortable living *for all the population* if only the evils of private property were abolished. Knowledge since then of economic history makes this faddish *Weltanschauung* of Rousseau, Godwin and Condorcet a ludicrously over-optimistic pipedream. Reasoned hopes for progress, yes; but attained technology sufficient for utopia, no. Such limited historical and statistical knowledge as could have been known to Karl and Friedrich at the time, if they looked for it, would not have rationally supported their unthinking self-confidence on the subject; and there is no evidence that they felt much need to test their empirical view.

This fallacy of 'plenty already here' is not unique to Marxians. It has long been widely held in many places. Among conservatives and reactionaries it can take the form: 'If only Milton Friedman's stipulations are followed, potential plenty will become actual plenty.' Psychologists say that the simplest fallacies tend to be the most persistent ones. Certainly this general one has persisted. In part, but only in part, it helps account for Marx's deliberate neglect of how his future utopias were to operate economically. (Lay people divide into those who exaggerate potential plenty and those who exaggerate inevitable exhaustion of non-renewable resources.)

FALLACY TWO: NEGLECTING OF NEED FOR LAND AND NATURAL RESOURCES

Labour to get all of product is a possible ethics and a natural wish. But that implies nothing valid about the cause-and-effect productivity of non-human inputs. Unlike their classical contemporaries, Marx and Engels were scathingly critical of the Malthusian algorithm. Capitalist apologists are not wrong to recognize the fact of the essential productivity of land input when it works with labour input – particularly in pre-twentieth-century times; though Marx, who if anything exaggerated the 'scientific' quality of Quesnay, oddly himself downplays the Physiocratic truth about land's peculiar *non*-sterility. The Irish question without land scarcity is Hamlet without the gloomy Dane; real North American GDP per capita superiority in 1880 to European, when abstracting from the copious geological endowment of the former, makes for shallow economic history.

And the fallacy is so unnecessary. The productivity of inputs privately owned by non-workers can be admitted without agreeing that their status quo owners have legitimate ownership and a legitimate claim to their competitive returns. Furthermore, even if workers were all endowed exactly alike and shared equally in the fruits of natural resources, land's important scarcity emasculates vitally the labour theory of value as applied to the relative prices of corn and cloth and mousetraps. It is no wonder that Marx (and even Ricardo!) never really understood this – inasmuch as the pens of Stigler, Sraffa, Hollander and Blaug have failed to spell out the needed understanding.

'But didn't Marx write extensively and authoritatively on land rent?' I will be asked. Yes, he did devote some manuscripts and notebooks to rent. But his rent analysis is grossly defective, even for a pre-1870 writer (see Howard and King 1992; Samuelson 1992). And Marx's tableaux of $c_j + v_j + s_j = c_j + v_j$ (1 + rate of surplus value) do ignore any special role for land and fail to generate an insightful theory of how labour gets 'exploited' and how the swag gets divided between landowners and tool owners.

The greatest fortunes in the past three centuries completely elude the paradigm that Marx thought was his most insightful one. The paradigm cannot touch the question: why is Japan in the OECD more egalitarian than France is?

Between the Napoleonic and First World Wars, world population doubled whereas European population quadrupled. Carlyle's dismal science of mainstream economics broadly explains these basics that escape the Marxian novelties.

The future problems of non-renewable resources and environmental deterioration fit smoothly into Walras–Fisher economics. Von Thünen's pages of 1850, which contrast starkly with those of the Marxian school, can also accommodate well to these issues.

So far I have been talking about Marxian economics as bad *positivistic* economics on these matters. It is equally damning as bad *normative* economics on issues such as planned parenthood and other policies relevant to people/land densities. (Mao's Malthusian China was in contrast here to, say, the Indian Communist Party line on absence of birth control as a factor in Indian poverty. But Mao did not use, or have need to use, *Das Kapital* as a bible in this regard.)

Marx and Engels were enthusiastic admirers of Charles Darwin, who never learned of their movement or doctrines. They liked his emphasis on change, but the Malthus they vilified was the writer who led both Darwin and Alfred Wallace independently to their conception of evolution by natural selection. Darwin would have been scathing on the sentimental notion that there would be plenty for all if only man's market etiquettes were not so vile, and even more scathing on the notion that lush living would last for ever after the withering away of the state. Neither Darwin nor neo-Darwinians like R. A.

Fisher (1930), however, predicted the successful potential of volitional preventive checks to population in a modern educated society.

FALLACY THREE: THE STERILITY OF DEAD LABOUR EMBALMED AS 'CAPITAL'

At first the young Marx rejected labour cost as the determiner of price. Later, after grappling with Ricardo's texts, he decided that relative prices could to an approximation be equated to relative (dated, marked-up!) labour costs. Although an early admirer of Quesnay's Physiocracy, with its *tableau économique* based upon land alone as non-sterile, Marx mostly ignored land scarcity as an important (and proper) value-added formulation in which price equals wage + rent + interest-profit, where the depreciation of the capital used up today includes in it the direct wage and land costs at earlier stages of production.

We can ignore land complications too if we concentrate on scenarios where land is redundant and free in newly settled continents. Suppose you start with a dogma (which, by definition, is a proposition not to be questioned): the only legitimate income is that earned by the sweat of the brow, the craft of the human hand, or the wit of the brain of *Homo sapiens*. What does the impersonal competitive market mechanism know of, or care for, such abstract ethical principles? Dr Pangloss and Adam Smith's palaver about Invisible Hands are also immaterial to the brute facts of ruthless Darwinian competition involving cents and dollars.

How do produced inputs enter into the time-phased price structure when labour produces the corn that works with labour to produce finished consumable bread? Smith understood the general notion of value-added accounting. To Marx's credit, he worried about what today we call input–output systems and the infinite (matrix) progressions that converge to stationary-state *real* prices: (P_{corn}/wage, P_{bread}/wage). And, in the singular but possible case, where the competitive market-clearing rate of interest-profit is zero, labour will get its ethical 100 per cent at the same time that positive-priced produced corn is being reimbursed for that amount of it used up in producing the loaf of bread. (Aside: Böhm-Bawerk also understood this. That is why he never accepted the positive productivity of tools as, by itself, an adequate proof of the necessity of a positive rate of interest. Something extra was needed to explain why there could be, or has to be, a posited time mark-up charged against *all* inputs.)

Capitalistic owners of tools useful in working with labour will receive steady-state positive interest-profit if the supply of needed tools is not forthcoming repeatedly at a zero interest rate. Capitalists have something that workers do not have. From the Darwin–Walras viewpoint, the enemy of worker A is worker B or worker Z. The enemy of tool-owner α is tool-owner β or ω. Those are the brute realistic facts about power in a market where 1,000 workers face each other and 100 tool-owners. It will be a miracle of singularity if the ruling conditions of supply and demand work out to a net resultant where the steady-state interest rate is Schumpeter's 0.00 . . . .

All this is oh-so-elementary. Has it failed to reckon with the *possibility* of there being a single input–output set of techniques? No. Has it overlooked 'double reswitching?' No. Has it failed to notice Wicksell effects? No.

Marie Antoinette said of the poor: Let them eat cake. Karl–Piero–Paul can say of the worker desirous of receiving all of the steady-state product that his labour can produce with the use of tools that are priced with *no* time mark-up in them: Go off and somehow get the tools you need; or, if you like, produce them yourself and maintain their supply in the steady state, then you will be able to consume *all* with no exploitative mark-ups or time discounts; of course if you can't catch the rabbit, you can't make this prescribed stew.

Why are these banalities of any relevance? It is because you cannot understand the 1950–90 growth of the Soviet Union if you fail to recognize that its progress early in this period was importantly conditional on its extraordinary accumulating of produced inputs relative to labour-force growth; and the deductive truth that extrapolating into the latter part of the period what would be necessary to assure comparable exponential growth will make implausible the prediction that Soviet growth rates would be maintainable. See Bergson (1973) and Weitzman (1970) for *ex ante* analysis of what was confirmed *ex post*.

Be resigned then to the sterility of the Marxian paradigm to interpret trends under communism. What about understanding the 1960–90 growth trends in, say, Singapore, Hong Kong, Haiti or the USA? Modern savants, rightly, study the statistics of the Singapore labour force, capital formation, raw material imports, and so forth. When they note an apparent difference between Hong Kong and Singapore, in which the former seems more impelled forward by technological change and the latter by increased produced-goods input, this suggests much that could be of interest in hypothesizing future trends.

CONCLUDING REFLECTIONS

It is ever difficult to try to separate ethical wishes of desiderata from positive descriptions and proposed models for explaining and understanding. But at the end of the day ethical goals are ill-served by mere wishful thinking. The facts do not tell their own true and unique story. They get perceived; and some perceptions tolerate deviations from reality more stubbornly than others.

Karl Marx had a high IQ and energetically studied writings of his predecessors and contemporaries. He began with great self-confidence, and amazingly his belief in the correctness of his novelties of analysis never weakened. (I have pondered over what alternative patterns of economic history might have altered the time profile of his beliefs, but with little in the way of conclusions.)

If Marx learned about problems of defining a Newtonian derivative in calculus, he left us manuscripts on the subject. Some of these are in some circles admired; when I present his words anonymously to a world-class mathematician and ask for a comparison of them with Bishop Berkeley's similar scribblings, he chills with faint praise. When Marx chanced upon works in commercial arithmetic – compound interest and all that – his preserved notebooks show him to have assayed better formulations: this failure to calibrate his own comparative advantages is illuminating. To avoid sterility and error a self-confident autodidact must be very lucky indeed.

John Morley observed: where it is a duty to worship the sun, the laws of heat will be ill-understood. He could as well have said, where it is a duty to abhor the sun, a correct thermodynamics will be delayed in coming. So it was with Karl Marx. He was not burdened with a belief in Adam Smith's Invisible Hand. But early on, Marx began with a prejudgement that market mechanisms were prejudicial to human welfare. Suspicion plays a useful role in nominating testings for analysis, empirical beliefs and doctrines. Yet when it hardens toward paranoia, suspicion shields the autodidact from recognizing and interpreting real-world trends.

Paul Baran, who was a leading Marxist writer at mid-century, can examplify Morley's points. Once, on the occasion of a visit to California, I chanced to have drinks with Baran at the Stanford Faculty Club. A remark of his quite astonished me, even though I had known him pretty well at Harvard in the interval between his Berlin studies and his sojourn in Washington at the Office of Strategic Services. 'Paul,' said Paul, 'if I could believe that the market mechanism accomplished something useful, I would cease to be a Marxist.' Of course, one is not under oath on such occasion, but I was genuinely amazed at his cavalier rejection of *any* trace elements of truth in Smith's Invisible-Hand mumblings. Legitimate suspicions would have been understandable (around, I suppose, 1955) that market efficiency must often be bought at the expense of intensified inequality of wealth, income and opportunity. But that anyone trained at Berlin and Harvard Universities, and with Baran's demonstrated IQ, could at that date be unaware of the improvements in welfare economics over Smith's apologetics – by Pareto, Barone, Pigou, Lerner, Bergson, Meade, Hicks, Little, and other welfare economists – did definitely surprise me. I could see that, at the moment, he believed in what he was saying.

Marx and Engels themselves, in the *Manifesto* and elsewhere, penned some eloquent lines on what the bourgeois era had been able to accomplish by way of aggregate material advance. But its market trappings, like the moulds employed in helping cement to set during construction, could apparently be shed by the mid-nineteenth century. The ripe technology of capitalism could rather easily be plucked and permitted to somehow run itself in the people's paradise to come. Lenin, too, in hiding between the 1917

February and October Revolutions, enunciated in Petrograd this same comfortable belief.

In the Age After Gorbachev we have to remind our grandchildren that even the clear-sighted Joan Robinson – perhaps fortified by reading the 1920–40 debates between Lerner–Lange and Mises – held a similar view: whatever the process by which capitalism had accumulated copious and varied plants, tools and inventories, after a successful people's revolution those stocks could be maintained while their total of returns were transferred once and for all from undeserving tycoons and *rentiers* to the people in fair shares. Her future utopia was the kibbutz writ large, and maybe this time without distorting Pigouvian externalities, imperfections of competition, and periodic fluctuations in effective demand.

This is not an ignoble vision. Nor is it a paradigm defective in inner logic. Alas, there is no simple study of experience that can clearly rebut or confirm it. (And I, who have limited patience with strong prescriptive models, will add by way of digression: the alternative model of a 100 per cent *laissez-faire* market-mechanism utopia in no scientific way dominates over it.)

In conclusion, a deeper study would do research into Marx's not necessarily earned self-confidence. And into his penchant for rhetorical paradoxes. (Instead of money buying goods, goods buy money: clever, maybe, but where does that leave you in the study of price-level inflation or possible underconsumption?)

The curse of the poor is their poverty. The curse of the lone-wolf heretic is his isolation. Ricardo had his Malthus to discuss with; and James Mill, and Colonel Torrens, and .... Marx had no semi-equal to give him acceptable criticism and nominate for him new tacks. You may ask yourself, why didn't Karl seriously study J. S. Mill on rent and thereby avoid gross error? Yes, why? Alas, the Marx that might have been is not the Marx, the only Marx, who actually was.

BIBLIOGRAPHY

Baran, P. (1957) *The Political Economy of Growth*, 2nd edition, New York: Monthly Review Press.
——— (with P. Sweezy) (1966) *Monopoly Capital: An Essay on the American Economic and Social Order*, New York: Monthly Review Press.
——— (1970) *The Longer View: Essays toward a Critique of Political Economy*, New York: Monthly Review Press.
Bergson, A. (1973) 'Soviet economic perspectives: toward a new growth model', in *Problems of Communism*, March–April, pp. 1–9.
Böhm-Bawerk, E. von (1896) *Karl Marx and the Close of His System*, Berlin: Haering. Translated into English (1898), London: Fisher Unwin.
Bortkiewicz, L. von (1907) 'On the correction of Marx's fundamental theoretical construction in the third volume of *Capital*', *Jahrbuch Nationalökonomie Statistik* 34: 370–85. Translated into English as an appendix by E. von Böhm-Bawerk to *Karl Marx and the Close of His System* and Rudolf Hilferding (1949), *Böhm-*

Bawerk's Criticism of Marx, ed. P. Sweezy, New York: August M. Kelley.

—— (1907) 'Value and price in the Marxian system', *Archiv für Sozialwissenschaft und Sozialpolitik* 25: 445–88. Reprinted (1952) in English in *International Economic Papers* 2: 5–60.

Darwin, C. (1859) *On the Origin of Species by Means of Natural Selection, or the Preservation of Favoured Races in the Struggle for Life*, London: John Murray.

Dmitriev, V. (1898) *Ekonomicheskie ocherki*, Vyp, I, 'Teoriya tsênnosti D. Ricardo (opyt' tochnago analyza)' [Economic Essays, Issue I, 'The theory of value of D. Ricardo, an attempt at a rigorous analysis'], Moscow.

Fisher, I. (1930) *The Theory of Interest*, New York: Macmillan.

Fisher, R. A. (1930) *The Genetical Theory of Natural Selection*, Oxford: Oxford University Press.

Hilferding, R. (1904) *Böhm-Bawerk's Criticism of Marx*. Translated into English (1949) in Sweezy, P. (ed.) *Karl Marx and the Close of His System by Eugen von Böhm-Bawerk and Böhm-Bawerk's Criticism of Marx*, New York: Augustus Kelley.

Howard, M. C. and King, J. E. (1992) 'Marx, Jones, Rodbertus and the theory of absolute rent', *Journal of the History of Economic Thought* 14: 70–83.

Kahn, R. (1931) 'The relation of home investment to unemployment', *Economic Journal* 41: 173–98.

Kalecki, M. (1933) *Próba teorii koniunktury*, Warsaw: Instytut Badania Koniunktur Gospodarczych i Cen. Translated into English as 'Essay on business cycle theory', in *Selected Essays on the Dynamics of the Capitalist Economy, 1933–70*, Cambridge; Cambridge University Press, 1966.

Keynes, J. M. (1919) *The Economic Consequences of the Peace*. Reprinted in *The Collected Writings of John Maynard Keynes*, vol. 2, London: Macmillan for the Royal Economic Society, 1971.

—— (1931) *Essays in Persuasion*. Reprinted in *The Collected Writings of John Maynard Keynes*, vol. 9, London: Macmillan for the Royal Economic Society, 1972.

—— (1933) *Essays in Biography*, New York: Harcourt, Brace and Co.

Marx, K. (1867, 1885, 1894) *Capital*, 3 vols.

—— (1935) *Value, Price and Profit*, New York: International Publishers.

Marx, K. and Engels, F. (1848) *Manifest der Kommunistischen Partei*. Translated into English as *Manifesto of the Communist Party*, in Marx, K. (1973) *Marx: The Revolutions of 1848*, Harmondsworth: Penguin.

Quesnay, F. (1759) *Tableau économique*.

Robinson, J. (1942) *An Essay on Marxian Economics*, London: Macmillan.

Russell, B. (1896) *German Social Democracy*, London: Longmans, Green & Co.

Samuelson, P. A. (1957) 'Wages and interest: a modern dissertation of Marxian economic models', *American Economic Review* 47: 884–912. Reproduced as ch. 29 in Samuelson, P. A. (1966) *The Collected Scientific Papers of Paul A. Samuelson*, vol. 1, Cambridge, MA.: MIT Press.

—— (1970) Foreword to Balinky, A., *Marx's Economics: Origin and Development*, Lexington, MA: D. C. Heath.

—— (1971) 'Understanding the Marxian notion of exploitation: a summary of the so-called transformation problem between Marxian values and competitive prices', *Journal of Economic Literature* 9: 399–431. Reproduced as ch. 153 in Samuelson, P. A. (1972) *The Collected Scientific Papers of Paul A. Samuelson*, vol. 3, Cambridge, MA: MIT Press.

—— (1974) 'Marx as mathematical economist: steady-state and exponential growth equilibrium', in G. Horwich and P. A. Samuelson (eds) *Trade, Stability and*

Economics, New York: Academic Press. Reproduced as ch. 225 in Samuelson, P. A. (1977) *The Collected Scientific Papers of Paul A. Samuelson*, vol. 4, Cambridge, MA: MIT Press.

—— (1992) 'Marx on rent: a failure to transform correctly', *Journal of the History of Economic Thought* 14: 143–67.

Schumpeter, J. A. (1942) *Capitalism, Socialism and Democracy*, Oxford: Oxford University Press.

Seton, F. (1957) 'The "transformation problem"', *Review of Economic Studies* 24: 149–60.

Sraffa, P. (1960) *Production of Commodities by Means of Commodities: Prelude to a Critique of Economic Theory*, Cambridge: Cambridge University Press.

Steedman, I. (1977) *Marx after Sraffa*, London: NLB.

Strachey, J. (1932) *The Coming Struggle for Power*, London: Gollancz.

—— (1935) *The Nature of Capitalist Crisis*, London: Gollancz.

Sweezy, P. M. (1942) *The Theory of Capitalist Development: Principles of Marxian Political Economy*, New York: Oxford University Press.

Thünen, J. H. von (1850) *Der naturgemässe Arbeitslohn und dessen Verhältniss zum Zinsfuss und zur Landrente*, 1st section, Rostock: Leopold.

Tugan-Barranowsky, M. (1905) *Theoretische Grundlagen der Marxismus*, Leipzig: Duncker & Humblot.

Walras, L. (1926) *Éléments d'économie politique pure*. Paris: R. Picon & R. Durand-Auzias; Lausanne: F. Rouge.

Weitzman, M. (1970) 'Soviet postwar economic growth and capital–labor substitution', *American Economic Review* 60: 676–92.

Wicksteed, P. (1933) *The Common Sense of Political Economy, and Selected Papers and Reviews on Economic Theory*, vols 1 and 2, London: C. Routledge & Sons.

17

MR KEYNES AND THE
ANTI-NEOCLASSICS

Christopher Bliss

INTRODUCTION

My title, a turn on that of the famous paper by John Hicks (1937), is intended
partly seriously. It is true that my exercise is almost the opposite of that
undertaken by Hicks. He set out to show that the theories proposed by Keynes
and that advocated by his classical opponents could both be encompassed by
a common model in which the two views reflected different assumptions
concerning Hicks's IS and LM curves. It was an exercise in reconciliation. Yet
it proposed a peace in which, in effect, the Keynesian side of the argument
took away the spoils of victory. First, the structure of the encompassing model
is absolutely Keynesian, in the sense that it is constructed from components
all of which may be found in Keynes (1973). For that reason the classical view
is demoted to a limiting special case of Keynes.

I am not concerned here with Keynes and his opponents. I look instead at
the relationship between Keynes's ideas, concerning particularly capital and
investment, and those of some of his self-styled disciples in the Cambridge
of the period, roughly 1950–70. Joan Robinson was the leading exponent of
the views which I shall examine. I call this school the anti-neoclassicals. My
argument, however, does not lead in the direction of reconciliation and
encompassing. The view that the quantity of capital cannot be measured, for
which reason the marginal product of capital is not a usable concept,
particularly for determining the level of investment, comes directly from
Keynes. However in developing this view in the direction of an essentially
sterile debate concerning the possibility of aggregating capital in what too
often were frankly equilibrium situations, the anti-neoclassicals ill served
their master. I argue that Keynes's doubts about the marginal product of
capital were to do with a rejection of, any view that investment (unlike
employment) could be determined by a calculation. And the root reason for
that view was not aggregation, which hardly concerns the individual investor,
but what in modern terminology would be called missing markets and
imperfect information.

Although in one regard what I do differs in kind from what John Hicks did, my approach is similar in the following respect. I construct a model of a highly simplified and stylized character which nevertheless, I believe, captures some of the spirit of Keynes's discussion of investment. To underline the point that capital and its measurement are really tangential to the important issues, I use a model in which aggregate capital plays no role. Investment takes the form of devoting output to building specific capital inputs. Investment is irreversible in the sense that once incorporated in a form of capital the output cannot be recovered. The model is a period model in which capital starts to produce output only in the period after it is constructed. So there is waiting, the essential feature of capital according to the Austrian School. Even so, discounting as such is a relatively unimportant issue. It could be dispensed with entirely were it not needed to bound infinite sums above and ensure that maximization is meaningful. According to my argument, problems of unobserved states and price uncertainty are what really matter.

It is appropriate to write about these questions in a volume dedicated to Geoff Harcourt. He managed to participate in the fevered debates of the time without ever adopting either the rancour or the hypocrisy which sometimes characterized the style of the anti-neoclassical school. The hypocrisy involved especially the measurement of capital, for whatever they proclaimed, everyone did it.[1] Broad-minded – in the anti-neoclassical school, but not 100 per cent of it – Geoff always recognized that even neoclassicals can do interesting work.[2] So a chapter which uses neoclassical techniques to look at Keynes's non-neoclassical conclusions feels right for Geoff Harcourt.

Where Keynes is concerned, just as with any economist, hagiography is stultifying and counter-productive. In building a model with a strong flavour of Keynes, I am in no sense attempting to vindicate Keynes or to show that Keynes got everything right. On the contrary, I believe that Keynes should have submitted more of his intuitive ideas to formal analysis, and that had he done so he would have seen that some kind of imperfect competition is necessary to his account of unemployment, and particularly of investment. It is probable that Keynes's unwillingness to include imperfect competition in his theory owed more to academic tactics than to an ultimate perception of the truth. He may have feared that including imperfect competition would encourage people to dismiss his theory of unemployment as just a demonstration that one of the inefficiencies resulting from monopoly would be unemployment. However, a consequence of Keynes's fully competitive specification has always been that it is nearly impossible to understand why unemployment is not accompanied by continuously falling wages. Equally, Keynes's discussion of wage bargaining makes little sense unless wage bargainers are seen as large in the economy. (See Keynes 1973: ch. 2 and Bliss 1992.)

Also, very importantly, a critic of an imagined imperfect competition Keynes would have been completely wrong to claim that classical economics was familiar with all the implications of the conclusion that monopoly causes unemployment. The classical analysis of the time was partial equilibrium and for that reason innocent of the principle of effective demand and of the invalidity of Say's law.

KEYNES ON THE MARGINAL EFFICIENCY OF CAPITAL

In discussing Keynes's views on investment and capital I draw almost exclusively on *The General Theory* (Keynes 1973). This does not simply reflect limited reading. Keynes's thoughts on investment developed very radically between the *Treatise on Money* (Keynes 1971), his previous major theoretical work, and *The General Theory*. It is from the latter work that the ideas with which I am concerned are taken.

In discussing the marginal efficiency of capital in ch. 11 of *The General Theory*, Keynes (1973) advances an argument which was to have far-reaching consequences for the importance which his followers were to attach to the measurement of capital. He writes:

> There is, to begin with, the ambiguity whether we are concerned with the increment of physical product per unit of time due to the employment of one more physical unit of capital, or with the increment of value due to the employment of one more value unit of capital. The former involves difficulties as to definition of the physical unit of capital, which I believe to be both insoluble and unnecessary.
>
> (Keynes 1973: 138)

Keynes goes on to discuss two further issues. One is whether the marginal efficiency of capital is an absolute number or a ratio. The other is the truly important issue, which Keynes explains as the uncertainty of the relationship between immediate returns on an investment and the future returns. It is hard to read this section of ch. 11 without taking away the impression that Keynes regarded the three points as having almost equal weight. Surely that is not the case. The moment we disaggregate capital it is obvious that we have to work in terms of values. That is the same as saying that equilibrium prices will have to enter investment calculations.[3] Equally, because capital input and outputs will not be the same goods, values as relative prices again enter calculations. The productivity of capital is not a pure number.

In any case, the impression at the point in the text discussed above that Keynes regarded all three points as of equal weight is shortly corrected. He writes: 'The schedule of the marginal efficiency of capital is of fundamental importance because it is mainly through this factor (much more than through the rate of interest) that the expectation of the future influences the present' (1973: 145).

If Keynes had only articulated some dissatisfaction with the way equilibrium conditions for the demand for capital were stated, his contribution would have amounted to rather little. It is Keynes's third point, that expectations of the future influence the present, that really shakes the classical view of the world. Keynes seemed to feel that the apparent vagueness of the concept of expectations prohibited its submission to formal analysis. Of course it is hard to capture everything in any simple formalization. Yet analysis in my view is both feasible and productive. One idea in particular demands formalization. Investment is an uncoordinated process with positive externalities. The more other producers invest, at least in the production of complements, the more profitable will be the investment of any particular agent. In orthodox Keynesian economics the demand multiplier is a major reason for investment externality. My model will generate something like a multiplier. However, it is not quite the Keynesian multiplier, which, as we know it, depends on some kind of price rigidity.[4]

A MODEL WITH INVESTMENT COMPLEMENTARITY

The model is as simple as it is possible to be, consistent with getting across the basic ideas. There are N firms which may be thought of as specialist capital builders. Although they produce different types of capital, firms are in every other respect in symmetrical situations. In other words, only the individual capital product type differentiates one firm from another. Firms are family-owned enterprises so that investment and saving are the same thing. Where aggregate quantities are concerned, no meaning attaches to aggregate saving. Investment involves applying output to build capital goods. We abstract from labour completely to concentrate on the investment decision. Therefore capital goods are robots which automatically cooperate with each other to produce output. Because capital lasts for ever, investment implies a critical irreversibility. With regard to production technology, the model is much simpler than that of Bliss (1968). However, capital is disaggregated, which is important for the treatment of investment.

Many readers will be tempted to think already that it is absurd to discuss Keynes and investment in a model which in effect assumes Say's law to be satisfied, and also abstracts from employment, and therefore necessarily from unemployment. Such readers should be patient. In deconstructing Keynes's various ideas it may be useful, even necessary, to dissociate various elements of Keynes's package. For Keynes a crucial feature of investment is that in aggregate it is not automatically coordinated with aggregate saving. That point seems not to have much to do with the aggregation and measurement of capital. The present model places its emphasis on the fact that different investments are not automatically *coordinated with each other*. This will be seen to raise serious problems of calculating the return on investment, an issue which on my interpretation is central to Keynes's concerns. Thus the model

202

which follows, if not performing a Keynes opera, is singing some of his tunes.

The level of aggregate product at time t is given by

$$Y(t) = F[k^1(t), k^2(t), \ldots, k^N(t)] \qquad (17.1)$$

where $k^i(t)$ ($i = 1, \ldots, N$) is the amount of capital of type i (made by firm i) at t, and $F[\ldots]$ is a concave differentiable constant returns to scale production function with associated minimum unit cost function:

$$c[r^1(t), r^2(t), \ldots, r^N(t)] \qquad (17.2)$$

where $c[\ldots]$ is the minimum cost of producing one unit of product when the rentals for the various types of capital are $r^1(t), r^2(t), \ldots, r^N(t)$.

The technology for the production of capital takes the following simple form. To add Δ units to capacity of any type of capital requires that Δ units of output be applied to its construction. This output must come from the family's own consumption as there is no capital market for the finance of investment.

For all its simple foundations, the model has the potential for considerable complications. This is because to invest, an agent has to increase capacity and lower current consumption in the expectation that future income, and therefore future consumption, will be increased sufficiently to make the investment worthwhile. This intertemporal substitution of consumption is mediated through the rental of capitals, which, because agents are not atoms in the economy, are themselves affected by investment decisions.

TWO CONCEPTS OF EQUILIBRIUM

A development of the economy starting without loss of generality at time 1 is defined by two infinite vector sequences:

$$k(1), k(2), \ldots, k(t), \ldots \qquad (17.3)$$

and

$$r(1), r(2), \ldots, r(t), \ldots \qquad (17.4)$$

where $k(t)$ is the vector of capital levels for the N types of capital good at t, and $r(t)$ is the vector capital rentals at t.

Consider two different senses in which such a sequence might be called an *equilibrium*. The first corresponds to a perfect-foresight equilibrium in which large agents act as Cournot–Nash quantity setters when choosing capacity levels. The second is a Nash equilibrium of the Markov game in which agents play strategies which relate investment rates functionally to the current state of the economy.

203

1   For all i, and given the other components of the sequence (17.3), the
values $k^i(t)$ maximize:

$$\sum_{t=1}^{\infty} \delta^{t-1} U[c^i(t)] \tag{17.5}$$

subject to

$$r^i(t) \cdot k^i(t) - k^i(t+1) + k^i(t) \geq r^i(t) \tag{17.6}$$

and i and t; and

$$F[k^1(t), k^2(t), \ldots, k^N(t)] \cdot \left[\frac{\partial c[r^1(t), r^1(t), \ldots, r^N(t)]}{\partial r(t)} \right] = k(t)$$

$$\tag{17.7}$$

This is called a *quasi-Walrasian equilibrium*. The quasi refers to the fact
that this is not a competitive equilibrium.

2   For each i there is a function, the same for all t:

$$k^i(t+1) = S^i[k(t)] \tag{17.8}$$

such that, given the S functions of all other agents, no agent i can improve
the value of expression (17.5) by altering his or her own function. Notice
that in calculating the consequences of such an alteration, the agent
assumes the satisfaction of conditions (17.6) and (17.7) at all values of
t. And equation (17.8) has a unique solution in $r(t)$, given the k values,
because the $r(t)$ vector is the marginal product of various capitals and
$f[\ldots]$ is differentiable.[5] This type of equilibrium is called a *Markov
equilibrium*.[6]

The two definitions are not equivalent to each other. Consider an agent in
quasi-Walrasian equilibrium deciding whether to vary own-capital holding.
By definition he will decide not to, but it is the nature of the calculation
employed which concerns us here. In determining the effect of a variation, the
agent takes other agents' capital holdings as given and recomputes equilibrium prices. At a Markov equilibrium the agent can consider a variation in
own-capital holding at a particular time. This can be done only by varying the
strategy function. To calculate the consequences of such a variation the agent
takes other agents' strategy functions as given. Therefore for given strategy
functions other agents will vary their capital holdings when an agent varies
his own.

EXISTENCE OF EQUILIBRIUM

No proofs of existence are offered. That is simply because, without specializing the model, none can be demonstrated. To explain why in detail would take the argument into too technical territory. The basic point is that when optimizing, the agents are constrained by demand functions, in this case for the services of a particular type of capital. In such circumstances we may encounter non-convexities and discontinuities, which means that standard existence proofs cannot be applied.[7]

Problems at least as bad for proving existence apply in the case of equilibrium in the Markov game. Another possibility for the Markov equilibrium is that no pure strategy equilibrium exists but there does exist a mixed strategy equilibrium. Uniqueness is yet another matter again, and is not guaranteed even if equilibrium exists, and not even if the structure of the model is completely symmetrical between agents. These issues will be set aside for the time being, but not so that we lose sight of them. Indeed, it will be argued below that the fact that equilibrium on very reasonable definitions may not exist and may not be unique supports in an unexpected way Keynes's idea that investment decisions cannot be reduced to calculations.

The definition of Markov equilibrium does not explain how the game is played. Specifically, it does not detail how the agents decide whether a strategy $x^i(t + 1) = S^i[x(t)]$ is or is not optimal given the strategies of other players. Ideally there is no problem. Well-specified strategies establish a grand mapping from $x(t)$ to $x(t + 1)$, denoted

$$x(t + 1) = \sum [x(t)] \qquad (17.9)$$

Then, given all strategies, any agent can *solve the model*. And once the model can be solved, any case can be evaluated. That does not tell us what the agent does if the model cannot be solved, as would be the case if no Markov equilibrium exists. There will be more on that point below.

EQUILIBRIUM AND INFORMATION

The relation between the two concepts of equilibrium is best explained by focusing on information. The first definition is essentially Walrasian equilibrium, in the Arrow–Debreu form with all futures markets present, adapted to cope with large agents. The second is in game theoretic style with the strategies expressed in strongly separable form, as is in principle made possible by the separability of the utility functions. In each case it is detailed what an agent will do at a point in time given certain information. That information differs considerably in the two cases.

In the case of the quasi-Walrasian equilibrium, the agent needs to know present and all future capital rentals. In the case of the perfect Markov equilibrium, the agent needs to know the present level of all capital holdings and the strategy functions of all other players. In the latter case one could argue, following the game theorists, that in a common-knowledge game the player does not need to know others' strategies to play Nash. Rather, a Nash equilibrium is the natural outcome for players to expect if they understand the game. This line of argument hardly shrinks the information demanded of the agent. Common knowledge means knowing everything about other players barring their strategies – so much, in fact, that strategies can be calculated. The calculation of equilibrium strategies requires that the consequences of strategies be known, which in turn demands forward solution of the difference equation implied by any particular strategies. Therefore these equilibrium concepts require that agents be informed about the world in which they act to a truly incredible extent.

The implication of these inflated demands for information for investment theory will be considered again below.

UNDER-INVESTMENT AND THE 'MULTIPLIER'

A major question which is thrown up by the theory of investment as expressed in the model is whether it can explain low-confidence or pessimistic situations in which, to put it simply, 'it makes no sense to invest because investment generally is low'. To express it another way, can we model low-investment equilibrium traps? The answer is surprisingly simple. Yes, if equilibrium according to either definition is non-unique. No, if equilibrium is unique. Naturally, in either case the existence of equilibrium is assumed.

This answer is circular, of course, as someone who believes in a low-level equilibrium trap surely believes in a multiplicity of equilibria. More illuminating is to consider that cross-effects from investment levels imply interdependence, but that this does not entail that low investment will fully justify similarly low investment levels. In the production function, imagine all capital holdings in one period of time to be lowered relative to equilibrium values by a certain percentage. By constant returns to scale, capital service prices are unaffected. However, the incentive to invest is lowered for each agent, because other capital inputs are low. This is the investment complementarity effect. Yet to note the existence of this effect is not to suppose that low capital holdings completely justify themselves to the extent that an x per cent lowering of all capital holdings will make every agent wish to hold x per cent less capital.

There is no necessity for a general reduction in capital holdings to disturb equilibrium conditions. Even so, when one takes into account that it is not possible to have a general reduction in capital holdings, because initial capital holdings are given and have to be respected, it will be seen that normally an investment-lowering multiplier effect is inconsistent with equilibrium. A word like 'normally' must seem dreadfully imprecise. However, its role is clear. It is certainly in principle possible that there will be multiple equilibria starting from the same initial conditions, and should one equilibrium show high investment relative to the other, one could describe the comparison between the equilibria using the language of multiplier effects. If our equilibria were strictly competitive we would know that each had to be Pareto optimal, which would rule out straightforward depression of economic activity bad for all. With imperfect competition not even that line of argument is available.

WHAT KEYNES REALLY SAID

In the introduction to *On Keynesian Economics and the Economics of Keynes* the author writes 'it is Keynes' *Gestalt*-conception of how a modern capitalist economy works, and not "what he really said," that we ultimately want to grasp' (Leijonhufvud 1968: 11). If this is conceded, it follows that it would be futile to conjure up Keynes's ghost to ask it which of the two ways of looking at investment discussed above comes closest to his own vision of the investment decision. Surely both are remote from the direction of Keynes's thought. All the agents considered so far are calculating, and calculating with what Keynes would surely have regarded as an absurdly large amount of information. Probably Keynes would recognize the quasi-Walrasian equilibrium as akin to the classical theory which he wished to overthrow, despite its evident non-competitive character. The present-based Markov game looks more Keynes-like. Yet the forward-looking common-knowledge Nash solutions would hardly appeal to a resurrected Keynes.

Keynes's concept of the investment decision is essentially non-algorithmic. The decision is subjective and depends upon non-analysable psychological urges (animal spirits). Of course the account of the issue provided in *The General Theory* is strongly tied up with the principle of effective demand, and particularly with uncertainty concerning future levels of effective demand. This is a different view from that entailed by the model of investment complementarity considered above, which was a model of perfect price flexibility. Obviously the quantity rationing constraints of the standard Keynesian model cannot be reproduced in a perfect price flexibility model. Setting the two types of model beside each other points up the contrast between two multipliers. There is Keynes's multiplier, which represents expenditure-driven relaxations of quantity constraints, leading to further expenditure-driven relaxations of quantity constraints, in a diminishing series. This is in contrast to what might be called the real multiplier, which means that high activity by agents in the economy calls forth high activity from all agents. When the agents are non-atomistic, as in the present treatment, what high activity does is to shift demand curves to the right, hence providing the incentive for high activity.

That brings the argument full circle; for a demand-curve is very similar to quantity constraint. True, there is no absolute quantity restriction. There is, however, a curve along which an agent can increase quantity sold only by taking a lower price. When the curve shifts, the effect is the same as if a quantity constraint had been relaxed. The conclusion is the familiar one that general-equilibrium imperfect-competition models behave in a Keynesian manner, even when, as non-monetary price-flexible constructs, they cannot strictly be considered Keynesian at all.

Our analysis of equilibrium shows agents with a great deal of knowledge of the model calculating outcomes and deciding on capital holdings accordingly. An implied question is: what do agents do if they lack all that information, or if, having it, they cannot compute equilibrium outcomes because no equilibrium exists? Naturally it is hard to say. The only secure presumption is that the agents will act, for even inaction is an act. Like stage players who have forgotten their lines they will ad lib, hoping for a prompt. This is the field of individual psychology, where instinct and intuition rule; or animal spirits, as one might put it.

DIXIT–PINDYCK POSTPONABILITY

In several important papers and an influential book, Avinash Dixit and Robert Pindyck[8] examine the consequences of the fact that the timing of investment is very often at the discretion of the investor. In a full-information model, or one soluble by calculation based on available information, this point has no important consequences. The point carries weight when the world is uncertain. Then the investor does not face the classic dichotomy of neoclassical investment theory: to invest or not to invest? Rather, the choices are to invest or to wait. Plainly irreversibility plays an essential role in a theory of this type. The reason why the investor is reluctant to commit resources to capital, but prefers to await the arrival of more information, is that a mistaken investment decision cannot be undone except at considerable cost.

Dixit and Pindyck's uncertainty is standard stochastic process uncertainty in which the nature of the stochastic process is known to the investor. In that context nothing is lost by considering small agents. The large-agent model of the present chapter introduces epistemological uncertainty concerning the nature and validity of model solutions, and particularly how other agents will act. The result may be paralysis, a situation in which the agent, unable to find any rational way of choosing an action, fails to act at all. The ass of a famous tale starved in a similar manner, because reason could not tell it for which of several equidistant bales of straw it should set out. The ass is not noted for its high intelligence, which is why it figures in this moral tale. One has to be incredibly stupid to be ultra-rational.

With irreversible investment, waiting to see what happens is not a mad choice. It has much to recommend it. Even if the investment is absolutely the right thing to do, the most that can be lost as a consequence of a one-period postponement is next period's capital rental multiplied by the size of the investment. If the investment is right, that is serious money. However, the discounted losses consequent on an investment which locks the agent into holding too much capital for what may be many periods are potentially far larger.

The trouble with waiting to see what happens is that when everyone does it what happens is affected by the waiting of many. Then something like the real multiplier results. We have seen that a real multiplier is unlikely to be the outcome of an equilibrium. When, however, agents, for whatever reason, are unable to compute equilibrium values, a low-level disequilibrium trap is a real possibility.

CONCLUDING REMARKS

One way of reducing the quantity of information available to agents is to make model parameters random. When that has been done, agents have no choice but to optimize under uncertainty. More than that, they may experience difficulty in recovering true values for model parameters even *ex post*. Lucas (1972) showed what is essentially the same point long ago. Such is not the route mapped out by Keynes. His is not a theory of rational calculating agents fully acquainted with the model and the data-generating process for stochastic variables. The argument above has shown that when agents are large in the economy one can model a great lack of clarity concerning the returns to investment without making the model explicitly stochastic. Should the model be stochastic, things get that much more complicated. For instance, agents will need to know the degree of risk aversion of other agents.

Despite complications not unlike these, Keynes believed that lower interest rates encourage investment. One might say that he held that, given animal spirits, lower interest rates encourage investment. There has to be enough stability and computability there to allow this simple and rational effect to make itself felt through the noise and indefiniteness of the investor's beliefs and calculations. There is every reason to suppose that such simple and rational effects may make themselves felt. No doubt the causes which make a person attractive are hugely complicated, multifarious and subtle. Yet that large eyes, a well-proportioned face and a trim figure can only help is what common sense and experience teach.

Finally, I return to the aggregation of capital. That has been avoided and it has been argued that in disequilibrium situations it is not the basic issue. Yet for the investment complementarity model to work as described it is important that different capital inputs should complement each other. This means that an increase in one capital input should increase the marginal product of other capital inputs. That would not be the case were the production function (17.1) to take the following special form:

$$Y(t) = F[k^1(t) + k^2(t) + \ldots + k^N(t)] \qquad (17.10)$$

Then all investors are adding to essentially the same capital stock. The conditions for perfect capital aggregation are satisfied, and an increase in one capital input lowers the marginal product of other capital inputs. That said, there is an investment coordination problem even in this special case. What happens is that high investment by others discourages own investment.

NOTES

1   For a case of Joan Robinson doing it see Robinson (1956: ch. 13). No real justification is offered for the use of the real capital ratio. Later analysis showed that it is no better as a capital aggregate than any other value measure. Nicholas Kaldor, who profoundly shifted his position from the time when he argued against Frank Knight in favour of capital aggregation (see 'The theory of capital' in Kaldor (1960)), used aggregate capital in his growth models.

2   For Harcourt's leading treatment of the capital controversies see Harcourt (1969).

3   Geoff Harcourt, along with several Cambridge economists at the time, including myself, was fascinated by the 'double switching' examples which showed that investors in two distinct economies, differing only by their equilibrium prices, could each find the same real investment decisions to be optimal, whereas investors in an economy between the two, in terms of the value of the rate of interest, would not find the same real investment decisions to be profit maximizing. Aside from any other implications of these examples, they show clearly that the return on investment must be a value-defined concept.

4   Imperfect competition, however, may lead to price rigidity sufficient to give multiplier effects. See Hart (1982).

5   Note that the $k(t)$ values are unique given the $r(t)$ values. Suppose not. Then there exist k and k' such that $F_k[k] = F_k[k'] = r$. Multiplying through by k and k', we see that output minus cost is the same for both k values. In that case, by concavity, neither input is profit maximizing.

6   This is a Markov equilibrium because it is the case, or it is assumed to be the case, that only capacity levels reached at a certain time matter for agents' actions, and not the history which describes when and how those capacity levels were arrived at. On Markov games see Fudenberg and Tirole (1991: ch. 13).

7   The point is well known. To show it, consider a simple example. A producer can generate output costlessly. Given the outputs produced by other agents, she maximizes sales revenue. Owing to variable elasticity of demand, two separate points on the demand curve generate equal maximal revenue. Now let another agent slightly vary output. Then neither the two points nor anything close to them may give equal revenue. This type of possibility generates discontinuities in response functions. In the present application the problem concerns whether the utility maximizing level of a capital holding, taking account of revenue and the cost of accumulating capital, will be a continuous in others' capital holding. There is no natural way to guarantee this.

8   The papers are cited in the book itself; see Dixit and Pindyck (1994).

REFERENCES

Bliss, C. (1968) 'On putty-clay', *Review of Economic Studies* 35: 105–32.

—— (1992) 'Nominal wage setting and the theory of games', in P. Dasgupta, D. Gale, O. Hart and E. Maskin (eds) *Economic Analysis of Markets and Games*, Cambridge, MA: MIT Press.

Dixit, A. K. and Pindyck, R. (1994) *Investment under Uncertainty*, Princeton, NJ: Princeton University Press.

Fudenberg, D. and Tirole, J. (1991) *Game Theory*, Cambridge, MA: MIT Press.

Harcourt, G. C. (1969) 'Some Cambridge controversies in the theory of capital', *Journal of Economic Literature* 7: 369–405.

Hart, O. D. (1982) 'A model of imperfect competition with Keynesian features', *Quarterly Journal of Economics* 97(1): 109–38.

Hicks, J. R. (1937) 'Mr Keynes and the Classics', *Econometrica* 5: 147–59.

Kaldor, N. (1960) *Essays on Value and Distribution*, London: Duckworth.

Keynes, J. M. (1971) *A Treatise on Money*, vol. 6 of *The Collected Writings of John Maynard Keynes*, London: Macmillan for the Royal Economic Society.

—— (1973) *The General Theory of Employment, Interest and Money*, vol. 7 of *The Collected Writings of John Maynard Keynes*, London: Macmillan for the Royal Economic Society.

Leijonhufvud, A. (1968) *On Keynesian Economics and the Economics of Keynes*, London: Oxford University Press.

Lucas, R. E. (1972) 'Expectations and the neutrality of money', *Journal of Economic Theory* 4(2): 103–24.

Robinson, J. (1956) *The Accumulation of Capital*, London: Macmillan.

18

KEYNES'S USE OF THE TERM 'INVOLUNTARY UNEMPLOYMENT'

A historical perspective

Bernard Corry

INTRODUCTION

One of the characteristics of Geoff Harcourt's approach to economics and in particular his work on economic policy has been his empathy with those who suffer misfortunes at the hands of the economic machine. In what follows I am concerned with unemployment and I dedicate my contribution to him for his concern with those unfortunate enough to endure long spells of unemployment.

However much we may argue today about the meaningfulness and usefulness of the concept of involuntary unemployment, there can surely be little doubt that for Keynes and for the early appraisers and reviewers of his *General Theory* (Keynes 1972: vol. 7)[1] the concept was of key central importance, and any argument that it was unnecessary would have been dismissed out of hand as having missed the whole point of his revolutionary ideas. The explicandum in *The General Theory* was the actual volume of output produced in a capitalist economy. From a theory of output Keynes assumed that, at least in the short run, he could map into a theory of employment. He asserted that with one or two notable exceptions – Malthus and Hobson being particular examples – economists had tended to assume that actual output was determined by supply-side considerations: by such variables as the state of technology, the stock of capital and other factor constraints.

Superimposed upon this 'long-run' view was another branch of traditional theory that tried to account for fluctuations in output and employment around this supply-determined trend of output. So theories of the trade cycle were developed. This, then, was the basic agenda of macroeconomics before the arrival of Keynes's *General Theory*. It is sometimes argued that prior to this date (1936), unemployment was not on the economists' research agenda. This is patent nonsense, as any historian of economics will know.[2] There is a vast pre-Keynesian literature on all aspects of unemployment – some of which I shall review below. But, and it is a most important but, Keynes was out to present a new theory of the 'normal' level of output where the system could remain for a long time unless shocks – planned or otherwise – occurred to move it to a new equilibrium.[3]

Keynes argued that this 'normal' or 'equilibrium' level of output and employment was typically determined, given the supply-side variables, by aggregate demand conditions. Given the supply conditions – the existing level of money wages, the degree of competition in product markets, the structure of industry, etc. – the volume of output was stated to be determined by the effective demand for it. The resulting output was a stable[4] equilibrium one that was not easily alterable by supply-side changes, especially not by wage flexibility, but crucially this equilibrium output would not necessarily be at full employment; indeed, there were good reasons for believing that less than full employment would be as common as full employment.

These shortfalls of output below capacity were, in Keynes's theory, due to a lack of effective demand, and the extra unemployment associated with this output was equally due to aggregate demand failure. To distinguish this 'type' of unemployment from unemployment due to the structure of demand or supply-side factors, Keynes used the term 'involuntary unemployment'.

Now this choice of terminology may have been unfortunate for several reasons, some of which were becoming apparent at the time, others having surfaced subsequently. In the first place, the term was not new! It already had a certain meaning and symbolism in economists' jargon and also in popular discourse. Second, the term 'involuntary' only too easily invited linguistic interrogation and scholastic debates about the distinction between involuntary and voluntary unemployment. Third, Keynes's economic analysis of the labour market contains a now familiar ambiguity that can fairly easily lead to the interpretation that this involuntary unemployment is really voluntary, or indeed, to the other extreme, that all 'genuine' unemployment is involuntary![5]

THE ORIGINS OF THE TERM 'INVOLUNTARY UNEMPLOYMENT'

The term 'involuntary unemployment' does not seem to have come into common usage by economists until the twentieth century. Indeed, the terms 'unemployed' and 'unemployment' themselves were only beginning to make their appearance towards the middle of the nineteenth century. Thomas Attwood, famed for his involvement in the Birmingham currency school, did define full employment as early as 1832 (Corry 1962: 86), but much of the early discussion of the topic was in terms of the under-utilization of capital – 'factories lying idle' – and the distress involved was related from a

213

capitalist's viewpoint rather than directly focused on the unemployment of labour.[6]

Until the 1880s the major social policy concern of economists, certainly in the UK and USA, was with the problem of poverty. The economic miracle of growth that had brought such prosperity to the Victorian business and professional classes had trickled through to skilled workers but had left vast reservoirs of poverty. Initially this poverty was not seen to be directly connected with unemployment. There may originally have been good grounds for this view: many in work were below measured poverty lines and many not in the labour force were in the same situation.[7]

Explanations of unemployment tended to be in terms of what may be called a characteristics theory of unemployment – an approach incidentally that has resurfaced at regular intervals in the literature of unemployment, not least in current discussion. Characteristics theory lays emphasis on personal characteristics of the unemployed: their failure to develop a capitalistic work ethic, their ill-health, lack of appropriate skill training (or any at all), etc. Public concern was expressed at this state of affairs but any suggestions of public aid for the unemployed was dismissed with the view that it would inevitably worsen the situation. As Harris, in her comprehensive study of the late Victorian and Edwardian period, has put the matter;

> Public employment and public relief for the unemployed were therefore regarded as both dangerous and futile; and lack of employment was seen either as a voluntary condition which working men incurred wilfully, or as an inevitable occurrence which they should predict and provide for out of their earnings whilst in employment.
>
> (Harris 1972: 1–2)

But by the end of the 1880s, mainly because the clear evidence produced by surveys of poverty (the famous examples being those of Booth (1902) and Rowntree (1901)), unemployment analyses began to be disentangled from the general poverty issue, and indeed could be said to have taken over, or at least to be on a par with it, as the major social problem to be investigated by economic enquirers.[8] It is at this time that the terms 'unemployed' and 'unemployment' begin to be used more frequently, although we still have phrases such as 'want of employment' 'work-shortage', 'non-employment', 'involuntary idleness', and other euphemisms. Efforts were also made to measure unemployment, and this inevitably involved more careful thought being given to the exact meaning of the word. In the UK, until the introduction of unemployment insurance in 1908 the only available way of measuring the number of unemployed people was to take trade unions records of payments to unemployed members and try to generalize from these records to the whole working population. This procedure brought in severe estimation biases, as contemporary commentators were well aware. Hobson argued that one should try to estimate the numbers unemployed 'by the inclusion of all forms of involuntary leisure suffered by the working classes (1895: 419). Later in the same contribution, he actually uses the term 'involuntary unemployment' (ibid.: 420). He also points out that the figure so estimated will differ from those obtained from trade unions estimates.[9]

Sidney and Beatrice Webb in their *Prevention of Destitution*, following very much the analysis and recommendations of the *Minority Report of the Poor Law Commission*,[10] advocated as an anti-destitution policy, 'a national policy dealing with every aspect of the problem, which, if deliberately pursued and experimentally developed, will progressively operate so as more and more to prevent the very occurrence of Involuntary Unemployment' (Webb and Webb 1911: 107). This unemployment involved the 'dismissal of thousands of workmen, from absolutely no fault or shortcoming of their own' (ibid.: III), and the Webbs note that these dismissals were due not to adverse personal characteristics, or 'choice', or changes in the structure of production, but to a general depression of trade 'which seem[s] to operate quite irrespective of seasonal fluctuations, industrial revolutions, or personal shortcomings' (ibid.). On the other hand, those workers who chose to be unemployed should receive no public support, indeed should be positively deterred. In the words of the Webbs again, 'it is essential, on grounds of economy, that there should be a searching out of all incipient cases and such a disciplinary supervision as will prevent persons from becoming destitute through neglected infancy, neglected childhood, preventable illness, and voluntary unemployment' (ibid.: 317).

There is clear evidence of the use of the term 'unemployment' in Cambridge economics before the First World War. Pigou uses the term freely: 'unemployment does not include all the idleness of wage-earners, but only that part of it which is, from their point of view and in the existing conditions at the time, involuntary' (1913: 14).[11] Those excluded from his definition are 'those who are idle, not from necessity, but from choice' (ibid.). In modern terminology, Pigou was defining involuntary unemployment as the difference – strictly measured in terms of hours of labour – between the supply and demand for labour at the current real wage. As he put the matter,

> the amount of unemployment ... which exists in any industry, is measured by the number of hours' work ... by which the employment of the persons 'attached to' or 'occupied in' that industry falls short of the number of hours' work that these persons would have been willing to provide at the current rate of wages under current conditions of employment.
>
> (ibid.: 16)

D. H. Robertson, whose thoughts on monetary economics were strongly intertwined with those of Keynes – at least until the *Treatise on Money* – also makes use of the concept of involuntary unemployment. This occurs in his *Study in Industrial Fluctuations*,[12] where we read:

For while an employer cannot easily compel a workman to work more than he wishes to, he can, through his control of the access to the instruments of production, effectually prevent him from working as much as he wishes to. It follows that the complaints of involuntary unemployment among the wage-earners need not make us doubt the correctness, as far as concerns the business classes, and therefore the course of industrial policy, of our diagnosis of the industrial malady.

(Robertson 1915 [1948]: 209)[13]

Again the Webbs, writing this time in 1929, state that 'Involuntary Unemployment is now a world-wide constant phenomenon in every industrial state' (Webb and Webb 1929: 634). And along the lines of their earlier use of the term, they mean by involuntary unemployment the inability immediately to find work.

We have shown so far that the term 'involuntary unemployment' was commonly used in the literature relating to unemployment prior to the 1930s. Although there is some ambiguity in the use of the term it generally relates to what would today count as the *Labour Force Survey* definition of unemployment: that is, those out of work who are actively seeking work at the current wage rate and are available immediately for work. That is what most people would think of as a reasonable definition of unemployment. This way of looking at involuntary unemployment is very common in current interpretations of Keynes's economics. But how in fact did Keynes use the term and how did he account for its existence? To these questions we now turn, for it is here that the great muddle begins.

KEYNES AND INVOLUNTARY UNEMPLOYMENT

From his earliest writings Keynes was concerned with what were later to be called macroeconomic issues, but there is not much before *The General Theory* that is explicitly focused on unemployment. His paper on fluctuations, given in 1913 to the Political Economy Club,[14] is mainly concerned with what he calls 'financial fluctuations' and barely refers to output or employment (Keynes vol. 13: 2–14). In *A Tract on Monetary Reform*, published in 1923 (Keynes vol. 4), Keynes is primarily trying to explain fluctuations in the general level of prices; the Wicksellian-type model that he uses to conduct his analysis puts the cause of most examples of macroeconomic instability at the door of price fluctuations: 'Unemployment, the precarious life of the worker, the disappointment of expectation, the sudden loss of saving, the excess windfalls to individuals, the speculator, the profiteer – all proceed, in large measure, from the instability of the standard of value' (Keynes vol. 4: V). There is little overt concern with the situation of the unemployed in periods of depression: 'the period of depression has exacted its penalty from the working classes more in the form of unemployment than by a lowering of real wages, and State assistance to the unemployed has greatly moderated even this penalty' (ibid.: 28).

In *A Treatise on Money*, published in 1930 (Keynes, vols 5 and 6), Keynes is still mainly concerned with the effects of changes in the general price level caused by divergences between saving and investment. A fall in the general price level creates a problem because labour costs do not fall in line with commodity prices, they only adjust with a time lag, and it is for this reason that we observe output and employment fluctuations in the face of price fluctuations. The analysis here is very 'classical', at least in the sense that it does imply that money wage stickiness is the factor that leads to output and employment fluctuations rather than just fluctuations in the general price level. Keynes writes:

> the entrepreneur, faced with prices falling faster than costs, had three alternatives open to him – to put up with his losses as best he could; to withdraw from his less profitable activities, thus reducing output and employment; to embark on a struggle with his employees to reduce their money earnings per unit of output – of which only the last was capable of restoring real equilibrium from the national point of view.
>
> (Keynes vol. 6: 163)

He further argues that long periods of unemployment are caused by the difficulty of lowering 'money-earnings per unit of the factors of production'; we often have to wait for 'increases in efficiency' to 'lower money-earnings per unit of output'. I make this point about the classical nature of Keynes's diagnosis of unemployment in the *Treatise* because I wish to bring out in starkest contrast his new approach in *The General Theory* and with it the key role of the 'Keynesian' concept of involuntary unemployment. It is not without interest that in the monumental *Encyclopaedia of the Social Sciences*, published in 1935, the long article on unemployment contributed by Karl Pibram does not mention Keynes nor reference him in the extensive bibliography.[15] But of course a lot was happening to Keynes's thinking between the *Treatise* and the publication of *The General Theory* in 1936. In terms of economic events, the beginning of the world recession began with the New York stock market crash of 24 October 1929, although the world implications were not immediately recognized.[16] At about the same time, the *Treatise* was sent to the printers.

Also at the same time – early November 1929 – Philip Snowden, Chancellor of the Exchequer in the Labour government, set up the Macmillan Committee to investigate the monetary and financial system of the UK.[17] Keynes was a member of the committee[18] and also gave evidence before it. Then in January 1930 the government set up the Economic Advisory Council of which Keynes was also a member,[19] and to that body was soon added a Committee of Economists which Keynes chaired.[20]

In his work for these bodies we have an ongoing record both of the changing analytical framework and the policy implications that this changing framework involved; what is clear is that Keynes displays increasing scepticism about the efficacy of a general reduction in money wages in lessening mass unemployment. His earlier arguments that a general reduction in wages would be difficult to engineer are beginning to be reinforced by the possibility that, even if the reduction were possible, it would not lessen unemployment. This position is strengthened once Keynes finally drops the analysis of the *Treatise* and works in terms of the model of *The General Theory*. To consider this point we have to take a stand on the essential break between the macroanalysis of the *Treatise* and other of Keynes's writings using that framework, and the analysis of *The General Theory*. Only then will the crucial importance of the concept of involuntary unemployment be apparent. As I shall seek to demonstrate, it is not a 'throwaway' concept or marginal to the main structure. It is, however, fraught with difficulties of interpretation, as commentators have long realized, but to jettison the concept, as many economists argue today that we should, is to miss the central point of *The General Theory*. We may have legitimate grounds, theoretical and empirical, for rejecting the economics of *The General Theory* – in part or *in toto* – but essential to any understanding of it is the concept of involuntary unemployment.

The main differences between the analysis of the *Treatise* and that of *The General Theory* are:[21]

1 the spelling out of a theory of effective demand;
2 the determination of equilibrium output (and hence equilibrium employment) where aggregate demand equalled aggregate supply;
3 the argument that the equilibrium so determined was stable; and
4 the argument that the equilibrium was not necessarily at full employment.

In summary, the central new feature of *The General Theory* is that, given supply conditions, equilibrium output is determined by effective demand, and this output is often at less than full employment output. So far, so good! But Keynes's problem was to translate this theory into orthodox classical labour market analysis so that the two systems of thought could be readily compared and contrasted. This is where the problem began. Perhaps Keynes should never have attempted such a translation. Now where does the concept of involuntary unemployment come in? If equilibrium output is below full employment output (another ambiguous concept!), then employment will be below full employment. The unemployment that this causes is involuntary unemployment. It is involuntary because it has not been caused by personal characteristics, or by trade union activity or government legislation, but by aggregate demand failure.

The new ideas in *The General Theory* did not, of course, appear overnight; Keynes went through a long period of modifying or, rather, throwing over the structure of the *Treatise*[22] to come up with his revolutionary ideas. The process by which he did this has been well documented in the literature, and here again I follow the interpretation pioneered by Patinkin, whose narration seems to fit best all the available facts. The actual term 'involuntary unemployment' makes its appearance in Keynes only late in the day – in rough drafts of *The General Theory* that date from 1932.[23] It was after he had discovered the theory of effective demand and worked out its implications for Say's law and the classical emphasis on voluntary unemployment.

APPORTIONING BLAME: INVOLUNTARY UNEMPLOYMENT IN *THE GENERAL THEORY*

The term first makes its appearance in ch. 2. We should recall here that after publication of *The General Theory* Keynes stated that this was the section of his book most in need of revision.[24] He discusses the classical postulate that *'the utility of the wage when a given volume of labour is employed is equal to the marginal disutility of that amount of labour* (Keynes vol. 7: 6; original emphasis). He notes the modifications necessary for imperfect competition in labour markets and remarks that this postulate is compatible with 'voluntary' unemployment:

> For a realistic interpretation of it legitimately allows for various inexactnesses of adjustment which stand in the way of continuous full employment: for example, unemployment due to a temporary want of balance between the relative quantities of specialised resources as result of miscalculation or intermittent demand; or to time lags consequent on unforeseen changes; or to the fact that the change-over from one employment to another cannot be effected without a certain delay, so that there will always exist in a non-static society a proportion of resources unemployed 'between jobs'.
>
> (ibid.)

But this is not the sum of voluntary unemployment! We read further that

> [in] addition ... the postulate is also compatible with 'voluntary' unemployment due to the refusal or inability of legislation or social practices or of a combination for collective bargaining or of a slow response to change or of mere human obstinacy, to accept a reward corresponding to the value of the product attributable to its marginal productivity.
>
> (ibid.)

Note that this is quite a list and takes us well beyond 'frictional' unemployment; it clearly is meant to include what we today would discuss under the headings of trade union monopoly models, insider–outsider models, efficient wage theory, etc. so what category is left for his new theory of unemployment? 'The classical postulates[25] do not admit of the possibility of the third category, which I shall define ... as "involuntary" unemployment' (Keynes vol. 7: 6). Notice at this stage that Keynes's earlier explanation of the persistence of unemployment after a shock had been that it was due to wage inflexibility or lags in the adjustment of money wages to a fall in prices, but he now classes it as part of voluntary unemployment – so that we do not now have the equating of involuntary unemployment with all those willing to work, seeking work, and unable to find it. This was the typical meaning given to the term by earlier writers – Cambridge and otherwise. The change in emphasis reflects Keynes's other major policy change from the *Treatise* to *The General Theory*. He no longer believes in the efficacy of wage reductions (even if politically possible) as a remedy for mass unemployment.

So how does Keynes define involuntary unemployment?[26] The ambiguities and misunderstandings that have plagued the interpretation of the concept begin with Keynes's famous and admittedly rather tortuous definition. It bears repeating in full because here is the origin of the post-*General Theory* part of the story.

> *Men are involuntarily unemployed if, in the event of a small rise in the price of wage-goods relatively to the money-wage, both the aggregate supply of labour willing to work for the current money-wage and the aggregate demand for it at that wage would be greater than the existing volume of employment.*
>
> (Keynes vol. 7: 15; emphasis in original)

He goes on to state that this definition, which I shall interpret shortly, is the 'same thing' as his other one, which looks at involuntary unemployment as full employment minus actual unemployment. Full employment is defined as 'a situation in which aggregate employment is inelastic in response to an increase in the effective demand for its output' (ibid.: 26). Let us return to that first definition. A standard interpretation of it is to translate the quoted passage into a neoclassical model of the labour market; it is usual to write:

$$Nd = f(W/P) \qquad f' < 0 \qquad\qquad (18.1)$$

$$Ns = g(W/P) \qquad g' > 0 \qquad\qquad (18.2)$$

$$Nd = Ns \qquad\qquad\qquad (18.3)$$

$$[W/P]^* = h(Nd - Ns) \qquad h' > 0 \qquad\qquad (18.4)$$

where Nd and Ns are the demand and supply of labour; W is the money wage rate; P is 'the' price level, assuming for simplicity that the same price is applicable to both demand and supply functions; $[W/P]^*$ is the rate of change of the real wage; and a prime following a symbol refers to the relevant derivative. Equation (18.1) is the demand for labour equation derived from standard cost-minimizing behaviour. Equation (18.2) is the labour supply equation; strictly speaking, it should be for hours (as should the demand function), but if we assume a fixed working week we may interpret it in terms of number of workers. Equation (18.3) is the market clearing equation and (18.4) is the market adjustment equation.

It would seem to follow from this framework, using the analytics of orthodox price theory, that if we are in a situation where $Ns > Nd$ or, in Keynes's words, a situation where 'the existing real equivalent of [the money] wage exceeds the marginal disutility of the existing employment' (Keynes vol. 7: 14), than either (a) we are in a temporary situation as wages fall to clear the market, or (b) wages are inflexible downwards and the disequilibrium will persist. Involuntary unemployment then becomes a symptom of wages being 'too high'.[27] But this interpretation is most emphatically not what Keynes intended. His many policy statements make that clear beyond doubt, but the ambiguity in interpretation has arisen because of Keynes's apparent acceptance of the first classical postulate, that, to repeat it, 'the wage is equal to the marginal product of labour' (Keynes vol. 7: 5). Commentators have interpreted this as a belief in the classical demand function for labour, with employment as a function of the real wage. Hence in order to show any difference at all between Keynes's vision of the labour market and that depicted in classical economic reasoning it has been assumed that the difference must lie in the treatment of labour supply. Keynes gave credence to this way of thinking by his 'acceptance' of the first postulate. What did Keynes have to say about labour demand in *The General Theory*? Well, in a very real sense that is what the whole of the book is about! But let us be more specific. The first thing to be clear about is that he did assume short-run falling marginal product to labour. From this it followed, in his simplified economy, that there was a negative relationship between employment and the real wage.[28] This is what Keynes meant by accepting the first postulate; as he elucidated his acceptance further, he stated:

> It means that, with a given organization, equipment and technique, real wages and the volume of output [and hence of employment] are uniquely correlated, so that, in general, an increase in employment can only occur to the accompaniment of a decline in the rate of real wages.
>
> (Keynes vol. 7: 17)

The key here is correlation, not, repeat *not*, a causation running from the real wage to employment. He continues his argument, 'Thus if employment increases, then, in the short period, the reward per unit of labour in terms of wage-goods must, in general, decline and profits increase' (ibid.). And again he reiterates, 'any means of increasing employment must lead at the same time to a diminution of the marginal product and hence of the rate of wages measured in terms of this product' (ibid.: 18). The causal sequence is absolutely clear: it is from employment to the real wage. The determinant of employment, given supply conditions, is given by effective demand:

The amount of labour which the entrepreneurs decide to employ[29] depends on the sum (*D*) of two quantities, namely *D*1, the amount which the community is expected to spend on consumption, and *D*2, the amount which it is expected to devote to new investment. *D* is what we have called ... effective demand.

(ibid.: 29)

CONCLUSION

I have shown that the term 'involuntary unemployment' was in use well before Keynes brought it to the fore. I have also presented my evidence for my earlier assertion that involuntary unemployment was part and parcel of Keynes's new effective demand theory of employment. He did produce it in a manner that could and did lead to a complete distortion of his intended meaning. Perhaps he should not have used the term; it had been used well before his contribution in a very different sense so perhaps there was bound to be confusion. Words used in economics are rarely ethically neutral and it may well be that Keynes used the term intentionally to take the blame for mass unemployment away from labour – organized or not – and to place it on the economic system itself.

There are some hopeful signs that this intention of Keynes has not entirely left the mind-set of today's economist!

NOTES

1 All references to Keynes's writings will be from the *Collected Writings of John Maynard Keynes*, published by Macmillan for the Royal Economic Society (Keynes 1971 onwards).
2 A useful reference here is provided by Garraty (1978).
3 The interpretation of the current UK unemployment situation from a Keynesian perspective is obvious!
4 Or, in the words of Robertson (1965: 440), 'a temporary underemployment quasi equilibrium'.
5 The ambiguity referred to is of course to be found in ch. 2 of *The General Theory*. Vast amounts have been written on this matter; for a reasonable account see Drobny (1988).
6 Ashton (1946) cites Bray (1847) [1957]) as the first nineteenth-century user of the term. There are in fact some isolated earlier usages much before this; see Anon. (1816); Anon. (1822); McCormac (1830); Anon. (1843).
7 There was also the problem of 'underemployment' – workers often on a restricted working week. This was a particular problem in the so-called casual trades where labour was hired on a daily basis, as for example was the case in dock work. Beveridge's early work, *Unemployment: A Problem of Industry* (1909), largely focused on this problem.
8 For example, in 1885 H. S. Foxwell wrote, 'it is my most rooted and settled conviction that, of all the many claims of labour, the most grave, the most

pressing, and the most just, is the claim ... for more regular employment' (quoted in Court 1965: 406).

9 He is not sure, however, whether the 'true' estimate will be greater or less than that derived from trade union data. A similar point was made later by Pigou (1913) and Beveridge (1909).

10 Beatrice Webb was a member of the Commission and a signatory, indeed main author, of the *Minority Report*. This *Minority Report* is also important in the history of the economic analysis of unemployment because it supported the idea – due to A. L. Bowley – that counter-cyclical public works should be used to offset the unemployment cycle.

11 That Pigou should have used the term is not without a certain irony because Keynes was later to castigate him for failing to deal with involuntary unemployment in his *Theory of Unemployment* (Pigou 1933).

12 This book began life as a Trinity College Fellowship dissertation submitted in 1913. It was initially unsuccessful (Keynes was one of the examiners!), but was successfully resubmitted in 1914.

13 In his study, Robertson cites an article by Charles Rist (Rist 1912); in this article, which is concerned with the correlation between unemployment, strikes and price movements, Rist states that 'le chômage volontaire est d'autant plus fort que le chômage involontaire est plus faible, et reciproquement' (Rist 1912: 756).

14 The paper was entitled 'How far are bankers responsible for the alternatives of crisis and depression?' It arose out of his thoughts on Robertson's Fellowship dissertation.

15 The article is dated 1934. Keynes is mentioned, though, along with Kahn, in the article on public works.

16 Not even by Keynes, who commented on the event on the following day in the columns of the *New York Evening Post* in a rather optimistic manner. (Keynes vol. 10: 3).

17 The actual terms of reference of the committee were; 'To inquire into banking, finance and credit, paying regard to the factors both internal and international which given their operation, and to make recommendations calculated to enable these agencies to promote the development of trade and commerce and the employment of labour.'

18 The other academic economist on the committee was T. E. Gregory.

19 On the work of the council see Howson and Winch (1977).

20 Robbins and Pigou were also members of the Committee and Kahn was one of the secretariat.

21 My interpretation here follows that of Don Patinkin (1976).

22 It is well known that Keynes was dissatisfied with the analytic core of the *Treatise* even before it was published. There is a clear contrast between the ideas implicit in *Can Lloyd George Do It?*, published in 1929 (Keynes vol. 10) and those of the *Treatise*.

23 See Keynes (vol. 13: 407). He was certainly using the phrase in his Cambridge lectures for the Michaelmas term of 1933 (Rymes 1989: 85).

24 Keynes wrote on the matter, 'In regard to his [i.e. Viner's] criticisms of my definition and treatment of involuntary unemployment, I am ready to agree that this part of my book is particularly open to criticism.' This is from a reply he wrote to some early reviews of *The General Theory*, it was published in the *Quarterly Journal of Economics* in February 1937 (Keynes vol. 14: 109 ff.).

25 In ch. 2, Keynes had listed two classical postulates. The first was one that 'the wage is equal to the marginal product of labour' (Keynes vol. 7: 5).

26 For an elaboration of this point see Corry (1986).

27 This is a very standard interpretation of 'Keynesian' economics in current macroeconomic textbooks. For example, Stevenson *et al.* write, 'the traditional approach, the so-called Keynesian "fixed wage" model, postulates downward rigidity in the money wage, and hence the failure of the labour market to clear. While this generates involuntary unemployment, no convincing rationale for wage stickiness and the consequent market failure was offered' (1988: 27–8). It is a fascinating story to trace the progress of this misinterpretation of Keynes after the Second World War. This is the subject of a further paper by the present author.

28 In a more complicated multisector economy, even with diminishing marginal product in each sector it is possible for 'average' marginal product to be constant or even rise as employment expands. It all depends on the changing structure of output.

29 His discussion here is of a pure capitalist economy.

REFERENCES

(Anon.) (By a member of the Dublin Society) (1816) *Suggestions submitted to the Consideration of the Nobility, Gentry and Magistrates of Ireland, anxious to support unemployed people, until work shall be provided for them.* Dublin: O'Neil.

(Anon.) (By a Retired Officer) (1822) *Emigration Recommended as a means of improving the Condition of the Unemployed and the Unproductively Employed.* Dublin: Courtney.

(Anon.) (1843) *The Unemployed, and the Proposed New Poor-Law: A letter from a Renfrewshire heritor, to the holders of real property in that county, and other manufacturing districts of Scotland.* Glasgow: J. Smith.

Ashton, T. S. (1946) 'The relation of economic history to economic theory', *Economica* 13: 81–96.

Beveridge, W. H. (1909) *Unemployment: A Problem of Industry*, London: Longman.

Booth, C. (1902–3) *Life and Labour of the People in London*, 17 vols, London: Macmillan.

Bray, J. F. (1848 [1957]) *A Voyage from Utopia*, ed. M. F. Lloyd-Pritchard, London: Lawrence & Wishart.

Corry, B. A. (1962) *Money, Saving and Investment in English Economics*, London: Macmillan.

——— (1986) 'Keynes's economics: a revolution on economic theory or in economic policy?', in R. D. C. Black (ed.) *Ideas in Economics*, London: Macmillan.

Court, W. H. B. (1965) *British Economic History, 1870–1914: Commentary and Documents*, Cambridge: Cambridge University Press.

Drobny, A. (1988) *Real Wages and Employment: Keynes, Monetarism and the Labour Market*, London: Routledge.

Garraty, J. A. (1978) *Unemployment in History: Economic Thought and Public Policy*, New York: Harper & Row.

Harris, J. (1972) *Unemployment and Politics: A Study in English Social Policy, 1886–1914*, Oxford: Claredon Press.

Hobson, J. A. (1895) 'The meaning and measurement of unemployment', *Contemporary Review* 67: 415–32.

Howson, S. and Winch, D. (1977) *The Economic Advisory Council 1930–1939*, Cambridge: Cambridge University Press.

Keynes, J. M. (1971–89) *The Collected Writings of John Maynard Keynes*, London: Macmillan for the Royal Economic Society. The writing of Keynes quoted in this paper are principally in the following volumes, originally published on the dates shown:

A Tract on Monetary Reform (1923) vol. 4.

Can Lloyd George Do It? (with Hubert Henderson) (1929) vol. 10.

A Treatise on Money (1930) vols 5 and 6.

The General Theory of Employment, Interest and Money (1936) vol. 7.

McCormac, H. (1830) *Plan for the Relief of the Unemployed Poor*, Belfast: Stuart & Gregg.

Patinkin, D. (1976) *Keynes' Monetary Thought*, Durham, NC: Duke University Press.

—— (1982) *Anticipations of the General Theory*, Oxford: Blackwell.

Patinkin, D. and Clark J. (eds) (1977) *Keynes, Cambridge and the General Theory*, London, Macmillan.

Pigou, A. C. (1913) *Unemployment*, Home University Library of Modern Knowledge, London: Williams & Norgate.

—— (1933) *The Theory of Unemployment*, London: Macmillan.

Pribram, K. (1935) 'Unemployment', in *Encyclopaedia of the Social Sciences*, ed. E. R. A. Seligman and A. Johnson, vol. 15, New York: Macmillan.

Rist, C. (1912) 'Relation entre les variations annuelles du chômage, des grèves et des prix', *Revue d'Économie Politique* 26: 748–58.

Robertson, D. H. (1915 [1948]) *A Study of Industrial Fluctuation*, Series of Reprints of Scarce Works on Political Economy 8, London: London School of Economics and Political Science.

—— (1963) *Lectures on Economic Principles*, London: Collins Fontana Library.

Rowntree, B. S. (1901) *Poverty: A Study of Town Life*, London: Macmillan.

Rymes, T. K. (ed.) (1989) *Keynes's Lectures 1932–35: Notes of a Representative Student*, London: Macmillan.

Stevenson, A. M. V. and Gregory, M. (1988) *Macroeconomic Theory and Stabilisation Policy*, Oxford: Philip Allan/Barnes & Noble Books.

Webb, S. and Webb, B. (1911) *The Prevention of Destitution*, London: Longman, Green & Co.

—— (1929) *English Poor Law History*: part 2, *The Last Hundred Years*, London: Longman, Green & Co.

19

THE GENERAL THEORY OF EMPLOYMENT, INTEREST AND MONEY AND PRICES

Omar F. Hamouda

Post-Keynesians have attempted in the past three decades to bring together various components from the works of Keynes, Sraffa and Kalecki, among others. One of the strongest proponents of such an approach was Joan Robinson. Elsewhere (Hamouda 1991) I have explained how on many occasions Joan Robinson stressed the idea of building on the theoretical components used by her most recent prominent predecessors. She was, however, also very sceptical that even the ensemble of all their ideas could offer a theoretical picture with applications to every situation. It has been argued by Hamouda and Harcourt (1988) that there is no unified post-Keynesian general theory acceptable to all, but rather a group of fragmented pieces that cannot be integrated into a coherent whole.

Post-Keynesians have thus spent a great deal of time discussing the interpretations and the similarities and differences of their three major forefathers, or trying to justify different components of each thinker or to piece the bits of the various theories together. However, except for a few contributions (for example, in the first generation, of Joan Robinson, Harrod, Kaldor and Shackle, and in the second generation of Pasinetti) very little, especially in the past two and half decades, has been done in terms of building up from the fundamentals in the unfinished work of the initiating three. (Of course, many have offered cosmetic changes here and there.) To illustrate, as much as Sraffa's theory of standard commodity was a major improvement over Ricardo's price theory, to this day the fundamentals of his addition are yet to be further improved. Except for the odd suggestion to segment off portions of Keynes's theory, Keynes's theory of value and Kalecki's theory of mark-up also remain virtually unaltered as to their fundamentals.

As an exercise for the purpose of this chapter, the case of Keynes's general theory will be considered. It has been often repeated, especially by economists of the dominant school, that the general theory is not as general as it sounds. Keynes himself went out of his way in the introduction to *The General Theory* to argue that his theory was general, and thereby to justify the title of the book. Indeed, if by 'general' is meant that the theory can explain situations of both full employment and unemployment, then Keynes's theory can indeed be seen as general; that is, one that encompasses what Keynes called the classical theory, which always assumed full employment. If, however, one were to understand 'general' in terms of a theory that can accommodate changes in both prices and quantities, one does not have to go far to realize that such a price theory is missing in Keynes. He himself explicitly said that *The General Theory*, or at least a great deal of it, assumed prices as constant. In this light, one might accept Hicks's interpretation that *The General Theory* is a general theory of output.

Keynes's neglecting to address prices as changeable from the outset of *The General Theory*, whether for convenience or not, can none the less be viewed as a major omission. It will be argued in this chapter that had Keynes supplemented part of his theory of prices from *A Treatise on Money* into the general theory, he would probably have produced a yet more general theory which would have included both short-term and long-term analyses (not to be confused with Keynes's mention of short-term and long-term expectations), which would have accommodated the situation of unemployment as a special case due to blockages in the economic process, and which would have incorporated into itself an explicit theory of the business cycle, instead of its being relegated to Chapter 22 of his *General Theory*. It is thus asked here why post-Keynesians have not picked up on this issue of the omission from Keynes's *General Theory* of his *Treatise*'s theory of value, why Keynes himself left his theory of value out of his general theory, and whether a theory of value can in fact be supplemented to Keynes's general theory without altering its character.

I

Why have post-Keynesians not picked up on the issue of the omission from Keynes's *General Theory* of his *Treatise*'s theory of value? In his *Treatise on Money*, Keynes provided an original sectorial price theory as well as an overall price theory to which he grafted the quantity theory of money. (More will be said about this below.) Given Keynes's adherence to the quantity theory of money in the *Treatise* and his expressed unhappiness with it in *The General Theory*, Keynes apparently distanced himself from the *Treatise*. Post-Keynesians consequently seem to have taken Keynes's introduction to his *General Theory* to the letter. Although Keynes overemphasized there his liberation from the *Treatise*, in point of fact in the introduction he meant only that in *The General Theory* he had freed himself from the quantity theory of money which haunted him for some time. Most post-Keynesians have none the less simply accepted Keynes's statement at the time as a rejection of the *Treatise* in its entirety and have therefore shown little interest in it, let alone in salvaging any part of it.

There are, however, a few recent theses and books dedicated to Keynes's transition from the *Treatise* to *The General Theory* in which the authors (Dimand 1986, 1988; Kahn 1984; Lerner 1974; Meltzer 1988; Moggridge 1973), as historians of thought, astutely explain the evolution of Keynes's ideas. For the most part, they do not concern themselves with the theoretical implications of Keynes's having abandoned, for example, the Fundamental Equations of the *Treatise*, nor do they posit counterfactual situations, such as what *The General Theory* might have become if the *Treatise*'s theory of value were to have been grafted on to it. They attempt instead an explanation of the difficulties Keynes experienced in articulating his concepts in his exchanges with his contemporaries, especially Robertson, Hawtrey and the members of the 'Circus'.

These recent works on Keynes's transition have been stimulated and made possible in substance by two sets of original documents. One set comprises the first half of the documents included in the publication in 1979 of vol. 29, *The General Theory and After*, a supplemental volume in *The Collected Writings of John Maynard Keynes*, which brought to light for the first time some notes and correspondence related to Keynes's lectures in the early 1930s leading to the writing of *The General Theory*. These documents contain a great deal of discussion about certain aspects of the *Treatise* as well as the embryo of what was to become *The General Theory*. The findings reproduced in vol. 29 created yet another interest: in the notes of Keynes's students' during the same period. Hence another stimulus to the discussion was the publication by Tom Rymes in 1989 of a composite set of students' notes from, among others, those of Lorie Tarshis, Robert Bryce and Marvin Fallgatter, each of whom attended Keynes's lectures in the early 1930s. All this new material will continue to give inspiration not only to the historians of thought who would like to explore in ever greater detail the how and the why of the evolution of Keynes's ideas, but, as the present exercise attempts to reveal, the texts may also be of interest to economic theorists who might use these past ideas as a springboard to enhance further theory.

II

Why did Keynes leave the *Treatise*'s theory of value (i.e. prices, in this context) out of his general theory? What is Keynes's theory of value, and is it any different from that of his predecessors? It has been known for a long time both that the quantity theory of money sets out to determine the price level overall, which is a macro relation, and that the determination of relative prices is found in the interaction of the forces of supply and demand on the micro scale, as Keynes reminded his reader in ch. 21 of *The General Theory*. Irving Fisher explained the relation of the two as follows:

The price level is not determined by individual prices, but ... on the contrary, any individual price presupposes a price level. We have seen that the complete and only explanation of the price level is to be sought in factors of the equation of exchange and whatever antecedent causes affect these factors. The terms 'supply' and 'demand', used in reference to particular prices, have no significance whatever in explaining a rise or fall of price *level*.

(Fisher 1911: 180)

In neoclassical economics, the relative prices of two goods in equilibrium are expressed as a ratio of either their corresponding marginal utilities or their marginal products. Outside equilibrium, very little can be said about relative prices. Although the elements of supply and demand are present in the short-term analysis of prices in the classical theory of value, its long-term prices of a commodity at least are determined by the cost of production which in turn can be reduced, theoretically and approximately, to an expression in terms of labour. Here too relative prices can be expressed as a ratio, however, of the direct and the indirect labour used to produce those commodities.

Keynes managed in the *Treatise* to develop a theory of sectorial prices (based upon Fundamental Equations), which in fact, on the one hand, allowed him to express the general overall price through averages (not marginal concepts), independently of the quantity theory of money, and, on the other hand, let him manage to construct sectorial prices, which can be seen in a sense as the result of a hybrid theory of partly neoclassical, partly classical inspiration. For example, in the *Treatise*, the sectorial price depends directly on the cost of production per unit of output and on the profit per unit of consumer goods produced. In his *General Theory*, on the other hand, Keynes changed his approach, saying that prices are governed partly by the 'marginal cost' and partly by the scale of output (1936: 292–307). Furthermore, as Lerner noticed shortly thereafter, 'the cost incurred in the production of any commodity constitutes the income out of which comes the demand for all the other commodities' (1939: 159). Therefore, whether in one form or the other, Keynes related prices in a particular way to cost, income and demand, with money wages, an important determinant of the overall price level.

Did Keynes think perhaps that his theory of value in *The General Theory* made his theory of prices of the *Treatise* redundant? It seems that he did not abandon his Fundamental Equations immediately upon completion of the *Treatise*. It has been reiterated (Dimand 1988: 24; Kahn 1984: 65, 68; Meltzer 1988: 63) that Keynes said, however, that they were built out of a truism and so felt therefore they did not have much to say. The recently edited Keynes correspondence and his students' notes reveal that well into the development towards *The General Theory* Keynes continued to retain the Fundamental Equations of the *Treatise* (e.g. Keynes 1979: 72). The host of reactions, criticisms and discussions about the various components of the Equations,

229

especially with regard to Keynes's use of *S* (savings) and *I* (investment), as well as his implied analysis at the secondary level, the impact of the various changes in certain variables in relation to others, must have brought him to postpone further discussion of prices. The discussion of prices does resurface in *The General Theory* but not before the very end, ch. 21, once all the essentials of the general theory have been established. In the interim, Keynes was placing exclusive emphasis on the quantities of his macro variables. None the less, his turning away from the *Treatise*'s Fundamental Equations was unlike the case of his leaving behind the quantity theory, for in the later case Keynes declared he was abandoning the quantity theory, while the Fundamental Equations he simply left in limbo.

III

In retrospect, could Keynes in fact have supplemented his theory of value in the *Treatise* to the general theory without changing its major contributions: a theory that can explain the situation in which an economy is stuck with less than full employment and a related apparatus of effective demand? Chapter 21 of *The General Theory* is devoted entirely to the theory of prices, where Keynes, as already mentioned, notes that price is determined by marginal cost and size of output. Unfortunately, in that chapter Keynes was much more concerned with the impact of the change in the quantity of money and effective demand on employment and prices than he was with elaborating price theory in line with the Fundamental Equations. Since in *The General Theory* Keynes was really concerned only with quantities and output, it is not surprising that he neglected the importance of price changes.

According to Keynes's students' lecture notes and other sources, the authors who have attempted to trace the transition of Keynes's ideas between the two works (e.g. Dimand, Kahn, Meltzer) have all argued that *The General Theory* evolved from the *Treatise*. Keynes in his early lectures started with the components of the Fundamental Equations. Since, as rightly stated by Dimand (1988), Keynes's concern was with moving from price adjustment to output adjustment, prices were left out of his discussion. Despite this fact, Keynes's abandonment of the Fundamental Equations seemed more like unfinished business set aside. Seen in retrospect, one can find in the *Treatise*, concerns with more than just price adjustment, as Hicks astutely noted:

> Keynes, I think, is contemplating a process of expansion (we had better not say monetary expansion, since that sounds as if the quantity of money must be involved, as he is anxious to insist it need not be) as taking place in three stages. In Stage One there is a rise in *flexible* prices (of capital goods or of consumer goods) without any change in output or in employment. In Stage Two comes the change in *real* activity (employment and output). In Stage Three comes the change in *real*

activity (employment and output). In Stage Three comes the rise in *rigid* prices (wages and so on). Of course, it is not maintained that every particular expansion will last long enough to work through to Stage Three; it may peter out before it gets there. . . .

The peculiarity of the treatment in the *Treatise* is the extreme concentration on what I have called Stage One. Stages Two and Three are there; they make their appearance, time and time again, in the verbal discussion. But it is Stage One alone that is closely analyzed; it is Stage One alone to which the Fundamental Equations essentially refer.

(Hicks 1977: 191–2; emphasis in original)

Indeed, not only was Hicks extremely perceptive, but Keynes himself was aware of the problem at the time of writing *The General Theory*. For example, in a reference to his *Treatise* in *The General Theory*, he remarked:

what now seems to me to be the outstanding fault of the theoretical parts of that work (namely, Books III and IV), [is] that I failed to deal thoroughly with the effects of *changes* in the level of output. My so-called 'fundamental equations' were an instantaneous picture taken on the assumption of a given output. They attempted to show how, assuming the given output, forces could develop which involved a profit-disequilibrium, and thus required change in the level of output. But the dynamic development, as distinct from the instantaneous picture, was left incomplete and extremely confused.

(Keynes 1936: vi–vii; emphasis in original)

It seems thus first of all that Keynes's passage reflects exactly the stages Hicks described in the quotation above and that Keynes himself was aware that in his theory he needed some kind of introduction of change in output to allow his process to go from Stage One to Stage Two, in Hicks's terminology. It was the lack of dynamism in Keynes's Fundamental Equations, to take into consideration the effect of changes in output, which made his theory deficient. That is to say, once one allows for a change in prices, some mechanism has to exist by which that change can have an impact on quantities; such a mechanism was missing from Keynes's theory. Therefore, should Keynes's theory of price and output be developed, some mechanism whereby the Fundamental Equations become dynamic would be required. One way of doing this would be to supplement the price equations with quantity equations, make the two sets interdependent and introduce some lag structure.

Another important element, relevant to the present discussion, which is related to the aforementioned dynamics and to *The General Theory* is the multiplier. According to Dimand,

At first, Kahn and other members of the 'Cambridge Circus' attempted to show that the multiplier was fully consistent with the theoretical framework of the *Treatise*. It soon became evident, however, that the multiplier process did not fit comfortably into the 'Fundamental Equations'.

(Dimand 1988: 87)

Indeed, according to the correspondence in the *Collected Works* vol. 29, there was a great deal of tedious discussion between Keynes on the one hand and the members of the Circus on the other about the impact of various changes in the components of the Fundamental Equations, and slowly the interest in continuing discussion either of the Equations or of their components simply faded away with a shift in focus. If Dimand's above claim about a perceived uncomfortable fit is correct, there was simply insufficient effort undertaken by the 'members of the "Cambridge Circus"' at the time to make the multiplier consistent with the Fundamental Equations. In a very simple way, by introducing the propensity to save out of income into the second Fundamental Equation, Hicks managed to construct 'a revised form of the Fundamental Equation' (1977: 197). Hicks berated Keynes for not giving this revised form of the Fundamental Equation explicitly, but insisted that it was in the *Treatise* to be inferred 'from the rhetorical passage about the Danaid Jar (p. 139) and from many other references'.

> The parallel between this multiplier and the famous multiplier of the general theory is very instructive. In the form I have just given to it it is like the 'Keynesian' multiplier of the *General Theory* in being the final stage of a process – for there can be no consumption out of profits until there are profits! It cries aloud to have a process analysis like that of the Kahn multiplier, applied to it.
>
> (Hicks 1977: 197)

Of course, Hicks was aware that his introduction of the multiplier into the Fundamental Equations was only a first step and that a more elaborated theory would be required before the full implications of such a process could be analysed.

For Keynesians in general, the introduction of the liquidity theory in Keynes's *General Theory* was pivotal. Although there is a perception that it is unique to *The General Theory*, however, those familiar with the *Treatise* would maintain that most of its ingredients can be found already in the *Treatise*. To understand that position and to get a sense of this connection, one has, first of all, to disregard the quantity theory and, secondly, to recognize, as Kahn did, that 'equation (2) [the Fundamental Equation of the overall price] represents a remarkable breakthrough. The price level of consumption-goods is equal to – Keynes actually wrote "determined" by – under normal conditions – money cost per unit of output' (1984: 70). It is interesting to see that some fifty years later Kahn came to realize that the Fundamental Equations were a breakthrough and that they did not need to be attached to the quantity theory of money. The quantity theory of money was to his mind actually redundant.

Indeed, in the *Treatise* the quantity theory was grafted unnecessarily on to the Fundamental Equations. Keynes's overall price is expressed entirely in terms of some macro-index of efficiency earnings and some aggregate level of profit which is derived from the difference between the value of new investment and savings (1930: 138). Now if one were to redefine investment as a function of the interest rate and savings as a function of income, and still bring in money through Keynes's liquidity theory as expressed in *The General Theory* $[M = M_1 + M_2 = L_1(Y) + L_2(r)]$ (Keynes 1936: 199), one could make Keynes's discussion of the liquidity theory and the spectrum of assets much richer and yet consistent with *The General Theory*. It seems thus that many of the ingredients necessary to rebuild (or at least to expand) the general theory on the basis of the Fundamental Equations without losing the main characteristics of the general theory can be found in the *Treatise*, including the important issues of confidence and the expectations of entrepreneurs.

In sum, it seems that Keynes felt the dynamics of the Fundamental Equations was not set right, and that too much emphasis had been placed on prices themselves, to the neglect of the impact of changes in prices on output. These deficiencies, as explained, can, however, be remedied. Hicks managed to introduce the multiplier into the Fundamental Equations. Kahn suggested that the Fundamental Equations themselves were breakthroughs and that they did not need to be related to the quantity theory of money. More importantly, the relation I to S, which is crucial to *The General Theory* is also essential to the *Treatise*. Also, in the *Treatise* there is much discussion about investment's dependence on profitability and expectations which is also the forerunner of the theory of expectations found in *The General Theory*. Given the characteristics of the Fundamental Equations, one can find embedded in them both a theory of distribution and a theory of fluctuation in relation to equilibrium. Such an amalgamated theory, which is very attractive to contemplate, is yet to be produced and put to the test.

One final note concerns the micro-aspect of the Fundamental Equations. If one were to redefine the sectorial prices of consumer goods and investment goods at a more disaggregated level and assume that these prices depend on the rate of efficiency earnings expressed in money wages and on the firm's rate of profit (these components would be expressed in money terms and calculated as averages), then one would avoid all the difficulties related to the measurement of physical labour and capital (as in Ricardo's theory) as well as those related to the concept of 'marginal' (as in the case of neoclassical economics). Such a theory of value would then constitute the microfoundation of the would-be newly expanded general theory. Of course, this avenue is yet to be contemplated.

IV

It has been argued in this chapter, as an exercise in counterfactuals, that if the Fundamental Equations and all the discussion related to aspects of the liquidity theory found in the *Treatise* were to be fused with the major ingredients of *The General Theory*, one would arrive at the much richer outcome of an enlarged, more encompassing theory. Furthermore, if prices were to be introduced at the outset, even with a special concentration on the case of less than full employment, however long such a situation would last, and if allowances for price fluctuations, no matter how small, were to be included, then the general theory would be general not only in Keynes's sense but also in a general sense.

REFERENCES

Dimand, R. W. (1986) 'The macroeconomics of the *Treatise on Money*', *Eastern Economic Journal* 12(4): 431–50.

—— (1988) *The Origins of the Keynesian Revolution*, Stanford, CA: Stanford University Press.

Fisher, I. (1911) *The Purchasing Power of Money*, New York: Macmillan.

Hamouda, O. F. (1991) 'Robinson's post-Keynesianism', in I. H. Rima (ed.) *The Joan Robinson Legacy*, New York: M. E. Sharpe.

—— (1993) *John R. Hicks: The Economist's Economist*, Oxford: Blackwell.

Hamouda, O. F. and Harcourt, G. C. (1988) 'Post Keynesianism: from criticism to coherence?', *Bulletin of Economic Research* 40(1): 1–33.

Hicks, J. (1977) *Economic Perspectives: Further Essays on Money and Growth*, Oxford: Clarendon.

Kahn, R. F. (1984) *The Making of Keynes' General Theory*, Cambridge: Cambridge University Press.

Keynes, J. M. (1930) *A Treatise on Money*, 2 vols, New York: Harcourt, Brace & Co.

—— (1936) *The General Theory of Employment, Interest and Money*, New York: Harcourt, Brace & Co.

—— (1979) *The General Theory and After*, in *The Collected Writings of John Maynard Keynes*, vol. 29, London: Macmillan for the Royal Economic Society.

Lerner, A. (1939) 'Saving and investment: definitions, assumptions, objectives', *Quarterly Journal of Economics*, 53: August.

—— (1974) 'From *The Treatise on Money* to *The General Theory*', *Journal of Economic Literature*, 12(1): 38–42.

Meltzer, A. H. (1988) *Keynes's Monetary Theory: A Different Interpretation*, Cambridge: Cambridge University Press.

Moggridge, D. E. (1973) 'From the *Treatise* to *The General Theory*: an exercise in chronology', *History of Political Economy* 5(1): Spring, 72–88.

Rymes, T. K. (ed.) (1989) *Keynes's Lectures, 1932–35: Notes of a Representative Student*, London: Macmilllan.

Seccareccia, M. S. (1983) 'A reconsideration of the underlying structuralist explanation of price movements in Keynes', *Treatise on Money*', *Eastern Economic Journal* 9(3): 272–83.

20

KEYNES AND FINANCIAL MARKET PROCESSES IN HISTORICAL CONTEXT

From the *Treatise* To *The General Theory*

Michael S. Lawlor

To me, Geoff Harcourt represents strength, humour and decency in a combination that seems sadly lacking in economics today. Geoff has the strength of his convictions, both politically and intellectually. He describes his politics as that of an old-fashioned Christian Socialist. His intellectual tastes run to the moral-philosophy style of doing economics that characterized Cambridge economics in its heyday: the Cambridge from Marshall to Keynes to Joan Robinson. As was the case with each of these figures, these political and economic convictions are intertwined in Geoff in an unashamedly open fashion. Not for him the timid public pronouncements of the modern 'positive' economist, couched in abstractions and qualified in such a way that any number of possible policy conclusions (or none) are left to be drawn. For a younger generation of economists with progressive political instincts, struggling in a seemingly ever more conservative professional and political climate, Geoff's example is a continuing source of strength and inspiration. But more important than this public persona to his many friends (of any stripe) is Geoff Harcourt's private abundance of personal charm, human warmth, good humour and common decency. Although many people have taken shots at his public pronouncements (and gotten back as much, I might add), all who have really come to know Geoff Harcourt personally cherish his companionship and friendship.

In what follows I offer a short essay in honour of the many contributions, both personal and professional, that Geoff Harcourt has made to the discipline of economics. Its Harcourtean dimensions flow from the intersection within it of three of Geoff's favourite themes: the importance of the historical context to an understanding of economic theory; the analysis of investment activity in a macroeconomic setting; and the fascinating contemporary relevance of the work of that amazing group of economists who made up Keynes's circle. More precisely, I am here following up a point first suggested by Geoff's

'Keynes's college bursar view of investment' (Harcourt 1983), where it was argued that the internal memoranda and reports by Keynes concerning investment advice to his college and business partners contained the germ of his more academic theory of investment. Prompted by this suggestion I have recently set out to document the development, over the whole course of his career, of this interplay between Keynes's other interest and activities – what Skidelsky (1992: ch. 1) calls the 'many lives of Keynes' – and his more formal economic analysis. I have previously argued (Lawlor 1994) for a widening of the search for sources relating to what has come to be considered the distinctively Keynesian views on speculation and asset market activity contained in *The General Theory of Employment, Interest and Money*. It was there shown that this financial outlook had many early antecedents in Keynes's education, in the prominent texts of the turn-of-the-century literature on financial markets with which he was familiar, in Marshall's unpublished (in his and Keynes's lifetimes) work on monetary analysis, in Keynes's own investigations in the philosophy of probability and in his growing experience as an investor and speculator.

This chapter starts where my paper (Lawlor 1994) left off, in 1923, and traces the evolution of Keynes's analysis of financial markets through to *The General Theory*. Again I wish to follow the simultaneous development of his experience as a speculator and as a theorist of speculation. In large part this leads to a comparison of the texts and contexts of the *Treatise on Money* and *The General Theory*.

KEYNES, 1924–30: SPECULATION, THE CREDIT CYCLE AND *A TREATISE ON MONEY*

Keynes's own investment activity over the period 1924–30 (roughly the gestation period of the *Treatise*) was marked by what he called the 'credit cycle' of investment theory (see Skidelsky 1992: 24–7). It implied an active strategy later described by Keynes as 'holding ... shares in slumps and disposing of them in booms' (Keynes vol. 12: 106).[1] This policy is predicated upon an ability to predict the turning points of the slumps and the booms. In view of my premise that Keynes's investment activity, his policy concerns and his work in economics were often intertwined, it is not coincidental that this same period saw Keynes seriously grappling with the economic theory of financial markets for the first time. His goal was to find a theory of the credit cycle which would illuminate the events of these turbulent years. The result was *A Treatise on Money* (Keynes vols 5 and 6). The *Treatise* can be seen, as Robert Skidelsky (1992: 314–19) has argued, as Keynes's 'summing up of the 1920s'. This is particularly apt when we come to realize that the *Treatise*, like the Roaring Twenties, which ended in bust, was a deeply conflicted and contradictory experience.

To describe the role of speculation in Keynes's *Treatise on Money* is a complicated task, involving as it does the panoply of theoretical and applied arguments he put forward there to analyse the 'credit cycle' and its relationship to monetary factors. The task is made even more difficult by the fact that the book seems to grow and transform itself as it goes along. Starting out firmly rooted in the quantity theory and the natural-rate tradition, the *Treatise* ends up pointing in crucial ways towards *The General Theory* (Keynes vol. 7). But a case can be made that the *Treatise* in many ways represents Keynes's most mature treatment of speculation, and in the all-important analysis of the actual operation of stock market speculation (as opposed to its macroeconomic implications) it loses little in comparison with ch. 12 of *The General Theory*. Furthermore, the *Treatise*, unlike *The General Theory*, offers the reader a more detailed breakdown of the various exchanges on which speculation is carried out in an organized fashion. One of its implicit themes, carried over from Emery (1896), is the need to separate the analysis of potential social risks (Emery termed this 'the evils of speculation') attached to the activities of commodity, currency and stock speculators.

In the *Treatise* these detailed treatments of the various exchanges are part of a central theoretical analysis of the trade cycle, though this is obscured by the extended excurisons Keynes is led into by his attempt to combine high theory with institutional realism. The central question that is continually returned to is the degree to which 'monetary' phenomena exacerbate and amplify the credit cycle, conceived as a movement away from a theoretically 'real' or 'fundamental' equilibrium. An important aspect of this argument concerns the lack of a social mechanism for automatically (and in a short span of time) restoring the equality between saving and investment (linked in the *Treatise* to the benchmark full-employment, natural-rate equilibrium). In fact, Keynes claims not only that cyclical changes in the production of capital goods are not offset by counterbalancing changes in the value of these goods, but that the reactions of prices and the financial system during the cycle actually exacerbate and prolong the disequilibrium.[2] With this in mind, it is not surprising that the treatment of speculation in the *Treatise* stresses the role speculation might or might not play in restoring the fundamental equilibrium once it has been upset by some real disturbance. We shall look at each exchange's role in this regard.

SPECULATION IN THE FOREIGN AND COMMODITY EXCHANGES IN THE *TREATISE*

The role of the foreign exchanges is the easiest to approach. In the *Treatise* Keynes virtually repeats the analysis of the *Tract on Monetary Reform* of the 'machinery' of the forward market.[3] In the *Tract* he had offered an insider's analysis of the relationship between exchange prices and international interest rates. He had also denigrated naïve attacks on foreign exchange speculation as demagoguery and superstition. Currency speculators, according to the

Tract, exert on the whole a positive influence. By anticipating, they accelerate the inevitable adjustments to exchange rates in a flexible rate world due to changes in inflation and interest rates across countries. In the *Treatise*, however, the practical question is how any one country can achieve autonomy in managing its bank rate when the exchanges tend to enforce equalization of rates of return across countries. Again, as in the *Tract* discussion, Keynes suggests that the central banks themselves should enter the forward exchanges to offset any temporary disturbances from abroad that might interfere with domestic policy. Furthermore, to give some latitude to the domestic monetary authorities, Keynes suggests maintaining as wide a gap in the 'gold points' as is possible. This policy would downplay the sensitivity of the exchanges to expectations of return by introducing a degree of 'doubt' on the part of the speculators in short-term 'hot' money. Thus it seems fair to conclude that as of 1930 Keynes's earlier positive view (see Lawlor 1994) of currency market speculation as a stabilizing force was still retained.

As for the commodity exchanges, there is also a large degree of overlap with the discussions of the early 1920s. But now we begin to see the outlines of a 'moral risk' argument along the lines of the *Treatise on Money* analysis.[4] The issue is clearly laid out as a matter of the goodness of the 'organic whole'. That is to say, whatever social function we know commodity speculation to have in its own market must be set off against the probable effect this 'micro' function will have on the total situation. In this regard the treatment of speculation in the *Treatise* begins to look forward to *The General Theory*.

Commodity markets form an integral, if small, part of the analytical framework of the *Treatise*. They represent the financial institutions that perform the social function of carrying stocks of 'liquid capital' over the course of the cycle. In his analysis of the real side of the cycle, and the crucial determinants of the rate of investment, an important issue to Keynes is the possibility that commodity markets might provide a counterbalance to fluctuating production of these goods by accumulating buffering stocks carried over between boom and bust. This had played a large role in Hawtrey's analysis of the cycle (see Keynes's discussion (Keynes vol. 6: 116–31, esp. 117–18), and in the *Treatise* (ibid.: 119) Keynes claims that after studying the statistics – data that he had personally compiled for the London and Cambridge Economic Service on commodity stocks – he had come to believe that 'the true surplus stocks of liquid capital, which at any time are existing, are too small to have any decisive influence on the replenishment of working capital' (Keynes vol. 6: 119). The question then is to explain why the commodity exchanges, to which Emery (1896) and Hawtrey (1919) had ascribed a smoothing effect on consumption, and to which they and Keynes ascribed a 'risk-bearing' function,[5] could not hold sufficient carryover stocks during the bust to provide the means of easily supplying the needs of the eventually succeeding boom. Keynes argues that because a volume of carryover large enough to provide the needed buffer represents such heavy 'carrying costs',[6] speculators would be able to bear it only if the spot price were brought down to such ruinous levels as to halt any further production. Notice that this does not indict commodity market speculation as such, it just dethrones it (in company with many financial markets in the *Treatise*) from a position as a social homeostatic device. Keynes's use of the risk-bearing argument to model the larger issue of the trade cycle demonstrates his ability to combine creatively his deep knowledge of both the empirical magnitudes and the institutional facts of a situation with a slight tweak or rearrangement of existing theoretical tools, and in so doing to throw a dramatic new light on a practical economic issue. Thus here, he turns in on itself Emery's (1896) influential doctrine of the positive risk-bearing function of commodity market speculation. It is just because the market can so accurately evaluate its own risk that it cannot perform an automatic equilibrating function for the economy as a whole:

> The conclusion of this section may be summarized by saying that our present economic system abhors a stock of liquid goods. If such a stock comes into existence, strong forces are immediately brought into play to dissipate it. The efforts to get rid of surplus stocks aggravate the slump, and the success of these efforts retard the recovery.
>
> (Keynes vol. 6: 131)

THE *TREATISE*: SPECULATION ON THE STOCK EXCHANGE

That leaves the stock exchange. It is worth emphasizing that in both the *Treatise* and *The General Theory* stock market speculation occupies centre stage. In fact, a problem we encounter in describing the historical evolution of Keynes's ideas between the *Treatise* and *The General Theory* is that in almost every matter of *detail* (as distinct from the theoretical frameworks in which these details are embedded) save one, the treatments of stock market speculation are *identical* in these books. The historian is thus presented a twofold task. First, it seems important to highlight both the fact of, and source of, Keynes's evident turn against stock market speculation around 1930. This is important as a historical corrective to the commonly held conception that Keynes invented the analysis in ch. 12 of *The General Theory* out of whole cloth. In documenting the context of this aspect of the *Treatise* we are actually providing neglected background to the later work. But there is a second task to be confronted, namely the identification of what is novel in Keynes's use and description of stock market speculation in *The General Theory*. To address this question I will draw a parallel between Keynes's early theory of practical reason and his later economics. In particular I will show that the issue revolves around the status accorded to the 'knowledge' utilized by traders speculating on the stock market. To put it in more Marshallian terms, the difference between the *Treatise* and *The General Theory* reflects an altered status accorded long-period normal values in each.

In the *Treatise*, organized stock market speculation plays a major role in Keynes's theory of the origin and dynamics of crises, or movements away from savings–investment equilibrium. This is one context (the bond market and the determination of the short-term rate of interest being the other) in which the 'two-views' analysis – that of the bulls and the bears – becomes crucial. And as many commentators have noticed, this is a view that remains compatible with *The General Theory*, some going so far (see Kahn 1954, Meltzer 1988) as to equate this analysis with the liquidity preference theory. The details of the 'two-views' analysis in the *Treatise* have been well described before (see Horwich 1964: 416–26; Leijonhufvud 1981). For our purposes, what is interesting about this discussion is that in the matter of the description of the informational context for stock market expectations, Keynes in the *Treatise* takes one large step towards what his view would be in 1936, but he fails to let the other shoe drop, so to speak. He clearly recognized by this period[7] that the day to day value ascribed to equities by the price fixed on the exchanges may bear little relation to the fundamental income-earning potential of a corporation (Keynes vol. 6: 322–4). Instead, he describes these values as a matter of public sentiment concerning the form in which to hold wealth – either securities or 'idle balances'. Since both are fixed in total quantity for the short run for all practical purposes by the volume of existing bank deposits and the outstanding 'old shares' traded on the stock exchange, the rate of interest and stock prices adjust to satisfy the portfolio preferences of the marginal bulls and bears (Keynes vol. 5: 127–31). 'Thus the actual level of security prices is ... the resultant of the degree of bullishness of opinion and the behaviour of the banking system' (Keynes vol. 5: 224).

This view of stock market speculation in the *Treatise* is embedded in a complex quantity theory view whereby changes in stock market activity interact with the rate of interest and the price level via changes in 'industrial and financial circulation' (Keynes's breakdown of the stock of money) over the cycle.[8] Although speculators may alter the interest rate (or conversely alter security prices) temporarily, and so cause saving and investment to diverge, they cannot do so indefinitely. Each stage of the cycle has a built-in (if slow and creaky) corrective in the *Treatise*:

> as soon as the prices of securities has risen high enough, relatively to the short-term rate of interest, to occasion a difference of opinion as to the prospects, a 'bear' position will develop, and some people will begin to increase their savings deposits.... Thus in proportion *as the prevailing opinion comes to seem unreasonable to more cautious people*, the 'other

view' will tend to develop, with the result of an increase in the bear position.

(Keynes vol. 5: my emphasis)

Note the fact that in the *Treatise* there is thus a 'reasonable' basis for the opinions of speculators. This is because in the *Treatise*, as opposed to *The General Theory*, there is still a long-period fundamental value for securities:

> In the long-run the value of securities is entirely derivative from the value of consumption goods. It depends on the expectation as to the value of the amount of liquid consumption goods which the securities will, directly or indirectly, yield.

(Keynes vol. 5: 230)

It is for this reason that Keynes is largely unconcerned in the *Treatise* with the level of security prices *per se*. Speculation on the exchanges is of concern only in so far as it causes swings in the amount of money needed to satisfy the financial circulation and thus possibly leaves an insufficient amount of money to satisfy the industrial circulation. This of course is the mechanism in the *Treatise* by which speculation might 'stimulate new investment to outrun savings, or contrariwise' (Keynes vol. 5: 230). From this view follows his fairly mild (by comparison with *The General Theory*) policy evaluation:

> I should say, therefore, that a currency authority has no *direct* concern with the level of value of existing securities, as determined by opinion.... The main criterion for interference with a 'bull' or 'bear' financial market should be, that is to say, the probable reactions of this financial situation on the prospective equilibrium between saving and *new* investment.

(Keynes vol. 5: 230; emphasis in original)

In the *Treatise*, then, speculation on the stock exchange might possibly influence economic activity. If the speculators, because of their reliance on non-fundamental short-run psychological motives, line up on the 'wrong side' of the two views during a transition to a new higher or lower 'real' rate of interest, they can exacerbate the 'credit cycle'. As of 1930 Keynes had not yet seen this market externality as anything but a transitional friction in the movement between real long-period equilibria. Interestingly, though, he does seem to have felt a degree of tension in his position with respect to the underlying philosophical presuppositions regarding the rationality of such speculative activity. Towards the end of the *Treatise* we find him explicitly addressing this issue:

> How far the motives which I have been attributing above to the market are strictly rational, I leave it to others to judge.[9] They are best regarded, I think, as an example of how sensitive – over-sensitive if you like – to the near future, about which we may think that we know a little, even

241

the best informed must be, because, *in truth, we know almost nothing about the more remote future*.

(Keynes vol. 6: 322; my emphasis)

The contradictory nature of the *Treatise* concerns the puzzle of how we are to reconcile this statement with the argument above that speculators' activities will eventually draw prices toward the long-run fundamental values. For if 'in truth, we know almost nothing about the more remote future', how can we ever know the 'long-run ... value of securities [which] is entirely derivative from the value of consumption goods'? One answer to this question is yielded by a close comparison of the *Treatise* with *The General Theory* on the subject of stock prices. For many of the elements of what has come to be referred to as the Keynesian theory of stock prices – a view which is conventionally attributed to the analysis of 'long-term expectations' in ch. 12 of *The General Theory* – received almost identical treatment in the *Treatise*. Thus one way to bridge this crucial period of transition in Keynes's thought is to identify what the two books have in common. This will leave us in a position to isolate what *is* new in *The General Theory* with respect to speculation. A side-by-side comparison of the discussion of stock market valuation of securities in the *Treatise* (Keynes vol. 6: 322–5) and *The General Theory* (Keynes vol. 7: 152–7) reveals a striking degree of similarity. All the themes often thought to be unique to ch. 12 of *The General Theory* are discussed in this passage from the *Treatise*: excess volatility of prices, the extreme over-reliance on the continuity of existing conditions and current news to judge future profitability, the large number of ignorant participants and the consequent psychological judgements about 'average opinion' that make up the activities of professional traders.

If we take this evident similarity of the analysis of how stock prices are determined as given, Keynes clearly had developed most aspects of his mature treatment of speculation *per se* by the end of the *Treatise*. But, as he wrote to his mother in 1930, it was an analysis that did not hang together well: 'Artistically it is a failure – I have changed my mind too much during the course of it for it to be a proper unity' (Keynes vol. 15: 176). On the one hand he had painted a picture of a financially dependent system in flux, where cyclical movements away from fundamental 'real' equilibria were more than just passing inconveniences. Speculation on the exchanges – particularly the seemingly irrational stock exchange – could exacerbate these cyclical movements. Nevertheless, there remained at the core of the natural rate analysis powerful attractive tendencies pulling the economy back toward long-period equilibrium. In the second volume of the *Treatise*, dealing with applied and historical analysis, however, what had been asides about speculation on the stock exchange in the more theoretical passages of vol. 1 grew into a philosophical disquisition on the fundamentally uncertain knowledge context of investors' and speculators' activities. Thus, by the end

242

of the book, there coexisted in an uneasy juxtaposition a 'classical Marsh-allian' view alongside a 'Marshallian Keynesian' view. The Marshallian–Keynesian view was a unique blend of Emery's (1896) workmanlike role for speculators and Marshall's (1871) optimizing investors equalizing expected returns in a sophisticated stock equilibrium setting. But the larger classical framework in which this, the most sophisticated and complex financial market analysis of Keynes's career, was set, conflicted with what he saw, on a different plane of reasoning, as the peculiar rationality of modern financial market practices.

KEYNES INVESTMENT STRATEGY IN THE 1930s: 'FAITHFULNESS'

This is not the place to provide a complete analysis of the role of speculation in *The General Theory*. But given the stress I have placed on the similarity of Keynes's analysis of asset markets in the *Treatise* with that in *The General Theory* I should end by noting some of the differences encountered in the latter work. In keeping with the story to this point I shall note both a change in Keynes's personal investment activity and a change in his view of the knowledge context of speculation. More important than these, though, is the 'general theory' itself. For he now had a theoretical framework, an economic system, which combined with his philosophical speculations about asset markets to form a proper artistic unity.

Keynes's own investment experience in the turbulent markets of the late 1920s and early 1930s is instructive more for his turn in philosophy than any spectacular crisis. Unlike Irving Fisher for instance, Keynes did not lose everything in the crash of 1929. In fact, he had very little *to* lose, his portfolio of US securities being very slim at the time.[10] But he did lose substantially during the late 1920s on some speculative commodity transactions which, being carried on borrowed money, forced him to liquidate some of his shares in the City during a bear market. This, plus the declining value of what he had left (mostly shares in the Austin Motor Company), meant that his net worth went from £44,000 in 1927 to £7,815 in 1929. Events of precisely this sort, including the Wall Street crash of 1929, were reflected in the *Treatise*. In any case, by 1930, he had come to regret the whole project of attempting to time the market according to the credit cycle theory and had begun a policy he variously referred to as 'duty' and 'faithfulness'. To use his *General Theory* terminology, in his own stock market investments Keynes turned from 'speculation' to 'enterprise'. Clearly, he meant this as more than just a slogan, though, and began a new policy of investing to hold based on long-term prospects. Moggridge (in Keynes vol. 12: 16–17), for instance, offers evidence of the extreme concentration this led to for his portfolio. Often half of his holdings were constituted by three or four issues.[11]

Additionally, there is much evidence of this change in strategy in his internal investment writings of the period. To investing partners, his life insurance colleagues and his fellow bursars at Cambridge, he repeatedly urged buying to hold as both the most responsible and the most profitable policy. In a 1938 memorandum for the Estates Committee of King's College, titled 'Post mortem on investment policy', he recounts the experience of the previous twenty years since he had 'first persuaded the College to invest in ordinary shares' (Keynes vol. 12: 106). Regretting his earlier mistaken belief in the 'credit cycle policy', he explains:

> As the result of these experiences I am clear that the idea of wholesale shifts is for various reasons impracticable and indeed undesirable. Most of those who attempt it to sell too late and buy too late, and do both too often, incurring heavy expenses and developing too unsettled and speculative a state of mind, which if it is widespread, has besides the grave social disadvantage of aggravating the scale of the fluctuations.
>
> (Keynes vol. 12: 106)

He then goes on to report the three principles upon which he now thinks successful investment depends. It is worth quoting these in full as they so accurately describe the policy he in fact followed from at least 1930 on:[12]

1   a careful selection of a few investments (or a few types of investment) having regard to their cheapness in relation to their probable actual and potential *intrinsic* value over a period of years ahead and in relation to alternative investments at the time;
2   a steadfast holding of these in fairly large units through thick and thin, perhaps for several years, until either they have fulfilled their promise or it is evident that they were purchased on a mistake;
3   a *balanced* investment position, i.e. a variety of risks in spite of individual holdings being large, and if possible opposed risks (e.g. a holding of gold shares amongst other equities, since they are likely to move in opposite directions when there are general fluctuations).

(Keynes vol. 12: 107)

CONCLUSION: A GENERAL THEORY OF A SPECULATIVE ECONOMY

The corresponding ideas in *The General Theory* are immediately apparent. What *was* different about the discussion of the stock market in ch. 12 of *The General Theory*, compared to the analysis in the *Treatise*, was a clear change in policy stance toward speculation. In *The General Theory* Keynes no longer saw the central bank as capable of offsetting the influence of speculation in all instances and went so far as to propose increased transactions costs to make frequent speculative purchases more difficult: 'The introduction of a substantial government transfer tax on all transactions might prove the most serviceable reform available, with a view to mitigating the predominance of speculation over enterprise in the United States' (Keynes vol. 7: 160).

But why did Keynes come to so suspect the influence of stock market speculation in *The General Theory*? The answer concerns the possible dramatic effect he suspected speculation could have on real investment in new capital goods, both through the yield that such investments would be expected to earn in times of high liquidity premiums and through the collapse of the prospective yields to new projects, primarily as a result of a collapse of investor confidence. Since investment drove output and employment, according to *The General Theory* any inhibition of investment was necessarily a social evil.

In this regard, the most fundamental advance of *The General Theory* concerns the rejection of the strong *attractive* and *equilibrating* tendencies Keynes had ascribed to fundamentals in the *Treatise*. In *The General Theory* this purpose was served by his analysis of the marginal efficiency of capital. This had an outwardly rationalistic appearance in the form of the simple Fisherian discounting formula that reduced the complexity of the investment decision to a single value to be compared with the current rate of interest. Yet it is emphasized time and again in *The General Theory* that the prospective yield that goes into this formula is *not* an easily ascertainable quantity. It is, in fact, in investigating the basis of prospective yield that Keynes is led to his philosophical disquisition on stock prices, confidence and long-term expectations just reviewed. In sum, in his 'psychologizing' of the basis of the prospective yield in ch. 12 Keynes stressed that these expectations are based on precariously little current knowledge, that they are not readily checked by experience and that the marginal efficiency of capital is therefore subject to wide swings connected to changes in the confidence with which estimates of it are held. In *The General Theory*, there is thus no natural rate, no long-term value to which this psychological value is returned, as there was in the *Treatise*. Thus in *The General Theory* (Keynes vol. 7: 48–9) Keynes defines the 'long-period' level of employment as the level of employment that would result from the continuation of a state of expectations for a period long enough so that all current investment is based on one unchanging set of expectations. It is not that he expects a state of long-term expectations ever to actually last for such a period, but he is replacing the similarly fictional concept of the Marshallian long period with one based upon a given psychological state among investors.

After *The General Theory*, Keynes (1937a, 1937b, 1937c) often remarked upon the importance he attached to his psychological analysis of financial market processes. These accounts should be taken seriously. Market psychology was integral to *The General Theory*, just as it was alien to the *Treatise*. The description of stock market trading is very similar in the two books. Yet the recognition in *The General Theory* of speculation's potential social impact, and the acknowledgment that its philosophical basis in knowledge is more tenuous, makes that work unique. It should now be apparent, though, that the development of this aspect of Keynes's thought had a long history prior to *The General Theory*.

NOTES

1 All references to *The Collected Writings of John Maynard Keynes* (Keynes 1971–89) will hereafter be referred to by 'Keynes' followed by the volume and page numbers.
2 For an excellent short summary description in non-technical language of what Keynes of the *Treatise* saw as the normal course of the cycle see Keynes (vol. 5: 271–3).
3 In fact he refers the reader back to the *Tract* discussion (Keynes vol. 6: 291, 298). For a complete analysis of this see my previous paper (Lawlor 1994).
4 This is also a theme I have earlier developed at length (Lawlor 1994: 207–15).
5 I have previously discussed Emery's book at length (Lawlor 1994: 197–204), as well as Keynes's use of his work in his writings about speculation (ibid.: 204–23).
6 In the form of '1 Allowance for deterioration . . .; 2 Warehouse and insurance charges; 3 Interest charges; 4 Remuneration against the risk of changes in the money value of the commodity during the time through which it has to be carried by means of borrowed money' (Keynes vol. 6: 121).
7 In fact, one can find a description by Keynes very similar to the 'fashion' model of stock prices going back as far as 1910. See his article 'Great Britain's foreign investments' (Keynes vol. 15: 46).
8 It is interesting to note that the distinction Emery (1896: 82–92) made between the method of speculation by fortnightly account in England, versus the method of borrowing and lending stock characteristic of the Wall Street clearing houses, shows up in the *Treatise* as an explanation of how much easier it is to ignite a speculative boom on Wall Street than in the City of London (Keynes vol. 5: 225; vol. 6: 175–7). The major reason for this is that the US system may free speculation from running into a lending constraint from the banking system much more than in the British case.
9 One might say his other 'general theory' self eventually provided this judgement.
10 Not that Keynes did not have his own troubles with stocks during these years. First, his commodity losses in 1928 and 1929 necessitated the sale of British securities during a bear market to rectify growing inadequacies in his commodity cover. He also eventually got into the US market in a big way in 1932 and thereafter continued large American dealings until his death (see Keynes vol. 12: 13, table 5). Like all those active in the US market during this period he suffered some ups and downs. But on average he seems actually to have done quite well once he adopted his policy of 'faithfulness' to a small selection of stocks. Thus Moggridge reports (in Keynes vol. 12: 9), 'in the years after 1929, his investments outperformed the market in 21 of 30 accounting years and did so cumulatively by a large margin'.
11 To an investment partner, F. C. Scott, Keynes writes in 1942: 'I am quite incapable of having adequate knowledge of more than a very limited range of investments. Time and opportunity do not allow more. Therefore, as the investible sums increase, the size of the unit must increase. I am in favour of

having as large a unit as market conditions will allow' (vol. 12: 82). Interestingly, just as in the definition of speculation advanced in his 1910 lectures (see Lawlor 1994), this strategy implies that, although he had forsaken attempts to predict the credit cycle by this point, Keynes still thought he knew better than the market. Thus 'faithfulness' is not equivalent to the modern efficient-markets view, since it implies special knowledge of *fundamentals*. But it is also not a fad theory – what Shiller (1991) calls 'popular' models.

12   Skidelsky (1992: 343) appears to date this change in Keynes's strategy to 1928, whereas Moggridge (in Keynes vol. 12: 9–15) appears to date it to 1929. In any case it is evident by 1930, both in his portfolio and in his writings (see Keynes vol. 12: 57, 78, 82–3, 97–9, 102–7). An interesting deep background source for this is a book review Keynes wrote for the *Nation and Athenaeum* in 1925, of *Common Stocks as Long-Term Investments* by Edgar L. Smith (Keynes vol. 12: 247–52). It reports the 'striking' results of a long-term comparison of the return to investing in Wall Street shares versus bonds over a fifty-year period. Using various selections of stocks, Smith found that the 'common stocks have turned out best in the long run, indeed, markedly so' (Keynes vol. 12: 247). This is an early report of what is now a commonplace verity of financial lore.

REFERENCES

Emery, H. C. (1896) *Speculation on the Stock and Produce Exchanges of the United States*, New York: Columbia University Press.

Harcourt, G. C. (1983) 'Keynes's college bursar view of investment', J. A. Kregal (ed.) *Distribution: Effective Demand and International Economic Relations*, New York: St Martin's Press.

Hawtrey, R.G. (1919) *Trade and Credit*, London: Longman.

Horwich, G. (1964) *Money, Capital and Prices*, Homewood, IL: Irwin.

Kahn, R. F. (1954) 'Some notes on liquidity preference', *Manchester School of Economics and Social Studies* 22(3): 229–57.

Keynes, J. M. (1937a) 'The theory of the rate of interest', in *The Lessons of Monetary Experience: Essays in Honour of Irving Fisher*, Reprinted in *The Collected Writings of John Maynard Keynes*, vol. 14, London: Macmillan for the Royal Economoic Society.

—— (1937b) 'Alternative theories of the rate of interest', *Economic Journal* 47: 241–52. Reprinted in *The Collected Writings of John Maynard Keynes*, vol. 14, London: Macmillan for the Royal Economic Society.

—— (1937c) 'The general theory of employment', *Quarterly Journal of Economics* 51: 209–23. Reprinted in *The Collected Writings of John Maynard Keynes*, vol. 14, London: Macmillan for the Royal Economic Society.

—— (1971–89) *The Collected Writings of John Maynard Keynes*, 30 vols, London: Macmillan for the Royal Economic Society.

Lawlor, M. S. (1994) 'On the historical origin of Keynes's financial market views', *History of Political Economy* 26, Annual Supplement, *Higgling: Transactors and Their Markets in the History of Economics*, ed. N. De Marchi and M. Morgan, pp. 184–225.

Leijonhufvud, A. (1981) 'The Wicksell connection: variations on a theme', in *Information and Coordination*, Oxford: Oxford University Press.

Marshall, A. (1871)'Money', in J. Whittaker (ed.) (1975) *The Early Writings of Alfred Marshall*, 2 vols, London: Macmillan.

—— (1899) 'The folly of amateur speculators makes the fortunes of professionals: the wiles of some professionals', reprinted in M. Dardi and M. Gallegati (1992)

'Marshall on speculation', *History of Political Economy* 24(3): 586–93.
Meltzer, A. H. (1988) *Keynes's Monetary Theory: A Different Interpretation*, Cambridge: Cambridge University Press.
Shiller, R. J. (1991) *Market Volatility*. Cambridge, MA: MIT Press.
Skidelsky, R. (1992) *John Maynard Keynes*: vol. 2, *The Economist as Saviour 1920–1937*, London: Macmillan.

21

DID KEYNES REVERSE THE MARSHALLIAN SPEEDS OF ADJUSTMENT?

Using Harcourt's method to resolve theoretical controversies and gain insight into the real world

Paul Davidson

Geoff Harcourt has been an amazingly prolific economist. His interest is not theory for theory's sake, but theory as a means of understanding the economic world in which we live. Some of his greatest contributions have been in synthesizing debates in economic theory and offering the fair-minded reader a vision of how not only to resolve the controversy but also to use the resolution to gain insights about the real world. For an excellent example, see Harcourt and Araujo (1993).

In this controversy, Joan Robinson argued that the economy could grow over time at Harrod's warranted rate of growth only if realized effective demand keeps the 'stock of plant over-utilised to just the extent that it grows' (Robinson 1962). In this case, Robinson argued, the realized rate of profit *exceeds* the equilibrium rate of profit, defined as the Marshallian supply price of capital. Shove countered with the argument that an expanding system is not logically inconsistent with the maintenance of an equilibrium rate of profit. As long as growth in aggregate demand was expected, a 'normal' equilibrium profit rate should be the rule. Dobb tended to agree with Robinson that abnormal profits would be the rule in any expanding system, but admitted that Robinson did not give any reasons to explain why this was so.

In providing a resolution to this controversy, Harcourt argued that 'Davidson's (1968, 1972) model provides a solution [to this controversy], one which suggests that Shove's result is a very special case.' The model Harcourt adopted is one where both stock and flow demand and supply curves are explicitly developed.

In this Harcourtian spirit, I wish to use the same stock–flow model to resolve the recent argument in the mainstream literature that Keynes's revolution in economic theory was achieved simply by reversing the Marshallian speeds of adjustment of price versus quantity.

IS THE ESSENCE OF UNEMPLOYMENT LESS THAN PERFECTLY FLEXIBLE PRICES?

Tobin (1992: 394) insists that the absence of 'perfectly and instantaneously flexible prices' is a necessary condition for Keynes's unemployment equilibrium, and that '[c]omplete price flexibility means instantaneous adjustment, so that prices are always clearing markets, jumping sufficiently to all demand and supply shocks'. Since Old as well as New 'Keynesians' typically start their analysis of Keynesian unemployment with an economy initially in full employment equilibrium (with less than perfect price flexibility), they are implicitly, therefore, asserting that perfect price flexibility is *not* a necessary condition for the existence of full employment equilibrium. It follows that for mainstream 'Keynesians', *perfect price flexibility is a sufficient condition for full employment*.

This sufficient condition view, however, is in direct logical conflict with Keynes's claim (1936: 245) that his general theory was applicable to 'any degree of competition' and therefore unemployment equilibrium can occur even with perfectly competitive flexible prices. Moreover, Keynes (ibid.: 269) insisted that 'To suppose that a flexible wage policy is a right and proper adjunct to a system which on the whole is one of *laissez-faire* is the opposite of the truth.' In Keynes's 'general' theory, therefore, *complete price flexibility is neither a necessary nor a sufficient condition for full employment equilibrium.*[1]

Nevertheless, when a prestigious Old Keynesian such as Tobin claims that perfect price flexibility is sufficient to assure full employment, his comment perpetuates the modern fable that Keynes's underemployment analysis requires a reversing of the Marshallian speed of adjustment of prices and quantities. In other words, for Tobin to claim that 'Keynesian' unemployment equilibrium requires less than instantaneous price flexibility implies that it is an imperfection in the ability of *supply* prices to adjust to a demand shock that is the ultimate cause of unemployment. Gordon's characterization of mainstream Keynesian macroeconomic developments in recent decades reinforces this view of unemployment as a supply-side problem. Gordon (1990: 1117) states that the 'entire demand side of the economy is omitted . . . topics on the demand side can be omitted simply because they are not at the heart of the conflict between new-Keynesian and new-classical macroeconomics'.

If Gordon and Tobin were correct, then as a matter of logic and despite Keynes's claim in ch. 3 *The General Theory* (1936: 24–6), unemployment cannot be attributed *solely* to the determinants of the aggregate demand function that are independent of aggregate supply determinants. Keynes, however, argued that what Gordon calls the 'heart' of the conflict between Keynes's 'general theory' and the classical analysis lay in the fact that in the classical analysis, aggregate demand had no determinants independent of aggregate supply; that is, 'supply creates its own demand'. Keynes insisted that 'the substance of the General Theory' required an exposition of the determinants of aggregate demand that are independent of the determinants of aggregate supply prices. Old and New Keynesian disagree.

THE KEYNES AGGREGATE SUPPLY AND DEMAND SYSTEM

Keynes's taxonomic attack on the classical system can be algebraically and geometrically demonstrated via figure 21.1. Let Z represent aggregate supply (or entrepreneurial expectations of sales receipts) in monetary terms, D aggregate demand (or planned expenditures) in money units, w the money wage rate, and N the number of person-years employed. The aggregate demand function is given by

$$D = f_d(w,N) \qquad (21.1)$$

The aggregate supply function is given by

$$Z = f_z(w,N) \qquad (21.2)$$

Say's law asserts that

$$f_d(w,N) = f_z(w,N) \qquad (21.3)$$

'for *all* values of N, i.e. for all values of output and employment' (Keynes 1936: p. 26). The aggregate demand curve, D, and the aggregate supply curve, Z, coincide (Figure 21.1(a)).

To challenge the applicability of Say's law, Keynes had to develop a model where the aggregate demand function $[D = f_d(w,N) = D_1 + D_2]$ and aggregate supply $[Z = f_z(w,N)]$ are not coincident (see Figure 21.1(b)). Given specific assumptions regarding the D_1 relationship (as embodied in equation (21.9) below, the D and Z functions would intersect at a unique point of effective demand (point E in Figure 21.1(b)).

Keynes accepted the 'age-old' normal (Marshallian) supply conditions based on the marginal cost function plus any monopoly mark-up as a micro-basis for the aggregate supply function of equation (21.2).

Keynes developed an expanded taxonomy for the components of the aggregate demand relationship to differentiate his general case from the classical special case. In the classical system, there is only a single category of spending. All demand expenditures are a function of (and equal to) income earned (supply). Keynes split aggregate demand into two categories, D_1 and D_2, i.e.

251

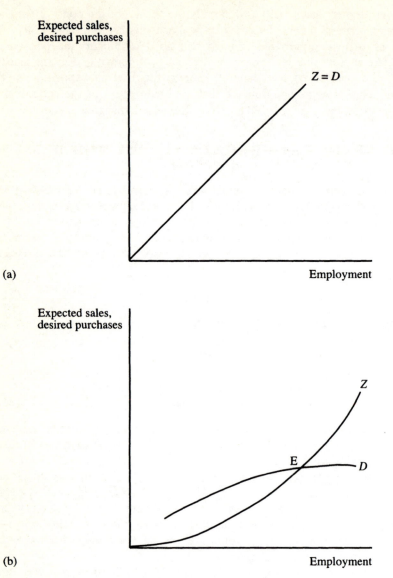

Figure 21.1 Aggregate demand and aggregate supply schedules

$$D = D_1 + D_2 = f_d(w, N) \qquad (21.4)$$

Keynes's D_1 demand category represented *all* expenditures which 'depend on the level of aggregate income and, therefore, on the level of employment N' (Keynes 1936: 28). That is

252

$$D_1 = f_1(w,N) \tag{21.5}$$

D_2, therefore, represented all expenditures *not* related to income and employment; that is

$$D_2 \neq f(w,N) \tag{21.6}$$

The microfoundations of the classical economics case assure us that all income is always spent on the products of industry.[2] In the simplest case, all current expenditures are related to current income and are therefore classified under D_1, which is immediately spent. The marginal propensity to spend out of current income is unity and any additional supply creates its own additional demand. (In an intertemporal setting with gross substitutability over time, agents plan to spend lifetime income on the products of industry over their life cycle; that is, the long-run marginal propensity to spend is unity.) Consequently, in either the short run or the long run, $f_d(w,N) = f_z(w,N)$ for all values of N and Figure 21.1(b) is relevant.

Keynes's second expenditure category, D_2, is not related to current income and employment by being equal to 'planned' savings (which can be defined as $[f_z(w,N) - f_1(w,N)]$. To demonstrate why D_2 is not equal to planned savings, Keynes assumed the existence of an uncertain future that cannot be either foreknown or statistically predicted by analysing past and current market price signals. In such a non-ergodic environment, future profits, the basis for current D_2 investment spending, can neither be reliably forecasted from existing market information, nor endogenously determined from today's 'planned' savings function $[f_z(w,N) - f_1(w,N)]$ (Keynes 1936: 210). Rather, investment expenditures depend on the exogenous (and therefore, by definition, sensible but not rational) expectations of entrepreneurs, or what Keynes called 'animal spirits'. Thus, in either the short run or the long run, D_2 expenditures cannot be a function of current income and employment, and equation (21.6) applies.

Explicit recognition of the possibility of two different classes of current demand for producible goods and services based on fewer axioms than required by the classical taxonomy makes Keynes's analysis the more general case. Classical theory, where Say's law prevails and where income-generating supply activities $[f_z(w,N)]$ create their own identical demand so that all markets clear, becomes 'a special case' (Keynes 1936: 3) where

$$D_2 = 0 \tag{21.7}$$

and

$$D_1 = f_1(w,N) = f_z(w,N) = Z \tag{21.8}$$

for *all* values of w and N.

The next logical task for Keynes was to demonstrate that 'the characteristics of the special case assumed by classical theory happen not to be those of the economic society in which we actually live' (Keynes 1936: 3). In other words, Keynes had to demonstrate that even if $D_2 = 0$, the D_1 function would not be coincident with his macroanalogue of the age-old supply function. To accomplish this, Keynes had to reject the special classical axiom of gross substitution as applicable to any economy that organizes on a money contractual basis in the face of an uncertain future. Under these more general conditions, some portion of an agent's income might be withheld from the purchase of producible goods. As long as producible goods are not gross substitutes for holding non-producible liquid assets (including money) for liquidity purposes, then no change in relative prices can induce income earners to buy producibles with that portion of income they wish to use to purchase additional security from holding liquid assets.

In an uncertain world, where money and all other liquid assets possess certain essential properties, agents can obtain utility (by being free of fear of possible insolvency or even bankruptcy) only by holding a portion of their income in the form of non-producible money or other liquid assets. As long as the gross substitutability between non-producible liquid assets (including money) and producible goods is approximately zero (Keynes 1936: ch. 17; Davidson 1983–4), then money is not neutral, even with perfectly flexible prices. Thus, the general case underlying the principle of effective demand is:

$$D_1 = f_1(w,N) \neq f_z(w,N) \tag{21.9}$$

and the propensity to save $[f_z(w,N) - f_d(w,N)]$ is equal to the amount out of current income that utility-maximizing agents use to increase their holdings of non-producible liquid assets.

By proclaiming a 'fundamental psychological law' associated with 'the detailed facts of experience' where the marginal propensity to consume is always less than unity, Keynes finessed the possibility that equation (21.8) was applicable to the real world. If the marginal propensity to consume is always less than unity, then $f_1(w,N)$ would never coincide with $f_z(w,N)$, even if $D_2 = 0$, and the special classical case is not applicable to 'the economic society in which we actually live' (Keynes 1936: 3).

Since Keynes apparently did not lay out the details of the Marshallian microfoundations, underlying his theory of effective demand, mainstream macroeconomists have concluded that Keynes's theory requires reversing the Marshallian speeds of adjustment at the level of analysing firm and industry supply behaviour.

ARE DIFFERING SPEEDS OF ADJUSTMENT OF PRICES VERSUS QUANTITIES RELEVANT TO KEYNES'S ANALYSIS?

The major difference between Old and New Keynesians involves the former's concept of nominal *stickiness* and the latter's notion of nominal *rigidities*

(Tobin 1993: 47–8). New Keynesians see rigidities – that is, unchanging nominal values for long periods of calendar time – as an essential aspect of Keynesianism, while Old Keynesians are willing to make a 'much less restrictive assumption' (ibid.: 46) regarding the time duration before prices adjust. This latter assumption 'leaves plenty of room for flexibility in any common sense meaning of the word' (ibid.). Between classical immediate flexibility and the New Keynesian long-term rigidity there are 'various speeds of price adjustment ... during which markets are not clearing' (Tobin 1992: 394). Tobin (1992: 394) claims that Old Keynesianism is the embodiment of reasonableness, since it 'owns the middle ground' between the polar New Classical and New Keynesian views on price flexibility.[3]

Was Keynes's entire anti-classical argument based solely on reversing Marshall's speed of adjustment argument? Keynes did not concede this. Rather, Keynes insisted that *as a logical conclusion of his analysis* no market price mechanism (including completely flexible prices) exists that ensures a self-righting full-employment equilibrium in a monetary economy. Despite Tobin's contention of what is the essence of Keynes's general theory, neither Old nor New Keynesians are able to engage classical theorists in any consistent logical debate using Keynes's principle of effective demand. Mankiw, at least (1992: 561), recognized this inability when he wrote, 'If new Keynesian economics is not a true representation of Keynes's views, then so much the worse for Keynes.'[4]

WHAT IS THE BASIS FOR REVERSING THE MARSHALLIAN SPEEDS OF ADJUSTMENT OF PRICES AND QUANTITIES ARGUMENT?

Ultimately Tobin's association of unemployment with less than perfectly flexible prices relies on Leijonhufvud's Walrasian interpretation of Keynes's economics. Leijonhufvud (1968) claimed that Keynes merely reversed the Marshallian speeds of adjustment of prices and quantities.

Friedman then argues that for Marshall's analysis

it takes time for output to adjust but no time for prices to do so. This assumption [of Marshall] has no effect on the final equilibrium position, but it is vital for the path to equilibrium ... Keynes ... deviated from Marshall ... in reversing the roles assigned to prices and quantities....

Keynes's assumption about the relative speeds of adjustment of prices and quantities is still the key difference in approach and analysis between those economists who regard themselves as Keynesians and those who do not.

(Friedman 1974: 17–20)

Post-Keynesian theory (e.g. Davidson 1972; 1974: 93–4), however, does not accept this speed of adjustment argument as an element of Keynes's legacy.

And even a major general equilibrium theorist disputes Leijonhufvud's proposition. Hahn writes that Keynes 'did not posit fixed prices. Rather the reverse. Nor did he seem to argue that prices change more slowly than quantities, as can be verified in the chapter which tells us why labour cannot control its real wage' (1977: 35). Hahn also agrees with the post-Keynesian view that if one argues that Keynes merely reversed the Marshallian relative speeds of adjustment, then 'there is not much left of the "revolution". For Keynes's contemporaries were all agreed that lack of perfect "price flexibility" was responsible for the trouble. I believe there is a good deal more to Keynesian economics than that' (ibid.: 32).

Although Leijonhufvud (1968) was the first to attribute to Keynes this reversal of Marshall's speed of adjustment argument, Leijonhufvud recanted after being a referee on an article of mine (Davidson 1974) that utilized the same stock flow analysis that Harcourt utilized in the Robinson–Shove–Dobbs controversy. Leijonhufvud stated:

It is *not* correct to attribute to Keynes a general reversion of the Marshallian ranking of relative price and quantity adjustment velocities. In the shortest of the short runs for which the system behavior can be defined in Keynes' model, output prices *must* be treated as perfectly flexible.

(Leijonhufvud 1974: 169)

Tobin may argue that the slow speed of adjustment of prices is a pragmatic rather than a logical issue and therefore, as a practical if not a theoretical matter, unemployment is inevitable in the real world. In this era of product bar codes and computers, however, it can take only a few nanoseconds for prices to be changed, whereas it takes some significant 'real time' to discharge workers and stop production flows. Even from a practical standpoint, therefore, the speed of price adjustment should be faster than the quantity adjustment speed.

UNDERSTANDING KEYNES'S USE OF MARSHALLIAN SPEEDS-OF-REACTION ANALYSIS

The Arrow–Debreu system assumes that all product demand curves are homogeneous of degree zero in terms of the product price level. Accordingly, a perfectly flexible price level assures that all product markets will always clear – simply because it ultimately assumes that the normal price level in the product market is independent of the money wage level and vice versa.

For Marshall this independence of product prices level and input price level is true during the *market period* where, by definition of 'market period', there is an existing supply (stock) of products that can neither be changed in quantity nor inventoried[5] for sale in a later period.

Keynes (1936: 25) explicitly claimed that the aggregate demand and supply curves in Figure 21.1(b) represents Keynes's 'substance of the General Theory of Employment' general theory. Accordingly, we should be able to relate this aggregate diagram to an underlying micro-stock-flow industry analogue to analyse the question that most mainstream Keynesians raise: what, if any, is the difference in the effect on employment of a hypothesized exogenous decline in aggregate demand when wages and prices do not instantaneously adjust compared to when there is perfect price flexibility?

Let us therefore assume an exogenous decline in the aggregate demand function (of say x per cent at each level of employment) from D_a to D_b in Figure 21.2(a); or, in nominal terms deflated by the money wage rate, from $D_a w_a$ to $D_b w_a$ in Figure 21.2(b), where w_a is the initial money wage rate. We wish to examine the effects of this hypothetical initial decline in aggregate expenditures (in real terms).

At the micro level, this decline in aggregate demand is perceived by entrepreneurs as, on average, a decline in the market-period demand curves for all producible goods and hence the demand curve facing the representatives firm (from d_a to d_b in Figure 21.3) relative to the existing and unchanged (stock) market-period supply of S_a in Figure 21.3. In Marshall's market period, there will be an instantaneous and perfectly flexible decline in all spot market prices (of x per cent, equal to the hypothesized proportionate decline in aggregate demand) from p_a^s to P_b^s, where the symbol p^s represents the market-period (spot) price of a product.

Keynes wrote that for any prospective change in demand, 'there is no escaping from the dilemma that if it [a change] is not foreseen there will be no effect on current affairs, while if it is foreseen, *the price of existing goods* will be forthwith so adjusted' (1936: 142; my emphasis). In Marshall's analysis, if the fall in market-period (spot) price is relative to the Marshallian short-run flow supply schedule ($s_a w_a$) in Figure 21.3, then output flow in each industry will decline from q_a to q_b (in Figure 21.3). Accordingly, entrepreneurs will lay off employees simultaneously in every industry. Unemployment will increase in this Marshallian representative firm analysis.

WHAT HAPPENS IF THE MONEY WAGE FALLS *PARI PASSU* WITH SPOT MARKET PRICES?

Classical theorists, however, carry Marshall's analysis one step further. They argued that if money wages are induced to fall *pari passu* with the proportionate fall in the initiating exogenous spot market demand for producibles, then Marshall's short-period flow supply curve would fall from $s_a w_a$ to $s_b w_b$ (in Figure 21.3), where w_b is the money wage after the assumed *pari passu* proportionate decline; that is $w_b = (1 - x)w_a$.

Classical theorists assume no further fall in the nominal market demand curve d_b in Figure 21.3. In other words, classical economists argued that a

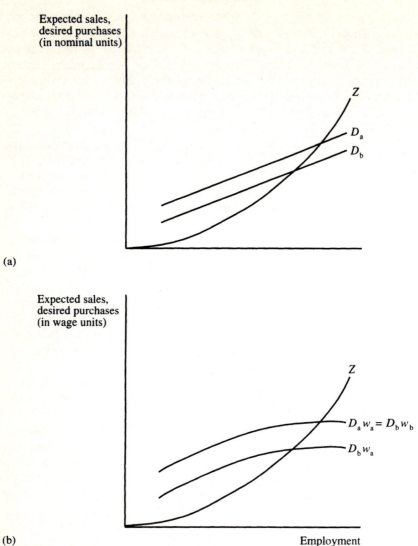

(a)

(b)

Employment

Figure 21.2 Aggregate supply and demand

pari passu fall in the money costs of production (including the supply price of entrepreneurs) results in a proportionate fall in nominal prices. This perfectly flexible price adjustment, it is claimed, restores aggregate real expenditures to their initial, hypothesized pre-exogenous demand decline, level. As a result, the representative firm reinstates its original (pre-demand change) production plan and produces q_a.

258

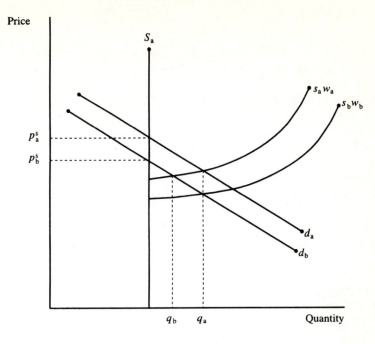

Figure 21.3 Micro supply and demand

In this analysis, the exogenous decline in demand has been rescinded miraculously by the induced fall in wages and prices. Accordingly, Old and New Keynesians accept the classical theorists' assertion that a perfectly flexible age–product price system will instantaneously restore the lower real aggregate demand function $D_b w_a$ to its pre-exogenous level of $D_a w_a$ merely by deflating the *assumed unchanged* nominal expenditures function D_b by a lower money wage, w_b. Perfect flexibility somehow ensures that the final aggregate demand curve $D_b w_b$ equals the initial $D_a w_a$ (in Figure 21.2(b)). *There is no change in real aggregate demand despite the hypothesized exogenous decline in aggregate demand.*

Keynes did not deny that a 'reduction in money wages is quite capable *in certain circumstances* of affording a stimulus to output as the classical theory supposes. My difference from this [classical] theory is primarily a difference of analysis' (1936: 257; my emphasis). He argued (ibid.: 259–60) that the classical theory's simplistic claim that a proportionate fall in all product prices and money wages will restore the real aggregate demand function by inducing proportionate declines in all micro-short-run flow supply functions without inducing any further change in micro-demand functions as an *ignoratio elenchi*; that is, a fallacy of offering a proof that is irrelevant to the proposition in question.

259

This fallacy involved transferring to an aggregate analysis Marshall's micro-argument that individual micro-demand and supply schedules can be constructed under the assumption that aggregate effective demand is given and unchanged no matter what the demand and supply conditions facing a single firm or industry. Yet this presumption is exactly what is at issue when mainstream economists enquire into economy-wide effects of a given decline in real effective demand. The question that must be analysed is whether any reduction in wages and product prices will be accompanied by the same demand when measured in money as that which would occur if wages and prices did not fall. Can the classical economist demonstrate that any exogenous decline in real effective demand is automatically neutralized by a perfectly flexible price system? As the earlier citation from Hahn indicated, the standard Walrasian/Arrow–Debreu fails to provide such a proof. Tobin and the New Keynesians have also failed to do so.

In terms of Figure 21.3, mainstream Keynesians as well as classical theorists merely invoke the names of Walras, Arrow and Debreu to presume they have proven that the exogenous decline from $d_a w_a$ to $d_b w_a$, inducing a proportionate simultaneous decline in the micro-flow supply function in each industry from $s_a w_a$ to $s_b w_b$, will restore production to q_a without any further feedback decline in the micro-money demand curve, d_b.

If, however, there is an initial exogenous decline in real spending at each N-level, then each micro-demand curve falls from $d_a w_a$ to $d_b w_a$. Anyone who believes in the beneficence of a perfectly flexible price system must then demonstrate that all real expenditures not directly related to employment (D_2, in equation 21.6) will increase sufficiently to exactly offset the hypothesized initial exogenous downward shift in the aggregate demand function. In terms of Figure 21.3, this implies that if the Marshallian flow supply function from $w_a w_a$ endogenously shifts downward by x per cent to $w_b w_b$ then the resulting reduction in nominal incomes flows *at each level of employment* has no further feedback effect on the Marshallian micro-demand nominal demand curves, $d_b w_a$. In other words, if prices and wages fall sufficiently to induce a proportionate fall in money incomes at each unemployment level, then the classical analysis presumes that money expenditure is the same at each employment level as it would be if there had been no decline in money wages and prices. The presumed fall in nominal income flows does have a macro-feedback effect of restoring real aggregate demand from $D_b w_a$ to $D_a w_a$ in Figure 21.2(b), whereas there is no presumed additional effect on the micro-demand function in Figure 21.3; that is, the micro-curve is the same whether all factor-flow supply prices (and hence money incomes) decline by x per cent at each N-level or remain at the initial levels.

Keynes explicitly rejected this Marshallian-type analysis which assumes that economy-wide micro-flow supply curves can decline without any impact on economy-wide micro-demand curves. He wrote:

For the demand schedules for particular industries can be only be constructed on *some fixed assumption* as to the nature of demand and supply schedules of other industries and *to the amount of [nominal] aggregate demand. It is invalid, therefore, to transfer the argument to industry as a whole* [i.e. Tobin's 'whole economy' argument (1992: 391)] *unless we transfer our assumption that aggregate effective demand is fixed.* Yet this assumption reduces the argument to an *ignoratio elenchi.* For whilst no one would wish to deny the proposition that a reduction of money-wages accompanied by the same aggregate effective demand as before will be associated with an increase in employment, *the precise question at issue is whether the reduction in money-wages will or will not be accompanied by the same effective demand as before measured in money* or, at any rate, by an aggregate effective demand which is not reduced in full proportion to the reduction in money wages (i.e., which is somewhat greater measured in wage-units). But *if the classical theory is not allowed to extend its conclusions in respect to a particular industry to industry as a whole, it is wholly unable to answer the question what effect on employment a reduction in money wages will have. For it has no method of analysis wherewith to tackle the problem.*

(Keynes 1936: 259–60; my emphasis)

Ultimately Tobin (1992: 397) falls back on a 'Keynes effect' in an attempt to provide the proof that Keynes demanded of classical economists. Keynes, however, anticipated such a response and argued that this 'Keynes effect' was not applicable to a monetary system with endogenous money supply:

the effect of a falling wage- and price-level on the demand for money that those who believe in the self-adjusting quality of the economic system must rest their argument ... [then] if the quantity of money is itself a function of the wage- and price-level, there is indeed, nothing to hope in this direction.

(Keynes 1936: 266)

Keynes admitted that if economists hypothesized a system where the money supply was truly exogenous, then there could be a Keynes effect by assumption. Nevertheless, even in such an unrealistic system, it would be pragmatically easier to obtain the same result of restoring the initial aggregate demand function via an economy-wide interest rate policy rather than trying to get all money wages to fall proportionately and simultaneously. He wrote: 'But if the quantity of money is virtually fixed ... we can ... theoretically at least, produce precisely the same effects on the rate of interest ... by increasing the quantity of money whilst leaving the level of wages unchanged' (Keynes 1936: 266).

NOTES

1 Keynes (1936: 245) insists that, as a theoretical matter, unemployment equilibrium is possible for 'any degree of competition' including perfect competition.

2 Classical microfoundations assume that the earning of income always involves disutility, and that the products of industry are the *only* scarce things which generate utility. It therefore follows that if future outcomes are knowable (i.e. ergodic), then utility maximizers will bear the irksomeness of engaging in income-producing activities only to the point where the marginal disutility of earning income equals the expected marginal utility of the products of industry that the agents 'know' they want to buy. All utility-maximizing agents are, on their budget constraint line, allocating *all* their income on purchasing producible goods and services. Given the classical postulates, any demand to hold non-producible money or other assets solely for liquidity purposes would be irrational. Even if it initially occurred, however, as long as producible goods are gross substitutes for money, then a change in relative prices could always induce utility maximizers to stop holding money and purchase the products of industry instead. Money is therefore merely a neutral veil!

3 Tobin apparently believes that the 'middle ground' is always the virtuous position. For example, see Tobin's (1974: 80) earlier debate with Friedman where he suggests that the absence of 'extreme' assumptions is somehow *per se* virtuous. Yet to obtain the middle ground often requires waffling on the essential logical issues.

4 Mankiw (1992: 560–1) continues, '*The General Theory* is an obscure book. I am not sure that even Keynes himself knew completely what he really meant ... *The General Theory* is an outdated book.... We are in a much better position than Keynes was to figure out how the economy works.... The long run is not so far away that one can cavalierly claim, as Keynes did, that "in the long run we're all dead".'

5 If the existing stock supply can be inventoried, then, as Wicksteed pointed out, the market period demand for products would include a reservation demand. This possibility of a 'reservation demand' can be implicitly included under Keynes's (1936: 53) concept of 'user costs' during the market (spot) period.

REFERENCES

Davidson, P. (1968) 'Money, portfolio balance, capital accumulation and economic growth', *Econometrica* 36: 291–321.
—— (1972) *Money and the Real World*, London: Macmillan.
—— (1974) 'Disequilibrium market adjustment: Marshall revisited', *Economic Inquiry* 12: 146–58.
—— (1983–4) 'Revising Keynes's revolution', *Journal of Post-Keynesian Economics* 6: 561–85.
Friedman, M. (1974) 'A theoretical framework for monetary analysis', in Gordon, R. J. *Milton Friedman's Monetary Framework*, Chicago: University of Chicago Press.
Gordon, R. J. (1990) 'What is new Keynesian economics?', *Journal of Economic Literature* 28.
Hahn, F. H. (1977) 'Keynesian economics and general equilibrium theory: reflections on some current debates', in Harcourt, G. C., *The Microfoundations of Macroeconomics*, London: Macmillan.
Harcourt, G. C. and Araujo, J. A. T. R. (1993) 'Accumulation and the rate of profit: reflections on the issues raised in correspondence between Maurice Dobb, Joan

Robinson, and Gerald Shove', *Journal of the History of Economic Thought* 15: 1–30. Revised version reprinted in Harcourt, G. C. (1995) *Capitalism, Socialism and Post-Keynesianism*, Cheltenham: Edward Elgar.

Keynes, J. M. (1936) *The General Theory of Employment, Interest and Money*, New York: Harcourt Brace.

Leijonhufvud, A. (1968) *The Economics of Keynes and Keynesian Economics*, London: Oxford University Press.

—— (1974) 'Keynes's employment function', *History of Political Economy* 6: 164–76.

Mankiw, G. (1992) 'The reincarnation of Keynesian economics', *European Economic Review* 36: 557–71.

Robinson, J. (1962) *Essays in Economic Growth*, London: Macmillan.

Tobin, J. (1992) 'An Old Keynesian counterattacks', *Eastern Economic Journal* 18: 387–400.

—— (1974) 'Friedman's theoretical framework' in R. Gordon (ed.) *Milton Friedman's Monetary Framework*, Chicago: University of Chicago Press.

—— (1993) 'Price flexibility and output stability: an Old Keynesian view', *Journal of Economic Perspectives* 7: 45–66.

22

J. M. KEYNES ON THE WORKING CLASS

Hans E. Jensen

In this chapter, I shall attempt to examine John Maynard Keynes's views on the working class and the relation of these views to his conception of the capitalist economy and his vision of its future development. My exploration is conditioned by two closely connected assumptions. The first is that Sir Austin Robinson was correct when he asserted that Keynes was a 'perfect "do-gooder", identifying the things that the world most needs to have done and using all his brains and persuasion to get them done' (Robinson 1975: 21–2). Among the things that should be done were corrections of the present society's 'failure to provide for full employment and its arbitrary and inequitable distribution of wealth and incomes' (ibid.). Second, Keynes therefore wrote *The General Theory* in order to show how the 'disease' of '"involuntary" unemployment' among the members of the working class, and their consequent 'poverty in the midst of plenty', might be cured (Keynes vol. 7: 372, 381, 6, 30).[1] As Keynes put it himself in 1940, he was working for 'an advance towards economic equality greater than any which we have made in recent times', which, among other measures, would include 'accumulation of working-class wealth under working-class control' (Keynes vol. 9: 368). It was therefore logical for Keynes to view himself as a practitioner of 'a moral science', namely that of an economics that employs 'judgments of value' (Keynes vol. 14: 297).

Keynes viewed the class structure of twentieth-century capitalist society as an offspring of technological developments that had had a fateful impact upon the institutions of that society. In 1930, he described these technological events as follows:

> From the sixteenth century, with a cumulative crescendo after the eighteenth, the great age of science and technical inventions began, which since the beginning of the nineteenth century has been in full flood – coal, steam, electricity, petrol, steel, rubber, cotton, the chemical industries, automatic machinery and the methods of mass production, wireless, printing ... and thousands of other things ... too ... familiar to catalogue.
>
> (vol. 9: 324)

'What is the result?' Keynes asked (vol. 9: 324). His answer was that society's institutions had been moulded by technological advances in such a manner that a triple class structure had emerged consisting of an 'investing class' of *rentiers*, a 'business class' of entrepreneurs, and an 'earning class' of workers (vol. 4: 4). The evolution of this class structure occurred in a process in which technology threw more and more people into 'a rapidly increasing' class of propertyless workers who earned their livelihood by selling their labour power to entrepreneurs (vol. 19, part 1: 128). Keynes called the working class an earning class because he wished to stress two things. First, in contradistinction to the 'unearned income' of the *'rentier'* (vol. 19, part 2: 846), the income of the worker is a truly earned one in the sense that it is a payment for efforts put forth. Second, the extent to which the members of the working class are able to earn incomes is determined by forces beyond their own control, namely the interlocking decisions of *rentiers* and entrepreneurs. In the 1930s, the entrepreneurs' expected rate of future profit, the 'marginal efficiency of capital', was approaching zero. Unfortunately, 'institutional and psychological factors ... [were] present which set a limit much above zero to the practicable decline in the rate of interest' that entrepreneurs had to pay the rentiers for access to their funds. Consequently, the transmission belt that transported investable funds from the *rentiers* to the entrepreneurs came to a grinding halt with the result that the entrepreneurs curtailed their expenditures drastically. This meant that the economy descended to a 'resting-place [far] below full employment' where it remained 'in a chronic condition of sub-normal activity' (vol. 7: 135, 218, 304, 249). The aforementioned massive involuntary unemployment of workers had become the order of the day.

Keynes's sympathy with the workers was not something new that was spawned by the economic catastrophe of the 1930s, however. It was a feeling that he had nurtured for a long time – a feeling that was based on a conviction that the historical evolution of institutions had placed the workers in an inferior economic and social position. Thus he observed in 1919 that the 'age which came to an end in August 1914' was so 'framed as to throw a great part of the increased income into the control of the class least likely to consume it', namely the property-owning class. As a result, the working class received such a small part of the national income that its members were forced to 'forgo so largely ... the comforts of life' (Keynes vol. 2: 6, 11, 13). Why did the workers acquiesce?

[Because] the labouring classes accepted from ignorance or power-lessness, or were compelled, persuaded, or cajoled by custom, convention, authority, and the well-established order of society into accepting, a situation in which they could call their own very little of the cake that they and nature and the capitalists were co-operating to produce.

(Keynes vol. 2: 11–12)

The 1920s saw no improvement in the workers' condition. On the contrary, they were increasingly chosen as the payers of the cost of economic policies and of institutional realignments in the private sector. For example, the British restoration of the gold standard in 1924 aimed at 'improving the foreign-exchange value of sterling up to its pre-war value in gold from being about 10 per cent below it'. Hence, said Keynes, 'whenever we sell anything abroad ... we have to accept 10 per cent *less in our money*' (vol. 9: 208; emphasis in original). Thus in order to remain competitive in the international market, the coal industry was forced to lower its export prices. In this situation, the

> colliery owners propose[d] that the gap [between price and current cost] should be bridged by a reduction of wages, irrespective of a reduction of the cost of living – that is to say, by a lowering of the standard of life of the miners. They are to make this sacrifice to meet circumstances for which they are in no way responsible and over which they have no control.
>
> (Keynes vol. 9: 222)

That 'this should seem to anyone to be a reasonable proposal,' said Keynes, 'is a grave criticism of our way of managing our economic affairs' (ibid.). He predicted, however, that the miners were 'bound to resist so long as they can; and it must be war, until those who are economically weakest are beaten to the ground' (ibid.: 211). And beaten they were. When the miners refused to accept a cut in wages, they were locked out in the spring of 1926 whereupon the 'Trades Union Council ... supported them with a General Strike'. When the strike collapsed after nine days, Keynes, whose 'feelings ... [were] with the workers', was 'not very cheerful about the future (vol. 19, part 2: 432, 545).

Keynes became increasingly alarmed in the closing years of the 1920s when his inspection of statistical indicators revealed that unemployment had 'never been less than one million' since 1923, and that in April 1929 '1,140,000 workpeople ... [were] unemployed' (Keynes vol. 9: 92). At first, he attributed this development to the 'imbecility' of public policies such as the return to gold and fiscal measures based on the '"Treasury view"' that 'money raised by the state for financing productive schemes must diminish *pro tanto* the supply of capital available to private industry' (Keynes vol. 19, part 2: 750; vol. 9: 147, 115).

As he pored over economic documents and listened to testimonies before committees of inquiry in the late 1920s and early 1930s, Keynes came to the conclusion, however, that imbecile governmental institutions had not caused the 'collapse of private investment' that ushered in the great depression. Rather, these institutions had merely failed to 'mitigate the consequences of the collapse' once it had occurred. Keynes was now of the opinion that the 'severe decline in the volume of investment' had its

266

origin in the institutions of capitalism itself (vol. 9: 147; vol. 13: 352). To be precise, the institution of rentiership had strangulated the economy by refusing to reduce lending rates sufficiently to enable the increasingly pessimistic entrepreneurs 'to call to the aid of their enterprises' those financial resources on which they depended as undertakers of new investments (vol. 4: 5).

To repeat, Keynes found that it was the working class that bore the bulk of the burden imposed on society by dysfunctioning economic institutions. He could think of only one effective means to the end of making it possible for the employable members of the working class to fetch a decent income in the labour market: 'a somewhat comprehensive socialization of investment' that would 'allow the growth of capital up to the point where it ceases to be scarce'. This would 'mean the euthanasia of the rentier, and, consequently, the euthanasia of the cumulative oppressive power of the [financier-]capitalist to exploit the scarcity-value of capital' (vol. 7: 378, 376).

The socialization of investment was therefore a measure whose employment Keynes suggested in order to bring about a more equal distribution of a full-employment national income. Hence he described himself as a 'leveller': 'I want to mould a society in which most of the existing inequalities and causes of inequality are removed' (Keynes quoted in Skidelsky 1992: 233). And then he asked rhetorically in a much-quoted statement:

> Ought I, then, to join the Labour Party? Superficially that is … attractive. But looked at closer, there are great difficulties. To begin with, it is a class party, and the class is not my class. If I am going to pursue sectional interests at all, I shall pursue my own. When it comes to the class struggle as such, my local and personal patriotisms, like those of every one else, except certain unpleasant zealous ones, are attached to my own surroundings. I can be influenced by what seems to me to be justice and good sense; but the *class* war will find me on the side of the educated *bourgeoisie*.
>
> (Keynes vol. 9: 297)

As Robert Skidelsky has pointed out, one of Keynes's criticisms of the Labour Party was directed toward its 'anti-elitism' (Skidelsky 1992: 234). Moreover, Keynes argued that 'doctrinaire State Socialism … is, in fact little better than a dusty survival of a plan to meet the problems of fifty years ago, based on a misunderstanding of what someone said a hundred years ago' (vol. 9: 290–1). On the other hand, he did not criticize socialism 'because it seeks to engage men's altruistic impulses in the service of society, or because it departs from *laissez-faire*, or because it takes away from man's natural liberty to make a million, or because it has courage for bold experiments. All these things I applaud,' said Keynes (ibid.: 290).

And Keynes was convinced that all these things and more could be

achieved if appropriate institutional adjustments were made. In this connection, he placed great faith in the abilities and social consciousness of those
'great modern businessmen' that he viewed as a class of superentrepreneurs
(Keynes vol. 9:319). Unlike the run-of-the-mill entrepreneurs, the superentrepreneurs had shed most of the traditional capitalist ideology and
motivations that still clung to the former. According to Keynes, the
superentrepreneurial function was shaped in a particular institutional mould,
namely that of the *large* 'joint stock institutions' (ibid.: 289):

> [T]he trend of joint stock institutions, when they have reached a certain
> age and size, [is] to approximate to the status of public corporations
> [such as the Bank of England or the Port of London Authority] rather
> than that of individualistic private enterprise. One of the most inter-
> esting and unnoticed developments of recent decades has been the
> tendency of big enterprise to socialise itself. A point arrives in the
> growth of a big institution – particularly a big railway or a big public
> utility enterprise, but also a big bank or a big insurance company – at
> which the owners of the capital, i.e. the shareholders, are almost entirely
> dissociated from the management, with the result that the direct
> personal interest of the latter in the making of great profits becomes
> secondary. When this stage is reached, the general stability and
> reputation of the institution are the more considered by the management
> than the maximum profit for the shareholders.
>
> (ibid.)

Keynes viewed this institutional development as 'a natural line of
evolution. The battle of Socialism against unlimited profit is being won in
detail hour by hour' (vol. 9: 290). The significant aspect of the self-
socialization of large enterprises is that the managers of these companies have
become institutionally adequate for entering into a working partnership with
the goverment in those organs of 'central planning' that Keynes in 1939
associated with an 'amalgam of private capitalism and state socialism' – an
amalgam that he viewed as 'the only practicable recipe for present conditions'
(vol. 21: 492). Thus the curse of unemployment could, and would, be
abolished if the superentrepreneurs were put in charge of planning for the
socialization of investment. It was this small élite of superentrepreneurial
'revolutionaries', as he called them (vol. 9: 319), that Keynes had in mind
when he included himself in the *educated* bourgeoisie. Once it is realized that
it was this kind of bourgeois personage with whom he identified himself, the
following declaration of his is not in conflict with the above-quoted
confession that the class war would find him on the side of the bourgeoisie:

> I am sure that I am less conservative in my inclinations than the average
> Labour voter; I fancy that I have played in my mind with the
> possibilities of greater social changes than come within the present

philosophies of, let us say, Mr Sidney Webb, Mr Thomas, or Mr Wheatley. The republic of my imagination lies on the extreme left of celestial space.

(Keynes vol. 9: 308–9)

As Keynes put it in 1937, this republic informed him that

[t]he natural evolution should be towards a decent level of consumption for everyone; and, when that is high enough, towards the occupation of our energies in the non-economic interests of our lives. Thus we need to be slowly reconstructing our social system with these ends in view.

(Keynes vol. 21: 393)

Hence Keynes looked forward to a day when the socialization of investment would bring forth that society in which 'we shall be free ... at last, to discard' all 'kinds of social custom and economic practice, affecting the distribution of wealth and of economic rewards and penalties, which we now maintain at all costs, however distasteful and unjust they may be in themselves' (vol. 9: 329). Thus, although he did not sympathize with the Labour Party, it was those who voted for that party's candidates that Keynes identified as the chief beneficiaries of such a development. It was to the furtherance of this kind of development that he dedicated his professional energies and efforts. As he is supposed to have said himself, 'he was possessed by "the *Verbesserungs* malady"' (Hession 1984: 203); that is, he 'believed in planning and contriving' as a means to the abolition of 'unemployment' and its associated 'social evils' (Harrod 1951: 192). He was convinced, however, that this could occur only in a state of 'liberal socialism', by which ... [he] mean[t] a system where we can act as an organized community for common purposes and to promote social and economic justice, while respecting and protecting the individual' (Keynes vol. 21: 500). This could hardly be thought of as a community that has all the institutional furniture that would be associated with a 'preservation of the *status quo*'; a preservation 'toward' which, it has been alleged, Keynes's work was 'oriented' (Dillard 1946: 152). As the above discussion should indicate, this 'is an incomplete portrait'. It may be 'true for the short term, but false for the long'. In the words of R. M. O'Donnell, 'as Keynes saw it, the ultimate goal was a decidedly non-capitalist utopia, a form of society with greater similarities to communist or left-wing utopias than to ideal societies built on capitalist or free market norms' (1989: 293). In Keynes's view, liberal socialism would be the only kind of society in which a working man would be fortunate enough to be 'faced with his real, his permanent problem – [namely] how to use his freedom from pressing economic cares, how to occupy his leisure, which science and compound interest will have won for him, to live wisely and agreeably and well' (Keynes vol. 9: 328).

Geoffrey C. Harcourt also considers himself a socialist, but 'a Christian socialist' (1986: 250). And like Keynes, he sees 'economics as very much a moral as well as a social science and very much a handmaiden to progressive thought' (ibid.: 5). Hence he believes that the purpose of economics is

> to make the world a better place for ordinary men and women, to produce a more just and equitable society.... [Economics] is really the study of the processes whereby surpluses are created in economies, how they are extracted, who gets them and what they do with them. All economies have created surpluses in one way or another. Capitalism does it in a particular way and that is the process in which I am most interested because I live in capitalist economies.
>
> (ibid.)

As he observed in 1986, however, Harcourt 'would like to help to create a society where the surplus is extracted and used in a way quite different from that of a capitalist society' (1986: 5). He was, therefore, in favour of putting 'nationalisation back on the agenda' (ibid.: 267). This would necessitate that planning be placed on the same agenda. But whereas Keynes envisioned that the superentrepreneurs would do most of the planning for the socialization of investment, Harcourt opined that planning for nationalization should be performed in the highest echelons of the civil service. Appointees to the 'key decision-making position' in the service should not only be 'highly intelligent' but also imbued with 'altruism and compassion and tolerance' (ibid.: 269). If these humanistic feelings are absent at the top of the civil service, there is no guarantee that plans will be 'implemented at key points without being frustrated by people who think that they are not necessarily practical or workable' (ibid.).

Harcourt, who developed his Keynesesque moral sentiments long before he became acquainted with the works of Keynes, has explained his intellectual development in the following words:

> When I first went to the University of Melbourne I still reflected the views of my [conservative] parents – but only for the first six months. For during those first six months I found out that not all the world was like 24 Faircroft Avenue [in Melbourne, where Harcourt grew up]. This converted me to socialism ... principally as a result of the Economic Geography lectures of Molly Bain and Bob Wilson....
>
> [O]ne of the things that really led me towards thinking about socialism was a description [in these lectures] of how oil wells were developed on the Californian oil fields by unfettered private enterprise. The wells were put down so close to one another that they let the gas out and so, much oil which otherwise could have been taken out, was lost forever.... [I]t seemed to me that we ought to develop institutions which allow us to take much longer horizons in planning the development of resources which are vital to the

community as a whole, not only the current generation but future generations as well.

(Harcourt 1986: 250, 268)

Given this outlook of his, Harcourt was in a receptive mood when he entered the University of Cambridge as a research student. Here he immersed himself in Keynes's 'writings and [in writings] about him' (Harcourt 1993: xii) at the same time as he became exposed to the ideas of some of Keynes's followers. When he returned to Cambridge as a faculty member after a sojourn to Australia, Harcourt worked closely with several Cambridge economists, some of whom had been Keynes's students and all of whom had been his colleagues: 'Richard Kahn, Joan Robinson, and also Nicholas Kaldor [and] Piero Sraffa' (Harcourt 1982: 387). These scholars, plus the 'late Michael Kalecki,' were the 'elder statespersons' in the 'Post-Keynesian school' with which Harcourt identifies 'more than [he does] with any other group' (ibid.).

Harcourt has made impressive contributions to the post-Keynesian corpus of knowledge. He has done so in two principal ways. In the first place, he has made analytical innovations in articles and books, and encouraged authors of theses to solve persistent problems in the post-Keynesian body of doctrine, and he has disseminated new knowledge in his lectures. Second, he has become *the* historian of post-Keynesian economics.

In conclusion, it should be pointed out that Harcourt's ingrained propensity to acknowledge his intellectual debt to other economists throws a veil over his own originality. He is a much more innovative scholar than one would suspect on the basis of a first reading of his theoretical and doctrine-historical publications. The impetus for this scholarly enterprise originated in Harcourt's experience as an undergraduate student at the University of Melbourne.

NOTE

1   All references to Keynes in this chapter are to the *Collected Writings* (Keynes 1971–89).

REFERENCES

Dillard, D. (1946) 'The pragmatic basis of Keynes's political economy', *Journal of Economic History* 6: 121–52.
Harcourt, G. C. (1982) *The Social Science Imperialists: Selected Essays by G. C. Harcourt*, ed. P. Kerr, London: Routledge & Kegan Paul.
—— (1986) *Controversies in Political Economy: Selected Essays by G. C. Harcourt*, ed. O. F. Hamouda, Brighton: Wheatsheaf.
—— (1993) *Post-Keynesian Essays in Biography*, London: Macmillan.
Harrod, R.(1951) *The Life of John Maynard Keynes*, London: Macmillan.
Hession, C. H. (1984) *John Maynard Keynes*, New York: Macmillan.

Keynes, J.M. (1971–89) *The Collected Writings of John Maynard Keynes*, 30 vols, London: Macmillan.

O'Donnell, R. M. (1989) *Keynes: Philosophy, Economics and Politics*, New York: St Martin's Press.

Robinson, A. (1975) 'A personal view', in Milo Keynes (ed.) *Essays on John Maynard Keynes*, Cambridge: Cambridge University Press.

Skidelsky, R. (1992) *John Maynard Keynes*: vol. 2, *The Economist as Saviour 1920–1937*, London: Macmillan.

23

KEYNES AND CHURCHILL

Heinz W. Arndt

In June 1944, the British economist Lionel Robbins, having observed Keynes negotiating with the Americans at the Bretton Woods conference, confided to his diary:

> I often find myself thinking that Keynes must be one of the most remarkable men that ever lived – the quick logic, the birdlike swoop of intuition, the vivid fancy, the wide vision, above all the incomparable sense of the fitness of words, all combine to make something several degrees beyond the limit of ordinary human achievement. Certainly, in our own age, only the Prime Minister [Churchill] is of comparable stature. He, of course, surpasses him. But the greatness of the Prime Minister is something much easier to understand than the genius of Keynes.
>
> (Howson and Moggridge 1990: 158)

More recently, the American economist J. K. Galbraith has drawn the same comparison in his usual caustic manner: In 1936 'Keynes, like his great contemporary Churchill, was regarded [in US official circles] as too clear-headed and candid to be trusted' (Galbraith 1975: 133).

Keynes and Churchill stand out as arguably the greatest British figures of this century. They were near-contemporaries, Churchill born in 1874, Keynes in 1883. Although born into and belonging to very different segments of British society – Churchill the aristocrat and politician, Keynes the middle-class intellectual – they had social contacts through most of their lives and for over twenty years worked with (and sometimes against) each other. Yet the vast literature on both of them contains no account of their relationship. To give such an account is the purpose of this chapter.

PARALLEL LIVES

From 1906 to 1908, Churchill was under-secretary at the Colonial Office in the Liberal government, while Keynes was a clerk in the India Office. But the two government departments were quite distinct, and there is no evidence, nor likelihood, that the Minister and the junior civil servant had anything to do with each other. From 1908 to 1910 Churchill was President of the Board of

Trade and, in close collaboration with Lloyd George, who was Chancellor of the Exchequer, initiated a radical programme of social reform. Spurred on by Beatrice Webb and assisted by the young William Beveridge, he introduced labour exchanges, unemployment and infirmity insurance. But during the very years while Churchill was 'one of the founders of the welfare state' (Addison 1994: 57), intensely concerned with the problem of unemployment which twenty years later would preoccupy Keynes, the latter was a young don at Cambridge, moving from philosophy to economics, but living the congenial life of an 'Apostle' among like-minded friends. The year 1909 saw Lloyd George's radical budget, the constitutional crisis over the House of Lords and troubles in Ireland. Keynes, we are told, 'was aware of these things, tangentially involved in some of them, but was basically indifferent to them' (Skidelsky 1983: 232).

In 1911, after a spell as Home Secretary, Churchill became First Lord of the Admiralty, and 'his radicalism faded' (Addison 1994: 65). For the next decade, he was wholly absorbed by political and military affairs, naval rearmament, the Dardanelles, active service in France, the Ministry of Munitions and the War Office. Thus, although Keynes from the outbreak of the First World War in August 1914 played an important role in the Treasury under the government of which Churchill was a member, their official paths did not cross, and this remained the case even during the Versailles peace conference of 1919. Keynes was in Paris as Treasury representative on the British delegation from January 1919, and Churchill visited Paris in February, but, as Keynes later mentioned, 'Churchill was little concerned with the conference' (Keynes vol. 10: 64),[1] and there is no evidence that they met there. When Keynes published his passionate denunciation of the Versailles settlement in his *The Economic Consequences of the Peace*, he sent a complimentary copy to Churchill, but we do not know whether it was acknowledged.

Until 1924, therefore, when Churchill became Chancellor of the Exchequer in Baldwin's Conservative government, Keynes and Churchill lived parallel lives, almost fortuitously unconcerned with each other's business. But this is not to say that they did not know each other and meet socially. Churchill's political and society circles and Keynes's Cambridge and Bloomsbury ones overlapped at a few points. One may have been the Webbs. Beatrice first met Churchill in 1903, when she dismissed him in her inimitable way as 'bumptious, shallow-minded and reactionary', but came to be much more favourably impressed when in 1908 he swallowed Sidney's scheme for labour and unemployment' (MacKenzie and MacKenzie 1977: 355). Keynes was on the fringe of Fabian activity at Cambridge. In 1909 he spoke to the Fabians on foreign investment, in 1911 at the Union in support of Sidney Webb (Moggridge 1992: 190). Among the Cambridge Fabians was his friend Rupert Brooke, who once, with Lytton Strachey, 'tried to explain Moore's ideas to Mrs Webb while she tried to convince us of the efficacy of prayer'

(MacKenzie and MacKenzie 1977: 381). It is difficult to believe that, through Brooke and the Webbs, and later in Bloomsbury, Keynes did not have social contact with Shaw, Wells and others, who in turn must have encountered Churchill, the Liberal politician.

The other possible *point d'appui* is Lady Ottoline Morrell, who liked to play hostess to Bloomsbury, on Thursday evenings at the Morrells' house at 44 Bedford Square and later at their Garsington country home. On 18 May 1911, she gave a party in honour of Churchill, who 'looked very fine in full-dress uniform' – he was going on to a ball at Buckingham Palace (Seymour 1992: 131). Keynes visited her for the first time a month later, though he had no doubt seen and heard of her before, and in the following years saw much of her, staying at Garsington many times, including quite a long stay to recuperate after his appendicitis operation in July 1915 (Moggridge 1992: 247). Again there is no record that Churchill and Keynes met through Lady Ottoline, but it is not unlikely. During the war, in 1916, we are told, 'Keynes continued to labour at the Treasury and his letters to his parents were full of a busy social life studded with the names of the Asquiths, the McKennas, Lady Ottoline Morrell and Mr Winston Churchill' (Keynes vol. 16: 177). In March 1916, he told his mother he had 'dined twice at Downing Street in the past fortnight' (Skidelsky 1983: 326). Whether at No. 10 or 11 he did not say, but Churchill may well have been present.

Between 1922 and 1924 Churchill was out of office and Parliament, and divided his time between fighting elections unsuccessfully, journalism and other writing. Keynes, intermittently involved in reparations and war debt diplomacy, commuted between Cambridge and Bloomsbury and divided his time between teaching, journalism and other writing. This phase ended dramatically when Baldwin resumed office as Prime Minister in November 1924. To Churchill's own and everyone else's surprise, he offered him the Chancellorship of the Exchequer. Churchill later commented, 'I should have liked to have answered "Will the bloody duck swim?" but as it was a formal and important occasion I replied "This fulfils my ambition"' (Clarke 1994: 79).

CHURCHILL'S CHANCELLORSHIP

Ever since he left the Treasury in 1919, Keynes had been much concerned with the central problem of British financial policy: whether Britain should return to the gold standard at the pre-war parity for sterling. At the end of the war, a Committee on Currency and Foreign Exchanges headed by the former Governor of the Bank of England, Lord Cunliffe, had recommended such a return. The Lloyd George government had accepted this recommendation in principle and had passed legislation which, following questions in Parliament, set 31 December 1925 as the deadline. Keynes's views fluctuated. In the early 1920s he had favoured a policy of securing domestic price stability by maintaining a flexible exchange rate and thus avoiding the deflationary policy needed to raise sterling to parity, with the adverse effects of such a policy on money wages and/or unemployment. He argued this case in 1923 in the *Tract on Monetary Reform* (*Collected Writings*, vol. 4) and in numerous articles. He again presented his views in July 1924 to a committee under Austen Chamberlain appointed by Snowden, the Chancellor in the short-lived first Labour Government. He now argued that there was no need for a deflationary policy since rising prices in the USA would see sterling rise to or above par. The committee seemed to agree with Keynes, rather than with the Treasury and the Bank of England, which regarded return to gold at the old parity as essential to the standing of London as the world's financial centre. But before they completed their report, the Labour government fell, and general elections in October 1924 brought Baldwin to power with Churchill as his Chancellor of the Exchequer (Moggridge 1992: ch. 17).

Churchill came to the Chancellorship without any formal training in economics and without any strong views except for a liberal attachment to free trade and sympathy for the unemployed. It is probably true, as Skidelsky has claimed, that 'Churchill understood modern no better than old-fashioned economics' (Skidelsky 1992: 197), but he had an acute intelligence and great power of application to any problem he had to deal with. Within weeks of assuming his new office he was presented by Montagu Norman, the governor of the Bank of England, with a plan to prepare for a return to gold at par before the end of 1925. He was worried about the domestic implications of which Keynes had warned in articles in *Nation* with which he was familiar. By 29 January he had written a substantial paper, dubbed 'Churchill's Exercise', setting out the objections to a quick return to gold. It led the head of the Treasury, Bradbury, to comment that 'he appears to have his spiritual home in the Keynes–McKenna sanctuary' (Skidelsky 1992: 426). There has been some doubt whether Churchill was expressing his own view or was merely provoking his official advisers into stating their case for the return to gold more forcefully. In this he was certainly successful, eliciting long and trenchant replies. But there is also no doubt that Churchill was genuinely perplexed and torn between the pros and cons. On reading another article by Keynes, 'The return towards gold', Churchill complained in another memorandum:

> The Treasury have never, it seems to me, faced the profound significance of what Mr Keynes calls 'the paradox of unemployment amidst dearth'. The Governor shows himself perfectly happy in the spectacle of Britain possessing the finest credit in the world simultaneously with a million and a quarter unemployed.
>
> (Moggridge 1992: 428)

In another attempt to resolve his doubts, Churchill arranged for a dinner on 17 March to which he invited, besides his private secretary (P. J. Grigg),

Bradbury and Niemeyer for the Treasury and Bank and Keynes and McKenna for the opposition. Till midnight and beyond, Keynes and McKenna argued that at the pre-war parity sterling would be overvalued by 10 per cent and that the adjustment to the higher rate would mean additional unemployment and industrial unrest over wage cuts, and Bradbury and Niemeyer again put their case. Churchill, 'ready to and anxious to be convinced as far as my limited comprehension of these extremely technical matters will permit' (Rose 1994: 174), asked McKenna:

> This is not entirely an economic matter; it is a political decision, for it involves proclaiming that we cannot, for the time being, complete the undertaking which we acclaimed as necessary in 1918, and introduced legislation accordingly. You have been a politician; indeed you have been Chancellor of the Exchequer. Given the situation as it is, what decision would you take?
>
> (Grigg 1948: 182–3)

McKenna is said to have replied: 'There is no escape; you have to go back; but it will be hell' (ibid.).

On 19 March Churchill agreed with Norman on the return to gold at the old parity and on 28 April he announced the decision in the Budget. In July Keynes published his pamphlet, *The Economic Consequences of Mr Churchill* (*Collected Writings*, vol. 9). Keynes was not now opposed to a return to the gold standard as a fixed exchange rate system. His ferocious attack was directed at the overvaluation of sterling implied in the return at pre-war par, because of its effects on unemployment and the balance of payments. Nor was it directed at Churchill personally. Churchill, he said, had made the disastrous decision partly because he 'has no intuitive judgement to prevent him from making mistakes; partly because, lacking this intuitive judgement, he was defeated by the clamorous voices of conventional finance; and, most of all, because he was gravely misled by the experts (Keynes vol. 9: 212). Neither did Churchill resent Keynes's criticisms. In Parliament, he charged Snowden with inconsistency in first urging the earliest possible return to gold and then attacking the government for taking this course, and contrasted Snowden's line with 'the position of Mr Keynes, who is, I suppose, by far the most distinguished and able exponent of opposition to the return to gold. He is the great advocate of a managed currency, the most powerful and persuasive advocate' (Churchill 1974: 3595).

On the day in September 1931 when the pound went off gold – an event which Keynes greeted with delight, 'chuckling like a boy' (C. H. Rolphe, cited in Skidelsky 1992: 397) – Keynes had lunch with Churchill. That evening the Webbs visited the Keyneses at Tilton, their country house. Keynes told Beatrice, as she later recorded in her diary, that during lunch Churchill had claimed he had never been in favour of the return to the gold standard (MacKenzie and MacKenzie 1985: 260). He called it his 'biggest blunder', and blamed Montagu Norman for it (Boyle 1967: 190).

Keynes's warnings about the economic and social consequences of the return to gold at par were soon borne out by the problems of the coal industry which led to the General Strike of 1926. When the coal owners, in the face of declining international competitiveness, sought to reduce wages, Keynes objected, and Churchill, as Chancellor, also adopted a conciliatory position, offering a subsidy which, he hoped, would maintain industrial peace. But once the miners secured the support of the TUC for a general strike, Churchill turned militant. Keynes had little sympathy with the rabid tone Churchill adopted as editor of the government's official strike journal, the *British Gazette*, and indeed with Churchill's increasingly conservative positions in the last three years of his chancellorship. In 1928, we find him writing a rude letter to Churchill: 'Dear Chancellor of the Exchequer, What an imbecile Currency Bill you have introduced!' Churchill replied courteously: 'My dear Keynes, Apologies for not replying sooner ... I will read your article enclosed and reflect carefully, as I always do, on all you say' (Keynes vol. 19: 749–50). In 1929, Keynes criticized Churchill's opposition to the programme for combating unemployment through public works put forward by Lloyd George and supported in a Liberal Party pamphlet, *We Can Conquer Unemployment*, to which Keynes had contributed. Churchill in his last Budget speech of April 1929 had put the orthodox 'Treasury view' that deficit-financed public investment would create little employment because it would crowd out private investment through higher interest rates. Keynes's refutation was the main theme of his *Treatise on Money* (*Collected Writings*, vols 5 and 6) on which he worked during those years.

From May 1929, when the Baldwin government fell, until September 1939, when Churchill once again became First Lord of the Admiralty, he was out of office and almost devoid of interest in economic matters, preoccupied first with India and then with Germany. Professional contacts with Keynes were few and far between. When Keynes in 1930 proposed a 10 per cent tariff on all imports, as an alternative to a devaluation of the pound, Churchill, in a dramatic departure from his attachment to free trade, expressed sympathy, converted, according to Grigg, 'by the blandishments of Keynes' (Grigg 1948: 233). When Churchill visited the USA in the following year, Brendan Bracken briefed him on events at home, sending him the views of Keynes on the world monetary situation (Lysaght 1979: 132).

There is no published record of Churchill taking any interest in the Keynesian revolution of the 1930s. Keynes, on the other hand, was all with Churchill in his onslaught on appeasement. In March 1938 he wrote to him, 'I have shared the general admiration of your magnificent speeches in the House of Commons' (Gilbert vol. 5: 955), and a few months later he referred in a letter to Kingsley Martin to 'anti-Chamberlain candidates supported by all of us, e.g. Winston' (Keynes vol. 28: 123).

But if professional contacts after 1925 were few, social contact was frequent, chiefly through the Other Club.

THE OTHER CLUB

The Other Club was founded by Churchill and F. E. Smith (the later Lord Birkenhead) in 1911 when, it is said, both had applied for membership of The Club, the exclusive club that went back to Samuel Johnson's day, and had been blackballed (Campbell 1983: 268). The object of the new club (as of the old) was 'dining and wagering'. It was to consist of not more than fifty members, of whom not more than twenty-four should be Members of the House of Commons. The rules, whimsically drafted by F. E. Smith, specified that the club was to meet on alternate Thursdays 'at 8.15 punctually' when Parliament was in session. The names of the Executive Committee 'shall be wrapped in impenetrable mystery'. 'Nothing in the Rules of Intercourse of the Club shall interfere with the rancour or asperity of party politics.' Dinners were generally held in the Pinafore Room of the Savoy and could go on late into the night. Churchill's chauffeur had many happy memories of these occasions when interviewed by Churchill's biographer: 'Winston never missed this if it was possible to attend, and he always enjoyed himself there, always coming out at around 2 am, give or take an hour, in a very happy frame of mind' (Gilbert vol. 5: 63, 506). Churchill's last public appearance in December 1964, aged 90, was at a dinner of the club (Rose 1994: 141).

Membership was by invitation. If a particularly eminent member was to be recruited, Lloyd George would join Churchill in issuing the invitation (Hazlehurst 1995). The list of members over the years reads like a *Who's Who* of Britain's political and intellectual élite, from Lloyd George, Smuts and Reading, to high brass such as Kitchener and Roberts, to press lords such as Beverbrook and Camrose, writers such as H. G. Wells, Arnold Bennett and P. G. Wodehouse, artists such as Lutyens and Munnings, scientists such as Lindemann (Lord Cherwell) and Cockroft, and judges (Coote 1971). But the chief qualification for membership appears to have been that 'Winston thought well of them' (Gilbert vol. 5: 63).

Keynes was invited in 1927, the invitation demonstrating that Churchill bore him no grudge over his *Economic Consequences*. Keynes attended the dinners whenever time allowed. 'It was a place of good talk and pleasant intimacy, more worldly in tone than the Bloomsbury gatherings in which he usually found recreation' (Harrod 1951: 396). Arnold Bennett encountered the new member at dinner in 1927 and found him 'very agreeable and rather brilliant' (Bennett 1935: 962). In 1929, Keynes lost £160 in bets on the general elections but won £10 from Churchill, no doubt at the club. When Churchill during his visit to New York, in 1931 was run into and severely hurt by a car, several of his Other Club friends, including Keynes, contributed to a £2,000 gift of a car (Manchester 1983: 882). On another occasion, in 1940,

Churchill's Other Club companions, including Keynes, presented him with a silver-gilt snuffbox that had belonged to Nelson (Gilbert vol. 6: 853).

Dinners at the Other Club gave Keynes opportunities to talk to Churchill and, particularly after the outbreak of the Second World War, to raise policy matters by-passing official channels. In October 1939, he tried (unsuccessfully) to persuade Churchill, then First Lord, to remove wheat from the list of contraband goods, partly to influence German and world opinion and partly to dissipate Germany's foreign exchange reserves (Moggridge 1992: 628). In July 1942, Keynes became concerned about the large sterling liabilities Britain was accumulating. When the India Office rejected any suggestion of blocking these balances, Keynes took his case to Churchill, now Prime Minister, at a meeting of the Other Club. The result was an 'Action This Day' minute to the Chancellor which began, 'Lord Keynes mentioned to me the other night' and asked for discussion in Cabinet (Moggridge 1992: 638). Keynes attended one more dinner of the club, exhausted after strenuous negotiations in the USA and amid numerous other commitments, three weeks before his death on 20 April 1946 (Rose 1944: 341).

THE SECOND WORLD WAR

From May 1940, Churchill led the country's war effort, daily preoccupied with national defence, domestic politics and high diplomacy. For most of the time, according to Austin Robinson, he was 'sublimely unaware in all but very occasional detail of what happened on the economic front' (Robinson 1975: 19). Brendan Bracken claimed he was 'always bored by unheroic money matters' (Lysaght 1979: 250). Keynes was sometimes inclined to agree with this view. In July 1941, he wrote to the Chancellor of the Exchequer, Kingsley Wood:

> The President [F. D. Roosevelt] ought to be left free to concentrate on issues of strategy, diplomacy and politics without having to consider the pressing and difficult details of economic policy, which he does not really care for any more than our own Prime Minister.
>
> (Keynes vol. 23: 155)

But there were many times when he found Churchill attentive to economic policy issues he put to him and at least once he gave him top marks. In April 1945, reporting in a personal letter on a dinner Churchill gave to a lot of finance people, including the Chancellor of the Exchequer and the Governor of the Bank of England, to hear the views of Roosevelt's emissary, Bernard Baruch, Keynes said: 'Winston was quite magnificent throughout, in his best form, taking a profound interest in our Treasury problems for once, thoroughly understanding the points at issue' (Keynes vol. 24: 302).

Keynes spent the first months of the war mainly at Cambridge, plagued by ill health after a severe bout of influenza, writing *How to Pay for the War*

(*Collected Writings*, vol. 10) and other aspects of war-economic policy. But he was soon drawn into official business and from August 1940 had an office and a secretary in the Treasury. Churchill soon made use of him. When Sir John Anderson was appointed Lord President of the Council with responsibility for overall control of the country's economic resources for the war effort, Churchill directed him, 'You should summon economists like Keynes to give their views to you personally' (Wheeler-Bennett 1962, 260). In June 1940 Keynes drafted for Churchill a statement of encouragement to the French (Keynes vol. 22: 180). In July 1941, just preceding the Roosevelt–Churchill meeting that yielded the Atlantic Charter, Keynes saw a draft of Article VII which, by proclaiming non-discrimination in trade as one of the Allies' war aims, appeared to preclude the maintenance of imperial preference. Keynes may have had a hand in the subsequent insertion of the saving clause 'with due respect for their existing obligations' (Amery 1988: 707–8), which later became the 'grandfather' clause in the GATT.

During and just after the war years, Keynes visited the USA five times on official business: in 1941 to help mobilize US financial resources for Britain, including Lend-Lease; in 1943 for preliminary negotiations about the Keynes and White plans for the IMF and World Bank; in 1944 for the Bretton Woods conference; and in 1946 for discussions on the terms and conditions of the US loan to Britain, and each time also on much else. Churchill was undoubtedly aware of these issues, though not closely involved. A draft of Keynes's plan for a clearing union was put to Cabinet in April 1942 (Moggridge 1992: 678). When it came to finding a name for the new international currency unit, Keynes proposed 'bancor' but at one point suggested that

> our Prime Minister and President Roosevelt could between them do better than most of us at this game, as at most other games, if they had the time to turn their minds to writing a new dictionary as well as a new geography.
>
> (Keynes vol. 25: 272)

D. H. Robertson suggested 'winfranks' (Keynes vol. 22: 302). On one occasion, Churchill and Keynes travelled back from America together (Gilbert vol. 8: 526). During the tense discussions of plans for post-war world trade early in 1944, Cherwell reported to Churchill that there were two factions in Treasury, one headed by Keynes, the other by Henderson, 'an economist with Schachtian aspirations' (Keynes vol. 25: 302). Again, early in 1945, Churchill asked Keynes to attend a meeting on the same issues with the Governor of the Bank of England and senior Ministers (Keynes vol. 26: 323).

There is little published evidence of other contacts between them during the war years, apart from dinners at the Other Club. The Prime Minister undoubtedly had a say in the appointment of Keynes as a director of the Bank of England in September 1941 and his elevation to the peerage in June 1942. Professor Moggridge tells me that Keynes's appointments book mentions, for

17 June 1942, '10 Downing Street' – to celebrate the latter event? Harrod refers to Keynes 'staying with Mr Churchill during the war', presumably at Chartwell (Harrod 1951: 471). In May 1946, a few weeks after Keynes's death, Churchill, almost as exhausted as Keynes had been, wrote to Cherwell: 'I am at what poor Keynes called in the last weeks of his life "saturation point"' (Gilbert vol. 8: 234).

TWO GREAT MEN

Public figures as prominent, clever, opinionated and combative as Churchill and Keynes inevitably attracted criticism all their lives. Margot Asquith once said, 'Winston has a noisy mind' (Leith-Ross 1968: 30). A recent biography of Churchill is a compendium of every criticism and abuse ever levelled at him (Rose 1994). Keynes was fiercely attacked over his *Economic Consequences of the Peace* (*Collected Writings*, vol. 2) and later by economists who disagreed with him. Montagu Norman referred to him as a 'clever dilettante' (Boyle 1967: 160), Lloyd George in his war memoirs as 'an entertaining economist whose bright but shallow dissertations on finance and political economy, when not taken seriously, always provide a source of innocent merriment to his readers' (Lloyd George 1933–6: 684). But even at the time, and certainly on a longer view, these aspersions were overwhelmingly outweighed by praise and admiration.

One of Churchill's senior officials in Treasury reminisced about his 'vitality, his keen imagination and critical appreciation of any proposal put to him and his grasp of administration in the office, together with his generous temperament and genial expansiveness at Chartwell [which] won him the affection of all of us' (Leith-Ross 1968: 118). One of his successors as Prime Minister described the Churchill of 1924–9: 'Unique, wayward, exciting, a man with a peculiar glamour of his own, that brought a sense of colour into our rather drab political life' (Macmillan 1966: 176). These testimonies could be multiplied from the large literature.

Panegyrics on Keynes, no less whole-hearted, abound. Bertrand Russell: 'The sharpest and clearest intellect that I have ever known' (Skidelsky 1983: 124). At the Bretton Woods conference:

> On our side, one name stands quite alone. Maynard's performance was truly wonderful.... His industry was prodigious, his resilience and continuous optimism constant wonder to those inclined to pessimism, while I doubt whether he has ever spoken with more lucidity and charm.
>
> (Lee 1975: 220)

And, finally, one of his former Cambridge students:

> He was so much ahead of the field in wisdom, intellect and power, wit,

in art, in generosity, in his range, and in the ease, gaiety and simplicity that went with all this, that I have never had any reverence left for any other famous men, economists or not, that I have since encountered.

(Bensusan-Butt 1980: 26)

In the heat of debate, Churchill and Keynes could be disparaging about each other. During the 1929 election campaign Churchill once referred to 'Professor Keynes' as 'the proprietor or controller of an extreme radical weekly newspaper' (Churchill 1974: 6442), and Keynes once declared a statement by Churchill to be 'feather-brained' (Keynes vol. 9: 240). But through most of their public lives, they expressed mutual regard. 'Keynes had not only an intellectual appreciation of Mr Churchill's gifts, but also: a certain warmth of sympathy for one whose type of mind was very different from his own' (Harrod 1951: 360). Keynes was not merely being polite when, in his review of Churchill's *The World Crisis*, he declared that 'Mr Churchill was, perhaps, the most acute and concentrated intelligence which saw the war at close quarters from beginning to end' and that 'Mr Churchill writes better than any politician since Disraeli' (Keynes vol. 10: 53). Nor was Churchill merely being polite when he referred to Keynes in 1925 as 'by far the most distinguished and able exponent of the opposition to the return to gold' who has argued his case in 'a series of searching and brilliant articles, formidable and instructive' (Churchill 1974: 3595).

Churchill's and Keynes's backgrounds, personalities and interests were very different. Their two major periods of substantial professional interaction, Churchill's chancellorship and the Second World War apart, the published literature allows us only glimpses of personal contact between them. But, as Skidelsky has said, 'the relations between the two men were friendly' (Skidelsky 1992: 690), and to know this, and to learn something about the relations between these two great men, cannot fail to give one pleasure.

ACKNOWLEDGEMENT

For helpful comments on an earlier draft I am indebted to Professor D. Moggridge and Dr L. D. Thomson.

NOTE

1   All references other than speeches to J. M. Keynes in this chapter are to the *Collected Works* (Keynes 1971–89).

REFERENCES

Addison, P. (1994) 'Churchill and social reform', in P. Blake and W. R. Louis (eds) *Churchill*, Oxford: Oxford University Press.

Amery, L. (1988) *The Empire at Bay: The Leo Amery Diaries, 1929–1945*, ed. J.

Barnes and D. Nicholson, London: Hutchinson.

Bennett, A. (1935) *Journal 1896–1928*, New York: Viking.

Bensusan-Butt, D. M. (1980) *On Economic Knowledge*, Canberra: Australian National University.

Boyle, A. (1967) *Montagu Norman*, London: Cassell.

Campbell, J. (1983) *F. E. Smith: First Early of Birkenhead*, London: Jonathan Cape.

Churchill, W. S. (1974) *Complete Speeches*, 8 vols, ed. R. R. James, London: Heinemann.

Clarke, P. (1994) 'Churchill's economic ideas, 1900–1930', in P. Blake and W. R. Lewis (eds) *Churchill*, Oxford: Oxford University Press.

Coote, C. R. (1971) *The Other Club*, London: Sidgwick & Jackson.

Galbraith, J. K. (1975) 'How Keynes came to America', in Milo Keynes (ed.) *Essays on J. M. Keynes*, Cambridge: Cambridge University Press.

Gilbert, M. (1976–88) *Winston Churchill*, 8 vols, London: Heinemann.

——— (1967–82) *Companion Volumes*, London: Heinemann.

Grigg, P. J. (1948) *Prejudice and Judgment*, London: Jonathan Cape.

Harrod, R. F. (1951) *The Life of John Maynard Keynes*, London: Macmillan.

Hazlehurst, C. (1995) 'The founders of the Other Club: an investigation', Canberra.

Howson, S. and Moggridge D. (eds) (1990) *The Wartime Diaries of Lionel Robbins and James Meade, 1943–45*, London: Macmillan.

Keynes, J. M. (1971–89) *Collected Writings*, 30 vols, ed. A. Robinson and D. Moggridge, London: Macmillan.

Lee, F.G. (1975) 'The international negotiator', in Milo Keynes (ed.) *Essays on J.M. Keynes*, Cambridge: Cambridge University Press.

Leith-Ross, F. (1968) *Money Talk: Fifty Years of International Finance*, London: Hutchinson.

Lloyd George, D. (1933–6) *War Memoirs*, London: Nicholson & Watson.

Lysaght, C. E. (1979) *Brendan Bracken*, London: Allen Lane.

MacKenzie, N. and MacKenzie, J. (1977) *The First Fabians*, London: Weidenfeld & Nicolson.

——— (eds) (1985) *The Diary of Beatrice Webb (1924–43)*, vol. 4, London: Virago.

Macmillan, H. (1966) *Winds of Change, 1914–1939*, London: Macmillan.

Manchester, D. (1983) *W. S. Churchill: Visions of Glory, 1874–1932*, London: Little, Brown.

Moggridge, D. (1992) *Maynard Keynes*, London: Routledge.

Robinson, A. (1975) 'A personal view', in Milo Keynes (ed.) *Essays on J. M. Keynes*, Cambridge: Cambridge University Press.

Rose, N. (1994) *Churchill: An Unruly Life*, London: Simon & Schuster.

Seymour, M. (1992) *Ottoline Morrell: Life on a Grand Scale*, London: Hodder & Stoughton.

Skidelsky, R. (1983) *J. M. Keynes: Hopes Betrayed, 1883–1920*, London: Macmillan.

——— (1992) *John Maynard Keynes: The Economist as Saviour, 1920–1937*, London: Macmillan.

Wheeler-Bennett, J. W. (1962) *John Anderson*, London: Macmillan.

24

COHERENCE IN POST-KEYNESIAN ECONOMICS

Stephen Pratten

INTRODUCTION

The origins of post-Keynesian economics are notoriously diverse: Smith, Ricardo, Marx, Marshall, Keynes, Kalecki and Sraffa are all perceived as important influences. Moreover, various relatively distinct branches of post-Keynesianism are often identified as emerging from these roots. Although certain general characteristics can be identified including an opposition to orthodox approaches and an emphasis upon the significance of institutions, the complexity of human agency and importance of uncertainty, numerous competing substantive positions are developed. A question that arises from the existence of such distinct approaches within post-Keynesianism is whether they can all be interpreted as mutually consistent and belonging to a coherent whole. In recent years this has become a somewhat controversial issue.

Some have claimed that any attempt to define, or consider the degree of coherence within, post-Keynesianism is a futile, even dangerously counter-productive, exercise. Thus, Harcourt and Hamouda write:

> the real difficulty arises when attempts are made to synthesize the strands [of post-Keynesian economics] in order to see whether a coherent whole emerges. Our own view is that to attempt to do so is vainly to search for what Joan Robinson called 'only another box of tricks' to replace the 'complete theory' of mainstream economics which all strands reject.
>
> (Harcourt and Hamouda 1988: 230–1)

In contrast, many suggest that a clear characterization of the essence of post-Keynesian economics may encourage its promotion over orthodox approaches. Some go on to claim that coherence can be identified at a substantive level[1] while others insist that it must be located at a methodological or philosophical level.[2] Especially prominent with respect this later view have been attempts to situate the coherence of post-Keynesianism within a shared adherence to a critical realist perspective.[3] In this chapter I wish to highlight the relative fruitfulness of, and implications which follow from, pursuing a philosophically informed account of post-Keynesianism.

IN SEARCH OF COHERENCE

Authors such as Harcourt and Hamouda, who express reservations regarding the search for coherence, seem particularly concerned that this project could mimic orthodoxy by imposing some narrow set of methods that must be followed slavishly or by promoting certain substantive results that must be accommodated. Any suggestion of sacrificing the rich diversity characteristic of post-Keynesian economics with its competing relatively distinct strands for a restricted, if compatible, set of positions is viewed with considerable suspicion. Unsurprisingly, the claim that the search for coherence can be counterproductive is often accompanied by a plea for pluralism. Coherence, however, need not necessarily imply universal adherence to particular substantive positions or specific methods. Rather, if, like those who link post-Keynesian economics with a critical realist position, one locates coherence at the level of a common methodological orientation, only a shared set of fairly abstract perspectives on, for example, the aims of science, the nature of human agency and the relationship between human agents and social structure may be implied, leaving considerable scope for divergence with regard to the appropriate methods to deploy as well as conflicting substantive results.

A particular conception of the role of methodology is being drawn upon here, one that those who see the project of isolating some essential definition of post-Keynesian economics as counterproductive, or those who identify the coherence of post-Keynesian economics at a substantive level, may contest. Therefore, before highlighting how critical realism can be seen as providing coherence for post-Keynesianism and outlining the consequences that follow, it is worth briefly setting out the presuppositions being made regarding the role of methodology.

According to critical realism, although philosophy is viewed as dependent upon, and indeed interwoven with, science and other social practices, it is also seen as 'retaining certain relatively autonomous prerogatives of its own' (Bhaskar 1993: 93). Central, here, is the idea of philosophy as a potential *under-labourer* for science. On this view, the main work of philosophy is to clear away the debris in the path of science. To elaborate, critical realism regards philosophy as addressing the question as to what the world, or aspects of it, 'must' be like for recognized scientific practices and human capabilities to be possible. The form of argumentation is thus *transcendental*. Philosophy examines the conditions of possibility of certain especially significant scientific, and other social, practices that we experience. In particular, experimental practices and the application of scientific results outside the experimental set-up constitute the premises for transcendental arguments in the philosophy of natural science. Such generally accepted features of scientific practice can be rendered intelligible by postulating that actual events and states of affairs are produced and governed by a multiplicity of equally real underlying structures, mechanisms, powers and tendencies; that is, the world is structured and essentially open. Meanwhile, the capacity of human intentionality and choice can act as premises for critical realism in the social realm. On this critical realist reading transcendental arguments merely constitute a subset of *retroductive* arguments, defined by the movement 'from a description of some phenomenon to a description of something which produces it or is a condition for it' (Bhaskar 1986: 11), which is characteristic of science more generally, and hence they have no special logic or any innate certainty associated with them.[4] Such transcendental arguments are characteristically accompanied by what Bhaskar terms 'transcendental refutations' which show the implausibility of alternative accounts. For example, a transcendental refutation of some proposed account of science is obtained if it can be shown to be inconsistent with the possibility of science, or of certain generally recognized scientific practices. Bhaskar provides just such a transcendental refutation of positivist-inspired philosophies of science; he shows that they are inconsistent with the very practices of science.

So what can be said of the relationship between philosophy or methodology and science on this account? Two features stand out. First, it is crucially important to recognize both that there can be no discourse on the methods of science in isolation from the sciences themselves, and that any substantive practice is always susceptible to methodological analysis and critique. That is, philosophy neither exists apart, nor contemplates a distinct realm of its own, but neither does it compete with science. On the contrary, it treats the self-same world but does so transcendentally. At the same time, underpinning all substantive inquiries are methodological and philosophical assumptions. Obviously these need not be easily recognizable. Rather, and more usually, they exist at a tacit level of general concepts and broad perspectives regarding the subject matter to be investigated and the forms of explanation appropriate for it.

Second, although philosophical assumptions are ubiquitous, philosophy cannot anticipate substantive theory; it does not produce radically new knowledge as science can, but renders explicit, knowledge already implicit, encrusted, in certain other practices. Philosophy can, for example, tell us that the world must be structured for science to be possible, but it cannot tell us what structures the world contains or how they differ; these are entirely matters for substantive theory. Thus, critical realism combines very strong *ontological* theses with extreme caution in respect to any particular scientific statements. Given the reservations concerning substantive definitions of post-Keynesian economics outlined above, it is important to note that critical realism cannot determine any specific research outcomes or specify in detail the methods to be deployed.

The critical potential of realist arguments in economics should now stand out. Methodology can attack the overt or covert philosophical premises of existing perspectives where these are rooted in erroneous conceptions of science and explanation. At the same time, critical realist arguments can be used to defend a theory or an approach from attack where such critiques are based upon naïve assumptions regarding the nature of science. More importantly, given our focus here, some authors have suggested that it is precisely at this level that the coherence of post-Keynesian economics can be identified – in that if anything can render intelligible the most important nominal features of post-Keynesian economics it seems that it must be something like a shared commitment to a broadly critical realist perspective. If the coherence of post-Keynesian economics is to be isolated in this manner a number of implications follow, some of which may be less than welcome for certain post-Keynesians. First, some methods utilized by individual post-Keynesians together with the justifications offered to support their deployment, and indeed whole strands traditionally classified within or close to post-Keynesian economics, may be seen to have more in common with an orthodoxy revealed as essentially connected to a misconceived conception of explanation. Second, it may be the case that just as post-Keynesianism can be shown to be consistent with critical realism, so too may competing approaches such as those of the old institutionalists and Austrians, suggesting in turn commonalities not apparent at a substantive level. In the remainder of this chapter I shall attempt to pursue some of these issues.

A PHILOSOPHICAL GROUNDING FOR POST-KEYNESIAN ECONOMICS

How then can critical realism account for the diverse nominal characteristics of post-Keynesian economics? The notion that post-Keynesianism stands in opposition to orthodox economics is, of course, generally recognized. In response to a widely perceived crisis within the orthodox theory project, numerous solutions have been put forward and certain transformations in particular substantive aspects of the project have been partially carried through. These various responses make it difficult for post-Keynesians to articulate at a substantive level what exactly they are objecting to regarding orthodox theory. Critical realists in isolating the inadequacies of orthodox theory in entrenched methodological misconceptions bring into focus precisely what post-Keynesians are opposing.

To summarize briefly, Lawson (1995) uses critical realism to situate the failings of orthodox theory, suggesting that orthodox economics is tied to a particular, essentially positivist, methodology. He argues that orthodox economists base their conception of what economics is and what it ought to be able to achieve upon a specific deductivist mode of explanation and, more generally, a view of science in which elaborating constant conjunctions of events – regularities of the form whenever event X then event Y – is regarded as the focus of science. This perspective, with its preoccupation with identifying and predicting event regularities, according to the realist position, fundamentally misrepresents science. The adherence to this flawed conception of science not only has implications at some, supposedly detached, methodological level but also has repercussions for substantive analyses. In fact, it is possible to render intelligible many features associated with orthodox economic theory by tracing through the implications of retaining such a methodological orientation. It is important to note that whereas it may be the case that when orthodox economists reflect upon their method they often borrow the rhetoric of the constant conjunction view, especially the related emphasis on prediction, the argument does not depend on orthodox economists openly and consistently elaborating this view. Indeed the attachment to this conception of science is often not fully recognized by economists themselves, and the repercussions of holding such a view are rarely perceived. It is more usual for the commitment to the constant conjunction view to manifest itself in more obscure ways. Especially useful in tracing out the influence of this view of science and showing how it informs the procedures adopted at a substantive level is the notion of closure and the related issue of the conditions which have to be satisfied for a closure to obtain.

If, on the constant conjunction view, science is about identifying exceptionless regularities and formulating laws which have predictive as well as explanatory power, then it follows that only where such strict regularities obtain and closed systems prevail can science get off the ground. Few such regularities have to date been uncovered in the social realm. If economists who hold such a view of theory and science wish to explain real phenomena the question that arises is what steps can be taken to ensure that an event regularity holds? Realists have usefully reflected upon the conditions which must hold if strict regularities are actually to occur.[5]

Many of the trajectories characteristic of orthodox economics can be interpreted as attempts to secure the satisfaction of the conditions for closure. The search for event regularities and the implicit recognition that certain conditions have to be in place before such regularities follow through encourages particular general perspectives on human agency, social institutions and change. So, for example, in order to ensure a constant event regularity a condition must be placed on the nature of the individuals of the analysis, one that can be formulated as the *intrinsic condition for closure*. The requirement here is that under any specified set of conditions the individual always responds to a given stimulus in the same sort of way. Any system including an agent which is complex enough to initiate action not fully determined by its immediate environment will be an open system; that is, a system in which constant conjunctions of events do not occur. Some guarantee or stipulation is required ensuring that in identically specified conditions the individual in question always responds in the same predictable way. The intrinsic condition for closure then requires either that the internal structure be constant or, in the limiting case, absent. Under what circumstances, then, is the intrinsic condition satisfied and how does this relate to orthodox economics? The most straightforward way of satisfying this condition, or rather of analytically restricting human behaviour in such a way that the condition is presumed always automatically satisfied, is to suppose that agents are only and always rational; that is, are economic maximizers. It is the tacitly recognized need to provide some basis for supposing the satisfaction of the intrinsic condition that this axiom has been so stubbornly maintained within the orthodox project. Until relatively recently it seems to have been thought by many orthodox economists that some variant of the rationality principle was uniquely capable of securing the satisfaction of the intrinsic condition. It is important to note that from this perspective the rationality postulate can be seen as only one, if very convenient, way of meeting the intrinsic condition. For, as Lawson (1995) observes, assuming agents always follow simple, fixed, context-dependent rules will do equally well.[6]

Although such conditions for closure are helpful in isolating the nature of the traditional positions and characteristic manoeuvres of orthodoxy, this is not to suggest that the goal of securing constant event regularities and closed systems can, in fact, be achieved in this manner. In the social realm, the internal complexity of human agents and the complex interactions of social systems prevent these conditions from being met. The social realm is open and cannot even provide the temporary artificial closures available through experiment in the natural realm. Once this is recognized, as Collier notes, 'Orthodox economics begins to look like "hunting for a black cat in a dark room where there is no cat" ... hunting, that is, for constant conjunctions in an open system where there are no constant conjunctions' (1994: 226).

Post-Keynesian aversion to orthodox theory can be seen, then, as constituting a reaction against these essentially positivist directives on how economics should be approached. It is not only the opposition to orthodoxy that can be rendered intelligible by operating at this level; so too can many of the positive characteristics of post-Keynesian economics. Critical realism not only discredits positivist-inspired approaches but promotes more plausible general conceptions, and it is precisely these broad perspectives which can be found to inform, implicitly, many of the themes associated with post-Keynesianism.

On the critical realist view, the aim of economics, and social science, is to identify the structures governing, the conditions surrounding, facilitating as well as being transformed through some human activities of interest. The constraints on the development of a more adequate social ontology dissolve as a realist orientation is adopted. Specifically, it becomes possible to enquire into the nature of potential objects of scientific study with the intention of using such insights to select those methods which are most likely to illuminate relevant aspects of reality. For example, the recognition that whereas people are very much products of their economic and social positions and the attached rules, norms, conventions, etc., the actual choice among possibilities remains open, highlights the importance of the study of agents' conceptions. Human behaviour is not determined, nor completely explained, by reference to some framework of social rules; the causal power of social forms is always mediated through human agency. All social practices depend upon intentional human agency so that reference to beliefs, opinions, interpretations and attitudes, although of course not sufficient, is clearly important for any adequate social explanation. Abandoning the constant conjunction view facilitates the accommodation and exploration of all the various facets of a structured and complex human agency. This, of course, ties in with post-Keynesian criticisms of orthodox accounts of human agency and sensitivity regarding the importance of agents' own conceptions.

A more adequate account of the link between human agency and social structure is also opened up by the abandonment of the constant conjunction view and adoption of critical realism. Specifically, a transformational view can be developed in which all social structures are viewed as being both produced through human agency and given to it. Social structures represent the materials for action and not only constrain but, in doing so, facilitate human action. At the same time, existing social structures are themselves reproduced or transformed through individual action taken in total. On this model, society would not exist without human activity, and society is a necessary condition for any intentional act but the one cannot be reduced to, or conflated with, the other. The post-Keynesian emphasis upon the importance of social institutions and dynamic historical processes can be seen as implicitly calling for the adoption of some such social ontology.

Now, it is important to appreciate that such a basis for post-Keynesian economics, rooted in a shared commitment to a set of fairly abstract perspectives, though leaving scope for competing substantive positions and contrasting methods, does carry real consequences for research. Post-Keynesians themselves, although implicitly drawing upon this realist position, typically do not consciously and systematically ground their work within it and thus do not always recognize the implications that follow from its adoption. That is to say, post-Keynesianism remains uneasily anchored within critical realism. This can lead to tensions not only with respect to individual authors' own work but also between strands typically considered within the post-Keynesian tradition. These implications can be usefully illustrated by returning to the contributions of Geoff Harcourt and, specifically, certain of his methodological commentaries.

Geoff often appears to advocate something approximating a realist orientation. For example, he suggests that both Joan Robinson and Kalecki adopted a 'horses for courses' approach, letting the specific characteristics of time and place talk to them *before* they attempted to model, explain and offer policy advice. They did not beg questions nor look at the world with a blinkered gaze – there *must* be an equilibrium out there (perhaps more than one), and it (or they) must be examined to see if it is (they are) locally or globally stable, the presumption being that *usually* it (they) would be.

(Harcourt 1992: 30; emphasis in original)

In distancing post-Keynesian economics from the dehabilitatingly narrow perspectives of orthodox economics Geoff suggests that the methods of economic analysis be fashioned sensitively to our insights regarding the nature of social reality. This, of course, is very much in line with the realist orientation sketched above.

These realist intuitions feed through into some further reflections on Kalecki's method. According to Geoff, Kalecki's

simplifying assumptions were used to allow him to bring out starkly the really crucial processes at work, 'a clearer presentation of the gist of the problems concerned', to establish in their purest forms results which nevertheless continued to dominate the analysis when the simplifying assumptions were removed.

(Harcourt 1991: 1610)

The argument here appears to be that in theoretical science the aim is not to explain happenings in the world in all their detail. Rather, the objective is to explain certain aspects of those happenings by abstracting, which is understood as the stripping away in thought all that is not relevant to the target of explanation. That is, in an open system, observed phenomena can be resolved into the different effects of various mechanisms, and to isolate one or a few such mechanisms is to abstract from the original phenomena. Crucially, on this essentially realist reading, abstraction is interpreted to be real – it is not any sort of fiction. Whether in the natural or social realm, the aim of science is to obtain knowledge of real mechanisms or structures which give rise to, or govern, the flux of events. Abstraction is concerned precisely with isolating the real mechanisms, structures, powers and processes at work.

Geoff, perhaps motivated by his concern to promote pluralism within post-Keynesian economics, tends not to pursue the critical implications of a realist orientation to their full extent, which generates a certain amount of ambiguity regarding his methodological recommendations. Thus, notwithstanding his generally realist interpretations, Geoff often appears to equate abstraction with a certain loss of realism. Thus he writes:

Often important conceptual problems can be discussed and analysed within the bounds of distinctly 'unrealistic', that is, highly abstract models. This has been recognised at least since the time of Ricardo and is reflected in some modern debates – for example the controversies in capital theory.

(Harcourt 1984: 197–8)

This is again suggested when he states that if

doctrinal debate is the issue – the robustness of a fundamental intuition or insight in a particular approach ... – it is right and proper to operate at a high level of abstraction, to use simple, very unrealistic models which are appropriate for capturing the essence of the problem but which exclude all other 'matters of the real world' as irrelevant for the purpose in hand.

(Harcourt 1995: 5)

This kind of association seems to imply that if one is not directly addressing events and actualities then one must in some sense be dealing with the *less* real. Such a prioritization of events and experiences is, of course, simply the reverse side of the failure to render explicit a realm of *equally* real structures, mechanisms and powers.

It is important to recognize that not all methods can be defended along realist lines. A realist orientation would, at the very least, imply that techniques chosen be defended by reference to their consistency with our ontological insights and ability to reveal real social mechanisms. Geoff, wishing to accommodate diversity, suggests that 'there is a host of relevant languages running from intuition and poetry through lawyer-like arguments to pure mathematics and formal logic, which are appropriate for different issues, and for different aspects of the same issues' (Harcourt 1992: 30). In the context of post-Keynesian economics it is this kind of argument that appears to be behind comments such as:

The important perspective to take away is ... that there is no uniform way of tackling all issues in economics and that the various strands in post-Keynesian economics differ from one another, not least because they are concerned with different issues and often different levels of abstraction of analysis.

(Harcourt and Hamouda 1988: 231)

We can now see that such remarks remain highly ambiguous. Although there may exist a variety of possible methods to deploy, if one is to pursue consistently a realist position then their merits should be considered in terms of, perhaps among other things, their relative sensitivity to our insights into the nature of social material and ability to illuminate significant features of social reality. If certain methods are in conflict with our basic insights into the nature of social reality it is not enough to invoke levels of abstraction or research focus. For example, if one is committed to the proposition that agents have real choice, this undercuts methods, such as formal equilibrium models, which presuppose closed systems, and if such models are to be retained then arguments should be forthcoming specifying how they can facilitate the elaboration of real social structures. Despite Geoff's realist intuitions, no systematic distinctions are drawn between methods and approaches which can be defended along realist lines and those which cannot.

A critical realist basis for post-Keynesian economics not only helps us identify certain tensions in post-Keynesians' reflections but may also necessitate a certain amount of redrawing of the boundaries. In particular, it may be found that some strands do not share these underlying philosophical perspectives despite common substantive concerns. Geoff writes regarding the methodological stance favoured by Garegnani:

> He is loath to scrap the lengthy tradition in which economic theory is concerned with the determination of natural or normal prices, including a uniform long-run natural or normal rate of profit, and a methodology which employs the comparison of long-run equilibrium positions. . . . To do so would be to confine 'the theory to short run equilibria and a dynamics made of a sequence of them . . . to a theory which becomes barren of definite results'.
>
> (Harcourt 1976: 138)

According to Harcourt, 'Garegnani is inclined to say that the orthodox theory is wrong, but its methodology (in so far as it consists of long period positions) is sound' (Harcourt 1981: 251). These kinds of comment are, of course, far from conclusive, but they are suggestive of certain correspondences between the methodological position adopted by such authors and that characteristic of orthodoxy. If the argument summarized above, locating the essential nature of orthodox theory at the level of a broad conception of explanation, is correct, and if these authors can be shown to share such a perspective, then it follows that, although traditionally considered within post-Keynesian economics, they may more appropriately be classified as confined in similar ways to orthodoxy. This suggestion is, of course, highly speculative and would require far more support than can be provided here.[7] Nevertheless, it may be found that those who do adopt a critical realist position within post-Keynesianism have more in common with competing heterodox approaches such as those of the old institutionalists and Austrians[8] than certain branches historically treated as within post-Keynesianism. Such conclusions may well generate considerable disquiet, but at least these distinctions are then not arbitrary, merely historical or based on the authority of crucial individuals but rooted in key methodological differences.

CONCLUDING REMARKS

This chapter has done little more than sketch out what is at stake regarding the issue of coherence in post-Keynesian economics. Although a common adherence to critical realism does render intelligible many of the nominal features of post-Keynesian economics, such as their characteristic concern with social institutions, process and agents' conceptions, and makes sense of the post-Keynesians' opposition toward orthodox approaches and yet remains consistent with diversity at a substantive level, certain possibly unwelcome implications follow. For example, once a realist orientation is adopted then the use of particular methods should be defended along the lines that they are consistent with our insights into social reality and facilitate the elaboration and illumination of social structures. Whereas such a realist orientation would still be compatible with debate regarding appropriate methods, it seems unlikely to legitimize at least some of the procedures certain post-Keynesians favour. Moreover, if a particular branch previously classified as within the post-Keynesian perspective does not in fact share these broad perspectives, then it should be acknowledged as different in an essential way from the rest of post-Keynesianism. Of course, if it is felt necessary to retain all strands traditionally associated with post-Keynesian economics then the search for coherence may have to be abandoned. To return to Geoff Harcourt once more, his contributions can perhaps be seen as representative of post-Keynesianism more generally in being caught between pursuing a consistent realist position with all the implications that may follow and attempting to accommodate competing positions that may be found to lie in fundamental methodological opposition to one another. His reluctance to pursue the project of identifying coherence within post-Keynesian contributions perhaps reflects an implicit recognition of these tensions.

ACKNOWLEDGEMENTS

I am grateful to Fred Lee for valuable discussions on some aspects of this chapter and to the editors of the volume for their comments.

NOTES

1   Kregel, for example, appears to locate coherence at a substantive level. He writes, 'My own position is that the only way to make progress is by attempting to use the monetary theory that we find in the *General Theory* ... to form a foundation for a post-Keynesian theory of *price* ... and to attempt to link this to the theory of prices and production which we find in the Sraffa model and within Professor Pasinetti's approach' (1991: 81; emphasis in original).

2   Dow notes, 'I feel quite strongly that the way one defines Post Keynesianism is methodological, and that's why I've always thought it was important to be quite explicit about methodology' (1995: 154). There are those who in characterizing post-Keynesianism incorporate both a methodological and substantive dimension, e.g. Lavoie (1992) and Chick (1995).

3   So, for example, Arestis (1990), Arestis *et al.* (1994), Dow (1990, 1995) and especially T. Lawson (1994) all point to the relevance of critical realism when considering the coherence of post-Keynesianism. Critical realism itself has been

stimulated to a large extent by the writings of Roy Bhaskar.

4   On this view philosophy makes no claim to be unrevisable; there may be rival transcendental arguments to explain the same thing, just as there are rival theories at the frontiers of science. This is suggestive of the distinctions between the critical realist use of transcendental arguments and their more traditional Kantian deployment.

5   See in particular Collier (1994: 128–9), and Lawson (1995).

6   Besides the intrinsic condition for closure, critical realists also note at least one other condition necessary for a closure to obtain; that is, the extrinsic condition for closure. Here, it must be ensured that the agents or mechanisms under investigation have been effectively isolated from the influence of those aspects of the environment not explicitly considered in the analysis. Whenever it is not possible physically to isolate the system these external factors must be eliminated either by internalizing them within the system or treating them as constant in their influence. Again the implicit recognition of the need for this condition to be satisfied can prove useful in rendering intelligible the characteristic contortions of orthodox theory.

7   This issue deserves further investigation not least because, even among those authors who acknowledge realism as an important aspect of the definition of post-Keynesian economics, there appears to be no consensus regarding the consequences that follow for the interpretation of neo-Ricardianism. Lavoie, for example, notes, 'some may doubt that there is any link between realism and neo-Ricardianism. This is not so', and goes on to quote Milgate's characterization of the neo-Ricardian method as involving the 'abstract characterisation of the actual economy' aimed at capturing 'the systematic, regular and persistent forces at work in the system' (1992: 9). Meanwhile, in Lawson's discussion of the nature of post-Keynesianism it is significant that in elaborating the most important nominal characteristics of post-Keynesianism he makes no reference to any of the leading neo-Ricardian writers. This may suggest a belief that this position is not consistent with a post-Keynesianism rooted in critical realism.

8   This would, of course, be dependent on its being shown that these approaches are at least at times consistent with critical realism. A degree of progress has already been made in this direction. See for example, C. Lawson (1994), S. Fleetwood (1995) and J. Runde (1993).

REFERENCES

Arestis, P. (1990) 'Post Keynesianism: a new approach to economics', *Review of Social Economy* 48(3): 222–46.

Arestis, P., Mariscal, I. and Howells, P. (1994) 'Realism in post-Keynesian quantitative analysis', in M. Glick (ed.) *Competition, Technology and Money*, Aldershot: Edward Elgar.

Bhaskar, R. (1986) *Scientific Realism and Human Emancipation*. London: Verso.

——— (1993) *Dialectics: The Pulse of Freedom*, London: Verso.

Chick, V. (1995) 'Is there a case for post Keynesian economics?', *Scottish Journal of Political Economy* 42: 20–36.

Collier, A. (1994) *Critical Realism: An Introduction to Roy Bhaskar's Philosophy*, London: Verso.

Dow, S. C. (1990) 'Post-Keynesianism as political economy: a methodological discussion', *Review of Political Economy* 2(3): 345–58.

——— (1995) Interview, in J. E. King, *Conversations with Post Keynesians*, London: Macmillan.

Fleetwood, S. (1995) *Hayek's Political Economy: The Socio-economics of Order*, London: Routledge.

Harcourt, G. C. (1976) 'The Cambridge controversies: old ways and new horizons – or dead end?', reprinted in Harcourt, G. C. (1992) *On Political Economists and Modern Political Economy: Selected Essays of G. C. Harcourt*, ed. C. Sardoni, London: Routledge.

—— (1981) 'Marshall, Sraffa and Keynes: incompatible bedfellows?', reprinted in Harcourt, G. C. (1992) *On Political Economists and Modern Political Economy: Selected Essays of G. C. Harcourt*, ed. C. Sardoni, London: Routledge.

—— (1984) 'Reflections on the development of economics as a discipline', reprinted in Harcourt, G. C. (1992) *On Political Economists and Modern Political Economy: Selected Essays of G. C. Harcourt*, ed. C. Sardoni, London: Routledge.

—— (1991) Review of *Collected Works of Michal Kalecki*, *Economic Journal* 101(409): 1608–10.

—— (1992) 'A post-Keynesian comment', *Methodus* 4(1): 30.

—— (1995) 'Doing economics', mimeo, University of Cambridge.

Harcourt, G. C. and Hamouda, O. F. (1988) 'Post-Keynesianism: from criticism to coherence', as reprinted in Harcourt, G. C. (1992) *On Political Economists and Modern Political Economy: Selected Essays of G. C. Harcourt*, ed. C. Sardoni, London: Routledge.

Kregel, J. A. (1991) 'The organising principle in post-Keynesian economics', in W. Adriaansen and J. van der Linden (eds) *Post-Keynesian Thought in Perspective*, Groningen: Wolters-Noordhof.

Lavoie, M. (1992) *Foundations of Post-Keynesian Economic Analysis*, Aldershot: Edward Elgar.

Lawson, C. (1994) 'The transformational model of social activity and economic analysis: a reconsideration of the work of J. R. Commons', *Review of Political Economy* 6(2): 186–204.

Lawson, T. (1994) 'The nature of post-Keynesianism and its links to other traditions: a realist perspective', *Journal of Post-Keynesian Economics* 16(4): 503–38.

—— (1995) 'A realist perspective on contemporary economic theory', *Journal of Economic Issues* 29(1): 1–32.

Runde, J. (1993) 'Paul Davidson and the Austrians', *Critical Review* 7(2–3): 381–97.

297

25

NOTES ON THE HISTORY OF POST-KEYNESIAN ECONOMICS IN AUSTRALIA

John E. King

That post-Keynesian thinking has obtained at least a toehold in the Australian economics profession is due, in very large part, to the influence of Geoff Harcourt. As I suggest in the first section of this chapter, respect for (and continuing contact with) Cambridge joined with a long-standing native tradition of macroeconomic heresy to create an intellectual environment favourable to the early propagation of Keynesian ideas. In the second section I assess Harcourt's own contribution, focusing on his first (pre-capital controversies) book and his joint editorship of the country's one truly international journal, *Australian Economic Papers*. The conflicting pressures of 1970s radicalism and the return – with Ivy League doctorates – of the neoclassical vampires are described in the concluding section.

1930–60: HOW KEYNES CAME TO AUSTRALIA

Australians might be excused for having taken a rather dim view of John Maynard Keynes, given his endorsement of a classical deflationary package for them, including a 10 per cent money wage cut (Keynes 1932). In fact *The General Theory* conquered Australia with a speed and thoroughness that would have impressed the Spanish Inquisition, and by 1945 there was no more totally Keynesian economics profession in the world. To some extent this must have reflected the intensity of the country's suffering in the Great Depression, but there was also a significant political and intellectual background. *Laissez-faire* had never taken hold in the Australian colonies. White settlement itself was the direct result of state intervention, and both the colonial and (after 1901) the Commonwealth governments played a major role in economic life, regulating the labour market – for example – to a degree almost unprecedented by international standards. Economic thought was appropriately pragmatic: if there were few Australian socialists, there were few pro-capitalist 'libertarians' either (Groenewegen and McFarlane 1990). There was, however, a tradition of popular underconsumptionism which owed much to the writings of J. A. Hobson and a long series of currency cranks, and this made demand-side explanations of economic crisis appear quite natural. Popular suspicion of monetary reformers was thus less acute than was often the case overseas (Kuhn 1988). At a more refined level there already existed by the early 1930s a lively and inventive school of Australian macro-economics, represented most famously by the Cambridge-educated L. F. Giblin, co-discoverer of the multiplier, and also by less celebrated but equally distinguished theorists like Douglas Copland and another Cambridge man, E. R. Walker (Cain 1984). Neatly poised between the plebeian radicals and the professors was the larrikin figure of R. F. Irvine, an academic with populist pretensions and a considerable following (McFarlane 1966).

Thus it was that *The General Theory* met with almost no resistance in Australia, which sent a steady stream of its brightest young economists to study in the Fens. Grant Fleming's careful analysis of citations in the *Economic Record*, at the time the country's only serious economic journal, reveals a preponderance of references to Cambridge sources both before and for some years after 1936 (Fleming 1994). The *Record* published one of the earliest, and undoubtedly one of the best, reviews of *The General Theory* by Brian Reddaway (1936), who was visiting Melbourne on a Bank of England scholarship at the time.[1] There was no opposition to Reddaway's very favourable exposition of the new ideas: Australia had no Pigou, no Hayek, no Viner, no Haberler. In January 1939, section G of the Australia and New Zealand Association for the Advancement of Science devoted its meeting to a discussion entitled 'Economic Theory and Monetary Policies with Special Reference to Australia and New Zealand'. The proceedings, published in the *Record* in April of the same year, demonstrate the well-nigh unanimous acceptance of *The General Theory* by the Australian profession, at least one of the papers, E. E. Ward's piece on Marx and Keynes, being as good as anything anywhere in the world on its chosen subject.[2] There was a simultaneous 'Keynesian Revolution' in economic policy, spearheaded by public servants of such high intellectual calibre as H. C. ('Nugget') Coombs and Leslie Melville, both propagators of *The General Theory* in the pages of the *Economic Record*. By 1945 the 'Treasury line' was unashamedly Keynesian, and would remain so for another three decades (Whitwell 1986).

This was undoubtedly reflected also in the teaching of macroeconomics at the seven Australian universities.[3] Peter Groenewegen's research reveals the predominance of British textbooks until the 1960s (Groenewegen 1995: 8–10), and this is confirmed by the recollections of my interviewees. As an undergraduate at the University of Western Australia just after the war, Keith Frearson remembers using Benham's *Economics* as the principal text, and finding the teaching rather uninspired. Geoff Harcourt's experience at Melbourne (where he arrived in 1950) was quite different. He was required to read two 'great books' in Economics I: Wicksteed's *Commonsense* and Keynes's *Tract on Monetary Reform*, the chapter on the forward exchanges being 'very hard ... but very challenging'. In the summer vacation at the end of his first year Harcourt read *The General Theory*, which was 'all the rage for Economics B', in which Don Cochrane and Joe Isaac taught it to a class of 700. Isaac also introduced honours students to the writings of Michal Kalecki. At Melbourne a few years later Peter Riach read *The General Theory*, Hansen's *Guide to Keynes*, Kaldor's 1940 article on the trade cycle, and Harrod and Domar on growth, along with Hicks and Lange on IS–LM.

At Adelaide in 1952 Michael Schneider studied first-year economics under Peter Karmel, using the proto-post-Keynesian *Elements of Economics* by Lorie Tarshis as the principal text; Harcourt also remembers seeing it as an undergraduate at Melbourne. Towards the end of the decade, at the University of Sydney, Peter Groenewegen learnt introductory macroeconomics from a series of British textbooks, including Benham, Cairncross's *Introduction to Economics* and the superior *Textbook of Economic Theory* by Stonier and Hague, which included the best formulation of aggregate supply and demand analysis available anywhere in the world at the time. Frearson and Schneider believe that Stonier and Hague was also in use at Monash in the early to mid-1960s, while Robert Dixon recalls its use there later in the decade, along with Brooman's *Macroeconomics*.

Apart from Hansen and Tarshis, these are all British texts; both Groenewegen and Schneider recall Samuelson's *Economics* being regarded with some condescension as very much a book for beginners. Groenewegen doubts whether any introductory US text was used at Sydney – as opposed to the University of New South Wales – before the late 1960s. At a higher level, Frearson used Alvin Hansen's *Guide to Keynes* and Dudley Dillard's *Economics of J. M. Keynes* at Melbourne in the late 1950s, Harcourt read Dillard's book earlier in the decade, and Groenewegen remembers using Kalecki, Robinson's *Accumulation of Capital* and Kenneth Kurihara's rather misleadingly titled *Post-Keynesian Economics* as an honours student. By the end of the following decade, US or US-inspired texts were infiltrating the introductory courses. Donald Whitehead insisted that Lipsey's *Positive Economics* was used from the outset (i.e. from 1967) at Melbourne's third university, La Trobe, and Michael White remembers Samuelson, and Ackley's *Macroeconomic Theory*, supplementing the 'more sophisticated' and 'highly Keynesian' *Economic Activity* (1967) by Harcourt, Karmel and Wallace at Monash in 1969. Even at Sydney, Ackley and Lipsey were in use by the beginning of the 1970s.

Two conclusions may be drawn from these recollections. First, there was no bastion of pre-Keynesian economics in Australia, no 'Chicago of the South'. Second, the Keynes who was taught in Australian universities was (at least before 1970) quite close to being the real thing. By comparison with macroeconomics in the USA, the 'grand neoclassical synthesis' was severely qualified Down Under. This is a question of degree, but it does seem that Australian economics graduates were educated in a way which made at least some of them more open to post-Keynesian influences than their North American contemporaries. Even at Monash, which was soon to enjoy a reputation as something of a neoclassical stronghold, Michael White remembers the elementary macroeconomics he learnt there as emphasizing the role of money and the causal primacy of investment over saving (and concluding with an analysis of the Swan diagram, subsequently taught only in later years). Fourteen years earlier, as a graduate student at Cambridge, Keith Frearson had faced no difficulty in understanding Joan Robinson's lectures, whereas his friend Tom Asimakopulos – soon, of course, to become a distinguished post-Keynesian theorist – found her teaching all very mysterious, on account of his neoclassical, North American, upbringing.

This points to one final, very important, factor: the continuing strength of the Cambridge connection. Between the wars Cambridge was the natural destination for a talented young Australian economist. Future professors of economics who went there soon after 1945 included Cochrane, Richard Downing and Peter Karmel, and the long-serving Professor of Economics at Melbourne, Wilfred Prest, was also a Cambridge graduate. This Cambridge link remained strong until Harvard and Chicago took over in the 1960s (cf. Groenewegen 1995: 6–8). In some cases (it would be interesting to know exactly how many) it was institutionalized, as with the Shell scholarship which took Michael Schneider to a guaranteed place at Christ's College. Arriving in Cambridge shortly after Harcourt, Schneider recalls, among his contemporaries there, seven economists who returned to have distinguished academic careers in Australia (three of them became professors) and another who became a senior public servant. Except for agricultural economists, American Ph.D.s were very uncommon before the 1970s. Some Australians, like Keith Hancock, Joe Isaac and Peter Riach, went to the London School of Economics, but this was a minority choice, and Riach's decision caused some surprise in Melbourne (King 1995: 114). The majority of young Australian economists acquired the pure milk of *The General Theory*, first-hand, from Robinson, Kaldor, Kahn and Sraffa.

1960–75: THE HARCOURT CONTRIBUTION

This is not the place for a comprehensive survey of Geoff Harcourt's writings, nor for a full assessment of his career. What I want to do in this section is much more modest: to comment on the textbook he wrote jointly with Peter Karmel and Bob Wallace, *Economic Activity*, as an indicator of his own thinking in the mid-1960s and of the state of Australian macroeconomics at that time, and to assess his influence on *Australian Economic Papers* between its establishment in 1963 and his departure to Cambridge in 1982.

As the preface indicates, *Economic Activity* originated in a first-year lecture course given by Karmel at the University of Adelaide from 1950 and inherited by the other two authors. It also contains theoretical material on monetary questions drawn from Wallace's second-year course at Adelaide. Harcourt wrote the bulk of the first draft, drawing heavily on the initial structure provided by Karmel; he used the final draft as the basis for first-year lectures at Cambridge in 1966 (Harcourt *et al.* 1967: v). 'The book is Keynesian in spirit' (ibid.), but precisely what is meant by this is difficult to establish. Much of the content is conventional short-run income–expenditure analysis, of the type found in the standard Keynesian textbooks of the day, and it is not surprising to find works by Ackley, Eckstein, Hansen, Lipsey and Schultze among the suggested reading (ibid.: 318–19). There is no discussion of income distribution, no hint of a Kaleckian alternative to the normal 'Keynesian' macromodel[4] and little more than a mention of the theory of economic growth (ibid.: 314–16); this, Harcourt recalls, was a deliberate simplification for first-year students. On monetary questions, the reader would have learnt (again from the preface) that 'the Hicks–Hansen LM–IS analysis which is widely used in British and American textbooks is not specifically used because, among other reasons, the assumptions which it implies about the capital market are not sufficiently applicable to the Australian situation' (ibid.: vi). These brief and rather cryptic remarks are supplemented by a footnote disclaiming any originality on these issues and concluding, unambiguously: 'The argument of chapter 13 is obviously rooted in Hicksian general equilibrium analysis' (ibid.: vi n1). Harcourt attributes this phase to Wallace, who had been Hicks's pupil at Oxford.

Chapter 13 deals with 'the interaction between planned expenditures and financial factors', and does indeed contain a verbal formulation of IS–LM to establish the necessity for simultaneous equilibrium in the goods and money markets. The quantity of money is exogenously given, an increase in aggregate demand raises the rate of interest, and this has a 'damping effect' on investment (ibid.: 260–2). But there is also a flavour of endogenous money, since 'changes in aggregate demand will affect the supply of money, as well as the demand for money' (ibid.: 262). This occurs in part through increased public use of overdraft facilities, against which possibility the banks hold substantial excess reserves (ibid.: 265 n1). Equally unorthodox (though possibly inspired by the UK Radcliffe Report) is the discussion in chapter 6 of the way in which 'potential spenders' obtain finance by converting fixed and savings deposits into money, and by drawing on overdraft entitlements (ibid.: 83; cf. p. 309). Adding to this the recognition that 'the Australian monetary authorities determine directly certain key rates of interest' (ibid.: 266), one could almost describe the young Harcourt, in Basil Moore's terms, as a 'horizontalist' with respect to the money supply (Moore 1988).

Other post-Keynesian elements are evident in the discussion of inflation in the penultimate chapter, which is notable for the first (and only) appearance in *Economic Activity* of aggregate supply and demand analysis. A very strange analysis it is, too. Unlike the contemporary formulations of Weintraub and Davidson,[5] the diagrams are in price–quantity space. Unlike the neoclassical texts of the 1990s, however (relatively flat), *micro* marginal and average variable cost curves are used as surrogates for the aggregate functions, very much in the manner of one of Harcourt's great heroes, Lorie Tarshis (Harcourt *et al.* 1967: 268–76).[6] Then mark-up pricing is introduced, together with the assumption of a constant average product of labour, to yield a horizontal aggregate supply curve up to the full-employment level of output (ibid.: 277–9). A modern post-Keynesian might well, at this point, be licking her lips in anticipation. Surely a firm statement of the theory of wage-push inflation must come next, followed by a detailed examination of the case for an incomes policy? After all, wages policy was the subject of heated discussion in Adelaide at this time, involving Hancock, Whitehead, Eric Russell and others; Harcourt has always acknowledged Russell's influence on him. Alas, the whole question is dealt with in one page. Money wage increases are simply listed, as a source of inflationary pressure, along with increased profit margins, higher import prices and increased rates of indirect taxation, and the discussion of wages policy is confined to a single paragraph summarizing the difficulties inherent in transforming the Australian arbitration system into an organ of anti-inflation policy (ibid.: pp. 306–7).

Economic Activity seems not to have been widely used as a text outside Adelaide and Cambridge, although it was translated into Italian. Very much a joint product of Adelaide and Cambridge, it reflects an ambivalence towards the neoclassical synthesis that seems to have been shared by many incipient post-Keynesians in the 1960s. Evidently it was not the work of someone who then believed that Michael Kalecki was the greatest economist of the twentieth century (Harcourt 1987: xi), nor even that Keynes had been traduced by his neoclassical, general equilibrium interpreters. Its treatment of money, of aggregate supply and demand, and of inflation did, however, point in a post-Keynesian direction. And the Australian student who pursued the suggestions for further reading would have encountered, in addition to the US Keynesians, Kahn's classic article on the multiplier, *The General Theory*, Austin Robinson's obituary and Harrod's biography of Keynes, not to mention pieces by Kalecki, E. F. Schumacher and Paul Wells.

The economics department at Adelaide was never a 'red base', a stronghold of economic heresy and political radicalism in the way that Amherst, the New School or the University of California (Riverside) have become. Michael White remembers the department as predominantly neoclassical, but eclectic and partly for this reason relatively open, liberal and tolerant. This openness, of course, is a Harcourt characteristic, and it carried over into his editorial work. He was one of the prime movers behind the foundation in 1963 of *Australian Economic Papers*.[7] By contrast with the *Record*, which was (and remains) very much the organ of the Australian and New Zealand profession, the new journal had a cosmopolitan outlook almost from the start, with the inevitable neoclassical articles offset by a perceptible Cambridge component. The second issue included Harcourt's own critique of Nicholas Kaldor, and his Adelaide colleague Hugh Hudson's paper on the integration of cycle and growth models. In the third, Keith Frearson's survey of Cambridge growth theory was followed by one of Joan Robinson's earliest onslaughts against the US Keynesians, 'Pre-Keynesian theory after Keynes' (Robinson 1964). This attracted (in the fifth number) a 'modest defence' of pre-Keynesian theory by David Bensusan-Butt and an unyielding response from Robinson. Before the 1960s were out, *Papers* had published articles by D. M. Nuti on the choice of techniques in Soviet industry, N. Okishio on technical choice and planning prices, E. J. Nell on money and barter, and Robinson again, this time on the theory of value.

The significance of the journal was probably at its peak in the early 1970s, when the leading US journals had become effectively closed to post-Keynesian ideas and the alternative outlets later provided by the *Journal of Post Keynesian Economics* (founded in 1978) and the *Cambridge Journal of Economics* (1977) had yet to emerge. Between 1970 and 1975 *Australian Economic Papers* published work by Asimakopulos, D. J. Harris, J. F. Henry, J. S. Metcalfe, E. J. Nell, P. A. Riach, A. Roncaglia, I. Steedman and D. Vickers. Harcourt's tolerance and eclectic taste were reflected in the subject matter, which ranged from technical appraisals of Marxian crisis models, Kaleckian and Kaldorian distribution theory, and Sraffian trade analysis, to Nell's widely quoted polemic 'The revival of political economy'. Although this was the period *par excellence* of crisis and self-questioning for mainstream economics, few, if any, prominent international journals would have welcomed such heresy – the *Economic Journal* in 1969–75 under Phyllis Deane's influence was a rare exception – and Australia's profile as a centre for the dissemination of post-Keynesian ideas was for a time very high. Between 1976 and 1980, *Papers* published another score of Sraffian, Marxian and post-Keynesian articles, with authors who included Asimakopulos, K. Bharadwaj, V. Chick, A. S. Eichner, H. Kurz, J. E. Roemer, N. Shapiro and Steedman.

The next three years, the last under Harcourt's editorship, yielded a further twenty heterodox papers from (among others) Asimakopulos, S. C. Dow, J. A. Kregel, K. W. Rothschild, Shapiro and Steedman, and featuring the very important English translation of Kalecki's review of *The General Theory* (Targetti and Kinda-Hass 1982). By this time many of the leading British, Italian and North American post-Keynesians had published in *Papers*, though among the fish who got away were large ones like Weintraub, Davidson and Minsky from one side of the Atlantic, Kaldor and Pasinetti from the other. The journal was also a valuable outlet for Australian post-Keynesians such as Robert Dixon, Peter Riach, Trevor Stegman and Martin Watts. After Harcourt's departure, *Australian Economic Papers* briefly retained some post-Keynesian affiliations under the (co-) editorship of Colin Rogers, but since the late 1980s it has become a purely mainstream journal.

AFTER 1975: RADICALS AND NEOCLASSICALS

It would be absurd to suggest that Harcourt's influence was exhausted by 1975. But this was a crucial year for Australian society, with stagflation newly established as the country's principal (and apparently intractable) economic problem and the Governor-General's dismissal of the Whitlam Labour government dashing social democratic hopes and opening up deep and bitter divisions inside and outside academia. Intellectually, too, the mid-1970s represent a divide, witnessing the rise both of radical economics and of a strident and aggressive neoclassical revival in more orthodox circles.

A good impression of the state of economic dissent towards the end of the decade can be obtained from Peter Groenewegen's 1979 survey of radical economics in Australia, which identified a number of reasons for the growth of dissatisfaction with the mainstream: a general political radicalization in the early 1970s, sharpened (crucially) by opposition to Australian involvement in the Vietnam War; the increasingly unsatisfactory performance of the national economy; the development of feminism, and awareness of the problems faced by Aboriginal people and migrants; and (again of paramount importance) the increasing sense of crisis in neoclassical economics worldwide (Groenewegen 1979b: 185–6). In addition there was the personal contribution of Geoff Harcourt, most obviously through his international prominence in the Cambridge capital controversies (ibid.: 187).

Groenewegen recognized the existence of several unorthodox schools of thought, including institutionalists, Marxists, neo-Ricardians and post-Keynesians, the divisions between them often somewhat blurred. The post-Keynesians, he suggested, sought to construct a new political economy 'on Keynes–Kaleckian lines' (Groenewegen 1979b: 174). 'Much of this group bases itself on the Marshallian Cambridge tradition, as revitalised by Keynes and Kalecki, and enriched by Sraffa's rehabilitation of classical political economy (that is, from the Physiocrats up to and including Marx)' (ibid.: 176). This is a very Australian – perhaps also a very Cambridge – definition of post-Keynesianism; it would not have appealed greatly to many North Americans (because it was too socialist), nor to many Italians (because it was too neoclassical). Indeed, as Groenewegen admits, it was already the subject of vigorous criticism from Australian Marxists (ibid.: 188–9).

Post-Keynesian economics had spread to Australia, Groenewegen suggests, very largely through the efforts of Harcourt, supported by a few economists outside Adelaide (though he mentions only Frearson at Monash, an infrequent publisher whose importance was stressed by several of my interviewers) and by economists/political scientists like Bruce McFarlane. It remained 'relatively underdeveloped' at the end of the 1970s. 'In fact, Groenewegen maintains, 'without Harcourt's contributions, there would have been little to survey', other than Riach's important resuscitation of Kaleckian microeconomics and critical appraisal of Kaldor's analysis (1979b: 205, 204).

Groenewegen himself regarded the Kaleckian model as offering the best hope for a coherent radical economic framework, and indeed had used it in his own well-received textbook on public finance (Groenewegen 1979a). His survey concludes on an upbeat, with the prediction that it was, of all the schools, the post-Keynesian in which

> the most important contributions to Australian radical economics will be made in the next decade, and by an increasing number of scholars. This exciting prospect is liable to eventuate because the best of the young talent in radical economics in Australia is being steered into this area of enquiry.
>
> (Groenewegen 1979b: 205)

For a while this prognosis appeared to be a reasonable one. Post-Keynesian theory was by this time taught at Adelaide and a number of other institutions. Groenewegen lectured on Sraffa and Kalecki at the University of Sydney, where third- and fourth-year students also learned post-Keynesian ideas from Jim Wilson and (somewhat later) Joseph Halevi. At the University of New South Wales the initiators were Geoff Fishburn, Bill Junor and Dave Clark (the latter now a famous apostate and advocate of neoliberalism), along with John Nevile; their work has been continued by Peter Kriesler and Trevor Stegman. In Melbourne, post-Keynesianism was strongest at Monash, where from the early 1960s Keith Frearson taught Robinsonian growth theory, Peter Riach lectured on income distribution and labour economics and Michael Schneider taught the history of economic thought. One of their students, Robert Dixon, took over an existing 'political economy' syllabus at the University of Melbourne and by the middle of the 1980s had converted it into a course on Marxian and post-Keynesian theory. At other universities, as for example La Trobe, post-Keynesian ideas insinuated themselves into courses on the history of economic thought and advanced macroeconomics. A series of dissertations with a post-Keynesian flavour began to emerge, in paticular from Adelaide, Perth and Sydney, where Groenewegen was an influential supervisor. The best of these was Kriesler's *Kalecki's Microanalysis*, which was published by Cambridge University Press in 1987, several years after earning its author a Sydney master's degree. And a steady trickle of Australian papers found their way into the *Journal of Post Keynesian Economics*.

Groenewegen would, however, be the first to admit that, despite all this activity, his 1979 prediction was much too optimistic. In fact radical economics of all descriptions went into a pronounced and continuing decline after 1980. The worldwide shift to the right in the economics profession was compounded, in the Australian case, by a number of local idiosyncrasies. One was the continuing repercussions of the Whitlam débâcle, not least the perceived fiscal laxity of the 1972–5 Labor government, which discredited Keynesian macroeconomic policy. Another was a strong business and academic reaction against the statist and protectionist tradition which I described at the beginning of this chapter. Finally, there was the accelerating Americanization of the economics profession, evident in changes in the recruitment, teaching, publishing and research degree practices of most (if not all) economics departments in Australia. The future lay with neoclassical theory, more specifically with the militantly deregulationist and anti-Keynesian variant of neoliberalism known locally as 'economic rationalism' (Pusey 1991). None of this was peculiar to Australia, of course, but these developments occurred more rapidly, and went further, than for example in the UK or Italy.

Moreover, post-Keynesianism never achieved the dominant position among dissenting economists that Groenewegen had anticipated, despite the declining influence of Marxism, which edged some of its previous advocates into the post-Keynesian camp. The remaining Marxians, and some of the Sraffians, tended to become more dogmatic and sectarian, not less. Meanwhile, the 'political economy' movement, which had briefly served as an umbrella for all the heretical tendencies, split into 'activist' and 'academic' strands, the latter increasingly under the influence of an atheoretical institutionalism which potential converts like the young Peter Kriesler found deeply unsatisfying. Post-Keynesian influence in the Sydney Department of Political Economy, which split from Economics in 1974, was always minimal, and very little post-Keynesian material has appeared in the movement's *Journal of Australian Political Economy*, now in its nineteenth year of publication. In Economics at Sydney, on the other hand, third-year courses in capital and distribution, and in economic growth, continue to attract about forty students each year.

Post-Keynesians survive in most other Australian universities, albeit generally as an embattled minority. One exception is among historians of thought, where there has always been a strong post-Keynesian presence. This is apparent both at the biennial conferences of the History of Economic Thought Society of Australia (which began in 1981) and in the pages of its journal, the *History of Economics Review*;[8] at the 1995 Brisbane conference there were seven papers (out of thirty-eight) on post-Keynesian themes. Specifically post-Keynesian conferences have been held at the University of New South Wales in 1988, with Basil Moore as a guest; at the University of Melbourne in 1989, associated with the visit of Hyman Minsky; at La Trobe in 1994, when Paul Davidson was a visitor; and at the University of Newcastle in 1995.[9] Two-thirds of the joint authorship of the forthcoming biography of Michal Kalecki are Australian (Kriesler and McFarlane: the third is Jan Toporowski). Supplementary volumes of Keynes's *Collected Writings* are in preparation by an Australian, Rod O'Donnell of Macquarie University. Thus life in the intellectual ghetto remains vigorous and diverse.

JOHN E. KING

ACKNOWLEDGEMENTS

As the title implies, this is very much 'work in progress', a provisional report on research which is continuing and ideas which are only part-formed. I have drawn heavily on interviews with Robert Dixon, Keith Frearson, Peter Groenewegen, Geoff Harcourt, Peter Kriesler, Peter Riach, Michael Schneider and Michael White, and comments by Grant Fleming and Peter Kenyon. Their assistance is gratefully acknowledged, but the usual disclaimer applies, very forcefully.

NOTES

1 The review contains (yet) another version of the IS–LM model (Reddaway 1936: 34–5). According to Geoff Harcourt, Reddaway was blissfully unaware of this until Harcourt and Warren Young pointed it out to him, decades later.
2 As can be seen by comparing it with contemporary articles published overseas and reprinted in Horowitz (1968: 103–202).
3 One in the capital city of each of the six states, plus the Australian National University in Canberra (established in 1946). Not until the foundation of the University of New South Wales (formerly a technical institute) in 1958, and Monash in 1961, did any state have a second university.
4 Though Kalecki's (1944) 'Three ways to full employment' is cited as suggested reading.
5 Neither of whom is referred to in the index, or features in the list of recommended reading.
6 Wallace taught for a term at Stanford in 1964–5, with Tarshis, and the second draft of *Economic Activity* was written there in the summer of 1965 by Harcourt and Wallace, with Karmel providing the final draft of the policy chapter.
7 The first editor (1962–4) was Hugh Hudson, who had worked with Kaldor in Cambridge; Harcourt was his assistant. In 1964–6 the journal was edited by Keith Hancock and Harold Lydall, with an editorial committee which included Harcourt. From 1967 Hancock and Harcourt were the co-editors.
8 Until 1991 known as the *HETSA Bulletin*.
9 Peter Kriesler organized a 'Post-Keynesian Day' at the 1990 Conference of Economists, with Harcourt and Nell among the speakers. Other prominent post-Keynesian visitors have included Joan Robinson (in 1967 and 1975), Sidney Weintraub (1974), Kurt Rothschild (1980), Paul Wells (1979–80), Henry Phelps Brown (1967 and 1975) and, at various times, Luigi Pasinetti, Paolo Sylos Labini and Victoria Chick.

REFERENCES

Cain, N. (1984) 'The propagation of Keynesian thinking in Australia: E. R. Walker 1933–36', *Economic Record* 60(171): 366–80.
Fleming, G. A. (1994) 'Some problems in interpreting citation practices in the *Economic Record*, 1925–1946', *History of Economics Review* 22: 1–15.
Groenewegen, P. (1979a) *Public Finance in Australia: Theory and Practice*, Sydney: Prentice-Hall.
——— (1979b) 'Radical economics in Australia: a survey of the 1970s', in F. H. Gruen (ed.) *Surveys of Australian Economics*, vol. 2, Sydney: Allen & Unwin.

—— (1995) *The Post 1945 Internationalization of Economics: The Australian Experience*, Working Papers in Economics 216, Sydney: University of Sydney.

Groenewegen, P. and McFarlane, B. (1990) *A History of Australian Economic Thought*, London: Routledge.

Harcourt, G. C. (1987) Introduction to Kriesler, P., *Kalecki's Microanalysis*, Cambridge: Cambridge University Press.

Harcourt, G. C., Karmel, P. H. and Wallace, R. H. (1967) *Economic Activity*, Cambridge: Cambridge University Press.

Horowitz, D. (ed.) (1968) *Marx and Modern Economics*, London: MacGibbon & Kee.

Kalecki, M. (1944) 'Three ways to full employment', in Oxford University Institute of Statistics, *The Economics of Full Employment: Six Studies in Applied Economics*, Oxford: Blackwell.

Keynes, J. M. (1932) 'The report of the Australian experts', *Melbourne Herald*, 27 June. Reprinted in *The Collected Writings of John Maynard Keynes*, vol. 21, London: Macmillan and Cambridge University Press for the Royal Economic Society.

King, J. E. (1995) *Conversations with Post Keynesians*, London: Macmillan.

Kriesler, P. (1987) *Kalecki's Microanalysis*, Cambridge: Cambridge University Press.

Kuhn, R. (1988) 'Labour movement economic thought in the 1930s: underconsumptionism and Keynesian economics', *Australian Economic History Review* 28(2): 53–74.

McFarlane, B. (1966) *Professor Irvine's Economics in Australian Labour History*, Canberra: Australian Society for the Study of Labour History.

Moore, B. J. (1988) *Horizontalists and Verticalists: The Macroeconomics of Credit Money*, Cambridge: Cambridge University Press.

Pusey, M. (1991) *Economic Rationalism in Canberra: A Nation-Building State Changes Its Mind*, Cambridge: Cambridge University Press.

Reddaway, W. B. (1936) 'The general theory of employment, interest and money', *Economic Record* 12: 28–36.

Robinson, J. (1964) 'Pre-Keynesian theory after Keynes', *Australian Economic Papers* 3: 25–35.

Targetti, F. and Kinda-Hass, B. (1982) 'Kalecki's review of Keynes's *General Theory*', *Australian Economic Papers* 21(39): 244–60.

Whitwell, G. (1986) *The Treasury Line*, Sydney: Allen & Unwin.

26

ROBERTSON AND THE POST-KEYNESIAN APPROACH TO GROWTH AND CYCLES

Lilia Costabile

INTRODUCTION

Robertson has not traditionally been a very popular author among economists in the Keynesian and post-Keynesian schools of thought. In view of what an authoritative eye-witness (Robinson 1947: 36) had to say on his contribution to the formation of the 'Cambridge' approach to macroeconomics in the 1920s, this suggests that some underevaluation may have occurred.

My interpretation is that this underevaluation may be due to the generalized habit of comparing Robertson's approach exclusively to that taken by Keynes in *The General Theory*. A more balanced appraisal would require that this theory be evaluated against the wider background of Keynesian and post-Keynesian macroeconomic dynamics. Here I focus on Robertson's role as a precursor of the post-Keynesian approach to the theory of growth and cycles. I try to show that, in the 1920s and early 1930s, Robertson was addressing some of the very questions which were later to be asked by Harrod, Domar and Kaldor, and that he provided some answers very similar to those given by these three writers. Moreover, his analysis was framed in terms of the interactions between real and monetary factors, a circumstance enriching his contributions with some interesting features, which are latent in the models of Domar, Harrod and Kaldor. I argue here that exclusive concentration on the debates which followed the publication of *The General Theory* has diverted our attention from Robertson's analysis of growth and cycles in a monetary economy, which is where, in my view, his major theoretical contribution lies. I hope to be able to convey the flavour, if not the essence, of his approach in the limited space of this chapter.

The chapter belongs to a 'tradition' proposing to rediscover Robertson's contributions[1] and to reappraise them. My interpretation is relatively novel, since even those authors (Keynesian or otherwise) who are sympathetic towards Robertson's contributions[2] have generally ignored, or not paid due attention to, the long-run dynamic nature of the main body of Robertson's theory, where the equality between saving and investment is regarded as a condition of *steady growth*. Thus, in many interpretations of his work, the links between money, economic fluctuations and growth have been unduly severed. This chapter tries to re-establish the links. The present interpretation is based in Robertson's writings in general, but specifically grounded on the following: *Banking Policy and the Price Level* (1926) and the revised version of this book (1932), *Money* (1922, 1928a), 'Theories of the banking policy' (1928b), 'Saving and hoarding' (1933a), 'Industrial fluctuation and the natural rate of interest' (1934) and some other of his writings from the 1920s, which will be quoted below. Moreover, I have considered two of his later writings which shed some light on the issues with which he had been dealing in the 1920s: his article 'Thoughts on meeting some important persons' (1954) and the third volume of his *Lectures in Economic Principles* (1956–9). The present interpretation is also corroborated, I hope, by the works of those interpreters who *did* recognize Robertson as a precursor of the theory of growth.[3]

THE CONDITIONS FOR GROWTH IN EQUILIBRIUM

Robertson's basic objective in chs 5–7 of his *Banking Policy and the Price Level*, and in related writings, was to isolate the abstract conditions for equilibrium in a growing economy, or for 'steady growth'. He distinguished between alternative types of economy, on the basis of their technology of exchange (barter and monetary economies) and on the basis of their ownership regime (cooperative economies and capitalist economies).[4] For reasons of space, here I will refer only to the model of a monetary capitalist economy. Although on occasion he adopted the simplifying assumption of a constant output, Robertson generally considered both output and price adjustments: as he stated, the effects of changes in monetary policies (and, I would add, of demand conditions) on prices and quantities depend upon the 'elasticity of supply', which he did not assume to be zero (Robertson 1949: xiii).

His basic analysis was based on the following assumptions: (a) all prices are flexible, but some money incomes, including wages, are relatively sticky; (b) all capital goods are considered as goods in process, or 'unready goods' (1928a: 103): these goods are also defined as 'circulating capital', and include the wage-goods (Robertson 1949: 42);[5] (c) all money takes the form of bank deposits, and all savings are kept in money balances (ibid.: 52); (d) all bank assets consist of loans to firms for working capital purposes (ibid.: 58 n1); (e) all circulating capital is provided by the banks (ibid.).

The objective is to isolate the conditions under which the economy will grow at a steady growth rate, but, for simplicity, the analysis starts with the equilibrium conditions in a 'stationary economy' (Robertson 1949: ch. 5, sections 6 and 9 and Appendix to ch. 5, sections 1 and 2); it is then extended to a steadily growing economy, while the general case of a 'steady economy', that is, an economy which is either stationary or steadily growing, is also dealt with (in ch. 5, sect. 2).

Robertson's stationary model in *Banking Policy and the Price Level* can be represented as follows.

Since all capital production is financed by the banks, and since all money takes the form of bank deposits, the value of circulating capital must be equal to the value of the money stock:

$$M_t/P_t = C_t \qquad (26.1)$$

where M_t is the money stock in the current period, C_t is circulating capital[6] and P_t is the price level.

The second equation is the famous 'Cambridge equation', in which Robertson encapsulated his assumptions concerning agents' saving behaviour. This equation specifies the real value of households' money holdings as follows:

$$M_t/P_t = kR_t \qquad (26.2)$$

where k is the fraction of their real incomes which households wish to save *and* keep in liquid form, and R_t is the community's real income in the period considered; in other words, kR_t is the real value of bank deposits.

From equations (26.1) and (26.2) it follows that:

$$k = C_t/R_t \qquad (26.3)$$

where C_t/R_t is the (circulating) capital : output ratio. This ratio was regarded by Robertson as a technical quasi-constant. Let us define v as being equal to C_t/R_t. Then we can rewrite the above equality as:

$$k = v \qquad (26.3')$$

This equation states the equilibrium condition that households (or, as Robertson said, the general public) save and (given the model's assumptions) keep in liquid assets a fraction k of real income exactly equal to the fraction v which is used as circulating capital in production, and hence is not available for consumption.[7] It should be stressed that this is a genuine equilibrium condition, not an identity; for, as Robertson stressed, k and v are determined by 'entirely independent forces' (1949: 57), since k reflects the public's preferences and habits regarding its saving and hoarding behaviour, whereas v is a technical quasi-constant. Therefore, even in a stationary society, they would be equal *ex-ante* by a mere fluke. As Robertson said, 'the preservation of even a stationary equilibrium would be something of a miracle' (1954 as reprinted in 1956: 77).[8]

Robertson's analysis here points towards the same problem that Domar (1946) was to raise at a later stage, namely the sustainability of the 'warranted' rate of growth. This link between Robertson's and Domar's models may be seen more clearly by developing Robertson's equations with reference to a growing economy. In order to do this, consider first that the real money stock in any given year is equal to the money stock inherited from previous years, plus that deriving from current savings (S_t), which, as already stated, in this model are entirely kept as money assets. Thus we can write

$$\frac{M_t}{P_t} = \frac{M_{t-1}}{P_{t-1}(1 + \pi)} + \frac{S_t}{P_t} \tag{26.4}$$

where $\pi = (P_t - P_{t-1})/P_{t-1}$.

Given the well-known Robertsonian hypothesis of a consumption lag, we write the saving function as

$$\frac{S_t}{P_t} = sR_{t-1} \tag{26.5}$$

Substituting equations (26.5) and (26.2) into (26.4), we obtain

$$\frac{M_t}{P_t} = \left(\frac{k}{1 + \pi} + s \right) R_{t-1} \tag{26.6}$$

From equations (26.2) and (26.6) we obtain

$$kR_t = \left(\frac{k}{1 + \pi} + s \right) R_{t-1} \tag{26.7}$$

Let us define g as the rate of growth of real output. From this it follows that $R_t = R_{t-1}(1 + g)$. Robertsonian 'equilibrium' requires price stability. We define g^* as the rate of growth that ensures $\pi = 0$ in equation (26.7). Hence, for this rate of growth of real output, equation (26.7) becomes

$$g^* = \frac{s}{k} \tag{26.8}$$

g^* is the rate of growth that preserves equilibrium; that is, price stability. Equation (26.8) defines the equilibrium rate of growth as equal to that ratio between the propensity to save and the fraction of their real incomes which people hold as liquid assets. Using the equilibrium condition (26.3′) (which states the equality between k and v in equilibrium), we get

$$g^* = \frac{s}{v} \tag{26.9}$$

which is identical to the celebrated 'Domar equation', and states that the rate

313

of growth must be equal to the ratio between the propensity to save and the capital: output ratio.

An alternative formulation of these equilibrium conditions is

$$k + s = v(1 + g^*) \tag{26.10}$$

This equation shows that dynamic equilibrium is preserved if the stock of capital held by the firms sector (on the right-hand side) grows exactly at the rate which guarantees the absorption of the fraction of real incomes which is not consumed by the community (on the left-hand side). This result leads us to an evaluation of the links between the real and the monetary forces in this model. The first basic difference between Robertson's and Domar's approaches is that the Robertsonian equilibrium condition requires that the real stock of money held by the saving public (not merely the portion of this stock deriving from the flow of their current savings) be equal to the real value of the stock of circulating capital held by the firms sector. The Robertsonian formulation, by focusing on the equilibrium between the household sectors' decisions as to their stock of liquid assets, and the firms' decisions concerning capital formation, sheds some interesting light on the interactions between real and monetary equilibrium conditions, which were not clarified in subsequent post-Keynesian models. It should also be stressed at this stage that, contrary to the Domar model, Robertson's is characterized by price flexibility (see the next section). Equilibrium in his model, meant lack of inflationary or deflationary pressures, as a consequence of the coherence between the 'general public's' intertemporal choices and firms' investment decisions.

There is a second important difference: Robertson's analysis of equilibrium growth mainly concerns the growth of circulating capital. This is so because, as a first approximation, Robertson considered investments mainly as the process of *producing* capital goods, and was interested in the financing of production, as opposed to the financing of the purchase of capital goods, although he also extended his model to deal with fixed capital and developed a similar analysis for this extended version (1949: ch. 7). Robertson himself acknowledged this difference between his 'basic model' and Domar's (1954 as reprinted in 1956: 78–9). Domar's formulation is more complete from this point of view, as it concerns both circulating and fixed capital. However, this difference, though relevant, does not invalidate the conclusion that Robertson anticipated the post-Keynesian analysis of 'steady growth', and the post-Keynesian awareness that the preservation of dynamic equilibrium would be problematic and purely casual.[9]

Robertson also anticipated some aspects of the Harrodian approach to the 'natural rate of growth' (Harrod 1939, 1948). He analysed separately the two exogenous factors of growth: population growth (1949: ch. 5, sect. 8; Appendix, sects 4 and 5) and technical progress (ibid.: ch. 5, sect. 7) and Appendix, sect. 3). He developed the condition of steady growth for an economy growing at an exogenous rate of $(1 + r)$, dictated by either population growth or technical progress (or both), as implying equality between the real value of the money stock and the capital:output ratio multiplied by $(1 + r)$. 'In Harroddese', he argued (Robertson 1954 as reprinted in 1956: 77), this is the condition that would 'enable the warranted rate of growth to be maintained and to correspond with the natural rate'.

GROWTH OUT OF EQUILIBRIUM

Having shown that his analysis included a proto-formulation of what would later be called the 'actual', the 'warranted' and the 'natural' rates of growth, and of their problematic relationships, it would be tempting to go on to the issues of instability and 'knife edges'. However, this would not be a faithful rendering of Robertson's thought on growth. The similarities between Robertson's analysis of dynamic equilibrium and the models by Harrod and Domar stop here: Robertson did not develop a diagnosis of 'instability' for capitalist economies. On the contrary, he was interested in the mechanisms through which capitalist economies grow, in spite of their lack of coordination between households' intertemporal consumption plans and firms' investment decisions. His idea was that entrepreneurs' investment decisions are motivated by their will to exploit new, profitable outlets opened up by technical progress, population growth, the opening of new markets, and the like, quite independently of the public's saving decisions. What happens when the amount of savings spontaneously generated by the market is less than the demand, and firms themselves are not able or willing to provide a required difference in order to realize their investment projects? The answer, Robertson argued, is to be found in the banking sector's willingness to finance firms' investment projects. Here monetary factors come to the forefront in the analysis of growth.

Suppose we are in a disequilibrium situation of the kind just described, i.e. with $v - k \neq 0$, this difference being an 'error signal' (as defined by Samuelson in his 1963 reading of Robertson's model). For instance, let us, for simplicity, think of an economy whose population's rate of growth rises from zero to a positive value r. Stimulated by this rise (possibly because they interpret it as a promise of an expanding market), firms decide to employ the new population. In order to do so, given the unchanged saving habits of the old population, they demand loans to the banking sector for the payment of wages to the new population, at the current wage rate, w. Under these hypotheses, investment (that is, the absorption of the new population into employment) is impossible if banks do not respond elastically to firms' demand. This proposition would not be true, of course, if the saving and hoarding decisions of the old population were to change at the firms' will. If we rule out such an extreme hypothesis, as well as the equivalent one that the rate of interest acts as a perfect equilibrating factor between saving and hoarding decisions and investment decisions,[10] then investment decisions will be converted into actual investments only if the supply of bank money rises at a rate equal to r, the rate of growth of population. In other words, money has to behave as an endogenous variable.

Assume that this elastic response occurs. Then, if, as Robertson hypothesized, the new population produces its output with a lag, and if the new population's saving and hoarding habits are the same as those of the old population, the demand for 'circulating capital' (that is, in this context, the consumption goods for the maintenance of the new workers) rises at the same rate as the population and the money supply, r. To see the *disequilibrium* consequences involved in this process, let us go back to our equation (26.3), which we now rewrite as

$$kP_tR_t = P_tC_t \tag{26.3''}$$

The right-hand side of this equation has now risen by a factor $(1 + r)$ due to the rise in population and in investment, whereas the left-hand side has not changed. In other words, our 'error signal'

$$kP_t - \frac{C_t}{R_t}P_t(1 + r)$$

is less than zero. Who is going to provide the required amount of savings? How is this disequilibrium situation going to be remedied? Notice that these are two distinct questions, implying different answers.

The answer to the first question is that wage earners, and fixed-income receivers in general, experience a *disequilibrium* situation, since their consumption falls below the planned level, because their real wages fall. This can be seen on the basis of the following Robertsonian lagged-consumption function

$$A_{wt} = a_{wt}(W_{t-1}/P_t^e) \tag{26.11}$$

where A_{wt} is the consumption of wage earners (for brevity I will omit mention of other fixed-income receivers and their earnings), a_{wt} is their average propensity to save, W_{t-1} is the wage bill in the previous period, $a_{wt}W_{t-1}$ are their money expenditures in the current period, and P_t^e is the level of prices which they expected to prevail today on the basis of their (adaptive) expectations ($P_t^e = P_{t-1}$). The essence of this process is a redistribution from fixed incomes to profits, since the latter rise exactly in proportion to the rise in the price level.

Thus workers' actual consumption differs from the level they had planned by an amount depending on the level of price inflation. What is the rate of price inflation? Since circulating capital, in this example, resolves entirely to 'advances to labour', then

$$C_t = \frac{W_t}{P_t} L_t$$

where L_t is the number of workers. Substituting this value into equation (26.3″) we get

$$kP_t R_t = P_t \frac{W_t}{P_t} L_t$$

Since L_t has increased by a factor $(1 + r)$, P has to rise at the same rate in order for the equality between the demand and supply of circulating capital to be re-established. Robertson, however, added that prices may for a while rise less than in proportion to the increase in the money supply, if entrepreneurs decided to devote part of their increased profits to restoring the real value of their money balances, thus performing 'Induced Lacking'.[11]

The difference between workers' planned consumption and their actual consumption is what Robertson called 'Automatic Lacking'. In a capitalist economy, workers' (and fixed-income receivers') automatic lacking (or, in plain language, their forced saving) is the source of capital accumulation, whenever the required amount of saving is not spontaneously made available by the intertemporal choices of capitalists, or by those of workers themselves. Forced saving is the result of a redistribution of income from wages to profits which the banking sector promotes through its credit policy. This is the essence of growth *out of equilibrium*. The equality between the demand and the *ex post* supply of circulating capital is not synonymous with equilibrium. Quite the contrary, in the inflationary context just described it is the result of the imposition of forced saving on workers and on all fixed-income receivers.

We can now answer the second question: how is equilibrium going to be re-established? The answer is that, if labour productivity is kept constant, at the end of the production period production will rise at the same rate as population and prices. If no other injection of money takes place, prices will now fall back to their original level, and the real wage rate will be restored. The economy will be in equilibrium again, with higher employment. The sacrifices imposed on the public have made capital accumulation possible (in this case, capital accumulation is of the 'extensive' variety).

The effects of technical progress, in Robertson's analysis, are similar to those of a rise in population. Suppose that, with a constant population, capitalists see an opportunity for profits in investments embodying technical progress. In order to produce the new capital goods, they will demand and obtain loans from the banking system. Since the new capital goods will produce their increased output only after a lag, in the interval prices will rise and the real resources to be devoted to a deepening of the accumulation process will be provided through the sacrifices imposed on workers and other

317

people receiving a fixed income. These categories of people 'finance', so to speak, capital accumulation whenever capitalists are not willing to do so themselves, and whenever the banking system accommodates their demands.

Eventually, the higher productivity of new investment will determine a permanent increase in the level of output. Robertson was also concerned with the distribution of the fruits of technical progress. How these will be distributed depends, once again, on monetary policy. If the money supply is kept constant in the face of the increased production, prices will fall and the fruits will be distributed 'even-handedly'[12] among the different classes. By contrast, if the money supply grows at the same rate as labour productivity, then prices will remain stable and capitalists will reap all the benefits of this progress. Robertson recommended that the first policy be adopted. This is what he meant when he argued that the 'right' policy is one that stabilizes the 'price of productive capacity' rather than the price level. (This point, made in Robertson (1932: ch. 5, sect. 7), was further developed by Robertson in the third volume of his *Lectures* (Robertson 1956–9)). The 'more scientific view', he argued in 1962 (making an interesting use of this expression), called for falling prices.

It is well known that post-Keynesian writers in the 1950s were trying to dispense with 'the awkwardly rigid conclusion' (Pasinetti 1974: 104) that, for any given natural rate of growth, there is only one saving rate which will keep the system on an equilibrium rate of growth. In other words, the problem is that of achieving the equality between the effective rate of growth and the 'natural' rate (under the assumption that the 'warranted' rate is equal to the natural one). It is also well known that the post-Keynesian solution, and more precisely, Kaldor's solution, was that the saving : output ratio adapts, via a change in the level of prices. The same problem arises in Robertson's model, and his solution, as we have just shown, was exactly the same as that chosen by Kaldor. Kaldor, in 1955–6, suggested that the seeds of his model may be sought in Keynes's *Treatise on Money*, and Kahn later (1978: 551) echoed this position. But the history of the development of this approach suggests that Robertson should at least share this tribute with Keynes.

CYCLES, MONEY AND GROWTH

In this section I summarize Robertson's arguments concerning the relationships between money, cycles and growth. My main objective is to distinguish Robertson's position from that of the Austrian School, to which it has sometimes been likened. Implicitly, this discussion will cast some doubts on those interpretations of Robertson, not discussed in this chapter, which are framed in terms of 'short-period' analysis.[13]

From the very beginning of his academic career, Robertson was interested in the theory of cycles, as his first book, *A Study of Industrial Fluctuation* (1915), would suffice to testify. Actually, he presented much of his argument concerning growth in the context of his discussion of cylical fluctuations, which, as he remarked, 'occur against a background of secular and structural change' (1937). The reason for this interlinked treatment of cycles and growth is one of substance: he thought that cycles are the necessary form of economic growth, not merely in a capitalist economy but in every economy (although, in his view, the economic and legal institutions of capitalism act as an aggravating factor of cycles). As we have seen, he thought that investments are basically determined by firms' autonomous decisions, reflecting their willingness to incorporate technical progress, or to increase the stock of capital to accommodate an expected increase in demand. Now, capital and its 'indivisibilities', as well as the discontinuous nature of technical progress, are the fundamental cause of cyclical fluctuations: more precisely, cyclical upturns are due to the indivisibilities in fixed capital and the discontinuous nature of technical progress, whereas the downturn is due to the temporary saturation of the demand for fixed capital which necessarily follows after the expansion (Robertson 1949: ch. 2). This is why Robertson thought that cycles were, to a certain extent, 'appropriate': any attempt at eliminating cycles would be equivalent to an attempt at eliminating growth itself, for the alternation of expansion and depression is due to the nature of investment itself.

Two main points distinguish Robertson's position from that of the Austrian School. First, for Robertson *real* factors are the ultimate cause of fluctuations,[14] not (as Hayek had it) the 'disequilibrating' interest rate policy of the banks, although this policy may sometimes act as an *additional* factor. Money enters the picture in a different way. Within limits, it may be used as the means to achieve secular growth (rather than crises and capital disruptions, as intimated by the Austrians), when equilibrium growth cannot be relied upon, owing to a discrepancy between saving decisions and investment decisions. Let me quote a passage from the third volume of Robertson's *Lectures on Economic Principles*, which clearly expresses his views concerning the role of money in the growth of capitalist economies:

> I have tried not to take it for granted that the preservation of monetary equilibrium should be in all circumstances the overriding objective of policy in the wider or strategic sense. Indeed my little book on *Banking Policy and the Price Level* was written thirty years ago partly in order to suggest the contrary. Looking back on the history of capitalism, I should myself find it difficult to say dogmatically that such episodes as the English railway mania of the 1849s, or the American railway boom of 1869–71, or the German electrical boom of the 1890s, each of which drenched the country in question with valuable capital equipment at the expense of inflicting inflationary levies and adding to the instability of employment, where on balance a 'bad thing'. And in these more enlightened days if a community,

even though making modest but steady progress, feels itself under an urgent need to equip itself rapidly with fixed capital instruments for purposes of defence, or for reaping the harvest of technical improvements in which it has for some reason lagged behind the rest of the world, the fact that a certain policy will involve monetary un-neutrality or disequilibrium cannot in my view be taken to be a decisive argument against it. As I suggested last term, we are far from being able to say that the amount of provision for the future which will be made by a free enterprise economy which preserves monetary equilibrium is in any absolute sense the 'right' amount.

(Robertson 1956–9: vol. 3, pp. 44–5)

Second, another important policy implication of Robertson's views on cycles is that deflationary monetary policy cannot be used to remedy the slump, as advocated by the Austrians. And, for that matter, Robertson would rather advocate an expensionary monetary policy, and even fiscal policy as a remedy.[15] As Samuelson put it, his 'gentle renunciation of Hayekian deflationism' always kept Robertson from 'being the darling of the libertarians'.

CONCLUSIONS

Robertson was concerned with the analysis of growth, and of the relationships between growth, money and cycles. Admittedly, his equations were very rudimentary. They show the extraordinary 'tension' which he imposed on the 'Cambridge equation', into whose simple symbols he initially grafted the equilibrium conditions for a stationary economy, then even the dynamic equilibrium conditions for a growing economy. This should not blind us to the fact that he anticipated many of the basic questions which were later to be asked by the post-Keynesian analysts of growth, and many of their answers too. Moreover, he regarded cycles not as temporary and irrelevant oscillations around an independent growth path, but as the necessary form of growth itself. Finally, he contemplated the possibility of growth out of equilibrium, and regarded bank money as an essential ingredient of this process.

Robertson asked three basic questions: (1) Under what circumstances is an economy capable of growth in equilibrium (or steady growth)? (2) Which variable 'adapts' when the conditions of steady growth are not spontaneously met? (3) What should the role of monetary policy be in a growing economy?

1   In his answer to the first question, he anticipated Domar's condition of equality between the actual and the 'warranted' rate of growth, as well as Harrod's 'natural' rate of growth.
2   In disequilibrium, saving decisions are simply frustrated, to the extent that they differ from the predetermined amount of investment: the

necessary equality between investment and saving being achieved via changes in the price level and, consequently, in the distribution of income from wages to profits, or vice versa (just as in Kaldor's model referred to above).[16]

3 Finally, monetary policy should not blindly promote the stability of prices, because that stability may hamper growth. Rather, monetary policy should be moderately accommodating in the expansionary phase, to the purpose of promoting the redistribution of income required for investment decisions to be realized; and it should subsequently allow prices to fall, in order to distribute the fruits of expansion, in the form of increased output, equally among capitalists and workers.

ACKNOWLEDGEMENTS

This chapter is an abridged version of my introduction (in Italian) to the Italian translation of Dennis H. Robertson's *Banking Policy and the Price Level, with Other of His Writings on Money*, which I edited in 1993. I am indebted to Geoff Harcourt, Bob Rowthorn and the editors of this book for their comments on this article. For comments on the Italian version, I thank Adriano Giannola, Augusto Graziani, Riccardo Realfonso and Claudio Ricci. I am responsible for any remaining errors.

NOTES

1 Frank Hahn (1986: xiii) once noticed that Robertson's contributions 'keep getting "rediscovered",' and he rightly (in my opinion) attributed this fact to the widespread tendency to forget about the history of economic thought. An additional reason may be that these 'rediscoveries' are one effect of the fact that, as Robertson himself wrote, 'highbrow opinion is like a hunted hare; if you stand in the same place, or nearly the same place, it may be relied upon to come round to you in a circle'. But Robertson could not foresee that one of the effects of this 'coming round in a circle' of highbrow opinion would be the periodical 'rediscovery' of him as a precursor of this and that theory.

2 Among these interpreters are Castellino (1983), Costabile (1983, 1985, 1993), Danes (1979, 1985), Dennison (1968), Goodhart (1990), Graziani (1981), Hahn (1955), Harcourt (1992), Kregel (1983: 55, 67), Laidler (1995), Pasinetti (1974: 51–3), Robinson (1947), Presley (1978, 1981, 1992), Wilson (1953), and those mentioned in note 3.

3 See Samuelson (1963), Hicks (1964: 312, 316), Fellner (1952), Gilbert (1982: 66–70) and Bigg (1990: 92). With the exception of Samuelson, these authors did not develop their arguments analytically. Samuelson did, but his analysis referred mainly to the problem of slumps.

4 Robertson did not use the label 'capitalist economy'; rather, he spoke of 'our wage and money systems', characterized by a 'disharmony of interest between "Capital" and "Labour"' (1949: 19–22). For these distinctions see Robertson (1949: chs 1 and 2, particularly pp. 7–8 and 19–23. Throughout this chapter I refer to the 1949 reprint of *Banking Policy and the Price Level*. The differences between the different editions were extremely minor, and did *not* involve the

passages quoted here. On Robertson's distinction beween different types of economies see also Danes (1979, 1985).

5 In *Banking Policy and the Price Level* Robertson argued that all capital goods (circulating capital and fixed capital) are alike from the point of view of the kind of saving which their *production* requires; that is, short-term saving. By contrast, the *purchase* of capital goods 'involves a further provision of saving, this time of the long variety' (1949: 85). Robertson was interested mainly in how saving is provided for *production* purposes, and *in this sense* his basic model includes only circulating capital. However, he extended his basic model (ibid.: ch. 7) to include fixed capital; that is, the puchase of fixed-capital goods. See also what he had to say on fixed capital in 'Thoughts on meeting some important persons' (1954 as reprinted in 1956: 76).

6 Notice that, for simplicity, I have substituted the symbol C for the expression qDR which Robertson used (1949: 57–8), where $q(= C/DR)$ is a technical quasi-constant, i.e. the capital : output ratio in the production period. According to Robertson, $q = 1/2$ in 'steady' conditions, but is subject to change during cyclical fluctuations. D is the production period. When $D = 1$ (e.g. 1 year) then q is exactly equal to the capital : output ratio, i.e. v (rather than q) in my notation. Robertson thought that, in reality, $D = 1$ year, both in the UK and the USA.

7 In Robertson's own formulation, this equation reads $k = qD$ (1949: 53). The two sides of this equation may be read either as fractions of real income or as periods, since k is the (inverse of) the period of circulation of money relative to *final* income and D is the period of production (hence qD is the ratio of circulating capital to output in the average period of production).

8 Samuelson (1963), in his interesting reconstruction of Robertson's model, grudgingly acknowledged that Robertson was dealing here with *ex ante* variables. His comment was: 'All this is very non-neoclassical, very non-Robertsonish.' For non-neoclassical as Robertson's model might have been, it is difficult to see how it could have been non-Robertsonish, since it was Robertson's own model; and, in my view, this point is essential to his views on money and growth (see the quotation from Robertson on pp. 319–20).

9 Marx anticipated this awareness. See Sardoni (1981).

10 In his 1949 preface to *Banking Policy and the Price Level* (p. xi), Robertson wrote, 'I think it is probable that my first draft (achieving in this a post-Keynesian modernity which I would now be the last to defend) made no mention of the rate of interest whatever.'

11 In Robertson's period analysis, time is split into 'atoms of time': in the first 'day' the rise in the price level imposes an 'automatic lacking' on capitalists, but this promptly disappears when their money incomes rise with the price level. In order to restore the real value of their money stock, however, they will perform 'induced lacking' from the second day until the end of the inflationary process. On induced lacking see Costabile (1985) and Laidler (1995).

12 Samuelson (1963: 532). Robertson overlooked the possibility that falling prices may determine bankruptcies. Keynes's alternative prescription was to raise money wages. (Geoff Harcourt reminded me of this point.)

13 Harcourt (1992) carefully noticed the relative irrelevance of the short-period in Robertson's *Lectures on Economic Principles*. For one short-period interpretation of Robertson see Milgate (1982).

14 As emphasized by Goodhart (1990).

15 See, for example, his review of Durbin (Robertson 1933b). See also Laidler (1995).

16 Two of Harcourt's articles (1963, 1965) which criticize and extend Kaldor's

model belong to the theoretical tradition which was cultivated in Cambridge in the 1920s, when Robertson and Keynes were working along common theoretical lines.

REFERENCES

Bigg, R. J. (1990) *Cambridge and the Monetary Theory of Production: The Collapse of the Marshallian Macroeconomics*, London: Macmillan.

Castellino, O. (1983) 'Keynes e Robertson', *Piemonte Vivo Ricerche*, Turin: Cassa di Risparmio di Torino.

Costabile, L. (1983) 'Note sulla relazione tra credito, accumulazione e risparmio in *Banking Policy and the Price Level* di D. H. Robertson', *Studi Economici* 21: 115–35.

—— (1985) 'Credit creation, capital formation and abstinence in the approach of D. H. Robertson', in R. Arena, A. Graziani and J. Kregel (eds) *Production, circulation et Monnaie*, Paris: Presses Universitaires de France.

—— (1993) 'Introduzione' to Robertson, D. H. (1993) *Politica bancaria e livello dei prezzi. Con altri scritti sulla moneta*, ed. L. Costabile, Naples: Edizioni Scientifiche Italiane.

Danes, M. J. (1979) 'Dennis Robertson and the Construction of Aggregative Theory', unpublished Ph.D. dissertation, London: London School of Economics.

Danes (Anadayke-Danes), M. J. (1985) 'Dennis Robertson and Keynes's *General Theory*', in G. C. Harcourt (ed.) *Keynes and His Contemporaries: The Sixth and Centennial Keynes Seminar Held at the University of Kent at Canterbury, 1983*, Basingstoke and London: Macmillan.

Dennison, S. R. (1968) 'Dennis Holme Robertson', in *International Encyclopedia of the Social Sciences*, vol. 13, London: Macmillan.

Domar, E. D. (1946) 'Capital expansion, rate of growth and employment', *Econometrica* 14: 137–47.

Fellner, W. (1952) 'The Robertsonian evolution', *American Economic Review* 42(3): 265–82.

Gilbert, J. C. (1982) *Keynes's Impact on Monetary Economics*, London: Butterworth.

Goodhart, C. (1990) 'Dennis Robertson and the real business cycles: a centenary lecture', Financial Markets Group Discussion Paper 92. Reprinted in Presley, J. R. (ed.) (1992) *Essays on Robertsonian Economics*, Basingstoke and London: Macmillan.

Graziani, A. (1981) *Teoria Economica. Macroeconomia*, Naples: Edizioni Scientifiche Italiane.

Hahn, F. H. (1955) 'The rate of interest and general equilibrium analysis', *Economic Journal* 65(1): 52–66.

—— (1986) Foreword to Henin, P. Y., *Macrodynamics: Fluctuations and Growth. A Study of the Economy in Equilibrium and Disequilibrium*, London: Routledge & Kegan Paul.

Harcourt, G. C. (1963) 'A critique of Mr Kaldor's model of income distribution and economic growth', *Australian Economic Papers* 2: 20–36.

—— (1965) 'A two-sector model of the distribution of income and the level of employment in the short run', *Economic Record* 41: 103–17.

—— (1992) 'Marshall's *Principles* as seen at Cambridge through the eyes of Gerald Shove, Dennis Robertson and Joan Robinson', in Harcourt, G. C., *On Political Economists and Modern Political Economy: Selected Essays of G. C. Harcourt*, ed. C. Sardoni, London: Routledge.

Harrod, R. F. (1939) 'An essay in dynamic theory', *Economic Journal* 49: 14–33.

——— (1948) *Towards a Dynamic Economics*, London: Macmillan.

Hicks, J. R. (1964) 'Dennis Holme Robertson, 1890–1963', in *Proceedings of the British Academy*, vol. 50, London: Oxford University Press.

Kahn, R. F. (1978) 'On some aspects of the development of Keynes' thought', *Journal of Economic Literature* 16: 545–59.

Kaldor, N. (1955–6) 'Alternative theories of distribution', *Review of Economic Studies* 23: 83–100.

Kregel, J. (1983) 'Effective demand: origins and development of the notion', in J. Kregel (ed.) *Distribution, Effective Demand and International Economic Relations*, Basingstoke and London: Macmillan.

Laidler, D. (1995) 'Robertson in the 1920s', *European Journal of the History of Economic Thought* 2(1): 151–74.

Milgate, M. (1982) *Capital and Employment: A Study of Keynes's Economics*, London: Academic Press.

Pasinetti, L. L. (1974) *Growth and Income Distribution*, Cambridge: Cambridge University Press.

Presley, J. R. (1978) *Robertsonian Economics: An Examination of the Work of Sir D. H. Robertson on Industrial Fluctuations*, London, Macmillan.

——— (1981) 'D. H. Robertson, 1890–1963', in D. P. O'Brien and J. R. Presley (eds) *Pioneers of Modern Economics in Britain*, London: Macmillan.

——— (ed.) (1992) *Essays on Robertsonian Economics*, Basingstoke and London: Macmillan.

Robertson, D. H. (1915) *A Study of Industrial Fluctuation: An Enquiry into the Character and Causes of the So-Called Cyclical Movements*, London: P. S. King & Son.

——— (1922) *Money*, Cambridge Economic Handbooks, London: Nisbet & Co.

——— (1926) *Banking Policy and the Price Level*, London: P. S. King & Son.

——— (1928a) *Money*, revised edition, Cambridge Economic Handbooks, London: Nisbet & Co.

——— (1928b) 'Theories of the banking policy', *Economica* 8: 131–46.

——— (1932) *Banking Policy and the Price Level*, revised edition, London: P. S. King & Son.

——— (1933a) 'Saving and hoarding', *Economic Journal* 43: 399–413.

——— (1933b) 'Monetary policy and the trade slump', *The Highway*, March 1933, 11–13.

——— (1934) 'Industrial fluctuation and the natural rate of interest', *Economic Journal* 44: 650–6.

——— (1937) 'The state and economic fluctuations', Harvard, 1937. Reprinted as 'The snake and the worm' in Robertson, D. H. (1940) *Essays in Monetary Theory*, London: P. S. King & Son, and Robertson, D. H. (1966) *Essays in Money and Interest*, selected with a memoir by Sir John H. Hicks, London: Fontana Library.

——— (1949) *Banking Policy and the Price Level* (reprinted with a new preface), New York: Kelley.

——— (1954) 'Thoughts on meeting some important persons', *Quarterly Journal of Economics*, May. Reprinted in Robertson, D. H. (1956) *Economic Commentaries*, London: Staples Press.

——— (1956–9) *Lectures on Economic Principles*, London: Staples Press.

——— (1962) *Memorandum Submitted to the Canadian Royal Commission on Banking and Finance*. Reprinted in *Essays in International Finance* no. 42, May 1943, Princeton, NJ: University of Princeton.

——— (1993) *Politica bancaria e livello dei prezzi. Con altri scritti sulla moneta*, ed. L. Costabile, Naples: Edizioni Scientifiche Italiane.

Robinson, E. A. G. (1947) 'J. M. Keynes', *Economic Journal*, 57:1–68.

Samuelson, P. (1963) 'D. H. Robertson (1890–1963)', *Quarterly Journal of Economics* 77(4): 517–36.

Sardoni, C. (1981) 'Multisectoral models of balanced growth and the Marxian schemes of expanded reproduction', *Australian Economic Papers* 20(37): 383–97.

Wilson, T. (1953) 'Professor Robertson on effective demand and the trade cycle', *Economic Journal* 43: 553–78.

27

POLITICAL ECONOMY, HOUSEHOLD ECONOMY AND THE PRICE OF LAND

Towards a decolonization of 'social science imperialism'

Christopher A. Gregory

AN ECONOMICS OF EVERYTHING OR A POLITICAL ECONOMY OF SOMETHING

The 'social science imperialists', to use Geoff Harcourt's (Harcourt 1982) memorable phrase, now have an economics of Everything: family life, child rearing, dying, sex, suicide, crime, politics, environment – you name it, nothing is excluded. Geoff has not only done us a great service in naming the all-conquering demon, but has also been a prominent member of the Cambridge team of logic-choppers who have slain it. The big question today, however, is why has neoclassical theory been able to live on to become bigger and more powerful than ever.

Part of the answer is that neoclassical economics has equipped itself with an antidote which renders it immune to criticism of its internal logic and its assumptions. But another part of the answer is that political economy in the Ricardo–Marx–Sraffa tradition is not 'imperialist' enough; it remains 'local' in the sense that it bears the marks of its birthplace in the nineteenth-century English and Western European countryside. This shows up in its theory of rent, which contains a number of implicit assumptions about the marketability of land. In this short essay I will compare and contrast Sraffa's and Marx's theory of rent in order to reveal these assumptions and to show how they reflect the particular conditions of English and Western European farm household economy respectively. Classical political economy locates itself on the factory floor, as it were, and from such a perspective household economy is part of the social datum of the analysis. I will suggest that if political economy is to provide a viable alternative to neoclassical economics today it must expand to include a theory of household economy.

THE PRICE OF LAND

The question of rent poses the more general question of the determinants of the price of land. For neoclassical economics this is a simple problem. Land is a scarce good whose value is determined by the laws of supply and demand, laws whose ultimate explanation is to be found in the utility-maximizing behaviour of individuals. Scarcity and consumption are natural facts of human existence for neoclassical economists and the question of the price of land raises no special problems. The neoclassical theory of goods is universal; it is simply a matter of applying the tools of the trade to the new problem at hand – and this can be anything from extramarital affairs through suicide to cups of tea. Value, from this perspective, is always and everywhere an expression of an individual's cognition, and this philosophical stance is the basis of the imperialistic tendencies of neoclassical economics.

For classical political economy, on the other hand, where value is seen as the expression of political relations between people in historically specific situations, the question of the price of land raises thorny theoretical problems because classical political economy is, first and foremost, a theory of value of reproducible commodities whereas land is the classic example of a scarce good. How does a theory of reproducible commodities explain the value of scarce goods? It is one thing to show, for example, that the exchange values of iron or wheat are an expression of the political relations between wage labour and capital; but the question of the value of land on which these commodities are produced raises altogether different questions because, among other reasons, land is not carried off to market for sale on a regular basis. Indeed, in many cases, if not most, it is not marketed at all.

The political economists approached this problem by means of a number of fine distinctions. This first is between *use value* and *exchange value*. The former is a people–nature relation, the latter is a people–people relation. The problem of use value raises questions of natural and technological history which lie beyond the scope of political economy. For example, the use value of agricultural land in Java differs from that in sub-Saharan Africa, and the reasons for this are to be found in the human history of land use and the natural history of ecology in both areas. The problem of exchange value raises the question of the wages, prices and profits, and the task of classical political economy has been to show how these interrelated phenomena are an expression of historically specific relationships between people by means of a labour theory of value or some form or other. Farmland creates problems for such a theory because it is not a commodity that can be produced by the expenditure of labour power. These problems are inherent in the notion of the price of land itself, which, from the point of view of political economy, is conceptualized as the capitalized value of rent. The following formula captures the essence of this definition.

Exchange value of land = rent/interest rate

327

If, for example, the annual rent of land of a given holding of 100 acres is £100 and the ordinary rate of interest is 5 per cent, then the marketable price of land is £2,000, or 'twenty years' purchase' as they used to say in England (Habakkuk 1952: 26). The exchange value of land in this 'per holding' sense is also its value as a land capital; on a 'per acre' basis an exchange value of £20 is implied.

This *marketable* exchange value of land is its 'long-run' or 'natural price' and it must be distinguished from the 'short-run' or *marketed* price. For a given rent, this difference shows up as one between the ruling rate of interest on money capital and the rate of return on land capital. In the classical theory of prices the former provided the 'centre of gravity' around which the latter was supposed to move. However, as the theoretical dispute between Child and Locke in the seventeenth century illustrates – see Habakkuk (1952) – the matter is not quite as straightforward as the theory predicts because the rate of return on land capital sometimes moves independently of the rate of return on money capital.

The question 'What determines the price of land?', then, is not a simple one. It immediately bifurcates into two new problems. What determines the rate of return? What determines the rental rate of land that is used for producing commodities using capitalistic methods? The rate-of-return question, in turn, raises the question of the differential rates of return on land capital and money capital and the relationship between them. The rent question divides into two further questions: What determines the rental value of land of different qualities? What determines the rental value of land of the same quality?

Sraffa and Marx restricted their analysis to the rent question; their factory floor perspective led to an answer which argues that rental values are an expression of the political relation between capital and wage labour. Their demonstrations are ingenious and their theories contain many important propositions; but, like the scientist who tries to discover the properties of fire by working under water, their theories only tell us part of the story because the value of land springs as much from the relations of household reproduction as it does from the relations of commodity reproduction.

SRAFFA'S THEORY OF RENT

In *Production of Commodities by Means of Commodities*, Sraffa (1960: 74–8) purges Ricardo's theory of rent of all reference to use value – a pre-given order in the natural fertility of land, for example – to yield two stunningly original propositions that, on first reading, test one's credulity. The first is that, in the case of rent on lands of different quality, the order of the fertility of land varies with changes in the distribution of income; that is, the order of fertility is not determined independently of price determination. The second is that, in the case where land is of the same quality, the rent is 'invisible' in the sense that the only evidence of scarcity is the existence of two methods of producing the commodities on the scarce land; as Sraffa (1960: 76) notes, 'if there were no scarcity, only one method, the cheapest, would be used on the land and there could be no rent'. Upon reflection it is apparent that these propositions are a logical extension of his general argument that *no* notion of capital – be it in the form of wheat, iron or land – can be looked upon as a measurable quantity independent of distribution and prices. His work, then, can be seen as a formal demonstration of Marx's argument that capital is a social relation of production: that behind the exchange values linking commodities lie relations between people.

Sraffa's terse prose, to say nothing of his counterintuitive propositions, tests the patience of even the most sympathetic reader. Many of his arguments, to borrow one of his phrases (1960: 60), look as if they are the 'freak result of abstract-mongering that can have no correspondence in reality'. However, if the reader does the hard work of placing his thought in the context of the history of thought and the history of capitalism the obscurity of his thought begins to yield dividends, as Geoff Harcourt pointed out many years ago. But it also reveals a hidden assumption which informs his analysis: *that land is not a marketable commodity.*

This assumption – a perfectly reasonable one for the England of Ricardo's time – is required if Sraffa's theory of scarce land capital is to make economic sense. Take the case of land of different qualities. Here the least fertile land yields no rent. Given that the value of land capital (i.e. the price of land) is equal to the capitalized value of rent, it follows that this land has zero value and becomes, as he puts, 'free' like all other natural resources. But this analogy does not hold because air and rain remain 'free' whatever the distribution of income, whereas land that was 'free' at one level of distribution may yield a rent at another. Now consider the case of rent on land of different qualities. Here rent is 'invisible' because it takes the form of dual methods of production. How can rent of this kind, which has no determinate value form, be capitalized? The implication of this is that the value of scarce capital in the form of land is either zero or indeterminate. To put it another way, land has a use value in Sraffa's theory but no exchange value: its use value derives from the fact that commodities can be produced from it; it has no exchange value in the sense that the landlords keep it off the market.

But how do the landlords keep land off the market? How do they stop this important use value from becoming a commodity? How is this scarce non-commodity reproduced? These questions cannot be answered within the narrow confines of Sraffa's theory of commodity reproduction. One requires a theory of household reproduction, or, to be more precise, a theory of household economy that is embedded in a theory of market (commodity) economy and the state. Classical political economy in the Ricardo–Marx–Sraffa tradition is exclusively concerned with market economy and the state; household economy was beyond its scope. My contention is that the determinant of the value of a scarce good like land cannot be understood without a theory of household reproduction and, further, that such a theory can only be derived from the comparative and historical evidence. In other words, if one wants to understand the social relations that determine the non-market exchange value of scarce goods then one must begin with an analysis of the historical and anthropological evidence on the reproduction of the landed family.

The relations of landed household reproduction are not uniform. A distinction must be made between those households who farm their land and those, the élite, that do not. England is unique in the sense that farmlands have traditionally been controlled by élite families who needed to keep land off the market in order to reproduce themselves. The development of capitalist agriculture in England owes much to the barriers to the free trade in land that these families set up.

The arrangements conformed to a standard pattern:

> In its essentials the marriage settlement first secured that the family estate should in each generation descend to the eldest son. It did this by limiting the interest in the estate of the father of the husband and, after him, of the husband himself, to that of life-tenant, and entailing the estate on the eldest son to be born of the marriage. Secondly, the marriage settlement empowered both the father and husband to raise jointures [i.e. money revenue] for their respective wives and portions, i.e. capital sums, for their daughters and young persons when they came of age.
>
> (Habakkuk 1950: 15)

Thus the eldest son received the farmlands, the wives money revenue, and the other children money capital. The eldest son also inherited the problem of finding the money for the jointures and portions. 'The prudent course,' noted Habakkuk, 'would have been to save, but the normal practice was to borrow.'

Figure 27.1 depicts these relationships in a sightly simplified form. The scheme shown here was the basic building block of a system whose dialectical complexity becomes apparent when it is realized, for example, that one man's wife is another man's daughter and that she gets money revenue from one and money capital from the other.

The role of the state was crucial in that it provided the legal framework for this particular system of household economy to work. Indeed, the development of this common pattern in the eighteenth century was to a considerable extent the result of technical changes in the land law (Habakkuk 1950: 16). Demography, too, played a crucial role, for it is obvious that the system presupposes that the male line reproduces itself.

From the perspective of market economy this system is a barrier to the free trade in land, a barrier that has its basis in the principles of household economy. Such a system is implicit in Sraffa's theory of rent. It is also implicit

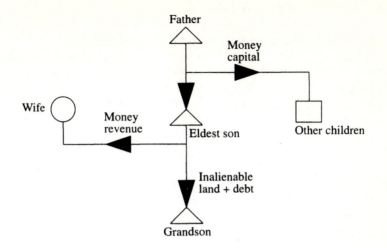

Figure 27.1 Marriage settlements in eighteenth-century England

in Ricardo's theory, but the evidence is that he understood it much better, as suggested by his oblique reference to a seller of land as being 'almost always under the necessity of selling' (1817 [1954]: 154). This 'necessity' has its logical basis in demographic failure of the male line, and the historical evidence suggests that this was the most important factor in bringing land on to the market (Clay 1968: 510, 517). For example, the period 1680–1750 saw many sales because the male reproduction rate in élite families fell below 1 throughout this entire period.

Élite families were not the only kind of landed family found in nineteenth century England but they were, it seems, the predominant one. As Marx noted, 'John Bright's assertion that 150 landlords own half of England, and 12, half the Scotch soil, has never been refuted' (1867: 322 n2). A brief history of primogeniture in England over the period from 1500, and the debates surrounding it, has been written by Thirsk, who notes that it was most common among the nobility in the sixteenth century

and seems to have been deemed by common consent the most acceptable practice for family and state reasons. It reduced strife among brothers when the eldest automatically took the leading position; it maintained the status of the family; and it preserved a class of rulers in society. In general it did not cause excessive hardship to younger sons because the nobility had the means to provide adequately for all. The hardships were felt most keenly among the gentry because their means were not sufficient to provide decently for younger sons.

(Thirsk 1984: 368)

331

'In the eighteenth century,' she adds,

> the aspirations of the gentry filtered down to the next class below, and produced yeomen who followed the rule of primogeniture and, in order to make the assurance doubly sure, settled their estates. Primogeniture gained ground among the middle classes and provoked another controversy, centring upon that class, in the nineteenth century.
>
> (ibid.: 372)

The system of primogeniture and entailments, then, kept land off the market in the England of Ricardo's time. This much is the social datum of Sraffa's rehabilitated Ricardian theory of rent; it gives meaning to his implicit assumption that farmland is not marketed. But it also means that Sraffa's theory of rent is applicable only to those situations where élite landed households of the English kind existed; that is, to England!

MARX'S THEORY OF RENT

If the Ricardo–Sraffa theory of rent reflects the specific conditions of late-eighteenth-century English agriculture with its implicit assumption that land is a non-commodity, then Marx's theory reflects the conditions prevailing in Western Europe in the early nineteenth century, for it contains the explicit assumption that land is a commodity that is actively marketed.

Marx's theory of rent differs from Ricardo's in one highly significant way: Marx has a theory of 'absolute rent'. This is the rent that arises on land of the lowest quality and it is created, he argues (1894: 737), by landed property. Absolute rent is a form of monopoly pricing, and it means that when marginal land reaches the market it will always have a price greater than zero under the capitalization principle of pricing. This innovation in the theory of rent was needed to account for the active land market that developed in Western Europe after the Napoleonic revolutions. Marx also discusses another important category of landlord not considered by either Ricardo or Sraffa, the 'peasant proprietor'. Again, this concept is an artefact of the particular conditions of European agriculture of Marx's time. Members of households of this type, according to Marx, were capitalists, landlords and workers rolled up in one. They paid rent in advance, as it were, when they purchased their land with the aid of a mortgage. A further defining characteristic of peasant proprietors was their smallholdings, which consisted of scattered parcelled plots. These, argued Marx, got even smaller because of inheritance practices which gave brothers equal claim to their father's land.

The conditions of reproduction of élite households of the English type is very different from that of 'peasant proprietors' and it is the latter that forms the social datum of Marx's analysis of rent. Table 27.1, which gives a statistical overview of some relevant factors relating to the market for land in

Table 27.1 Arable land market from selected decades

	1700–9	1740–9	1780–9	1820–9	1860–9
Total arable (Morgen)	1,029	1,029	1,029	1,029	927
Percentage arable sold	12	14	26	30	16
Price/Morgen (florins)	31	54	109	127	564
Mean population/decade	340	455	516	738	924

Source: Sabean 1990: 361
Note: 1 Morgen = 0.78 acres = 0.32 hectares

a village in southern Germany over the period 1700–1869, helps us to contextualize Marx's theory.

The significant features to note in this table are the Malthusian contradiction between the trebling in the size of the population and the constancy in the area of arable land, the 'overheating' of the land market in the nineteenth century as measured by the increase in the quantity sold in the period 1820–9 and in the increase in land prices generally in the period to 1869. During the nineteenth century the price of land 'rose at a rate which far outstripped the price of labor or that of any other commodity' (Sabean 1990: 20). It was during this period that Marx developed his theory of 'peasant proprietorship' in land parcels which tells the sad tale of ever-increasing debt brought about by these rapidly rising land prices.

But, as Sabean's meticulous work reveals (1990: 47), this tale tells only part of the history of peasant production during this period because the peasantry did not disappear as Marx's evolutionary theory predicted. On the contrary, the catastrophic pauperization of the early part of the century was followed by the reconstruction of, in the words of a contemporary observer, a 'prosperous peasantry' (ibid.: 415). If the principles of market and national economy could be said to be behind the pauperization, then the principles of household economy were behind the reconstruction. In the period 1820–9 the land market was more active than at any other time during the nineteenth century owing to the economic dislocation following the Napoleonic Wars when villagers went bankrupt and a significant amount of property was sold at forced public auction. Increased population led to a greater intensity of land use and to a demand for land that, thanks to the new laws that abolished entailments and other impediments to the free marketing of land, was able to be met through an increased supply. This was a crucial difference from the English situation. In England élite landlord families managed to keep land off the market. They also managed to enlarge their holdings by means of the infamous enclosure movement.

The effect of this was to send dispossessed peasants off to the labour market in big numbers. In other words, whereas forces of commercialization in England created a market for labour by means of barriers to the free trade in land, the same forces in Western Europe created an active free trade in land. There were, of course, countervailing tendencies to the process of proletarianization in England and 'peasantization' elsewhere in Europe but the general point holds. The reasons for these differences are to be found in the history of the political relations between household economy, the market and the state in the two cases.

But what was the process that created a 'prosperous peasantry' by the end of the century? To understand this it is necessary to go beyond the relationship between employer and employee on the factory floor to the politics of the family relations. This requires an investigation of the complicated relation-ships created by the vertical vector of lineage descent, the horizontal vector of marriage alliance, and the fragile circle of siblingship. These social relations of family creation, preservation and destruction, which are under-written by biological relations of human reproduction, work in unpredictable ways and often in opposition to the 'laws of the market'. The value of scarce goods such as land can never be properly understood unless these 'social data' become part of a broader theory of value.

It is beyond the scope of this chapter to develop this point here, but some of the issues at stake can be grasped by briefly considering the work of Sabean, who has analysed the family labour relations behind every transaction in Table 27.1 in painstaking detail. His general conclusions are as follows. First, there was no change in the distribution of wealth despite a population increase of about 350 per cent over the 170-year period: in 1710 the upper 10 per cent owned 29 per cent of the wealth and the lower 50 per cent owned 17 per cent; in 1790 the corresponding figures were 28 per cent and 18 per cent; in 1870 33 per cent and 14 per cent (1990: 454). Second, wealthy families created lines of connection with poor families through marriage. Third, access to property 'was almost completely a matter of descent, and most of it was either inherited, given, or sold to nuclear kin' (ibid.: 420). Of particular interest is his observation that the price of land sold to brothers and sisters and children was much lower than the market rate; this price was called 'family price' (ibid.: 403).

Thus the relations between people in the land market in the village studied by Sabean were not like the alienated relationships that characterize those between buyer and seller in the supermarkets of today; they were relations between kin that were able to counter the dissolving market forces to produce the paradoxical effects that Marx and others were totally unable to predict because of their ignorance of the principles of household economy.

The workings of farm household economy in capitalist countries such as Australia suggests that 'family pricing' is not something that is restricted to peasant households. In the Murrumbidgeee Irrigation Area of Australia, the

Water Conservation and Irrigation Commission of New South Wales exercises rigorous control over irrigated land ownership and use. The area is divided up into small horticultural blocks of around 20 ha each and into large-area rice farms of around 200 ha. No family can own more than one farm and no subdivision is permitted. The area under crop is also fixed by quota, and regular aerial surveys ensure that these regulations are observed. The effect of this has been to ensure the reproduction of large consolidated plots of land by, in effect, rendering illegal the principles of household economy. Thus when someone dies the land is either given to a selected son or, as is more usual, sold on the market. Sometimes the land is sold by a group of heirs at a kinship price. This ensures that all siblings share in the estate equally and that the buyer, one of the siblings, is not burdened with a lifelong debt through having to pay the market price for the farm. The pattern of land sales in Griffith since the irrigation area was established at the beginning of the century tells a very interesting tale. Soldier-settlers of English descent were granted the land after the war and many of them proved to be inefficient farmers. As their lands entered the market they were purchased by Italians with experience of smallholder ('peasant') farming. The rules of inheritance enabled these poor ex-peasant proprietors to reproduce themselves as relatively wealthy capitalist farmers, first on the small horticultural farms and later on the bigger rice farms. These migrants encouraged their relatives to migrate and now the farmland is owned mainly by Australians of Italian descent. An interesting feature of this migration is that relatives were prepared to pay prices well in excess of market rates to be near their next of kin. For example, in 1969 a rice farm in Griffith cost twice the price of an equivalent rice farm in Leeton some 60 km away. When a real-estate agent pointed this fact out to a prospective buyer his response was, 'I've already migrated once; I don't want to migrate again' (Huber 1977: 70). Here, then, we have the principles of household economy working to create a kinship price that diverges from 'usual' market rate, but this time the price is higher than expected.

These examples are sufficient to suggest that the value of a scarce good such as farmland springs from the social relations of consanguinity, affinity and contiguity of household reproduction and not from the social relations of industrial production; they also suggest that when goods like this become commodities, their market price is influenced in unpredictable ways by the social relations of scarcity in the household. Scarcity, then, is not a natural fact of life, as neoclassical theory would have it; it is a social relation of household reproduction that can be grasped only by examining historically specific forms of reciprocal recognition within households.

CHRISTOPHER A. GREGORY

GOODS, COMMODITIES AND THE INDETERMINATE PRICE OF LAND

Let me now try to draw the threads of my argument together. From the perspectives of household economy, land, for the landed family, is first and foremost a *good* that produces *commodities* for sale on the market. Moreover, it is a good that can sometimes assume the form of a commodity. These contradictions create problems for the classical theory of value because of its exclusive focus on reproducible commodities and its neglect of household economy. The formal expression of this, in Sraffa's work, is a theory of land capital where the price of land is indeterminate. This comes about, I argued, because a good, by definition, has no price of production – no primary or 'natural' price – because it is scarce.

The value of land as a scarce good springs not from an individual's cognition, as marginal-utility theory would have it, but from historically specific relations of consanguinity, affinity and contiguity which are the product of reciprocal recognition. In other words, scarcity is a social relation of household reproduction, not a matter of individual choice. Inheritance is a relationship between the dead and the unborn created by the living. Relationships between the living create mutually recognized obligations that are often enforced by the state, as the English system of primogeniture and entailment shows. Three generic forms of household economy can be distinguished: the élite landlord family of the English type, the farm family of the Australian type, and the small farm family of the European type. Land is the supreme good in household economies of these types and it assumes the physical form of large consolidated plots in the first two cases and relatively small holdings of parcelled land in the third. The principles regarding the valuation of commodities produced by these goods vary in each case. The principles regarding the valuation of marketed land – the commodity form of a good – also varies. As a marketable commodity, the price of land is the capitalized value of its annual rent but its marketed value may be more or less than this; to put it another way, the rate of return on land may be more or less than the long-term rate of interest and the reasons for this unsystematic variation are to be found in the principles of household and national economy in question.

In the ideal case land, as the supreme good, is not marketed. In other words, a good, as a non-commodity, does not have a price. When it is completely controlled by the family it is unpriced or priceless and it is valued as a good. The unpriced/priceless value of a scarce good is something that a landed family must fight to defend by whatever political means it can.

There is room, then, for another theory of goods. Political economy must expand to become a theory of the *production of commodities by means of commodities and goods*. This will require an analysis of the social relations of household reproduction. This is not a simple matter of adding equations

336

and unknowns. Political economy began as a method of comparative and historical analysis and this method is in urgent need of rehabilitation. Sraffa's theory should, I believe, be seen as a prelude to this task, which, alas, is beyond the ability of a single person.

AUSTRALIAN RULES OK

Sraffa has partially rebuilt the logical and mathematical foundations of classical political economy, and the work of Geoff and his colleagues in Cambridge has enabled us to understand the theoretical and political significance of Sraffa's hieroglyphics. If this line of thinking is to continue, then, as Geoff has rightly stressed, Sraffa must be linked to his ascendants Marx, Ricardo, Quesnay so that the descendants can continue the work set. The task is not a simple matter of adding household economy to political economy but of reasserting the primacy of the *political* in a *political* economy that includes household economy, market economy and the imperial state. This can be done only by taking a comparative and historical approach to the politics of relations between family, market and the nation-state. This will not produce an economics of Everything but will produce an economics of something substantial with which to do battle with the social science imperialists. Our aim should not be an economic theory of Everything but a modest theory of something that has clearly defined historical and geographical limits. Humility and a sense of humour are our best weapons against the arrogant pride of the imperialists, who, having theoretically conquered almost every human problem on the globe, are fast running out of things to explain. Geoff Harcourt, Scholar, Gentlemen, Joker and Citizen of the World – but, alas, no longer a resident of Oz – is a wizard when it comes to wielding the weapons of a theoretical critique. He has kicked a few Behinds, many Six-Pointers, and taken some superb High Marks; he is having a great game and it's only in its sixty-fifth minute.

ACKNOWLEDGEMENT

I wish to thank Georg Elwert and Judith Robinson for helpful comments on an earlier draft.

REFERENCES

Clay, C. (1968) 'Marriage, inheritance, and the rise of large estates in England, 1660–1815', *Economic History Review* 21(3): 503–18.

Habakkuk, H. J. (1950) 'Marriage settlements in the eighteenth century', *Transactions of the Royal Historical Society* 33: 15–30.

—— (1952) 'The long-term rate of interest and the price of land in the seventeenth century', *Economic History Review* 5(1): 26–45.

Harcourt, G. C. (1982) *The Social Science Imperialists*, London: Routledge & Kegan Paul.

Huber, R. (1977) *From Pasta to Pavlova: A Comparative Study of Italian Settlers in Sydney and Griffith*, St Lucia: Queensland University Press.

Marx, K. (1867) *Capital*: vol. 1, *A Critical Analysis of Capitalist Production*, Moscow: Progress.

—— (1894) *Capital*, vol. 3, Moscow: Progress

Ricardo, D. (1817 [1954]) *On the Principles of Political Economy and Taxation*, Cambridge: Cambridge University Press.

Sabean, D. W. (1990) *Property, Production, and Family in Neckarhausen, 1700–1870*, Cambridge: Cambridge University Press.

Sraffa, P. (1960) *Production of Comomodities by Means of Commodities: Prelude to a Critique of Economic Theory*, Cambridge: Cambridge University Press.

Thirsk, J. (1984) *The Rural Economy of England: Collected Essays*, London: Hambledon Press.

28

THE NOBEL PRIZE IN ECONOMICS[1]

A. W. Bob Coats

Historically speaking, the Nobel Prize in Economics has a somewhat ambiguous status, which may indeed seem appropriate to those sceptics who have questioned whether economics is a bona fide science.[2] Alfred Nobel could conceivably have shared this scepticism, for economics was not included in his will as one of those (genuine?) sciences (like physics, chemistry, physiology or medicine) whose practitioners could be expected to produce 'discoveries', inventions' or 'developments' justifying the award of prizes 'to those who have conferred the greatest benefit on mankind'.[3] It was not until 1969, sixty-eight years after the first Nobel awards, that the 'Bank of Sweden Prize in Economic Sciences [sic] in Memory of Alfred Nobel' was inaugurated to celebrate the Bank's tercentenary. Economics is the only subject to have been added to the original Nobel list (which included two unambiguously non-scientific subjects: literature and peace), and like physics and chemistry (but not physiology or medicine) it is supervised by the Royal Swedish Academy of Sciences.[4] The monetary value is the same as for the other Nobel prizes, and as far as possible the same procedure for selecting laureates has been employed.

Despite some initial resistance, and the special circumstances of its birth, the economics prize quickly gained international recognition and much of the prestige associated with the other science prizes. During the past quarter-century there have been twenty-six awards to a total of thirty-seven individuals, for prizes have been shared on nine occasions, usually between two persons but twice (1990 and 1994) between three[5] – the maximum permitted in any one year under the Nobel rules. Unlike the natural science prizes, the economics prize has been awarded every year; indeed, the number of individuals honoured has increased more rapidly in the past decade than in the early years, although there was said to be a backlog of worthy contenders.

Thirty-seven awards obviously constitutes an insufficient basis for generalizations about the recent history of economics. Nevertheless, they inevitably stimulate speculation about the state of economics and the changing characteristics of major achievements in the subject, as judged by the slowly changing personnel of the Prize Committee and, behind them, the large but ever-changing pool of professionals whose views have been either sought or offered gratuitously.

THE SCOPE OF ECONOMICS

Several of the Nobel prizes have acknowledged the merits of interdisciplinary or multidisciplinary work, which some economists may consider beyond the proper domain of their subject. Thus the Coase (awarded 1991) and Becker (1992) prizes can be viewed as rewards for 'trespassing', to use Albert Hirschman's evocative term; yet they provoked no reactions comparable to the shock expressed in some quarters at the award in 1978 to Simon, a polymath who could be classified as a political scientist, sociologist or even a business economist.[6] (If so, he would have been the first of that species to be ennobled.) Moreover, his severe attacks on the rational maximization postulate could be said to have undermined one of the central pillars of economic orthodoxy.

SHARED PRIZES AND THE PROBLEM OF COLLABORATION

The task of assigning credit for innovations in economics is much less difficult than for the other Nobel science prizes, where teamwork is nowadays common, even across national boundaries.[7] The joint economics prizewinners have seldom worked together even when their researches were parallel or complementary.[8] In some instances, e.g. Hicks and Arrow (awarded 1972) or Ohlin and Meade (1977), the recipients were of different generations, so that the younger man could have known and built upon his predecessor's work. With Kantorovich and Koopmans (1975), however, despite similarities in their contributions, the former's work remained unknown in the West for many years owing to his scientific and political isolation in the Soviet Union. Miller's prize (1990) is especially intriguing, for his joint work with Modigliani (M–M) on capital costs and the determination of corporate values was officially recognized both then and five years earlier, when Modigliani was ennobled. Admittedly the latter's award also acknowledged his earlier research on household savings and the life cycle hypothesis, whereas Miller's prize recognized his significant developments and extensions of the M–M foundations, which apparently merited an additional award. Even so, it is reasonable to wonder why Miller was not fully recognized in 1985, especially as the prize is supposed to be awarded for a specific contribution rather than a lifetime's achievement.[9]

Among successful laureates modesty is *de rigeur*, and generous acknowledgement of indebtedness to colleagues is a standard, no doubt sincere, feature of their Nobel lectures.[10] Several have warned of the dangers of overemphasizing any single individual's achievement, thereby obscuring the work of others 'whose researches have been crucial to the development of the field' (Coase 1992: 714). Friedman doubted that the Nobel Prizes did any good, either in economics or the other sciences (Friedman 1990: 91), and Hayek worried that unlike the natural sciences, where influence is judged mainly by the laureate's fellow experts, in economics any influence was likely to be felt among politicians, journalists, civil servants, and the public generally. He therefore suggested that the prize committee should demand from the laureates 'a sort of Hippocratic oath never to exceed in public pronouncements the limits of their competence' (see Machlup 1976: xviii). How many economists, one wonders, would be willing, or even able, to accept this constraint?

According to Solow, 'any successful line of analysis is almost certain to be a group product' (Solow 1987 [1992]: 211), and Stigler has emphasized the difficulty of doing 'creative work if one is not in a congenial environment', citing as examples episodes of intense scientific progress in economics in Cambridge, Vienna and Chicago (1990: 101). Two historians of science have even formulated a general rule of scientific innovation: RPRT (the importance of being in the right place at the right time – Stephen and Levin 1992: 158–9). Yet there are exceptions. For instance, according to the official announcement, Leontief was 'the sole and unchallenged creator of the input–output technique' (*Swedish Journal of Economics*, vol. 75, 1973, p. 428), and Harry Johnson cited Meade and Coase as typical examples of the British tradition of lone scholarship (Johnson 1979: 65).

AGE AND ACHIEVEMENT

In her fascinating study *The Scientific Elite*, Harriet Zuckerman calculated that the mean age at which natural science Nobel laureates (1901–72) did their prizewinning research was 38.7 years, with the prize award coming on average 13.5 years later (Zuckerman 1977: 161, 218). A rough calculation for the economics prize yields comparable figures of 35.6 and 29.5 years respectively. According to Assar Lindbeck, an influential member of the Prize Committee, it usually takes longer in economics to evaluate any new contribution because empirical tests are more unreliable than in physics or chemistry, and 'new results may be relevant only to a particular transient set of circumstances' (1985: 51). Stigler, the laureate best qualified in the history of economics, is more cynical, arguing not only that new ideas are difficult to evaluate, but that 'quite possibly all of the new ideas of a period will prove to be sterile' (1983: 536). Indeed: 'Most "new" ideas are not new at all, only unfamiliar, and most new or unfamiliar ideas are mistaken or infertile' (1990: 104). So much for cumulative progress in economics!

The greater delay in recognizing economics achievements may be due to the fact that most economics awards are for theoretical 'developments', as against the 'discoveries' or 'inventions' credited to the natural scientists. This delay reduces the likelihood that Nobel awards will have a large or lasting impact on new research since they represent contributions of some three decades earlier which will have been assimilated into the subject.

As noted earlier, the average age of economics prizewinners has not fallen over time as might have been expected; and whereas intellectual precocity may generally be found earlier among theorists, Tinbergen, Kuznets, Leontief, Klein and Stone all produced heavily empirical prizewinning work in their thirties (cf. the theoretical contributions of Nash: 22; Arrow and Sharpe: 30; and Samuelson: 32). Kantorovich, Markowitz and Becker produced prizewinning work in their twenties, and so did Coase – that is, if we date his achievement from his 1937, rather than his 1960, article.

THE CRITERIA OF AWARDS

The roster of economics laureates has often been criticized for various reasons, most notably its lack of imagination, and it seems clear that the Prize Committee's desire to achieve unanimity has led to the exclusion of mavericks and dissidents.[11] No Marxist or woman has been honoured – though many economists believed Joan Robinson should not have been passed over[12] – and only one institutionalist, Myrdal (possibly Lewis might be added here), and one Austrian, Hayek, have been selected. The most outspoken and powerful attack on the proceedings and the resulting decisions came from Myrdal, a member of the Swedish Academy, who complained that the Prize Committee's 'draconian rules of secrecy' effectively excluded other Academicians from its discussions. The politicization process, he claimed, was clear from the 'balancing act' of 1974, when he and Hayek shared the prize,[13] and two years later Friedman's award provoked Myrdal's lengthy protest in the Swedish press, denying that economics was a positive science, and arguing that the economics prize was a mistake, and should be abolished![14] Yet ironically Myrdal had been one of the most enthusiastic and effective supporters of its initiation! Friedman's prize was undoubtedly the most controversial, inspiring a militant protest at the awards ceremony on the grounds that he had supported the brutal Pinochet regime in Chile.[15] Myrdal considered that this award had seriously damaged the prize's scientific standing; and it certainly provoked discussion of the interrelationship between 'positive' and 'normative' economics.

ECONOMIST LAUREATES' CRITIQUES OF THEIR DISCIPLINE

Unlike the literature and peace prizes, the natural science awards have seldom if ever been the target of political accusations. Nor, it seems, have they ever evoked fundamental insider critiques of the kind economists have made of their subject. In part these critiques may reveal the innovator's idiosyncratic nonconformity, and a number of criticisms reflect the generation gap, with elder statesmen deploring recent scientific trends. This certainly applies to Frisch's derogatory term 'playometrics', and Ohlin's, Coase's and others' protests against excessive abstraction. Leontief asserted that 'formulas are mere playthings, while real economics begins with operational concepts and, above all, real "numbers"' (Dorfman 1973: 431; also Leontief 1971: 1–7; 1982: 104–5). Buchanan depicts himself as a severe critic of prevailing economic orthodoxies, attacking the 'allocating–maximizing paradigm' (1989: 87) and scathingly dismissing 'Keynesian macroaggregation absurdities' (ibid.: 105; see also Buchanan 1992: 104–5; Szenberg 1992: 131[16]) thereby putting himself in direct opposition to Solow, a Keynesian, who asserts that macroeconomics is the heart of economics; 'what it's all about' (1989: 25). Against Arrow and Debreu's general equilibrium work there is Tobin's blunt rejection of the 'Walrasian Auctioneer fairy tale' (Sichel 1989: 75). Lewis's and Schultz's joint award seems odd, given their flatly contradictory accounts of the role of labour in developing countries, and Tobin's and Friedman's work in monetary analysis and policy are, in important respects, in direct conflict.

Perhaps the most radical Nobel economist attack on late-twentieth-century economics was by Hayek, who stressed the limitations of quantification in economics, and the contemporary obsession with 'scientism', by which he meant the failure to grasp the essential differences between the social and the natural sciences. On the whole, he concluded, 'We have at the moment little cause for pride; as a profession we have made a mess of things' (Hayek 1975: 433, 434, 438).

CONCLUSIONS

Looking at these profound insider criticisms one wonders whether there is any effective mechanism for resolving basic disagreements in economics; and, if not, whether this wrecks economics' claim to be a bona fide science?

This is not the place, if indeed there is one, for an unlaureated commentator to pontificate on the Economics Prize in Memory of Alfred Nobel. As Karl Brunner, an official commentator, observed:

> Authoritative measures of the importance [or value] of research results are non-existent. If we are invited to make such assessments we are inevitably driven to the experts, those who as a result of their own research are recognized as best qualified to render judgment.
>
> (Brunner 1982: 7)

There is, of course, an inescapable element of circularity in this, especially if the group of experts in question is small, tightly knit and relatively homogeneous.[17] As surviving Nobel prizewinners in economics are consulted during the selection process, and as Americans predominate, American conceptions of 'good' economics will inevitably be disproportionately influential. Of course the economics profession is much larger in the USA than elsewhere, but the fact that economics has increasingly become an American science may mean that leading economists in other countries are more liable to be overlooked.[18] And, incidentally, the selection procedure may recently have worked in favour of Chicago economists.

Some observers have suggested that the Prize Committee not only has set out to choose the 'best' economists not already honoured (for there apparently has been no serious consideration of a second award to any individual), but also has aimed to shape the future development of the discipline. However, there is no evidence of any such intentions; and any attempt to do so would be an arrogant, and probably fruitless, endeavour. It is no surprise that the sequence of awards reveals trends in the subject as well as its heterogeneity. Thus Keynesian economics, econometrics, mathematical economics and development economics were much more fashionable in the early post-1945 decades, whereas the recent intellectual and ideological shift away from interventionism or planning towards an enhanced faith in and reliance on market forces is reflected in the number of awards in microeconomics. The shift away from the earlier economists' preoccupation with problems of poverty and inequality has been accompanied by a constriction of focus and a concomitant abstract and technocratic professionalism which is not yet fully recognized in the more recent awards.[19] As noted above, these generally reflect the work of some three decades ago and the newer wave may appear in future selections.

The Nobel prizewinners in economics are selected by academics, for whom academic (that is, theoretical and technical) values are predominant, and there is apparently no way by which the prizes can recognize that economics is preeminently a policy science; that most economists are employed outside academia; and that the discipline's public reputation depends largely on the economists' contributions to policymaking, rather than their more esoteric intellectual products. And in this respect the economics prizes may have contributed to the crisis in graduate education which has been the subject of growing concern within the profession in recent years.

NOTES

1　This chapter is a substantially revised and drastically abbreviated version of an essay previously published in German (Coats 1994). See also for background, Harcourt (1984), Katz (1989) and Zahka (1992).

2　Apparently a number of non-economist members of the Royal Swedish Academy of Science opposed the inauguration of the economics prize.

3　Fortunately it is unnecessary to consider here whether, and if so how far, the development of economics has conferred benefit on mankind – e.g. in terms of progress in economic policies. Nobel's narrowly positivistic conception of scientific progress 'as an accumulation of many hard little pellets of empirical knowledge, to be shaken free of any conceptual matrix in which they are unaccountably embedded' is inappropriate to economics. (Cf. Fleming 1966, in Zuckerman 1977: 52–3).

4   The physiology or medicine prizes are awarded by the Royal Caroline Medico-Chirurgical Institute; the literature prize by the Swedish Academy at Stockholm; and the peace prize by a committee appointed by the Norwegian Storting (parliament).

5   An appendix to this chapter contains a list of prizewinners, with a brief extract from the official announcement about the prizewinning work. In writing the chapter I have drawn heavily on these announcements, the Nobel Lectures and official commentators' assessments, as well as various laureates' public statements about the prize and/or their work.

6   At the time when Simon's award was announced he had never been an officer, or even a member, of the American Economic Association (AEA), and many economists (who should have known better) did not know his name, let alone his research. Simon later recalled that his selection as a Distinguished Fellow of the AEA, in 1976, was treated as a 'step on the way to a Nobel nomination' (Simon 1991: 321–3). However, there is no direct evidence of any regular connection between these two honours.

7   The problems of assigning credit to innovators in the natural sciences are treated by Zuckerman (1977: 138–43, and 176–8).

8   The cases of Harsanyi and Selten are an exception to this generalization.

9   The official terminology is 'specific achievements rather than outstanding persons'. Yet this is not always easy to interpret unambiguously. Friedman, for example, was cited for a variety of contributions, whereas Klein was said to have published prizewinning work 'over a number of years'. Another of the original conditions, that prizes were to be awarded for contributions in the year preceding the prize award, has never been strictly enforced.

10 A remarkable exception is Allais, the only economics laureate claiming to be self-taught. He believed he possessed 'one *very exceptional* advantage, that of never having been conditioned by university training and the constant repetition of established truths' (Mäler 1992: 234–5; emphasis in original). See also Allais (1992b).

11 Lindbeck conceded that in the early years the prizewinning authorities tended to 'play safe', overlooking new trends in economic research. His expectation that in later years the emphasis would shift somewhat from established to new research results, and perhaps younger laureates, has not been borne out (Lindbeck 1985: 55). Take, for example, however deserving, the awards to Fogel and North, Nash, Harsanyi and Selten. Of course, some observers might consider a mainstream that included such diverse figures as Hayek, Myrdal, Simon, Buchanan and Becker already quite broad enough!

12 For an exploration of the possible reasons why Joan Robinson was denied a Nobel prize, see Turner (1989: 214–21). It may be significant that she repudiated *The Economics of Imperfect Competition*, the early book that many regard as her principal claim to recognition. Paul Davidson, a supporter, suggested that the Prize Committee would have been acutely embarrassed had some newspaper reporter discovered the views she expressed in her second edition. Incidentally, very few women have won natural science Nobel Prizes.

13 One distinguished economist, Charles Kindelberger, described this award as a 'perhaps malicious decision' (1987: 401), and Paul Samuelson termed it 'a bad joke, destined [*sic*] to make two people desperately unhappy. That's chalk and cheese' (Turner 1989: 217). A contemporary joke claimed that when the decision

was announced both Hayek and Myrdal nearly had a heart attack: the former because he had won the prize; the latter because he had to share it!

14 An English-language version was published in 1977 in *Challenge* 89: 50–2.
15 For fascinating background material on the Friedman award see Frazer (1988: vol. 1, chs 3 and 10). The author is an uncritical admirer of Friedman.
16 Cf. Allais's attack on 'the tyranny of the dominant ideas generated by the "establishment"' which posed obstacles to discoverers of genius (1988: 245–6; emphasis in original).
17 A number of official commentators have acknowledged their inability to judge even substantial parts of their subject's research. This is eloquent testimony to the range and complexity of the discipline, and the high degree of specialization prevalent nowadays.
18 For stimulating, albeit impressionistic, discussion of the question: 'Is there a European economics?' see the symposium in *Kyklos* 1995, pp. 185–311. See also the forthcoming special issue of *History of Political Economy* on *The Post-1945 Internationalization of Economics*, edited by the present writer.
19 For severe criticism, see Hutchinson (1992, *passim*).

REFERENCES

Allais, M. (1992a) Autobiographical sketch, in K.-G. Mäler (ed.) *Nobel Lectures: Economic Sciences 1981–1990. Including Presentation Speeches and Laureates' Biographies'*, Singapore: World Scientific.
—— (1992b) 'The passion for Research', in M. Szenberg (ed.) *Eminent Economists: Their Life Philosophies*, Cambridge: Cambridge University Press.
Brunner, K. (1982) 'Ronald Coase – old fashioned scholar', *Scandinavian Journal of Economics* 94(1): 7–17.
Buchanan, J. M. (1989) 'The state of economics', in W. Sichel (ed.) *The State of Economic Science: Views of Six Nobel Laureates*, Kalamazoo, MI: W. E. Upjohn Institute for Employment Research, 1992.
—— (1992) 'From the inside looking out', in M. Szenberg (ed.) *Eminent Economists: Their Life Philosophies*, Cambridge: Cambridge University Press.
Coase, R. (1992) 'The institutional structure of production', *American Economic Review* 82: 713–19.
Coats, A. W. (1994) 'The Nobel Prize in Economics', in K. D. Grüske (ed.) *Die Nobelpreisträger de Ökonomischen Wissenschaft*: vol. 3, *1989–93*, Düsseldorf: Verlag Wirtschaft und Finanzen.
Dorfman, R. (1973) 'Wassily Leontief's contribution to economics', *Scandinavian Journal of Economics* 75(4): 430–9.
Frazer, W. (1988) *Power and Ideas: Milton Friedman and the Big U-Turn*: vol. 1, *The Background*, Gainesville, FL: Gulf-Atlantic Publishing Co.
Friedman, M. (1990) 'My evolution as an economist', in W. Breit and R. W. Spencer, *Lives of the Laureates: Ten Nobel Economists*, Cambridge, MA: MIT Press.
Harcourt, G. (1984) 'Reflections on the development of economics as a discipline', *History of Political Economy* 16(4): 489–517.
Hayek, F. A. von (1975) 'The pretence of knowledge', *Swedish Journal of Economics* 77(4): 433–42.
Hutchinson, T. W. (1992) *Changing Aims in Economics*, Oxford: Blackwell.
Johnson, H.G. (1979) 'James Meade's contribution to economics', *Scandinavian Journal of Economics* 81(I): 64–85.
Katz, B. S. (ed.) (1989) *Nobel Laureates in Economic Sciences: A Biographical Dictionary*, New York: Garland.

Kindelberger, C. P. (1987) 'Gunnar Myrdal', *Scandinavian Journal of Economics* 89(4): 393–403.

Leontief, W. (1971) 'Theoretical assumptions and nonobserved facts', *American Economic Review* 61: 1–7.

—— (1982) Letter to the Editor, *Science* 217: 104–5.

Lindbeck, A. (1985) 'The prize in Economic Science in memory of Alfred Nobel', *Journal of Economic Literature* 23: 37–56.

Machlup, F. (1976) *Essays on Hayek*, New York: New York University Press.

Mäler, K.-G. (ed.) (1992) *Nobel Lectures: Economic Sciences 1981–1990. Including Presentation Speeches and Laureates' Biographies*, Singapore: World Scientific.

Sichel, W. (ed.) (1989) *The State of Economic Science: Views of Six Nobel Laureates*, Kalamazoo, MI.: W. E. Upjohn Institute for Employment Research.

Simon, H. (1991) *Models of My Life*, New York: Basic Books.

Solow, Robert (1987 [1992]) 'Growth theory and after', in K.-G. Mäler (ed.) *Nobel Lectures: Economic Sciences 1981–1990. Including Presentation Speeches and Lauretes' Biographies*, Singapore: World Scientific.

—— (1989) 'The state of economics', in W. Sichel (ed.) *The State of Economic Science: Views of Six Nobel Laureates*, Kalamazoo, MI: W. E. Upjohn Institute for Employment Research.

Stephan, P. E. and Levin, S. G. (1992) *Striking the Mother Lode in Science: The Importance of Age, Place and Time*, New York and Oxford: Oxford University Press.

Stigler, G. J. (1983) 'The process and progress of economics', *Journal of Political Economy* 91(4): 529–45.

—— (1990) 'My evolution as an economist', in W. Breit and R. W. Spencer, *Lives of the Laureates: Ten Nobel Economists*, Cambridge, MA: MIT Press.

Szenberg, M. (ed.) (1992) *Eminent Economists: Their Life Philosophies*, Cambridge: Cambridge University Press.

Turner, M. S. (1989) *Joan Robinson and the Americans*, Armonk, NJ: M. E. Sharpe.

Zahka, W. J. (1992) *The Nobel Prize Economics Lectures: A Cross-Section of Current Thinking*, Aldershot: Avebury.

Zuckerman, H. (1977) *The Scientific Elite: Nobel Laureates in the United States*, New York: Free Press.

APPENDIX

Table 28.1 Nobel Prize awards for Economy, 1969–94

Year	Laureate	Field	Prize citations
1969	Frisch, Ragnar Oslo University Tinbergen, Jan The Netherlands School of Economics	Macroeconometrics	Developing and applying dynamic models for the analysis of economic processes
1970	Samuelson, Paul Massachusetts Institute of Technology	General equilibrium theory	Developing static and dynamic economic theory and actively contributed to raising the level of analysis in economic science
1971	Kuznets, Simon Harvard University	Development economics	Empirically founded interpretation of economic growth which has led to new and deepened insight into the economic and social structure and process of development
1972	Hicks, John R. All Souls College, Oxford Arrow, Kenneth J. Harvard University	General equilibrium theory	Pioneering contributions to general economic equilibrium theory and welfare theory
1973	Leontief, Wassily Harvard University	Input–output	Development of the input–output method and its application to important economic problems
1974	Myrdal, Gunnar University of Stockholm von Hayek, Friedrich August University of Freiburg	Macroeconomics and Institutional economics	Pioneering work in the theory of money and economic fluctuations and penetrating analysis of the interdependence of economic, social and institutional phenomena
1975	Kantorovich, Leonid Academy of Sciences, Moscow Koopmans, Tjalling C. Yale University	Normative allocation theory	Conributions to the theory of optimum allocation of resources

Year	Laureate	Field	Prize citations
1976	Friedman, Milton University of Chicago	Macroeconomics	Achievements in the fields of consumption analysis, monetary history and theory, and demonstration of the complexity of stabilization policy
1977	Ohlin, Bertil Stockholm School of Economics Meade, James University of Cambridge	International economics	Path-breaking contribution to the theory of international trade and international capital movements
1978	Simon, Herbert A. Carnegie-Mellon University	Administration science	Pioneering research into the decision-making process within economic organizations
1979	Schultz, Theodore W. University of Chicago Lewis, Arthur Princeton University	Development economics	Pioneering research into economic development, with particular consideration of the problems of developing countries
1980	Klein, Lawrence R. University of Pennsylvania	Macroeconomics	Creation of econometric models and their application to the analysis of economic fluctuations and economic policies
1981	Tobin, James Yale University	Macroeconomics	Analysis of financial markets and their relations to expenditure decisions, employment, production and prices
1982	Stigler, George J. University of Chicago	Industrial organization	Seminal studies of industrial structure, functioning of markets and causes and effects of public regulation

Table 28.1 cont.

Year	Laureate	Field	Prize citations
1983	Debreu, Gerard University of California, Berkeley	General equilibrium theory	Incorporation of new analytical methods into economic theory and rigorous reformulation of the theory of general equilibrium
1984	Stone, Richard University of Cambridge	National income accounting	Fundamental contributions to the development of systems of national accounts and consequent great improvement of the basis for empirical economic analysis
1985	Modigliani, Franco Massachusetts Institute of Technology	Savings and financial markets	Path-breaking analysis of the savings function
1986	Buchanan, James McGill George Mason University	Political and economic decision theory	Development of contract theoretical bases of economic and political decisions
1987	Solow, Robert MIT	Growth of production and increase of social welfare	Work on theory of economic growth
1988	Allais, Maurice École Nationale Supérieure des Mines, Paris	Equilibrium balance and efficiency criteria	Path-breaking achievements in the theory of markets and efficient resource use
1989	Haavelmo, Trygve Universitat Oslo	Econometric theory	Development of the probabilistic foundation of econometric method, and analysis of simultaneous economic structures
1990	Markowitz, Harry CUNY Miller, Merton University of Chicagto Sharpe, William Stanford University	Financial markets	Path-breaking achievements to the theory of financial markets

Year	Laureate	Field	Prize citations
1991	Coase, Ronald University of Chicago	Institutional economics	Discovery and clarification of the significance of transactions costs and the economic rights for institutional structures and the functioning of economic systems
1992	Becker, Gary University of Chicago	Microeconomics	Contribution to extending microeconomic theory to a wide range of human relations and cooperation, even outside of markets
1993	Fogel, Robert University of Chicago North, Douglas C. University of Washington, St Louis	Institutional economics	Revival of research in economic history by the application of economic theory and quantitative methods to interpret economic and institutional change
1994	Harsanyi, John C. University of California at Berkeley	Theory of non-competitive games	Analysis of games of incomplete information
	Nash, John F. Princeton University		Development of equilibrium concept for non-competitive games
	Selten, Reinhardt Rheinische Friedrichs-Wilhelms-Universität, Bonn		Refinement of the Nash equilibrium concept for analysing strategic interaction

29

THE SPLIT LEGACY OF WILFRED SALTER, AUSTRALIAN ECONOMIST EXTRAORDINARY

Andrea Maneschi

The transatlantic debates on capital theory produced a great sense of excitement in the economics profession in the 1960s and early 1970s. The controversies pitting Cambridge (England) against Cambridge (Massachusetts) were admirably expounded in a survey which Geoffrey Harcourt was commissioned to do for the *Journal of Economic Literature* (Harcourt 1969, subsequently expanded into Harcourt 1972). Graduate students at my own university, though far from Massachusetts, became intrigued with the notion that there was something to debate in economic theory after all, even regarding fundamental matters. On their own initiative they organized seminars to present and discuss chapters in Geoff's book. Of course I wanted then to meet the author himself, and a family visit to Australia gave me that opportunity, combining tourism in Adelaide with a memorable visit to the university. Further encounters with Geoff followed in Cambridge, England, where I spent parts of two leaves of absence. Professionally, the spotlight on the Cambridge controversies stimulated my interest in and self-study of the history of economic thought, of whose importance they had convinced me. Who first conceived of an aggregate production function depending on a variable representing an economy's entire capital stock? How had this been justified? How Ricardian was Sraffa's *Production of Commodities by Means of Commodities*? Geoff's book introduced me to the weird and wonderful world of capital reversing, Wicksell effects (price and real), double-switching, surrogate production functions, jelly and fossilized capital, basic and non-basic commodities, standard systems, the Kaldor and Pasinetti growth-and-distribution models.

Among the economists with whose work I became better acquainted through Geoff's book was a certain W. E. G. Salter, whose *Productivity and Technical Change* (Salter 1960) I recalled from my graduate student days. He made an appearance in connection with embodied versus disembodied technical change in Ch. 2 of Harcourt (1972), where Geoff stated that 'both

patriotism and judgement lead me to select the late W. E. G. Salter's work . . .
as one of the finest – and earliest – examples of the embodiment hypothesis'
(ibid.: 54–5). He noted that Salter had carried out his research in Cambridge,
England, over the years 1953–5 and that his basic ideas were contained in his
Ph.D. dissertation submitted in 1955. 'The consequent lag [in publication] has
tended until recently to rob Salter of proper recognition in the literature' (ibid.
55), in light of the fact that, working independently of him, Johansen (1959,
1961) had also developed models based on vintages of capital stock with
substitutability between factors *ex ante* but not *ex post*. Geoff added the
accolade that

> Salter's work is a model which all aspiring (and established) economists
> profitably could have before them. Its characteristics are a flair for
> formulating relevant *theory* which, clearly, neatly and excitingly
> expressed, is carried no further than the requirements of the problem at
> hand – and is immediately tested against the facts.
>
> (Harcourt 1972: 55; emphasis in original)

Salter's book was lucidly summarized in Harcourt's (1962) review article.

Harcourt's admiration for Salter is also apparent from a number of his
articles which have been handily collected in anthologies. Part III of *The
Social Science Imperialists* (Harcourt 1982) is devoted to Salter's work,
containing a review of Salter's 1960 book *Productivity and Technical Change*
(Harcourt 1962) and two papers on empirical estimates of production
functions and investment decision criteria which derived directly from
Salter's work. However, Salter's contributions could not be neatly segregated
into one part of the book, since references to them spill over into four other
chapters. Similarly, no fewer than ten of the twenty-one chapters of *On
Political Economists and Modern Political Economy: Selected Essays of G.
C. Harcourt* (Harcourt 1992) contain references to Salter.

The fates decreed that Wilfred Salter's life (1929–63) was to be tragically
short. In his obituary notice, Trevor Swan stated that

> seldom has an international academic reputation been won with so little
> braying of the academic trumpet; Salter never held a permanent post in
> any university. To his mind the work he did in a few fruitful years was
> essentially by way of preparation. Despite his already great achieve-
> ments, the name of Wilfred Salter invokes the echoes of 'unfulfilled
> renown'.
>
> (Swan 1963b: 487)

Other points noted by Swan were the period Salter spent as a Research Fellow
at the Australian National University, during which he wrote up his
Cambridge research into book form. Subsequently he appeared as an expert
witness on wages for the Australian Council of Trade Unions, was Assistant
Secretary in the Economic Section of the Prime Minister's Department, and

held a temporary appointment with the Harvard Advisory Group as Economic Adviser to the Government of Pakistan, the office in which he died.

Wilfred Salter and Geoff Harcourt (along with Heinz Arndt, Trevor Swan, Murray Kemp, Max Corden and Stephen Turnovsky) share the honour of being identified as one of 'seven internationally prominent economists operating in Australia from 1950' whose biographies are presented by Groenewegen and McFarlane (1990: ch. 8). Among the few works which Salter was able to complete in his lifetime, his book (Salter 1960) has become a classic of the literature on technical progress and productivity change.[1] His other papers, listed by Swan (1963b) and Fisher (1987), complement the book in various ways, with one notable exception which is *sui generis*, his paper on internal and external balance (Salter 1959). The latter contains what has become known as the 'Salter diagram', consisting of a transformation curve showing the trade-off between traded and non-traded goods, and illustrates the role of public policy in attaining balance-of-payments equilibrium and full employment in an economy which cannot influence its terms of trade. The type of model developed by Salter and other Australian economists such as Trevor Swan and Max Corden is now known as the 'Australian model' of trade. Admirers of Wilfred Salter can be divided into two distinct sets who appear to be unaware of each other, those who praise his work on productivity and technical change, and those who praise his Australian open-economy model. It is useful to remind Salter's admirers of his diverse contributions to the field of economics. This chapter hopes to make a modest effort in this direction, first comparing Salter's neo-Ricardian model to the Ricardian one, noting similarities and differences, then looking at the enduring influence which Salter's open-economy modelling has had on international economists.

RICARDIAN RENT AND SALTER'S NEO-RICARDIAN MODEL

The theoretical framework undergirding Salter's vintage model is set out in Salter's book (Salter 1960, especially chs 4–6), and in his last paper (Salter 1965). The latter, notable for its elegance and mature expression of his thought, not only presented Salter's model in mathematical form, but went beyond the earlier version by adding interesting amplifications of its underlying assumptions. Salter stressed that output depends on 'the fossilized history embedded in the capital stock' and that his model 'does not involve the measurement of capital', adding that 'this is important, not so much in itself, but because it offers a means of escape from the tyranny of the aggregate production function, $Y_t = F_t(N_t, K_t)$' (ibid.: 273, 275). It is clear where Salter's sympathies lie in the Cambridge capital controversy, since his 'capital' is the antithesis of a blob of jelly or Swan-like Meccano set components, being instead 'a "who's who" of individual items of plant and equipment' (ibid.: 276). It plays the role of 'the repository of [the economy's] recent history', whereas 'the assumption of fluid capital effectively cuts off an economy from its own past history' (ibid.: 266, 268). The advantage of 'breaking away from the notion of a self-contained present' is the ability to introduce 'historical restraints' in addition to technical ones as determinants of the economy's output, wages, profits and average productivity (ibid.: 276). An interesting implication is 'a kind of historical "echo effect". Today's events are influenced by events e years ago; and these in turn will influence events e' years in the future' (ibid.: 285).

Salter had earlier pointed out the close relationship between his model and the Ricardian one postulating lands of differential fertility, arguing that

> when technology is continually improving, we can apply the concept of the Ricardian extensive margin to the existing capital stock with very few modifications. Capital goods in existence are equally as much a part of the economic environment as land or other natural resources. Both are gifts: natural resources are the gift of nature, capital goods are the gifts of the past. The fertility of land corresponds to the level of technical knowledge embodied in capital equipment; modern capital equipment embodying recent best-practice techniques is analogous to the most fertile land, and older capital equipment embodying less advanced techniques corresponds to land of decreasing fertility as the margin of cultivation is approached.... And in both cases the margin of use is determined by the ability to show a surplus or rent; no-rent land corresponds to capital equipment that has just been abandoned.
>
> (Salter 1960: 61)

He reinforced this analogy by calling his model 'a neo-Ricardian model' (Salter 1965), although this nomenclature should be distinguished from that which has been applied to Sraffian models. His view of capital as 'a "who's who" of individual items of plant and equipment' which cannot (and need not) be measured as an aggregate capital stock allows a treatment which 'more or less parallels that of land in the Ricardian model, in which it is not necessary to measure the amount of land since this underlies the function relating output and employment' (ibid.: 276).

The Ricardian extensive margin model doubtless inspired Salter's construction of his neo-Ricardian model, aptly illustrating the advantages of applying historically derived insights to a new context. The rest of this section compares these models to show that the contrasts between them are just as meaningful and instructive as the similarities. This comparison is facilitated if we represent the two models graphically as shown in Figures 29.1 and 29.2. Figure 29.1 plots labour productivity in terms of 'corn' on the vertical axis and employed labour (or doses of labour and shovels) on the horizontal. The employment of N_i labourers results in output O_i on land of the ith quality. If the total agricultural labour force equals the

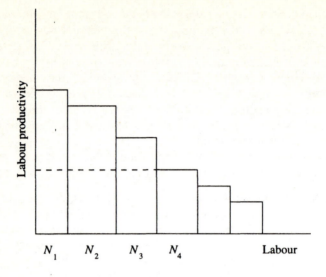

Figure 29.1 The Ricardian model

sum of N_1 to N_4, land of the fourth quality is the marginal no-rent land and Ricardian rent payments in terms of corn are measured by the areas of the first three rectangles contained above the dashed line. If the population expands further, the extensive margin is pushed out to lands of the fifth or lower qualities.

Salter (1960: chs 4–5) represented his neo-Ricardian model diagrammatically by plotting on the vertical axis the unit labour requirement L_n for plants built in period n, and on the horizontal axis the capacity output O_n of such plants. To make his diagram congruent with Figure 29.1, Figure 29.2 (which corresponds to Fig. 6 in Salter 1960: 59) plots vertically the inverses of unit labour requirements – that is labour productivities – of plants in operation, and horizontally the labour employed in them. The areas of Salter's rectangles, given by $L_n O_n$ for plants of period n, thus correspond to the bases of the rectangles in Figure 29.2, which equal employment N_n ($= L_n O_n$) in these plants, and the areas of the rectangles in Figure 29.2 correspond to the bases On of Salter's rectangles. The plant showing the highest labour productivity pertains to the current period n and is built using the best-practice technique available at prevailing factor prices, whereas the oldest plant in use dates from period $n - t$. Its labour productivity, $O_{n - t}/N_{n - t}$, equals the real wage, w, and the quasi-rents of the inframarginal plants are represented by the areas of the rectangles contained above the dashed line lying at a distance w from the horizontal axis. The average product of labour in the oldest plants in use is thus equal to the marginal product of labour in this industry. In period $n + 1$ a new technique becomes available with productivity shown by the

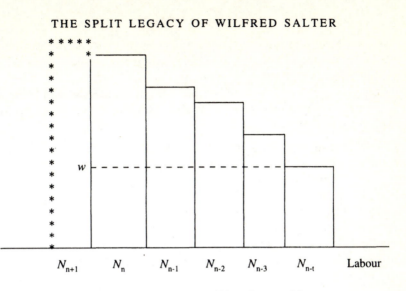

Figure 29.2 Salter's neo-Ricardian model

starred rectangle corresponding to output O_{n+1} and employment N_{n+1}. The condition for the introduction of these plants is that the capitalized value of the quasi-rents earned on them at the current interest rate should equal their investment costs. After their construction the real wage may rise, causing plants of period $n - t$ to become obsolete even though their physical life is not over. The wage thus determines 'how much of the fossilized history embedded in the capital stock influences present total output and productivity' (Salter 1965: 273).

A major difference between the two diagrams and their underlying models is that in the Ricardian case there is a single marginal land, whereas in Figure 29.2 there are two margins, one on the right referring to obsolete or obsolescent plants, the other on the left referring to newly built plants. Both margins, which Salter calls the 'moving frontier' (or forward margin) and the 'rearward frontier' (or margin), shift over time as new techniques are developed and old ones abandoned. The moving frontier 'is the only part [of the capital stock] in harmony with the present; the remainder has been outmoded by the march of events'. The plants which cannot earn a surplus above operating costs become 'the rearward frontier of the capital stock, the capital equipment which has become obsolescent' (Salter 1960: 64). This suggests the beam of a searchlight slowly moving from right to left in Figure 29.2, revealing new, improved plants on the left while allowing obsolescent ones on the right to fall into obscurity. An important distinction between these two margins is that different concepts of cost apply to them: 'for the forward margin total costs are relevant, while for the rearward margin only operating costs are significant.... Price = total costs of marginal new capacity = operating costs of marginal existing capacity' (Salter 1960: 74–5). The first

357

is a long-term equilibrium condition for new capacity, whereas the second is a short-term one for existing plant unable to earn any surplus over operating costs.

There is no counterpart for the forward margin in the Ricardian model, and its rearward margin moves from left to right rather than vice versa. As Salter pointed out,

> in terms of the analogy with land, the flow of new best-practice techniques corresponds to the discovery of land of continually increasing fertility, while gross investment is equivalent to the opening up of such land. As newly discovered fertile land may draw inwards the margin of cultivation through its influence on wages and prices, so also gross investment forces the scrapping of the more outmoded portions of the capital stock. But, unlike land, the process does not end. The frontier of technical knowledge knows no limit so that the system is always expanding.
>
> (Salter 1960: 64)

Only in a Garden of Eden can the continual discovery of ever more fertile lands be imagined. Outside it, there is no reason why hitherto unutilized lands should be the sole beneficiaries of improved techniques of cultivation, allowing them to become more productive than the most fertile land currently under use. Despite agricultural improvements, a Ricardian economy eventually heads for the stationary state, a scenario which contrasts sharply with the optimistic one of an ever-expanding and more productive system traced out by Salter.

A second difference relates to the manner in which capital accumulation leads the onward 'march of events' in the two models. What Harcourt refers to as a 'Salter isoquant' shows the best-practice techniques which are available *ex ante* in that model. The choice between them, and hence the chosen capital intensity, depends on prevailing factor prices. The higher the gross investment, the greater the incorporation of the current best-practice techniques into the capital stock. The rate of gross investment over time determines 'how far the past is allowed to intrude into the present' (Salter 1960: 72); that is, the rate at which obsolescent plants are scrapped. It is clear from Figure 29.2 that if the industry in question had consistently experienced a higher rate of investment, the rectangles on the left-hand side would be wider and hence fewer in number, so that the average productivity of labour and the wage rate would both be higher.[2] The evolution of a Ricardian system is also governed by the rate of capital accumulation, but this now interacts with the rate of population growth via the Malthusian mechanism. A rise in the rate of capital accumulation causes the wage rate and, with a lag, the growth rate of population to increase, pushing out the extensive margin of cultivation and bringing the stationary state closer. Instead of the rectangles in Figure 29.1 being widened by a higher rate of investment, as in the Salter model, its consequence would be a faster descent of the steps on the right and a narrowing of the gap between the average product of labour on marginal land and the subsistence wage rate.[3]

A third difference between the two models is that the height of each rectangle in Figure 29.1, in the absence of technical change, remains constant because of Ricardo's quaint belief in the 'original and indestructible powers of the soil' (Ricardo 1821 [1951]: 67). Although land is not allowed to show signs of exhaustion, Salter permitted wear and tear in machines, so that the heights of the rectangles in Figure 29.2 contained between the forward and rearward margins are likely to change over time. Salter also recognized that some types of technical change need not be embodied in new machines but benefit existing ones, providing another reason for these rectangles to change in size.

Finally, both the Ricardian and the Salter models can have a 'stationary state' as their equilibrium outcomes. The Ricardian one is an unhappy state of affairs for everyone except the landlord class. For Salter (1965: 285) the stationary state was a theoretical curiosum marked by 'unchanging technical knowledge, zero "net saving", a "balanced" age-composition of the capital stock and a constant labour force'. Neoclassical economists who investigated vintage-type models after Salter focused much of their attention on the properties of the steady state characterized by all variables growing at a constant rate. This dynamic counterpart of the stationary state did not hold much interest for Salter as compared to the 'long and tortuous path' (ibid.: 286) followed by a real-world economy as it lurches from one long-run equilibrium to the next without ever reaching it.

To summarize the similarities between the Ricardian model and Salter's neo-Ricardian one: both models eschew the aggregation of heterogeneous factors of production such as different types of capital equipment or lands of different fertility. The only important relationship in each case is that between the different age-groups of capital equipment (or qualities of land) and the output and employment associated with them. Both models generate Ricardian rent (or, in Salter's case, Marshallian quasi-rent) on plants or plots of land other than the obsolescent or marginal ones. The driving force in both cases is the rate of capital accumulation, which sets the trajectory the economy follows and determines how the allocation of labour changes over time between new and existing plants, or lands of different quality. Both models can have a stationary state as the long-run equilibrium they tend to, although its welfare connotations are markedly different.

The two models have been shown to differ chiefly in the following respects:

1   The Salter model has two margins, a forward one relating to the best-practice techniques currently implemented so that the price of the commodity covers both operating and capital costs, and a rearward

margin where the price covers only the labour or operating costs. Ricardo's model features only the second of these margins.

2   Higher rates of capital accumulation cause the capital stock to modernize at a faster rate in the Salter model, so that the rectangles in Figure 29.2 are wider, fewer in number and of a greater average height or labour productivity. In the Ricardian model the consequence is instead an accelerated move to lands of inferior fertility, so that labour productivity declines more rapidly.

3   As a result of technical change and physical deterioration, all the rectangles in Figure 29.2, and not only those corresponding to the forward and rearward margins, are undergoing continuous modification. In the Ricardian case the rectangles of Figure 29.1 can change only as a result of technical change.

4   A final and important difference relates to income distribution. The changes in the shares going to workers, capitalists and landlords in an evolving Ricardian economy are dramatic in nature and have clear policy implications such as free trade in corn to avert the onset of the stationary state. In the case of Salter's model the distributive consequences are of subsidiary interest since the focus is on individual industries rather than the economy as a whole. Salter showed in the empirical Part II of his book that these consequences are much more benign than those flowing from the Ricardian model.

A CHANGE OF HATS: SALTER'S OPEN-ECONOMY AUSTRALIAN MODEL

During his time at the Australian National University, Wilfred Salter interacted with economists such as Trevor Swan and Max Corden. This group became internationally known, in part because of their work on the role played by price and expenditure effects in achieving external and internal balance in a small open economy such as the Australian one. Their model is denoted by a variety of labels such as 'Australian', 'dependent economy', 'non-traded goods' or 'small open-economy' model. Although Salter had time to make only one contribution to its elaboration, it was a fundamental one which immortalized him as the author of the 'Salter diagram'. As Groenewegen and McFarlane (1990: 196) have argued, 'this paper ... shows the importance of the contemporaneous presence at the Australian National University of a small band of economists whose work interacted as a cumulative process of inspiration'.

International trade diagrams typically represent an economy which produces and consumes two commodities in different proportions, giving rise to exports and imports. For some purposes, however, one must recognize the existence of a third type of commodity which is not traded, whether because of transport costs or trade restrictions. But the graphical portrayal of a trade model containing three commodities is daunting at best. The stroke of genius underlying the Salter diagram shown in Figure 29.3 was his decision to collapse all traded goods into one composite commodity consisting of exportables and importables. Implicitly applying the Hicksian criterion for a composite good, Salter realized that his procedure was 'quite legitimate so long as the terms of trade are unaffected by events inside Australia' (Salter 1959: 226), which is the small-economy assumption.

Salter proceeded to characterize an economy's internal and external equilibrium as the point of tangency between an indifference curve and a transformation curve in the space of traded and non-traded goods. Equilibrium is shown at B in Figure 29.3, where an indifference curve (not drawn) is tangential to the transformation curve TT'. The slope of their common tangent tt' yields the equilibrium price ratio of traded goods in terms of non-traded goods, now known as the real exchange rate. Salter went on to examine various cases where equilibrium is not attained because the point of consumption does not coincide with that of production. If B remains the point of production, the consumption point must then be located in one of the four zones marked off by drawing vertical and horizontal lines through B. These zones correspond to the four 'zones of unhappiness' identified by Swan in an

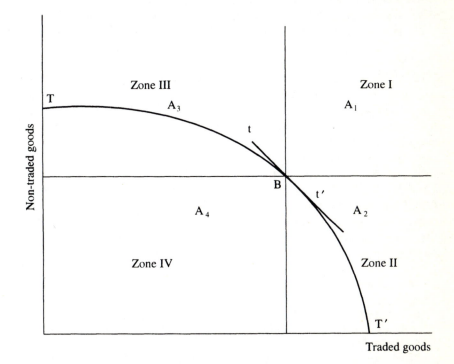

Figure 29.3 The Salter diagram

361

influential paper written in 1955 but published much later (Swan 1963a).[4]

Internal (or external) balance implies equality between the demand and supply of non-traded (or traded) goods. If the point of consumption in Figure 29.3 is A_1 (or any point in Zone I), there is excess demand for both traded and non-traded goods, that is, a balance of payments deficit and 'over-full employment'. Similarly, consumption points in Zone II like A_2 imply underemployment and a balance-of-payments deficit; those in Zone III like A_3, over-full employment and a balance-of-payments surplus; and those in Zone IV like A_4, underemployment and a balance-of-payments surplus. Recognizing that full equilibrium 'is a rare and delicate creature' (ibid.: 229), Salter went on to analyse different forms of disequilibrium such as a level of aggregate demand in excess of income, an exogenous increase in traded goods prices or a capital inflow. In each case a combination of expenditure policy and price adjustment (via deflation or devaluation) can restore full equilibrium.[5]

CONCLUDING OBSERVATIONS

Wilfred Salter has all the hallmarks of a true pioneer in the economics profession. He launched (together with Leif Johansen) a generation of vintage models and showed how an industry's output and productivity are determined by the 'petrified chronicle' embedded in its capital stock. His approach was technically far superior to the neoclassical attempt to measure output via a production function having aggregate capital stock as one of its arguments. His depiction of an economy via the Salter diagram in the space of non-traded goods and a composite traded good blazed a trail which international economists followed. It has continued to pay dividends, being applied to areas which Salter could not have envisaged such as economies with booming sectors (Corden and Neary 1982).

One of Geoff Harcourt's intellectual biographies has honoured 'Eric Russell, 1921–77: a great Australian political economist' (Harcourt 1982). If there is a Valhalla of great Australian economists, there can be little doubt that Wilfred Salter also belongs there. Geoff Harcourt would surely agree, given his heartfelt admiration for the work Salter completed in his brief lifetime. It is devoutly to be hoped that Geoff's own passage into this Valhalla (which can also be prophesied with confidence) is still far in the future.

NOTES

1 A second edition of his book (Salter 1966) was completed by the supervisor of Salter's Ph.D. dissertation in Cambridge, W. B. Reddaway. The original text was left intact, but in an addendum Reddaway extended the data series to 1963. His conclusion was that 'like [Salter's] own independent test through the use of American data, this one adds strength to one's belief in the fundamental rightness of his ideas'. Reddaway prefaced these remarks by noting that 'Wilfred Salter's

untimely death in 1963 deprived the world of a first-class economist who had the supreme gift of combining theoretical insights and the power to apply his ideas; of all the research students whose work I have supervised he certainly taught me the most, and made me do the greatest amount of hard work' (Reddaway, preface to Salter 1966: xiii).

2 Salter (1960: 67) illustrated these two alternative scenarios in panels (a) and (b) of his figure 7.

3 A more complete representation of the Ricardian model would allow for the intensive as well as the extensive margin of cultivation, though this would not alter the qualitative conclusions reached.

4 This paper and its 'Swan diagram' (as it subsequently became known) were critiqued by Corden (1960). As Arndt (1976) has pointed out, there were five versions of Swan's paper, the first of which was written in 1952 but never published. The second version, written in 1953, was published as Swan (1960). The 'dependent economy' in its title is probably the origin of one of the labels by which the Australian model has become known. Swan (1963a) is the third version.

5 The eleven specimens of the 'Salter diagram' in Salter (1959) depict a variety of equilibrium or disequilibrium situations by means of transformation and indifference curves, but do not show the four zones identified in Figure 29.3.

REFERENCES

Arndt, H. W. (1976) 'Non-traded goods and the balance of payments: the Australian contribution', *Economic Record* 52(137): 104–7.

Corden, W. M. (1960) 'The geometric representation of policies to attain internal and external balance', *Review of Economic Studies* 28(1): 1–22.

Corden W. M. and Neary, J. P. (1982) 'Booming sector and de-industrialisation in a small open economy', *Economic Journal* 92: 825–48.

Fisher, M. R. (1987) 'Salter, Wilfred Edward Graham (1929–1963)', in J. Eatwell, M. Milgate and P. Newman (eds) *The New Palgrave: A Dictionary of Economics*, London: Macmillan.

Groenewegen, P. and McFarlane, B. (1990) *A History of Australian Economic Thought*, London: Routledge.

Harcourt, G. C. (1962) 'Review article of W. E. G. Salter, *Productivity and Technical Change*', *Economic Record* 38(83): 388–94.

—— (1969) 'Some Cambridge controversies in the theory of capital', *Journal of Economic Literature* 7(2): 369–405.

—— (1972) *Some Cambridge Controversies in the Theory of Capital*, Cambridge: Cambridge University Press.

—— (1982) *The Social Science Imperialists*, ed. P. Kerr, London: Routledge & Kegan Paul.

—— (1992) *On Political Economists and Modern Political Economy: Selected Essays of G. C. Harcourt*, ed. C. Sardoni, London: Routledge.

Johansen, L. (1959) 'Substitution versus fixed production coefficients in the theory of economic growth: a synthesis', *Econometrica* 27: 157–76.

—— (1961) 'A method for separating the effects of capital accumulation and shifts in production functions upon growth in labour productivity', *Economic Journal* 71: 775–82.

Ricardo, D. (1821 [1951]) *On the Principles of Political Economy and Taxation*, in *The Works and Correspondence of David Ricardo*, vol. 1, ed. P. Sraffa, Cambridge: Cambridge University Press.

Salter, W. E. G. (1959) 'Internal and external balance: the role of price and expenditure effects', *Economic Record* 35(71): 226–38.

—— (1960) *Productivity and Technical Change*, Cambridge: Cambridge University Press.

—— (1965) 'Productivity growth and accumulation as historical processes', in E. A. G. Robinson (ed.) *Problems in Economic Development: Proceedings of a Conference Held by the International Economic Association*, London: Macmillan.

—— (1966) Productivity and Technical Change, 2nd edition with an addendum by W. B. Reddaway, Cambridge: Cambridge University Press.

Swan, T. W. (1960) 'Economic control in a dependent economy', *Economic Record* 36(73): 51–66.

—— (1963a) 'Longer-run problems of the balance of payments', in H. W. Arndt and W. M. Corden (eds) *The Australian Economy: A Volume of Readings*, Melbourne: Cheshire Press.

—— (1963b) 'Obituary: Wilfred Edward Graham Salter: 1929–1963', *Economic Record* 39(88): 486–7.

30

J. NEVILLE KEYNES
A dedicated Victorian don
Phyllis Deane

THE UNDERGRADUATE EXPERIENCE 1869–75

John Neville Keynes was born in Salisbury in 1852, the only son of a Nonconformist floriculturalist. At the age of 17 he left the small private boarding school which had inspired him to aim at an academic career, and took the advice of his father's friend, Henry Fawcett, then Alfred Marshall's predecessor as Professor of Political Economy at the University of Cambridge. Although he had already won a scholarship to University College, London (on the strength of his first-class performance in the matriculation examination), Neville's long-term goal was an Oxbridge fellowship which could give him a modest income for life. Fawcett himself had followed what was virtually the only route into the University of Cambridge currently open to ambitious young men whose entry had not been lubricated either by one of the major public schools or by family wealth and influence. In his case it had led, via a first class in the Mathematical Tripos, to a Trinity Hall fellowship and later a chair – leaving him free to pursue an active political career as a Liberal MP and, ultimately, Postmaster-General. His advice and example encouraged J. N. K. to take up his scholarship, and while reading for a London B.Sc., to enter for one or more Cambridge open-scholarship competitions. Thus, after having won the top mathematical scholarship to Pembroke College, J. N. K. was admitted to Cambridge in October 1872 as an undergraduate in a relatively small college with strong Anglican traditions.

At first he experienced a severe cultural shock. Fresh from the open-minded ambience of University Hall (a residential college avowedly established to maintain the sanctity of private judgement in matters of religion), he found himself the first and only Dissenter in an Anglican community.[1] Accustomed, moreover, to the wide-ranging menu of studies enjoyed by London undergraduates, he was alienated by the suffocatingly restrictive Cambridge examination system through which candidates for college fellowships were expected to pass with high honours. True, he had so often distinguished himself in maths examinations that he could reasonably expect to achieve a sufficiently high ranking in that subject to win a Pembroke fellowship. His problem, however, was not only that his intellectual horizons had been seductively widened at University College, but also that the Cambridge Mathematical tripos was simply ' a trial of memory and nerves'.[2] The prospect of three years' hard labour in what seemed an intellectual blind alley was intolerable, and during his first term J. N. K. seriously contemplated dropping out of Cambridge altogether. He then realized that if he joined the small band of maverick students reading for the Moral Sciences tripos, he could draw intellectual stimulus and direct personal instruction from a group of leading modern scholars (including Henry Sidgwick, Alfred Marshall and John Venn). In contrast, candidates for the Maths tripos were largely dependent on a miscellany of hard-pressed specialist coaches whose prime function was the intensive drilling of undergraduate minds for success in certain highly competitive written examinations. There was an alternative, however. By focusing almost exclusively on mathematics for the college examinations in May of his first year, he obtained Pembroke's top mathematical scholarship – which effectively guaranteed his place in the college, even if he switched to a tripos as low in the Cambridge hierarchy of disciplines as moral sciences.

Armed then with practical advice from Venn (the logician and fellow of Caius), and with a faculty-recommended reading list, J. N. K. went eagerly into residence for the long-vacation term of 1873 and began reading J. S. Mill's *Principles of Political Economy*, the basic text for that section of the Tripos. Having already made a friend of James Ward,[3] nine years older than himself, who held a Trinity scholarship in moral science, he now had a stimulating walking companion with whom to explore the thought-provoking ideas to which he was now being introduced for the first time. In summer 1873, then, J. N. K. embarked on a course of study that differed radically from all his previous experience at school or university. It was less rigorous in the specificity of its demands than any of the mathematical or classical or scientific subjects which he had studied so far. At the same time it was more challenging in its intellectual range and in the extent to which it called for original judgement and analytical skills rather than technical expertise, or mental gymnastics, or detailed recall of book work. He had two years to prepare himself for a written examination, where he would be required to address a selection of the questions posed in twelve three-hour papers on four related, but distinct, branches of knowledge: Moral and Political Philosophy; Mental Philosophy; Logic; and Political Economy. The moralist undergraduate had no need to hire the kind of coaches required by honours men reading mathematics or classics. For each branch he had a list of twelve to twenty books recommended by the Board of Studies for Moral Sciences – books which he was encouraged to read carefully and critically (though not necessarily exhaustively). Attendance at lectures was optional, and, for each course he chose to audit, he could get from the lecturer (for a fee of £1 per term) a set of questions, his answers to which would be read and assessed by the lecturer himself. The Moral Sciences tripos thus gave the candidate for honours maximum freedom to plan his own work programme. He could decide for himself each term which of the listed books he would read, which of the recommended lectures he would attend and which of the dons might be expected to give him personally the most helpful advice on how to tackle the kind of questions that could appear in the final examination. At each lecture he found himself one of a rather small audience (usually less than ten men), most of whom wrote answers to the questions set by the lecturer and had their answers criticized in front of the group. Each candidate rapidly became well known personally to the dons who regularly taught (and took turns in examining for) the Tripos.

In the event, it was not until the Saturday morning before the start of his third term as a moralist that Neville introduced himself to Alfred Marshall. J. N. K.'s diary for 18 April 1874, for example, records that he 'called on Marshall of John's, lecturer in Pol. Econ. – found him in his tub'. This laconic entry nicely illustrates the pleasant informality of the relationship between the new generation of dons and their honours students.

Meanwhile, having decided – against all conventional wisdom – to switch to Moral Sciences, a tripos which most Cambridge dons did not regard as a full-time occupation for honours men, J. N. K. urgently needed to acquire extra credits if he was to win his fellowship in a competitive election. It was not enough to win the accolade of Senior Moralist by topping the list of candidates in the 1875 tripos. So, being still a full member of University College, J. N. K. set about raising his academic standing by taking the first part of the London B.Sc. in summer 1873, the second in autumn 1874, and the London MA in summer 1876. Apparently undergraduate moralists really did have time to spare, for he managed to cover successfully a range of other (mainly scientific) subjects for the London B.Sc. By the time Pembroke's fellows voted him unanimously into a fellowship in August 1876, Cambridge's 1875 Senior Moralist had scored a high first class in the final London B.Sc. and won the gold medal for an outstanding performance in the London MA.

FELLOW OF PEMBROKE 1876–83

At that stage of his career, with his feet firmly on the first rung of the academic ladder, J. N. K. saw himself primarily as a university teacher – a role idealized for him by the modern generation of dons who had directly inspired him over the past three years. In principle he was equipped to teach any of the subjects covered in the Moral Sciences tripos. In practice, his strengths and his interests lay in two of them: logic and political economy. He was then happy to teach either or both. As far as Pembroke was concerned, the new Fellow had acquired enough academic honours to add lustre to the college's reputation for scholarship; its Anglican tutor (who positively discouraged undergraduates from reading Moral Sciences) was indifferent as to which branch he chose. In effect, his teaching function concerned only the Moral Sciences Board. When J. N. K. first learned his tripos results, in a letter from James Ward (the 1874 Senior Moralist who had been taken into the 1875 examiners' confidence), he transcribed part of it into his diary for 13 December 1875:

> It was agreed unanimously that, as Marshall puts it, you have a very clear mind: for the rest the Logic and Economy people rate you the highest. Jevons said that you floored the Logic papers and that your answers were a pleasure to read. I shd fancy that you pleased him better in Logic than in Economy; he evidently doesn't believe much in Marshall and was amused by your curves. Foxwell praises your precision, but says you shirk difficulties and lack originality in philosophy.... All are agreed that Pembroke ought to give you a Fellowship and Marshall thinks you ought to lay yourself out for Economic History, a subject that wants treating thoroughly both for the Moral and the History man.

At that time, however, there was a more than sufficient supply of reputable lecturers willing and able to teach political economy to the small number of moralists (rarely more than eleven in the 1870s) reading it for honours. As for the women students, their lectures on political economy were now competently supplied by Newnham's first resident lecturer, Mary Paley. Meanwhile, Marshall's notion that his most promising economic disciple should teach economic history had been simply an empire-builder's fantasy. It was the History Board rather than the Moral Sciences Board which organized lectures in economic history and it already employed V. J. Stanton (a Trinity Fellow, twentieth Wrangler in 1870) who had worked up the kind of elementary course on political economy, combined with economic history, that the historians thought they needed. So even if J. N. K. had wanted to specialize in economic history – and his diary offers no evidence that he ever did – the prospects of the historians inviting a recently graduated Marshallian to teach in that area were remote.

In the event, during his first year as a don, J. N. K. undertook a conscientiously limited teaching and examining programme. That involved thrice-weekly lectures in logic to women students (organized by Sidgwick), a similar course to honours men (as deputy for Venn), various *ad hoc* sessions of personal tuition (in either logic or political economy) with undergraduate men, or Girton women reading for the tripos, and examining in the Trinity scholarship examination at Sidgwick's invitation. He refused an invitation to lecture on Descartes to Girton women, perhaps because he did not wish to teach philosophy, but ostensibly because he has as many new lectures to prepare as he could satisfactorily deliver. After at first accepting W. Besant's invitation to write a primer on political economy, he wisely backed out of the commitment on hearing that Marshall's fiancée, Mary Paley, was writing a political economy textbook for University Extension students.

Marshall persuaded J. N. K. to compete for the Cobden Essay Prize, but the latter was uninspired by the set topic – 'the effect of machinery on wages' – and discouraged by the cast of examiners. Cliffe Leslie, the external examiner, was an Irish historical economist of international repute who represented a tradition of thought totally alien to the Ricardian/Marshallian orthodoxy then taking shape in Cambridge. The other two examiners were Henry Fawcett – J. N. K's friend, but not the kind of economist to impress a disciple of Marshall – and Samuel Phear, then Master of Emmanuel, a theologian who was there as Vice-Chancellor's representative. In this group of three the external examiner was obviously destined to dominate. 'The chief part of what I have already written is in direct opposition to Cliffe Leslie', groaned J. N. K. to his diary on learning the names of the adjudicators; but he resisted Marshall's worldly wise advice simply to delete all the passages that might affront Cliffe Leslie.

In the end, his first attempt at a sustained thesis on political economy was an instructive failure. He had difficulty in meeting the deadline and in keeping the essay to a suitable length, and he was beaten by one of his own pupils. After reading J. L. Nicholson's summary of his entry for the Cobden Prize J. N. K. confided to his diary on 8 July, 'I feel sure he will get the prize.' As indeed he did.

The diary makes it clear that J. N. K. was dedicated to becoming an effective teacher. He spent a great deal of time in reading widely for his lectures, in expounding them clearly and accurately, in setting testing questions for each of the various groups to whom he lectured, and in one-to-one discussion with students who had submitted written answers for him to assess. He referred frequently in his diary to the reception each lecture got from his audience and he anxiously sought individual comments on his performance – either directly, or indirectly through other dons in whom they confided. Most of his summer vacations were spent revising his lecture courses – in the light of further reading, or of critical comments, or of the levels of understanding revealed by students' classwork or examination papers. It is unlikely that the diffident, unassertive young Neville Keynes was ever a charismatic lecturer, but there is plenty of evidence in the diary to suggest that women students especially, and honours men generally, found his orderly, methodical approach to formal logic particularly helpful for examination-focused undergraduates and were explicitly grateful for the time and effort he put into giving advice and explanations to individuals.

Partly as a result of the relative scarcity of moral scientists competent to teach logic, and partly because J. N. K. was determined above all to improve his teaching performance, most of his lectures during the first few years of his fellowship were in that area. True, he could have resumed his political economy lectures to women when Marshall's departure to Bristol (after marrying Mary Paley) took away Newnham's resident lecturer. But J. N. K. was still so obsessively concerned to bring his logic course up to his own standards of excellence that when Sidgwick, in 1877, offered him the option of lectures on political economy to Newnhamites he refused. It was not until 1880 that he felt able to extend his load by lecturing to them on political economy as well as logic. However, by the time Marshall was elected to the Cambridge chair of political economy in December 1884, J. N. K. was spending more time on economics than on logic. His logic lectures were well under control, though he diligently kept his reading of the subject up to date. He had already published an undergraduate's manual which he described as his 'small book of problems and exercises in logic'. The first edition of it appeared in February 1884, under the title *Studies and Exercises in Formal Logic* (See Keynes 1906). In 1883 he had been appointed Examiner in Political Economy in the University of London and in September that year he acted as joint secretary (with Foxwell) for the Economic Section of the British Association for the Advancement of Science. In April 1884 he was elected to the University of Cambridge's first Moral Science lectureship and now lectured regularly, not only on logic, but also on political economy to women as well as to Indian Civil Service candidates[4] and to honours men who needed help in getting to grips with Marshall's curves. So, when the Marshalls returned to Cambridge J. N. K. was disappointed to be told by Sidgwick that he should consider his university lectureship as being in logic and not in political economy. 'I am rather coming to the conclusion that Sidgwick is open to the charge of wanting to regulate too much', he grumbled to his diary on 29 January 1885, in a rare burst of irritation with Henry Sidgwick.

THE SCOPE AND METHOD OF POLITICAL ECONOMY

Marshall, of course had other plans for the man who was currently his most promising disciple. He wanted to get J. N. K. into the Oxford lectureship he was himself vacating. When the Marshalls called at the Keynes family home to find its head away on Local Examinations work (he was now Assistant Secretary to the University of Cambridge Local Examinations Syndicate), Neville's devoted wife passed their message on, in a letter transcribed in the diary for 18 December 1884. Florence wrote:

> I must first of all tell you that I do not wonder at your enthusiasm for him. He *is* a most delightful man ... he said such nice things about you and seemed so genuinely interested in all that concerned you.... Of course we shd both very much dislike the thought of leaving Cambridge – but your work must be considered most of all – and you might have more congenial work at Oxford. At any rate you wd be able to devote

yourself to Political Economy which is the subject I believe you are really most interested in. And so long as we had each other and the boy[5] we could get on happily anywhere.

But J. N. K. was not persuaded that he would find Oxford a congenial place of work, or that (as Marshall hinted) he had a good chance of getting an Oxford chair within a few years. In spite of a barrage of letters from, and long talks with, Marshall he absolutely refused to be considered for the post, although he did eventually agree to commute weekly to Balliol to give a course, on his own choice of topic, the next Easter term. It was the Oxford lectures that provided the starting point for his book *The Scope and Method of Political Economy* (Keynes 1930) which dominated his vacations for the next quinquennium. Marshall had tried hard to persuade J. N. K. that if he accepted the invitation to repeat the Oxford lectures the following year, he would improve his chances of being elected to the Drummond Chair (then held by Bonamy Price) when it next became vacant. But by summer 1885, Neville was the happily married parent of two children (Maynard and Margaret) and the time-consuming weekly trip to Oxford had not inspired him with any enthusiasm for the place: the Balliol fellows had made no effort to welcome the stranger at their table, and the only Oxford don who displayed a kindred spirit was L. R. Phelps. Meanwhile, J. N. K. was enjoying the administrative job he had recently acquired in Cambridge – Assistant Secretary to the Local Examinations Syndicate – and saw an attractive future for himself as Chief Secretary. Moreover, he was realistically convinced that his chances of a chair in political economy – wherever and whenever a suitable opening arose – would hinge crucially on his having published a scholarly book in the relevant field. There was, he knew, no better place than Cambridge in which to write a monograph on the new economics. True, when he told Nicholson that he proposed to write a book on method he was scoffed at, on the grounds (according to his diary) that 'anyone could write such a book as that ... what we want is useful *applications* of the right method'. Nevertheless, Nicholson (by then Edinburgh's Professor of Political Economy) was one of the circle of Cambridge-trained economists to whom J. N. K. sent the proofs of *Scope and Method* for critical comment.

Overall, of course, it was Alfred Marshall whose influence on *Scope and Method* was greatest and who wrote detailed comments on each chapter – first in manuscript and then in proof. So their two books developed side by side, as it were, J. N. K. having also read Marshall's *Principles of Economics* (Marshall 1890) in its manuscript and proof stages, was heavily indoctrinated with its ideas from the outset and extremely sensitive to his master's criticisms even when he did not take his advice. In the end Marshall's *Principles* appeared first – in July 1890 – and J. N. K's *Scope and Method* six months later. Both men saw themselves as representatives of 'the new generation of economists' and both reacted against the methodological

371

controversies of the 1860s and 1870s that threatened to discredit the scientific credentials of political economy. They were also at one in their belief that what was then needed to end the tedious *Methodenstreit* of the past two and a half decades was an exposition that was judicious instead of polemic, moderate rather than extreme, expository more than argumentative. Hence the tone of J. N. K's preface:

> I have endeavoured to avoid the tone of a partisan and have sought in the treatment of disputed questions to represent both sides without prejudice. Whilst making no attempt to bring about a complete reconciliation between opposing views, I have been able to show that the nature of the opposition between them has sometimes been misunderstood and its extent consequently exaggerated.
>
> (Keynes 1930: vi)

In his introductory chapter J. N. K. reviewed the recent methodological debates in terms of two polar views of the scope and method of his discipline, one seeing it as a positive, abstract and inductive science, the other as an ethical, realistic and deductive science. He then set out to show that it was all of these things by distinguishing three types of economic enquiry:

1 'a positive science', i.e. 'a body of systematized knowledge concerning what is',
2 'a normative or regulative science', i.e. 'a body of systematized knowledge relating to criteria of what ought to be and concerned therefore with the ideal as distinguished from the actual', and
3 'an art as a system of rules for the attainment of a given end' (Keynes 1930: 34–5).

The object of this classification scheme was to distinguish assumptions and findings about what *is* (which constitutes the scientific core of political economy) from, on the one hand, statements about what ought to be (which also have scientific validity in so far as ethics is a rational discipline, a moral science), and, on the other hand, prescriptions for achieving desired ends. It permitted the economic theorist to insulate his or her fundamental theorems from accusations of ideological bias, or immorality, or relativity, as well as from the failures of economic policies derived from these theorems. In effect, the normative science and the art of political economy provided a protective belt for the hard core of neoclassical theory that emerged from the marginal revolution. The protective belt could absorb the attacks of historicists, socialists and nationalists and so shift the battlefield of methodological or doctrinal dispute away from fundamental principles:

> If political economy regarded from the theoretical standpoint is to make good progress, it is essential that all extrinsic or premature sources of controversy should be eliminated; and we may be sure that the more its

principles are discussed independently of ethical and practical considerations, the sooner will the science emerge from the controversial
stage.

(Keynes 1930: 52)

Scope and Method was well received by leading economists in Britain and
elsewhere, being favourably assessed in general. F. Y. Edgeworth, for
example, reviewed it first in *Nature* and afterwards (at length) in the
Economic Journal and set the tone for many later reviews. Among the extracts
from the *Nature* review which J. N. K. quoted happily in his diary for 28
February 1891 was the following:

> On a subject which it is undesirable always to be reopening, it may be
> hoped that Mr Keynes's work will prove final. It may be expected that
> his second logical treatise will enjoy the same popularity as his first; for
> it deserves the same rare encomium that if a reader is under the necessity
> of confining himself to a single book on the subject the single book had
> best be that of Mr Keynes.

J. N. K. was also sufficiently pleased with Bonar's review in *The Academy*
to quote chunks from it in his diary for 7 March 1891, e.g.:

> In a sense it is true that his book merely sums up the views about scope
> and method which have in the last twenty years been gradually taking
> shape in the minds of English and American economists under the
> influence of Jevons, Marshall and Walker.

This of course was the essence of Keynes's *Scope and Method*. It analysed,
in painstakingly clear, deliberately uncontroversial prose, the substance and
rationale for the methodological consensus of a new orthodoxy, the new
economics for which Marshall's *Principles* was the authorised text. However,
those who write treatises on what sort of study economics is and what it is all
about must resign themselves to the fact that it is a topic which the majority
of economists committed to a progressive research programme are content to
ignore.[6] So, although J. N. K.'s monograph figured on many honours
students' reading lists, and went into several editions, it was rarely quoted by
practising economists. It remained literally the last word on its subject until
the 1930s, when a new generation of economists – among whom Neville's son
Maynard was a leading member – were articulating powerful doubts
concerning the relevance of orthodox Marshallian theory to current economic
problems. It was then that Lionel Robbins responded with his *Essay on the
Nature and Significance of Economic Science* (Robbins 1930); but that
monograph focused on a narrower conception of the discipline than most
practitioners were prepared to swallow and it intensified rather than allayed
methodological controversy.

ACKNOWLEDGEMENT

The principal primary sources for this paper are the full and frank manuscript diaries kept by J. Neville Keynes almost continuously from his schooldays in the late 1860s to 1917. I am grateful to the Keeper of Manuscripts for permission to quote from the Keynes Diaries, which are the property of the Cambridge University Library (Add. MSS. 7827–7867).

NOTES

1   It was not until the University Tests Act of 1871 finally removed the statutory obligation on Masters and Fellows of colleges and Professors and Readers of the University to sign a formal declaration of uniformity with the Church of England that Nonconformists were free to aspire to a full academic career in the ancient English universities of Cambridge and Oxford.
2   On the Cambridge Mathematical tripos in the second half of the nineteenth century see Annan 1984: 24–5.
3   James Ward subsequently became Cambridge's Professor of Mental Philosophy.
4   J. N. K. read as much as he could find of books on the history of India and political, economic and social conditions there in an effort to make his political economy lectures relevant for the young men who were being groomed for the Indian Civil Service.
5   The boy was J. N. K's first-born, J. Maynard Keynes, born June 1883.
6   Sixty years later, D. H. Robertson, who had begun reading for the Economics tripos in 1910, referred thus to the subject of J. N. K's monograph: 'This is a topic which when I started to read economics in Cambridge in 1910, it was not I think fashionable among us to think much about.... To us, it seemed a topic more suitable for discussion by Germans than by Englishmen. There was on our reading list what I have since come to regard as a good, if dry book about it, J. N. Keynes's *Scope and Method of Political Economy*, but to be quite honest I doubt if many of us read it. We thought we knew pretty well what sort of things we wanted to know about and were glad enough to take the counsel given by Marshall himself near the beginning of the *Principles*, "the less we concern ourselves with scholastic enquiries as to whether a certain consideration comes within the scope of economics the better".' (Robertson 1951: 112).

REFERENCES

Annan, N. (1984) *Leslie Stephen*, London: Weidenfeld & Nicolson.
Keynes, J. N. (1906) *Studies and Exercises in Formal Logic*, 4th edition, London: Macmillan.
—— (1930 reprint) *The Scope and Method of Political Economy*, London: Macmillan.
Marshall, A. (1890) *Principles of Economics*, London: Macmillan.
Mill, J. S. (1848) *Principles of Political Economy*, London, Longman.
Robertson, D. H. (1951) 'Utility and all that', *Manchester School of Social and Economic Studies*, 19.
Robbins, L. (1930) *Essay on the Nature and Significance of Economic Science*, London: Macmillan.

31

SMITHIAN FOUNDATIONS OF THE MARKET ECONOMY

Alessandro Roncaglia

INTRODUCTION

In his *Donald Horne Address*, 'Markets madness and a middle way', Geoff Harcourt discusses the conditions for a well-functioning market economy, referring for two of them to Adam Smith. First, 'The thrust of the argument [of Smith's *Theory of Moral Sentiments*] is the need to design institutions which allow altruism, or "sympathy", to prevail'. Second, 'Smith, a wise person, recognized that one of the essential conditions for competitive markets to function in a "socially desirable" manner was that economic and political power should be widely diffused' (Harcourt 1992: 3). Smith – and Harcourt – thus point to the fact that moral and political aspects condition the working of a market economy. (Similar interpretations of Smith have been proposed by a number of authors, from Macfie (1967) to Pack (1991); cf. also Roncaglia (1989, 1995).)

This viewpoint implies a notion of what a market is – the classical notion – different from that prevailing in contemporary economics. In my opinion, the dominance of this latter, mainly marginalist, redefinition of the notion is responsible for the oblivion of the moral and political preconditions for a well-functioning market economy. In this paper I will first recall in the next section the classical notion of the market as a social set of interrelations between producers (and, eventually but not necessarily, consumers). The marginalist notion of the market – as a point in time and space where supply and demand meet – is then briefly recalled. A subsequent section discusses the role attributed by Smith to the moral foundations of a market economy and to institutions. A distinction between an all-out *laissez-faire* and Smithian liberism, and its connection with political liberalism, is then considered, and the final section briefly draws a few conclusions.

ALESSANDRO RONCAGLIA

WILLIAM PETTY: THE CLASSICAL NOTION OF THE MARKET

Schumpeter (1954) considered 'conceptualization' as the first stage of economic analysis, preceded by the 'pre-analytical' stage (where the problems to be dealt with are identified and some starting hypotheses are suggested), and followed by the stage of model-building. The stage of conceptualization is a crucial one, defining the substantive content of the economic variables utilized in building formal analytical models. Different theoretical approaches generally imply differences in the meaning of concepts designated by the same name. Thus, for instance, the 'reproduction' price of the classical–Sraffian approach is a different concept from the 'scarcity' price of the marginalist approach (Roncaglia 1978). This is true for the crucial notion of 'the market' as well.

In order to give a brief and tentative sketch of the classical notion of the market, we will concentrate attention on William Petty (1623–87), who in a short paper, 'Dialogue of diamonds', unpublished in his lifetime, provides a very interesting discussion of the market as a set of interrelationships between producers (for a broader discussion of Petty's ideas, see Roncaglia (1985: esp. 73–6)). The protagonists of the dialogue are Mr A, representing Petty himself, and Mr B, an inexperienced buyer of a diamond. The latter vaguely perceives the existence of some sort of 'rule of the market', asking whether he had paid too much or too little for the specific diamond which he bought. This means that there is a connection between different acts of exchange involving diamonds, though each act of exchange differs from any other because of the differences in time and place, in the actors involved, in the way the dealing takes place, and in the specific good object of the exchange. (Any diamond is different from any other diamond, so that the individuality of each act of exchange may seem a characteristic peculiar to this market; however, this is in fact rather frequent, even in markets for mass-production commodities: what exactly is 'a CD player'?) Thus, we need some common elements, some 'regularities', in order to connect a set of individual acts of exchange into a unified 'market'.

In search for 'regularities', without which no theoretical model could be constructed, Petty proposes a methodological rule: to leave aside those causes 'that depend upon the mutable Minds, Opinions, Appetites and Passions of particular Men', considering 'only such Causes, as have visible Foundations in Nature' (Petty 1963: 244). This means ignoring the specific circumstances of each individual act of exchange and concentrating attention on objective elements, in our case the physical characteristics of the goods exchanged (such as weight, dimension, colour, defects). The expert Mr A is capable of pointing to 'rules' concerning these characteristics; for example, 'The general rule concerning weight is this that the price rises in duplicate proportion of the weight' (ibid.: 627).

Our problem here, of course, is not the way in which the economist determines the theoretical price (natural price) of the commodity under consideration. Rather, we are concerned with the way in which 'the working of the market' is represented. In Petty's conceptualization of the market, there is no unique time and place where all demands and supplies meet. Each act of exchange is isolated both in time and space. The unifying element integrating in a single world market all individual acts of exchange is the 'knowledge' on the side of the experts of the objective elements which exert a systematic influence in the market. The experts, quite sensibly, are identified with the regular participants to the market: 'the great merchants of jevels all the world over doe know one another' (Petty 1963: 625). (Recent discussions on the role of 'middlemen' for the good functioning of commodity markets point in the same direction.)

Let us note, in passing, that parallel to such a definition of the market there is a (implicit) definition of 'the commodity' not as 'the atom of exchange', as it is interpreted in intertemporal contingency general equilibrium models, but as a concept already involving a certain degree of abstraction, and hence of aggregation: as when Petty (ibid.: 89) speaks of 'Corn, which we will suppose to contain all necessaries for life, as in the Lords Prayer we suppose the word Bread doth'. (This also explains why classical economists did not feel the need for a clear-cut distinction between 'the market' and 'the industry'.)

Petty's notion of the market (and of the commodity) is typical of the whole stream of classical economists from Adam Smith to John Stuart Mill, and including Karl Marx. Namely, the market is conceived as connecting dispersed individual acts of exchange into an integrated set because of the 'knowledge' and mutual interdependence of producers, reinforced by competition on the side of the buyers, and possibly by a web of professional middlemen. This is especially true when not only selling, but also buying, is a regular activity, as when considering produced and reproducible means of production and subsistence, the prices of which in classical theory are in fact determined by 'regularities' in their production (their 'difficulty of production', often summarized in terms of labour contained, with an implicit reference to a 'dominant technology'; see Roncaglia 1978: 27–9).

FROM THE CLASSICAL TO THE MARGINALIST NOTION OF THE MARKET

Parallel to the classical interpretation of the market as a web of relations connecting habitual participants to it, there is a different definition which runs through the centuries-long history of political economy. According to this view, most likely derived from the experience of medieval fairs, the market is conceived as a point in time and space where buyers and sellers meet. This notion is implicit, for instance, in some scholastic discussions of the 'just price'.

This in turn leads quite easily to the idea of a 'market price' determined by the opposite forces of supply and demand. This very simple idea does not (at least, not necessarily) imply the notion of well-specified (respectively decreasing and increasing) functions connecting quantities demanded and supplied to the commodity's price. Pre-classical and classical economists conceive demand and supply as categories including the most disparate elements, both casual and systematic, affecting the quantities offered by sellers and the money-backed intentions to buy. Theories of exchange value need to isolate among these disparate elements those acting in a systematic way, while leaving aside the irregular and contingent ones. Thus classical economists isolate 'difficulty of production' (summarized in 'labour contained') and the 'competition of capitals' leading to the assumption of a uniform rate of profits as the elements acting in a systematic way, and concentrate on such elements for the determination of their theoretical variable, 'natural prices' (or prices of production). On the contrary, the 'market price', though a notion already incorporating a certain degree of abstraction (because, as discussed in the previous section, it implies the identification of a set of exchange acts as included in a single market, and relating to a single commodity), is not conceived in classical political economy as a theoretical variable. It is the result of the whole group of systematic and casual elements included under the headings of supply and demand. The vague idea of scholastic authors of a market price as 'equilibrating' supply and demand should be interpreted not as arithmetic equality, but as connected to the idea of a 'just price', corresponding to a situation in which both buyers and sellers are satisfied as far as possible with the conditions of the exchange.

It is with the advent of marginalist economics that the idea of the market price as a theoretical variable, determined by the equilibrium between supply and demand, in turn conceived as 'well-behaved' functions of price, makes its appearance. This involves the introduction of a host of notions which were unnecessary in classical political economy, such as the idea of utility maps and the postulate of decreasing marginal utility behind demand curves, and some sort of law of production behind supply curves. (As Sraffa (1925) shows, the 'laws of returns' are introduced because of analytical necessity within the marginalist conceptual scheme, not for some alleged improvement they might supposedly contribute to the representation of economic reality; this analytical necessity persists in modern general equilibrium theory, with the assumptions of convexity of preference sets and production sets.)

The marginalist approach to price theory also involves a different view of the functioning of the market, where the primitive term of reference of the market fair is substituted by a new one, more rigorous and precise: the stock exchange. Here we have, in fact, a clear-cut example of a market as a point in time and space where demand and supply meet and determine an equilibrium price defined by their equality. Obviously, there are different possible ways of organizing the stock exchange; it is interesting to note that Walrasian price analysis, with its *deus ex machina*, the auctioneer, corresponds to the rules of Continental stock exchanges based on call auctions, whereas Marshallian analysis is rather to be related to the Anglo-Saxon stock exchanges based on continuous trading.

This point has been duly noticed. Thus Jaffé (1973: 117n) recalls that Walras's 'operational definition of the competitive market was further elucidated in a subsequent article, "La bourse, la spéculation et l'agiotage"' (Walras 1880 [1898]), which 'describes the operations of the Paris stock exchange as precluding not only nonuniformity of price but also any trading at "false prices"'. Kregel (1992: 532) proposes the above-mentioned comparison between the Walrasian notion of the market based on the Paris bourse and the Marshallian one based on the London stock exchange.

Another of the 'fathers' of marginalism, Jevons, after recalling the common-language definition of the market as 'any body of persons who are in intimate business relations and carry on extensive transactions in any commodity' (so that 'markets may or may not be localized'), proposes his own 'scientific' definition, so strict as not to apply even to stock exchanges, though they are the nearest real example for it:

> By a market I shall mean two or more persons dealing in two or more commodities, whose stocks of those commodities and intentions of exchanging are known to all. It is also essential that the ratio of exchange between any two persons should be known to all the others. It is only so far as this community of knowledge extends that the market extends.
>
> (Jevons 1871 [1970]: 132–3)

This notion of the market is not meant to be a 'stylistic' representation of reality. It is a logical necessity, in an analytical framework directed to determining equilibrium values for all economic variables, and where such values are derived from the comparison between scarce resources (supply) and human needs and desires (demand). The market is the abstract logical site where this comparison takes place.

The point to be stressed here is that the marginalist notion of the market is a very specific one, quite different in this respect from the vague reference to village fairs which historically preceded it in attributing to supply and demand the crucial role in price determination. One should then ask whether such a specific notion, using such terms of reference as highly organized financial markets, is an adequate conceptualization of manufactured goods markets in a developed industrialized economy. Doubts increase when, as in Jevons's case, we are confronted with an idealized representation of such markets. We may notice, in this respect, that even in stock exchanges the set of interrelations connecting agents – customs, habits, norms and moral values – are essential to the good functioning of the market; representing it as the point where well-behaved demand and supply functions meet means ignoring these essential elements.

Perhaps the classical conceptualization of the market should then be preferred, since it opens the door to keeping into account such elements, and allows greater flexibility in the analysis of the working of a market economy. As we shall see in the following sections, the classical (and, more specifically, Smithian) notion of the market involves moral and political prerequisites which seem to have been largely forgotten in marginalist as well as in modern mainstream analysis.

SMITH ON THE MORAL AND INSTITUTIONAL FOUNDATIONS OF A MARKET ECONOMY

According to Smith, human beings are essentially social animals. Hence, the division of labour originates in their propensity to enter into relations with each other through bargains. When the division of labour, which is the basic force behind the progress of nations, develops, and each person or group of persons specializes in the production of a commodity or group of commodities, each economic system (each nation-state) becomes characterized by a complex but sufficiently regular web of flows of commodities, from producers to utilizers. Political economy, as the analysis of developed human societies based on the division of labour, has as one of its crucial objects of study the way in which these flows of commodities are regulated, namely – in Smith's society – the market.

Thus the market economy appears in Smith, very much as in Petty, as a web of repetitive acts of exchange between sellers and buyers of the different commodities. There is no unique time and place, and auction mechanism, through which the exchanges are regulated so as to ensure the equality between supply and demand; the links connecting the participants to the market are provided by the forces of customs and habits and by the – greater or lesser, but always imperfect – knowledge of past events and current conditions on the side of the protagonists.

These protagonists, Smith stresses, are driven in their behaviour not by benevolence but by their self-interest. In a simplistic interpretation, this crucial idea gives origin to the marginalist notion of the 'economic man' who translates every economic problem into one of maximization of utility under constraint. In Smith, on the contrary, this notion of self-interest is grounded in a complex view of human beings and societies.

Following the tradition of the Scottish Enlightenment, Smith considers human beings as an imperfect and varied mixture of passions and interests. From this observation, he develops both a theory of ethics and a theory of

380

institutions, which constitute a necessary background to his political economy.

The theory of ethics is developed in his first book, *The Theory of Moral Sentiments* (Smith 1759 [1976]). The role of institutions is stressed both there and in books III and V of *The Wealth of Nations* (Smith 1776 [1976]), and is the subject of the *Lectures on Jurisprudence*, lecture notes collected by students and published posthumously (Smith 1978). Let us recall in brief the main characteristics of these two aspects of Smith's analysis of human societies, beginning with ethics.

Let us notice that self-interest, not selfishness, is the basic motive for human actions considered by Smith in *The Wealth of Nations*. Behind it there is the principle of self-approbation, whereby each individual considers whether his or her actions would be approved by an 'impartial spectator' judging them from the viewpoint of society's members, according to the 'moral principle of sympathy' developed by Smith in *The Theory of Moral Sentiments*. Selfish behaviour is checked by the moral duty to take into account the consequences of each action for others: this provides the basic ground for a 'civilized' market society, where rules of behaviour are respected not only because of legal but also because of moral constraints. In fact, as Smith stresses, without a sufficiently widespread acceptance of common moral rules no system of law could subsist. At the same time, since human beings are imperfect, laws and public institutions for the prevention of crime and the administration of justice are necessary, as well as support for education. Without laws and state administration of justice, 'the immense fabric of human society ... must in a moment crumble into atoms' (Smith 1759 [1976]: 86; cf. also p. 163).

Thus we should not interpret in isolation Smith's famous sentence, 'It is not from the benevolence of the butcher, the brewer or the baker, that we expect our dinner, but from their regard to their own interest' (Smith 1776 [1976]: 27). Underlying this sentence, there is the assumption of a civilized society, where the moral principle of sympathy generally prevails, and where moreover it is duly supported by public institutions. Among these, Smith considers not only those relating to defence, justice and government (which correspond to the extreme liberal idea of the 'minimal state'), but also 'publick works and institutions for facilitating the commerce of society' (a heading under which he discusses, among other things, transport infrastructures such as roads, channels and bridges, and chartered companies such as the East India Company – Smith 1776 [1976]: 723–57), and – most important for him, as a way to counter the negative effects of the division of labour – 'institutions for the education of youth', from elementary schools to universities (Smith 1776 [1976]: 758–87).

ALESSANDRO RONCAGLIA

LIBERISM AND LIBERALISM: THE POLITICAL FOUNDATIONS OF THE MARKET ECONOMY

A well-functioning market economy by definition requires free economic initiative. Equally true, but much less obvious, is the fact that it requires political freedom. The relationship between liberism (economic freedom) and liberalism (intended, as it meant originally, as individual self-determination or political freedom) is the object of a centuries-old debate. We will consider briefly only an aspect of it, again referring to Adam Smith.

To begin with, let us recall that there are different kinds and degrees of both liberism and liberalism; moreover, they can be combined in different ways. On both accounts, Smith's choice of the field is uncontroversial; again on both accounts, he is far from being an extremist.

'Every man is, no doubt, by nature, first and principally recommended to his own care; and as he is fitter to take care of himself than of any other person, it is fit and right that it should be so' (Smith 1759 [1976]: 82; this point is repeated, in nearly the same wording, on p. 219 – a very rare occurrence for such a polished writer as Smith). This passage is a clear statement in favour of individual self-determination. It is also, however, a very guarded statement: Smith does not say that 'every man is fitter than any other person to take care of himself'. This would have been compatible with such awkward ideas as that one should not trust a doctor for treating an illness (I owe this point to Raffaelli (1994), who also noticed that the two contemporary Italian translations of the *Theory of Moral Sentiments* go wrong on this point). Thus Smith's liberalism, though clear and, in a sense, a matter of principle, does not have the 'purity' which it assumed among French intellectuals of the period.

Smith's liberism is also rather different from extreme *laissez-faire*. It is not based on the identification of the interests of the community with the sum of the interests of its individual components: 'methodological individualism' cannot be attributed to Smith. It is not based on perfect, fully rational and fully informed economic agents endowed with independent preference maps. It is based, on the contrary, on the very idea of imperfect human beings: rational but not fully so, with a complex mixture of passions and interests motivating their actions, sufficiently well informed in their own business but never fully so, and poorly informed of matters not belonging to their daily life. These imperfections, however, are attributed not only to the subjects of a state, but to their rulers as well, and with resolute strength (see, for example, Smith 1759 [1976]: 232–3) to intellectuals designing abstract supposedly perfect schemes of how society should be organized and how individuals should behave. (This latter element should be noticed, since it runs counter to the dominant Enlightenment idea of the positive role of an absolute monarchy ruled by an enlightened and benevolent sovereign supported by the philosophers' good advices.)

Smith is certainly in favour of free economic initiative, especially in reaction to the constraints intrinsic in the remnants of feudalism; but he is also in favour of state intervention, not only in the obvious fields of 'common goods' (defence, police, justice) but also in fields belonging to 'social welfare' such as education, and most noticeably in the very working of the market economy, in order to counter the development of concentrations of economic power. He is also in favour of rules constraining market behaviour in the general interest: for instance, constraints on banking activity, which are compared to 'the obligation of building party walls, in order to prevent the communication of fire' (Smith 1776 [1976]: 324). (Viner (1927) provides an impressive list of Smith's interventionist proposals; let us add that Smith reaches the point of guarding against 'merchants and master manufacturers' undertaking a political role: see Smith (1776 [1976]: 266–7).)

By a curious fate, the interpretation of Smith's liberism-cum-liberalism was distorted by events which could rather have supported his moderate position. The extremist views on 'freedom, equality, fraternity' during the French Revolution, and especially the Terror, alienated liberalism to large strata of Great Britain's cultured classes; Smith's writings were thus the object of growing diffidence in the years immediately following his death, but came back again into fashion once reinterpreted as liberism-without-liberalism, *laissez-faire* devoid of political implications, with an interpretative cleavage between his economic and his political-moral thought which persisted over time. (The vicissitudes of the interpretations of Smith's thought on this point are illustrated by Rothschild (1992).)

Economic and political-moral elements can be separated, in Smith's thinking, only for the sake of expository simplicity – as happens in his own writings. At least implicitly (and in a sufficiently explicit way in Book III of *The Wealth of Nations*), Smith suggests that only free citizens can acquire the habits and customs of a responsible morality and – possibly by trial and error – the capabilities and knowledge required to quasi-rational economic agents in a well-functioning market economy.

CONCLUSIONS

In classical theory, markets are a social institution based on customary relationships. They involve knowledge based on habitual participation and on sufficiently regular commodity flows between sectors. They also involve a sufficient degree of mutual trust and supportive political and juridical institutions, ensuring the predominance of socially acceptable behaviour among imperfect human beings. Thus, in analysing the progressive or regressive state of the wealth of nations, Smith stresses the interrelations between cultural-political climate, legal institutions and economic development.

A 'civic' society is one where 'decent human beings' (to use one of Geoff

Harcourt's favourite expressions) are not a sparute minority. It is a society in which a code of public morality prevails: so that, for instance, compliance with tax payments is not considered an act of heroism or a demonstration of madness. It is a society in which political freedom strengthens a feeling of participation to the common weal and the readiness to provide collaboration and support to other fellow citizens. These are the preconditions for a well-functioning market economy; when they prevail, the wealth of nations is most likely to be in a progressive state, and this in turn ensures a helpful background for the society's civic development.

It should be stressed, however, that these preconditions are not, once established, automatically self-sustaining. History is full of examples of retrogressions towards barbarity, implying in the long run economic retrogression as well. Thus a vigilant attitude and active intervention, on the side of both citizens and their collective institutions, is continuously necessary. It is a great merit of classical economists such as Smith to have brought this point to the fore. In this tradition, the economist cannot consider her or himself a technician, dedicated to model-building and forgetful about the social (moral and political) foundations in which the model's variables are embedded. The risk, otherwise, is that of neglecting aspects which are in fact essential not only for our understanding of the working of a market economy, but also for the very survival of a free society.

ACKNOWLEDGEMENT

Thanks for comments and suggestions on a previous draft are due to Mario Tonveronachi.

REFERENCES

Harcourt, G. C. (1992) 'Markets, madness and a middle way', *Second Donald Horne Address*, Clayton: Monash University, National Centre for Australian Studies.

Jaffé, W. (1973) 'Léon Walras's role in the "Marginal Revolution" of the 1870s', in R. D. Collison Black, A. W. Coats and C. D W. Goodwin (eds) *The Marginal Revolution in Economics*, Durham, NC: Duke University Press.

Jevons, W. S. (1871 [1970]) *The Theory of Political Economy*, Harmondsworth: Penguin.

Kregel, J. A. (1992) 'Walras's auctioneer and Marshall's well-informed dealers: time, market prices and normal supply prices', *Quaderni di storia dell'economia politica* 10: 531–51.

Macfie, A. L. (1967) *The Individual in Society: Papers on Adam Smith*, London: Allen & Unwin.

Pack, S. J. (1991) *Capitalism as a Moral System: Adam Smith's Critique of the Free Market Economy*, Aldershot: Edward Elgar.

Petty, W. (1963) *Economic Writings*, New York: A. M. Kelley.

Raffaelli, T. (1994) 'Dalla teoria delle passioni al nuovo ordine: mercato e capitalismo in Adam Smith', *Moneta e Credito* 47: 203–31.

Roncaglia, A. (1978) *Sraffa and the Theory of Prices*, New York: Wiley.

—— (1985) *Petty: The Origins of Political Economy*, Armonk: Sharpe.

—— (1989) 'Italian economic growth: a Smithian view', *Quaderni di storia dell'economia politica* 7: 227–34.

—— (1995) 'Introduzione', in A. Smith, *La ricchezza delle nazioni*, Rome: Newton Compton.

Rothschild, E. (1992) 'Adam Smith and conservative economics', *Economic History Review* 45: 74–96.

Schumpeter, J. (1954) *History of Economic Analysis*, London: Allen & Unwin.

Smith, A. (1759 [1976]) *The Theory of Moral Sentiments*, Oxford: Clarendon Press.

—— (1776 [1976]) *An Inquiry into the Nature and Causes of the Wealth of Nations*, Oxford: Clarendon Press.

—— (1978) *Lectures on Jurisprudence*, Oxford: Clarendon Press.

Sraffa, P. (1925) 'Sulle relazioni tra costo e quantità prodotta', *Annali di Economia* 2: 277–328.

Viner, J. (1927) 'Adam Smith and laissez-faire', *Journal of Political Economy* 35: 198–232.

Walras, L. (1880 [1898]) 'La bourse, la spéculation et l'agiotage', in L. Walras, *Études d'économie politique appliquée*, Lausanne: Rouge.

32

HISTORY VERSUS EQUILIBRIUM

John Eatwell

It is customary in volumes of celebration to focus on those themes in the work of an admired colleague which are regarded not simply as representative of a productive career, but also as providing the starting point for positive new lines of development. In this essay I will focus on what has certainly been a major theme in Geoff Harcourt's work, but it is a theme with which I happen to disagree. I hope that I can shed some light on the analytical roots of our disagreement, and if I am successful this might prove to be the starting point for future agreement.

Joan Robinson's famous distinction between 'history' and 'equilibrium' was deployed primarily, but not solely, as a critique of neoclassical economics. The concept of substitution is fundamental to the structure of neoclassical theory, and substitution is meaningless without the ability to 'change proportions', whether proportions of goods consumed, or the proportions in which inputs are used in production. Consider, however, a situation in which two techniques consist of inputs of labour and a large number of produced means of production: 'The two lists of inputs and outputs are made up of items in different proportions and there may be some item in the second list that did not appear in the first' (Robinson 1978b: 134). In other words, two techniques which are 'close' to one another in the ordering of cost minimization as a function of input prices may none the less consist of radically different inputs, one a set of steel machines (for example) and the other a set of brass machines. 'Moving' from one to the other makes no sense. Indeed, it may be physically impossible. Each technique exists, so to speak, on a separate island: 'On each island a particular rate of profit obtains, and each has the stock of machines appropriate to its own rate of profit. There is no way of moving across a switch point from one island to another' (Robinson 1975: 38). Robinson concludes that 'The long wrangle about "measuring capital" has been a great deal of fuss about a secondary question. The real source of trouble is the confusion between comparisons of equilibrium and the history of a process of accumulation' (Robinson 1978b: 135). But this critique is not reserved for neoclassical economists alone:

The specification of a self-reproducing or self-expanding system such as that of Sraffa or von Neumann exists in logical time, not in history. Any point on it entails its past just as completely as it entails its future. To confront it with a question such as 'What would happen if demand changed' is nonsensical.

(Robinson 1978b: 128)

This association of Sraffa's analysis (in *Production of Commodities by Means of Commodities*) with what are characterized as the ahistorical failings of neoclassical theory is rather puzzling. For in the same essay Robinson praises the structure and content of classical theory:

The main preoccupation of the classical economists was with an historical process of accumulation in a capitalist economy and its relation to the distribution of the product of industry between the classes of society.... As soon as the uncertainty of expectations that guide economic behaviour is admitted, equilibrium drops out of the argument and history takes its place. The post-Keynesian theory reaches back to clasp the hands of Ricardo and Marx.

(ibid.: 126)

But what was *Production of Commodities* about, other than the logical vindication of the classical theory of value and distribution? How can a proposition in the hands of Sraffa be decried as 'not in history' and the very same proposition in the hands of Ricardo or Marx be lauded as a key element in the study of 'an historical process of accumulation'?

In fact, the indictment of Sraffa's analysis is but part of Joan Robinson's more general hostility to 'the confusion of comparisons of equilibria with processes'. This hostility was evident as early as her 'Lecture at Oxford by a Cambridge economist', given in 1953 (reprinted in 1978):

Never talk about *getting into* equilibrium, for equilibrium has no meaning unless you are in it already. But think of a system *being* in equilibrium and having been there as far back towards Adam as you find it useful to go so that every *ex ante* expectation about today ever held in the past is being fulfilled today. And the *ex ante* expectation today is that the future will be like the past.

(Robinson 1978a: 144)

Hence, all models of long-run equilibrium – classical, Marxian or neoclassical – are relegated to the status of academic exercises of distinctly dubious relevance. Instead, economic analysis should be located in ' historical time', and needs to include 'the whole story about the behaviour of the economy when it is out of equilibrium, including the effect of disappointed expectations on decisions being taken by its inhabitants' (Robinson 1978b: 130). This position has been reiterated by Geoff Harcourt in his description of the writing of *Some Cambridge Controversies in the Theory of Capital* (1972):

There were two main themes: the critique of the conceptual basis of price as an index of scarcity in the theory of distribution and the methodological critique emanating from Joan Robinson of the error of using differences to analyze changes; this was to become her dominant critique of neoclassical economics. Looking back now (May 1995) I think she went too far in playing down the first theme ('The unimportance of reswitching', 1975) – the conceptual basis of an approach *is* a legitimate target for criticism – *but was spot on with her insistence on the second critique.*

(Harcourt 1995: 242; the latter emphasis added)

In contrast with Geoff Harcourt's view, I believe that virtually all the steps in Joan Robinson's argument are incorrect:

1   the problem she identifies in neoclassical theory, 'the confusion between comparisons of equilibrium and the history of a process of accumulation', in fact derives from the inability to 'measure capital' and is not independent of that inability;
2   the term 'historical time' has no coherent analytically meaning and, far from providing the basis of a more concrete economics, is a source of theoretical nihilism;
3   and, finally, the analysis of long-period positions requires neither that the economy should have been in equilibrium since the beginning of time, nor that the impact of expectations upon the economy must be ignored.

I will deal with these points in turn, working from last to first.

Economic models are necessarily abstractions. To incorporate all the information pertinent to given circumstances would be to draw a map on the scale of one to one. The economist therefore abstracts from the myriad of circumstances those facts and relationships which he or she believes to be the most important and relevant to the matter in hand. These are then assembled into a model, the better to explore their interrelationships.

In fact there are two analytical exercises involved. First, the phenomenon to be explained (say, the price of apples) must be expressed in sufficiently generalized terms for propositions of broad significance to be made about it. Second, a theory is required to explain what determines the magnitude and behaviour of the phenomenon under consideration (e.g. what is the price of apples relative to the price of bread). It is the first of these problems which is addressed by the concept of long-period positions.

LONG-PERIOD POSITIONS

Of course, what exactly is an apple can be very finely calibrated (an Australian golden delicious in Cambridge market on a wet Tuesday afternoon in January). The finer the calibration, the nearer the scale tends to one to one,

388

and the less informative any explanation is likely to be. It was Adam Smith who broke through the detailed description which characterized eighteenth-century political arithmetic (Smith [1776] 1976: ch. 7). His category of 'natural price' and the associated quantity 'effectual demand' were derived from the systematic tendency in a competitive economy for the same commodity to sell at the same price, and, equivalently, for each distinct quality of labour to receive the same wage, each quality of land the same rent, and for there to be a uniform rate of profit on the capital invested in every line. Smith made it clear that if means of production were not fully mobile between alternative uses (the essential condition of competitiveness in classical terms – see Eatwell 1982, 1987), then wages, rents and rates of profit may not tend to uniformity. And he also recognized that any *actual* price or quantity will equal the natural price only by a fluke.

Without Smith's general definition of what was to be explained (the natural prices and associated quantities) the economic *analysis* of value and distribution simply could not begin. Quesnay struggled to develop concepts of price as the starting point for an analysis of the operation of markets. But, lacking any clear notion of the competitive general rate of profit, he was left with a plethora of not entirely consistent definitions (see Vaggi 1987a, 1987b). As John Stuart Mill argued, it is competition which endows economic variables with the necessary regularity and consistency that permits the formulation of the 'principles of broad generality and scientific precision . . . according to which they will be regulated' (Mill 1848 [1909]: II, iv, sect. 1, p. 147). Of course if there are good reasons to suppose that the competitive process is inhibited, by systematic barriers to entry for example, then a description of those systematic barriers should be included in the specification of the economy's 'centre of gravitation'.

So the 'long-period position' is simply the position which the forces of competition will, in any given set of circumstances, tend to establish. And the simplest version of that given set of circumstances (in the absence of any specific additional information which would suggest that the mobility of resources is inhibited) would result in a tendency to a uniform rate of profit and the associated prices. There is nothing in this conception to lead us to suppose that this long-period position is ever attained. There is nothing to make us suppose that it will not itself continuously change as circumstances change (Ricardo expected the normal prices of agricultural goods to rise as accumulation forced production onto land of inferior quality, and the normal prices of industrial goods to fall as accumulation and the increase in 'the extent of the market' stimulated an ever wider division of labour). There is nothing that decrees that, if the information is available, the long-period position should not be in part determined by the process by which it is approached (that is, it might be path-dependent). And there is nothing which requires that the economy should have been in that long-period position 'as far back as Adam'.

Since a uniform rate of profit entails that the structure of means of production be adjusted to the structure of demand, movement toward the 'centre of gravitation' will undoubtedly be affected by the expectations which guide entrepreneurs' investment decisions. Sometimes they will get things hopelessly wrong and market prices will diverge wildly from normal long-period prices. At other times they will get things right and the dispersion of profit rates will be low. The essential assumption made by Adam Smith is that in general the forces of competition (which were, after all, far more limited in 1776 than they are today) will tend to prevail, and that cumulative spirals away from the centre of gravitation will be the exception rather than the rule. The modern corporation is essentially a device for increasing the mobility of resources, and hence minimizing the downside risk of all forms of uncertainty. Competition in the classical sense is thereby enhanced, not diminished (Clifton 1977).

In this respect it should be remembered that the theory of value and distribution is necessarily a general, not a partial, phenomenon. It makes no sense at all to develop a theory of price at the level of the firm, or even the industry. One firm's mark-up is another firm's cost, and in turn a cost for the first firm. The theory of value accordingly requires that all the consequential intersectoral ramifications be taken into account. The long-period position, defined by uniformity of the rate of profit and associated prices, is just the simplest and most general representation of those ramifications. If we cannot construct a coherent theory to explain how the magnitude of that rate of profit is determined, then it is folly to attempt to explain the determination of prices under more complex characterizations of markets.

Adam Smith's natural prices (or prices of production, or long-period normal prices – however they are labelled they are conceptually all the same) are defined independently of the theory which exposes their determinants. Competition simply ensures that there will be a tendency toward normal prices. It does not determine whether the rate of profit is 10 per cent or 25 per cent or whether a loaf of bread is worth 8 apples or only 3. The past 220 years have produced two theories of the determination of normal prices and the associated rate of profit: the classical theory (which we now know works), and the neoclassical theory (which does not).

HISTORICAL TIME

Once we have defined, at a suitable level of generality, what is to be explained, a theory must be constructed to provide the explanation. This involves characterizing economic behaviour in terms of a number of parameters (say, the set of available technologies, or the size and distribution of endowments) and a number of behavioural relationships (say, the utility function, or the propensity to consume). These parameters and relationships are presumably chosen because they are believed to be the dominant factors in the determination of the variable which is to be explained. It is obvious that no theory or model represents an exhaustive inventory of all the factors affecting any given variable, and it is also obvious that all models contain an element of spurious precision. But none the less, if the model is well constructed then it should encompass the dominant determining factors. Accordingly, the solution of the model should be a 'centre of gravitation' in the determination of the phenomena being examined. What this means is that, on average, the factors which have been left out of the model's inventory are indeed of relatively minor importance, and do not tend to produce systematic deviation of the actual state of the world from the model solution.

The two notions of 'centre of gravitation', that of the long-period positions and that of the model, are formally independent of one another. None the less, good economics requires the presence of both. The competitive tendency to establish normal prices implies that any deviation of the rate of profit from uniformity will set up competitive forces which will tend to re-establish that uniformity. The impact of a phenomenon not included in the model which causes the rate of profit to deviate from the determined 10 per cent will be short-lived, and duly overwhelmed by the dominant forces of the model. The first is about deviations from the centre of gravitation. The second is about deviations of the centre of gravitation.

The importance of the presence of both notions may be demonstrated by consideration of the Arrow–Debreu model of intertemporal equilibrium (Debreu 1959; Arrow and Hahn 1971). In this model an equilibrium is defined as the competitive resolution of individual attempts to maximize utility over time, subject to the constraints of endowment and intertemporal production possibilities. In other words, the equilibrium which is to be determined is defined in terms of the model. In contrast with the case of long-run equilibrium, it is not possible to write down a definition of equilibrium prices and quantities other than in terms of the model itself. Any difference in the specification of the model will change the specification of the equilibrium. The notion of the solution of this model as a 'centre of gravitation' makes no sense at all. The deviations from the equilibrium position which are a necessary consequence of the fact that the specification of the model cannot, by the very nature of abstraction, be exhaustive will not be met by a tendency to re-establish the same equilibrium. Instead they will define a new intertemporal path. It is no accident that the expressions 'long-run' and 'short-run' are nowhere to be found in the world of intertemporal equilibrium. In that setting they have no meaning. The only sense that can made be of the model is that the authors suppose it to be a complete statement of the world or, more modestly, just the solution of a set of equations which may be of interest in its own right. The idea that it is an abstraction from a more complex economy, that it is a centre of gravitation, is notable by its absence. This is why the analysis of intertemporal equilibrium has produced a large catalogue of models, no one of them more general than the rest.

Given that a map on the scale of one to one would be useless, even if it could be constructed, any and all analyses of economic phenomena are constructed in terms of some sort of model. The solution of the model may be a rate of profit, or a rate of growth, or a sequence of outputs and prices modelled within a dynamic framework. Whatever the model might be, if it is any good it will necessarily be a centre of gravitation, for inevitably some of the factors which affect outputs and prices from time to time will have been left out of the model, considered to be relatively unimportant. This is equally true of models which are (misleadingly) defined as 'disequilibrium dynamics'. The element of disequilibrium arises from the fact that the specification of the model includes dynamic interactions between, say, prices and quantities in one time period, and changes in prices and quantities in the next time period. But even in this case, if the model is not presumed to be a exhaustive description of the world then its solution (the path of prices and outputs through time) should be a centre of gravitation.

How then can 'equilibrium drop out of the picture and history take its place'? If we are to be able to talk about any phenomenon whatsoever, abstractions will need to be made, and solutions worked out which, if the model is indeed well constructed, will be centres of gravitation. And the only way to assess the impact of changes in any parameters of the model will be to compare alternative solutions. In this particular context, 'history is bunk'.

The mistake arises from identifying the absence of 'historical' data with the characterization of normal prices. It is not the specification of the long run *per se* which is ahistorical. It is the model used to explain the determination of the equilibrium which may be ahistorical. A distinguishing characteristic of the classical theory of value and distribution is that the data of that model – the size and composition of output, the technology, and the real wage – form a core around which other explanations must be assembled (Garegnani 1987). The theory of value and distribution does not, for example, embody an explanation of the determination of composition of output. Moreover, even in the core, an important element, the real wage, is to be determined by what Marx called 'moral and historical circumstances'. Even when Sraffa dropped the real wage, and instead expressed the wage simply as a price, he turned for the determination of the rate of profit to the monetary policy of the state, another 'historical phenomenon'. So even the theoretical core of the analysis of value and distribution requires an input from the concrete institutional circumstances of the day; from, if you like, history.

The same is true of Keynes's theory of effective demand. Not only is it impossible to think about Keynes's analysis other than in the institutional context of a modern capitalist economy with a fully developed monetary system, but also the theory of output, once stripped of Keynes's inadequate theory of investment, requires 'historical' information. The determination of investment by means of an elastic schedule of the marginal efficiency of capital is logically flawed. Keynes's own explanation of why aggregate investment should be an inverse function of the interest rate is unsatisfactory, and his appeal to the authority of Irving Fisher's rate of return over cost aligns his argument with the now well-known errors of neoclassical capital theory (see Garegnani 1978). Stripped of the marginal efficiency of capital schedule, the 'core' of Keynes's principle of effective demand is the multiplier and an 'exogenously' determined level of investment. History, in the form of the concrete circumstances defining the process of accumulation, and hence the level of investment at any particular time, intrudes into the theoretical core of the model.

So a necessary location within the institutions of a capitalist economy, and the intrusion of those institutions and their concrete consequences into the theoretical core of the model, are common attributes of classical and Keynesian analyses.

The neoclassical theory of value and distribution is very different. The data of the theory, preferences, the technology and the size and distribution of the endowment exhaust the domain of economics. They are the axiomatic data which define the starting point of economic analysis. There are, of course, some models of the formation of preferences, for example, but these are simply formal extensions of the same data set. No further data are required for the determination of prices, outputs and the technique in use. Moreover, although the theory is of a market economy, it is apparently 'universal'. Institutions are imperfections, other than in the case in which the formation of institutions is reduced to a problem of utility-maximizing choices.

The neoclassical theory of value and distribution and the neoclassical theory of output and employment are one and the same theory. That theory defines an equilibrium in which the prices determined are those which clear markets, including the market for labour. Theories of unemployment require that there be market failure. Some imperfection, such as sticky wages or sticky prices, or the impact of uncertainty upon decision-making and behaviour, is required to prevent prices and outputs gravitating toward market clearing levels (Eatwell and Milgate 1983). In this context, uncertainty, if it disrupts the normal operations of market, can be the basis of a theory of unemployment. Uncertainty is imposed upon an otherwise perfectly functioning neoclassical model.

In Keynes's analysis, in which investment is an exogenous variable, factors such as expectations, which might affect the level of investment, are an important element in the determination of the level of output and employment. Expectations and uncertainty, and the manner in which the institutions of modern capitalism attempt to minimize the negative impact of uncertainty, are integral parts of the normal operation of the Keynesian model – not, as in the neoclassical model, imperfections imposed on an otherwise harmonious world.

JOHN EATWELL

COMPARISONS AND PROCESSES

The concept of normal long-period positions requires that the composition of output be adapted to the scale and composition of demand. This is the normal reaction of profit-maximizing entrepreneurs to changes in the composition of demand. To suppose, as in the extreme example outlined above, that adaptation is impossible because an economy is only capable of producing steel machines whereas brass machines are required, makes nonsense of the very definition of 'an economy'. One of the defining characteristics of an economy is the range of goods which it can possibly produce, and that includes the range of capital goods.

In neoclassical models of non-capitalistic production and exchange (apples and bread produced by means of land and labour), the proposition that production is adapted to demand poses no theoretical difficulty. If the composition of demand changes in favour of apples, then land and labour are transferred from bread to apple production. After a period in which the transfer is incomplete and prices deviate from normal long-period prices, a new normal equilibrium will be attained. The same argument, as far as the adaption of capacity to demand is concerned, holds for a model of capitalistic production in which apples and bread are (improbably) produced by labour and machines. A change in the structure of demand will require labour to be shifted from one activity to the other, and the composition of the stock of machines to be altered. The process of change may be quite complicated, but, in the absence of other information, there is no reason to suppose the economy will not tend to gravitate to a new position in which production, and the stock of capital goods, is adjusted to demand.

The essential difference between these two models is that in the land and labour case the endowment of the two factors may be specified as given magnitudes, and the change in the structure of demand analysed as a reallocation of those given factor stocks. In the capital and labour case there is no sense (other than in a one-commodity world) in which the stock of capital can be taken as given quantity which is reallocated. In the land and labour example, the change in the composition of demand will (presuming that apples and bread are produced by different proportionate inputs of land and labour) result in changes in relative factor prices. That change will result in the substitution of one input for the other. In the model which includes capital goods the idea of the substitution of capital for labour has no meaning. That is the core problem. The fact that if techniques are arrayed along a wage–profit frontier, 'adjacent techniques' cannot be characterized as portraying the substitution of capital, for labour is independent of the physical specification of the adjacent techniques. Even if it were the case that adjacent techniques comprised the same produced means of production and that the transformation of one set of capital goods into the other could proceed relatively smoothly, there would still be no sense in the idea of capital–labour substitution. Joan Robinson's problem of comparisons and processes derives from the capital theoretic difficulties of neoclassical theory. It is not, as she supposed, an independent critique.

In this respect the distinction which Robinson draws between Marshallian and Walrasian models is not very helpful. In all neoclassical models, the endowment of factor services must be defined in a manner which is appropriate for cost-minimizing choice of technique. It is this choice of technique which is, of course, the vital link between demands for produced commodities and the determination of excess demand for factors. If, on the one hand, cost is to be minimized with respect to a set of factor prices which includes the rate of profit, then the only consistent specification of the endowment is as a quantity of value. This is clearly inadmissible. If, on the other hand, the endowment is expressed as a list of factor services, as is done by Walras, then there is no reason why market-clearing rentals should conform with the condition that the prices of producible means of production should equal their costs of reproduction; that is, that there will be no such thing as the rate of profit and the clearing equilibrium will not be a long-period for the economy. (On Walras, see Garegnani 1960; Eatwell 1987.) To both Marshall and Walras the fundamental problem is the specification of the endowment in a manner which is compatible with the determination of normal, long-period prices and the associated rate of profit.

SUMMING-UP

Trying to guess why people adopt particular intellectual positions is a fairly fruitless exercise. Why did Ricardo, for example, insist on analysing the problem of the relationship between labour values and prices in terms of the fact that prices change when distribution changes, whereas labour values do not? This led him to embark on the totally futile search for a invariable standard of value. If only he had started from the proposition that relative labour values and relative prices are different, he would have avoided that blind alley.

Exactly why Robinson should have developed her 'comparisons versus processes' approach to the critique of neoclassical theory is equally mysterious. The argument first appears at the same time as she launched her critique of the production function (Robinson 1953), which of course predated the full understanding of capital theoretic problems following the publication of Sraffa's *Production of Commodities* in 1960. But then her attachment to critique became more pronounced, as was evident in the two articles 'History versus equilibrium' and 'The unimportance of reswitching' (Robinson 1975, 1978b). Her references to Keynes's *QJE* article of 1937 suggest that she may have been following Keynes's argument that ubiquitous uncertainty renders precise economic calculation impossible. This is a peculiarly nihilistic position. For if Keynes were right, then even his own principle of effective demand would be worthless. If uncertainty makes systematic decision-making impossible, including the decision as to what proportion of income to consume, then the multiplier is a notion as empty of meaning as any abstract price theory. The *QJE* article was, I believe, Keynes's reaction to the tendency toward full employment which he had inadvertently imported into his general theory (Keynes 1936), via the marginal efficiency of capital schedule. Uncertainty was a device to prevent the price mechanism working. But once the deficiencies of his analysis of investment are recognized there is no need to follow Keynes down this defensive path.

Of course, my puzzlement stems from the fact that I believe Robinson's position to be fundamentally flawed. Others, including Geoff Harcourt, clearly think otherwise. I hope that this article has at very least helped clarify exactly what the logical foundations of this difference of opinion might be.

REFERENCES

Arrow, K. J. and Hahn, F. (1971) *General Competitive Analysis*, San Francisco: Holden-Day.

Clifton, J. A. (1977) 'Competition and the evolution of the capitalist mode of production', *Cambridge Journal of Economics* 1(2): 137–51.

Debreu, G. (1959) *Theory of Value: An Axiomatic Analysis of Economic Equilibrium*, New York: Wiley.

Eatwell, J. (1982) 'Competition', in I. Bradley and M. Howard (eds) *Classical and Marxian Political Economics*, London: Macmillan.

—— (1987) 'Walras's theory of capital', in J. Eatwell, M. Milgate and P. Newman (eds) *The New Palgrave: A Dictionary of Economics*, 4 vols, London: Macmillan.

Eatwell, J. and Milgate, M. (eds) (1983) *Keynes's Economics and the Theory of Value and Distribution*, London: Duckworth.

Garegnani, P. (1960) *Il capitale nelle teorie della distribuzione*, Milan: Giuffre.

—— (1978) 'Notes on consumption, investment, and effective demand, I', *Cambridge Journal of Economics* 2(4): 335–53.

—— (1987) 'Surplus approach to value and distribution', in J. Eatwell, M. Milgate and P. Newman (eds) *The New Palgrave: A Dictionary of Economics*, 4 vols, London: Macmillan.

Harcourt, G. C. (1972) *Some Cambridge Controversies in the Theory of Capital*, Cambridge: Cambridge University Press.

—— (1995) 'Recollections and reflections of an Australian patriot and a Cambridge economist', *Banco Nazionale del Lavoro Quarterly Review* 48(194): 225–54.

Keynes, J. M. (1936) *The General Theory of Employment, Interest and Money*, London: Macmillan.

—— (1937) 'The general theory of employment', *Quarterly Journal of Economics*, 51.

Mill, J. S. (1848 [1909]) *Principles of Political Economy; With Some of their Applications to Social Philosophy*, 6th edn, London: Longmans, Green & Co.

Robinson, J. V. (1953) 'The production function and the theory of capital', *Review of Economic Studies* 21: 81–106.

—— (1975) 'The unimportance of reswitching', *Quarterly Journal of Economics* 89: 32–9.

—— (1978a) 'A lecture delivered at Oxford by a Cambridge economist', in J. V. Robinson, *Contributions to Modern Economics*, Oxford: Blackwell.

—— (1978b) 'History versus equilibrium', in J. V. Robinson, *Contributions to Modern Economics*, Oxford: Blackwell.

Smith, A. (1776 [1976]) *An Inquiry into the Nature and Causes of the Wealth of Nations*, Oxford: Oxford University Press.

Sraffa, P. (1960) *Production of Commodities by Means of Commodities: Prelude to a Critique of Economic Theory*, Cambridge: Cambridge University Press.

Vaggi, G. (1987a) *The Economics of François Quesnay*, London: Macmillan.

—— (1987b) 'Natural price', in J. Eatwell, M. Milgate and P. Newman (eds) *The New Palgrave: A Dictionary of Economics*, 4 vols, London: Macmillan.

33

SHORT-PERIOD ECONOMICS IN RETROSPECT

Maria Cristina Marcuzzo

The distinction between short period and long period is a time-honoured tradition in economics. However, different justifications have been given to the common-sense perception that certain effects persist for longer than others and, accordingly, different authors have ascribed different weight to short-period analysis. For instance, in classical political economy its importance was underrated, in Keynesian economics it was stressed; later, in the neoclassical synthesis, its role increasingly shrank and eventually faded with the advent of the New Classical and neo-Keynesian macroeconomics.

The relevance of short-period analysis is a dividing issue also between neo-Ricardians and post-Keynesians. The former argue that only long-period positions can be made the object of an economic theory, since they are the outcome of permanent as opposed to temporary forces. They argue that while in Ricardo (and in classical political economy) the theory allows the determination of natural or long-period values for prices, profits and wages, in Marshall and, in general, in marginalist authors, long-period values cannot be consistently determined because of an inherent flaw in the theory of distribution based on supply and demand of factors of production. According to this interpretation, the difficulty of determining the normal rate of profit forced marginalist authors to abandon the *method* based on long-period positions. Short-period analysis is thus seen as a device for getting rid of the assumption of the uniform rate of profit (Garegnani 1976).

On the other hand, post-Keynesians stress the role of uncertainty in a monetary economy in preventing the economy from ever getting into long-run equilibrium; hence the irrelevance and possibly the misleading nature of a method based on long-period positions (Asimakopulos 1990). Thus, although post-Keynesians provide a reason why short-period analysis should be preferred to long-period analysis, they do not offer an explanation of how this change in approach came about.

In this chapter a rationale is provided of the origin of short-period economics: I argue that it is to be found in the change which occurred from Ricardo – through Marshall and Kahn – to Keynes in what it is believed can or cannot be made the object of an economic theory.

RICARDO

In Ricardo's theory a distinction is made between 'permanent' and 'temporary' causes of economic events. A permanent cause is interpreted as a sufficient condition for something to happen: its effects are certain regardless of the time interval necessary for their implementation. Permanent causes are sufficient but not necessary conditions, since the same effects could be brought about by other causes that are said to be 'temporary'; thus, they are neither necessary nor sufficient. They are not sufficient because their effects are not certain, and may well be offset by the working of more permanent forces, and they are not necessary because a given effect cannot be unambiguously imputed to them.

When permanent forces prevail, the value assumed by certain variables, such as prices, rate of profit, wages and the quantity of money, is called by Ricardo their 'natural' value. For instance, a change in the conditions of production of a given commodity is a 'permanent' cause of a change in its price, which means that the price will certainly change, although not every variation in commodity prices can be imputed to variations in the conditions of production. By contrast, a change in demand is a 'temporary' cause of a change in prices, not because its effect does not last long enough, but because it is not certain.

Similarly, when discussing natural wages, Ricardo granted that money wages can be pushed downwards when the supply of labour grows faster than demand, but, he said, if there is at the same time a change in the conditions of production of wage goods, making them more difficult to produce, their money prices rise and the overall effect is an increase, not a decrease, in money wages. The former can be taken as an example of a temporary cause whereas the latter – an increase in the price of wage goods – is a permanent cause of wage increases (Rosselli 1985).

Ricardo's definition of the natural quantity of money is given by analogy with the definition of natural wages and natural prices. The quantity of money is at its 'natural' level whenever the market price of the standard shows no deviation from the official price, that is to say whenever the purchasing power over the standard is kept constant. If gold is the standard, the quantity of money is kept at its natural level by a market mechanism; an increase in the quantity of money immediately lowers the exchanges, making the purchasing power of the standard in terms of the domestic currency higher abroad than at home, thereby making the export of gold profitable. The ensuing reduction in the quantity of gold brings the quantity of money back to its natural level. Thus, changes in the quantity of money involving changes in its purchasing power in terms of gold at home and abroad are 'temporary', because market mechanisms will bring the quantity of money to its natural level, thereby restoring the equality of the purchasing power of money at home and abroad. Changes in the quantity of money deriving from a change in the conditions of production of gold, on the other hand, are permanent, because they cause a change in its natural level.

The question in Ricardo's theory is, then, not one of measuring 'for how long' or 'to what extent' an observed consequence follows from a given cause, before deciding whether it is a short- or a long-run effect. The question is one of deciding which causes can be made the object of a theory, namely whether from a given cause consequences can be derived which are certain.

To Ricardo, the distinction between short and long run pertains to the question of which *causes* are eligible to become part of a theory, and not to the question of which *effects* endure or fail to endure. Ricardo takes permanency as a property independent of the length of time during which causes exercise their influence because the definition of a permanent cause is given not by the length of the duration of its effects but by its place in the structure of the theory.[1]

MARSHALL

Marshall presented his theory as an 'improvement' over Ricardo's theory and not as a change of approach.[2] However, the continuity is far from obvious. First, there is a change in terminology, in itself revealing of a change in meaning, from the use of 'natural' to that of 'normal' values. Second, for the classical authors, natural value, as opposed to what they term 'market value', is interpreted as the 'average value' which would prevail in a stationary state (Marshall 1964: 289). Marshall's criticism is that it is a 'fact that the general conditions of life are not stationary', the reason being that 'we cannot foresee the future perfectly. The unexpected may happen; and the existing tendencies may be modified before they have had time to accomplish what appears now to be their full and complete work' (ibid.). Therefore something different from the method employed by the classical authors must be envisaged. It follows that 'it is to the persistence of the influences considered, and the time allowed for them to work out their effect' that we should refer 'when contrasting Market and Normal price' (ibid.). Marshall asserts that 'the term normal implies the predominance of certain tendencies which appear likely to be more or less steadfast and persistent in their action over those which are relatively exceptional and intermittent' (ibid.: 28).

The contrast with Ricardo's approach is clear. It is apparent that Marshall's distinction aims to qualify causes according to the persistence of their effects in time, whereas Ricardo's aims to single out causes which can provide a sufficient explanation of given effects. For Marshall it is the *persistence in time* of a known cause which is the criterion for attributing the term 'normal' to the value assumed by a given variable, but for Ricardo it is the *certainty of their effects* that leads to identification of those causes which are responsible for 'natural' values.

Since the purpose of economic analysis is, according to Marshall, to determine the 'immediate and ultimate effects of various groups of causes' (Whitaker 1975: 97) through an accurate study of the element of time, the distinction between short and long period is derived not from the nature of the forces determining observed effects, but from the length of time necessary for the *same* forces to work their effects. Since the forces which govern the economic system are supply and demand, the crucial factor becomes 'the period of time which is allowed to the forces of demand and supply to bring themselves into equilibrium with one another' (Marshall 1964: 274).

Producers adapt the level of production to expected demand if, and only if, the expected supply price is sufficient to make it worthwhile to produce that quantity. The price 'the expectation of which is sufficient and only just sufficient' (Marshall 1964: 310) to produce that quantity is the 'normal' supply price. Given his definition, not surprisingly Marshall applies the term 'normal supply price' *equally* to the short and to the long period (ibid.), the only difference being that in the long period 'supply means what can be produced by plant, which itself can be remuneratively produced and applied within the given time' (ibid.: 315).

In conclusion, the distinction between short and long period is based on the *nature of the decisions* involved, which reflects what individuals take as given and what they expect in different periods of time. He wrote:

> For short periods people take the stocks of appliances of production as practically fixed; and they are governed by their expectations of demand in considering how actively they shall set themselves to work those appliances. In long periods they set themselves to adjust the flow of these appliances to their expectations of demand for the goods which the appliances help to produce.
>
> (Marshall 1964: 310–11)[3]

It is the nature of the decisions involved, characterized by the time horizon to which they apply, that sets the boundary between the long and the short period. Accordingly, economic theory can take as constant those factors over which decision can be postponed and take them as variables only when describing situations in which they are a matter of decision by economic agents.

KAHN

The economist who perhaps more than any other was concerned with giving a precise definition of short period was Richard Kahn, who chose it as the title of his Fellowship dissertation, 'The economics of the short period'.[4] Although the dissertation turned out to be more concerned with imperfect competition, we find in it the building blocks of what a few years later Robertson, was to refer to, in a letter to Keynes, as 'your and Kahn's s[hort] p[eriod] method' (Keynes 1979: 17).

From Marshall's definition of short period – as the situation in which machinery and the organization of production are assumed to be constant – Kahn drew a further implication. The possibility of considering them as constant from the point of view of the short period arises from the fact that in both cases the decision to alter them is the same and depends on whether demand conditions are or are not considered 'normal'. Accordingly, depending whether changes in demand are believed by entrepreneurs to be transitory or permanent, as compared with the level considered as normal, the decisions to modify the plant or the organization will or will not be taken.

Although short period cannot be 'shorter' than the length of the productive process or longer than the time necessary to modify productive capacity, the time necessary to modify productive capacity depends not only on technological factors, but also on prevailing conditions – depression or boom – which mould expectations regarding the return to 'normal' conditions of demand. The point of Kahn's dissertation is to prove that an equilibrium at less than full capacity may arise, in the event that the fall in demand is *not* expected to last, when the market is imperfect (Marcuzzo 1994).

In the following two or three years – when the 'multiplier' was also developed – Kahn presented his thoughts on short-period economics in a book bearing the same title as the dissertation, which, however, remained unfinished and is still unpublished.[5]

The nature of the short period is seen not as a conceptual experiment but as a question of fact, namely that the life of fixed capital is considerably greater than the period of production (Kahn 1932: ch. 2, p. 2; 1989: xiii).

If there were a complete range of continuous variation in the lives of the different means of production, the notion of short period could not be employed. But, in reality, as far as the range of variation is concerned:

> Between raw materials, on the one hand, and productive plant, on the other hand, there is a desolate and sparsely populated area. As a general rule, the life of physical capital is illustrated either by the mayfly or by the elephant.
>
> (Kahn 1989: xiii)

One aspect of the rationale for an 'economics of the short period' is, therefore, rooted in the nature of the production process, which gives meaning to a time interval where productive capacity is given and only its utilization varies. In fact, there are changes that occur rapidly (such as output and employment) and others that occur only slowly (such as alterations in fixed plant) (Kahn 1932: ch. 2, p. 6).

The other aspect characterizing the short period is rooted in expectations of changes in demand relative to the level perceived as 'normal'. The level of demand which individuals take as 'normal' is the benchmark against which observed variations are evaluated and expectations about its future course are formed.

The two aspects are combined to explain why in the short period productive capacity is not altered. This is so because a change in the conditions of demand is not perceived as permanent. In fact, the 'ideal' short period is defined as a situation where 'any change that occurs is not expected to be permanent' (Kahn 1932: ch. 2, p. 10). In a depression, however, short-period equilibrium implies expectations that demand will return to its normal level, since suspending production or reducing the productive capacity to zero would require the belief that demand continued to be permanently low. In a boom, by contrast, short-period equilibrium implies that expectations are such that an increase in production is preferred to building up capacity until the increase in demand is perceived as 'permanent'.

Since what matters are expectations about the normal values of certain variables, in particular the level of demand, it follows that the short period need *not* be a 'short' time interval or only a temporary state before the long-period forces work out their effects. It is rather a position which is maintained as long as the set of decisions, depending upon the expected values of selected variables, does not change (Dardi 1996).

When the demand for an industry's output alters, according to Kahn, there are changes where responsiveness is immediate and changes where responsiveness is slow, but there is no continuous range of variation between 'responsiveness' and 'irresponsiveness'. Changes that occur rapidly (output and employment) 'do not very much depend on what has occurred in the past or what is expected to occur in the future' (Kahn 1932: ch. 2, p. 12). They are reversible changes as opposed to changes 'which by definition have not time to occur in the short period [and which] depend on what has occurred in the past and what is expected to occur in the future' (ibid.).

In conclusion, according to Kahn, we have causes which have different effects according to whether they are *perceived* by economic agents as permanent or persistent on the basis of what is believed to be the normal value of a given variable. However, if what matters is the divergence between the expected and the 'normal' values of selected variables, the crucial question becomes whether one still needs a theory to explain how these normal values are determined or whether we can take them as being characterized simply by their repetitiveness.

KEYNES

Keynes further developed the short-period approach with the more general purpose of developing economic theory in order to explain decisions taken under different conditions of knowledge. Different conditions of knowledge reveal themselves in what individuals take as 'normal' in any given situation.

In a departure from Ricardo, economic theory is asked to capture the effects of decisions taken in an 'uncertain' environment and provide an explanation not of 'permanent causes', but of 'motives, expectations, psychological uncertainties' (Keynes 1973a: 300). Thus, whereas for Ricardo the predictive power of the theory is enhanced by severely limiting its domain, in Keynes – since 'the material to which it [economics] is applied is, in too many respects, not homogeneous through time' (ibid.: 296) – it is the search for permanent causes which is severely limited. In fact, according to Keynes:

The object of a model is to segregate the semi-permanent or relatively constant factors from those which are transitory or fluctuating so as to develop a logical way of thinking about *the latter*, and of understanding the time sequences to which they give rise in particular cases.
(Keynes 1973a: 296–7; my emphasis)

In a famous letter he then added:

One has to be constantly on guard against treating the material as constant and homogeneous. It is as though the fall of the apple to the ground depended on the apple's motives, on whether it is worth while falling to the ground, and whether the ground wanted the apple to fall, and on mistaken calculations on the part of the apple as to how far it was from the centre of the earth.

(ibid.: 300)

Whereas for Ricardo the aim of scientific enquiry is the search for permanent causes from which general laws can be derived,[6] the object of economic theory for Keynes is to develop a logical way of thinking about factors which are 'transitory and fluctuating', because they are the material to which economics must be applied.

The role assigned to expectations in *The General Theory* is to explain the possibility of an equilibrium at less than full employment. This equilibrium is not described as a situation characterized by 'wrong' expectations since 'the theory of effective demand is substantially the same if we assume that short-period expectations are always fulfilled' (Keynes 1973a: 181). Thus, the short period is not a situation where expectations are not fulfilled, but a situation in which expectations generate 'a state of things' (Dardi 1994) which conforms to it.

It follows that Keynes's approach to the distinction between short period and long period is radically different from the line taken later in macroeconomics by both monetarist and New Classical economists.

Friedman explains short-run fluctuations in output and employment as being due to 'wrong' expectations about the true level of inflation, arising from asymmetric information on the part of workers. This led to the well-known criticism by Lucas – the impossibility of sustained error – and therefore to the need to adopt a 'rational' mechanism of expectation formation. This criticism, however, did not lead to a change in the justification for the distinction between short- and long-run effects. Abandoning the argument based on wrong expectations in favour of unanticipated or noncredible economic policy simply meant shifting the burden of the informational asymmetry from the workers, *vis-à-vis* the entrepreneurs, to the public, in general, *vis-à-vis* the policymakers. The overall implication remains the same: short period means temporary effects and long period means permanent effects.

CHANGE IN METHOD

In order to illustrate the switch in the distinction between short and long period, it may be useful to compare the change in approach to monetary theory between Ricardo and Keynes, brought about by a change in method.

It is common opinion that Ricardo's theory represents the position according to which money is neutral; that is, variations in the nominal quantity of money have an effect on nominal variables, but only in the short period on real variables. Thus Ricardo is seen as the champion of the quantity theory of money and of long-period analysis.

If the quantity theory is interpreted as the proposition that a necessary and sufficient condition for a change in money price is a proportional increase in the money supply, it is certainly true that Ricardo never thought that any variations in prices necessarily implied a variation in the quantity of money. In other words, whereas the quantity of money always affects prices, variation in the quantity of money is not a necessary condition for a variation in prices. Price increases may just as well be caused by a decrease in the value of the standard, a rise in wages or tax increases. In fact, Ricardo advocated a policy of reduction in the quantity of money only in case of depreciation measured in terms of gold, and never in the case of an increase in prices, as we would expect if he held the strict quantity theory.

But is the change in the quantity of money a sufficient condition for a proportional change in money prices? The only proportionality factor to be found in Ricardo lies between the quantity of money and the price of gold, since any increase in the quantity of money above the natural level brings about an exactly equal decrease in its purchasing power in terms of gold.

As a consequence, but only as a consequence of this proportionality, if the relative values of commodities in term of gold are assumed to remain constant, then the monetary prices of commodities vary in proportion with the quantity of money. But if the relative values of commodities vary, for instance because there is a change in the conditions of production, then the proportionality between variations in prices and variations in the quantity of money disappears.

Thus, the non-neutrality of money in the short period conceived by Ricardo cannot be interpreted as a temporary effect, namely as something which is not destined to last. Rather, it should be interpreted as an uncertain effect because, in the absence of a theory to deny the validity of Say's identity, the level of output is given. Alternatively, the non-neutrality of money in the short period

405

should be interpreted as an effect which is offset by others deriving from a permanent cause. This is why temporary causes cannot be part of the theory: not because their effects are not recognized as part of reality, but because their effects are uncertain and volatile and can be offset by more certain and permanent ones (Marcuzzo and Rosselli 1994).

Keynes's approach is radically different. The quantity theory of money is first criticized in the *Treatise on Money* for being 'ill-adapted' for the purpose of exhibiting 'the causal process by which the price level is determined, and the method of transition from one position to another' (Keynes 1971: 120). The content of the theory is definitively rejected with the writing of *The General Theory*, where it is finally substituted by the liquidity preference theory (Kahn 1984); there the 'normal' interest rate is presented as exhibiting a 'conventional' nature, meaning that it is governed by the prevailing views as to what its particular value is expected to be.[7]

The liquidity preference, the propensity to consume, the marginal efficiency of investment, the wage unit and the quantity of money are presented by Keynes as the 'ultimate independent variables' of his theory. He denies, however, that the distinction could ever be general; on the contrary, the division is said to be quite arbitrary from any *absolute* standpoint (Keynes 1973b: 247).

Keynes's point is that there are no grounds for ascribing necessity and generality to the distinction between causes, because this distinction is contingent on particular, ever-changing circumstances. He wrote:

> The division must be made entirely on the basis of experience, so as to correspond on the one hand to the factors in which the changes seem to be so slow or so little relevant as to have only a small and comparatively negligible short-term influence on our *quesitum*; and on the other hand to those factors to which *the changes are found in practice* to exercise a dominant influence on our *quesitum*.
>
> (Keynes 1973b: 247; my emphasis)[8]

The reason why in economics 'we cannot hope to make completely accurate generalizations' (ibid.) is because the economic system is not ruled by 'natural forces' that the economist can discover and order in a neat pattern of causes and effects. The task of economics is rather to 'select those variables which can be deliberately controlled and managed by central authority in the kind of system in which we actually live' (ibid.).

The General Theory explains why the level of employment oscillates around 'an intermediate position' below full employment and above the minimum subsistence employment (Keynes 1973b: 254). However, Keynes adds:

> we must not conclude that the mean position [of employment] thus determined by 'natural' tendencies, namely, by those tendencies which

406

are likely to persist, failing measure expressly designated to correct them, is therefore established by laws of necessity. The unimpeded rule of the above conditions is a fact of observation concerning the world as it is or has been, and *not a necessary principle* which cannot be changed.

(Keynes 1973b: 254; my emphasis)

My conclusion is that the change in method from Ricardo initiated by Marshall[9] (normal values as average occurrences rather sufficient causes), continued by Kahn (values *expected* or *believed* to be normal) and pushed further by Keynes (normal as conventional) meant giving pre-eminence to short-period economics, with far-reaching consequences for economic theory and economic policy. This may explain why neo-Ricardians and post-Keynesians are still divided on this issue.

ACKNOWLEDGEMENTS

This chapter was presented as a paper at the European Conference on the History of Economics, Rotterdam 1995; at the Malvern Political Economy Conference, 1995 and at a seminar held at the University of Roma III in 1995. I wish to thank the participants for comments and suggestions. I also thank David Papineau, literary executor of R. F. Kahn, for permission to quote from Kahn's unpublished, unfinished book 'The economics of the short period'.

NOTES

1   The sections on Ricardo draw on work I did jointly with A. Rosselli (see Marcuzzo and Rosselli 1994).
2   '[T]he foundations of the theory [of value] as they were left by Ricardo remain intact; ... much has been added to them, ... must has been built upon them, but ... little has been taken from them' (Marshall 1964: 417).
3   Marshall provides a rough measure of the length of the periods: short period is measured as 'a few months or a year', and long period is referred to as 'several years' (Marshall 1964: 314–15).
4   The dissertation was written between October 1928 and December 1929. It was first published in Italian in 1983 and in English only in 1989. Kahn was elected a Fellow of King's College, Cambridge, in March 1930.
5   Of the eleven planned chapters, on the evidence of the contents list, chapters 1, 3 and 4 remained unwritten, and chapter 7 was left unfinished. The extant copy, which was found among Kahn's papers in King's College archives, can be dated to the last quarter of 1932 (Marcuzzo 1996).
6   In a letter to Malthus of 4 May 1820, Ricardo wrote, 'My object was to elucidate principles, and to do this I imagined strong cases, that I might show the operation of those principles' (Ricardo 1955: 184).
7   The switch in meaning – 'normal' interpreted as 'conventional' – has been interpreted as an instance of Keynes's previous rejection of the 'principle of the uniformity of nature' (Carabelli 1991) presented in the *Treatise on Probability*.

8 The *quesitum* is 'what determines in any time the national income of a given economic system and (which is almost the same thing) the amount of its employment' (Keynes 1973b: 247).
9 The point that Marshall is the true initiator of the change in method is stressed also by De Carvalho (1990).

REFERENCES

Asimakopulos, A. (1990) 'Keynes and Sraffa: visions and perspectives', in K. Bharadway and B. Schefold (eds) *Essays on Piero Sraffa*, London: Routledge.

Carabelli, A. (1991) 'The methodology of the critique of the classical theory: Keynes on organic interdependence', in B. W. Bateman and J. B. Davis (eds) *Keynes and Philosophy*, Aldershot: Edward Elgar.

Dardi, M. (1994) 'Kahn's theory of liquidity preference and monetary policy', *Cambridge Journal of Economics* 18: 91–106.

Dardi, M. (1996) 'Imperfect competition and short-period economics', in M. C. Marcuzzo, L. L. Pasinetti and A. Roncaglia (eds) *The Economics of Joan Robinson*, London: Routledge.

De Carvalho, F. J. C. (1990) 'Keynes and the long period', *Cambridge Journal of Economics* 14: 277–90.

Garegnani, P. A. (1976) 'On a change in the notion of equilibrium in recent work on value and distribution', in M. Brown, K. Sato and P. Zarembka (eds) *Essays in Modern Capital Theory*, Amsterdam: North-Holland.

Kahn, R. F. (1932) '*The economics of the short period*', unpublished manuscript.

—— (1983) *L'economia del breve periodo*, Turin: Boringhieri.

—— (1984) *The Making of Keynes's General Theory*, Cambridge: Cambridge University Press.

—— (1989) *The Economics of the Short Period*, London: Macmillan.

Keynes, J. M. (1971) *A Treatise on Money*, in *The Collected Writings of John Maynard Keynes*, vol. V, ed. D. Moggridge, London: Macmillan for the Royal Economic Society.

—— (1973a) 'The general theory and after: defence and development', in *The Collected Writings of John Maynard Keynes*, vol. XIV, ed. D. Moggridge, London: Macmillan.

—— (1973b) *The General Theory of Employment, Interest, and Money*, in *The Collected Writings of John Maynard Keynes*, vol. VII, ed. D. Moggridge, London: Macmillan.

—— (1979) 'The general theory and after: a supplement', in *The Collected Writings of John Maynard Keynes*, vol. XXIX, ed. D. Moggridge, London: Macmillan.

Marcuzzo, M. C. (1994) 'R. F. Kahn and imperfect competition', *Cambridge Journal of Economics*, 18: 25–40.

—— (1996) 'Joan Robinson and Richard Kahn: the origin of short period analysis', in M. C. Marcuzzo, L. L. Pasinetti and A. Roncaglia (eds) *The Economics of Joan Robinson*, London: Routledge.

Marcuzzo, M. C. and Rosselli, A. (1994) 'Ricardo's theory of money matters', *Revue Économique* 45: 1251–67.

Marshall, A. (1964) *Principles of Economics*, 8th edn, London: Macmillan.

Ricardo, D. (1955) Letters, 1819–June 1821, in *Works and Correspondence*, vol. VIII, ed. P. Sraffa, Cambridge: Cambridge University Press.

Rosselli, A. (1985) 'The theory of natural wage', in G. Caravale (ed.) *The Legacy of Ricardo*, Oxford: Blackwell.

Whitaker, J. K. (1975) *The Early Economic Writings of Alfred Marshall, 1869–1890*, London: Macmillan.

34

THE LIMITATIONS OF THE ECONOMIC POINT OF VIEW

John K. Whitaker

I seek in what follows to characterize broadly the 'economic point of view', to highlight some difficulties in employing it outside the traditional domain of the economist, and to itemize more briefly some limitations of its power even within this domain.[1]

I

I define the economic point of view in its most general form as the presumption that certain social phenomena are the consequence of deliberate and freely accepted agreements – explicit or implicit – among self-interested individuals. Such individuals need not be narrowly egotistic or materialistic, but their concern is only for a relatively small group in which they take a special interest and not for the well-being of those with whom agreement is sought, or of society as a whole.

Since at least the time of Adam Smith a vision of spontaneous and self-regulating social order produced by free and deliberate agreement among self-interested individuals has played a central role in economic analysis. The trading of goods and services and the establishment of markets for such exchanges have been central to this vision, but the economic point of view is potentially capable of much wider application. The past thirty years have seen energetic attempts to extend it to areas such as law, politics, sociology and demography, which have traditionally been dominated by quite different approaches, a development sometimes termed 'economic imperialism'. Such extensions have met with some success, but also some resistance, even derision. Few would accept the claims that every face of human behaviour is reducible to the deliberate or rational pursuit of consistent goals, and that all social interactions represent a mutually agreeable exchange of *quid pro quo*. But the outer limits to the scope of such Napoleonic ambitions remain uncertain.

The economic approach rests on the assumption that individuals exhibit the following general characteristics:

1   They are endowed with stable and well-defined preferences over the set

of possibilities they might conceivably face.

2 They always choose from the set of options apparently available to them that option most preferred according to their own preferences.

3 They perceive the available set of options with reasonable accuracy.

4 They have a reasonable comprehension of the likely consequences of choosing any option.

Perfect knowledge or astonishing powers of calculation are not required for (3) and (4), rather a 'reasonable person' standard. But a belief in the efficacy of love potions, say, would probably violate characteristic 4.

It is sometimes claimed that this approach to explaining individual behaviour does not seek to describe the actual process of decision-making, only its consequences. Individuals are to be viewed as 'black boxes' which behave 'as if' they met the above conditions, but any enquiry into a box's inner workings is to be left to psychiatrists, neurobiologists, and suchlike.[2] However, precisely because it mirrors the kind of rationality which we hope prevails in intellectual discourse, the economic approach possesses a heuristic appeal somewhat at odds with such self-abnegating claims. This becomes obvious when questions of social policy are addressed. The welfare of an unanalysed black box is hardly a meaningful concept, so that normative economics is prone to take the economic approach literally rather than metaphorically – while, even for positive issues, there is a natural tendency for economists to come to believe, by long familiarity, in the descriptive validity of their assumptions, a transmutation of 'as if' into 'as'.

In countering critical reactions to their intrusions into new areas of individual and social life, economists do hold one extremely strong card. Whatever may be the springs of human action, it seems incontrovertible that opportunity-cost effects are omnipresent, even in areas of life far removed from pecuniary calculation. Protestations of the kind 'No amount of money would make me do that' are rarely tested by the response 'Here, if a million won't do take ten million and think of all the good you could do with it.' It is true that even within the economists' framework, lexicographic preferences could insulate higher-order aspects of behaviour from opportunity-cost considerations involving lower-order aspects (honour or conscience before wealth, and so on). But one need not be overly cynical to doubt the ubiquity of such insulation.

Non-economists tend to lack awareness of the subtle ways in which opportunity-cost considerations can creep into all areas of life, and indeed are prone to deny indignantly that they do so. Such a reaction is particularly common when health, and life itself, are at stake.

Economists are then in an ambivalent position, espousing an approach which often seems oversimplified and descriptively inaccurate but yet highlights important and easily overlooked forces that shape action, even if through little-understood channels and by individual adaptations that may be largely unconscious or unconsidered. This tension doubtless accounts for the typically puzzled reaction of non-economists to the forays economists make outside their traditional domain. There is evident plausibility to the economists' claim that considerations of worldly advantage have wide-ranging effects, yet the economists' explanation of why this is so comes in a guise that seems implausible and even risible to the unindoctrinated.

II

At this point I leave generalities and consider examples dealing with religion, extramarital affairs, suicide and marriage, which bring into focus various types of difficulty. These examples are rather extreme and perhaps represent the high-water mark of an ebbing economic imperialism, but their very extravagance helps highlight the points at issue.[3]

The first example, provided by Azzi and Ehrenberg, deals with a family's allocation of time to church attendance. The approach is characterized as follows:

> most religions promise their members some form of an afterlife. Furthermore, the expected afterlife benefits are often viewed by individuals as being at least partially related to their lifetime allocation of time to religious activities. This suggests that household participation in church-related activities should be analysed in the context of a multiperiod household-allocation-of-time model which allows for 'afterlife consumption', with this variable being at least partially a function of the household's investment of members' time in religious activities during their lifetime.
>
> (Azzi and Ehrenberg 1975: 28)

This 'salvation' motive, as it is termed, may be supplemented by a 'consumption' motive (people just like to go to church) or a 'social pressure' motive (going to church will help you succeed in business). But these additional motives get little attention, and the possibility that charitable donations may earn afterlife benefits is neglected. A married couple is assumed to know (or believe in) the production function by which church-going is converted to afterlife consumption. They also know that they will share equally in the latter and that they will have a subjective rate of time preference in the afterlife, so that the infinitely prolonged utility stream received there will have a finite present value. They are able to compare this present value with the utility of consumption occurring at any date in the present life. The available time in each period can be allocated freely between churchgoing, work for wages, or household activity. Maximization of utility (both here and hereafter), subject to the usual constraints, current and expected wage rates, etc., yields optimal current and planned future allocations of time and consumption in this life and an optimal expected utility stream in the afterlife.

The purpose of the model is, of course, to predict the response of current time-allocation decisions to changes in objective parameters, and to account for certain purported tendencies for churchgoing habits to differ by sex and age. Consider the latter first. How is the model supposed to explain the fact that women tend to spend more time churchgoing than do their husbands? By the fact that women's wages are lower, so that they can produce afterlife consumption at lower opportunity cost. But this is really no explanation, since it relies on unverifiable assumptions about the production process for afterlife benefits. Similarly, the tendency of churchgoing to rise with age is explained by the existence of a positive interest rate in the present life, on the quite gratuitous extra assumption that the rate of return on religious investment is less than this interest rate.

At this point we may prefer to view the model as an 'as if' one, to be judged by its success in prediction – to be precise, in predicting variation in churchgoing behaviour between individuals or groups of individuals. The available data are not ideal and the brute realities call for the inclusion of many extra explanatory variables on *ad hoc* grounds. The 'strong support' for their model claimed by the authors (p. 51) on the basis of their statistical analysis appears to rest upon the significance of age, sex and 'belief in an afterlife' as influences on churchgoing, even after other control variables are added. Also, and perhaps more to the point, data on average church attendance suggest that low-wage US states are more religious (although I doubt whether all the considerable sociocultural differences between low- and high-wage states are adequately controlled for).

But what if these results had come out differently? Would the model have been rejected, or would some of the quite arbitrary supplementary assumptions have been adapted to the facts? One suspects the latter. That would mean the model was not predictive after all, so that its value would have to be justified by the insight it gives into 'how and why' people go to church – not something on which I would give it high marks. Its defects in this regard are, I think, obvious. It takes a situation to which Keynes's strictures (1937: 124) about the invocation of expected utility in the face of fundamental uncertainty apply with a vengeance.[4] And it ignores many of the social and emotional pressures which surround religion and make the assumption of deliberate choice based upon stable independent preferences inappropriate. 'Guilt' is one of many words that simply do not enter the economist's lexicon.

My second example (Fair 1978) is also concerned with an individual's allocation of time. The focus is on extramarital affairs and the paper deals with the decision of a married individual to spend his or her time with a paramour. As Fair observes, the paramour could be replaced by a social club, or even a church group, and the theory would be essentially the same. It could hardly be indicated more pointedly that the theory is devoid of significant psychological or sociological content and concerned only with a formal representation of choice outcomes.

The theory involves three persons, termed Spouse, Individual and Paramour. They may be of either sex, although perhaps Spouse and Individual might be assumed to be of opposite sex. The theory focuses on Individual's decision to allocate his or her time. Individual is supposed to make this decision on the presumption that the actions of Spouse and Paramour will be quite unaffected by Individual's choice. (Oddly, Paramour and Individual may spend quite different amounts of time on the affair.) As Fair himself notes (p. 51), the situation might be more convincingly viewed as one of interactions in a three-person strategic game, a kind of problem that economists and game theorists have not succeeded in handling adequately.

The theory as formulated does impose certain restrictions on the way Individual's behaviour responds to changes in the parameters he or she faces. However, Fair's statistical application, based on inadequate and perhaps biased data, is unable to test for the fulfilment of these restrictions.

He finds that frequency of extramarital intercourse is significantly reduced by age and the self-reported degrees of marital happiness and religiosity, and significantly increased by the reported duration of marriage, findings which can be rationalized in terms of the theory but are hardly implied by it.

The ability of the theory to constrain the data interestingly remains quite unproven, whereas its inability to give insight into motivation is blatant. Extramarital affairs are often very unlike grocery shopping and can produce guilt, remorse, depression, and other strong psychological reactions, which suggest that the decision was hardly one of a calmly considered balancing of competing attractions based on adequate knowledge of the consequences. On such aspects of marital infidelity one would learn more from reading John Updike.

A paper on suicide (Hamermesh and Soss 1974) presents a model which implies that everyone would commit suicide at any age if made sufficiently poor, and conversely could always be induced not to commit suicide by being given enough money. Non-economic variables enter this decision calculus only by helping to determine the parameters of the preference function and the utility threshold at which the individual takes his or her quietus. The theory suggests that suicide rates will tend to decrease with income and increase with age. The latter effect follows from two rather arbitrary assumptions: that the current utility of income declines with age, and that the threshold is triggered, not by a low current rate of flow of utility, but by a low sum of current and expected future utility. Thus, someone might commit suicide now because of a sufficiently adverse event expected in the remote future.

The statistical results do show that age and income have the predicted effects and also that suicide rates rise with unemployment, although this is interpreted as an income effect rather than a consequence of the depression, feelings of worthlessness, and so on, that often accompany job loss. On some occasions suicide does apparently result from a calmly considered and balanced appraisal of a person's adverse future prospects – although the threat of poverty may be only a minor element compared to expected impairment of physical and mental functioning. But suicide which results from overwhelming fear and despondency can hardly be deemed rational in any but the trivial sense which equates voluntariness and rationality by definition.[5]

My final example is Gary Becker's pioneering analysis of marriage (Becker 1973–4; reprinted in Becker 1976). Becker observes that marriage is voluntary and that there are many potential mates, so that there is a kind of marriage market, although not usually an explicit one. He assumes, however, that the outcome will be the same as it would have been with an explicit market which operated perfectly to produce a unique 'sorting' or pairing of spouses. Marriages are made, not in heaven, but by the invisible hand.

The theory is premised on the assumption that a couple produces as a team an output of intangibles which can be reduced to a scalar and compared between households. The unique equilibrium sorting of mates is the one maximizing the total amount of this output over all households. To achieve this sorting it is necessary for each couple to have a contract, explicit or implicit, governing the division of the couple's output between themselves. Each individual 'joins' the marriage that provides him or her *as an individual* with the most output. The situation is exactly analogous to one with a marketed output in which the wives are hired by the husbands at specified wages to assist with production and a full competitive equilibrium is achieved. To soften the corners, Becker introduces the possibility of 'caring', as he terms it. Couples who care are more productive as a team. Thus, if they care sufficiently the optimal sorting will always pair them together. Moreover, since they care they may not adopt the market-dictated division of their joint product.

Specific implications follow only if specific restrictions are imposed upon the unobservable production functions for the intangible output, restrictions which it is difficult to justify independently of the phenomena to be explained. My main objection, however, is to the assumption that the marriage market attains equilibrium. Search for a potential spouse has high opportunity cost so that most individuals explore only a relatively small number of possibilities. Also, 'caring' is not something that exists in the abstract. One cannot take a pair at random and measure in advance the caring that might develop between them as a couple. Caring manifests itself only during the search process. Not only will the market fail to reach equilibrium, this equilibrium itself becomes strongly path-dependent once caring is admitted. If we are to analyse the 'marriage market' successfully it will have to be as a market very far from having achieved the analogue of a full competitive equilibrium.

The analysis of markets in disequilibrium is hardly one of the success stories of economics. A general framework for analysing the adjustment to equilibrium of a system of competitive markets is still lacking after a hundred years of effort, and for oligopolistic markets even less has been accomplished.

III

Applications of the economic point of view to, for example, planned pregnancy, or investment in education and trainir.g, show that the economists' tools can make valuable contributions beyond the traditional domain of markets and resource allocation problems. The decisions involved in such cases have a clear element of deliberateness and involve significant economic costs and benefits. Extensions to other areas, such as those described in Section II, may seem less compelling, and this for several possible reasons. So far as individual decisions are concerned, impulsiveness – often regretted – or social pressure may be the driving force. Or justifiable knowledge of the costs and benefits of the various alternatives may be lacking and perhaps even inconceivable. When group outcomes are in question, strategic behaviour may dominate, or group equilibrium may be non-unique or never attained.

With regard to the first class of problems, that involving explanation of individual behaviour, progress may lie in integrating the insights of economists – especially the insight that opportunity cost influences behaviour in subtle ways – with approaches to human behaviour developed by disciplines such as psychology, sociology and anthropology. Economists have been prone to live in a compartment hermetically sealed against such influences, and it remains to be seen whether useful syntheses with other approaches can arise.

IV

It is important to recognize that the economic point of view meets limitations in its own domain and not only in the extension of its grasp to novel areas. As already indicated, satisfactory treatments of market disequilibrium, strategic interaction and fundamental uncertainty are still lacking. Difficulties arise in part because of economists' penchant for assuming rationality, which makes for a reluctance to bound agents' rationality, or the knowledge on which it is exercised, in ways that are not themselves demonstrable to be rational at a deeper level. Yet the more incredible the tasks hypothetical agents are supposed to accomplish, the less plausible is the claim that human 'black boxes' can mimic agents' behaviour, despite our inability to explain how this might be accomplished.

Perhaps more important is the recognition that the economic point of view is unable to provide a self-contained analysis of society, or even of society's economic life. The difficulties focus on two aspects: preferences and institutions. Sufficient evidence that preferences, as opposed to animal needs, are socially formed is provided by the remarkable case of the wolf-boy of

Aveyron (Shattuck 1980). If economists take preferences as data then they obviously cannot claim to provide a self-contained analysis, or even an accurate one, whenever preferences are altered as a result of analysed economic changes.[6] Attempts by economists to dig down to more fundamental stable preferences, by interposing either a rational selection process for higher-level preferences (e.g. choosing to develop a taste for opera) or an internal technology which transforms ostensible objects of choice into more fundamental desiderata, generally seem unpersuasive and question-begging. It is difficult to imagine that the formation of preferences can be explained without the aid of other social sciences.

The problem of institutions is a dual one. First is the difficulty, indeed impossibility, of self-interested agreements not to cheat. The desire to preserve a reputation purely for selfish future benefit can only work if a relationship lasts literally for ever. In other cases the incentive to cheat will ultimately undermine any basis for cooperation, and that undermining reflects back to the present if myopia is absent. Agreements to penalize cheating must themselves be enforced by penalties which must in turn be enforced, leading on to infinite regress. At some level, socially responsible behaviour – trust, honesty, etc. – must be assumed as a necessary basis for cooperation, or else a governmental enforcer must be invoked, which opens up the whole question of the creation of government. Of course, economists can always endow individuals with an unexplained taste for socially responsible action, just as supposition of a taste for voting can account for the prevalence of voting when it is costly and the probability of affecting the outcome is negligible. But such a subterfuge hardly provides a compelling explanation.

The institutional framework involves informal understandings, customs, conventions, mores, and so on, as well as formal organizations and explicit contracts. Such implicit understandings will often be difficult to amend. Even when they can be given a plausible contractarian basis as tacit agreements to cooperate for mutual benefit, they will often be anachronisms based on the conditions of a distant past. This is the crux of the second difficulty with institutions. Since such tacit agreements cannot be continually renegotiated to attune them to current conditions they will become a *constraint* on current social adaptation rather than a consequence of it. This opens the door to, and may necessitate, more evolutionary, historical, institutionalist, even sociological, approaches to explaining current economic arrangements.

NOTES

1 I hope that the present chapter complements Harcourt's 'The social science imperialists' (Harcourt 1978). It draws upon Whitaker (1983), which I never got round to publishing despite Geoff Harcourt's urging. See also Ben-Porath (1982).

2 Friedman (1953) provided an influential treatment of the 'as if' approach.

3 Blinder's (1974) paper is an evident spoof and it is possible that the papers to be

discussed here were written tongue in cheek, although they certainly seem to be intended seriously.

4   Iannacone (1995) focuses on the industrial organization of the 'firms' supplying religious experience to consumers who are responding rationally to religious uncertainty. The consumers' side is not analysed in detail, but appears to involve maximization of expected utility. Application of expected utility to religious decisions goes back to Pascal's wager, but the common refusal to act on his logically impeccable argument suggests that the expected-utility framework is inappropriate.

5   Any voluntary act can be construed as the maximizing of some utility function subject to some perceived constraints, but if the preferences reflect the passion of the moment and the constraints are misperceived then there is little connection to stable features of personality or environment.

6   This is, of course, true of anything economists take as data, including technology. But the centrality of preferences to the economic point of view, their clear connection to social circumstances and their pertinence to welfare evaluations all combine to make endogenity of preferences the most significant instance.

REFERENCES

Azzi, C. and Ehrenberg, R. (1975) 'Household allocation of time and church attendance', *Journal of Political Economy* 83: 27–52.

Becker, G. (1973–4) 'A theory of marriage: part I', *Journal of Political Economy* 81: 813–47; 'A theory of marriage: part II', *Journal of Political Economy* 82 (Supplement): 11–26.

—— (1976) *The Economic Approach to Human Behavior*, Chicago: University of Chicago Press.

Ben-Porath, Y. (1982) 'Becker's *A Treatise on the Family* – Match or Mismatch', *Journal of Economic Literature* 20: 52–64.

Blinder, A. (1974) 'The economics of brushing teeth', *Journal of Political Economy* 82: 887–91.

Fair, R. C. (1978) 'A theory of extramarital affairs', *Journal of Political Economy* 86: 45–61.

Friedman, M. (1953) 'The methodology of positive economics', in M. Friedman, *Essays in Positive Economics*, Chicago: University of Chicago Press.

Hamermesh, D. S. and Soss, N. M. (1974) 'An economic theory of suicide', *Journal of Political Economy* 82: 83–98.

Harcourt, G. C. (1978) 'The social science imperialists', Annual Lecture to the Academy of the Social Sciences in Australia, Canberra, 1978. Reprinted in Harcourt, G. C. (1982) *The Social Science Imperialists*, London: Routledge & Kegan Paul.

Iannacone, L. R. (1995) 'Risk, rationality, and religious portfolios', *Economic Inquiry* 33: 285–95.

Keynes, J. M. (1937) 'Some economic consequences of a declining population', *Eugenics Review* 29: 13–17. Reprinted in *Collected Writings of John Maynard Keynes*, vol. 14, London: Macmillan for the Royal Economic Society.

Shattuck, R. (1980) *Forbidden Experiment: The Story of the Wild Boy of Aveyron*, New York: Farrar, Straus, Giroux.

Whitaker, J. K. (1983) Bateman Lecture, University of Western Australia, unpublished.

418

35

THOUGHTS INSPIRED BY READING AN ATYPICAL PAPER BY HARCOURT

Robert M. Solow

It should be understood that I was looking for an atypical article in the first place. Experience has taught me that a pleasant and productive way to contribute to a Festschrift is to write a sympathetic but serious commentary on an early work of the festee. This proved to be more complicated than I had expected in the case of Geoffrey C. Harcourt. His earliest papers were primarily applications of accounting theory to problems of economic interpretation; I did not think that I could say anything useful about them. But the later papers tend to be about the so-called 'Cambridge controversy' in one way or another. I wanted to avoid that topic. The main feeling I remember from those days is exasperation. My current view of the whole episode is, if possible, even more jaundiced. I have no wish to rain on what will no doubt be a parade of papers on that subject in this volume. So I kept looking.

In the end, I found an atypical paper of thirty years ago to discuss. It is even especially appropriate, because the paper of Harcourt (1966) is a comment on an earlier article in which I have a one-quarter equity interest (Arrow, Chenery, Minhas and Solow 1963). I will refer to these papers as GCH and ACMS respectively, because Harcourt is not really outnumbered.

ACMS introduces and analyses the class of two-input production functions with a constant elasticity of substitution between the inputs. (There are well-known extensions to many inputs.) Suppose labour is one of the inputs. Then it is shown first that cost minimization implies that the elasticity of output (value added) per worker with respect to the wage is exactly the elasticity of substitution, whether it is constant or not. Now suppose that the logarithm of output (value added) per worker, $\log (V/L)$, is in fact a linear function of the logarithm of the wage rate, $\log W$. In principle, then, the slope of that line is an estimate of the constant elasticity of substitution (CES) provided, of course, that one can defensibly assume the observations to have arisen from approximate cost minimization.

ACMS does just this, using as observational raw material census data covering some twenty-four industries in as many as nineteen countries. Indeed, the paper actually begins by showing that very many of these industries yield linear cross-section regressions of log (V/L) on log W, and then deduces the CES function as the only family of production functions with this property.

From this description, it will be clear that ACMS assumes implicitly that the observed (V,L,W) for a particular industry in a particular country represents the cost-minimizing input–output combination along a well-behaved production function, with full *ex post* substitutability. From that point of view, the use of international cross-sections for each industry is an advantage. Large differences in factor prices can be taken as more or less durable features to which each industry can be expected to have adapted. One could no doubt wonder whether the knitting-mills of Norway and Colombia have access to a common production function. ACMS wonders too. The paper can allow for neutral differences in efficiency, but that is all. In retrospect, that procedure looks at least defensible. If technological change in the most advanced countries appears to be roughly neutral over time, it may not be unreasonable to assume that other countries have access to the same technology with a lag that may be long or short depending on institutional differences, the volume of foreign direct investment, and other things as well. Today's cross-section modellers and convergence testers seem to have no qualms at all about taking it for granted that exactly the same technology is simultaneously available everywhere from Arizona to Zanzibar. We are now beginning to see some econometric evidence that the assumption of a common aggregate production function in international cross-sections is rejected by the data (see Canning *et al.* 1995). A different point of view seems to emerge from Islam (1995). To my mind, that is only to be expected, especially at the aggregate level, if only because different countries have different industry mixes, let alone for deeper reasons. ACMS does not go that far, and they are dealing with much less aggregated industries.

Harcourt comes along to ask a perfectly natural question. Suppose the underlying observations are generated not by a smooth technology with both *ex ante* and *ex post* substitutability, but instead by some sort of vintage structure with limited *ex post* flexibility or none at all. What sort of biases will the ACMS procedure tend to produce? I say 'perfectly natural' because I was then engaged in very similar investigations, though not in exactly the same context (see Solow 1963).

The first step is easy. The ACMS regression says that

$$\log (V/L) = a + b \log W$$

and interprets b as an estimate of 'the' (constant) elasticity of substitution. For ease of notation, I will replace V/L by v. In the vintage case with limited *ex post* substitutability, Harcourt points out, the parameter one really wants to know about is the *ex ante* elasticity of substitution that was available when the most recently installed technique was chosen in the country at hand, with whatever factor proportions and productivity were then cost-minimizing. To put it most clearly, what one would like to have on the left-hand side of the regression is not log v but log v^*, where v^* is value-added per worker on the most recent vintage of equipment in use in the country at hand. Let $v = cv^*$. The normal expectation is that $c < 1$ because technological progress is taking place, and the latest vintage ought to be more productive than the weighted average of past vintages. That does not have to be so, because the wage rate might have been so much higher in the past that much more capital-intensive techniques were consistently chosen. This effect, with consequently higher output per worker, could in principle outweigh the advance of technology. But it seems safe to ignore that possibility.

Then the 'true' relationship is log $v^* = a + b$ log W and the regression actually estimated by ACMS is

$$\log v = a + b \log W - \log c$$

The unobserved quantity c is not a simple parameter. It will differ from country to country and industry to industry, depending on the history of investment, and therefore the weight of recent and remote vintages, and probably on the history of factor prices as well. The biases in the ACMS estimates will depend on the country-to-country variation in c within each industry. The key question, as Harcourt points out, is whether c is correlated with W across the country observations making up each regression sample. If not, then only the estimate of a will be biased. If it is, then the estimate of b will be biased as well. What should one expect?

There are some straightforward qualitative things to be said. In a particular industry in a particular country, the parameter c will be small if the overall level of labour productivity is low compared with the level of labour productivity using the current best-practice cost-minimizing technique. And that, in turn, will be the case if the rate of technological progress is fast, or if the average age of the capacity in use is great, or if the wage is now much higher than it used to be.

To get any further requires the specification of a precise model. In fact, the third of those qualitative statements is just the point of ACMS: the sensitivity of productivity to the wage is measured by the elasticity of substitution in the non-vintage case. Harcourt's argument calls attention, quite rightly, to the bias that is introduced if the non-vintage approach is applied to data generated by a vintage structure.

But now we can see a little further. Bias occurs if c is correlated with W. We have just argued that choice of technique generates a correlation between c and the *change* in W, something not even observed in the ACMS contemporaneous cross-section regressions.

Think of a particular industry; Harcourt uses the cement industry in some of his calculations. The wage is higher in country A than in country B. Is it likely that wages in A have been rising faster than in B? That is certainly possible, but it is not necessarily the case. To the extent that convergence is occurring, to take an up-to-date idea, wages in low-wage countries might be gaining on the high-wage countries. The direction of bias in the ACMS regression, at least from this source, depends on which of those descriptions is closer to fact.

GCH does not discuss this chain of causation at all. Maybe it was not on his mind. Probably it was a sound decision. The cross-sectional data do not allow a judgement anyway; in practice one would need a fairly long run of data to isolate this effect. And since the effect could go either way, varying from case to case, there might be little to isolate.

The approach actually taken by GCH is quite different. He focuses on the other two lines of causation, and treats them by way of a series of 'stylized' numerical examples. The key parameters are taken to be, first, g, the growth rate of productivity from vintage to vintage; second, G, the growth rate of investment from vintage to vintage; and third, n, the number of vintages actually in use. Obviously n functions as a surrogate for the average age of the capacity in operation. The five cases are differentiated by stylized assumptions about the allocation of labour and output across vintages. For example, in the first case to be considered, it is simply assumed that '[t]here are balanced stocks of vintages in the relevant industry of each country, each containing the same number of vintages'. The constant labour supply in each country is distributed equally over the active vintages; thus the contribution of each vintage to the value-added of the industry just mimics the productivity path. In yet another case it is assumed that each vintage contributes the same share to total value added in the industry, with a constant decline in labour requirements from vintage to vintage. Since the number of active vintages is again arbitrarily chosen, total employment in the industry must be falling. There are other combinations, five in all, but these will give the flavour.

Each of these stylized cases gives rise to a table of values of c (actually c^{-1}, but no matter) for different combinations of the underlying parameters. There are no surprises. In all cases, c turns out to be less than 1, as expected. There is no countervailing force and, even if there were, it would almost certainly be weak. The variation of c with parameters such as g and n is also quite intuitive: c is smaller if g and n are larger. G, the rate of growth of investment, is a bit trickier, with the effect on c depending on the rule for allocating labour to vintages.

All this still leaves open the crucial question of the cross-sectional correlation of c with w. Something has to be assumed. At this point, GCH verges on the inscrutable. Harcourt uses data on the cement industry from Minhas (1963), combines them in some way with the c-values in his stylized scenarios, and with incompletely described assumptions about wages, to correct Minhas's ACMS-like estimates for the implied bias. For example, in one calculation he says: 'If n is smaller and G is greater, the higher is w, then (at least within the range of values estimated) the estimates of *b* are biased *upwards* in all five cases.' And then GCH cites the results for two of the five cases (stylized scenarios): they give values of *b*, and thus of the elasticity of substitution, equal to 0.70 and 0.86, to be compared with Minhas's 0.92.

Then a couple more experiments are mentioned. In one of them, it is assumed that the average age of capacity-in-use is great in both very poor and very rich (presumably very low- and very high-wage) countries, and less so in the middle. In that case, the two scenarios reported suggest that ACMS would underestimate the value of *b*, with GCH giving 1.05 and 1.01 as against Minhas's 0.92. The exact reverse assumption, with old capacity predominating in the middle and young capacity predominating in both rich and poor countries, leads to *b* = 1.02, and a case where higher-wage countries have older capacity yields a very high estimated elasticity of substitution, namely 1.38.

GCH concludes agnostically, and no doubt correctly: if the vintage structure with *ex post* fixed proportions is a more plausible description of an industry's technology than the case of relatively free *ex post* substitutability, then the ACMS method can lead to biased estimates of the elasticity of substitution. The direction of the bias can in principle go in either direction, and might be large or small. A priori reasoning cannot tell us. Harcourt rather thinks that the numbers just reported represent large biases, but I am not even sure I would know how to interpret an answer, pragmatically speaking. If you had concluded that the *ex ante* elasticity of substitution between labour and other inputs in the cement industry were 0.9, and then learned that it might actually be 0.75 or 1.05, would you live your life differently?

GCH goes on to suggest that further research into the characteristics of best-practice technologies (and presumably next-best as well) could usefully take the form of sample surveys at the plant level, such as were then being done by W. E. G. Salter, and have since been carried out by Zvi Griliches and others. All that seems very reasonable, and I am predisposed to agree. As an early proponent of the vintage model, and a natural-born believer that technical progress must ordinarily be embodied in investment, I have been puzzled that those ideas somehow never took off (and seem in no danger of doing so now). Vintage models, especially those with *ex ante* flexibility and *ex post* fixity of factor proportions, are hard to handle, both in theory and in practice. But I think the surviving authors of ACMS would join the author of GCH in thinking that mere messiness is not a good reason for neglecting whatever insights the vintage structure confers, including those that can be distilled from the calculations in GCH.

With that in mind, I would suggest that the GCH setup could have been developed further. In the article, the parameters *g*, *G* and *n*, defined earlier, are treated as independent. They are prescribed in various combinations in order to calculate a value for *c*, which is then itself combined with some (at best) qualitatively described pattern for *W* to give the final result. But almost anyone would agree that all those things are endogenously interconnected. To put this at its simplest, any story that prescribes a path for productivity, investment and wages will imply some particular pattern of allocation of labour to vintages, and a particular path for n. The least productive vintage in use will be at the zero-rent margin, with the going wage exhausting the value-added per worker. If GCH had told that kind of story, the bias from ignoring the vintage structure could have been related to historically meaningful patterns of evolution.

To put the point differently, there is real advantage in embedding this kind of question in a dynamic model, because doing so will impose a certain consistency on the hypothetical 'data' from which inferences are made. There is a possible disadvantage too: the model may be inappropriate and the inferences irrelevant or worse. Yes, but there is no way to avoid that risk. It is equally present for stylized scenarios that do not rest on a worked-out model.

What have I learned from this brief expedition to 'the way we were' thirty years ago, in the company of Geoff Harcourt? For one thing, there is much merit in experimentation. If one cannot do 'real' experiments, there are always numerical experiments with something to teach us. And precisely what they can teach us is to score theories on a scale that ranges from fragility to robustness. Anyone who clings to a frail theory must have a lot of confidence in its particular assumptions, and owes the rest of us some good reasons why we ought to accept them too. Robustness, on the other hand, is its own reward. A model that can stand up under the sort of exercise that I have just described has the powerful advantage that it does not have to defend the indefensible proposition that things are just so. They almost never are, of course. I do not know if GCH realized he was teaching that lesson thirty years ago. He probably does not know either. But that is what I learned.

REFERENCES

Arrow, K., Chenery, H., Minhas, B. and Solow, R. (1963) 'Capital–labor substitution and economic efficiency', *Review of Economics and Statistics* 43: 225–50.

Canning, D., Dunne, P. and Moore, M. (1995) 'Testing the augmented Solow and endogenous growth model', Working Paper 53, Queen's University of Belfast, June.

Harcourt, G. C. (1966) 'Biases in empirical estimates of the elasticities of substitution of CES production functions', *Review of Economic Studies* 33: 227–33.

Islam, N. (1995) 'Growth empirics: a panel data approach', *Quarterly Journal of Economics* 110: 1167–70.

Minhas, B. (1963) *An International Comparison of Factor Costs and Factor Use*, Amsterdam: North-Holland.

Solow, R. (1963) 'Heterogeneous capital and smooth production: an experimental study', *Econometrica* 31: 623–45.

36

IN THE BEGINNING ALL THE WORLD WAS AUSTRALIA...

Heinz D. Kurz and Neri Salvadori

HARCOURT v. LOCKE

Both of us had the privilege to attend several lectures and seminars by Geoff Harcourt dedicated to a variety of themes in which he adopted different methods of analysis and used different tools. However, there was one common element in all these lectures and seminars: Geoff's emphasis on the specificity of Australian football rules. For many years we joined in the laughter of others when Geoff made his jokes. However, laughing must not be mistaken for understanding. In fact, neither of us ever had the slightest clue how the often abstract argument under consideration related to the down-to-earth problem of Australian football rules.

It was only recently that we felt we had finally seen through the story to its true meaning. The miraculous event happened when we had to prepare a talk for the 1994 Siena workshop on 'Endogenous Growth and Development'. In this context one of us came across John Locke's *Second Treatise of Government*, published in 1690, which contains, among other things, an early version of a four-stage theory of socioeconomic development (see also the discussion in Meek 1976). The elaboration of this theory was stimulated by the discovery of the New World and the people inhabiting it: the American Indians. This discovery challenged many of the prevailing views about religion, social organization and government, and led to speculations about how contemporary European society may have evolved over time from certain 'primitive' forms. According to the four-stage hypothesis society 'naturally' progressed over time through the following more or less distinct and consecutive stages: hunting, pasturage, agriculture and commerce. Each of these stages was defined in terms of a different mode of subsistence to which corresponded different institutions relating to property, law and government, and different cultures; that is, sets of ideas, morals and customs. Locke maintained that in the earliest stage men 'for the most part, contended themselves with what un-assisted Nature Offered to their Necessities'. The things which 'the necessity of subsisting made the first Commoners of the World look after', Locke asserted, are the same as those which the then contemporary

American Indians were concerned with. He cast his hypothesis about the origins of modern society in the formula: 'In the beginning all the World was *America*' (Locke 1690 [1953]: 341–3).[1]

As we see it now, Geoff Harcourt implicitly challenged the view of Locke, who apparently had overlooked *the* most important indicator of the level of a nation's civilization: the football rules it followed. These rules, Geoff appeared to contend, were an unerring measure of civilization, and comparing the Australian football rules with the rules followed elsewhere it was clear: 'In the beginning all the World was *Australia*.' Not America. This was the hidden message in Geoff's talks. But it was not the whole thing. Indeed, there was a second and equally hidden message which came close to putting Locke's proposition upside down: 'In the end all the World might be *America*.' This aspect of the message was less opaque since Geoff never left any doubt about his political leanings and that he did not think highly of unfettered North American capitalism. In the end all the world might very well be North America if compassionate people, including intellectuals, don't prevent it from happening. His position is expressed with great clarity in his marvellous 'Recollections and reflections of an Australian patriot and a Cambridge economist' (Harcourt 1995).

This potentiality cannot, of course, be dealt with in a short space, as is available here – if it can be dealt seriously with at all. Here we shall focus attention on a much less grandiose issue, which reflects, however, a small aspect of the trend under consideration: the Americanization of economics.[2] More precisely, we shall focus attention on some recent developments in the theory of economic growth and development. Although ten years ago it would have been only a moderate exaggeration to maintain that the subject was dead and buried, today it would be a similarly moderate exaggeration to say that the subject does not belong to the most active fields in economic analysis. Given the burst of activity in theoretical and empirical research on economic growth and development which is reflected in a large and still mounting wave of publications, one can indeed speak of the revival of growth economics. Moreover, it is argued by some of the practitioners of the 'new' growth theory (NGT) that the 'new' growth models (NGMs) will revolutionize the way economists think about certain problems (Grossman and Helpman 1994). It is also claimed that the revolution will not be restricted to the periphery of economic analysis but will affect its core. In their view we are confronted with what may be called a 'basic innovation' in the way economists theorize which leaves its mark on virtually every aspect of analytical economics.

In this chapter it will be argued that these claims are not warranted. It will rather be shown that in terms of substance there is 'nothing new under the sun'. Indeed, what the NGMs contain are but old ideas in a new garb. The ideas put forward can be traced back to the 'classical' economists from Adam Smith to David Ricardo. What is new is the bold attempt to put these complex ideas into some simple algebra. In doing so, the old wine of classical vintage has been put in neoclassical bottles and sometimes even oxidized to neoclassical vinegar.

The structure of the chapter is the following. First the approach of the classical economists to the theory of distribution and growth will be summarized. The emphasis is on those aspects in the writings of Smith, Ricardo and their followers which bear a close resemblance to salient features of the NGMs. Obviously, only a synthesis of the classical approach can be given, leaving out all differences between different authors. Attention will focus on the way the classical economists dealt with *non-accumulable* factors of production such as labour and land, because it is in this regard that the NGMs can be said to be essentially 'classical', despite the different forms in which the argument is dressed. We then deal with four different kinds of NGM. It will be shown that these models determine the rate of profit by technology alone, or, if there is a choice of technique, via the profit-maximizing behaviour of producers. This is a consequence of an assumption about 'labour' which is very similar to, even if not identical with, an assumption we find in Ricardo. The difference is that now 'labour' is given a different name. With the rate of profit ascertained in this way, the rate of growth is then determined endogenously in terms of some assumption about saving behaviour. Contrary to widespread opinion, it turns out that increasing returns to scale are not indispensable in order to generate endogenous growth. The chapter finishes with some concluding remarks.

ENDOGENOUS GROWTH IN THE 'CLASSICAL' ECONOMISTS

Accumulation *vis-à-vis* diminishing returns in agriculture

The problem of economic growth and income distribution was a major concern of Adam Smith and David Ricardo. Ricardo's argument about what he called the 'natural' course of the economy contemplated an economic system in which capital accumulates, the population grows, but there is no technical progress: the latter is set aside. Hence the argument is based on the (implicit) assumption that the set of (constant returns to scale) methods of production from which cost-minimizing producers can choose is given and constant. Assuming the real wage rate of workers to be given and constant, the rate of profit is bound to fall: owing to extensive and intensive diminishing returns on land, 'with every increased portion of capital employed on it, there will be a decreased rate of production' (Ricardo 1817 [1951]: 98). Profits are viewed as a residual income based on the surplus product left after the used-up means of production and the wage goods in the support of workers have been deducted from the social product (net of rents). The 'decreased rate of production' thus involves a decrease in profitability. On the premise that there are only negligible savings out of wages and rents, a falling rate of profit involves a falling rate of capital accumulation. Hence, as regards the dynamism of the economy attention should focus on profitability. Assuming that the marginal propensity to accumulate out of profits, s, is given and constant, a 'classical' accumulation function can be formulated

$$g = \begin{cases} s(r - r_{min}) & \text{if } r \geq r_{min} \\ 0 & \text{if } r \leq r_{min} \end{cases}$$

where $r_{min} \geq 0$ is the minimum level of profitability which, if reached, will arrest accumulation (see Ricardo 1817 [1951]: 120). Ricardo's 'natural' course will necessarily end up in a stationary state.[3]

Clearly, to Ricardo the rate of accumulation is endogenously determined. The demand for labour is governed by the pace at which capital accumulates, whereas the long-term supply of labour is regulated by the Malthusian law of population.[4]

Assuming for simplicity a given and constant real wage rate, Ricardo's view of the long-run relationship between profitability and accumulation and thus growth can be illustrated in terms of Figure 36.1, which is a diagram used by Kaldor (1956). The curve CEGH is the marginal productivity of labour-cum-capital. It is decreasing since land is scarce: when labour-cum-capital increases, either less fertile qualities of land must be cultivated or the same qualities of land must be cultivated with processes which require less land per

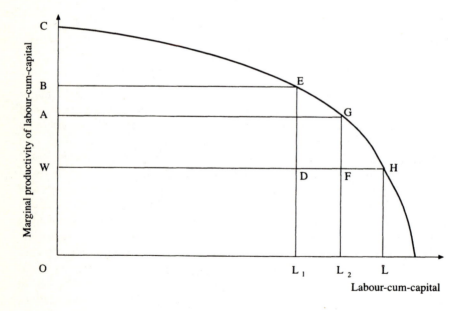

Figure 36.1 Diminishing returns to labour-cum-capital

428

unit of product, but are more costly in terms of labour-cum-capital. Let the real wage rate equal OW. Then, if the amount of labour-cum-capital applied is L_1, the area $OCEL_1$ gives the product, $OWDL_1$ gives total capital employed, and BCE total rent. Profit is determined as a residual and corresponds to the rectangle WBED. As a consequence, the *rate* of profit can be determined as the ratio of the areas of two rectangles which have the same base and, therefore, it equals the ratio WB/OW. Let us now consider the case in which the amount of labour-cum-capital is larger, that is, L_2. Then $OCGL_2$ gives the product, $OWFL_2$ the capital, ACG the rent, and WAGF profits. The rate of profit has fallen to WA/OW. Obviously, if a positive profit rate implies a positive growth rate (i.e. $r_{min} = 0$), the economy will expand until labour-cum-capital has reached the level $\bar{L}$. At that point the profit rate is equal to zero and so is the growth rate. The system has arrived at a stationary state. Growth has come to an end because profitability has.

The required size of the workforce is considered to be generated essentially by the accumulation process itself. In other words, labour power is treated as a kind of producible commodity. It differs from other commodities in that it is not produced in a capitalistic way by a special industry on a par with other industries, but is the result of the interplay between the generative behaviour of the working population and socioeconomic conditions. In the simplest conceptualization possible, labour power is seen to be in elastic supply at a given real wage basket. Increasing the number of baskets available in the support of workers involves a proportional increase in the workforce. In this view the rate of growth of labour supply adjusts to any given rate of growth of labour demand without necessitating a variation in the real wage rate.[5] Labour can thus put no limit to growth because it is 'generated' within the growth process. The only limit to growth can come from other non-accumulable factors of production: as Ricardo and others made clear, these factors are natural resources in general and land in particular. In other words, to the classical economists there is only endogenous growth. This growth is bound to lose momentum as the scarcity of natural factors of production makes itself felt in terms of extensive and intensive diminishing returns. (Technical change is of course envisaged to counteract these tendencies.)

Production with land as a free good

For the sake of the argument let us try to think about Ricardian theory without the problem of land. Setting aside land in Ricardo's doctrine may strike the reader as something similar to Hamlet without the prince. However, the only purpose of this thought experiment is to prepare the ground for a discussion of the NGMs in the next main section. If there were no land, or rather, if land of best quality were available in abundance – that is, a free good – then the graph giving the marginal productivity of labour-cum-capital would be a horizontal line and therefore the rate of profit would be constant whatever the

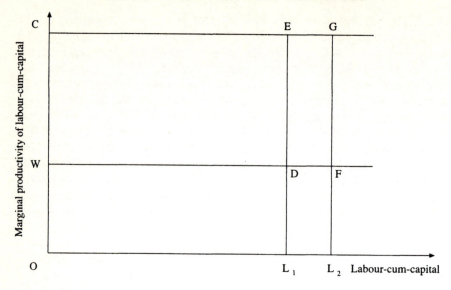

Figure 36.2 Constant returns to labour-cum-capital

amount of labour-cum-capital. This case is illustrated in Figure 36.2. As a consequence, the growth rate would also be constant: the system could grow for ever at a rate that equals the given rate of profit multiplied by the propensity to accumulate.

Production with a 'backstop technology'

However, to assume that there is no land at all or that it is available in given quality and unlimited quantity is unnecessarily restrictive. With the system growing for ever, the point will surely come where land of the best quality becomes scarce. This brings us to another constellation in which the rate of profit need not vanish as capital accumulates. The constellation under consideration bears a close resemblance to a case discussed in the economics of 'exhaustible' resources; that is, the case in which there is an ultimate 'backstop technology'. For example, certain exhaustible resources are used to produce energy. In addition, there is solar energy, which may be considered an undepletable resource. A technology based on the use of solar energy defines the backstop technology mentioned. Let us translate this assumption into the context of a Ricardian model with land.

The case under consideration would correspond to a situation in which 'land', although useful in production, is not indispensable. In other words, there is a technology which allows the production of the commodity without any 'land' input; this is the backstop technology. With continuous sub-

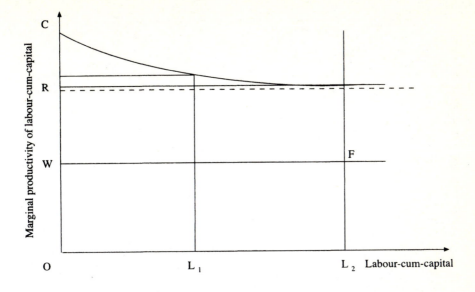

Figure 36.3 Returns to labour-cum-capital, bounded from below

stitutability between labour-cum-capital and land, the marginal productivity of labour-cum-capital would be continuously decreasing, but it would be bounded from below. This case is illustrated in Figure 36.3, with the dashed line giving the lower boundary. In this case the profit rate and thus the growth rate would be falling, but they could never fall below certain levels, which are positive. The system would grow indefinitely at a rate that would asymptotically approach the product of the given saving rate multiplied by the value of the (lower) boundary of the profit rate. In Figure 36.3 the latter is given by WR/OW.

Increasing returns to labour-cum-capital

Finally, we may illustrate the case of increasing returns to labour-cum-capital (see Figure 36.4), as it was discussed, following Adam Smith's analysis of the division of labour, by authors such as Allyn Young (1928) and Nicholas Kaldor (1957). Taking the wage rate as given and constant, the rate of profit and the rate of growth are bound to rise as more labour-cum-capital is employed. (In Figure 36.4 it is assumed that there is an upper boundary to the rise in output per unit of labour-cum-capital given by OR.) In order to be able to preserve the notion of a uniform rate of profit, it has to be assumed that the increasing returns are *external* to the firm and exclusively connected with the expansion of the market as a whole and the social division of labour. This implies that whereas in the case of decreasing returns due to the scarcity of

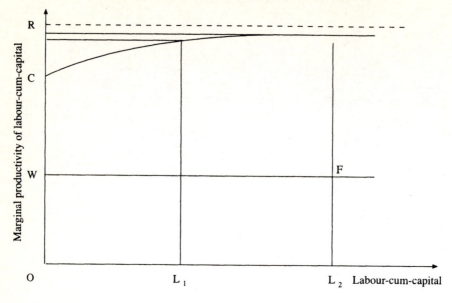

Figure 36.4 Increasing returns to labour-cum-capital

land (Figures 36.1 and 36.3) the product was given by the area under the marginal productivity curve, now the product associated with any given amount of labour-cum-capital is larger than or equal to that amount multiplied by the corresponding level of output per unit of labour-cum-capital. It is larger, if there is still scarce land; it is equal to it, if there is not. In any case, the sum of profits and wages equals the product of the given amount of labour-cum-capital multiplied by the corresponding level of output per unit of labour-cum-capital.[6] Hence, in the case in which labour-cum-capital is L_2, the product is given by the corresponding rectangular. As a consequence, the product is larger than the area under the marginal productivity curve. The cases of decreasing and increasing returns are therefore not symmetrical. It goes without saying that in this case a rising real wage rate need not involve a falling general rate of profit.

Finally, it is to be stressed again that the 'Ricardesque' endogenous growth illustrated in Figures 36.1–36.4 are intimately related to the fact that labour is envisaged as a commodity which is in some sense 'produced' by using corn and nothing else. The real wage rate is considered 'on the same footing as the fuel for the engines or the feed for the cattle'. The straight line WF in the various figures can indeed be interpreted as the 'average cost function' related to the production of labour. If the wage rate were to depend on the amount of labour employed, then the average cost function would not be a straight line, but substantially the same argument would apply. Put in a nutshell, the 'secret' of the endogeneity of growth in the work of the classical authors consisted of the assumption of a 'technology' producing labour. We will see in the next section that essentially the same 'secret' is at the heart of the NGT.

There is, however, another possible way of interpreting the diagrams. In order for this interpretation to hold, we have to remove labour from the scene. If this is done, a picture emerges in which corn is produced by using only corn and, eventually, land. The curve that was previously interpreted as the marginal productivity of labour-cum-capital can now be interpreted as the marginal productivity of corn (as an input); the straight line WF would therefore be located at a distance from the horizontal axis of exactly one unit (WO = 1). All the other elements of the argument developed above would remain exactly the same. We shall see in the following section that this interpretation provides a key to understanding an important aspect of the NGT.

THE 'NEW' GROWTH MODELS

A classification

The concept of 'endogeneity' employed in the NGMs is specified by Barro and Sala-i-Martin in their recent book *Economic Growth* as follows: long-run growth is determined '*within the model*, rather than by some exogenously growing variables like unexplained technological progress' (Barro and Sala-i-Martin 1995: 38; our emphasis). They add: 'The key property of endogenous-growth models is the absence of diminishing returns to capital' (ibid.: 39). Therefore, the way or mechanism by means of which diminishing returns to capital are avoided provides a criterion by which to classify the NGMs (see also Kurz and Salvadori 1995b). We may distinguish between the following types of model:

1   'linear models' or 'AK models' (Rebelo 1991; King and Rebelo 1990);
2   models in which returns to capital are bounded from below (Jones and Manuelli 1990);
3   the model by Lucas (1988), which focuses attention on the accumulation of human capital; and
4   the model by Romer (1986), which emphasizes the generation of new knowledge in the research and development activities of firms.

We shall deal with these different models in turn.

Linear or 'AK' models

First, there are models which set aside all non-accumulable factors of production such as labour and land and assume that all inputs in production are accumulable, that is, 'capital' of some kind. The simplest version of this class of models is the so-called 'AK model', which assumes that there is a linear relationship between total output, Y, and a single factor capital, K, both consisting of the *same* commodity

$$Y = AK \qquad (36.1)$$

where $1/A$ is the amount of that commodity required to produce one unit of itself. Because of the linear form of the aggregate production function, these models are also known as 'linear models'. The rate of return on capital, r, is given by

$$r + \delta = \frac{Y}{K} = A \qquad (36.2)$$

where δ is the exogenously given rate of depreciation. The saving–investment mechanism and the assumption of a uniform rate of growth, that is, a steady-state equilibrium, then jointly determine a relationship between the growth rate, g, and the rate of profit, r. Rebelo (1991: 504, 506) obtains either

$$g = \frac{A - \delta - \rho}{\sigma} = \frac{r - \rho}{\sigma} \qquad (36.3)$$

or

$$g = (A - \delta)s = sr \qquad (36.4)$$

Equation (36.3) is obtained when savings are determined on the assumption that there is an immortal representative agent maximizing the following intertemporal utility function

$$\int_0^\infty e^{-\rho t} \frac{1}{1 - \sigma} [c(t)^{1-\sigma} - 1] dt$$

subject to constraint (36.1), where ρ is the discount rate, or rate of time preference,[1] $1/\sigma$ is the (constant) elasticity of substitution between present and future consumption ($(1 \neq \sigma > 0)$,[2] $Y = c(t) + \dot{K}$, and $\dot{K}$ is the derivative of K with respect to time. Equation (36.4) is obtained when the average propensity to save, s, is given. Hence, in this model the rate of profit is determined by technology alone and the saving–investment mechanism determines the growth rate.

This model is immediately recognizable as the model dealt with at the end of the previous section, in which labour was set aside, on the assumption that the technology to produce corn is that illustrated in Figure 36.2. Even the saving-investment mechanism is essentially the same: in the case of equation (36.3) $\sigma = 1/s$ and $\rho = r_{min}$ (provided that $r > r_{min}$); in the case of equation

(36.4) r_{min} = 0. Hence, the version of the 'new' growth theory under consideration is but the most elementary of all classical models. No classical economist can be accused of having taken that model too seriously.

A slightly different avenue was followed by King and Rebelo (1990). Instead of one kind of 'capital' they assumed that there are two kinds, real capital and human capital, both of which are accumulable. There are two lines of production, one for the social product and the real capital, which consist of quantities of the same commodity, and one for human capital. The production functions relating to the two kinds of capital are assumed to be homogeneous of degree one and strictly concave. There are no diminishing returns to (composite) capital for the reason that there is no non-accumulable factor such as simple or unskilled labour that enters into the production of the accumulable factors, investment goods and human capital.[7] As in Rebelo's model, the rate of profit is uniquely determined by the technology and the maximization of profits which, because of the non-substitution theorem,[8] implies that only one technique can be used in the long run. The growth rate of the system is then endogenously determined by the saving–investment equation. The larger the propensities to accumulate human and physical capital, the larger is the growth rate.

Comparing the latter model with the classical theory, we can draw the following conclusion: the role played by 'labour' in the classical authors is assumed by 'human capital' in King and Rebelo (1990). Both factors of production are taken to be producible; with constant returns to scale, as in King and Rebelo (1990) and in the case depicted in Figure 36.2, the rate of profit and, therefore, the rate of growth are determined and constant over time. The linear NGMs thus simply replicate in elementary terms the logic of the classical approach to the theory of distribution and growth.

Returns to capital bounded from below

Next there are models which preserve the dualism of accumulable and non-accumulable factors but restrict the impact of an accumulation of the former on their returns by a modification of the aggregate production function. Jones and Manuelli (1990), for example, allow for both labour and capital and even assume a convex technology, like the Solow model (Solow 1956). However, a convex technology requires only that the marginal product of capital is a decreasing function of its stock, not that it vanishes as the amount of capital per worker tends to infinity. Jones and Manuelli assume that

$$h(k) \geq bk \qquad \text{each } k \geq 0$$

where $h(k)$ is the per capita production function and b is a positive constant. The special case contemplated by them is

$$h(k) = f(k) + bk \qquad (36.5)$$

where $f(k)$ is the conventional Solovian production function. As capital accumulates and the capital : labour ratio rises, the marginal product of capital will fall, approaching asymptotically b – its lower boundary. With a given propensity to save, s, and assuming capital to be everlasting, the steady-state growth rate, g, is endogenously determined: $g = sb$. Assuming on the contrary intertemporal utility maximization, the rate of growth is positive provided the technical parameter b is larger than the rate of time preference ρ. In the case in which it is, the steady-state rate of growth is given by equation (36.3) with $r = b$.

It is not difficult to recognize that the difference between the model of Jones and Manuelli (1990) and that of Rebelo (1991) is the same as that between the cases illustrated by Figures 36.3 and 36.2 above.

Human capital formation and its externalities

Finally, there is a large class of models which contemplate various factors counteracting any diminishing tendency of returns to capital. The models can be grouped in two categories. In both kinds of models, *positive external effects* play an important part: they offset any fall in the marginal product of capital.

Models of the first group attempt to formalize the role of human capital formation in the process of growth. Elaborating on some ideas of Uzawa (1965), Lucas (1988) assumed that agents have a choice between two ways of spending their (non-leisure) time: to contribute to current production or to accumulate human capital. It is essentially the allocation of time between the two alternatives contemplated that decides the growth rate of the system. For example, a decrease in the time spent producing goods involves a reduction in current output; at the same time it speeds up the formation of human capital and thereby increases output growth. With the accumulation of human capital there is said to be associated an externality: the more human capital society as a whole has accumulated, the more productive each single member will be. This is reflected in the following macroeconomic production function

$$Y = AK^{\beta}(uhN)^{1-\beta}h*^{\gamma} \tag{36.6}$$

where the labour input consists of the number of workers, N, multiplied by the fraction of time spent working, u, multiplied by h, which gives the labour input in efficiency units. Finally, there is the term $h*$. This is designed to represent the externality. The single agent takes $h*$ as a parameter in his or her optimizing by choice of c and u. However, for society as a whole the accumulation of human capital increases output both directly and indirectly, that is, through the externality. Here we are confronted with a variant of a *public good* problem, which may be expressed as follows. The individual optimizing agent faces constant returns to scale in production: the sum of the partial elasticities of production of the factors he or she can control – that is,

436

his or her physical and human capital – is unity. Yet for society as a whole the partial elasticity of production of human capital is not $1 - \beta$, but $1 - \beta + \gamma$.

Lucas's conceptualization of the process by means of which human capital is built up is the following

$$h = \upsilon h(1 - u) \tag{36.7}$$

where υ is a positive constant. (Note that equation (36.7) can be interpreted as a 'production function' of human capital by means of human capital: the average product is constant and equals υ.)

Interestingly, it can be shown that if there is *not* the above-mentioned externality, i.e., if γ in equation (36.6) equals zero, and therefore returns to scale are constant and, as a consequence, the non-substitution theorem holds, endogenous growth in Lucas's model is obtained in essentially the same way as in the models of Rebelo (1991) and King and Rebelo (1990): the rate of profit is determined by technology and profit maximization alone; and for the predetermined level of the rate of profit the saving–investment mechanism determines the rate of growth. Hence, as Lucas himself has pointed out, the endogenous growth is positive *independently* of the fact that there is the above-mentioned externality; that is, independently of the fact that γ is positive. For a demonstration of this fact, see Kurz and Salvadori (1995b: 13–19). Therefore, though complicating the picture, *increasing returns do not add substantially to it: growth is endogenous even if returns to scale are constant.* As is well known, if returns to scale are not constant then the non-substitution theorem does not apply. Therefore, neither the competitive technique nor the associated rate of profit are determined by technical alternatives and profit maximization alone. Nevertheless, these two factors still determine, in steady states, a relationship between the rate of profit and the rate of growth. This relationship together with the relationship between the same rates obtained from the saving–investment equation determines both variables. Thus, although the analysis is more complex, essentially the same mechanism applies as in the models dealt with in the subsection dealing with linear or 'AK' models (pp. 433–5). Once again the concept of 'human capital' has assumed a role equivalent to the role of the concept of 'labour' in classical economics. However, although most contemporary economists would presumably be hostile to the idea that 'labour' could be treated as a produced factor of production, they appear to have had no difficulty in accepting the idea that there is a technology producing 'human capital'.

Endogenous technical change

Models of the second group attempt to portray technological change as generated endogenously. The proximate starting point of this kind of model was Arrow's paper on 'learning by doing' (Arrow 1962). Romer (1986) focuses attention on the role of a single-state variable called 'knowledge' or 'information'. It is assumed that the information contained in inventions and discoveries has the property of being available to anybody to make use of at the same time. In other words, information is considered essentially a non-rival good. However, it need not be totally non-excludable; that is, it can be monopolized at least for a time. It is around the two different aspects of publicness (non-rivalry and non-excludability) that the argument revolves. Discoveries are made in research and development departments of firms. This requires that resources be withheld from producing current output. The basic idea of Romer's model is that 'there is a trade-off between consumption today and knowledge that can be used to produce more consumption tomorrow' (ibid.: 1015). He formalizes this idea in terms of a 'research technology' that produces 'knowledge' from forgone consumption. Knowledge is assumed to be cardinally measurable and not to depreciate: it is like perennial capital.

Romer stipulates a research technology that is concave and homogeneous of degree 1:

$$\dot{k}_i = G(I_i, k_i) \tag{36.8}$$

where I_i is an amount of forgone consumption in research by firm i and k_i is the firm's current stock of knowledge. (Note that equation (36.8) can be interpreted as a production function describing the production of 'knowledge' by means of 'knowledge' and the forgone consumption good.) The production function of the consumption good relative to firm i is

$$Y_i = F(k_i, K, x_i) \tag{36.9}$$

where K is the accumulated stock of knowledge in the economy as a whole and x_i is a vector of inputs different from knowledge. Romer assumes that 'factors other than knowledge are in fixed supply' (ibid.: 1019). This implies that 'knowledge' is the only capital good utilized in the production of the consumption good. (The forgone consumption good is a capital good used in the production of knowledge.) Spillovers from private research and development activities increase the public stock of knowledge, K. It is assumed that the function is homogeneous of degree 1 in k_i and x_i and homogeneous of a degree greater than 1 in k_i and K.

Assuming, unlike Romer, that the above production function (36.9) is homogeneous of degree 1 in k_i and K involves a constant marginal product of capital: the diminishing returns to k_i are exactly offset by the external improvements in technology associated with capital accumulation. In this case it can be shown that, as in the models previously dealt with, the rate of profit is determined by technology and profit maximization alone, provided, as is assumed by Romer, that the ratio K/k_i equals the (given) number of firms. The saving–investment relation then determines endogenously the growth rate. Once again endogenous growth does not depend on an assumption about increasing returns with regard to accumulable factors.

Growth would not be 'more endogenous' if increasing returns were to be assumed. Such an assumption renders the analysis a good deal more complicated. In particular, a steady-state equilibrium does not exist unless the marginal product of capital is taken to be bounded from above. This is done by Romer in terms of an *ad hoc* assumption regarding equation (36.8) (ibid.: 1019). This assumption is not different from the one used in drawing Figure 36.4, where the marginal product of corn is shown to be increasing with the scale of production, but is bounded from above.

CONCLUDING REMARKS

This chapter has shown how in some of the best-known NGMs endogenous growth is generated. Notwithstanding their many differences, it is a striking common feature of these models that the rate of profit is determined by technology alone, or, if there is a choice of technique, by the profit-maximizing behaviour of producers. With the rate of profit determined in this way, the task of the saving–investment mechanism is restricted to the determination of the steady-state growth rate. With a given saving rate, the growth rate is simply the profit rate multiplied by the saving rate. With intertemporal utility maximization things are slightly more complicated and the saving rate is endogenously determined. It has also been shown that contrary to widespread opinion increasing returns are not an indispensable ingredient in order to obtain endogenous growth. The profit rate is determined by technology because it is assumed that there is a technology producing 'labour'. In order to render this fact acceptable to a twentieth-century audience, the factor has been given new names and enters the stage either as 'human capital' or 'knowledge'. Exactly as in the Ricardian analysis, in this way the profit rate is determined. The readers of *Production of Commodities by Means of Commodities* by Piero Sraffa (1960) will immediately recall that when at the beginning of ch. 2 wages are regarded as entering the system 'on the same footing as the fuel for the engines or the feed for the cattle', the profit rate and the prices are determined by technology alone. On the contrary, when workers get a part of the surplus, the quantity of labour employed in each industry has to be represented explicitly, and the profit rate and the prices can be determined only if an extra equation determining income distribution is introduced into the analysis. The additional equation generally used by advocates of neoclassical analysis is the equality between demand and supply of 'capital', which requires the homogeneity of this factor. But no extra equation is required in the NGT since, as in Ricardo and at the beginning of ch. 2 of Sraffa's book, there is a technology producing 'labour'.

Finally, it should be noted that the NGT has revived *long-period* analysis, centred around the concept of a uniform rate of profit. However, the kind of long-period argument put forward in the NGT falls way behind the present state of the art in this field of research. In particular, it appears to us to be anachronistic to attempt to develop a theory of growth that focuses on product innovations, new 'industrial designs', etc. in terms of a model which preserves several of the disquieting features of the neoclassical growth theory of the 1950s and 1960s, including the setting aside of the diversity of behaviour and the heterogeneity of goods and particularly of capital goods. These latter assumptions the NGT shares with Knight's famous Crusonia plant, in particular, a homogeneous capital jelly (cf. Kurz and Salvadori 1995b). There is no need and indeed no justification whatsoever to continue to dwell on such fairy tales; first, because the structure of the theory does not require such an assumption since distribution is *not* determined by the equality of the demand and supply of 'capital', and second, because modern long-period theory of 'classical' derivation might offer an alternative that allows a better understanding of the phenomena under consideration.

We hope to have shown that many of the interesting aspects of the NGMs are related to the classical perspective their authors (unwittingly) take on the problem of growth, whereas some of their shortcomings derive from the lack of solutions to the problems of the neoclassical theory of growth which were put into sharp relief during the 1960s. It has also been hinted that in some non-neoclassical approaches to the theory of accumulation and growth, the endogeneity of the growth rate has always been taken for granted (cf. Kurz and Salvadori 1995c). A brief look into the history of economic thought shows that from Adam Smith via David Ricardo, Robert Torrens, Thomas Robert Malthus, Karl Marx up to John von Neumann, Evsey Domar, Roy Harrod, Joan Robinson and Nicholas Kaldor both the equilibrium and the actual rate of capital accumulation and thus both the equilibrium and the actual rate of growth of output as a whole were seen to depend on agents' behaviour, that is, endogenously determined. In this regard there is indeed nothing new under the sun.

ACKNOWLEDGEMENTS

Neri Salvadori gratefully acknowledges financial support from MURST (the Italian Ministry of University and Technological and Scientific Research) and CNR (the Italian National Research Council).

NOTES

1   Later authors replaced this classification of economic stages of society, and the reasons given for why one such stage should give way to another, by other classifications and other explanations of the dynamics of transition. Marx, for example, saw a sequence leading from the feudal via the capitalist to the socialist and finally communist society, and representatives of the German historical school suggested still other social stages. However, it is a common feature of all these different conceptualizations that they start from the idea of a 'normal' development of society in terms of a sequence of states through which society

must progress, where each of these states can be characterized by its peculiar institutional features, its 'mode of production' (Marx), including the way in which the product is distributed. Given the specificity of each stage an economic analysis peculiar to it is required in order to come to grips with differences in time and space. For example, socioeconomic systems that are predominantly governed by custom and command are to be dealt with differently from economies that have already experienced the rise of the market and of the exchange economy (see Hicks 1969).

2   Geoff coined the term 'social science imperialism' (see Harcourt 1982, esp. part VII); see also his 'Reflections on the development of economics as a discipline', reprinted in Harcourt (1986: ch. 1).

3   This path must not, of course, be identified with the *actual* path the economy is taking because technical progress will repeatedly offset the impact of the 'niggardliness of nature' on the rate of profit.

4   Real wages may rise; that is, the 'market price of labour' may rise above the 'natural' wage rate. This is the case in a situation in which capital accumulates rapidly, leading to an excess demand for labour. As Ricardo put it, 'notwithstanding the tendency of wages to conform to their natural rate, their market rate may, in an improving society, for an indefinite period, be constantly above it' (1817 [1951]: 94–5). If such a constellation prevails for some time it is even possible that 'custom renders absolute necessaries' what in the past had been comforts or luxuries. Hence, the natural wage is driven upward by persistently high levels of the actual wage rate. Accordingly, Ricardo's concept of 'natural wage' is a flexible one and must not be mistaken for a physiological · minimum of subsistence. For Smith's view on wages and the growth of the workforce, see Kurz and Salvadori (1995a: ch. 15).

5   In the more sophisticated conceptualizations underlying the arguments of Smith and Ricardo, higher rates of growth of labour supply presuppose higher levels of the real wage rate. But the basic logic remains the same: in normal conditions the pace at which capital accumulates regulates the pace at which labour grows.

6   Let $x = f(L, L^*)$ be the product of the last unit of labour-cum-capital when L represents the amount of labour-cum-capital employed and the division of labour is artificially kept fixed at the level appropriate when the amount of labour-cum-capital employed is L^*. Obviously, $f(L, L^*)$ as a function of L alone is either decreasing as in Figures 36.1 and 36.3 (if land is scarce) or constant as in Figure 36.2 (if land is not scarce). The product at L^* equals $\int_0^{L^*} f(L, L^*)\, dL$; that is, the area under the curve $f(L, L^*)$ in the range $[0, L^*]$. If

$$\frac{\partial f}{\partial L^*} > -\frac{\partial f}{\partial L} \qquad \text{for } L = L^*$$

then the curve $x = f(L, L)$, which is the curve depicted in Figure 36.4, is increasing, but the product is, as stated in the text, larger than or equal to the sum of profits and wages, which equals the product of the given amount of labour-cum-capital multiplied by the corresponding level of output per unit of labour-cum-capital.

7   The assumption that the formation of human capital does not involve any unskilled labour as an input is not convincing: the whole point of education processes is that a person's capacity to perform unskilled labour is gradually transformed into his or her capacity to perform skilled labour. Adam Smith, for

441

example, was perfectly aware of this. For an analytical treatment of the problem of human capital, taking Smith's discussion as a starting point, see Kurz and Salvadori (1995a: ch. 11).

8   We need a special case of the non-substitution theorem because no primary factor (or a primary factor with a zero remuneration) is assumed; see Kurz and Salvadori (1994).

REFERENCES

Arrow, K. J. (1962) 'The economic implications of learning by doing', *Review of Economic Studies* 29: 155–73.

Barro, R. J. and Sala-i-Martin, X. (1995) *Economic Growth*, New York: McGraw-Hill.

Grossman, G. M. and Helpman, E. (1994) 'Endogenous innovation in the theory of growth', *Journal of Economic Perspectives* 8: 23–44.

Harcourt, G. C. (1982) *The Social Science Imperialists: Selected Essays*, ed. P. Kerr, London: Routledge & Kegan Paul.

—— (1986) *Controversies in Political Economy: Selected Essays of G. C. Harcourt*, ed. O. Hamouda, New York: New York University Press.

—— (1995) 'Recollections and reflections of an Australian patriot and a Cambridge economist', *Banca Nazionale del Lavoro Quarterly Review* 48: 225–54.

Hicks, J. R. (1969) *A Theory of Economic History*, Oxford: Clarendon Press.

Jones, L. E. and Manuelli, R. (1990) 'A convex model of equilibrium growth: theory and policy implications', *Journal of Political Economy* 98: 1008–38.

Kaldor, N. (1956) 'Alternative theories of distribution', *Review of Economic Studies* 23: 83–100.

—— (1957) 'A model of economic growth', *Economic Journal* 67: 591–624.

King, R. G. and Rebelo, S. (1990) 'Public policy and economic growth: developing neoclassical implications', *Journal of Political Economy* 98: 126–50.

Kurz, H. D. and Salvadori, N. (1994) 'The non-substitution theorem: making good a lacuna', *Journal of Economics* 59: 97–103.

—— (1995a) *Theory of Production: A Long-Period Analysis*, Cambridge: Cambridge University Press.

—— (1995b) 'What is "new" in the new theories of economic growth? Or: Old wine in new goatskins', revised version of a paper presented at the workshop 'Endogenous Growth and Development' of The International School of Economic Research, University of Siena, Italy, 3–9 July 1994. To be published in the workshop proceedings, London: Macmillan.

—— (1995c) 'Theories of "endogenous" growth in historical perspective', paper given at the Eleventh World Congress of the International Economic Association, Tunis, 17–22 December 1995. To be published in the conference proceedings.

Locke, J. (1690 [1953]) *Two Treatises of Government*, 2nd edition, ed. P. Laslett, Cambridge: Cambridge University Press.

Lucas, R. E. (1988) 'On the mechanics of economic development', *Journal of Monetary Economics* 22: 3–42.

Meek, R. L. (1976) *Social Science and the Ignoble Savage*, Cambridge: Cambridge University Press.

Rebelo, S. (1991) 'Long run policy analysis and long run growth', *Journal of Political Economy* 99: 500–21.

Ricardo, D. (1817 [1951]) *On the Principles of Political Economy and Taxation*, vol. 1 of *The Works and Correspondence of David Ricardo*, ed. Piero Sraffa with the collaboration of M. H. Dobb, Cambridge: Cambridge University Press.

Romer, P. M. (1986) 'Increasing returns and long-run growth', *Journal of Political Economy* 94: 1002–37.

Solow, R. M. (1956) 'A contribution to the theory of economic growth', *Quarterly Journal of Economics* 70: 65–94.

Sraffa, P. (1960) *Production of Commodities by Means of Commodities*, Cambridge: Cambridge University Press.

Uzawa, H. (1965) 'Optimum technical change in an aggregate model of economic growth', *International Economic Review* 6: 18–31.

Young, A. (1928) 'Increasing returns and economic progress', *Economic Journal* 38: 527–42.

37

HARCOURT AS A HISTORIAN OF ECONOMIC THOUGHT

John B. Davis

In his first year at Cambridge to study for a Ph.D. in economics, Geoff Harcourt locked himself away for the better part of a term from friends, family and the temptations of Cambridge to read and study Joan Robinson's newly published *The Accumulation of Capital* (1956). He later testified that

> *The Accumulation of Capital* had a profound effect on me. It presented a 'vision' of how capitalism works over time and, more tentatively, a conceptual framework with which to think about the processes involved and which made sense of what I saw happening around me. It formed the core from which my own work and teaching was from then on always to start.
>
> (Harcourt 1992: 3)

He went on to add that one of the great virtues of Robinson's work was that she was able to synthesize the work of Smith, Ricardo, Marx, Marshall, Keynes, Kalecki, Kahn and, in her later work, Sraffa. The history of economic thought, seen through this Robinsonian lens, would form the backdrop for Harcourt's own thinking and many contributions to post-Keynesian theories of investment, pricing, employment and the distribution of income. It was also from this Robinsonian perspective that Harcourt wrote and continues to write the history of post-Keynesian economic thought, covering the Cambridge capital controversy, the post-Keynesian revival of classical political economy, contemporary post-Keynesian theory, and finally the history of 'Joan Robinson and her circle'.

It seems fair to say that no one has approached Harcourt's facility and insight in explaining how the different strands of post-Keynesianism weave together to produce a distinct and identifiable modern form of economic analysis and thinking. His advantage in this has in part been due to his having been at Cambridge at the time of the initial emergence of post-Keynesianism in the 1950s when it first began to become clear that Keynes's own thinking – as opposed to hybrid Keynesianism of the Samuelsonian sort – would not, and perhaps could not, be widely accepted by an economics profession fundamentally conservative in nature. Led by Robinson, Kahn, Kaldor and Sraffa, Cambridge then began to train a new generation of economists who were conscious of the fact that they were producing theory following new pathways, though with origins more than a century old in classical political economy. Harcourt was a member of this new generation; a member, as he puts it, of the class of 1955–8. But Harcourt's advantage in explaining post-Keynesianism and its history is also due to his talent as a historian of ideas, which has enabled him to survey the structure and significance of contemporary economic ideas, especially in their relation to the issues facing modern economies. It was this that enabled him to make his initial foray into the history of thought in his definitive and unequalled history of the Cambridge capital controversy. Writing the history of the debate practically as fast as it happened, Harcourt demonstrated a gift in grasping the present as history.

This chapter outlines Harcourt's contributions to the history of post-Keynesian economics both to draw attention to the scope of his achievements as a historian of ideas, and to help explain the nature of post-Keynesianism itself. It is important to understand the latter objective to appreciate the former. Post-Keynesianism's different currents sometimes create the impression that the term 'post-Keynesian' lacks an identifiable referent. Post-Keynesian economics may none the less be identified as the product of a succession or accumulation of theoretical innovations in economics aimed at helping us understand modern industrial, monetary economies. Harcourt has focused upon the quarter-century history of the emergence of post-Keynesianism at Cambridge influenced most by Keynes, Sraffa and Kalecki. That history was first told in terms of the Cambridge capital controversy (see below), was next deepened through discussion of the post-Keynesian revival of classical political economy traditions (the subject of a section starting on p. 448), was then broadened by a gathering of related movements in the identification of post-Keynesianism as an approach and method (see p. 450), and is currently being re-examined from the perspective of the original contributions of 'Joan Robinson and her circle' (p. 452).

THE HISTORY OF THE CAMBRIDGE CAPITAL CONTROVERSY

The Cambridge capital controversies had their origin in Robinson's critique of the aggregate production function (1953–4), drew inspiration from Sraffa's classic work (1960), and climaxed in the reswitching and capital-reversing debates of 1965–7. The controversies surely represent one of the more paradoxical episodes in the history of economic thought. Two different groups of some of the world's best-known and talented economists representing two different long-standing traditions in the history of economic thought engaged in a protracted, intense intellectual exchange for nearly ten years over one of the most important issues in economic theory and in capitalism, but none the less largely misunderstood one another, often failing to communicate at all, with the result that though the debates arguably produced a reasonably clear set of conclusions, few economists today either recognize their importance or grasp their implications for current economic theory. Indeed, many of the participants in the debates confined themselves to citing the errors of their opponents. Harcourt, however, drew valuable conclusions about the significance of the debates for post-Keynesian economic thinking and economics generally.

The lack of communication and misunderstanding between the two Cambridges was in good part due to the fact that the Cambridge, England, critique of marginal productivity theory specifically targeted the aggregate production function. One response from Cambridge, Massachusetts, was that this did not preclude consideration of the marginal products of individual capital goods, and thus that no serious critique of marginal productivity theory was involved. Throughout the later debates over reswitching and capital reversing, this point remained unresolved, with Cambridge, Massachusetts, insisting more and more as the flaws of aggregate production function thinking became apparent that marginal productivity theory had its principal home in general equilibrium analysis, and Cambridge, England, insisting that aggregate analysis was central to any understanding of the economy as a whole.

What explained this breakdown in communication between the two sides? Harcourt drew on Robinson, who had argued that the problem was not about the measurement of capital but rather about its meaning, where this involved specifying the nature of a capitalist economy in terms of its institutions and rules, one of which would presumably be that in a system in which one class owned the means of production, a uniform rate of profits had to be paid on all capital goods. Harcourt thus commented in his 1976 'Cambridge controversies' review of the debates:

> What is involved is the relevant 'vision' of the economic system and the historical processes associated with its development. In particular, stress is laid by the Cambridge (England) school on production and distribution as involving underlying social relations, especially their implication for production and distribution, accumulation and growth.
>
> (Harcourt 1992: 133)

Cambridge, Massachusetts, however, insisted, in the words of Frank Hahn, that what all one needed to do, or could do, was 'to get the purely technical argument right' (Hahn 1972: 2; quoted in Harcourt 1992: 132). Importantly, this presupposed that in the social sciences ideology and analysis could be easily and clearly separated, a proposition that Cambridge, England, following the lead of Dobb 1973: 4–7), firmly rejected. This methodological disagreement, Harcourt recognized, had concrete implications for the progress of the debates. Because Cambridge, Massachusetts, believed that ideology and analysis could and ought to be kept separate, it came to conclude that the unwillingness of Cambridge, England, to keep them separate demonstrated an ideological rather than scientific motivation. This ultimately also justified the attitude that ultimately many assumed in the Cambridge, Massachusetts, tradition toward the debates, namely, that they had never involved a truly scientific exchange, and ought accordingly to be ignored – along with, for that matter, all the thinking associated with Cambridge, England.

The effect on Cambridge, England, and the future of post-Keynesian thinking was decisive. Whereas once in the respectably scientific and highly influential tradition of Keynes, the thinking of Cambridge, England, abruptly became outcast in the mid-1970s, its ideas increasingly proscribed from the economics curricula of major universities, first in the United States and then gradually elsewhere, on the supposed but largely unexamined grounds that it was methodologically corrupt and unscientific.[1] This could not but have surprised Cambridge, England, economists, who had not only correctly identified important flaws in marginal productivity thinking as an account of the modern industrial economy only to have them disregarded, but who had had good reasons worth discussion rather than simple dismissal for maintaining the connectedness of ideology and analysis. Post-Keynesianism, then, first emerged as a distinct form of economics as a result of these developments, in that its body of theoretical and methodological assumptions acquired an inadvertent unity and relative autonomy by virtue of their outcast status. Subsequent development of post-Keynesian thinking, then, not only built upon the theoretical foundations established by Cambridge, England, in the debates, but did so with an awareness of the importance of the methodological positions involved. One of Harcourt's most important judgements regarding the Cambridge controversies emphasized this latter point.

Although lack of communication and misunderstanding characterized much of the debates between the two Cambridges, their most ironic aspect, Harcourt concluded, was that their 'climax itself was not very satisfying, because it occurred in the wrong – or at least not in the most important or fundamental – areas' (1992: 130). Were one to suppose that the Arrow and Hahn general equilibrium theory was the only viable form of marginal productivity theory,

> the sorts of questions that the classical political economists were attempting to answer, in particular, the determination of relative shares of profits and wages as capital goods accumulate over time, and what happens to the living standards of broad class groupings, to the rate of profits (the uniform, long-run, natural or normal rate of profits, that is) and to the techniques of production in the process – broad, aggregative,

sociological questions associated with the 'laws of motion' of capitalist
societies – would end up unaddressed

(ibid.: 135)

One reason for this, Harcourt explained, is that general equilibrium theory is
'not explanatory ... nor a descriptive hypothesis, principally because it cannot
handle historical time' (ibid.: 136). Throughout the capital controversies
Robinson had always insisted that at root in Cambridge, Massachusetts,
thinking was 'an error in methodology – a confusion between comparisons of
imagined equilibrium positions and a process of accumulation going on
through history' (Robinson 1974: 11). Real-world economies did not operate
in logical time, however, but through causal processes in historical time.

> The Keynesian method is to describe a set of relationships (intended to
> correspond ... to the relevant features of the economic system) and to
> trace the effects in the immediate and further future of a change taking
> place as an event at the moment of time.

(Robinson 1975: 92)

That there was no communication on this issue, Harcourt saw, meant that
there could be no resolution of the many different points in contention
between the two Cambridges. The particular effect this had on the future
development of post-Keynesianism, however, was for Cambridge, England,
economists to grasp clearly that economic methodology required attention to
real, causal, historical processes, which created a basis for investigation of
those 'broad, aggregative, sociological questions associated with the "laws of
motion", of capitalist societies' investigated in classical political economy.
This meant that early post-Keynesians next set out to re-explore and revive
the assumptions of that mode of thinking.

THE REVIVAL OF CLASSICAL POLITICAL ECONOMY

Harcourt's most important contribution in this regard was his 1975 *Economic
Record* review essay of four books (Harcourt 1975a), Dobb's *Theories of
Value and Distribution* (1973), Hahn's *The Share of Wages in the National
Income* (1972), Hicks's *Capital and Time* (1973) and Johnson's *The Theory
of Income Distribution* (1973). Dobb (1975), Hahn (1975) and Hicks (1975)
later responded to the review, and Harcourt (1975b) replied to their
comments.[2] His initial premise was that each of the four was essentially
'concerned with the great problems of the classical political economists –
distribution and the theory of value, allied with the process of accumulation
of capital goods over time in a decentralized economy, usually competitive,
capitalist economy' (Harcourt 1992: 101). What distinguished the four
authors, however, was the prominence or neglect each accorded distribution

and production, and specifically, whether one held to 'the dependence of the price structure on distribution', or favoured 'the converse dependence of distribution on a demand-determined price-structure' (Dobb 1973: 266; quoted in Harcourt 1992: 112). Here Harcourt found invaluable Dobb's understanding of the history of economic thought in terms of two competing traditions, which differently conceived the relationship between analysis and ideology, and which disagreed on the scope of political economy. These issues linked to the question of whether one reasoned in terms of universal general laws, or adopted a historical-relativist position which emphasized institutions and time.

For Harcourt, Hahn represented an interesting case on account of his employing a simultaneous-equations methodology to add an account of the distribution of income to Keynesian analysis of overall economic activity. In response to Harcourt's charge that this ran counter to Keynes's and Kalecki's emphasis upon the idea of a one-way process of direction from investment to savings, Hahn reasserted the themes of mathematical mutual dependence, suggesting in the process that post-Keynesian economists were guilty of the most incomprehensible mistakes in reasoning. A better example of Dobb's thesis of two competing (and non-communicating) traditions in economic thinking might not be found. As Harcourt noted in his reply, the real problem here seemed to be that post-Keynesians were concerned with classical questions – accumulation over time, the distribution of income between classes, the role of a uniform natural rate of profits in a capitalist economy – which were matters that modern general equilibrium theory was never intended to address. 'Hahn has ignored the criticism that the wrong approach may have been used to model the world for particular questions' (Harcourt 1992: 126), and this meant that misunderstanding and lack of communication were likely to prevail.

Hicks, interestingly, took the occasion of his comment to emphasize the historical methodology intentionally applied in his later work generally, a feature which he believed Harcourt had not appreciated in reviewing *Capital and Time*, and which he allowed was missing from his earlier, better-known work. Given this, he then argued that economies out of equilibrium may none the less be understood to converge to equilibrium when certain simplifying assumptions are adopted. One of Harcourt's original concerns was which such simplifying assumptions might justifiably be made, specifically regarding whether wages are fixed or variable, when one was trying to understand the role of the surplus in modern economies. But Hicks's view of history required an equilibrium concept. It was an excellent example of a framing concept that Dobb would term ideological.

Interestingly, after Dobb's book had appeared, Hutchinson (1974) had argued that Dobb was wrongheaded in attempting to justify a role for 'individual motivation' in economic analysis. Dobb thus replied in his comment that his emphasis on ideology rather concerned 'the extent to which the shaping of any model, or set of abstract propositions in a subject ... is inevitably influenced ... by what may be termed a larger conceptual framework of ideas about the nature of existing society and its history' (quoted in Harcourt 1992: 118). This restatement of Dobb's view was seconded by Harcourt in his own reply. It reflected his recent experience over the reception to his comments on ideology in his book on the capital controversies (Harcourt, 1972), where it was clear that there was very little sympathy for considering any possible role the concept of ideology might have in theoretical disputes. It may also have been behind Johnson's unwillingness even to reply to Harcourt's original review on the grounds that Johnson thought that Harcourt simply did not like his book – an interpretation of ideological differences reduced to personal motivation.

Thus again, not only did deep-seated differences divide economists from different traditions, but individuals from these traditions were also unable to communicate about fundamental methodological issues. The great virtue of the exchange that came out of Harcourt's *Economic Record* review essay, however, was to make clear that there were these very different traditions, that post-Keynesianism with its interest in the 'broad, aggregative sociological questions' facing economies had natural roots in classical political economy, and that there was unlikely to be much overlap of interest between post-Keynesianism and the economics of Hahn, Hicks and Johnson. What needed to be done, then, was to map out the distinctive contours of this tradition with its classical political economy antecedents in its contemporary development in connection with modern industrial economies.

THE BROADENING OF POST-KEYNESIANISM AS A DISTINCTIVE TRADITION

In an often-cited paper, (Hamouda and Harcourt 1988), Harcourt turned to the task of explaining the nature of post-Keynesianism *per se* (see also Harcourt 1982). Despite the many papers already on the subject, the controversial character of the issues, the diversity of theories and the ideological suspicions of many in the economics profession still left it unclear to many just what post-Keynesianism involved. Harcourt, however, chose to explain post-Keynesianism as a single approach according to the different routes by which it had come out of classical political economy. He discerned three strands of thinking distinguishing major groups of thinkers, and also identified a collection of outstanding individual figures who defied classification within any one strand. Emphasizing the continuity with classical political economy made the surplus approach central to theories of value and distribution. The classicals had also sought an analysis of gravitational natural prices rather than supply-and-demand market prices, and treated money as a veil via the quantity theory over a real economy governed by Say's law. Clearly, these basic ideas allowed for different elaborations in the context of modern industrial economies.

One strand led to Marshall. Marshall preserved the classical dichotomy between value and distribution, on the one hand, and money, on the other (though abandoning surplus thinking by explaining long-period normal prices in terms of supply and demand). Keynes pursued the money side of this classical vision and, though retaining the classical emphasis on broad, sociological relationships, ended up throwing over the quantity theory, Say's law and the classical dichotomy for an analysis of a monetary production economy. North American post-Keynesianism (Weintraub, Tarshis, Davidson, Minsky) took up this conception, and added an account of the aggregate supply function. The latter took firm price or sales proceeds expectations (according to the form of competition assumed) as a starting point, and investigated how entrepreneurs would react if these short-period expectations went unfulfilled. Analysis of the economy as a monetary production economy emphasized uncertainty, the centrality of the money wage, the properties of money liquidity, and financial instability.

A second strand of post-Keynesianism, a neo-Ricardian one, derives from Sraffa's rehabilitation of the surplus approach, emphasizes the importance of a long-period approach to income and employment, and firmly rejects any elements of a subjective theory of value. Sraffa's work laid the basis for the critique of aggregate production function analysis central to the Cambridge capital controversies. It also led to important disagreements with those post-Keynesians attached to Keynes's downward-sloping marginal efficiency of capital and investment schedules, which were regarded as inconsistent with the main results of the capital theory debates. This conflict suggested to some that neo-Ricardian economics was fundamentally different in nature from other strands of post-Keynesianism. Putting aside questions of semantics, Harcourt's strategy was to show that in terms of Dobb's two competing traditions, neo-Ricardianism and monetary production post-Keynesianism none the less shared the same classical heritage.

The third strand Harcourt distinguishes passes through Marxian economics, stressing the significance of social relationships in the sphere of production, the technical structure of production, and the potential surplus available at any moment of time. The real wage is determined in class conflict, and whether the potential surplus is realized depends upon the interplay between an accumulation function (in the sense of Robinson's 'animal spirits' function) and a savings function reflecting the distribution of income. Kalecki was especially influential here in combining Keynes's effective-demand analysis and Marx's reproduction schemes. Robinson represented the two-sided relationship between accumulation and profitability with her famous banana diagram. The micro-foundations of the approach were developed from Kalecki's degree of monopoly mark-up view by a variety of individuals. Contributors have none the less differed over the relative importance of long-run and short-run factors in explaining price-setting.

Finally, Harcourt takes Kaldor, Goodwin, Pasinetti, Shackle and Godley to be beyond classification. Yet all share classical presuppositions in their work, and are consequently labelled post-Keynesian. Harcourt's survey of post-Keynesianism, then, demonstrates the existence of a shared orientation across very different types of thinkers based on their common concern with 'concrete situations, the historical experience and the sociological character-istics of the economies' they study (Hamouda and Harcourt 1988: 231). All, it might be said, sought to fit theories to the facts they found rather than fit facts to pre-held theories – a formalist trait characteristic for Dobb of the other great tradition in economics that emerged after classical political economy. Given this distinction, to attempt to place all types of post-Keynesian thinking in a single schema is a misplaced exercise. Different levels of abstraction and different issues necessarily produce different types of theories. This methodo-logical conviction is specifically post-Keynesian.

'JOAN ROBINSON AND HER CIRCLE'

Harcourt's largest and most recent project in writing the history of post-Keynesian economic thought involves explaining the thought of 'Joan Robinson and her circle', the first economists who were self-consciously post-Keynesian. Robinson, Kahn, Kaldor and Sraffa were not only the first to see that Keynes's and Kalecki's work departed in fundamental ways from Marshallian thinking, but also to see that it did so by reintroducing classical questions and concerns into modern economics. They were also the first to see that new divisions within the economics profession – initially brought about by Keynes's rejection of Say's law and the quantity theory of money, and then over the competing conceptions of the proper domain of economics produced in the Cambridge capital controversy – were likely to persist in the future.

Of course Harcourt's choice of Robinson as the central figure in this group naturally reflects his own commitments and interests in economics. Other post-Keynesians accord Sraffa greater importance (or Kalecki for that matter, though he was not really part of the post-Keynes 'circle' or in Cambridge for very long). Still, it is probably fair to say that the combination of Robinson's combative personal character and the hostile reception of post-Keynesianism by the majority of economists did make her a pivotal figure in the emergence of post-Keynesianism, and that any history of this emergence ought to ascribe to her a key role. Harcourt, however, puts his finger on something probably even more important: Robinson, especially in her *Accumulation of Capital* (1956), provided 'a "vision" of how capitalism works over time and, more tentatively, a conceptual framework with which to think about the processes involved' (Harcourt 1992: 3). In this respect, she very much was a follower of Keynes, who also emphasized the significance of economists' vision of the economy: 'Keynes himself (and others on his behalf, notably Joan Robinson) claimed that he tried to change our *method* of doing economics as well as our way of *seeing* how our economies work' (Harcourt and Sardoni 1994: 132; emphasis in original). Thus it is Robinson's particular 'vision' of both the operation of the economy as a whole and the way of approaching its explanation that we need to attend to in order to understand Harcourt's history of the beginnings of post-Keynesianism.

That vision matured in *The Accumulation of Capital*, and combined Keynesian thinking about investment, animal spirits and finance with Marxian ideas regarding reproduction and realization via Kalecki to create an understanding of capitalism as a historical process (Harcourt and King 1995: 40–2). It was heavily influenced by Sraffa's work on Ricardo and the concept of the surplus, and affirmed the distinctiveness of classical political economy. Indeed, Harcourt suggests that one of Robinson's virtues was her ability to synthesize hers and others' ideas, and that she was less concerned about getting credit for things than getting things right. This meant that, at least for a time, Robinson's vision reflected the Cambridge, England, view (especially for those at Cambridge, Massachusetts), so that telling the history of 'Robinson and her circle' is simply telling the history of the circle. Much the same might be said about the earlier 'Cambridge circus' (despite Kahn's special role in communicating with Keynes).

Sadly, the passing of Robinson, Sraffa, Kaldor and Kahn by the mid-1980s has left Cambridge with few post-Keynesians, and, lacking a single, prominent university location and the notoriety of the original followers of Keynes, post-Keynesianism has struck some as less substantial as an alternative method and body of economics than it in fact is. Yet not only are the number of active post-Keynesians and the range of new developments based on the work of 'Robinson and her circle' quite extensive, but post-Keynesians today are generally aware that they share a distinct tradition in the history of economics with specific methodological commitments to a historically informed analysis of modern economies. Harcourt's history of post-Keynesian origins counts as an important contribution to the development of this understanding.

CONCLUDING NOTE

Harcourt's claims for Joan Robinson emphasize her vision and capacity as a synthesizer of ideas. In this respect he has always very much been her student both in having a vision of post-Keynesianism as a distinct and original tradition of thought, and in being able to explain the coherence of the range of post-Keynesian ideas. These talents, it turns out, are rarer than one might suppose, since few others seems to possess them. Indeed, in this respect post-Keynesianism may find itself in a rather enviable position in that Dobb's other main tradition in economic thought seems to lack a figure comparable in talent and insight to Harcourt.

NOTES

1   It is arguable that the decline of Keynesian macroeconomics in later years also had its origins in this development, since neoclassical-synthesis Keynesians were wedded to aggregate production analysis. New classical macroeconomics is based on a fully disaggregated, Walrasian analysis of the economy.
2   The original papers and later exchange are reprinted in Harcourt (1992: 101–29).

REFERENCES

Dobb, M. H. (1973) *Theories of Value and Distribution since Adam Smith: Ideology and Economic Theory*, Cambridge: Cambridge University Press.

—— (1975) 'Revival of political economy: an explanatory note', *Economic Record* 51(135): 357–9. Reprinted in Harcourt, G. C. (1992) *On Political Economists and Modern Political Economy: Selected Essays of G. C. Harcourt*, ed. C. Sardoni, London: Routledge.

Hahn, F. H. (1972) *The Share of Wages in the National Income: An Enquiry into the Theory of Distribution*, London: Weidenfeld & Nicolson.

—— (1975) 'Revival of political economy: the wrong issues and the wrong argument', *Economic Record* 51(135): 360–4. Reprinted in Harcourt, G. C. (1992) *On Political Economists and Modern Political Economy: Selected Essays of G. C. Harcourt*, ed. C. Sardoni, London: Routledge.

Hamouda, O. F. and Harcourt, G. C. (1988) 'Post-Keynesianism: from criticism to coherence?', *Bulletin of Economic Research* 40: 1–33. Reprinted in Harcourt, G. C. (1992) *On Political Economists and Modern Political Economy: Selected Essays of G. C. Harcourt*, ed. C. Sardoni, London: Routledge.

Harcourt, G. C (1972) *Some Cambridge Controversies in the Theory of Capital*, Cambridge: Cambridge University Press.

—— (1975a) 'Decline and rise: the revival of (classical) political economy', *Economic Record* 51(135): 339–56. Reprinted in Harcourt, G. C. (1992) *On Political Economists and Modern Political Economy: Selected Essays of G. C. Harcourt*, ed. C. Sardoni, London: Routledge.

—— (1975b) 'Revival of political economy: a further comment', *Economic Record* 51(135): 368–71. Reprinted in Harcourt, G. C. (1992) *On Political Economists and Modern Political Economy: Selected Essays of G. C. Harcourt*, ed. C. Sardoni, London: Routledge.

—— (1976) 'The Cambridge controversies: old ways and new horizons – or dead end?', *Oxford Economic Papers* 38(1): 25–65. Reprinted in Harcourt, G. C. (1992) *On Political Economists and Modern Political Economy: Selected Essays of G. C. Harcourt*, ed. C. Sardoni, London: Routledge.

—— (1982) 'Post Keynesianism: Quite wrong and/or nothing new?', *Thames Papers in Political Economy*, London: Thames Polytechnic.

—— (1992) *On Political Economists and Modern Political Economy: Selected Essays of G. C. Harcourt*, ed. C. Sardoni, London: Routledge.

Harcourt, G. C. and King, J. (1995) 'Talking about Joan Robinson: Geoff Harcourt in conversation with John King', *Review of Social Economy* 53(1): 31–64.

Harcourt, G. C. and Sardoni, C. (1994) 'Keynes's vision: method, analysis and "tactics"', in J. Davis (ed.) *The State of Interpretation of Keynes*, Boston and Dordrecht: Kluwer.

Hicks, J. (1973) *Capital and Time: A Neo-Austrian Theory*, Oxford: Clarendon Press.

—— (1975) 'Revival of political economy: the old and the new', *Economic Record* 51(135): 365–7. Reprinted in Harcourt, G. C. (1992) *On Political Economists and*

Modern Political Economy: Selected Essays of G. C. Harcourt, ed. C. Sardoni, London: Routledge.

Hutchinson, T. W. (1974) *The Cambridge Version of the History of Economics*, Occasional Paper 19, Birmingham: Faculty of Economics and Social Sciences, University of Birmingham.

Johnson, H. G. (1973) *The Theory of Income Distribution*, London: Gray-Mills.

Robinson, J. V. (1953–4) 'The production function and the theory of capital', *Review of Economic Studies* 21: 81–106.

—— (1956) *The Accumulation of Capital.* (Second edition, London: Macmillan, 1969.)

—— (1974) 'History versus equilibrium', London: Thames Polytechnic.

—— (1975) 'Letter to the editor', *Cambridge Review* 97: 91–2.

Sraffa, P. (1960) *Production of Commodities by Means of Commodities: A Prelude to a Critique of Economic Theory*, Cambridge: Cambridge University Press.

38

ECONOMICS AND SOCIAL CONSCIENCE

The Harcourt case

Mark Perlman

INTRODUCTION

My experience as both a contributor to and an editor of Festschriften is that their chapters, if there is a common theme at all, tend to cluster either around the fields in which the person being honoured has taught and worked or around the idiosyncratic interests of a circle of admirers whose offerings fall into no special category. This chapter falls in the latter class, and I worry about identifying adequately this volume's audience.

My chapter is meant to focus on the underpinnings of most of Geoffrey Harcourt's work,[1] which are often more apparent in his conversations than in his writings. In short, I wish to enquire as to the nature of his economics, and the reason his creative and systemic influence has been so regularly overlooked by the 'mainstream'. Is it his failing or theirs; what does he offer that they do not appreciate?

My answer is to turn to the manner in which our discipline has been oriented, and why it chooses to frame questions the way it does. In so doing, I think I can shed some light on the reason why, some, such as Harcourt, seem out of step, including the unique focus of their questions and the apparent 'strangeness' of their answers. However, let me add one other line of thought. Many economists have drawn a line between 'practical economics', sometimes called 'Political Economy' or (as in Germany) 'Economic Policy', and something called the Economic Science.

This distinction was often used in the late nineteenth century. More recently Joseph A. Schumpeter once harkened to it in his 1914 (translated in 1954) *Economic Doctrines and Method*, and Lionel Robbins wrote what recent generations considered to be the definitive statement in his 1934 *An Essay on the Nature and Significance of the Economic Science*. Others have the same view, a view predicated on the existence of an ontological economics. Schumpeter later repudiated his earlier view, holding that economics was not apart from, but rather actually involved, sociology.[2] Robbins's reformulation, presented at the 1980 Denver meetings of the

American Economic Association, was, though less specific, no less total (Robbins 1981). These recantations notwithstanding, 'mainline' economists – that is, the orthodox followers of 'Hicks–Samuelson neoclassicism'[3] – have instrumentally all but accepted that economics is a science, and that sciences do not have 'human faces'.

This thinking leads us to a consideration of the 'Harcourt problem'. The Harcourt problem is that his economics seems to be built on a humanism, one which I think is probably compatible with much earlier reasoning in the discipline, even though it is alien to what is now *à la mode*.

THE PREMISES OF WESTERN (ENGLISH AND FRENCH) ECONOMICS

Two early premises

Economics as we generally know it was built initially on two piers: one was Hellenistic and dealt with the criteria for approval; the other was Judeo-Christian and dealt with the nature and failings of man. The Hellenistic divide was between the abstractions of Plato and the empirical generalizations of Aristotle – between 'theory' (if you will) and a mixture of direct observation, cogitation about what had been seen, and eventually generalization and even an abstract statement of the generalized point. Put explicitly, the Hellenistic tradition focused on choice of method (appropriately termed 'methodology'), and that tradition is much in style these days.

The Judeo-Christian tradition, by contrast, starts not with a methodological division but with the story, the story of the Fall of humankind. From it two questions can be seen to emerge: what was the Sin and what was the Punishment? About these questions there developed parallel but different answers. The first is that of Thomas Aquinas, who, following the other Church fathers, saw the Sin as essentially a series of immoral seductions of the weaker character by the stronger; in the end, humankind's Punishment was hard labour – production through fatigue, the strength of the back, and by the sweat of his brow for Adam; and the pains of childbirth (women's production) for Eve. Scarcity became the rule, and the days of 'free-loading' were over.

The second answer was given by another medieval Aristotelian, Moses Maimonides. Maimonides saw the Sin as Faustian: excessive human curiosity leading to disobedience. For Maimonides, the Punishment was something worse than scarcity; it was Uncertainty. As he saw it, the knowledge necessary for Adam's and Eve's decisions, granted them previously, was gone, and what they had to rely on was their opinions – not much of a substitute.

From these contrasting Judeo-Christian approaches we draw two conclusions about the premises of economics: they involve Scarcity and Uncertainty.

Given these ancient legacies, is there more to what we have? The answer is clearly yes.

The premises dominant after the seventeenth century

The answers to Hobbes

Granted the early theological efforts, it was Thomas Hobbes who introduced the questions which shape much of modern economics. In his seminal *Leviathan*, among the derivatives of the many ideas he presented were three which shaped most English economics until after the hegemony of Marshall at the *fin de siècle*. Hobbes was, if not the first, certainly the most successful to suggest the methodology of empiricism, where belief was in ontological observation – material things as facts. Second, Hobbes denied divine purpose as the basis of social organization, substituting for it a combination of power and shrewdness (not exactly identical with logic, or what others would call 'reason'). Third, there was the ultimate derivative of individualism with implicit effort at what Bentham was later to call the seeking of pleasure and avoidance of pain.

Despite his cachet, there were few writers, aside from Bernard Mandeville, who sought to uphold the Hobbesian changes to the traditions of the Judeo-Christian religions. Most went in the other direction, 'correcting' Hobbes by substituting natural law, something quite compatible with biblical revelation. Such is true for the case of John Locke's vision of limited government and the inalienable rights of the individual. Or, as in the case of Anthony Ashley Cooper, life was not inherently 'nasty, brutish, and short', but, rather, good because men were normally born good. Or most clearly of all, of Adam Smith, who thought first (as in *The Theory of Moral Sentiments*) that Hobbes's observations were faulty, and that man was not simply individualistic but also had strong communitarian predilections. Smith complemented this first view by showing that, even if some men were individualistic, empirically they could realize that, through specialization, cooperation with other men reduced the fatigue, eased the strain on the back, and soothed the brow. Smith's *Wealth of Nations* became, quite probably unintentionally, the gospel of individualism because it revealed that a taste for plenty was enough to end the 'war of every man against every man'. But if its hull was individualism, its (natural law) superstructure was perfect competition.

It is not appropriate in this chapter to point out how complex were Jeremy Bentham's views; it is sufficient, however, to note that James Mill simplified them, and the unqualified hedonistic utilitarianism we wrongly associate with Bentham was, as Murray Rothbard has recently pointed out, a dour, Scottish (he said Presbyterian) version – a *reductio ad absurdum* – but one that caught on (Rothbard 1995). It assumed and explicitly ennobled the ideas of individualism and economic competition.

Another answer, one coming from natural law

The Scholastic tradition in economics complemented divine revelation as seen in the Gospels and/or by the Church fathers by offering a doctrine of natural law, this being a set of principles not specified in the theological documentation but nonetheless just as valid. Obviously the trouble with the natural-law approach was the same as the trouble with religious revelation: it was impossible to prove through empirical observation. Yet this need not lead us to dismay, as there were and are bright men and women who live by faith.

Most identify René Descartes as the one who popularized the natural-law approach to observation. He postulated that all phenomena are related (an act of faith) and that their relationships and functions can ultimately be described in a common language, viz. mathematics. Mathematics came (not by his explicit intent) to replace theology as the Queen of Knowledge, and formal mathematical formulation became the preferred method of demonstration. The balance between Aristotle and Plato was retipped, and Plato's star began to rise.

Among the great devotees of natural law were the French Physiocrats, brilliant men schooled in Cartesian thinking. Whether Quesnay drew his *tableau économique* correctly is less important than its underlying assumption: that the economy could best be illustrated through a formal analogue. Because of the discontinuities of France's political system, the Physiocrats' direct influence was short-lived. But well within their reforming camp were August Cournot, Leon Walras, and others like Jules Dupuit, who, living about a century later, presented the natural-law legacy as a formal (mathematical) statement of how economic systems could work if some fashion of efficiency were the sole criterion.

Living about the time of the Physiocratic upheaval was the political theorist Jean Jacques Rousseau, who offered both a substitute theory of government of basic social organization and its formal government; underlying optimal social organization and its formal government was fraternal love and respect, with government, itself, based on an abstraction, the 'general will'. Rousseau rejected Hobbes's view of man's inherent concern with personal (or familial) survival, and his 'general will' rejected the 'Lockian' legacy of individualism, substituting for it a new legacy of communitarianism. To this legacy we shall return a bit later.

ECONOMICS AS A SCIENCE

For most economists it is a commonplace that the economics discipline began to acquire its current modern or scientific character around 1871 at the time of the introduction of marginal analysis, particularly as it was presented by William Stanley Jevons[4] and Léon Walras.[5] Such a commonplace, of course, betrays profound ignorance of earlier formal (often, mathematical) writers, such as Richard Cantillon, Johann von Thünen, August Cournot and a host of others whose claims may be genuine but not as broad.[6] But a discipline is what it is said to be, and few these days express much interest in what seems to be mostly antiquarianism. Old names matter very little.

Our question is, when did economists start to consider themselves proper scientists? But even before that hour, there was the question of just what was meant by science and scientific. One explanation was that of Francis Bacon, the lawyer-turned-philosopher, who described what he called the 'scientific method' as a technique of reducing observations to testable hypothesis and then, through trial and error, reducing these hypotheses to a bare truth – this being a hypothesis which could not be reduced further by repeating subsequent empirical testing.

A second explanation lay in the science of Isaac Newton, as opposed to that of Charles Darwin. Newton held that a theory worked out cognitively was true, even if preliminary observations were non-confirmatory. Their kind of science depended upon Cartesian reductionism and the test of immanent criticism (no logical flaws within its statement or the logical ramifications). Darwinian science was of a *post hoc, ergo propter hoc* nature. Yet it too was considered scientific.

For economists, the preferred or prototypical science came to be physics, particularly as the subject had been initially organized around the now largely outmoded Newtonian principles of equilibrium and later revised by limited theoretical speculation checked by improved empiricism (physical observation). Again, as with biology, there were some who argued that Newton's explanations were limited to endogenous analyses only, but these views, occasionally mentioned but rarely considered, did little to remind economists, enthusiastic about Walrasian general-equilibrium analysis, that their quarry was small fry. Walras was not interested in exogenous analysis, and neither were they.

CAMBRIDGE'S INFLUENCE

Marshall's contributions

For economists trained in the British Marshallian (then called 'neoclassic') tradition, there was a built-in excuse. Marshall's partial-equilibrium approach made sense if one knowingly accepted his premise, stated clearly, that economics dealt with decisions made by the manager of a firm or the head of a consuming household. What Marshall offered was: (a) a splendid explanation in prose, in geometry and, later ('at the end of the book'), in the calculus, of what he clearly labeled a *static* approach; (b) an explanation which assumed clearly the prevalence of perfect competition (albeit he did acknowledge Cournot's and others' efforts to explain oligopolists' pricing policies); (c) an abstract 'model' based on the prevalence of eventual increasing costs;[7] and (4) a shrewd choice of 'real-world' (empirically generally true) examples to illustrate his theoretical abstractions.

Industry and Trade, presumably the ultimate realization of the once-promised vol. 2 of his *Principles of Economics*, was not as widely read as the *Principles*. For one thing, *Industry and Trade* did not pretend to be universal; that is, 'scientific'. It offered shrewd observation, not demonstrable models, and it seemed to suggest that, as against tendencies towards stability (equilibrium), there were profound unpredictable centrifugal forces. Unlike his *Principles*, *Industry and Trade* was time and place bound, not universal. It eschewed formal statements; that is, geometry or the calculus. In a word, it did not advance the scientific side of the economics discipline. It seemed on that score retrogressive, and in recent decades (say, since 1940) it has been ignored by mainline types.

Pigou's influence

It was Arthur C. Pigou, Marshall's personally chosen successor, who shaped the development of mainline Cambridge economics until the mid-1930s. Pigou's initial impact (a decade before the First World War) was to establish the Economics tripos as a working institution. Later, it was his interest in public welfare which dominated both his attention and the Cambridge curriculum. That interest in public welfare shifted the focus from the manager of a firm or a householder as decision-maker to the community as decision-maker; from the standpoint of an individual to the standpoint of a community. Pigou's attention had always been pinned to industrial (labour) relations and by the mid-1920s it focused mostly on unemployment as the principle social evil. It may come to some as a surprise, but as late as the 1950s graduate students not part of the various Keynesian contingents still selected 'welfare economics' as their major point of concentration, and what they meant was more likely the Pigovian interest in tax and subsidy policies, usually coupled with an interest in unemployment and other aspects of labour economics, than the abstract kind of optimization processes formulated according to Pareto Lerner–Kaldor–Hicks/Samuelson principles.

Keynes's revolution

In one sense Keynes's revolution in the 1930s was more against Marshall than Pigou. I see the shift in his acceptance of Pigou's principal focus on communitarian social decision-making. If Keynes seems to have abandoned his interest in monetary policy as the principal tool even before his *Treatise on Money* had cooled from the press, even that two-volume study was predicated on Pigovian rather than the Marshallian *Principles* 'premises' – the critical economic decisions were not those of the firm or of the household, but rather those of some central or governmental bureau; by the time of *The*

General Theory, decision-making concern was the taxing authority.

Accordingly, in terms of the Bible story (Genesis 27), Keynes's voice may seem to have been the voice of the later-patriarch 'Jacob' Marshall, but the hand was really the hand of 'Esau' Quesnay; the Physiocratic legacy had managed to cross the Channel. Surely, the dominant English theorist of that period, aside from Maynard Keynes, was John R. Hicks, who had also come to a communitarian approach, albeit through a general equilibrium approach fashioned by Leon Walras and greatly improved by Vilfredo Pareto. The legacy of communitarianism, of social responsibility and social planning, appeared side by side with the previously dominant seventeenth-century Locke–*Wealth of Nations* legacy.

I suggest, however, that there were two kinds of communitarianism apparent. One was 'lower-case' communitarianism, the kind of thing fashioned by policy 'wonks' like Maynard Keynes. The other was a 'higher-case' communitarianism of which Hicks and Samuelson are two leading examples. The former was essentially Pigovian, political and directed to concrete social problems of which redistribution of wealth, full employment and economic growth were the most important. The other offered sets of scientific (abstract) principles. The era of Keynes referred mostly to the time when the voices of the policy wonks dominated. But after the 1960s, the 'higher-case' writings of the scientists came to dominate academia.

THE RECENT SCENE

Generally

Since the 1970s the policy wonks have largely abandoned their attachment to the Keynesian communitarian approach. Why? Because in its stead there arose two Ezras – prophets leading the Chosen People back from their imposed exile to their proper land: 'Ezra'-Margaret and 'Ezra'-Ronald.[8] These two Ezras, like the original Ezra, taught the Chosen People that the Old Faith, revealed to Adam Smith the Teacher and confirmed by James Mill (Master of the Simple Truth), involved going back to the original Locke–*Wealth of Nations*–Smith cultural legacy, the legacy of individualism, perfect competition and utilitarianism.

As the record reflects all too strongly, academic-economists-cum-policy wonks have now all but abandoned the Keynesian communitarism. They have followed their appropriate Ezra back to the appropriate milk-and-honey Holy Land and are born-again rational-expectation individualists. Others, including several Nobel Laureates, have not renounced their faith in communitarianism; rather they have lifted it to the level of scholarly abstraction. As their language is formal (and the non-economist policy wonks do not grasp its principles, much less its nuances) they are seen as ivory-towered scientists which to quote Francis Bacon, 'much good is to be expected'. In so far as they

462

proselytize, their converts speak in the modern language of tongues (symbolic logic or advanced maths) and they present no immediate social nuisance and are considered best left alone by the born-again individualists.

The rise and fall of Geoffrey Harcourt

As should now be evident, our honouree, Geoffrey Harcourt, has been faithful to a Keynesian legacy in several senses. For one, like Keynes, he has been fascinated by the economics of epistemical uncertainty. Hence his seeming weakness of defining Sin in terms of the illicit nature of expecting to find Infinite Knowledge; he accepts the Punishment of accepting the reality of his being opinionated.

Second, like the Keynes of *The General Theory*, he built on the Pigovian trading of 'lower-case' communitarianism – an interest in wonkish centrally developed plans – for coping with the problems of income redistribution and growth.

So long as the age of Keynes flourished, so did Harcourt's leadership. He preached well, influenced many people,[9] and clearly admitted to his priesthood a large number of acolytes, namely Ph.D. graduate students. But with the rise of the prophets 'Ezra-Margaret' and 'Ezra-Ronald' and their organized march back to the Holy Land of individualism, utilitarianism and perfect competition, he has become unsuccessful as a proselytizer among the young and innocent. Many one-time possible graduate student devotees, not wishing to follow the crowd back to that Holy Land, have not seen the light of 'lower-case' ameliorative communitarianism; but rather have turned to the study of the cabbala.[10]

CONCLUSION

People of the calibre of Harcourt tend to be overlooked by the current crowd of young economists. Modern economics journals cater to the truth as revealed by 'St John Hicks' and 'St Paul Samuelson'. If their journals are occasionally corrupted by the publishing of articles of interest to policy wonks, they restrict most of their pages to the message of the two Prophets, Ezra-Margaret and Ezra-Ronald.

In the nineteenth century Frederick Maurice created at Cambridge a tradition which focused students' attention on social evils and on the need to try to ameliorate (if not to erase) them. I would put Harcourt into that Maurice tradition. He comes to it quite openly; as Maurice was, so is he a Christian socialist. Knowledge and ambition were to be put to service of the community.

He also comes to it possibly because of a less well-known reason. His devotion to the policy assumptions found in the later career and works of Joan Robinson is well known. Mrs Robinson, incidentally, was the great-granddaughter of Maurice. So perhaps no small part of Harcourt's search for palliative truth can be explained by saying that the Maurice–Robinson apple did not fall far from the tree – or, to shift metaphors, that some oaks have a tremendous capacity to shed acorns. This is, of course, not to suggest that there is anything nutty about Harcourt; on the contrary, it suggests that whether he is taken more or less seriously at the present, mighty oaks will grow from the old Maurice–Robinson and new Harcourt acorns.

Even Hobbes, in some real sense the father of utilitarianism, saw that life without social regulation was 'nasty, brutish, and short.' Harcourt fits into our cultural legacy quite easily.

NOTES

1 Before I first met Harcourt I was told by his earliest mentor, Professor Wilfred Prest, that Geoff was a strongly religious man – that he had been moved to conversion to Christianity, but that he saw human improvement as associated not with the individualism strand in our heritage but with the communitarian one. Let me return to this theme later at the end of this chapter (cf. Harcourt 1995).

2 This point is what separates most clearly Schumpeter from Pareto. In his 1949 essay on Pareto (Schumpeter 1949) and in his posthumous *History of Economic Analysis* (1954), Schumpeter made this point. He accepted what Pareto called 'residuals' as being essential to economic understanding. True, Schumpeter endorsed some mathematization of economics, but was sceptical of finding appropriate techniques. In the end he was clearly no longer confident that economic reasoning had only objective and logically compatible assumptions.

3 As is so often the case, the actual patrons of a view are less dogmatic than their followers. I am less than confident that Sir John Hicks (as he termed himself and his views during the last decade or so of his life), for one, would have accepted as the economic science what had been rightly attributed to John R. Hicks (which he claimed were an earlier, more imperfect intellectual incarnation).

4 From my standpoint it was Wicksteed, rather than Jevons, whose work is preferable as the exemplar of the scientific approach. But the modest Wicksteed announced that he was Jevons's disciple, and because Wicksteed was a parson (albeit a Unitarian one) we should take him at his word.

5 Again, I would prefer Pareto as the better exemplar. But even though Pareto was an ungenerous man (and resented Walras, for whom he seems to have had only reasons for gratitude), where he excelled was not in the conceptualization (that was Walras's forte, by Pareto's own admission) but in the technical exposition. So it is appropriate to credit Walras. Another factor was that Walras was a social reformer (a point ignored completely by those who have heard the title of his work but who have never looked at it); Pareto's intellectual journey took him to many 'ideological' spas but he never remained long enough to take any one of their full cures. In the end he had sampled liberalism, socialism, some even say fascism, and abandoned rational (simple, systematic) economics for non-rational (complex, questionably systematic) sociology.

6 Of course there are several, particularly Ludwig von Mises's students and followers, who think of praxeology as really the true science. And for them it is Carl Menger, even more than Jevons or Walras, who deserves the patriarchal mantle as the Discovering Scientist.

7 It is clear from the mathematical appendix to Marshall's *Principles of Economics*

that Marshall realized the fragility of the assumption of increasing costs. However, few of his students handled calculus that well, and even fewer realized that this former wrangler told the 'greater truth' only to those who had both the ability and the desire to handle that appendix.

8　For those not schooled in the prophets, both major and minor, Ezra (a minor prophet) lived at the time of the Jews' return from Babylonian exile. He preached resumption of the previous rituals, which many of those who had not been exiled no longer practised.

9　He actually has official recognition. The government of his native country awarded him its Order of Australia for services to the economics discipline.

10　Cabbala, a subtle and intricate study of Jewish mysticism, was developed in the Middle Ages. Presumably its subtlety and intricacy make it non-available for those who are 'common-sense wonks'.

REFERENCES

Harcourt, G. C. (1995) 'Reflections of an Australian patriot and a Cambridge economist', *Banca Nazionale del Lavoro Quarterly Review* 48(194): 225–54.

Robbins (1981) 'Economics and political economy', *American Economic Review* 71(2): 1–10.

Rothbard, M. N. (1995) *Classical Economics: An Austrian Perspective of the History of Economic Thought*, vol. 2, Aldershot: Edward Elgar.

Schumpeter, J. A. (1949) 'Vilfredo Pareto', *Quarterly Journal of Economics* 63: 147–73.

—— (1954) *History of Economic Analysis*, New York: Oxford University Press.

39

ECONOMICS AND RELIGION

Sheila C. Dow

INTRODUCTION

Geoff Harcourt has always made it clear that his economics is inextricably bound up with his politics and his religion. Thus, for example, he describes himself as a Christian socialist (Harcourt 1994), and he discusses the evolution and interdependence of his religious, political and economic views in his autobiographical statement (Harcourt 1992). This interdependence is also evident from the social concern underlying all his theorizing. Geoff Harcourt has expressed the motivation underpinning his economics as follows: 'to make the world a better place for ordinary men and women, to produce a more just and equitable society.... I see economics as very much a moral as well as a social science and very much a handmaiden of progressive thought' (Harcourt 1986).

Thinking of politics and religion as a value system, Geoff Harcourt falls squarely in the tradition of those others who have seen economics as a moral science. It was only with the efforts, beginning in the nineteenth century, to model economics on classical mechanics (see Mirowski 1994), that economics began to be presented as value free. This project never succeeded. Drakopoulos (1991) has demonstrated how the philosophy of hedonism has consistently underpinned orthodox economics, in spite of attempts to make economics value free. I would suggest that it is the predominant view in heterodox economics that values are endemic to economic theory. The case for this view has been put in a variety of ways. Myrdal (1953) developed the argument in terms of ideology. Eichner (1985: ch. 2) made the point from the perspective of institutionalism. Davidson (1972: ch. 1) made the point by suggesting a political pattern to distinctions between approaches to economics. Indeed, the perspective that there are legitimate alternative approaches to economics implies the possibility that differences between approaches may stem at least partly from differences in value systems; this is implicit in the concept of paradigm as something shared by a social grouping of scientists, and even more in the rhetoric approach to economics. Thus, for example, it has been suggested that different approaches to political economy be distinguished from each other in terms of their respective visions of the economic process (see Dow 1990). It is hard to understand 'vision' without reference to value systems. Finally, the argument that economics cannot be divorced from (religious) values has also been made by some contributors to Brennan and Waterman (1994). These arguments are not uncontroversial, but they are taken as given here. For the purposes of my argument, it is taken as given that economics is a moral science.

The question to be addressed here instead is whether there is anything distinctive about religious values rather than, say, humanist values, as far as economics is concerned. Given that any values fundamentally condition the economics within which they are embedded, are religious values different in kind? I concentrate my attention on religion in the Judeo-Christian tradition. There are potentially many avenues through which religious belief may influence economic thought. The particular approach to this question adopted here is to consider the connection between religious belief and knowledge.

ECONOMICS AND KNOWLEDGE

The connection between religious belief and knowledge is an old one; in ancient literature, knowledge was seen as something that was acquired, from God, through grace. Barry Gordon (1994) has presented a fascinating discussion of the relationship between economics and ancient views on religion in these terms. He explains the different views as to the consequences of the Fall of humankind, which was understood as a withdrawal of knowledge. In particular, this lack of knowledge threatened the capacity of humankind to continue the ideal, communal, form of economic organization. Some saw the lack of knowledge as not fundamentally impeding humankind in performing the role of assistant manager to God; others saw the withdrawal of knowledge as absolute. Gordon argues that it is the later view which predominated. Of particular interest among those who took the later view is Saint Augustine of Hippo. Saint Augustine provided a rationale for the monastic system in terms of superior knowledge, the scope for which was limited to those devoting their lives to the monastic orders. It was only through benefit of their access to superior knowledge that the religious orders could set up a communal style of economic organization; those without access to this knowledge must rely on the market as the best available form of economic organization. It is this association between knowledge and belief which provides a clue as to the particular role of religious belief in economics.

Modern economics had its origins in the work of Adam Smith. The Scottish Enlightenment of which Smith was a part constituted a challenge to the authority of religious orthodoxy. But this by no means indicates that the Scottish Enlightenment was an irreligious development of thought; far from it (see Sutherland 1982). The Enlightenment was fuelled by attempts to address burning moral issues with reason. Indeed, this was the product of another manifestation of Protestantism in Scotland: the promotion of general literacy by the Church of Scotland in order to improve general knowledge of the Bible and thus strengthen belief. There was thus a long tradition of viewing knowledge and reason as a necessary part of the process of enhancing a particular belief system. Nevertheless, human sinfulness meant that full knowledge was not attainable. For all that Smith in some ways turned his back on religion, he still absorbed this traditional understanding of knowledge in his theory of science (Smith 1795 [1980]). Indeed, the Scottish Enlightenment was distinctive, partly as a result of the nature of the education system, for its historically contingent view of knowledge creation, given the intrinsic human incapacity to identify truth (or at least to know that it has been identified). Thus Smith's theory of science (following Hume) sees scientists as motivated by psychological factors (Skinner 1972). The purpose of theories is to lull the disquiet aroused by unexplained events; theories are more appealing the more they put forward connecting principles to explain events. They are appealing if they appeal to the imagination. Successful theories are thus psychologically satisfying rather than true.

Smith's economics was archetypically moral science. The underlying analysis of human behaviour was inextricably tied up with social value systems (see Smith 1759 [1976]), contrary to the modern misinterpretation of Smith's concept of self-interest as selfishness. But the important aspect of Smith's economics for our purposes is his theory of knowledge. Knowledge is enhanced by reason, but it is beyond human understanding to arrive at ultimate truth. Smith's theorizing draws heavily on the concept of the Deity. The notion of the invisible hand in particular draws on the belief in a Deity who has perfect knowledge, such that the unintended consequences of human actions lead to a favourable social outcome. Thus the motivation of acquisitiveness, which Smith ascribes to the Deity, has the unintended consequence of promoting economic growth. The spending of the wealthy has the unintended consequence of making the distribution of income more equal (Heilbroner 1986: 60–1). Smith does not presume to represent a complete system on the part of the Deity. The self-deception he identified with acquisitiveness and the potential for damaging unintended consequences of market activity in the form of monopoly power are not fully explained in terms of the deliberate design of the Deity.

Post-Keynesian economics derives its theory of knowledge from Keynes (1921 [1973]), where he analysed the grounds for rational belief. Keynes used the term 'belief' for knowledge, in the Cambridge tradition. It should also be noted that Keynes, like Smith, had been influenced by a religious upbringing (Brown 1988). Like Smith, Keynes lived in an environment which, even in its rejection of traditional religious values (or indeed because of this rejection), nevertheless was in the process deeply concerned with moral issues. Like Smith, Keynes denied that science in general could lay claim with certainty to truth. For Keynes, little knowledge was held with certainty; certainty was confined to logically necessary statements, statements known to be true through direct knowledge, and statements of quantifiable probability drawn from repeated observation where there is limited independent variety. Because Keynes had an organic vision of the economic process (Carabelli 1995), he saw the scope for certain knowledge as being very limited and accordingly he paid it scant attention. Most knowledge is held with uncertainty. Yet methods of acquiring knowledge are employed as the basis for action. This knowledge is built up from a combination of evidence, theorizing, convention and intuition. The role of the latter two sources of knowledge assumes greater importance the less the availability of relevant evidence and the less the scope for theorizing about underlying causal structures; that is, the greater the uncertainty. Further, there are differences in the degree to which uncertainty is recognized, a matter in which psychology must play an important part (Dow 1995).

Post-Keynesian theory based on this theory of knowledge can be contrasted with orthodox theory which is based rather on the concept of information. The term 'information' conveys the notion of a given set of facts which is knowable, at least in principle; if not known, the facts are waiting to be discovered. This distinction was drawn out by Loasby (1983) in contrasting Shackle's notion of created knowledge with Kirzner's notion of information discovery. The concept of knowledge, rather than information, conveys the notion of an endemic unknowability, even in principle. Nevertheless, unknowability does not entail an absence of knowledge, but rather directs attention to the basis on which (uncertain) knowledge is built up. One significant basis for knowledge is conventions which evolve to provide a basis for action, in the absence of complete knowledge. Farmer (1995) has persuasively argued that knowledge is thus social; analysis based on individual knowledge, referring to some unattainable complete set of knowledge, is inappropriate for economic analysis.

Unknowability is central to much post-Keynesian theorizing. It explains the importance of conventions in general, and particular conventions such as money; it explains the role of liquidity preference (Runde 1994) and the potential instability of investment (Lawson, 1995). But the existence of conventions and animal spirits as the foundation for belief in turn forms the basis for action. Post-Keynesianism thus avoids the nihilism of methodological individualistic interpretations of unknowability (as depicted critically by Coddington (1982) and favourably by Amariglio and Ruccio (1995). Keynes indeed is best understood as being concerned with belief with a view to action (Carabelli 1988). This is surely also what drives Geoff Harcourt's fascination with economics and his policy activism.

THE SIGNIFICANCE OF RELIGIOUS BELIEF

Since Keynes used the term 'belief' to refer to any knowledge, what difference does it make whether or not that belief is religious? The argument

I would like to put forward here is that, among other things, religious belief involves a belief in the existence of perfect knowledge, in the person of the Deity. It is important that some distinctions be made clear. First, the fact that perfect knowledge exists does not make it accessible to humanity. Indeed, endemic sinfulness is identified with a lack of knowledge. When I refer to 'perfect knowledge', therefore, I do not use the term in the same sense as 'perfect information' in orthodox economics as something which is in principle accessible to humans. On the other hand, perfect knowledge and unknowability are not being presented here as a dual; there is scope for humans to acquire more knowledge, even if perfect knowledge is inaccessible. Finally, faith provides a bridge between perfect knowledge and human lack of knowledge. Just as Keynes argued that knowledge can be derived from a variety of sources and in a variety of ways, religious belief can be seen as adding another dimension to the build-up of knowledge. In the Scottish theological tradition, for example, reasoned argument and belief are not regarded as separable, so that belief is seen as part of the more general knowledge structure.

The significance of a belief that perfect knowledge does exist, I would suggest, is that it puts human lack of knowledge in a different light. It has always been difficult, but necessary, for post-Keynesian economics to spell out the various middle grounds it inhabits. One such middle ground is that between certainty and uncertainty. There has been something of a crisis of confidence in orthodox macroeconomics for a variety of reasons. But one of these reasons is an awareness, acquired from neo-Austrian influences, of the limits to our knowledge at the macro level. This has been in part a reaction to the overconfidence with which fine-tuning came to be applied in the 1960s and 1970s. The economic stability (to which Keynesian policy activism had contributed) had been taken to imply that Keynes's theory of uncertain knowledge and its implications for economic behaviour was no longer relevant. As a result this theory was not available in the consciousness of economists when the need arose. 'Keynesian' policies were thus seen as inadequate to deal with the supply shocks of the 1970s and their aftermath. Even Keynes had doubts about policymaking on the grounds that its consequences could not be known with confidence (O'Donnell, 1989). This has all encouraged tendencies to withdraw from policy activism at the macro level.

Post-Keynesians, Harcourt notable among them, have argued consistently for policy activism in spite of the extent of our ignorance, on the basis that what knowledge we have (albeit held with uncertainty) supports such activism, relative to the human cost of policy passivism. I would suggest that the optimism generated by a belief in a Deity with perfect knowledge, to which we have some access through belief, provides added confidence in arguing for action even in the absence of full knowledge. This argument is not altogether straightforward. It cannot be taken far in any particular context without addressing the contents of belief in addition to the knowledge of the Deity. There is scope, for example, for belief that the market system is part of a grand plan resulting from the perfect knowledge-base of the Deity; that is, the belief that policy activism is unwarranted. Within that belief system, there is scope for differences between, say, the neo-Austrian approach on the one hand, which emphasizes human knowledge limitations, and general equilibrium theory on the other hand, which does not. Further, belief as to the beneficence or otherwise of God is relevant: faith, or trust, is generated only when there is belief that perfect knowledge is being employed for good ends. My argument here is that, where an approach to economics supports activism, as does post-Keynesian theory, it does make a difference whether there is belief in a benchmark of perfect knowledge, even when that benchmark is not directly accessible to humans. The difference arises from the sense of optimism which the belief in the existence of that benchmark provides when combined with trust in God.

McCloskey (forthcoming) has pointed to the dangers of claiming a transcendent truth, which he identifies with modernism. He classifies the modernist theory of knowledge as élitist in justifying policies to be applied to others by means of claims to truth; he identifies it equally with an earlier aristocracy, with paternalistic scientists and philosophers and with Marxism, whereby one class lays claim to knowledge by which policies are applied to another class. Post-modernism, he suggests, is the theory of knowledge of the bourgeoisie, which doubts any claims to truth (a theory of knowledge which has antecedents in the Scottish Enlightenment).

Clearly, from this perspective, by evoking religious belief it may seem that I have introduced the potentially dangerous notion of a transcendent truth as the determinant of action. Certainly the scope for reference to truth entailed by religious belief does *seem* to take us away from considerations of unknowability. But the significance of religious belief and the existence of perfect knowledge depends on the underlying theory of knowledge. If that theory is one which sees human knowledge as fundamentally limited, then, even if truth is revealed through religious belief, there is ultimately no way of being sure that it is truth; we are still in the realms of reasoned argument (of which belief is a part). Applied to a theory of knowledge which allows truth to be recognized by humans, religious belief and belief in the existence of perfect knowledge have quite different implications.

CONCLUSION

My purpose here has been to consider whether religious belief played a role in economic thought any different from that of values in general. I concluded that it is through the theory of knowledge that religion's particular role emerges. Even though economic processes are ultimately unknowable as far as humans are concerned, this does not provide grounds for pessimism, and particularly policy pessimism, if there is belief in a beneficent Deity who embodies perfect knowledge. Starting from a theory of knowledge which recognizes the necessarily limited knowledge attainable by humans, but which nevertheless accepts mechanisms for reducing uncertainty, religious belief can fit easily into the knowledge structure. Whereas for any individual the relevance of religious beliefs for economics depends on the particular nature of the beliefs, their primary relevance in general is in maintaining the optimism which arises from recognition that God embodies perfect knowledge.

This argument is still particular in that it has been presented from the perspective of a Keynesian theory of knowledge and a particular religious tradition. There is much scope for extending the discussion to refer to other theories of knowledge and other religious traditions. But the argument should serve at least to demonstrate that religious values have the potential to have a distinctive effect on economics when compared to non-religious values. Further, as far as the post-Keynesian theory of knowledge is concerned, the argument suggests that the notion of perfect knowledge may have relevance, although in a fundamentally different way from its relevance to orthodox economics.

ACKNOWLEDGEMENT

I am grateful to Ian Steedman for helpful comments and suggestions.

REFERENCES

Amariglio, J. and Ruccio, D. (1995) 'Keynes, postmodernism, uncertainty', in S. C. Dow and J. Hillard (eds) *Keynes, Knowledge and Uncertainty*, Aldershot: Edward Elgar.

Brennan, H. G. and Waterman, A. M. C. (eds) (1994) *Economics and Religion: Are They Distinct?*, Boston: Kluwer.

Brown, N. (1988) *Dissenting Forebears: The Maternal Ancestors of J. M. Keynes*, Chichester: Phillimore.

Carabelli, A. (1988) *On Keynes's Method*, London: Macmillan.

—— (1995) 'Uncertainty and measurement in Keynes: probability and organicness', in S. C. Dow and J. Hillard (eds) *Keynes, Knowledge and Uncertainty*, Aldershot: Edward Elgar.

Coddington, A. (1982) 'Deficient foresight: a troublesome theme in Keynesian economics', *American Economic Review* 72: 480–7.

Davidson, P. (1972) *Money and the Real World*, London: Macmillan.

Dow, S. C. (1990) 'Post Keynesianism as political economy: a methodological discussion', *Review of Political Economy* 2(3): 345–58.

—— (1995) 'Uncertainty about uncertainty', in S. C. Dow and J. Hillard (eds) *Keynes, Knowledge and Uncertainty*, Aldershot: Edward Elgar.

Drakopoulos, S. (1991) *Values and Economics Theory*, Aldershot: Gower.

Eichner, A. S. (1985) *Towards a New Economics*, London: Macmillan.

Farmer, M. (1995) 'Knowledgeability, actors and uncertain worlds', in S. C. Dow and

J. Hillard (eds) *Keynes, Knowledge and Uncertainty*, Aldershot: Edward Elgar.

Gordon, B. (1994) 'Theological positions and economic perspectives in ancient literature', in A. M. C. Waterman and H. G. Brennan (eds) *Economics and Religion: Are They Distinct?*, Boston: Kluwer.

Harcourt, G. C. (1986) 'Introduction', in Harcourt, G. C., *Controversies in Political Economy: Selected Essays by G. C. Harcourt*, ed. O. F. Hamouda, New York: New York University Press.

—— (1992) 'Introduction', in Harcourt, G. C., *On Political Economists and Modern Political Economy: Selected Essays of G. C. Harcourt*, ed. C. Sardoni, London: Routledge.

—— (1994) 'Comment', in A. M. C. Waterman and H. G. Brennan (eds) *Economics and Religion: Are They Distinct?*, Boston: Kluwer.

Heilbroner, R. L. (1986) *The Essential Adam Smith*, Oxford: Oxford University Press.

Keynes, J. M. (1921 [1973]) *A Treatise on Probability*, in *Collected Writings of John Maynard Keynes*, vol. 8, London: Macmillan for the Royal Economic Society.

Lawson, T. (1995) 'Economics and expectations', in S. C. Dow and J. Hillard (eds) *Keynes, Knowledge and Uncertainty*, Aldreshot: Edward Elgar.

Loasby, B. J. (1983) 'Economics of dispersed and incomplete knowledge', in I. M. Kirzner (ed.) *Method, Process and Austrian Economics: Essays in Honor of Ludwig von Mises*, Lexington, MA: Lexington Books.

McCloskey, D. (forthcoming) 'The genealogy of postmodernism: an economist's guide', in J. Amariglio, S. Cullenberg and D. Ruccio (eds) *Postmodernism, Economics and Knowledge*, London: Routledge.

Mirowski, P. (ed.) (1994) *Natural Images in Economic Thought*, Cambridge: Cambridge University Press.

Myrdal, G. (1953) *The Political Element in the Development of Economic Theory*, London: Routledge.

O'Donnell, R. M. (1989) *Keynes: Philosophy, Economics and Politics: The Philosophical Foundations of Keynes's Thought and Their Influence on His Economics and Politics*, London: Macmillan.

Runde, J. (1994) 'Keynesian uncertainty and liquidity preference', *Cambridge Journal of Economics* 18(2): 129–44.

Skinner, A. S. (1972) 'Adam Smith: philosophy and science', *Scottish Journal of Political Economy* 19: 307–19.

Smith, A. (1759 [1976]) *The Theory of Moral Sentiments*, ed. D. D. Raphael and A. L. Macfie, Oxford: Clarendon.

—— (1795 [1980]) 'History of astronomy', in W. P. D. Wightman (ed.) *Essays on Philosophical Subjects*, Oxford: Clarendon.

Sutherland, S. R. (1982) 'The Presbyterian inheritance of Hume and Reid', in R. H. Campbell and A. S. Skinner (eds) *The Origin and Nature of the Scottish Enlightenment*, Edinburgh: John Donald.

Geoff Harcourt: A Bibliography

ARTICLES, NOTES AND CHAPTERS IN BOOKS

1 (with D. Ironmonger) 'A pilot survey of personal savings', *Economic Record*, vol. 32, May 1956, pp. 106–18.
2 'The quantitative effect of basing company taxation on replacement costs', *Accounting Research*, vol. 9, January 1958, pp. 1–16.
3 'Pricing policies and inflation', *Economic Record*, vol. 35, April 1959, pp. 133–6.
4 (with A. D. Barton) 'Investment allowances for primary producers', *Australian Journal of Agricultural Economics*, vol. 3, December 1959, pp. 12–18.
5 (with J. W. Bennett) 'Taxation and business surplus', *Economic Record*, vol. 36, August 1960, pp. 425–8.
6 'Pricing policies and earning rates', *Economic Record*, vol. 37, June 1961, pp. 217–24.
7 'The payment of prisoners', *Australian Quarterly*, December 1961, pp. 86–9.
8 Review of W. E. G. Salter, *Productivity and Technical Change*, *Economic Record*, vol. 38, September 1962, pp. 388–94.
9 'Investment and initial allowances as fiscal devices', *Australian Accountant*, September 1962, pp. 473–7.
10 (with D. H. Whitehead) 'The wool textile industry', ch. 13 of A. Hunter (ed.) *The Economics of Australian Industry*, Melbourne: Melbourne University Press, 1963, pp. 419–59.
11 'A simple Joan Robinson model of accumulation with one technique: a comment', *Osaka Economic Papers*, January 1963, pp. 24–8.
12 'Taxation and primary production', *Farm Policy*, March 1963, pp. 101–5.
13 'A critique of Mr Kaldor's model of income distribution and economic growth', *Australian Economic Papers*, vol. 2, June 1963, pp. 20–36.
14 (with R. L. Matthews) 'Company finance', ch. 9 of R. R. Hirst and R. H. Wallace (eds) *Studies in the Australian Capital Market*, Melbourne: F. W. Cheshire, 1964, pp. 377–424.
15 (with V. G. Massaro) 'A note on Mr Sraffa's sub-systems', *Economic Journal*, vol. 74, September 1964, pp. 715–22. Reprinted in French in G. Farcarello and P. de Cavergne (eds) *Une nouvelle approche en économie politique? Essais sur Sraffa*, Paris: Economica, 1977, pp. 53–61.
16 (with V. G. Massaro) 'Mr Sraffa's *Production of Commodities*', *Economic Record*, vol. 40, September 1964, pp. 442–54.
17 'Incomes policy and the measurement of profits', *Banker's Magazine*, December 1964, pp. 361–4.
18 'The accountant in a golden age', *Oxford Economic Papers*, vol. 17, March 1965, pp. 66–80. Reprinted in R. H. Parker and G. C. Harcourt (eds) *Readings in the Concept and Measurement of Income*, Cambridge: Cambridge University Press, 1969, pp. 310–25.

19 'A two-sector model of the distribution of income and the level of employment in the short run', *Economic Record*, vol. 41, March 1965, pp. 103–17.

20 (with G. Whittington) 'The irrelevancy of the British differential profits tax: a comment', *Economic Journal*, vol. 75, June 1965, pp. 373–8.

21 'The measurement of the rate of profit and the bonus scheme for managers in the Soviet Union', *Oxford Economic Papers*, vol. 18, March 1966, pp. 58–63.

22 'Biases in empirical estimates of the elasticities of substitution of CES production functions', *Review of Economic Studies*, vol. 33, July 1966, pp. 227–33.

23 'Cash investment grants, corporation tax and pay-out ratios', *Bulletin of the Oxford University Institute of Economics and Statistics*, vol. 28, August 1966, pp. 163–79 and vol. 29, February 1967, pp. 87–93.

24 'Investment-decision criteria, capital-intensity and the choice of techniques', *Czechoslovak Economic Papers*, no. 9, 1967, pp. 65–91, and ch. 14 of J. T. Dunlop and N. P. Federenko (eds) *Planning and Markets*, New York: McGraw-Hill, 1969, pp. 190–216.

25 'Investment-decision criteria, investment incentives and the choice of technique', *Economic Journal*, vol. 78, March 1968, pp. 77–95.

26 'The macroeconomic implications of Christie Kurien's core sector model', in *The Relevance of the Social Sciences in Contemporary Asia*, World Student Christian Fellowship Federation, 1968, pp. 126–9.

27 'Some Cambridge controversies in the theory of capital', *Journal of Economic Literature*, vol. 7, June 1969, pp. 369–405. Reprinted in Italian in G. Nardozzi and V. Valli (eds) *Teori dello Sviluppo Economico*, Etas Kompass, 1971.

28 'A teaching model of the "Keynesian" system', *Keio Economic Studies*, vol. 6, no. 2, 1969, pp. 23–46.

29 'G. C. Harcourt's reply to Nell', *Journal of Economic Literature*, vol. 8, March 1970, pp. 44–5.

30 (with A. S. Watson and P. D. Praetz) 'The CET production frontier and estimates of supply response in Australian agriculture', *Economic Record*, vol. 46, December 1970, pp. 553–63.

31 (with A. S. Watson and P. D. Praetz) 'Reply to Powell and Gruen, and Byron', *Economic Record*, vol. 46, December 1970, pp. 574–5.

32 'G. C. Harcourt's reply to Ng', *Journal of Economic Literature*, vol. 9, March 1971, pp. 69–70.

33 'Las parábolos neoclásicas y la función agregade de producción', *Cuadernos de Económica*, June 1973, pp. 46–62.

34 'The rate of profits in equilibrium growth models', *Journal of Political Economy*, vol. 81, September–October 1973, pp. 1261–77. Reprinted in French in C. Berthomieu and J. Cartelier (eds) *Ricardians, Keynesians et Marxistes*, Nice: CORDES, 1974, pp. 51–75.

35 (with A. Asimakopulos) 'Proportionality and the neoclassical parables', *Southern Economic Journal*, vol. 40, March 1974, pp. 481–3.

36 'The Cambridge controversies: the afterglow', in M. Parkin and A. R. Nobay (eds) *Contemporary Issues in Economics*, Manchester: Manchester University Press, 1975, pp. 305–34. Reprinted in French as 'Les controverses cambridgiennes: après la tourmente', in G. Grellet (ed.) *Nouvelle critique de l'économie politique*, Paris: Calman, Levy, 1976, pp. 35–76.

37 'The social consequences of inflation', *Australian Accountant*, October 1974, pp. 520–8.

38 'Capital theory: much ado about something', *Thames Papers in Political Economy*, Autumn 1975, pp. 1–16. Spanish version, 'Las controversias de los economistas i un mar de irrelevancias?', *Económica*, 1974, pp. 27–53.

39 'Decline and rise: the revival of (classical) political economy', *Economic Record*, vol. 51, September 1975, pp. 339–56.

40 'Revival of political economy: a further comment', *Economic Record*, vol. 51, September 1975, pp. 368–71.

41 'The Cambridge controversies: old ways and new horizons – or dead end?', *Oxford Economic Papers*, vol. 28, March 1976, pp. 25–65.

42 (with P. Kenyon) 'Pricing and the investment decision', *Kyklos*, vol. 29, fasc. 3, 1976, pp. 449–77.

43 'The theoretical and social significance of the Cambridge controversies in the theory of capital: an evaluation', *Revue d'Économie Politique*, vol. 87, 1977, pp. 191–215. Reprinted in J. Schwartz (ed.) *The Subtle Anatomy of Capitalism*, California: Goodyear, 1977, pp. 285–303.

44 'Eric Russell, 1921–77: a great Australian political economist' (the 1977 Newcastle Lecture in Political Economy) Research Report no. 36, iii + 26 pp.

45 'On theories and policies', ch. 4 of J. P. Nieuwenhuysen and P. J. Drake (eds) *Australian Economic Policy*, Melbourne: Melbourne University Press, 1977, pp. 40–52.

46 'Maurice Dobb 1900–1976', *Economic Record*, vol. 52, 1976, pp. 395–6.

47 'Eric Russell, 1921–77: a memoir', *Economic Record*, vol. 53, December 1977, pp. 467–74.

48 'Policy and responses for Australia', *Economic Papers*, no. 60, December 1978, pp. 61–69.

49 'The social science imperialists' (the 1978 Academy Lecture, November 1978), *Politics*, vol. 14, November 1979, pp. 243–51.

50 'Non-neoclassical capital theory', *World Development*, vol. 7, October 1979, pp. 923–32.

51 'Robinson, Joan', in David L. Sills (ed.) *International Encyclopedia of the Social Sciences, Biographical Supplement*, vol. 18, New York: The Free Press, 1979, pp. 663–71.

52 (with P. M. Kerr) 'The mixed economy', ch. 14 in J. North and P. Weller (eds) *Labor*, Sydney: Ian Novak, 1979, pp. 184–95.

53 'Discussion', *American Economic Review*, vol. 70, May 1980, pp. 27–8.

54 'A post-Keynesian development of the "Keynesian model"', ch. 9 of E. J. Nell (ed.) *Growth, Profits and Property: Essays in the Revival of Political Economy*, Cambridge: Cambridge University Press, 1980, pp. 151–64.

55 'Introduction to Symposium on Income Distribution', *Journal of Post Keynesian Economics*, vol. 4, Winter 1980–1, pp. 155–7.

56 'Marshall, Sraffa and Keynes: incompatible bedfellows?', *Eastern Economic Journal*, vol. 5, January 1981, pp. 39–50.

57 'Notes on an economic querist: G. L. S. Shackle', *Journal of Post Keynesian Economics*, vol. 4, Fall 1981, pp. 136–44. A longer version is the introduction to S. F. Frowen (ed.) *Unknowledge and Choice in Economics*, London: Macmillan, 1990, pp. xvii–xxvi.

58 'The Sraffian contribution: an evaluation', in I. Bradley and M. Howard (eds) *Classical and Marxian Political Economy: Essays in Honour of Ronald L. Meek*, London: Macmillan, 1982, pp. 255–75.

59 'Notes on the social limits to growth', *Economic Forum*, Summer 1981, pp. 1–8.

60 'An early post Keynesian: Lorie Tarshis (or: Tarshis on Tarshis by Harcourt)', *Journal of Post Keynesian Economics*, vol. 4, Summer 1982, pp. 609–19.

61 'Reflections on the development of economics as a discipline' (the 1982 G. L. Wood Memorial Lecture, June 1982), published in *History of Political Economy*, vol. 16, no. 4, 1984, pp. 489–517.

62 'Making socialism in your own country' (the 1982 John Curtin Memorial Lecture, August 1982), pp. 28.

63 'Post Keynesianism: quite wrong and/or nothing new?', *Thames Papers in Political Economy*, Summer 1982, pp. 1–19, Reprinted as ch. 6 in P. Arestis and T. Skouras (eds) *Post Keynesian Economic Theory: A Challenge to Neo-classical Economics*, Brighton: Wheatsheaf, 1985.

64 Review of T. Balogh, *The Irrelevance of Conventional Economics, Social Alternatives*, vol. 3, March 1983, pp. 61–2.

65 'A man for all systems: talking to Kenneth Boulding', *Journal of Post Keynesian Economics*, vol. 5, Fall 1983, pp. 143–54.

66 'On Piero Sraffa's contributions to economics', in P. Groenewegen and J. Halevi (eds) *Altro Polo Italian Economics Past and Present*, Frederick May Foundation for Italian Studies, University of Sydney, 1983, pp. 117–28.

67 'Harcourt on Robinson', in H. W. Spiegel and W. J. Samuels (eds) *Contemporary Economists in Perspective*, Greenwich, CT: JAI Press, 1984, pp. 639–58.

68 'Keynes's college bursar view of investment', in J. A. Kregel (ed.) *Distribution, Effective Demand and International Economic Relations*, London: Macmillan, 1983, pp. 81–4.

69 Summary of discussion in G. D. N. Worswick and J. Trevithick (eds) *Keynes and the Modern World*, Cambridge: Cambridge University Press, 1983.

70 'The end of an era: Joan Robinson (1903–83) and Piero Sraffa (1898–1983)', *Journal of Post Keynesian Economics*, vol. 6, Spring 1984, pp. 466–9.

71 'John Hicks', in A. Kuper and J. Kuper (eds) *The Social Science Encyclopedia*, London: Routledge & Kegan Paul, 1985, pp. 355–6.

72 'Nicholas Kaldor', in A. Kuper and J. Kuper (eds) *The Social Science Encyclopedia*, London: Routledge & Kegan Paul, 1985, pp. 422–3.

73 'James Meade', in A. Kuper and J. Kuper (eds) *The Social Science Encyclopedia*, London: Routledge & Kegan Paul, 1985, p. 509.

74 'Joan Robinson (1903–83)', in A. Kuper and J. Kuper (eds) *The Social Science Encyclopedia*, London: Routledge & Kegan Paul, 1985, p. 713.

75 'Piero Sraffa (1898–83)', in A. Kuper and J. Kuper (eds) *The Social Science Encyclopedia*, London: Routledge & Kegan Paul, 1985, p. 816.

76 'Foreword', *Cambridge Journal of Economics*, vol. 7, no. 3/4, September/December 1983, p. 209.

77 'A twentieth century eclectic: Richard Goodwin', *Journal of Post Keynesian Economics*, vol. 7, Spring 1985, pp. 410–21.

78 (with T. J. O'Shaughnessy) 'Keynes's unemployment equilibrium: some insights from Joan Robinson, Piero Sraffa and Richard Kahn', in G. C. Harcourt (ed.) *Keynes and His Contemporaries: The Sixth and Centennial Keynes Seminar Held at the University of Kent at Canterbury 1983*, London: Macmillan, 1985, pp. 3–41.

79 'The influence of Piero Sraffa on the contributions of Joan Robinson to economic theory', *Supplement to the Economic Journal*, vol. 96, 1986, pp. 96–108.

80 (with M. H. I. Dore) 'A note on the taxation of exhaustible resources under oligopoly', *Economic Letters*, vol. 21, no. 1, May 1986, pp. 81–4.

81 'Bastard Keynesianism', in J. Eatwell, M. Milgate and P. Newman (eds) *The New Palgrave: A Dictionary of Economics*, vol. 1, London: Macmillan, 1987, pp. 203–4.

82 'Post-Keynesian economics', in J. Eatwell, M. Milgate and P. Newman (eds) *The New Palgrave: A Dictionary of Economics*, vol. 3, London: Macmillan, 1987, pp. 924–8.

83 'Smithies, Arthur (1907–81)', in J. Eatwell, M. Milgate and P. Newman (eds) *The*

New Palgrave: A Dictionary of Economics, vol. 4, London: Macmillan, 1987, pp. 375–6.

84 'Reddaway, William Brian (born 1913)', *The New Palgrave: A Dictionary of Economics*, vol. 4, London: Macmillan, 1987, pp. 108–9.

85 'Theoretical methods and unfinished business', in D. A. Reese (ed.) *The Legacy of Keynes*, Nobel Conference XXII, San Francisco: Harper & Row 1987, pp. 1–22. Also in Portuguese, 'O legado de Keynes: métodos teóricos e assustos incabados', ch. 4 of E. J. Amedeo (ed.) *John M. Keynes: cinqüenta anos da teoria geral*, Rio de Janeiro: INPES/IPEA, 1989, pp. 45–62. A shorter version is reprinted as 'On Keynes's method in economic theory', in M. Sabastiani (ed.) *The Notion of Equilibrium in the Keynesian Theory*, Basingstoke: Macmillan, 1992), pp. 99–105.

86 'Comment arcos sobre o ensaio do Prof. Marglin', in E. J. Amadeo (ed.) *John M. Keynes: cinqüenta anos da teoria geral*, Rio de Janeiro: INPES/IPEA, 1989, pp. 119–22.

87 'Comment on Garegnani', in K. Bharadwaj and B. Schefold (eds) *Essays on Piero Sraffa*, London: Unwin Hyman, 1990, pp. 141–4.

88 (with O. F. Hamouda) 'Post Keynesianism: from criticism to coherence?', *Bulletin of Economic Research*, vol. 40, January 1988, pp. 1–33.

89 'Introduction', *Cambridge Journal of Economics*, vol. 12, 1988, pp. 1–5.

90 'Nicholas Kaldor, 12 May 1908 – 30 September 1986', *Economica*, vol. 55, May 1988, pp. 159–70.

91 'Robinson, Joan Violet (1903–1983)', in Lord Blake and C. S. Nichols (eds) *The Dictionary of National Biography, 1981–1985*, Oxford: Oxford University Press, 1990, pp. 346–7.

92 'Sraffa, Piero (1898–1983)', in Lord Blake and C. S. Nichols (eds) *The Dictionary of National Biography, 1981–1985*, Oxford: Oxford University Press, 1990, pp. 381–2.

93 (with G. Whittington) 'Income and capital', ch. 7 of J. Creedy (ed.) *Foundations of Economic Thought*, Oxford: Blackwell, 1990, pp. 186–211.

94 'On the contributions of Joan Robinson and Piero Sraffa to economic theory', ch. 3 of M. Berg (ed.) *Political Economy in the Twentieth Century*, New York and London: Philip Allan, 1990, pp. 35–67.

95 'Different approaches and uncomfortable critiques: Joan Robinson and the economics profession', *Cambridge Review*, vol. 111, no. 2308, March 1990, pp. 27–32.

96 'Joan Robinson's early views on method', *History of Political Economy*, vol. 22, no. 3, 1990, pp. 411–27.

97 (with B. McFarlane) 'Economic planning and democracy', *Australian Journal of Political Science*, vol. 25, November 1990, pp. 326–32.

98 'R. F. Kahn: a tribute', *Banco Nazionale del Lavoro Quarterly Review*, vol. 176, March 1991, pp. 15–30.

99 Review of Turner, M. S., *Joan Robinson and the Americans*, and Feiwel, G. R. (ed.) *Joan Robinson and Modern Economic Theory*, vol. 1 and *The Economics of Imperfect Competition and Employment: Joan Robinson and Beyond*, vol. 2 *History of Political Economy*, vol. 23, Spring 1991, pp. 158–64.

100 'Marshall's *Principles* as seen at Cambridge through the eyes of Gerald Shove, Dennis Robertson and Joan Robinson', in M. Dardi, M. Callegati and E. Pesciarelli (eds) *Alfred Marshall's 'Principles of Economics', 1890–1990*: vol. 1, *Quaderni di storia dell economia politica*, vol. 9, 1991, pp. 355–72.

101 'Athanasios (Tom) Asimakopulos, 28 May 1930 – 25 May 1990: a memoir', *Journal of Post Keynesian Economics*, vol. 14, no. 1, Fall 1991, pp. 39–48.

GEOFF HARCOURT: A BIBLIOGRAPHY

102 'Joan Robinson', in T. Bottomore (ed.) *A Dictionary of Marxist Thought*, 2nd edition, Oxford: Blackwell, 1991, pp. 483–4.

103 'G. C. Harcourt (born 1931)', in P. Arestis and M. Sawyer (eds) *A Biographical Dictionary of Dissenting Economists*, Aldershot: Edward Elgar, 1992, pp. 232–41.

104 'Joan Robinson (1903–1983)', in P. Arestis and M. Sawyer (eds) *A Biographical Dictionary of Dissenting Economists*, Aldershot: Edward Elgar, 1992, pp. 454–63.

105 (with A. Singh) 'Sukhamoy Chakravarty, 26 July, 1934 – 22 August 1990', *Cambridge Journal of Economics*, vol. 15, 1991, pp. 1–3.

106 (with B. J. McFarlane) 'A reply to Osiatynski', *Australian Journal of Political Science*, vol. 26, no. 3, November 1991, pp. 355–6.

107 'Markets, madness and a middle way', *The Second Annual Donald Horne Address*, Melbourne, 1992, also published in *Australian Quarterly*, vol. 64, no. 1, pp. 1–17 and, in a revised version, in 'Viewpoint', *Cambridge Review*, vol. 14, no. 2320, February 1993, pp. 40–5.

108 'Kahn, Richard [Ferdinand], Baron Kahn of Hampstead (1905–1989)', *DNB* (forthcoming).

109 'A post Keynesian comment', *Methodus*, vol. 4, no. 1, June 1992, p. 30.

110 'Kahn and Keynes and the making of *The General Theory*', *Cambridge Journal of Economics*, vol. 17, February 1994, pp. 11–23.

111 'Is Keynes dead?', *History of Economics Review*, no. 18, Summer 1992, pp. 1–9.

112 'George Shackle: a tribute', *Review of Political Economy*, vol. 5, no. 2, 1993, pp. 272–3.

113 (with J. A. T. R. Araujo) 'Maurice Dobb, Joan Robinson and Gerald Shove on accumulation and the rate of profits', *Journal of the History of Economic Thought*, vol. 15, Spring 1993, pp. 1–30.

114 'A Large G & T', *ALR*, no. 148, March 1993, pp. 34–6. A longer version was published as 'Macroeconomic policy for Australia in the 1990s', in *Economic and Labour Relations Review*, vol. 4, no. 2, December 1993, pp. 167–75.

115 'Reply to Gerard Henderson and Ross Gittins', *Australian Quarterly*, vol. 64, no. 4, Summer 1992, pp. 463–4.

116 'The Harcourt plan to "save" the world', *At the Margin*, issue 1, Lent 1993, pp. 2–5.

117 'John Maynard Keynes, 1883–1946', ch. 6 of R. V. Mason (ed.) *Cambridge Minds*, Cambridge: Cambridge University Press, 1994, pp. 72–85.

118 'On mathematics and economics', to be published in a volume of the Science and Human Dimension Conference, 'Mathematics: what should non-mathematicians know?' to be edited by J. Cornwell and published by Cambridge University Press. Published in Harcourt, G. C., *Capitalism, Socialism and Post-Keynesianism: Selected Essays of G. C. Harcourt*, Cheltenham: Edward Elgar, 1995, pp. 201–17.

119 'What Adam Smith really said', *Economic Review*, vol. 12, no. 2, November 1994, pp. 24–7.

120 (with A. Hughes and A. Singh) 'Austin Robinson, 20 November 1897 – 1 June 1993: an appreciation', *Cambridge Journal of Economics*, vol. 17, no. 4, December 1993, pp. 365–8.

121 (with M. Kitson) 'Fifty years of measurements: a Cambridge view', *Review of Income and Wealth*, series 39, no. 4, December 1993, pp. 435–47.

122 'What Josef Steindl means to my generation', *Review of Political Economy, Josef Steindl Memorial Issue*, vol. 6, no. 4, 1994, pp. 459–63.

123 'Krishna Bharadwaj, 21 August 1935 – 8 March 1992: a memoir', *Journal of Post*

Keynesian Economics, Winter 1993–4, vol. 16, no. 2, pp. 299–311.

124 'Josef Steindl, 14 April 1912 – 7 March 1993: a tribute', *Journal of Post Keynesian Economics*, Summer 1994, vol. 16, no. 4, pp. 627–42.

125 'The capital theory controversies', in P. Arestis and M. Sawyer (eds) *The Elgar Companion to Radical Political Economy*, Aldershot: Edward Elgar, 1994, pp. 29–34.

126 'The structure of Tom Asimakopulos's later writings', in G. Harcourt, A. Roncaglia and R. Rowley (eds) *Income and Employment in Theory and Practice*, London: Macmillan, 1994, pp. 1–16.

127 (with C. Sardoni) 'George Shackle and post Keynesianism', to be published in S. Boehm, S. F. Frowen and J. Pheby (eds) *Economics as the Art of Thought: Essays in Memory of G. L. S. Shackle* (London: Routledge, forthcoming).

128 (with Claudio Sardoni) 'Keynes's vision: method, analysis and "Tactics"', in J. Davis (ed.) *The State of Interpretation of Keynes*, Norwell, MA: Kluwer, pp. 131–52.

129 (with Gabriel Palma) 'Introduction', *Cambridge Journal of Economics*, vol. 18, February 1994, pp. 1–2.

130 "Keynes, John Maynard', in G. Hodgson, W. J. Samuels and M. R. Tool (eds) *The Elgar Companion to Institutional and Evolutionary Economics A–K*, Aldershot: Edward Elgar, 1994, pp. 442–4.

131 'Robinson, Joan', in G. Hodgson, W. J. Samuels and M. R. Tool (eds) *The Elgar Companion to Institutional and Evolutionary Economics L–Z*, Aldershot: Edward Elgar, 1994, pp. 442–6.

132 'Comment', in H. G. Brennan and A. M. C. Waterman (eds) *Economics and Religion: Are They Distinct?*, Boston, Dordrecht and London: Kluwer, 1994, pp. 205–12.

133 'Taming speculators and putting the world on course to prosperity: a "Modest Proposal"', *Economic and Political Weekly*, vol. 29, 17 September, 1994, pp. 2490–2.

134 'Joan Robinson, 1903–83', *Economic Journal*, vol. 105, September 1995, pp. 1228–43.

135 'Lorie Tarshis, 1911–1993: in appreciation', *Economic Journal*, vol. 105, September 1995, pp. 1244–55.

136 'Recollections and reflections of an Australian patriot and a Cambridge economist', *Banco Nazionale del Lavoro Quarterly Review*, vol. 48, September 1995, pp. 225–54. (Also in Italian: *Moneto e Credito*, vol. 48, September 1995, pp. 299–329).

137 'Some reflections on Joan Robinson's changes of mind and their relationship to post-Keynesianism and the economics profession', ch. 26 of M. C. Marcuzzo, L. L. Pasinetti and A. Roncaglia (eds) *The Economics of Joan Robinson*, London: Routledge, 1996, pp. 317–29.

BOOKS

1 (with P. H. Karmel and R. H. Wallace) *Economic Activity*, Cambridge: Cambridge University Press, 1967. Italian edition 1969.

2 (with R. H. Parker (eds)) *Readings in the Concept and Measurement of Income*, Cambridge: Cambridge University Press, 1969. Second edition, with G. Whittington, Oxford: Philip Allan, 1986.

3 (with N. F. Laing (eds)) *Capital and Growth: Selected Readings*, London: Penguin, 1971, reprinted 1973. Spanish edition 1977.

4 *Some Cambridge Controversies in the Theory of Capital*, Cambridge: Cambridge University Press, 1972. Italian edition 1973; Polish edition 1975; Spanish edition 1975; Japanese edition 1980. Reprinted, Gregg Revivals Series, ed. M. Blaug, 1991.

5 *Theoretical Controversy and Social Significance: An Evaluation of the Cambridge Controversies*, Edward Shann Memorial Lecture. University of Western Australian Press, 1975.

6 (ed.) *The Microeconomic Foundations of Macroeconomics*, London: Macmillan, 1977.

7 *The Social Science Imperialists. Selected Essays by G. C. Harcourt*, ed. P. Kerr, London: Routledge & Kegan Paul, 1982.

8 (ed.) *Keynes and His Contemporaries: The Sixth and Centennial Keynes Seminar Held in the University of Kent at Canterbury 1983*, London: Macmillan, 1985, vi + 195 pp.

9 (with R. H. Parker and G. Whittington (eds)) *Readings in the Concept and Measurement of Income*, 2nd edition, Oxford: Philip Allan, 1986, vii + 371 pp.

10 (with Jon Cohen (eds)) *International Monetary Problems and Supply-Side Economics: Essays in Honour of Lorie Tarshis*, London: Macmillan, 1986, viii + 162 pp.

11 *Controversies in Political Economy: Selected Essays by G. C. Harcourt*, edited O. F. Hamouda, Brighton: Wheatsheaf, 1986, 293 pp.

12 *On Political Economists and Modern Political Economy: Selected Essays of G. C. Harcourt*, ed. C. Sardoni, London: Routledge, 1992.

13 *Post-Keynesian Essays in Biography: Portraits of Twentieth Century Political Economists*, Basingstoke: Macmillan, 1993.

14 (with M. Baranzini (eds), *The Dynamics of the Wealth of Nations: Growth, Distribution and Structural Change. Essays in Honour of Luigi Pasinetti*, Basingstoke: Macmillan, 1993.

15 (with A. Roncaglia and R. Rowley (eds)) *Income and Employment in Theory and Practice*, Basingstoke: Macmillan, 1994.

16 *Capitalism, Socialism and Post Keynesianism*: *Selected Essays of G. C. Harcourt*, Cheltenham: Edward Elgar, 1995.

FORTHCOMING

1 (with C. Sardoni) 'George Shackle and post Keynesianism', in S. Boehm, S. F. Fowen and J. Pheby (eds) *Economics as the Art of Thought: Essays in Memory of G. L. S. Shackle*, London: Routledge.

2 (with P. Riach (eds)) *A 'Second Edition' of The General Theory*, London: Routledge.

3 (with P. M. Kerr) 'Marx, Karl Heinrich (1818–1883)', in M. Warner (ed.) *International Encyclopedia of Business and Management*, London: Routledge.

4 (with W. Bradford) 'Units and definitions', chapter in G. C. Harcourt and P. Riach (eds) *A 'Second Edition' of The General Theory*, London: Routledge.

5 (with P. Riach) 'Introduction' to G. C. Harcourt an P. Riach (eds) *A 'Second Edition' of The General Theory*, London: Routledge.

6 'How I do economics', chapter in S. G. Medema and W. G. Samuels (eds) *Exploring the Foundations of Research in Economics: How Should Economists Do Economics?*, Cheltenham: Edward Elgar.

7 Entry on 'John Maynard Keynes', in T. Cate *et al.* (eds) *The Encyclopedia of Keynesian Economics*, Cheltenham: Edward Elgar.

8 (with D. Spajic) 'The post-Keynesian school', in C. Sardoni (ed.) volume on Economics in *Storia de XX Secolo*, Rome: Istituto della Enciclopedia Italiana, 40 pp.

INDEX